OBAMA
on the
HOME FRONT

OBAMA
on the
HOME FRONT

Domestic Policy Triumphs and Setbacks

JOHN D. GRAHAM

Indiana University Press
Bloomington and Indianapolis

This book is a publication of
Indiana University Press
Office of Scholarly Publishing
Herman B Wells Library 350
1320 East 10th Street
Bloomington, Indiana 47405 USA

iupress.indiana.edu

The paper used in this publication meets the minimum requirements of
the American National Standard for Information Sciences—Permanence
of Paper for Printed Library Materials, ANSI Z39.48-1992.

Manufactured in the United States of America

Library of Congress Cataloging-in-Publication Data

Names: Graham, John D. (John David), [date] - author.
Title: Obama on the home front : domestic policy triumphs and setbacks / John D. Graham.
Description: Bloomington : Indiana University Press, 2016. | Includes bibliographical
  references and index.
Identifiers: LCCN 2016017100 (print) | LCCN 2016017719 (ebook)
  | ISBN 9780253021038 (cl : alk. paper) | ISBN 9780253021151 (e-book)
Subjects: LCSH: United States—Politics and government—2009- | Obama, Barack.
Classification: LCC E907 .G729 2016 (print) | LCC E907 (ebook) | DDC 973.932092—dc23
LC record available at https://lccn.loc.gov/2016017100
Fron

1 2 3 4 5 21 20 19 18 17 16

CONTENTS

PREFACE

From 2001 to 2006 I served President George W. Bush in the Executive Office of the President as a Senate-confirmed official in the US Office of Management and Budget (OMB). My role, dubbed "regulatory czar" by the *New York Times*, was to oversee the regulatory, statistical, and information-policy functions of the federal government. In this capacity, officially known as administrator of the Office of Information and Regulatory Affairs (OIRA), I supervised a staff of fifty career civil servants and collaborated with the key White House offices, including the president and vice president, on virtually every domestic policy issue from homeland security to environmental protection.

One of the lessons I drew from my rewarding experience inside the government is that the power of the president to shape public policy on domestic matters, while substantial, is quite constrained. That was the intention of the framers of the Constitution, but the informal powers of the presidency grew enormously in the twentieth century, creating the so-called imperial presidency.

A new development has accentuated the limitations of presidential power: the polarization of the Congress on party lines. America has gone through several bouts of intense polarization in its history, but the current one has lasted longer and affected more issues than the previous ones. It appears that there is no end in sight, meaning that future presidents are also likely to govern under conditions of polarization along party lines.

As President Barack Obama's two-term presidency comes to a close, I am struck by a disheartening phenomenon that both Bush and Obama experienced. In football it is an infraction called "piling on," but in politics there is no penalty for this behavior. I refer to the ease with which blame is assigned to whomever is the current president for virtually everything bad that happens in Washington, DC, or even in the country or world at large. That blame comes not simply from the president's partisan opponents but from members of the president's party as well. The campaign for the next US president, to be elected in November 2016, has already begun, and candidates in both parties are jockeying for an early advantage by establishing exploratory committees and reaching out to donors and volunteers. It is as if the country will move to the next president without ever learning from Obama's significant accomplishments, setbacks, and mistakes.

In this book I call for a "time out" to consider what we should learn from the Obama presidency about how presidents should go about getting things done. As in my previous book, *Bush on the Home Front: Domestic Policy Triumphs and Setbacks* (Indiana University Press, 2010), the focus is less on the question of whether President Obama's policies were good or bad for the country and more on the question of whether he was effective at accomplishing his agenda, and why. The goal is to shed light on how presidents can overcome—or cope with—the intense polarization that has characterized our politics for the last twenty-five years or more.

The audience for this book is first and foremost students and scholars of the American presidency, although anyone with an intellectual appetite for American politics should find the book of interest. It is also aimed at a wide variety of practitioners: professional supporters and critics of the Obama administration, reporters who cover the White House and Congress, members of Congress and their staffs, governors and mayors, party activists, campaign strategists, business and NGO (nongovernmental organization) leaders who lobby the president and Congress, judges, donors to political causes, and the many people who served in the federal government during the Obama administration. The case studies in chapters 3 through 9 will also appeal to readers with special interests in the subjects of economic policy, health care, energy/environment, and immigration.

This is a book for readers who are interested in an assessment of Barack Obama's track record as domestic policy maker and party leader. What did Obama pledge to do in domestic policy, and what did he actually accomplish? Why did some initiatives succeed and others fail? Did Obama's policies, and the efforts to enact them, contribute to the large losses experienced by the

Democratic Party in 2010 and 2014? If Obama had refined his policy agenda and modified his political strategies, could he have accomplished even more of his agenda without hurting his party? What lessons should future presidents draw from Obama's presidency? In the course of answering these questions, particular attention is paid to the complications posed by polarization, including the emergence of the Tea Party.

This is not a book about the inner workings of the Obama White House. Nor is it a book about the internal politics of the Obama administration or the personalities of those who served in that administration. Those who were on the inside are in the best position to offer reflections on how the Obama White House operated and who was most influential on various issues.

My interest in writing this book arose out of the April 19, 2012, conference "Change in the White House? Comparing the Presidencies of George W. Bush and Barack Obama," sponsored by the Peter S. Kalikow Center for the Study of the American Presidency at Hofstra University (New York). At this conference my co-author, Ronnye Stidvent, and I presented a working paper titled "Presidential Policy Making in a Polarized Era: Comparing the GW Bush and Obama Administrations," which examined the relative success of Bush and Obama at accomplishing their domestic agendas. I therefore thank Ronnye for helping me to get started thinking about the Obama presidency. I offer an especially warm thanks to Professor Meena Bose of Hofstra University for inviting us to the conference, for supplying comments on the conference paper, and for encouraging me to contribute to the literature on the American presidency.

Several anonymous peer reviewers commissioned by Indiana University Press offered constructive guidance when the book was at the prospectus stage. I also recognize with appreciation additional peer reviews by scholars and practitioners (Elisabeth Andrews, Heather Campbell, James E. Campbell, Diana Epstein, Lee Hamilton, Jeffrey Holmstead, Baron Hill, Frances E. Lee, David Orentlicher, Dennis Paustenbach, Bert A. Rockman, Scott Segal, Mike Tschudi) whom I commissioned to help me refine the case studies and sharpen the overall argument of the book. In addition I solicited several anonymous reviews from officials who worked in the Obama administration. I thank them for their insightful suggestions.

As the book progressed through various stages of development, I received extremely helpful research assistance from several students at Indiana University. Those students include Yi Cui, Alyssa Julian, Matt Irick, and Emilee

Sanchez. These individuals contributed some insightful analysis as well as detailed documentation and references. Devin New and Maggie Pearson provided invaluable assistance in preparing the manuscript for IU Press. My editor Rebecca Tolen at Indiana University Press was a constant source of encouragement and also helped me set deadlines for the enterprise. Any residual errors are my responsibility.

OBAMA
on the
HOME FRONT

1

BARACK OBAMA'S ASSETS
AND CONSTRAINTS

The record of any American president attracts attention, but Barack Obama is of special interest. As the first African American president in the nation's 240-year history, he is certainly a symbolically significant figure. The symbolism is not simply about America's bid for progress in overcoming its history of slavery but also about the opportunity that America offers to talented individuals born to families of mixed race, limited means, and family dysfunction. After all, Obama's writings reveal that he grew up without any meaningful relationship with his father and that at key points during his childhood his mother relied on relatives to raise him.[1]

The symbolism was not necessarily beneficial to President Obama as he strove to accomplish his policy agenda. His rapid rise in American politics was frightening to many conservatives and reactionaries, triggering a groundswell of grassroots opposition that is referred to loosely as the "Tea Party."[2] There has been much political energy in this movement, particularly in Republican primary races for the House and Senate. In fact, Obama confronted many Republican members of Congress who perceived danger in even modest efforts to collaborate with him. As a result, he faced not only the intense congressional polarization that Bill Clinton and George W. Bush experienced but also an exacerbation of that polarization due to the rise of the Tea Party.

Fortunately, Barack Obama brought some substantial talents to the challenge. He is an intellectual, a community organizer, a legal authority on the US Constitution, a gifted orator, a skilled campaigner, and a politician with experience at both the state and federal levels of government. Michelle Obama is an impressive and appealing spouse, and Obama is father to their two lovely children. In terms of temperament, he is described as a leader who is more inclined to seek resolution than confrontation—a realist who "keeps lines of communication open and does not burn bridges."[3] Throughout his political career, he has had few personal scandals and is seen as a man of integrity, even by Republican senators.

One certainly cannot argue with Obama's academic credentials. After starting his undergraduate studies in California at Occidental College, he graduated with a BA in political science from Columbia University in 1983. He then devoted several years to church-based community organizing on the South Side of Chicago before being admitted to Harvard Law School. Obama was elected president of the *Harvard Law Review* in his second year, a role that tested his mediation skills, because the *Law Review* was struggling with ideological conflict during this period. After law school he taught constitutional law for twelve years (1992–2004) as a lecturer at the University of Chicago Law School.

For three terms (1997–2004) Obama served as an elected Illinois state senator. In 2000 he lost a primary challenge for a US House seat to Congressman Bobby Rush, but he later ran for the US Senate. After winning Illinois' Democratic nomination for US senator in March 2004, he accepted an invitation to deliver a keynote speech at the Democratic National Convention, a speech that proved to be such an inspiring and memorable address that it helped launch his national political career. Obama was elected senator in November 2004 and served only a brief period until he launched his quest for the presidency in 2007. He served as a senator until he was elected president of the United States in November 2008 and was sworn into office in January 2009.

There is an unusual aspect of Barack Obama's background compared to all presidents since Lyndon Baines Johnson (LBJ): the absence of experience as an executive. From Richard Nixon through George W. Bush, all presidents had previously served as a governor or as vice president. Obama was also the first sitting senator elected president since John F. Kennedy.[4]

In contrast to George W. Bush, whose decision making was described as intuitive and decisive, Obama is described as a cautious, analytical, and deliberative decision maker who draws on a progressive value system.[5] Moreover, his value system is liberal, but his temperament is moderate, even conservative.[6]

On occasion Obama has taken some nonprogressive positions on issues. As a senator in the 1990s, he, like many Democrats, opposed ratification of the Kyoto Protocol on climate change engineered by Vice President Al Gore. More recently, he annoyed environmentalists as US senator and president with his support of "clean coal" and "fracking" for oil and gas (see chapters 7 and 8).

On most issues, however, Obama's stances have been on the progressive side of America's political spectrum. He was ranked by *National Journal* as the sixteenth most liberal senator in 2005, the tenth most liberal in 2006, and the most (number 1) liberal in 2007 on a composite score that includes key roll-call votes on economic, social, and foreign policy issues.[7] During the Democratic nominating process for president in 2008, Obama generally ran to the left of Hillary Clinton, the mainstream candidate favored by much of the Democratic establishment.[8] Thus, in both 2008 and 2012 America elected a progressive candidate for president, arguably the first progressive since Franklin Delano Roosevelt.

The Obama presidency offers fresh evidence of the challenges faced by a non-centrist—a progressive insurgent rather than an establishment Democrat —occupying the White House. In this respect Obama's challenges resemble those faced by Ronald Reagan, an insurgent from the right, more than they resemble the challenges facing more centrist presidents such as Gerald Ford, Jimmy Carter, George Herbert Walker Bush, Bill Clinton, or even George W. Bush. An interesting question that the Obama presidency raises is to what extent—and how—can a president from one of the ideological wings of the American political spectrum move the country's policies in the direction that he or she prefers, given that the center of the American electorate is generally considered moderate or even conservative-moderate?[9]

The Obama presidency is of special interest for yet another reason: Obama came into office as the American economy was careening into the worst downturn since the Great Depression of the 1930s. The general election contest of

2008 between Obama and the Republican nominee, Arizona senator John Mc-
Cain, was quite competitive coming out of the Republican National Convention in August. In fact, some polls were reporting that McCain had a slight
lead, even after his controversial vice presidential nomination of Governor
Sarah Palin of Alaska.[10] The McCain campaign (which was touting the basic
soundness of the nation's economic situation) was undermined by the unexpected housing bubble that rippled throughout the country, ultimately leading
to the collapse of the financial system.[11] Some argue that Obama would have
defeated McCain anyway; others say that he was handed the election—and an
extremely difficult start to his presidency—by the rapid and frightening onset
of the "Great Recession."[12]

OBAMA THE CANDIDATE

As a presidential campaigner Obama's track record was remarkable.[13]
He overcame the conventional wisdom that the moderate-conservative American electorate will vote for Democratic presidential candidates only if they are
moderate Southerners like Bill Clinton or Jimmy Carter. Obama's two presidential campaigns were known for impressive ground games: it is estimated
that in 2008 he had four times as many grassroots campaign volunteers as
John Kerry in 2004 or Al Gore in 2000, and the multiple was even larger in
the battleground states.[14] Obama's campaign also compiled a list of 13 million
e-mail addresses of small donors and sympathetic activists and deployed new
social and media technologies in precedent-setting ways.[15] In addition, Obama
motivated millions of people (especially youth and minorities) with weak ties
to the political system to vote and to urge others to vote.[16]

The vote tallies speak for themselves. In 2008, against McCain, Obama
won the two-party popular vote 53.7–46.3 percent and the Electoral College by
an even more decisive margin of 365–173. In 2012, despite a sluggish economic
recovery and an arguably stronger Republican opponent in Massachusetts governor Mitt Romney, he won the two-party popular vote 52–48 percent. Romney actually defeated Obama among independents, yet Obama overwhelmed
Romney with votes from young people and nonwhites.[17] Obama's second Electoral College victory (332–206) was basically a rerun of the first one, except that
during the second race he chose not to campaign in Indiana and he lost North
Carolina by the slimmest of margins.

Some observers question how Obama could have been reelected in 2012 when the US economy was in such poor shape. In fact, Obama's reelection confirms two long-term patterns in American politics. First, when the rate of unemployment drops significantly in the period before a presidential election, the incumbent president wins reelection.[18] In other words, what matters politically is not so much the absolute condition of the economy but how it is trending. Moreover, Americans are highly likely to reelect their president to a second term when the president was elected after a president from the other party has served. Since 1900 that has happened eleven out of twelve times (Jimmy Carter, who was not reelected in 1980, is the exception). In a sense, the American electorate seems inclined to eight-year terms after a party switch in the White House.[19]

When we assess why Obama was victorious in the Electoral College when his party's predecessors (John Kerry and Al Gore) lost to George W. Bush, the answer resides in some of the key battleground states. Obama won Florida, Ohio, Virginia, Colorado, Iowa, and Nevada in both 2008 and 2012, all states (except Iowa) that Bush had won in both 2000 and 2004.[20] One could argue that the Republicans McCain (2008) and Romney (2012) lost not so much because they were weaker candidates than George W. Bush (2000, 2004), but because Obama was a stronger candidate than Gore and Kerry and because he was able to exploit the unpopularity of Bush at the end of his presidency.

If we entertain the notion of presidential coattails, Obama had them. In the Senate the Democratic Party gained eight seats in 2008 and two seats in 2012. The House gains for Democrats were twenty-three seats in 2008 and eight seats in 2012. Obama was particularly effective at motivating occasional voters to vote, and they voted disproportionately for Democratic candidates. Without question, candidate Obama helped the Democratic Party in both 2008 and 2012.

OBAMA'S POLITICAL STANDING

From the perspective of presidential studies, Obama's first term is of special interest. His political standing, defined as the sum of his popular vote (measured as a percent), Electoral College vote (percent), and job approval rating (percent), was strong in January 2009, but was considerably less impressive in January 2013 (see table 1.1).

Table 1.1. Political Standing of Postwar US Presidents

President	Popular Vote (%)	Electoral Vote (%)	Job Approval (%)	Total	Rank
Johnson (1964)	61	90	71	222	1
Eisenhower (1956)	57	86	76	219	2
Reagan (1984)	59	98	62	219	2
Eisenhower (1952)	55	83	78	216	4
Nixon (1972)	61	97	51	209	5
Reagan (1980)	51	91	57	199	6
Obama (2008)	53	67	75	195	7
Bush 41 (1988)	53	79	57	189	8
Kennedy (1960)	50	56	77	183	9
Clinton (1996)	50	70	62	182	10
Carter (1976)	50	55	66	171	11
Clinton (1992)	43	69	58	170	12
Nixon (1968)	43	56	59	158	14
Obama (2012)	51	62	52	165	13
Bush 43 (2000)	50	50	57	157	15
Bush 43 (2004)	51	53	51	155	16

Source: Charles O. Jones. *The Presidency in a Separated System* (Washington, DC: Brookings Institution, 2005), 52, table 3.3.

Note: Popular vote is share of two-party vote. Job approval is upon entering office.

Weary of the Iraq War and the politics of George W. Bush, the American electorate—in 2006 and 2008—awarded the Democratic Party progressively larger majorities in Congress. As a result, no president since LBJ began his first term with the favorable partisan circumstances that Obama enjoyed: a decisive (if not landslide) victory in the Electoral College, a relatively high favorability rating in public opinion polls (around 70 percent), a large majority in the House of Representatives, and an almost filibuster-proof majority in the Senate.

LBJ was one of the most productive lawmaking presidents in American history, and Obama began with LBJ-like advantages. Thus, the expectations for the Obama presidency were quite high, indeed dangerously high, since unrealistic expectations are a precursor to public disappointment and diminished presidential job approval ratings.[21]

Obama's second term is less interesting from a lawmaking perspective, because he faced a conservative Republican majority in the House of Representatives, a filibuster-vulnerable Democratic majority in the Senate from 2013 to 2014, and a Republican majority in the Senate from 2015 to 2016. Like Bill Clinton and George W. Bush, Obama played defense as much as offense in legislative matters during his second term.[22]

An assessment of Obama's performance is also of interest because his standing was never compromised by any major personal scandal involving himself, high-ranking officials in his cabinet, or his White House staff.[23] There was no Watergate mess and no sex-related scandal. As a result, the public reaction to the Obama administration was primarily a reflection of attitudes about the economy and Obama's policy agenda.

THE RISE OF THE TEA PARTY

The seeds of the contemporary Tea Party movement are a matter of some dispute. Some suggest that the followers of Ross Perot in the early 1990s were precursors to the Tea Party. The movement can certainly be traced to a strong belief of some conservatives that President George W. Bush betrayed the conservative movement with his profligate spending habits and his refusal to veto any spending bills that were championed by Republicans in Congress. An event that "lit the brushfires of tea-party fervor" was the $700 billion Troubled Asset Relief Program (TARP) engineered for Wall Street in the fall of 2008 by the Bush administration and the Democratic Congress.[24]

Accounts differ as to when the first modern Tea Party protest occurred, but each account puts the movement's birth after the election of Barack Obama. On January 24, 2009, a "Tea Party" protest was organized in New York to counter new taxes being imposed by the Democratic governor of New York, David Paterson. On President's Day 2009 a twenty-nine-year old woman (Keli Carender), who was angered by what became the $787 billion Recovery Act ("stimulus") package, organized "The Anti-Porkulus Protest" that attracted more than one hundred people to Westlake Park, Seattle. She recalls, "It didn't make sense to me to be spending all this money when we don't have it."[25] Three days later the movement gained a national foothold when a business editor for CNBC, Rick Santelli, broadcasting live from the floor of the Chicago Mercantile Exchange, slammed the Obama administration's new refinancing plans for mortgages on the grounds that they promote "bad behavior." His "rant," which included a call for "Tea Party protests," went viral in multiple media.[26]

An initial wave of protests occurred on February 27, 2009, in dozens of cities across the country, with the focus being TARP and the stimulus package.[27] With a boost from Fox News, a much larger protest—hundreds of thousands of people—occurred on April 15, 2009 ("Tax Day"). Meanwhile, without any central direction or leader, but spurred by Internet communication, local activists launched roughly one thousand Tea Party groups in communities around the country. Later, with funding and organizational support from national conservative groups, Tea Party activists dominated numerous August 2009 town hall meetings and challenged local congressmen and senators about President Obama's plans on spending, health care, and climate change.

A good illustration of the rise of Tea Party influence is the 2010 Senate race in the state of Kentucky. The establishment Republican candidate, Congressman Trey Grayson, was defeated for the Republican nomination by Ron Paul's third son, Rand Paul. As with many Tea Party candidates, it is easier to describe what Rand Paul was against (big government) than what he supported, although he championed Austrian economics, a precursor to libertarianism.[28]

Social scientists who have studied the Tea Party agree that it is a populist, grassroots movement reflecting anger about the state of the country, fear about what Obama was planning to do, and a desire to "take back our country."[29] Among Tea Party supporters in April 2009, 88 percent disapproved of President Obama's performance, and 92 percent said his policies were leading the country to "socialism."[30]

Much of the movement's focus started on fiscal issues and matters of liberty, but its scope proliferated to encompass many issues of concern to populist conservatives, such as illegal immigration, environmental regulation, gay marriage, abortion, and secularism.[31] There were tensions within the Tea Party movement (e.g., libertarians versus social conservatives), but its members rallied in unison against Obama and his specific policy initiatives.

Among those sympathetic to the Tea Party, misperceptions about Barack Obama were quite common. He was variously seen as not native born (and therefore ineligible to be president), a Muslim, a man with ties to terrorists, a socialist, and a secret member of the Black Panthers.[32] Factual misperceptions are probably widespread among left-wing movements (e.g., MoveOn.org) as well, but the misperceptions about Obama made it difficult for the White House to deal with the Tea Party without seeming dismissive. Thus, in addition to the growing partisan polarization faced by Bill Clinton and George W. Bush, Obama confronted an intensifying Tea Party movement.

THE STRENGTH OF OBAMA'S CO-PARTISANS IN CONGRESS

A president's success in lawmaking is strongly related to the partisan composition of the Congress, both the House and Senate. Other things being equal, a Democratic member of Congress is more likely to vote in favor of an Obama initiative than is a Republican member of Congress. Thus, in assessing how much Obama accomplished in his relationships with the Congress, we need to consider the partisan mix of Congress throughout his presidency. In 2009 the Democrats in Congress started very strong in both chambers, but that strength lasted much longer in the Senate than it did in the House.

When President Obama was elected in 2008, the Democrats picked up twenty-three seats in the House of Representatives, enlarging his party's majority to 256–178 (with one vacancy). The Democrats lost their House majority in 2010 after a political earthquake that enabled the Republicans to gain sixty-four seats and a 242–193 majority (see chapter 10 for the causes of the earthquake). In 2012 the Republican margin in the House was reduced slightly, to 234–201, but it was enlarged to 248–187 after the Republican gains in the 2014 midterm elections. Thus, President Obama enjoyed only two years of his party's possessing a majority in the House. This simple fact should sharply curtail any expectation of his success with progressive legislative initiatives in years three through eight of his two-term presidency.

In the Senate, Obama's 2008 election was accompanied by a net gain of eight Democratic seats, bringing the Democratic majority to 59–41 (counting two independents as Democrats, since they caucus with the Democrats on a regular basis). The Democrats held sixty of one hundred seats in the Senate for a brief period,[33] but the critical sixtieth Democrat was lost in a stunning special election in January 2010. Republican Scott Brown, who became an instant darling of the Tea Party due to his opposition to "Obamacare," captured the seat that became vacant when veteran Massachusetts senator Ted Kennedy passed away.

As if the Brown victory foreshadowed doom, the Democrats lost six Senate seats in 2010 (reducing the party's margin to 53–47), regained two in 2012 (for a Democratic margin of 55–45), but then lost nine in 2014 (ceding a 54–46 majority to the Republicans). Thus, President Obama enjoyed a Democratic majority in the Senate for six of eight years. Nonetheless, the size of the Senate majority was small enough that the White House was typically in desperate need of some Republican crossover votes to surpass the sixty-vote threshold necessary to overcome a filibuster threat.

Before turning to a theory of presidential effectiveness in chapter 2, it is useful to summarize the procedural tools and constraints that President Obama confronted. They are basic features of our Constitution and congressional procedures that newly elected presidents are not entitled to change. In effect, they are the rules of the game.

UNILATERAL EXECUTIVE ACTION

A president has some formal authority in domestic policy, and as President Obama's second term came to a close, he sought to bypass the Republican Congress by using executive powers to pursue several of his policy priorities. This pattern raises a more general question: when should a president favor executive lawmaking over requests for new legislation from Congress? The latter is generally the definitive and durable approach to lawmaking, but it is also much harder to accomplish given the 535 strong-willed members of Congress and the filibuster threat in the Senate. The sequence of the two types of lawmaking also requires consideration. If legislation fails, the president may be able to pursue executive action to achieve at least partial success. Alternatively, the president can avoid expenditure of political capital in Congress by taking executive action and then pursue legislation only if executive action proves to be ineffective, unlawful, or insufficient.

Executive powers are less well understood by the public and reporters, but they can be quite potent. There are numerous types of executive action,[34] but the two most important instruments of formal executive lawmaking are the presidential executive order (EO) and rule making, which produces regulation.[35] There are a variety of types of executive action similar to an EO (e.g., presidential memoranda) that Obama used to engage in policy making.[36]

An EO covers only the operations of the federal government, but the ripple effects of the EO may induce change in society at large.[37] President Clinton used an executive order in 1999 to compel language assistance for people with limited English proficiency. The order has directly and indirectly led to changes in the behavior of organizations throughout American society.[38]

A rule making, which is undertaken by one of the agencies or bureaus of the executive branch, may be sufficient to accomplish some or all of the president's policy objectives. A rule is legally binding on covered organizations or individuals and is enforceable in a court of law. The secretaries of cabinet departments serve at the pleasure of the president, and they often possess authority, through existing congressional authorization, to issue regulations.[39] As a result, cabinet agencies generally take instructions—sometimes reluctantly—from the White House unless Congress has specifically made the agency independent of White House control (e.g., the Federal Reserve Board chairman, though appointed by the president, serves a fixed term and does not serve at the pleasure of the president).

The exercise of executive power has important limitations compared to enactment of legislation. Opponents of an executive action are permitted to challenge the action through litigation. (Lawsuits can also be initiated against legislation but are usually quite difficult to win.) The courts could rule that the president lacks the necessary legal authority under existing law, including the Constitution. In that case the president, typically acting through a cabinet department, is compelled to revise the executive action to satisfy the court's opinion (in which case the action may be reissued), or the White House may need to go to the Congress seeking authorization to act. In reality, federal judges usually defer to the expertise of executive branch agencies, and presidential executive orders are rarely overturned in federal court.[40]

In theory Congress could override an executive action (e.g., through new legislation or through a resolution of disapproval in both chambers under the Congressional Review Act), but the president may counter with a presidential veto. The two-thirds requirement for overriding a veto is almost always impossible for opponents in Congress to overcome. Alternatively, the Congress may use (or threaten) riders on appropriations bills to block regulatory initiatives by the president; however, those bills are also vulnerable to a veto. In practice, Congress rarely overrides executive actions.[41]

Executive actions may be more temporary than legislation. A future president, through unilateral executive action, may modify or repeal a previous executive action, assuming the modification or repeal can survive judicial scrutiny. Legislation, on the other hand, is much more difficult to revise or rescind once it is enacted.

The frequency with which one president alters or revokes a previous president's actions is not as great as one might think, even when the two presidents are of different parties. Toward the end of 2000, the outgoing Clinton administration issued numerous new regulations. Most of them were not modified or repealed by the incoming George W. Bush administration, even though the "midnight rules" upset many Republicans in Congress.[42] Presidents may tend to preserve their political energy for their own agendas.

In chapters 3 through 9 I look closely at when and how President Obama used executive power to accomplish his domestic policy agenda. I also consider whether he might have been well advised to rely more heavily on executive action rather than focus primarily on persuading Congress to pass legislation.

FUNDS FOR WHITE HOUSE INITIATIVES

When a president's policy initiative is costly, it may be financed with public funds or through an "unfunded mandate" on nonfederal organizations (e.g., businesses, labor unions, or state and local governments). The White House can often accomplish unfunded mandates without legislation from Congress through the rule-making process. The better-known financing method, expenditure of federal funds, requires use of monies appropriated by Congress. In cases for which a president's initiative requires public funds to be appropriated for a specific purpose, it is very difficult or impossible for the White House to achieve the policy objective without some authorizing legislation or appropriations language from Congress. The framers of the US Constitution gave the Congress, not the president, the ultimate power of the public purse.

A probing, impartial legal analysis is necessary to determine how much of the president's agenda on a policy issue can be accomplished without legislation. Attorneys in the White House, at the agencies, and at the Justice Department are available to offer legal analysis to the president. Since the federal judiciary has also become polarized on party lines, the fate of a president's executive action may hinge on a key factor that the White House cannot control:

the partisan orientation of the federal judge (or the partisan mix of a panel of federal judges) who is assigned to resolve a particular case.[43]

RULES OF THE LEGISLATIVE PROCESS

Like all presidential administrations, the Obama White House confronted a Congress that operates according to procedural rules. In order to enact a bill into law, the White House must (1) persuade at least one House member and at least one senator to introduce the bill for consideration, (2) persuade the House leadership and the majority leader of the Senate to permit a floor vote to be taken on the bill, and (3) secure at least a majority of votes in favor of the bill in each chamber. Filibusters are not permitted in the House, but if a filibuster is threatened in the Senate, a supermajority vote of at least sixty out of one hundred senators is necessary in order to limit the allowed time for floor debate.[44] In recent decades the minority party in the Senate has increasingly used the filibuster threat to block initiatives favored by the majority party.[45]

Most presidents have only dreamed about a filibuster-proof majority in the Senate. Prior to Obama, only three presidents in modern history have enjoyed votes from sixty or more senators from their party (Kennedy, 1961–1962; Kennedy/LBJ, 1963–1964; LBJ 1965–1968; and Carter, 1977–1978).[46] Obama enjoyed sixty votes in the Senate but for only several months in 2009–2010.

Committee deliberations are important,[47] but they have become less influential as party leaders in Congress have exercised more control over the selection of committee chairs and committee activities.[48] In most cases the White House needs success in at least one House committee prior to floor action. Success in committees typically entails sympathetic committee chairs, a majority vote in each committee that is granted jurisdiction over the bill, and a majority vote from a House-Senate conference committee (if the House and Senate pass different versions of the bill that need to be reconciled).

Only when the basic rules of congressional procedure are satisfied does a bill desired by the White House come to the Oval Office for the president's signature. Unlike some parliamentary systems in Europe, where a prime minister is the leader of the legislature, the president of the United States is not a member of Congress, does not introduce or vote on legislation, and is actually responsible for an entirely separate branch of the federal government.[49]

HOW THE PRESIDENT SHAPES
DOMESTIC LEGISLATION

The framers of the Constitution were not very generous to the president when it comes to formal lawmaking powers in domestic affairs.[50] They were aware that the Articles of Confederation had not even mentioned the executive branch, and sought to respond to John Locke's case for a stronger executive.[51] Nonetheless, Article I of the Constitution grants sweeping lawmaking powers to the Congress while Article II mentions presidential powers and responsibilities only briefly.[52] The president is authorized to convene the Congress, to recommend legislation to the Congress, to veto acts of Congress, to deliver a State of the Union address to the Congress, and—pursuant to a vague "vesting clause" in Article II—to supervise the executive branch.[53]

Lacking formal lawmaking power, presidential influence over legislation occurs in two ways: agenda setting at the start of the process and vote-centered strategies at the congressional endgame.[54] When the president influences the congressional agenda, he is helping shape decisions about which issues are debated and which policy alternatives are considered. Later in the process, vote-centered strategies are aimed at influencing the outcomes of roll-call votes on specific legislative proposals.[55] There is rich literature demonstrating presidential influence through both of these avenues.[56]

Presidents are rarely considered effective in domestic policy unless they prove, early in their administration (and repeatedly thereafter), that they can work the Congress to obtain desired legislation. A president who relies heavily on executive actions rarely builds a strong legacy as a lawmaker.[57]

If the White House seeks to keep a low profile on an issue, the president's staff may communicate quietly with allies on Capitol Hill, urging them to introduce and move a bill. If the bill begins to move, the White House will decide when the best time is to signal public support for the initiative. On campaign pledges that give rise to legislative proposals, the White House typically goes public at the start, since the president can build credibility with party activists and donors by publicly honoring his campaign pledges.

The president's annual budget request of Congress and the annual State of the Union address are good forums for setting a legislative agenda for the Congress. In this role the president has the power to persuade, but it is ultimately the Congress that decides whether an item on the White House's agenda will be considered and enacted. Since World War II, presidents have been remarkably effective in pushing issues on to the legislative agenda, even if the opposing party has a majority in Congress.[58]

When the Congress passes legislation that the president dislikes, the president can veto the legislation. Even if a veto is rarely executed, the president may threaten a veto in order to compel key members of Congress to negotiate on an issue. The veto is a potent negative power but it is not very helpful when Congress simply refuses to act on a presidential request.

THE "CROSS-PARTISAN" STRATEGY

A legislative initiative by the White House can unfold in three ways: bipartisan cooperation, in which the president reaches out to leaders of both parties in Congress in a consensus-building effort; partisan lawmaking, in which the president's party in Congress is asked to pass the president's agenda without seeking cooperation or votes from the opposing party in Congress; or the "cross-partisan" strategy—sometimes referred to pejoratively as "cheap bipartisanship"[59]—in which the White House combines votes from the president's party with a limited number of votes from members of the opposing party but without seeking support from leaders of the opposing party in Congress.[60]

When the two parties are polarized and of roughly equal strength in the Congress, a partisan strategy cannot work and the leadership of the opposing party can block bipartisanship.[61] Thus, the cross-partisan strategy may be the White House's only hope for legislative success. The 2012 movie *Lincoln* featured our most revered president executing a cross-partisan strategy in the Congress in order to pass the Thirteenth Amendment to the Constitution, the one that abolished slavery.

The cross-partisan technique is extremely important in our modern era of polarization, for the leaders of the opposing party in Congress have strong strategic incentives to oppose a presidential priority (regardless of its substantive content).[62] Party leaders in the Senate have become particularly suspicious of cross-partisan efforts, especially when they help a senator from the opposing party look good back home. Limited cross-partisan support was central to most of George W. Bush's legislative successes[63] because the Republican Party lacked sixty votes in the Senate and Bush typically faced defections from at least a few senators from his own party.[64]

OBJECTIVE OF THIS BOOK

Barack Obama was clearly a winner on the presidential campaign trail. Should he also be considered a winner as a presidential policy maker and party leader? Those are questions that this book seeks to answer. In short, I assess the record of President Obama in domestic affairs in conjunction with his record as leader of the national Democratic Party.

Building on my previous book, which assessed the domestic record of President George W. Bush,[65] this book contributes to knowledge of the American presidency by (1) developing a theory of presidential effectiveness under conditions of congressional polarization and (2) applying the theory's prescriptions through a comparison of what Obama pledged to accomplish to what he was actually able to accomplish in domestic policy. Counterfactuals are analyzed to suggest ways that Obama might have been even more effective than he was and at less political cost to his party. Thus, the book is a blend of theory and empiricism in presidential politics, with an eye toward offering practical insight to future presidents and their advisors.

As a former Senate-confirmed official in the White House of George W. Bush (2001–2006), I am acutely aware of the challenges facing any occupant of the Oval Office and the limited powers that the Constitution grants the president in domestic affairs. I share the view of many political scientists that presidential influence on domestic policy is overestimated.[66] Making presidential campaign pledges is much easier than delivering policy reforms through durable legislative or executive action.[67] Ambitious White House plans can be foiled as a result of public apathy, partisan stonewalling, interest group opposition, or other factors.

There is a small but growing literature on the Obama presidency. Useful journalistic accounts have covered Obama's first and second years with emphasis on internal White House deliberations and conflicts, how the Obama White House dealt with the Wall Street crisis, and the struggle to pass the 2009 stimulus package.[68] The pathway to health care reform has been recounted and interpreted,[69] as has the failure of Obama's ambitious energy/climate proposal.[70] A variety of edited volumes exist in which authors touch on various themes of the Obama administration, some in foreign policy and some in domestic affairs.[71] However, there is no other comprehensive account of Obama's successes and failures in domestic affairs and no theoretical framework that would permit consideration of some improved counterfactuals.

I go beyond the framework used in my earlier book on Bush 43 by adding an additional assumption: that the president, as a national leader of his political party, seeks to protect and enhance his party's electoral interests, particularly in the Congress. As I demonstrate in chapter 10, it is unusual for a president to make progress on his policy agenda while simultaneously advancing—or at least not hurting—the electoral fortunes of his co-partisans in Congress. As the Obama presidency underscores, this is a topic in urgent need of inquiry by scholars and practitioners.

It no longer seems plausible that a president can operate, as Dwight Eisenhower did at times, above the fray of partisan politics. In an era of the permanent campaign, the president is seen as the national leader of his political party.[72] Bush 43 was certainly seen that way, despite his "uniter" campaign rhetoric in 2000.[73] Indeed, Bush 43's 2004 reelection strategy—aimed at energizing his base—dispensed with any notion that he was a uniter. Obama strove to be a "post-partisan" president, but, as we shall see, that was easier said than done.[74]

In a polarized environment, party activists expect the president to be a national leader of their party, which means they expect him to conduct his daily affairs—and make policy decisions—in ways that are favorable to the fortunes of his party. If the president is from the opposing party, party activists will perceive him—and frame him—as the leader of the enemy.[75] This is a modern reality that presidents grudgingly come to accept.

THE MAIN ARGUMENT

The main argument of the book is as follows. Despite the strong status-quo bias in the US Constitution's separation of powers, a bias that has been exacerbated by the post-1990 period of polarization and the recent rise of the Tea Party movement, President Obama made significant progress on his domestic policy priorities. He was not always successful (e.g., his energy/climate initiative failed to reach the Senate floor), and he was forced to make some big compromises (e.g., health care reform did not include a single payer plan or even a "public option"), but he can claim major victories on economic stimulus, Wall Street reform, improved access to health care, restructuring of the domestic auto industry, cleaner new cars and electric power plants to curb climate change, a revitalization of the oil and gas industry in the United States, and repeal of the Bush tax cuts for high-income households.

Most of Obama's legislative achievements occurred during his first two years in office, when the Democratic Party enjoyed big majorities in both the House and Senate. His executive record includes a variety of less visible (yet important) achievements that occurred throughout his presidency. "Success" and "achievement" are judged here by whether Obama accomplished what he set out to do, without any claim about the substantive merits of his policies. The ultimate consequences of the policies are not assessed.

A major question surrounding the Obama presidency is the extent of his responsibility for the huge losses that the Democratic Party suffered in the November 2010 and November 2014 midterm elections. Significant losses were unavoidable, as indicated by the historically poor track record of the president's party in midterm contests. Nonetheless, the cumulative loss of seventy-six House seats and fifteen Senate seats in 2010 and 2014 was much larger than expected, based on the post–World War II history of two-term presidents.

I conclude that President Obama might have accomplished even more of his domestic agenda, and with significantly less risk to the Democrats in Congress, if he had made some different decisions. In 2009–2010 the Obama White House should have coupled his progressive initiatives with some centrist policy proposals (e.g., corporate tax reform or regulatory reform).[76] To protect cross-pressured Democrats in Congress, some of the president's progressive priorities (e.g., climate policy) should have been accomplished with executive authority instead of through legislative proposals. (Indeed, some of Obama's executive proposals in his second term probably should have replaced failed legislative proposals in his first term). The health care plan should have been stripped of its more radioactive provisions (e.g., the public option and the individual mandate) from the start, and in fact Obama has made creative use of executive power in his second term to reduce some of the political damage from the Affordable Care Act. In this way he would have complicated the task of his opponents, including Tea Party activists, who were seeking to frame him as an extremist.[77]

The strategy might have protected Obama's approval ratings among independents, reduced the number of risky roll-call votes cast by moderate Democrats in Congress, and increased the number of votes where centrist Democrats could have collaborated with moderate Republicans on pro-business, pro-growth initiatives. Politically, President Obama also could have taken his role as national party leader more seriously by actively campaigning in 2010 for vulnerable Democrats in the House, as George W. Bush did with some success for Republicans in 2002. If Obama's first term had proceeded in this modified way, the partisan approach to health care reform—which was the only realistic path, given the progressive nature of the proposal—could have been executed with less overall risk to the president's popularity and to the reelection prospects of moderate Democrats in the Congress.

In a book about the presidency it is natural to explore causal hypotheses that relate to presidential choice. Yet we know that presidents sometimes succeed or fail for reasons that are unrelated to their choices. Hitler made it easy for Roosevelt to enter the European theater by declaring war on the United States; the Japanese attack at Pearl Harbor certainly helped Roosevelt persuade a sleepy America that we needed to get into the war. Obama's triumphs and setbacks are not all related to his choices, and it is difficult to distinguish presidential leadership or incompetence from presidential luck (good or bad). Thus, in the case studies in chapters 3 through 9 I seek to provide a rich enough context for Obama's choices so that non-presidential explanations as well as Obama-related ones are available for the reader's consideration.

COUNTERING MISPLACED CRITIQUES

In the course of offering this nuanced critique I reject a variety of alternative critiques that have been leveled against the Obama White House. Some have suggested that Obama should have focused exclusively on the economy, deferring action on health care and other domestic issues until his second term.[78] I counter that such a timid strategy would have created too much vulnerability for President Obama among his progressive base while missing a once-in-a-century opportunity to accomplish major reform of the health care system.

The Obama White House was not guilty, as alleged, of pursuing too many of its numerous 2008 campaign pledges, as there is clear evidence that priorities were set (e.g., stimulus, Wall Street reform, and health care reform), and many pledges were not acted upon during his first term (e.g., minimum wage legislation) due to the unanticipated collapse of the economy and the need to focus on a handful of big initiatives.[79] The second term also had some clear priorities (e.g., gun control and immigration), although I question whether they were legislatively unrealistic.

Nor do I subscribe to the view that Obama did not make sufficient use of the bully pulpit to advance his agenda.[80] Presidential attempts at public persuasion—even by an extremely skilled communicator like Barack Obama—are unlikely to produce mass changes in popular opinion on a major domestic issue.[81] If a policy proposal is already popular, the president can enhance the probability of its enactment by designating it a presidential priority (e.g., Wall Street reform), but there is no evidence that a modern-day president, through speeches, can turn divisive or unpopular proposals into popular ones.[82] Obama gave plenty of fine speeches in support of his agenda; the key problems were the content of the agenda and the choice of lawmaking strategy (executive versus legislative) rather than a poor rhetorical case made for the agenda.[83]

There is yet another view—popular among liberal commentators, bloggers, and grassroots progressive activists—that Obama was too eager to find compromise early in his presidency, that he bargained away his progressive principles too quickly on the early decisions about the economic stimulus, health care reform, and the torture of suspected terrorists.[84] As the case studies in this book reveal, this progressive critique ignores the fact that Barack Obama was not just dealing with an obstructionist minority party. His progressivism pressured influential moderates from his own party, such as Max Baucus of Montana (health care), Kent Conrad of North Dakota (the federal budget), Mary Landrieu of Louisiana (energy/climate), and Ben Nelson of Nebraska (numerous issues). Joe Lieberman of Connecticut (health care) was technically an independent but was part of the highly touted sixty-vote Democratic Senate majority that was supposed to be filibuster-proof. It is no secret that Lieberman would not accept a single payer plan or even a public option on health care.[85] Obama ultimately compromised with these senators because he had no choice other than to do so, not because he was timid or overly oriented toward compromise.

As explained in table 1.2, the notion that President Obama enjoyed a sixty-vote majority in the Senate from January 2009 to January 2011 is a myth. The reality is that he enjoyed sixty Democratic votes for only a brief period, primarily the fall of 2009. Those sixty Senate Democrats (including the two independents, Lieberman and Bernie Sanders of Vermont, who caucused with the Democrats) worked for only seventy-two days when Congress was in session. The implication is profound: the Obama White House almost always needed one or more Senate Republicans to overcome a filibuster threat.

Table 1.2. Obama's Fleeting Sixty-Vote Senate Majority, 2009–2010

Date	D	R	V[1]	Event
Late 2008	50	49	1	Balance prior to November 2008 election
January 26, 2009	58	41	1	Result of November 2008 election and Gillibrand (NY) appointed to replace Clinton (NY)
April 30, 2009	59	40	1	Specter (PA) switches parties R to D
July 7, 2009	60	40	0	Franken (MN) replaces Coleman (MN) after lengthy recount
August 25, 2009	59	40	1	Kennedy (MA) dies in office
September 9, 2009	59	39	2	Martinez (FL) resigns
September 10, 2009	59	40	1	LeMieux (FL) appointed to replace Martinez (FL)
September 25, 2009	60	40	0	Kirk (MA) appointed to replace Kennedy (MA)
February 4, 2010	59	41	0	Brown (MA) takes Kennedy (MA) seat after special election
June 28, 2010	58	41	1	Byrd (WV) dies in office
July 16, 2010	59	41	0	Goodwin (WV) appointed to replace Byrd (WV)
January 26, 2011	53	47	0	Balance after November 2010 election

Source: United States Senate, "Party Divisions in the Senate, 1789–Present," 2015, http://www.senate.gov/history/partydiv.htm.

[1]Vacant

I also reject the (mutually inconsistent) criticisms that President Obama devoted too much or too little political energy to recruiting Republican support for his initiatives. By temperament Obama always preferred a more consensus-oriented path, and he worked hard, at least early in his presidency, to gain Republican collaboration. Indeed, his outreach to Republicans (which many progressive Democrats found distasteful) was, in several instances, vital in attracting pivotal Republican votes in the Senate, such as those for the stimulus package and Wall Street reform. It also helped recruit the support of moderate Democrats, since even limited Republican support provided some political cover for the difficult votes that moderate Senate Democrats cast in favor of Obama's progressive initiatives. Had President Obama not engaged in his efforts to persuade Republicans, moderate Democrats in Congress would have been even more likely to defect on critical votes when Obama desperately needed their support.

If Obama had advanced an ideologically more diverse policy agenda in his first year, one that highlighted some of his centrist as well as progressive inclinations, his presidency could have unfolded quite differently. His image as a political leader would have been more difficult to stereotype,[86] the decline in his popularity (especially among independents) may have been attenuated, his party's losses in 2010 might have been diminished, and his reelection mandate in 2012 might have been significantly stronger than it ultimately was. Under those improved conditions, he might have been able to exert an even broader and deeper impact on domestic affairs throughout his eight years in office.

In other words, Obama needed to be a more astute politician early in his presidency, as his public image was being shaped, in order to protect his popularity and advance the interests of his party in Congress. Unlike Bill Clinton, who advanced moderate views on welfare reform, crime, trade, and fiscal restraint, there was little in Obama's first-term legislative agenda that was appealing to centrists or conservatives.[87] And the near-complete focus on a progressive agenda played into the hands of Obama's critics (the Tea Party, conservative bloggers and talk-show hosts, and Republican Party leaders), who portrayed Obama as an ideological extremist.

For the impatient reader who likes the bottom line up front, here are the two key conclusions of this book.

1. Despite the risks of gridlock, the Obama administration was often effective in moving America's domestic policy in a direction consistent with his 2008 campaign pledges and his State of the Union speeches. Much of this reform occurred during his first two years, when he enjoyed large Democratic majorities in the House and Senate, but it also included some major executive accomplishments throughout his presidency.

2. The key success story of the Obama presidency is not health care reform —the jury is still out on its longevity, and as designed and mishandled it was politically toxic to the Democratic Party—but economic policy: potential avoidance of a Great Depression through several (often unpopular) measures (fiscal stimulus, industry bailouts, and collaboration with the Federal Reserve Board on easy money), a restructuring and revival of the domestic auto industry coupled with a new generation of clean cars and trucks, a revitalization of

the oil and gas industry in the United States through hydraulic fracturing and horizontal drilling, and a (painfully slow yet) sustained economic recovery that protected the poor and the long-term unemployed from undue hardships.

SCOPE AND METHODS

The scope of this book is large but carefully delimited. The focus is domestic policy, since Obama faced arguably the biggest domestic challenges since the Great Depression of the 1930s. Foreign affairs and defense policy raise different issues in presidential studies because the president's constitutional authority in these areas is far greater,[88] and the international issues—though extremely important—tend not to be the dominant issues in the eyes of many voters. In fact, Obama faced an Iraq-weary public who had even less interest in foreign policy than is typical.[89] The merits of Obama's domestic policies are not examined here, only whether he was successful in accomplishing what he set out to do and why.

My case studies cover a number of the most critical issues that defined Obama's two presidential campaigns: the economy, taxes and spending, health care, energy/climate, and labor/immigration. Since it is not possible to analyze every area of policy in detail in a book of this kind, I have omitted areas that were important secondary themes, including education, agriculture, transportation, gay rights, and drug abuse. With the exception of the financial crisis and the Great Recession, which I argue are the central issues of Obama's presidency, I touch only lightly on how Obama reacted to unanticipated external events during his presidency, such as the Deepwater Horizon oil spill in the Gulf of Mexico (April 2010), the earthquake and tsunami in Japan (March 2011), and the Sandy Hook shootings (December 2012). The White House reaction to unexpected crises is a distinct dimension of presidential effectiveness, one that I do not take up in this book in any detail.

The two dominant methodological traditions in presidential studies are formal modeling and qualitative case studies. I have chosen the case-study method for this book because I believe the richness and political dynamics of a president's efforts at policy making are best captured through case studies. On the other hand, I draw extensively from the predictions of formal models (especially models of Congress) to guide my construction of the case studies and my search for patterns in congressional voting. In the final chapter I also draw some insights from the case studies that should be helpful to formal modelers as they refine their contributions to the study of Congress and the presidency.

The data I have used are drawn entirely from publicly available sources. Campaign pledges are drawn from the 2008 Obama-Biden campaign website and campaign speeches as covered by the mainstream press.[90] Obama's legislative priorities are identified in public statements made by the White House (e.g., the president's annual State of the Union addresses and the annual budget requests sent to Congress by the US Office of Management and Budget). Public actions by Congress and the executive branch are drawn from national news accounts. *Congressional Quarterly* is the source for information on roll-call votes in the Congress. Major regulatory initiatives are drawn from the OMB's annual report to Congress on regulation and formal agency notices published in the *Federal Register*. I make extensive use of national news publications (*Wall Street Journal, New York Times, Washington Post,* and *USA Today*) to help recreate the chronology of key events and present the case studies as coherent stories.

I cover the first seven years of Obama's two terms, acknowledging that much can happen in the last twelve months of a second term. George W. Bush, for example, collaborated with a Democratic Congress on a variety of major pieces of legislation as his presidency came to a close, and Obama is making aggressive use of executive power as this book goes to press. History suggests, however, that lame duck presidents rarely build their legacies during their last two years in office.[91] When presidents have a big impact in their last two years, it tends to be in foreign affairs.[92]

Throughout the book the term "Obama White House" is used as if the unitary theory of the executive branch is descriptively accurate.[93] Thus, no distinctions are drawn between the agendas of particular executive offices or personalities (e.g., Vice President Joe Biden and chair of the National Economic Council, Larry Summers). Nor is the interplay between the White House and the cabinet agencies covered, since they are all—at least in theory—under Obama's leadership. Accounts of intra-campaign and intra-administration deliberations are valuable (and intriguing) but best written by those possessing firsthand knowledge of what happened.

What matters for my inquiry is that Obama's domestic agenda was established at the start of his first term and pursued with various modifications thereafter. It is feasible to determine whether the agenda was accomplished or not and to explore whether the agenda—even if accomplished—might have been accomplished in a different way and possibly at less political cost. It is also feasible to analyze modifications to the agenda from the perspective of their possible impact on Obama's popularity and the well-being of his party in Congress.

A key inference question becomes how to suggest possible improvements in President Obama's effectiveness, given that we observe only the outcomes (policy and electoral) that occurred with the agenda he established. Drawing from the theoretical reasoning in chapter 2 and the case material in chapters 3 through 9, I develop some promising counterfactuals—basically conjectures or speculations about what might have happened (policy-wise and electorally) if Obama had made some different choices.[94] In the final chapter the promising counterfactuals are integrated into an alternative vision of what he could have done, realistically, to accomplish more of his agenda while reducing the carnage among his co-partisans in Congress.

Why engage in counterfactuals? The Obama presidency will not be rerun. Even if it could be rerun, the philosophies and personalities of Barack Obama, John Boehner, Nancy Pelosi, Mitch McConnell, and Harry Reid cannot be reconfigured. The answer is that we are seeking lessons for future presidents, and without any insightful counterfactuals about the Obama presidency, all we can do is describe what happened. Counterfactual reasoning helps us learn from President Obama's mistakes and missed opportunities, the kinds of insights that may be especially valuable to the science of presidential studies and to future presidents and their advisors.

There is much risk of cognitive bias in this endeavor. Psychologists, for example, refer to hindsight bias as the "knew-it-all-along-effect."[95] To minimize hindsight bias, the analyst needs to start by suspending the temptation to view all observed outcomes as inevitable (determinism). The analyst also needs to be open to alternative courses of action that might have produced different outcomes than those that have been observed. When assessing alternative possibilities, the analyst forecasts outcomes using only information—and all relevant information—that was available to the decision maker at the relevant time (or information that could have been obtained with plausible effort). The reasoning process I am describing is prevalent in a branch of management science called decision analysis.[96]

A related literature in history urges analysts who consider counterfactuals to place some strict boundaries on those counterfactuals in order to constrain the infinite number of possibilities and to avoid unrealistic scenarios. In chapter 2 some of those strict constraints are defined: Barack Obama occupies the Oval Office after his two victorious presidential elections; he enters an environment of partisan polarization in Congress that has been building for more than twenty years; he confronts the same constitutional powers and checks and balances that all modern presidents have faced; he possesses particular talents and experiences; and he has developed a significant but fairly limited set of relationships at power centers in Washington, DC.

What can be adjusted in the counterfactuals are the precise content and timing of Obama's domestic agendas, the mix of legislative and executive strategies, Obama's role in campaigning for members of Congress, his communications activities, and the White House's approach to the public administration aspects of the executive branch (such as appointments to agency posts). In other words, the fundamentals Obama faced are unchanged, but the strategic and tactical choices that he made beginning in January 2009 could have been different.

A danger is that there are so many possible counterfactuals—and combinations of counterfactuals—that the exercise could proliferate to an infinite number of possibilities. Following the advice of historians, I try to discipline the counterfactuals by limiting them to those that are proximate in time, holding most other variables constant.[97] Their validity cannot be tested definitively, but their degree of credibility depends on the extent to which they draw from—or are at least consistent with—the theoretical propositions outlined in chapter 2. I do not attempt a very different type of counterfactual that entails imagining that Hillary Clinton or John McCain had been elected instead of Barack Obama, since those thought experiments cause too many variables to change. Given what Obama had reason to know at the time he made his decisions, the book searches for alternative decisions that might have worked better for his policy agenda and for the political standing of Obama and the Democratic Party.

2

PRESIDENTIAL EFFECTIVENESS WHEN CONGRESS IS POLARIZED

In this chapter I advance a prescription for presidential effectiveness that is tailored to the specific challenges a president faces in domestic policy when Congress is polarized along partisan lines. For example, given that President Obama faced determined GOP opposition to his policy agenda, how should he have pursued his policy interests in economic stimulus, health care, green energy, and immigration reform? The theory is constructed based on knowledge of presidential power, congressional behavior, party politics, administrative law, voting behavior, and American politics more generally. Specifically, my theory builds on the Moe-Howell thesis of unilateral presidential power, which emphasizes the president's underappreciated power to make law on his own.[1] I share Eric Posner and Adrian Vermeule's normative stance that an ambitious view of the president is consistent with the US Constitution.[2]

To heighten practical insight, my prescriptive theory is framed as a series of "propositions" (or suggestions) for White House behavior in domestic policy. These could be framed as falsifiable predictions of rational presidential behavior under conditions of partisan polarization in Congress. The suggestions are used to guide development of the issue-specific case studies in chapters 3 through 9 and to address some of the prominent criticisms that have been directed at President Obama's domestic policy making. The theory is also used in chapter 11 to suggest some alternative agendas and strategies that might have worked better for Obama, given his policy goals and partisan interests.

The chapter starts with some basic assumptions about any president's goals as a politician and then defines what is meant by the president's policy agenda. The key policy tools for achieving the agenda—legislation and executive lawmaking—are then explored. Next, the importance of competent public administration to successful implementation of the president's agenda is considered.

With that as background, I proceed to the theoretical prescriptions for presidential effectiveness in the face of polarization. The central question is how a president should counter "opposition politics," the strategic opposition to the president's initiatives that is expected by leaders and members of the opposing party in Congress. I then consider the independent voter and why the president needs to keep cultivating independents. The chapter concludes with a short review of why legislators vote as they do, since that helps explain the modest expectations that the president should have about influencing roll-call votes in Congress.

THE PRESIDENT'S GOALS

Any investigation of effectiveness requires an identification of goals. I simplify by assuming that a president has three basic goals: (1) to accomplish his policy agenda (and thereby build a legacy), (2) to enhance his prospects of reelection (if he is in his first term), and (3) to advance the electoral interests of his co-partisans in Congress (in both the two midterm elections and during the president's reelection bid, assuming two terms in office). The relative weight given to the three goals varies from president to president and may fluctuate as a president's term of office unfolds (e.g., the president's reelection motive may predominate in his third and fourth years).

In his second term, when he will not face reelection again, a president is assumed to have only two objectives: (1) to accomplish his agenda and (2) to advance the electoral interests of his party. A president's interest in the welfare of his party colleagues may also wane in the second term as he focuses more on his policy agenda and his legacy.[3] But the midterm election in a president's second term will sustain some partisan interest, since the partisan mix in the Congress in the last two years remains an important factor in the president's ability to move his agenda through Congress. In fact, a president's supporters are more likely to complain about him during his second term, so presidents must continue to cater to the base to some extent.[4]

THE PRESIDENT'S POLICY AGENDA

The policy agenda refers to the changes in public policy that a president seeks to accomplish.[5] With the assistance of White House staff and other leaders in the administration, the policy agenda is crafted in accordance with the president's policy preferences but also gives prudent consideration to the agenda's impact on the his prospects for reelection and the possible electoral ramifications of the agenda for his political party.[6]

The agenda is typically derived from the president's campaign pledges but may also arise in response to changing conditions, events, crises, or opportunities that emerge once the president has taken office. Each year, in the State of the Union message and in the related budget documents prepared for Congress, the president lays out his agenda for the coming year. Thus, the policy agenda is revisited at least eight times over the president's maximum tenure of eight years.

The president's policy agenda is more specific and prioritized than the entire portfolio of administration policies. A secretary or assistant secretary of a cabinet agency may, at any time, launch an administration initiative with (or sometimes without) explicit approval of the White House. Administration policies of this sort are quite numerous and do not qualify as part of the president's policy agenda.

A key difference between an item on the president's policy agenda—sometimes called a presidential priority—and any other item of administration policy is that an item on the president's agenda typically reflects some personal deliberation and approval by the president or his most senior staff. The entire administration agenda—legislative and executive—may be quite large (since it covers hundreds of issues at numerous cabinet departments and agencies), but there are usually fewer than a dozen policy initiatives that are truly presidential priorities at any one time.

A presidential legislative priority is an initiative that will consume much of the energies of the White House legislative affairs team, buttressed by some of the president's personal time. Relevant cabinet departments may also be engaged to advance a legislative initiative, involving both the career staff and political appointees at the departments. The designation of presidential legislative priority also implies that the White House is signaling that members of Congress should consider the initiative. From 1949 to 2006 the president was able, on average, to win fewer than ten legislative requests from Congress per session.[7]

It is sometimes ambiguous whether an administration initiative is also a presidential priority. The White House may be floating a trial balloon through a cabinet department before deciding whether to put the prestige of the president behind the initiative, or the White House may simply be throwing a bone to interest groups with no intention of making a strong push with White House resources.[8] (Such "position taking" is not the same thing as lawmaking.[9]) Alternatively, the White House may be downplaying personal presidential involvement, since that could trigger greater opposition from the leadership of the opposing party in Congress.[10]

The president's agenda inevitably creates some political difficulties for members of his party in Congress. Those difficulties are sometimes referred to as "cross-pressures," as a member of Congress from the president's party may wish to support the president, but key interest groups or popular opinion in his or her district or state may provide countervailing reasons against such support.[11]

The president is concerned about the electoral fate of members of Congress from his political party, if only because the partisan mix of the Congress strongly influences the ability of the White House to execute a future legislative agenda.[12] Nonetheless, a president may choose to proceed with some items in his agenda, despite cross-pressures on his co-partisans in Congress, since the president is motivated to accomplish his agenda and build a legacy. And presidential success at legislation tends to help his party in Congress at subsequent elections, as voters seem to reward members of Congress who are aligned with a productive president.[13]

The White House also recognizes that an overly controversial agenda is perilous for the president's party and for his future opportunities to influence lawmaking in Congress. Reagan, for example, proposed such large cuts in popular federal spending programs that he put Republicans in Congress at risk of defeat if they voted for his spending cuts. The worst situation for the president is to submit a controversial proposal, hurt the president's image, and hurt the reelection prospects of his co-partisans in Congress, but fail to secure enactment of the controversial proposal. If a president is to offer a controversial proposal, he should obtain some policy or political gain to justify the controversy.

Even if a president does not appear to be allowing electoral considerations to determine the content of his policy agenda, the White House allows—sometimes explicitly—electoral politics to shape related choices: the timing or sequence of his initiatives, the choice of executive action versus legislation, public administration methods, and political/communications strategies. Moreover, the president may capitalize on unexpected events during his tenure and on any errors committed by the opposing party.[14] The result may be modifications to his original policy agenda as he seeks to seize policy opportunities and buttress his credibility with the electorate, interest groups, and the Congress. Thus, the president's policy agenda and electoral considerations are expected to interact with each other as the president, facing polarization, wrestles with leaders of the opposing party in Congress.

Developing a policy agenda is a crucial aspect of presidential leadership, and it requires a blend of vision, political risk taking, and realism.[15] Since the president has the ability to define the agenda and refine it over time, based on changing circumstances, the ultimate fate of the agenda is an important indicator of presidential performance.

PUBLIC OPINION AND THE PRESIDENT'S AGENDA

As the president formulates his policy agenda, he weighs public opinion and considers how the electorate might react to the agenda. It may seem obvious that the president will care about the public's reaction, but by considering voter ideology we can be more precise about whose opinions the president should care about.

We can crudely classify voters into three ideological categories: liberal, moderate, and conservative. Ideology can be described on a single issue, a group of issues, or as a general attitude. The latter approach is taken here for illustrative purposes. The electorate is not nearly as polarized ideologically as are party activists and members of Congress.[16] Since 1972, self-reported liberals have accounted for about 20 percent of the electorate, although there is some evidence that they have increased as a share in recent years, perhaps to 25 percent.[17] Self-reported conservatives have grown from 30 percent of the electorate in 1972 to somewhere between 35 and 40 percent of the electorate, with some evidence of a slight decline in the most recent years.[18] The largest category is the moderates,[19] defined as self-reported moderates plus those who report not knowing how to classify themselves. As a share of the electorate, moderates have declined from almost 50 percent in 1972 to about 40 percent in recent years, though some analysts believe their share has been almost constant.[20] Such data are the basis of the well-accepted conclusion that the modern American electorate is "unmistakably center-right."[21]

When a president is elected, he can determine with some precision his coalition of voters. The "base" is defined as voters who identify with the president's party, who are ideologically disposed to the party (e.g., conservative Republicans or liberal Democrats), and who voted for their party's winning presidential candidate. "Centrists" in the president's coalition are those who voted for the president and are either self-described moderates (Republicans, Democrats, or independents) or do not know how to classify themselves. The president's voting coalition also includes a small number of people who voted for the president but hold ideological views that are opposite from the president's base (e.g., liberals who voted for George W. Bush). They are defined here as centrists because they are not in the president's base and have demonstrated that they are flexible enough to make a surprising vote.

Presidents differ in their mixes of base and centrist voters. George W. Bush derived nearly equal shares from base and centrist voters. Bill Clinton derived roughly two-thirds of his votes from centrists. Obama's coalition is more similar to Clinton's than to Bush's. In 2008 Obama derived 62 percent of his votes from centrists and 38 percent from his base.[22] In general, Democratic presidents rely more on centrists than Republican presidents do, because the number of conservatives in the American electorate is greater than the number of liberals.[23] Moreover, "strong Republicans" are much more inclined to describe themselves as "conservative" than "strong Democrats" are to describe themselves as "liberal."[24] But neither party can reliably win presidential elections without tapping into the large pool of moderate voters.[25]

Self-described moderates are not necessarily centrists on any particular issue. Indeed, they often have very conservative or very liberal views on specific issues. What makes them moderate is that they do not consistently espouse liberal or conservative positions across issues.[26]

If public opinion were all that mattered to a president, then one might predict that the president's policy agenda should reflect some initiatives for his base and some for centrists, perhaps in rough proportion to the electoral support he receives from each.[27] In reality this prescription understates the importance of the base. The base contains the lion's share of the party activists who are the ground troops in a campaign as well as the donors who provide the monies to hire campaign workers, purchase paid advertising, and so forth. Nonetheless, it is difficult to escape the conclusion that, even when the president is an ideological insurgent from the right or left, it would be wise to devise a policy agenda that has some significant elements that appeal to centrists.

As a president governs in a polarized era, he seeks to nurture his popularity, as measured by job approval ratings, with his base and centrist voters. There is a tendency for the president's approval ratings to decline gradually after he is elected or reelected, but both Reagan and Clinton rebounded from postelection declines in their job approval ratings.[28] The White House seeks to boost the president's image through speeches, events, media appearances, and international travel, although there is not much evidence that the frequency of such activities has a big effect on job approval ratings.[29] External events outside the president's immediate control (e.g., economic trends such as changes in fuel prices or employment conditions) influence the president's popularity, but public perceptions of the president's policy agenda—and his perceived rate of progress accomplishing it—also play a role.

IMPLEMENTING POLICIES

To accomplish the presidential agenda, a president may request lawmaking by the Congress or engage in lawmaking through unilateral action, typically exploiting executive powers such as a presidential executive order or rule making. As important as lawmaking is, there is another aspect of presidential accomplishment that is often overlooked: implementation of new laws and programs.[30]

As the leader of the executive branch, the president and his team oversee the process of public administration that is essential in translating a new law or program into measures that have a meaningful impact on the day-to-day lives of citizens and organizations. Competent public administration has many facets—from agency appointments and budgetary controls, to information technology and outreach, to scientists and other technical experts.[31] It also entails successfully defending presidential programs when challenged by opponents in the courts. Thus, presidential success in policy making requires practical implementation as well as vision, clear priorities, and lawmaking success through legislation or executive action.

There is a temptation for presidents and the White House staff to treat public administration as secondary to politics. Or the White House may consider public administration as a job for career civil servants rather than politicians. Woodrow Wilson was a respected political scientist (as well as a president) who sought to draw a sharp conceptual distinction between public administration and politics.[32] But Wilson's plausible-sounding distinction has not stood the test of time among scholars who recognize that public administration and politics are intertwined.[33]

In the modern world of polarized American politics, the president is seen as the leader of the executive branch. After all, he appoints the secretaries and deputy secretaries of all the cabinet agencies. Through the OMB and the White House staff, the president also oversees the day-to-day decision making of the executive branch agencies.

Whenever a mistake is committed in the bureaucracy, the media and the president's partisan adversaries usually seek to portray the mistake as poor performance by the president and his team. If an error in public administration is related specifically to implementation of the president's agenda, the White House as well as the relevant agencies are likely to be seen as accountable. In short, it is not easy for the White House to distance the president from poor performance by public administrators in the executive branch of the federal government.

PRESIDENTS AS PARTY LEADERS

Modern presidents, whether they like it or not, assume their party's leadership.[34] They also handpick the national chairperson of their party and other leaders of the national committee. If intra-party conflicts arise, the president exercises final authority over the party's national activities.

Presidents are not the only political figures who engage in party building, but they can have a potent impact. They typically raise more money at a single fund-raiser than any other party leader.[35] Since World War II, and especially since 1980, presidents have often behaved at least as much as party leaders as national leaders.[36]

Presidents vary in how much time they engage in nuts-and-bolts party building. Whereas FDR and Truman gave priority to such efforts, Clinton had relatively little interest in them until later in his presidency.[37] In 2002 George W. Bush was an avid fund-raiser for Republican House candidates, even though midterm elections are difficult for the party occupying the White House. Overall, the pattern seems to be that presidents are the most motivated to engage in party building when their party is weakest and least motivated when their party is strongest.[38] One might therefore predict that Obama would not be an energetic party builder until later in his tenure.[39]

How should we judge whether a president is an effective party leader? A variety of criteria and metrics might be considered. Everything the president does, from personal behaviors to the policy agenda, reflects to some extent on his party.[40] The bottom line, however, at least from the party's perspective, may be whether the party's electoral outcomes in Congress have been positive or negative during the president's tenure. If this is the key performance metric, one must conclude, based on historical data, that presidents have been very poor party leaders, and thus I examine whether the president's policies may be part of the explanation.

Consider table 2.1, where I compare the electoral outcomes for the president's party in Congress using three different methods. The first column assumes the president is responsible for the electoral outcomes in Congress for five elections, beginning with the election prior to the president's first State of the Union address and extending to the election immediately prior to the president's departure from the Oval Office. This is the most inclusive measure and is considered the "fairest way" to measure a president's overall impact on his party.[41] The second column excludes the electoral outcomes in Congress when the president is first elected. This method ignores the president's initial coattails but may be most relevant to assessing the impact of the president's policies on the partisan makeup of Congress. The third column ignores the first and last election, focusing on three elections: the two midterm contests and the president's reelection year. The case for excluding the last election is that the campaign proficiency of the president's successor—not the president's policies—may have the strongest impact on congressional outcomes.

Table 2.1. Electoral Outcomes for the President's Party in Congress in the Post–World War II Period Using Three Different Methods

Presidential Administration	Net Change in Senate Seats			Net Change in House Seats		
	Method 1	Method 2	Method 3	Method 1	Method 2	Method 3
Truman[1]	−10	−10	−9	−9	−21	1
Eisenhower	−13	−14	−15	−24	−46	−68
Kennedy/LBJ	−10	−12	1	−34	−12	−7
Nixon/Ford	2	−4	−5	−44	−49	−48
Carter[2]	−15	−15	−3	−48	−49	−15
Reagan	3	−9	9	15	−19	−17
GHW Bush[3]	−1	−1	−1	0	2	−10
Clinton	−6	−6	−10	−65	−55	−56
GW Bush	−11	−8	0	−47	−43	−19
Obama[4]	−6	−14	−14	−45	−68	−68

Source: Gerhard Peters, "Seats in Congress Gained/Lost by the President's Party in Mid-Term Elections," American Presidency Project, 2015, http://www.presidency .ucsb.edu/data/mid-term_elections.php.

[1] four elections only; Truman begins in 1945 upon Roosevelt's death

[2] three elections only

[3] three elections only

[4] four elections only; term ends January 2017

For simplicity, Kennedy and LBJ are combined into one administration and Nixon and Ford into another. All nine administrations are eight years in length except Jimmy Carter and George H. W. Bush, who served only four years, and Barack Obama, who has served only seven years as of this writing.

The data tell a clear story: the electoral track record for the president's party is abysmal.[42] Using the most inclusive method (method 1), the president's party lost seats in the House and Senate during eight of the ten administrations. The average magnitude of loss is not trivial. In the Senate the average loss was 7.4 seats; in the House it was 36 seats. Note that the net losses do not occur in one election; they accumulate over the five elections (three presidential and two midterm) that define a two-term president's tenure in office (or over three elections in the case of Carter and Bush 41).

The second method (column 2) is most relevant to assessing how a president's policies may have impacted electoral outcomes in the Congress. Using this method, the Obama presidency stands out as the most toxic to the president's party since World War II. A similar insight emerges from the third method (column 3), which corrects for the fact that the election at the end of Obama's two terms has not yet occurred.

Using the first method the evidence suggests that a similar seat-loss pattern is occurring in both the pre-polarization (1952–1992) and post-polarization (1993–2013) periods. The post-polarization trio of Clinton, Bush 43, and Obama experienced an average loss of 6.7 seats in the Senate and 48 seats in the House (as of this writing Obama still has another election to go to complete this comparison).

If most of the losses incurred by the president's party are concentrated in the election at the end of his second term, then one might argue that the adverse party impacts are of little concern to the president. The opposite is the case. There are some losses in the last election, but they are relatively minor (Bush 43 is an exception) compared to the losses at the midterm elections.

Specifically, during the presidential administrations from Eisenhower through Obama, the president's party lost (net) a cumulative total of 325 House seats. A surprisingly modest net loss of 23 seats occurred in the elections at the end of the each president's service. (The two one-termers, Carter and Bush 41, were –35 seats and +9 seats in their reelection bids, respectively).[43] In the Senate the president's party lost (net) a cumulative total of 67 Senate seats. Of those losses, 18 were lost in the elections at the end of the president's service. Thirteen of those losses were during the two one-termers, Carter and Bush 41.

Some losses must be seen as inevitable (see chapter 10). When presidents win, they typically have coattails in Congress that dissipate over time. Presidents have tremendous difficulty living up to the (often excessive) expectations of voters, and their co-partisans in Congress bear the brunt of the disappointment. Perhaps frightened opponents of the president mobilize more effectively in reaction than they do in favor of their candidates. One point is for sure: presidents should not presume that, once elected, their margins in the Congress will improve over time—they need to "strike while the iron is hot."

The adverse historical experience also suggests that presidents need to find creative ways to pursue their policy agenda without unnecessarily hurting the electoral chances of their party in Congress.[44] The point is not that the president's party in Congress performs better in subsequent elections when the president is an ineffective legislative leader; the opposite is generally the case.[45] Nor is the point that the president should be altruistic toward the members of his party in Congress. Historically, a president's success rate with legislative requests is much higher when his party controls the Congress (and especially the House of Representatives) than when the opposing party has a majority in Congress.[46] Presidents need votes in Congress to pass their agendas, and because those votes are much more likely to come from members of their own party than from members of the opposing party, the president should assiduously avoid unnecessary controversy that might directly or indirectly curtail his party's strength in the Congress.[47] The prescriptions that follow are designed to help a president in both his role as party leader and his role as policy maker.

PRESCRIPTIONS FOR PRESIDENTIAL POLICY MAKING

In the design of domestic policy the president and his staff may consider the major problems facing the country, the range of possible solutions, and the merits and downsides of alternative policy choices. This might be considered the White House's policy-analytic role, where the president has the national interest squarely in his sights. While there is a legitimate role for policy analysis, the president's domestic policy agenda will also be designed with regard to its political appeal. In other words, the president utilizes his domestic agenda to advance his own prospects for reelection and his party's electoral performance.

Drawing from the building blocks established earlier in this chapter and in chapter 1, I suggest nine prescriptive propositions for presidential policy making in domestic affairs. Each proposition is aimed at helping the president achieve his goals in a polarized environment while protecting his party's electoral prospects.

1. The president should begin a four-year term with one or more initiatives that appeal to his base.

No president wins a general election contest without first winning his party's nomination. To acquire the nomination, the candidate competes in numerous primary elections and caucuses where party activists do the grassroots work for campaigns and comprise a substantial share of the voters.[48] In some states, independents and members of the opposing party are not even permitted to vote in a primary election or caucus.

As a result, the most loyal subgroups of voters and activists are predictable.[49] Democratic candidates for president focus on appealing to labor union officials and their members, environmental advocates, gay rights leaders, teachers, women's rights advocates, plaintiffs' attorneys, and African American and Hispanic leaders. Republican candidates for president focus their appeals on religious evangelicals, libertarians, businessmen, antitax enthusiasts, the affluent, pro-marriage and pro-gun activists, current and former military personnel, anti-immigrant groups, and senior citizen groups.

Party activists from the two parties are becoming more polarized over time.[50] They care about issues and they listen carefully to what candidates promise. Party activists may also be connected to donors, particularly donors who are sympathetic with the ideological stances of party activists. And party activists are often affiliated with single-issue interest groups (e.g., civil rights, pro-gun, business, or labor groups).[51] Thus, the priorities of the "political class" are different from those of ordinary voters, and they exert a disproportionate influence in political decisions.[52]

The behavior of presidential candidates, whether Republican or Democrat, during the nominating process is quite predictable: they generally take positions on issues that please the party activists, and activists seek to constrain (pin down) the candidates.[53] Indeed, a credible candidate for president is frequently a veteran party activist who later transitioned to the status of an elected official (governor or senator) before running for president.[54]

If presidential candidates do not cater to the preferences of party activists and instead espouse nuanced or eclectic positions, they risk losing the nomination to candidates on their extreme right or extreme left flank. Party activists are notoriously unimpressed by the argument that their presidential candidate should moderate his issue stances in order to appeal to the general public. Moderation may have advantages later, in the general election, but presidential candidates must first win the nomination of their party. And once presidential candidates have made issue pledges to party activists, they are expected—if they are elected—to lead, to work hard, and to deliver on those pledges.

As soon as a president is elected and seeks to govern, party activists are not bashful about reminding the White House of the president's campaign promises. Activists also confront the president and his staff, reminding them of how hard they worked for the president's campaigns. Thus, as the White House defines its policy agenda and works with Congress to enact the agenda, the White House tends to be quite sensitive to the viewpoints of party activists as well as donors and influential interest groups.[55]

The president's base-pleasing initiatives typically have their origins in pledges the president made during his campaign for election or reelection. As a president's campaign team is transformed into a presidential administration, his campaign pledges to his base should be given serious consideration as first-year priorities. And since there are multiple segments of a president's base with different interests, the agenda needs to have multiple planks that appeal to different interests. As explained above, the wishes of the president's base are expected to have disproportionate influence in the White House.

It may be impossible for the White House to honor all of the president's base-pleasing pledges, but presidents who take their bases for granted are vulnerable to primary challenges when they run for reelection. President Jimmy Carter was damaged by Senator Ted Kennedy's unsuccessful progressive campaign for the Democratic presidential nomination in 1980. Conservative Patrick Buchanan damaged George H. W. Bush's 1992 reelection prospects by exposing Bush's vulnerability among conservative voters.

Politically, the president's first order of business in domestic policy is to deliver—or at least try to deliver—in significant ways for his base. Without such efforts (and preferably victories), the president's viability as a politician may be short-lived.

2. The president should begin a four-year term with one or more initiatives that appeal to centrists, especially initiatives that facilitate collaboration between pragmatists from both parties in the Congress.

Centrists in Congress often represent districts or states where it can be politically beneficial to be seen collaborating with members of Congress from the opposing party. If a Democratic president announces a legislative priority that fosters bipartisan collaboration among centrists in Congress, it may be quite beneficial to centrist Democrats, since their constituents will see them working with Republican members of Congress and they can tout their bipartisan accomplishments at home. Alternatively, if the White House advances only progressive (or only conservative) initiatives, the centrist members of the president's party in Congress may have little to run on when they make their case at home for reelection.

Does this mean that President Obama was required to include some initiatives that appealed to mainstream conservative Republicans? No. Regardless of what Obama does, a high proportion of conservative Republicans vote for Republican candidates for president and Congress. A proposal that appeals to centrists in the two parties does not necessarily have to appeal to conservatives or progressives.

Over time the president may need to adjust the ideological composition of his domestic agenda based on changing circumstances, such as how much of his initial agenda is accomplished and how his job approval rating is trending among different factions of his constituency. If the president's partisan adversaries are gaining traction by framing him as an ideological extremist, he may wish to complicate their framing task by making (or emphasizing) an ideologically centrist proposal. Likewise, if the president senses that his reputation among progressives is suffering and that he is vulnerable to a primary challenge from a prominent progressive, he may wish to make a highly visible progressive proposal to shore up his vulnerability. Thus, before each of his State of the Union addresses, the president should reconsider how his domestic agenda can promote his political standing and the popularity of his co-partisans in Congress.

3. The president should begin a four-year term with one or more legislative initiatives that have a high probability of enactment.

It is crucial for presidents to build some momentum early in a four-year term, since that momentum energizes the president's party while the opposing party is put on the defensive. One of the best ways to establish some early credibility and momentum is to persuade Congress to enact a legislative priority before the president's first midterm election and preferably during the president's first year in office. An early legislative victory is significant on its own terms, and it may also generate momentum, through enhanced political credibility, that can be translated into additional legislative successes.[56] When a president does not accomplish any of his legislative priorities before the first midterm election, his job approval rating may suffer, his base may become disenchanted, and his partisan opponents in Congress may be energized to engage in additional obstructionism. Thus, getting off to a victorious start in Congress is quite important for the credibility of the White House.

To garner the benefits of a good start, the president should select at least one legislative initiative that has a high probability of enactment. It is sometimes difficult to gauge whether a proposal is likely to be received favorably by Congress. Fortunately, clues are often available: votes in previous congresses on similar issues, established positions on the issue by influential interest groups, the inclinations of key committee chairs in the Congress, and strong indications of support or opposition from public opinion polls.

Unless the president's party enjoys a filibuster-proof margin in the Senate, a purely base-pleasing initiative is unlikely to have a high probability of enactment, since leaders of the opposing party can readily mobilize unified opposition. In fact, a president may need to choose an initiative with very strong appeal to some members of the opposing party in order to ensure a high probability of enactment in Congress.

In his first year the president can expect a high degree of unity from members of Congress from his party, at least with respect to one or two major legislative initiatives. But support from his party alone usually cannot get the job done. As a practical matter, a high probability of enactment means that some crossover votes from members of the opposing party need to be obtained, particularly in the Senate.

Much has been written about the fact that Republican leaders Mitch McConnell (Senate) and John Boehner (House) were determined to deny Barack Obama any bipartisan legislative victories.[57] In a polarized environment that is predictable behavior. The challenge for the White House is to advance some proposals that are so enticing to segments of the opposing party that the opposing leaders cannot accomplish 100 percent party discipline.

During the first year of George W. Bush's presidency, many Democrats in the House and Senate found it appealing to work with him on No Child Left Behind, presumably because Bush's K–12 education initiative resonated with values that many Democrats share and because Bush was willing to funnel more federal funds to troubled urban school districts represented by Democratic politicians. In some cases the president's partisan opponents in Congress may be reluctant to oppose a popular initiative. Both Ronald Reagan and George W. Bush found some Democrats eager to collaborate on popular tax cuts in their first years in office, even though the leadership of the Democratic Party in Congress sought to accomplish unified Democratic opposition. Thus, even though Congress is polarized, it may be feasible for the White House to attract some crossover votes from members of the opposing party.

Presidential lawmaking success prior to the president's first midterm election is certainly not an automatic boost for his co-partisans in Congress. It depends on the substance of the new laws, especially how the new laws are perceived by elites and voters. But an ineffective president is more likely to hurt than help his co-partisans in Congress.

4. When choosing a small number of legislative priorities, the president should favor those initiatives that cannot be accomplished with executive power and disfavor those initiatives that can be accomplished (in whole or significant part) through executive action.

In some situations a president has no choice but to seek legislative action to accomplish his policy goal. The president may need new appropriations or new legal authority from Congress; neither can be supplied with executive powers. Initiatives that require congressional action merit special consideration when the White House sets legislative priorities.

There are many situations where the president already has some relevant legal authority or some flexible appropriations or other means to finance a policy initiative such as a regulation of business or state and local governments. In such cases the White House has a choice as to whether the policy goal should be accomplished though legislative or executive action.

Since there can be only a limited number of White House legislative priorities at any given time, it is typically advisable for the president to proceed with executive action on those issues where executive power can accomplish all or much of his agenda. A White House legislative priority should typically be reserved for an issue that truly requires congressional action.

5. The president should lean toward executive over legislative action when legislative failure may hurt his job approval ratings or cross-pressure more members of his party than members of the opposing party.

Given a viable choice between executive and legislative action, the president should consider which choice would be superior for his job approval rating and for the electoral prospects of his co-partisans in Congress. Prudence in the

White House is warranted because (1) a failed legislative proposal can be harmful to the president's job approval rating, and (2) a failed legislative proposal may force members of the president's party to cast damaging roll-call votes without any benefit in terms of accomplishing his agenda. Thus, the president has incentives to avoid possible defeats in Congress in settings where executive action could have accomplished much or all of the president's policy goals.

Initiating policy change through executive action has a variety of other advantages: it may be accomplished with less "noise" (media coverage) than a legislative action, which typically requires high-publicity committee and floor action in both chambers of Congress; it may be accomplished faster or with higher probability than legislation; and it can be pursued without cross-pressuring members of Congress from the president's party, since those members will not need to take a roll-call vote on the issue. In fact, the president may prefer executive action precisely because some members of his party can be "released" to (or not punished for) publicly criticizing his initiative if that is electorally helpful among their constituents.

Thus, in some cases a prudent strategy may be to start with executive action and pursue legislation at a later point only if the executive policies run into trouble in the courts or prove to be insufficient, given the president's policy goals. Executive action is particularly appropriate when a relatively large number of members of Congress from the president's party are likely to be cross-pressured by legislative deliberations and voting. The president should not ask members of his party to "walk the plank" when he could have accomplished his policy goal with executive action. For example, a crucial issue in Barack Obama's presidency is whether he should have pursued climate policy via executive action instead of legislative action in 2009–2010.

Executive action is not a universal panacea. As discussed in chapter 1, executive actions are vulnerable to judicial delay or reversal. In unusual circumstances, opponents in Congress may muster sufficient strength to repeal an executive order or rule making through legislative action. Or a future president may reverse a predecessor's executive action. Moreover, when the president bypasses Congress through the use of executive power, the White House is vulnerable to the criticism that the president is behaving like a czar rather than a leader of a democracy. Thus, the advantages and disadvantages of executive versus legislative lawmaking need to be weighed carefully on a case-by-case basis.

6. The president, in collaboration with his allies in Congress, should consider carefully whether a legislative proposal should start in the House or Senate, making sure that members of his party do not cast controversial votes when passage of the proposal in the other chamber is highly unlikely.

The rules of legislative procedure require that some types of legislation originate in the House (e.g., tax legislation). In most cases, however, legislation can start in either the House or Senate. If the president's party enjoys a majority in both chambers of Congress, careful consideration should be given to whether a bill requested by the White House is passed first in the House or the Senate. In circumstances where a roll-call vote may be controversial and electorally sensitive for members of the president's party, he and his party leaders in Congress should make a thoughtful decision as to where the votes should be taken first.

Conventional thinking is that the more challenging chamber (usually the Senate, with its sixty-vote requirement) should act second. The theory is that a favorable vote for the president's bill in the House may help pressure a reluctant Senate into action. There are exceptions, however. If a bill is highly unlikely to pass the Senate, it may make the most sense to start in the Senate, thereby sparing House members a risky vote unless the Senate delivers.

The House-first strategy tends to be oversold because House action does not necessarily exert much pressure on the other chamber. Because of statewide jurisdictions, senators have different constituencies than House members. Senators also have different time horizons (since House members serve two-year terms rather than the six-year terms of senators). Moreover, the Senate is more responsive to the interests of the less populated regions of the country, since each state is provided two senators (regardless of the state's population). And senators, who tend to be more independent from the White House than House members, are not necessarily impressed with legislation that passes the House, even legislation that is seen as a White House priority.[58]

From the president's perspective, it may also be more important to protect his co-partisans in the House than his co-partisans in the Senate, assuming a controversial vote has to be taken in one chamber first. At each election only one-third of the Senate is at risk of defeat, whereas all members of the House are at risk of defeat at each election. Moreover, it is virtually impossible for a president to advance a legislative request through the House once the opposing party has a majority and has captured the key leadership positions (i.e., Speaker of the House, chair of the House Rules Committee, and so forth). Ronald Reagan collaborated with a Democratic House in 1981–1982, but in the new era of partisan polarization the prospects for such leadership collaboration are minimal.

The rules of the Senate are more flexible, and thus the president may be able to move a preferred bill through the Senate, even though his party is in the minority, assuming a filibuster threat can be overcome. In short, when a president's party has a majority in the House, the president should favor sequencing decisions that give special consideration to protecting his party's majority in the House.

7. The president may conclude, on occasion, that a legislative proposal is advisable, even if it is unlikely to be enacted by the Congress.

Making a legislative proposal may have political value for the president or his party, even if opponents can muster the votes necessary to prevent the proposal from being enacted into law. By making a legislative proposal, the president may honor a commitment to campaign supporters or signal sympathy to an important base constituency.

Another situation in which a losing proposal may have political value is when congressional voting on a proposal cross-pressures more members of the opposing party than members of the president's party. Under these conditions the president may choose to make the proposal in an election year, seeking to gain maximum political benefit by forcing an uncomfortable vote by members of the opposing party.

8. When seeking to attract (minimize) crossover votes from members of the opposing (president's) party in Congress, the president should target members representing states or districts where voting behavior was favorable (unfavorable) to him.

Legislative success or failure for the president hinges on minimizing defections from members of the president's party and attracting some crossover votes from members of the opposing party. The "pivotal" votes come from members of Congress whose identities are typically known well in advance of the vote.

Formal models of congressional behavior, including those that encompass a role for presidential influence, have highlighted the concept of "pivotal" members of Congress.[59] In the Senate, if members are ranked from most likely to least likely to vote for a presidential initiative, the member who would cast the 60th vote is considered the pivotal member, because it takes 60+ votes to overcome a filibuster threat. All members near the 60th position are likely to receive special attention from the White House, since they are also the members most likely to succumb to overtures from opposing forces in Congress.[60] In the House, where majority rule prevails on the floor, the pivotal member is at the median of the chamber's preferences, the 218th vote.

When Obama enjoyed his big Democratic congressional majority (2009–2010), he did not benefit from a large number of Republican senators who felt an electoral incentive to collaborate with him. Nonetheless, there were eight Republican senators representing states that Obama carried in 2008: Susan Collins and Olympia Snowe of Maine, Arlen Specter of Pennsylvania (who soon switched to the Democratic Party), Charles Grassley of Iowa, Judd Gregg of New Hampshire, George Voinovich of Ohio, Richard Lugar of Indiana, and Scott Brown of Massachusetts (2010 only). Seven out of forty Republicans may seem like a small pool of potential crossover votes, but the Obama White House did not need a large number of Republican votes in 2009–2010. There was no point in making policy concessions to ten or twenty conservative Republicans in the Senate when the Obama White House needed the votes of only a few Republicans to overcome a filibuster threat.

As the Republican Party profited from the backlash against Obama and gained strength in Congress (2011–2016), the president had a larger pool of Republicans to consider as possible crossover candidates. By then, however, the House of Representatives was no longer in Democratic control and thus Obama's chances of legislating were quite limited.

In general, one should expect the risk of defection from Obama's agenda to be elevated among those Democratic members of Congress who represent states where Obama's electoral performance was relatively poor in the most recent presidential election. As table 2.2 indicates, those senators are primarily from the South and Midwest. Note that several of those Democratic senators from GOP-leaning states were veterans: Max Baucus of Montana, Ben Nelson of Nebraska, Jay Rockefeller of West Virginia, Byron Dorgan and Kent Conrad of North Dakota, Mary Landrieu of Louisiana, and Timothy Johnson of South Dakota. Persuading these veterans to support Obama's progressive agenda was no easy task.

Table 2.2. "Pivotal" Senators in the Obama Years Based on Obama's
Electoral Performance in Their States in 2008 or 2012, Democrats

Name	State	Obama's Share (%)		Member's Vote Share (%) (Year)
		2008	2012	
Begich	Alaska	38%	41%	48% (2008)
Pryor	Arkansas	39%	37%	80% (2008)
Lincoln	Arkansas	39%	37%	56% (2004)
Landrieu	Louisiana	40%	41%	52% (2008)
Nelson	Nebraska	42%	38%	64% (2006)
Rockefeller	West Virginia	43%	36%	64% (2008)
Manchin	West Virginia	43%	36%	61% (2012)
Dorgan	North Dakota	45%	39%	68% (2004)
Conrad	North Dakota	45%	39%	69% (2006)
Johnson	South Dakota	45%	40%	62% (2008)
Baucus	Montana	47%	42%	73% (2008)
Tester	Montana	47%	42%	49% (2012)
McCaskill	Missouri	49%	44%	55% (2012)
Bayh	Indiana	50%	44%	62% (2004)
Donnelly	Indiana	50%	44%	50% (2012)
Hagan	North Carolina	50%	50%	53% (2008)

In the case studies in chapters 3 through 9, we should expect the senators listed in table 2.2 to play critical roles on multiple occasions. A similar analysis can be conducted for the 435 members of the House of Representatives.

The White House Office of Legislative Affairs should be expected to expend most of its limited energies on members who will cast pivotal votes. It is a misallocation of resources to devote large amounts of time on members who are highly likely to vote for (or against) a president's proposal. (An exception to this principle is key committee chairs; they merit sustained attention because of their special powers over the president's proposals). The White House is especially aware of which members from the two parties are seeking reelection in the near future and are likely to face serious opposition. Those members are particularly sensitive to how any roll-call vote might affect their probability of reelection, and the president should be similarly sensitive if the member is a co-partisan.

Table 2.2. (*cont.*)

Name	State	Obama's Share (%)		Member's Vote Share (%) (Year)
		2008	2012	
Johnson	Wisconsin	70%	68%	52% (2010)
Kirk	Illinois	62%	58%	48% (2010)
Scott Brown	Massachusetts	62%	61%	52% (2010)
Collins	Maine	58%	56%	61% (2008)
Snowe	Maine	58%	56%	69% (2014)
Heller	Nevada	55%	52%	46% (2012)
Grassley	Iowa	54%	52%	64% (2010)
Ernst	Iowa	54%	52%	53% (2014)
Gregg	New Hampshire	54%	52%	66% (2004)
Ayotte	New Hampshire	54%	52%	60% (2010)
Toomey	Pennsylvania	54%	52%	51% (2010)
Portman	Ohio	53%	51%	57% (2010)
Martinez	Florida	51%	50%	49% (2004)
LeMieux	Florida	51%	50%	Appointed 2009
Rubio	Florida	51%	50%	49% (2010)
Voinovich	Ohio	51%	50%	64% (2004)
Coats[1]	Indiana	50%	44%	55% (2010)
Burr	North Carolina	50%	50%	55% (2010)

Source: Michael Barone and Chick McCutcheon, *The Almanac of American Politics, 2014*, (Washington, DC: National Journal Group, 2013).

Note: Based on electoral data, table 2.2 reveals which senators the Obama White House should have seen as potentially pivotal on the president's legislative priorities. Among Republicans a promising source of crossover votes are those members who represent states where Obama's electoral performance was relatively strong.

[1] Years of service prior to the start of Obama's presidency in January 2009. Coats served twice; the second time began in 2010.

9. *The president should give priority to the public administration aspects of governance not only for the good of the country but also because good public administration reassures the public, protects the president's job approval rating, and indirectly protects the political welfare of members of his party in Congress.*

After winning a competitive general election contest, there is a tendency for the incoming president and his White House staff to focus their energies on overtly political matters. A danger of this orientation is that it may neglect the public administration aspects of executive branch leadership.

Many public policies do not accomplish their goals because they are not implemented properly.[61] Even when goals are achieved, the accomplishments may result from implementation strategies that are unnecessarily costly or that impose unintended side effects on influential stakeholders. Moreover, failures in public administration, though they may seem to be the responsibility of career-level bureaucrats, are often blamed on the White House, since the president is the leader of the executive branch. In a competitive, polarized environment, adversaries of the president seize on administration errors as ammunition to question the president's competence and drive down his job approval ratings.

When the federal government failed to respond effectively to the aftermath of Hurricane Katrina, the job approval ratings of President George W. Bush suffered. The point is not that Bush should have behaved as a public administrator rather than a politician. What Bush and his advisors should have done was to make sure that competent leadership was in place at the Federal Emergency Management Agency (FEMA). Competence may encompass political aspects, but it also involves expertise in the technical, communications, and managerial aspects of running a federal agency. The White House, even more so than Congress, is seen as responsible for making sure that a federal agency has the proper leadership, resources, and authority necessary for effective implementation of the president's policies.

THE BIG COMPLICATION: POLARIZATION

From the perspective of presidential policy making, polarization of members of Congress along partisan lines has some profound implications. In the House, growing polarization has helped the president's agenda when his party has a majority in the House, but polarization has damaged his success rate in the Senate, regardless of which party has a majority.[62] Thus, a danger for the president is that congressional paralysis and gridlock will become the norm,[63] which presents him with the dismal prospect of a slim legislative legacy.

Each newly elected president is tempted to perceive that he can work around the polarization. Bill Clinton and George W. Bush, both Southern governors with records of bipartisan collaboration, had grand visions of co-operative bipartisanship. They were ultimately proven to be overly optimistic as the reality of Washington politics set in.[64] Obama began his presidency with promises of transformational "post-partisan" leadership, promises he had difficulty delivering on due to the rise of the Tea Party and GOP unity.[65]

Previous bouts of polarization have occurred in American history, but they have tended to divide the parties on a single issue (e.g., war or tariffs) and for only a relatively brief period of time. The current bout of polarization, which began after the Watergate scandal in the 1970s and intensified around 1990,[66] has been nastier and longer than previous ones, has witnessed greater use of the filibuster threat in the Senate,[67] and has curtailed the number of centrist legislators.[68] There is no end in sight.[69] Exacerbating the polarization has been profound changes in the mass media, including the development of "partisan media" outlets and a fragmentation of outlets that permits listeners to have their prior beliefs reinforced on a day-to-day basis.[70] A key distinguishing feature of today's polarization is "conflict extension," meaning that the two parties are unified in opposition to each other on numerous issues rather than only a few,[71] and the emergence of the Tea Party has contributed to the conflict extension.[72]

Indices of ideology suggest that there is no longer much ideological overlap between members of Congress from the two parties.[73] In 2012, for example, no Republican in the Senate had a more liberal voting record than the most conservative Democrat, and no Democratic senator had a more conservative voting record than the most liberal Republican. In the House only ten Democrats had a more conservative voting record than the most liberal Republican, and only five Republicans had a more liberal record than the most conservative House Democrat.[74] There is some evidence to suggest "asymmetric polarization," which means the average Republican member of Congress has shifted further to the right (ideologically) than the average Democratic member has shifted to the left.[75]

Under such conditions of polarization (with party and ideology highly correlated), roll-call votes in Congress proceed with a clear pattern: most rank-and-file members of Congress vote in accordance with the wishes of their party leadership (or the wishes of the president, if their party occupies the White House).[76] On many issues a majority of the members of one party vote against the majority position of members of the other party. Party unity is rising as bipartisan collaboration among members of Congress is declining.[77]

The trend toward party unity in roll-call votes does not entirely reflect more ideological polarization; it also reflects each of the parties working together better internally as teams, regardless of issue content.[78] Members of Congress in the president's party know they must run on the president's record as well as their own record, which provides them a clear incentive to help the president succeed.[79] Compared to thirty years ago, members of Congress today are more inclined to want to support the leaders of their political party (and especially "their" president) and stay unified.[80]

Indeed, some members of Congress now fear that party activists may choose to condemn them for collaborating with members of the opposing party or, worse yet, with a president from the opposing party. Polarization has been exacerbated by new campaign groups whose mission is to fund primary challenges to incumbents who are perceived as too inclined to compromise. The Tea Party and other conservative groups, in particular, are eager to support a primary challenger to a Republican incumbent who engages in too much bipartisan behavior. Overall, the statistical risk of an incumbent member of Congress losing a primary challenge is quite small, but that is partly because incumbents cast votes to discourage such challenges. The adverse consequences of such a loss by an incumbent are devastating.[81]

Among incumbents who lose to challengers from the opposing party, there are numerous instances for which the losing incumbent makes a comeback in a subsequent election. Defeat in a primary is different. Once a sitting member of Congress is defeated in a primary by a less moderate candidate from the party, the member's career as an elected official is typically ended (i.e., the defeated member finds it virtually impossible to run again and be victorious), unless he or she takes the perilous path of switching parties or running as an independent. Thus, the consequences of defeat in a primary election are so damaging that incumbents are becoming extremely wary of engaging in acts of bipartisan collaboration that are likely to be criticized by party activists in their states or districts.[82]

Under these conditions, polarization has reduced the number of laws enacted by Congress, particularly laws addressing the critical issues facing the country. Even the most basic functions of the legislature, passing annual budgets and raising the debt limit, are caught in the paralyzing syndrome of polarization. The two parties in Congress now have chronic difficulty working out their differences and advancing compromise legislation. In short, "compromise" has become a very bad word in Washington, DC, a phenomenon that is exacerbated by the tendency of the media to cover politics as a boxing match, with the compromiser framed as a loser.[83]

The current pattern of congressional polarization is in sharp contrast to the era of Lyndon Johnson or even Ronald Reagan, when bipartisan coalitions in Congress were common and seen as a positive.[84] During those years the president could often reach out to members of the opposing party in Congress to help stimulate a bipartisan coalition or to acquire some of the critical votes needed to pass a presidential initiative.[85]

The presence of polarization does not mean that ideologically centrist members of Congress are an endangered species. Their numbers have declined, but the more important factor is the growing reluctance of members to collaborate with a president from the opposing party or with the president's allies in Congress. Thus, partisan polarization in Congress is a serious complication faced by a White House seeking to accomplish the president's agenda.[86] Fortunately, the White House is not completely helpless in the face of a polarized Congress, but leaders of the opposing party in Congress *should be expected to obstruct* while blaming the resulting paralysis on the White House.

OVERCOMING "OPPOSITION POLITICS"

If a president succeeds in persuading Congress to enact legislation, a credit-claiming opportunity is created for the White House.[87] Members of the president's party in Congress have an interest in making their president look good, if only because high presidential approval ratings by the public boost the reelection prospects of members of Congress from the president's party. No member of Congress is as important as the president in defining the public image of a political party, and thus the political incentives for loyalty to the president are significant among his co-partisans in Congress.[88]

On the other hand, members of Congress from the opposing party have a political interest in denying the president credit-claiming opportunities.

Indeed, when a president declares that a specific legislative proposal is a White House priority, that declaration can be expected to trigger partisan controversy and an even wider gap between the two parties on the specific proposal than otherwise would be predicted.[89] The intensification of partisan conflict due to presidential involvement has been shown to be stronger for some issues (e.g., social welfare, education, defense, health, and international affairs) than for others (transportation, agriculture, public lands, energy, and the environment), in part because members of Congress see a "bring home the bacon" character to the latter issues, which tempts members of Congress to defect from the party line.[90]

When congressional leaders of the rival party in Congress oppose a presidential initiative on partisan grounds, as opposed to ideological or substantive grounds, they are engaging in "strategic opposition."[91] Such opposition is rooted in a simple fact of political life: almost anything that makes the president look good is harmful to the political interest of the opposition party in Congress.[92] Strategic opposition to the president is particularly likely when the two political parties are competitive in Congress (i.e., neither party is dominant), when a congressional election will occur soon and is hotly contested, and when majority control of the House or Senate "hangs in the balance."[93] The stark reality is that it is simply not in the opposition party's interest for the president to succeed with his legislative agenda, regardless of the substantive content of the agenda.

When the president senses that leaders and members of the opposing party may engage in "opposition politics," the president is not helpless. A variety of strategies can be deployed to counter strategic opposition and dissuade some members of the opposing party from undermining the president's initiative.

Direct Outreach to Legislators, Recruiting the Best Sponsor

Direct communication between the White House (the staff and the president) and key legislators is essential. The White House may identify who they want as the champion of their proposal, discuss the matter with leaders of the president's party in Congress, meet with that targeted member and her staff, and discuss what the White House can do to persuade that person to champion the issue. Recruitment of a legislative sponsor may entail some cashing in on chits or offering some benefits in the future on unrelated matters.[94] The primary sponsor is typically a member of the president's party, but members of the opposing party may also be considered.

When the White House needs co-sponsors for their legislative priority, which is common, member-to-member communication in the Congress can sometimes be even more effective than appeals from the White House. Thus, once a legislative champion has been recruited from the president's party, the champion and his staff are tasked with reaching out to possible co-sponsors and supporters in both parties. Over time, some legislators build a reputation for being effective at building legislative coalitions, including bipartisan ones. The president cherishes the opportunity to collaborate with the relatively few members of Congress who are effective at building reliable bipartisan coalitions.

When the White House confronts opposition from leaders of the opposing party in Congress, it should not be assumed that rank-and-file members of the opposing party will also oppose the president. Members of Congress in both parties are quite sensitive to how well the president ran as a candidate in their district or state.[95] The White House can identify potential crossover votes by listing those members who represent states or districts where the president won the popular vote in the most recent general election.[96] If necessary, the list can be lengthened by adding districts or states where the president came close to capturing a majority of the vote. The length of this possible crossover list serves as a rough upper bound on the number of crossover votes that are "gettable" when an issue is polarized. That count can be compared to the number of possible defections from the president's party.

When crossover votes are needed to support the president, the White House may find it fruitful to reach out directly—via staff or direct presidential communication—to those members of Congress from the opposing party who might be enticed. But the direct approach, by itself, may not lead to support or even a definitive answer. The leadership of the opposing party typically works to discourage collaboration with the president or at least delay indications of possible crossover support. Additional techniques (described below) may be required to "smoke out" the position of a member of Congress from the opposing party.

Harnessing the Resources of Sympathetic Interest Groups

Some interest groups typically stand to benefit from a presidential initiative. One of the most promising strategies for the White House is to reach out quietly to sympathetic interest groups and collaborate with them in an effort to build support for an initiative in the Congress.[97] Interest groups already have established networks with legislators from both parties, and accessing those networks can be both effective and efficient for the White House.

A related technique is to reach out to opposing interest groups and discuss ways to modify the president's initiative so that the intensity of opposition softens.[98] Interest groups rarely want to be on the bad side of the White House, since they may need the president's support on another issue down the road. Thus, many interest groups work cooperatively with the White House to find a way through their policy differences.

Exploiting Unexpected Opportunities for Bipartisanship

Some presidential scholars argue that effective presidential leadership of the Congress primarily consists of exploiting event-driven opportunities that provide a window of opportunity for bipartisanship.[99] The unexpected event is typically a tragedy or crisis of one sort or another.

After the terrorist attacks of 9/11, a bipartisan opportunity was created for legislation to create the new Department of Homeland Security. Senator Joe Lieberman and (after some foot-dragging) President George W. Bush exploited the powerful public emotion of the terrorist attacks to reorganize the relevant agencies in the federal government.

The president typically needs to act promptly to seize the moment, as the window of opportunity may close quickly. Bush had a burst in his job approval rating after 9/11 that it made it difficult for congressional Democrats to oppose him on terrorism-related issues. But that burst in popularity was temporary and did not extend to many issues other than terror.

If leaders of the opposing party do not provide explicit or tacit support for the president after a crisis or tragedy, those leaders may become vulnerable to public criticism that they are being political obstructionists on an urgent issue that merits bipartisan cooperation. Thus, when US military forces are endangered abroad, the president can usually request—and receive—bipartisan support from the Congress to reinforce US forces. Unfortunately for the president, bipartisanship to address crises or tragedies occurs less often in domestic affairs than it does in foreign policy.

Going Public, the National Approach

The White House can try to mobilize public opinion nationally in support of a presidential initiative and expect the public to pressure Congress into action.

Among all politicians the president is best positioned to draw attention to a proposal, whether during a special radio, television, or Internet address or during his annual State of the Union address. Working with an expert communications staff, the president can conduct press conferences, grant exclusive interviews on television shows with high viewership (e.g., *60 Minutes*), and even schedule a televised address to the country on a specific issue.[100] Sometimes the White House plans a series of media events and speeches around the country to focus public attention on a proposal. The White House can also coordinate the speeches of cabinet officials and the vice president, thereby magnifying public awareness of the president's proposal.

This so-called bully pulpit strategy has been used effectively in limited circumstances.[101] Presidential rhetoric may be crafted to unite the public or inflame issue-specific or partisan feelings.[102] When an issue is salient and a proposal is popular, a "go public" strategy by the president can pressure an indifferent or reluctant Congress into placing the idea on the legislative agenda.[103] That process of "priming" the public, by spotlighting an issue, is different from persuasive efforts to change public preferences, which is far more difficult.[104]

Presidents, by going public, tend to have more influence on budgetary matters than on new lawmaking.[105] Even if the president was not a significant factor in a legislative victory, the bully pulpit can also be used—during or after passage—to take credit for legislation.[106] It is important, though, to consider why it is quite difficult for the president to change votes in Congress by changing public opinion.[107]

Public opinion on many issues is ephemeral and difficult to change in a short period of time. Presidents in particular do not have a strong track record of using the bully pulpit to change public opinion on major issues.[108] Many members of Congress reside in "safe" seats, which means they may not be influenced much by changes in public opinion. Even if the president can convert some undecided citizens to be favorable, the converted may not be motivated enough to contact their member of the House of Representatives or senator.

In the days when three television networks dominated the mass media, the White House could engage in some degree of message control. Today's fragmented media is more difficult for the White House to manage, especially since the newer media (blogs, talk radio, social media, and cable news) often carry immediate commentary that challenges the legitimacy of a presidential message. Critics may take the opportunity to challenge the president's motives for making a reform proposal or to question the president's intelligence or ethics.[109] When a president goes public, he actually invites and stimulates push-back, criticism, and opposition. And the president may not be a credible advocate on some issues, at least in the eyes of undecided voters.[110]

If a legislative idea is unpopular, there is a wealth of evidence that communications by the president are unlikely to transform the idea into a popular one.[111] George W. Bush's controversial proposal to privatize Social Security did not become more popular, despite extensive communications from Bush throughout 2005.[112] Ronald Reagan, often considered a much better communicator than Bush 43, also failed to accomplish privatization of Social Security with a "go public" strategy.[113] When presidential speeches do move public opinion, it tends to be on issues of foreign rather than domestic policy, since voters are less knowledgeable on foreign affairs, interest groups have less influence, and citizens and members of Congress are more likely to defer to the White House on international affairs.[114]

If a desired legislative reform is unpopular, the White House is advised to work discreetly with trusted legislators.[115] Under some conditions, going public on an unpopular issue may end up delivering a perverse legislative outcome (i.e., a policy less close to the president's preferred outcome than would have occurred if he had worked quietly).[116] Considering when to work quietly and when to go public is crucial if a White House is to maximize its influence on congressional deliberations.[117]

When a "go public" strategy fails to persuade enough members of the opposing party to secure enactment, the president can pivot to a "blame the opposition" message. By framing the opposing party as "obstructionists," the president can drive down the public image of the opposing party. Unfortunately for the president, messages from the opposing party may lead the public to believe that the president deserves some (or all) of the blame for a legislative failure.

Going Public, Targeted Local Efforts

Sometimes a legislator from the opposing party may need more than an invitation from the White House to be cooperative. The White House can stage a local media event in the member's district or state, possibly coupled with a presidential visit, during which the White House makes clear that the president is seeking cooperation from the member of Congress in question.[118] In

2001 George W. Bush put pressure on Democratic senator Max Baucus by visiting Baucus's home state of Montana and discussing publicly with local media how he needed the senator's support on tax cuts.[119] At the time, Baucus was chair of the Senate Finance Committee, and Bush was popular in Montana.

The tactic of using local media does not always work by itself, but it does turn up the heat on the legislator from the opposing party. If sympathetic interest groups also turn up the heat on the legislator, the probability of support increases further. George W. Bush was not a highly popular president on a nationwide basis, but he was popular in some states and regions. He repeatedly used local-media techniques and sympathetic interest groups to help recruit critical Democratic crossover votes for his initiatives.[120] In doing so, he simply bypassed the leadership of the Democratic Party in Congress.

Instead of Making the Proposal a White House Priority,
Let Some Influential Members of Congress Take the Lead

When presidents tout a legislative initiative as their signature effort and campaign around the country for its passage, they may make it more difficult for some members of the opposing party to support it. Sometimes, as noted above, it is preferable for the president to settle for operating "behind the scenes," without publicly associating himself with an initiative, at least at the early stages of legislative deliberation. This can be considered the "quiet" approach to attracting bipartisan support.[121]

Permit or Support Additions or Modifications to the Presidential
Initiative That Are Ideologically or Regionally Attractive to
Members of the Opposing Party

If the White House senses that the leaders of the opposing party may be able to unify their caucus in opposition to an initiative, they may authorize additions or modifications to the initiative that entice some defections from the opposing party. From 2001 to 2004 George W. Bush could not move his energy bill through Congress because of strong Democratic opposition in the Senate. In 2005 Bush supported an alternative version of the energy bill that included an ethanol mandate that appealed to senators from both parties from the corn-producing Midwest states. The ethanol mandate was not an ideal policy from Bush's perspective, but it proved to be effective bait to entice the support of a sufficient number of crossover Democrats in the Senate to pass the energy bill.

The White House looks closely for situations in which a member of Congress from the opposing party is engaging in strategic opposition to a proposal, which means the voters in that member's state or district would likely favor the president's initiative. Rather than accept defeat in Congress without a vote, the White House can force the issue by persuading the leadership in Congress to make the opposing member cast an unpopular vote. When the member seeks reelection, the unpopular vote will become ammunition for a challenger.

In the 2001–2004 congressional debates on energy, Senate majority leader Tom Daschle was framed by the Republican Party as putting the interests of the Democratic Party above the interests of his home state of South Dakota, due to his alleged failure to work with George W. Bush on an energy bill with an ethanol mandate. Daschle was defeated for reelection in November 2004, in part because his leadership of "opposition politics" in the Senate did not play well with his constituents at home.

Making adjustments to policy to attract votes is not always a good idea. The White House needs to consider whether the additions/modifications to the initiative are so unattractive that the initiative is no longer worth enacting. Moreover, if the additions/modifications are likely to cause many defections among members of the president's party, the approach is not advisable.

In summary, the White House is in a different branch of government than the Congress, but in order for the president to be effective in domestic policy, the White House must be able to persuade the Congress to enact some of the president's legislative priorities. Leaders of the opposing party can be expected to engage in strategic opposition, but the White House can act to complicate efforts at opposition politics. Without an effective strategy to counter opposition politics, the White House will be unable to overcome one of any president's biggest fears: gridlock in the Congress.[122]

KEEPING AN EYE ON INDEPENDENT VOTERS

Independent voters are defined in various ways: as voters who express no affiliation with either political party, who do not see themselves as closer to one party than another, who declare themselves as independent, or who do not always vote for candidates of the same party.[123] They are certainly not activists in the Republican or Democratic parties. As a group, independents often lack a coherent ideology and thus tend to focus on factors such as the personality of candidates, including their integrity, and on the incumbent's reputation for getting things done.[124]

Many respondents in polls who say they are independent are actually "leaners," meaning they vote for the same party most or all of the time.[125] Truly ("pure") independent voters are becoming a smaller share of the American electorate over time, but they may comprise 5 to 10 percent of general election voters for president.[126] Since the number of voters with self-reported Republican and Democratic affiliations is roughly equal, and since the president typically wins at least 90 percent of the voters affiliated with his party, the median voter in a general election is likely to be a self-declared, pure independent.[127]

In the 1970s the Democratic Party held a large advantage in party identification, but in those days party and ideology were not highly correlated. The Democratic advantage has steadily eroded,[128] in part because growth in the number of Southern Republicans has more than offset growth in the number of Northeastern Democrats.[129] This gradual process of "sorting"—in other words, Southern conservatives moving to the Republican Party and Northern liberals to the Democratic Party—is seen as one of the key explanations for the growing polarization in American politics.[130] In effect, the sorting process is pushing the Republican Party to the right (on military and social as well as economic issues) while the Democratic Party is being nudged to the left. Pure independents confuse the situation because they are more likely than a strong Democrat or strong Republican to lack a coherent ideology.

If there were no independent voters, then the general election would boil down to a contest of which presidential campaign can do a better job of turning out their party-affiliated and ideological voters. Some campaign strategists favor a focus on party-affiliated and ideological voters for a simple reason: pure independents are difficult to persuade.[131] They tend to have limited interest in politics; they tend to find bitter partisan disputes distasteful; they may or may not vote; and they are difficult to attract with pledges on the issues, because they lack a coherent ideological orientation and such pledges aimed at them run a risk of offending party activists and donors.[132]

As a president engages in partisan battles to move his agenda through a polarized Congress, he must keep an eye on his job approval ratings, especially among independent voters. Although poorly represented in Congress (as Congress is dominated by the two major parties), independents play an influential role during an incumbent president's general reelection campaign and in midterm election contests for Congress.[133] There are too many pure independents to ignore them, especially since the two parties are often equally balanced with party-affiliated voters.[134]

The challenge for presidents is to devise ways to appeal to independent voters without revoking or weakening the issue pledges they have made to party activists. Politicians may do so in part by echoing the concerns of independent voters in their speeches and campaign commercials, but without making specific issue pledges. Instead, presidents pledge efforts at uniting the country and working with both parties on common goals, since that is important to independents. The Obama campaign highlighted this focus: a fifty-state campaign strategy (signaling a concern for national welfare rather than a singular focus on battleground states) and promises of a "post-partisan" presidency.[135] Soon after his election, Obama made a variety of overtures to underscore his willingness to work with Republicans: he appointed two Republicans as cabinet secretaries (Robert Gates at Defense and Ray LaHood at Transportation) and attempted, without success, to recruit a third at the Commerce Department (Republican senator Judd Gregg of New Hampshire).[136]

Obama's efforts have a sound rationale: pure independents tend to prefer politicians who seem eager to work with both parties.[137] Insofar as a president develops a reputation for being honest, ethical, pragmatic, and capable of working with leaders from both parties, he has a decent chance of securing the votes of many independents when he is up for reelection.[138] On the other hand, the leaders of the opposing party in Congress know that independents like a president who gets things done, so their incentives for obstructionism are quite strong, especially if they can blame the gridlock on the president's poor leadership skill.

In summary, the president seeks bipartisan legislation not only to build a legacy but also to appeal to independents, since they find partisan fighting and gridlock distasteful. The leaders of the opposing party in Congress look for fights on the president's agenda, because if the agenda is stalled, the president's base will become frustrated and independents will become disenchanted with the president's leadership skills. Much is at stake in the battle to persuade the independents.

HOW DO LEGISLATORS DECIDE HOW TO VOTE?

Before we consider how effective President Obama has been in dealing with the Congress on specific issues, it is useful to consider the perspective of the member of Congress. How a member decides to vote on a bill is a topic of intense interest among political scientists and practitioners.

Four basic explanations have been offered: the member's policy preferences, the member's desire to enhance his chances of reelection, the member's desire to please her party leaders, and the member's desire to please the president.[139] The explanations overlap to some extent, but the Office of Legislative Affairs in the White House often seeks to tease them apart, in order to understand the member's sensitivities.

Preferences about policy may be rooted in an instinctual sense of what is right or wrong, in an explainable ideological preference, in the results of a staff-level review of evidence and opinions on an issue, or in a tendency of the member of Congress to respect the policy preferences of his constituents. The deference to constituent opinion may be with an eye toward enhanced popularity and reelection, or it may simply be the member's conception of proper behavior by an elected official in a representative democracy.[140]

A reelection motive for a roll-call vote could operate in a variety of ways: a desire to seek favor with individual donors or grassroots party activists, a desire to seek favor with interest groups that have political power in the form of campaign resources, or a desire to seek favor with segments of her electorate who cast important votes in tight district or state-wide races.

The desire to please party leaders in Congress may be related to reelection interests, since the party is a critical source of campaign funds and other campaign assistance, but there are other party-related motives as well. A member respected by his party may be more likely to obtain good committee assignments or be appointed committee chair; he or she may also find it easier to have one's legislative proposals placed on the legislative calendar for floor consideration.[141]

Party-oriented voting on issues is not simply a product of top-down pressure from congressional party leaders; it reflects (voluntary) recognition by members that if the party holds together on issues, the results will benefit rank-and-file members in many ways.[142] And members of Congress from the president's party see presidential successes in Congress as in their interest. As a consequence, the president and other party leaders have gained more power in Congress because rank-and-file members of Congress have seen value in strong party leaders.[143] In short, as polarization has intensified, members of Congress have become more sensitive about—and responsive to—the needs of the party.[144]

To create an extreme image of party-line voting, imagine this behavior on the floor of the House or Senate: members of Congress vote "yes" if the party leader's thumbs are up and "no" if the party leader's thumbs are down. Such nonthinking behavior may not be irrational. By taking cues from his party leadership (instead of studying and weighing the merits of each bill), the member can save valuable time and focus his efforts on other valued matters (e.g., constituent service, a committee role, or raising money for colleagues or for his next campaign). When party pressures are strong, the rank-and-file member may give relatively less weight to other voting motives, such as his policy beliefs or constituency preferences.

A member's desire to please or curry favor with the White House can arise for multiple reasons. Members of either party may wish to establish a good relationship with the White House so that they can later use that relationship to seek support for favored policies, budgetary considerations, or an opportunity to be heard on unforeseen future issues. When the president is popular in the member's district or state, an issue alignment with the president may protect or boost the member's popularity at home. If the member is of the same party as the president, she will view the president as a national party leader and thus see a good relationship as an avenue for additional campaign resources at reelection time. And the member will want to support the president because, by doing so, she boosts the legislative effectiveness of the president, thereby boosting the popularity of the president and his party.[145]

Statistical research on congressional roll-call voting indicates that a high level of presidential job approval helps the president secure passage of his legislative agenda in Congress, significantly so in the House and marginally so in the Senate.[146] The influence occurs with members of Congress from the opposing party as well as members from the president's party.[147] More recent research suggests that the president's job approval rating among his base voters is an even more important predictor of legislative success in Congress than his overall job approval rating.[148]

In light of the above, we should not expect President Obama—or any president—to be potent in his influence on the voting behavior of rank-and-file members of Congress. The preferences of the president are only one factor among several that a member of Congress will consider.

∽

In the case studies that follow in chapters 3 through 9, I explore whether President Obama and his administration accomplished the policy goals that he established. In the course of describing Obama's triumphs and setbacks, I also uncover whether he adhered to the nine-point prescription for presidential effectiveness described above. In the last chapter of the book, I return explicitly to these nine propositions in order to offer constructive criticism of the Obama presidency.

My ultimate aim is to show that President Obama might have accomplished even more of his policy agenda than he actually did while exposing the Democrats in Congress to less political damage than was incurred. Hard proof cannot be provided, at least not with case studies alone, but the theory building and cases together are exploited to offer an optimistic message: the president need not be helpless in the face of polarization or highly toxic to his co-partisans in Congress. This type of counterfactual reasoning sets the stage for providing, in the last chapter, some general lessons for future presidents.

3

PREVENTING COLLAPSE, STIMULATING RECOVERY

No new president since FDR has confronted a frightening economic crisis on the scale that President Barack Obama inherited at the onset of his first term. It was not apparent at the time, but the United States was in the midst of what we now call the "Great Recession." Most of Obama's key short-term policies did not emerge from his campaign positions. The Great Recession deepened so rapidly in the fall of 2008 that neither the Republican nor the Democratic presidential campaign had sufficient time to advocate well-considered near-term policies. Indeed, the gravity of the financial and economic crises of 2007–2009 was not apparent until the financial firm Lehman Brothers collapsed less than a month before voters cast their ballots for president in November 2008.

In this chapter I explore how successful President Obama was in delivering the short-term economic policies he believed were necessary to prevent economic collapse (in the form of a repeat of the Great Depression) and stimulate recovery of the economy. Although he was not able to enact all of the short-term measures he requested, his record in short-term economic policy was impressive. Deploying both executive and legislative powers, Obama took aggressive steps to ease the fiscal and economic crises that he inherited. The tools of both monetary and fiscal policy were employed, and although the causality questions will be debated for decades, the economy did recover gradually, albeit sluggishly, throughout his presidency.

With regard to the theory in chapter 2, readers are encouraged to consider the following issues in this case study: How effective was Obama in using the stimulus to reward his political base? Did the stimuli create any electoral cross-pressures for moderate House Democrats, and were all of the cross-pressures necessary to accomplish his agenda? Did Obama make adequate overtures for at least limited GOP support of his stimulus measures? And how well did Obama exploit his executive powers to supplement his legislative request for fiscal stimulus? Answers to these questions are pursued at the end of this chapter and in chapter 11.

I begin by describing what is currently known about the causes of the Great Recession and then trace the rescue of financial institutions engineered by Bush, Obama, the Federal Reserve Board, and the Congress. Then I explore how Obama reaffirmed "easy money" policy, in part by reappointing Ben Bernanke as chairman of the Federal Reserve Board. The chapter goes on to focus on Obama's efforts to persuade Congress to enact three fiscal stimulus packages: the first in early 2009, the second in late 2010, and the third request in 2011–2012. Finally, I examine Obama's bold use of executive powers to rescue General Motors, Chrysler, and their suppliers, along with his more limited measures to assist home owners who were struggling to meet their monthly mortgage payments. The conclusion of the chapter explores several counterfactuals and sets the stage for considering Obama's long-term challenge: how to accelerate long-term growth while reducing the rate of income inequality in America (covered in chapter 4).

CAUSES OF THE GREAT RECESSION

The period from December 2007 to July 2009 is called the "Great Recession" because it was the longest recession (eighteen months) since the Great Depression of the 1930s (forty-three months), much longer than the average duration of recessions (eleven months) in the post–World War II period.[1] The starting and ending points of a recession are typically defined based on monthly changes in the size of the national Gross Domestic Product (GDP), but the human suffering typically starts during the recession and extends for many months after it is over.

The official rate of unemployment has some flaws as an indicator of the degree of hardship, but it is watched closely by the political class and covered intently by the mass media. From a baseline rate of 4.4 percent in December 2006 (considered virtually full employment for the US economy), unemployment grew steadily during the Great Recession and continued to rise after the Great Recession ended until reaching a peak of 10.6 percent in January 2010. When the rate of involuntary part-time employment is added to the rate of unemployment, one obtains the overall rate of underemployment of human labor in the economy. It reached a peak of 20 percent in April 2010, suggesting that one in five adult Americans could not find the amount of work they desired. Of even greater concern was the elevated number of long-term unemployed (six months or more), which rose from a low of 1.09 million in December 2006 to a peak of 6.43 million in December 2010.[2] All of these figures are conservative, because when people are discouraged and stop looking for work, they are no longer counted in the official rate of unemployment. Thus, the extent of hardship was even greater than official figures suggested.

The events preceding the Great Recession include an initial spike in world oil prices, a correction in US housing prices, and a surge in the rate of foreclosures on home mortgages. Those events were followed by a financial crisis, disruptions of liquidity in financial markets, and abrupt declines in housing and auto sales. Layoffs ensued and both business and consumer confidence plummeted. The links between home prices, foreclosures, and the financial crisis are particularly important to appreciate, since those links help explain what happened and why the ensuing recovery was so slow.[3]

From the late 1990s to 2006, home prices in the United States, adjusted for inflation, climbed an average of 85 percent, while more than doubling in some cities (Minneapolis, Naples, Phoenix, Sacramento, Salt Lake City, and Tucson). Rates of home ownership climbed rapidly during this period, often financed through large mortgages with zero or small down payments, weak income verification, and interest rate schemes that put the squeeze on households a few years after purchase. Mortgage brokers were being compensated based on the number of mortgages written, not for minimizing risk or future defaults.[4]

Once written, mortgages were bundled together, securitized (made tradable), and sold to investors around the world with little disclosure of risk. Many of the transactions occurred at relatively large unregulated financial institutions such as investment and commercial banks, real estate investment trusts, hedge funds, and money market funds.[5] Meanwhile, the government-sponsored insurers of secondary mortgages, Fannie Mae and Freddie Mac, were exempt from typical capital-reserve requirements and seemed to be more focused on expanding home ownership rates in low-income and minority communities than in ensuring the safety and soundness of the housing finance system.

Rating agencies were not of much assistance. They were assigning triple-A ratings to mortgage securities that were later shown to be quite risky.[6] And they were earning consulting fees from clients the rating agencies were supposed to be evaluating for risk, a clear conflict of interest.

This basic story is widely understood now, but in 2000–2006 warnings about the interaction of these developments were rare on Wall Street, in Washington, DC, and in academia. Housing prices had increased for decades and were expected to continue their upward march, so there seemed to be little cause for worry.

When the unexpected correction in housing prices began in 2006–2007, a rapid proliferation in mortgage foreclosures occurred around the country. Simply put, families could not afford to make their mortgage payments, and the strategy of borrowing against the rising value of their home was no longer viable. Losses mounted rapidly at banks and other financial institutions. Before Washington policy makers fully realized it, the entire financial system—in both the United States and abroad—came under severe stress, as exemplified by the demise of Lehman Brothers weeks before the 2008 presidential election. It was the largest bankruptcy filing in the history of the United States.

OBAMA'S RELIEF FOR WALL STREET

As the financial sector began to collapse, the cries for help from Wall Street were louder than they have been since the 1930s. A plan called the Troubled Asset Relief Program (TARP) was hastily put together by the Bush administration. The basic aim was to provide the Department of the Treasury $700 billion in liquidity that could be used to rescue otherwise viable financial institutions.[7]

Members of Congress were in no mood to subsidize Wall Street and had little confidence in a plan put together by the unpopular Bush administration. Initially, the House of Representatives voted against the package by a margin of 228–205. Republicans were opposed 133–65 and were joined by many Democrats who were offended by so much money going to protect financial institutions that had made bad investment decisions.

On the day of the negative vote in the House, the Dow Jones Industrial Average dropped 778 points (–7 percent), and similar losses rippled through stock markets throughout the world. President Bush and the Democratic leaders of the Congress pleaded with rank-and-file members to pass relief in a last-ditch effort to avoid a complete financial collapse. Four days later the House passed TARP—which had been sweetened with some popular tax relief and spending programs—on a bipartisan vote of 263–171. Action in the Senate was less controversial, as TARP passed 74–25, with opponents comprised of fifteen Republicans and ten Democrats.

A key feature of TARP would eventually lead to President-elect Barack Obama's being linked to the unpopular program. Monies were to be allocated for TARP in two $350 billion chunks, the second chunk allocated only after a presidential request of Congress and then only after Congress had been given fifteen days to deny permission.

Implementation of TARP proved to be extremely controversial. With hindsight, it certainly appears that the program served its purpose of stabilizing large financial institutions and boosting confidence on Wall Street.[8] But the process was not pretty. One large insurance company used TARP money to help finance millions of dollars in bonuses for corporate officers.[9] Obama's chief economic advisor, Larry Summers, was later quoted as saying, "Just wars have unintended victims and appropriate bailouts have regretted beneficiaries."[10]

Some of the initial TARP monies were simply used by banks to improve their balance sheets rather than to make more loans available to consumers. There was much second-guessing about why the Department of the Treasury rescued some institutions while letting others fold. Charges were made that too many funds went to foreign banks. And the high levels of executive compensation at some recipient banks sparked outrage. As stories about alleged mismanagement of TARP monies were spreading, the Bush administration made the unpopular executive decision to allow TARP monies to be used to bail out cash-strapped General Motors and Chrysler (covered later in this chapter).

Once the Bush administration had allocated the initial $350 billion, it was questionable whether Congress would approve release of the second chunk of funding. The public and Congress were much more interested in finding ways to help troubled home owners with their mortgage payments than in bailing out Wall Street. Before leaving office President Bush requested release of the second $350 billion, but Bush's credibility with Congress was at a low point.[11]

Behind the scenes, economic officials in the outgoing Bush administration were working closely with officials in the incoming Obama administration. When Bush made his request, President-elect Obama made it clear that he was supportive of the request, and he made calls to key members of the Senate to reassure them that the funds would be used responsibly.[12] President Obama later supported funding of a special inspector general to expose and punish misuse of TARP monies.[13]

Reflecting the widespread public discontent with TARP,[14] a measure was introduced in the Senate by Republican senator David Vitter of Louisiana to deny permission for the second installment of $350 billion. It was defeated 52–42 when a large majority of Senate Democrats voted together with six Republicans, in effect allowing Bush and Obama to begin spending the second $350 billion.[15] Nine Senate Democrats voted against Obama's plea to spend the monies.[16]

As a result of this action, the unpopular TARP program became as much a Democratic scheme as a Republican one, and Barack Obama became known as a defender of big Wall Street institutions. Rank-and-file congressional Democrats who voted for TARP had little trouble in November 2008, when they shared the ballot with a victorious Obama, but they wore the TARP vote around their necks in the difficult November 2010 midterm elections. The Tea Party story line on Obama's "socialism" often included his support of bank bailouts as one of the key points of evidence. Incredibly, surveys administered in July 2010 (four months before the 2010 midterm elections) revealed more Americans thought TARP was an Obama program (47 percent) than a Bush program (34 percent).[17]

The authority to expend TARP monies expired on October 2, 2010, but Treasury officials never tapped the full $700 billion. The big beneficiaries were banks ($245 billion), auto companies ($80 billion), and the insurer AIG

($68 billion).[18] While $470 billion was committed, some of the money began to be repaid (with interest) as Wall Street stabilized and the economy began to recover. By Obama's second term the Department of the Treasury reported that over 90 percent of the TARP obligations had been repaid,[19] and eventually the Treasury turned a profit on the bank bailouts.[20] Critics of TARP claim that the program simply facilitated big tax write-offs of losses at bailed-out firms,[21] but even some critics of TARP acknowledge that more TARP money was repaid to the Treasury than was ever anticipated.

THE BERNANKE-OBAMA COLLABORATION

As important as TARP may have been, the Federal Reserve Board (commonly referred to as "the Fed") was taking even bigger steps to restore liquidity and improve investor confidence. The engineer of the Fed's efforts was Ben Bernanke, an economist who was trained at MIT and Harvard and taught at Princeton before being appointed by President George W. Bush as a governor of the Federal Reserve System in 2002. In 2005 Bernanke moved over to the White House, where he served briefly as chair of Bush's Council of Economic Advisers. In 2006 Bush appointed Bernanke to succeed veteran Alan Greenspan as chair of the Federal Reserve Board, a nomination that was well received in the Senate, as only one senator—Republican Jim Bunning of Kentucky—voted against Bernanke's confirmation.

As it happened, Bernanke brought to the Fed a specialized line of expertise that proved to be quite helpful in the post-2007 period. He was a scholar of the Great Depression who clarified the role of "financial acceleration"—how a run on banks can turn a mild recession into a much more severe one.[22] Bernanke has acknowledged that he, like most experts, was slow to recognize the breadth and severity of the financial crisis, but he took dramatic unilateral steps toward the end of the Bush administration to avert a repeat of the Great Depression.[23]

The Federal Reserve under Bernanke pumped huge volumes of money into the nation's credit system by essentially expanding the money supply. He also supervised a smaller effort to support lending by consumers and small businesses.[24] During Bernanke's first term (2006–2010), the size of the Fed's balance sheet roughly doubled to an unprecedented $2 trillion. One result of the Fed's action was a sharp and sustained drop in interest rates, an outcome that played an important role in reviving the troubled housing and auto sectors of the US economy.

In theory the chairman of the Federal Reserve Board is independent of the White House, because the chairman does not serve at the pleasure of the president as a cabinet secretary does. And there is a long history of the Fed asserting its independence from the White House. On the other hand, the Fed chairman is appointed by the president for a fixed term of five years and cannot serve additional terms without renomination by the president and confirmation by the Senate. More importantly, the Fed chairman must constantly wrestle with members of the banking and finance committees of the Congress. It would be difficult for the Fed chairman to do his job if he were also under constant public criticism or questioning by the White House.

A fruitful collaboration unfolded in which Obama supported Bernanke's efforts to rescue Wall Street, ease the money supply, and raise investor confidence while Bernanke supported Obama's efforts at fiscal stimulus. In October 2008, before Obama was elected, Bernanke had already testified in favor of the need for a significant fiscal stimulus (i.e., some combination of additional federal spending and tax cuts). Indeed, Bernanke irritated Republicans with silence as to whether the Bush tax cuts should be made permanent.[25] But he ultimately went further than general support of fiscal stimulus and supported the effort at a large stimulus proposed by Obama and fashioned by the Democratic leaders in Congress.[26] As a result, the Bernanke-Obama collaboration produced a coordinated economic response to the financial meltdown: easy money at the Fed and fiscal stimulus by the Congress.

With Bernanke's term slated to end on January 31, 2010, Obama faced an important executive decision in 2009 as to whether to reappoint Bernanke to another five-year term. Bernanke was popular on Wall Street and well respected in the academic community, but he was a Republican and a holdover from the George W. Bush administration. There were plenty of qualified economists—some of them strong Democrats—Obama could have nominated: Princeton professor Alan S. Blinder, Janet Yellen (president of the Federal Reserve Bank of San Francisco), or his own economic advisor Larry Summers (on leave from Harvard).[27]

There was precedent for a president renominating a Fed chair who was affiliated with the opposing political party. Paul Volcker, a Democrat, was originally nominated by President Jimmy Carter in 1979 but was renominated by President Ronald Reagan in 1983 for a second term. And Volcker was controversial because his tight money policy—though seen as effective in fighting inflation—was also seen as exacerbating the painful 1980–1982 downturn.

In mid-2009, as the credit crisis appeared to be easing, the White House decided to announce President Obama's intention to nominate Bernanke for a second term. Bernanke's term did not expire until January 2010, but the White House saw political value in an early announcement, in part because it would be reassuring to markets and in part because it would offset some of the bleak near-term news about the deficit and the economy.[28] Some journalists speculated—brashly—that "Obama really had no choice but to reappoint Bernanke."[29] As it turned out, the White House had to work hard to secure Bernanke's confirmation.

Few paid much attention when the progressive Independent senator Bernie Sanders of Vermont and the conservative Republican senator Jim Bunning of Kentucky announced their intentions to oppose Bernanke's confirmation. What should have been noticed is that their rationales for opposition were rooted in popular sentiment.

The first major sign of trouble occurred at Bernanke's December 2009 confirmation hearing before the Senate Banking Committee. Committee chair Christopher Dodd of Connecticut indicated qualified support for Bernanke, but the senior Republican on the committee, Richard Shelby of Alabama, was sharply critical of the nomination (though he did not disclose his voting intentions). Ultimately the committee voted 16–7 in favor of confirmation, revealing more opposition than was anticipated.

Before the Senate floor debate, activists on both the left and right took aim at Bernanke's confirmation based on a perception that he was more worried about million-dollar investors on Wall Street than ordinary home buyers who could not pay their mortgages. On the right, the Tea Party attacked Bernanke as a champion of bank bailouts and pressed their case that the Fed should be abolished.[30] On the left, MoveOn.org initiated an online campaign against Bernanke's nomination for similar populist reasons (i.e., his focus on Wall Street instead of the welfare of "Main Street").

The second sign of trouble occurred in January 2010 when two senior liberal Democrats up for reelection in November 2010, Barbara Boxer of California and Russ Feingold of Wisconsin, announced publicly their intentions to oppose Bernanke's confirmation. Boxer and Feingold were reflecting the wave of populist sentiment against Wall Street that was revealed in the Democratic Party's loss of Ted Kennedy's Senate seat in Massachusetts. Bernanke was seen as favoring Wall Street over Main Street, and these senators, reluctant to be aligned with Bernanke, advocated a change in leadership at the Fed.[31]

Recognizing these challenges, the White House moved aggressively to save the nomination. A reluctant Harry Reid of Nevada, majority leader of the Senate, indicated publicly that he would support Bernanke, but based on a quick head count in his party, he determined that he might not have the necessary votes in his caucus. And since Sanders and Bunning were willing to put a hold on the nomination (threatening a filibuster), securing the nomination would require sixty votes rather than a simple majority.

To make a long story short, the White House secured the nomination through a 77–23 vote to limit debate on the Senate floor. The final vote on the merits supported Bernanke's confirmation 70–30. It was the narrowest confirmation margin in the history of the Fed. (The previous record of "nay" votes occurred in 1983 at Paul Volcker's 84–16 confirmation vote.) The seventy votes favoring Bernanke's confirmation were comprised of forty-eight Democrats and twenty-two Republicans. An additional six Democrats and one Republican voted to limit debate, per a White House request, but then voted against Bernanke's confirmation.[32]

In summary, although the Federal Reserve Board is technically independent of the White House, President Obama was an informal collaborator with Bernanke on a wide range of policies that were aimed at stabilizing financial markets and stimulating the recovery. Obama not only nominated Bernanke for a second term in 2009 but also deployed White House resources to secure his uncertain confirmation in the Senate. The result was six years of informal economic policy collaboration between Obama and Bernanke.

OBAMA'S FISCAL STIMULI

The Obama White House made three determined runs at fiscal stimulus: a successful one at the beginning of Obama's first year in office, another qualified success after the November 2010 midterm elections, and a third—unsuccessful—one in 2011–2012, during the run-up to his reelection bid. The largest, and least controversial, was the second one, since it was negotiated with the House Republican leadership and was passed with big bipartisan votes in the Congress.

Stimulus #1

Less than one month after being sworn in, the Democratic Congress responded to President Obama's request for a large fiscal stimulus, delivering a $787 billion package aimed at ending the Great Recession and stimulating recovery. The Congressional Budget Office (CBO) later upped the deficit impact of the package to $830 billion between fiscal years 2009 and 2019, with 50 percent of the fiscal impact incurred in fiscal year 2009 and 85 percent incurred by the end of fiscal year 2010.[33] The American Recovery and Reinvestment Act, commonly known as the Recovery Act, was a blend of spending and tax cuts, consistent with Bernanke's 2008 recommendation.

Approximately 70 percent of the package was new spending, including assistance to the states to pay for Medicaid, expanded unemployment compensation, grants to schools and colleges, funds for bridge and highway repairs, and food/health assistance for low-income families. The remaining 30 percent was tax relief, including general tax credits to individuals and businesses and targeted measures to promote renewable energy, energy efficiency, clean coal technologies, home and vehicle purchases, and plug-in vehicle purchases. Roughly three-quarters of the funds were to be spent within eighteen months, the goal being to put America back to work repairing the nation's infrastructure.

Much to Obama's dismay, no bipartisan recovery act emerged.[34] The White House catalyzed numerous opportunities for Republicans in Congress to get to know the president: dinners, parties, visits to Capitol Hill, and meetings in the White House complex.[35] Despite the dire condition of the economy, Obama's big win at the polls in November 2008, and multiple efforts by Obama to seek Republican support, no bipartisan bill emerged.[36] The Republicans practiced "opposition politics" (see chapter 2), thereby making the president and his fellow Democrats responsible for the consequences of the Recovery Act. When the final votes were taken, the Recovery Act was ultimately closer to losing the support of moderate Democrats in Congress than it was to attracting a significant number of Republican votes.

Obama did not start by making a comprehensive proposal. Instead, he gave Congress broad flexibility to design the package. He did call for a 60–40 percent split in new spending versus tax cuts (although House Democrats decided on more spending), and he indicated some policy preferences regarding the kinds of spending and tax cuts.[37]

The House Republican leadership was not necessarily opposed to a stimulus. A House Republican Economic Recovery Group met several times in January 2009, aiming to develop an alternative plan to what House Democrats were engineering.

Three days after Obama's inauguration, in a private meeting in the White House Cabinet Room, House Republican leader Eric Cantor handed out a one-page report titled "House Republican Economic Recovery Plan." It called for the following: (1) an immediate reduction in the two lowest individual income tax rates (affecting 100 million tax returns), (2) a tax deduction of 20 percent on income of all small businesses, (3) making unemployment insurance benefits tax free, and (4) a home buyer's credit of $7,500 for those who make a down payment of at least 5 percent of the value of a home. The House GOP plan stipulated that there must be no tax increases and that "any stimulus spending should be paid for by reducing other government spending."[38] Cantor did not commit to an overall size of the Republican stimulus.[39]

With the possible exception of the small business tax relief, Obama indicated that the provisions of the Cantor plan were not acceptable. The president objected to the income tax relief, because people who earn too little money to pay income taxes would not receive any benefit. Those people do pay Social Security and Medicare taxes, and they would benefit under the tax-credit approach that Obama and House Democrats were developing.[40] The administration was also concerned that tax cuts for higher-income taxpayers do not stimulate the economy, because those taxpayers are more likely to save the money than spend it.

Republican leaders in the House and Senate decided very early on that they would oppose the stimulus plan, in part for strategic political reasons (see the discussion of "opposition politics" in chapter 2), regardless of the precise content of the plan. On this account the Republican leaders did not necessarily believe they could stop the plan, but they could try to make Obama own it without any bipartisan support.[41] That was what their party activists, including the nascent Tea Party, were demanding.[42]

Reacting to a draft plan released by House Democrats, Republican minority leader John Boehner explained his concerns to Obama. The large size of the package would exacerbate the deficit, the public works projects were too slow and cumbersome to have a fast-acting stimulus effect, and many of the provisions were base-pleasing goodies for the Democrats rather than real stimulus.[43] Boehner was in effect warning Obama of the onslaught that occurred several months later: reports from conservative groups and members of Congress showcasing hundreds of cases of "waste" in the "Obama stimulus package."[44]

For moderate Republicans in the House, there may have been some temptation to vote for the stimulus, but the political danger of defection was also high. The Republican Policy Committee in Congress was apparently "taking names" of disloyal GOP members, and conservative groups were raising the prospect of primary challenges to any Republican defectors.[45]

When the House Democratic leadership tried to move the stimulus plan to the House floor, it became apparent that House Republicans were not the only source of potential opposition. A block of fifty-two "Blue Dog" (moderate) Democrats were worried about the plan, and a majority of them were planning on voting against it. If that happened, Obama would lose his first major legislative priority, since few Republican votes were expected.[46]

Democratic congressman Allen Boyd of Florida explained to the White House that the stimulus package was too big and included numerous items that were not really stimulus measures. He also wanted a "pay-as-you-go" (PAYGO) provision, which would mean that in the future Congress would have to finance any new spending programs with new higher taxes or cuts in existing spending programs.[47]

Obama agreed to meet with the Blue Dogs and some refinements were made to the plan, including a pledge to support PAYGO in the future. Their full set of concerns, however, could not be addressed. In the final House vote, forty-three of the fifty-two Blue Dogs voted in favor of the stimulus package, helping to deliver their new Democratic president his first major legislative victory.[48]

The original $819 billion stimulus package passed by the House was somewhat larger than the final $787 billion package. It passed 244–188, with no Republican votes and a total of eleven Democratic defections.[49]

If the stimulus was difficult to pass in the House, the Senate looked even dicier. Democratic senator Ben Nelson of Nebraska expressed publicly his concern that the House plan contained too much spending that was not really stimulus-related.[50] As a result, a somewhat different version of the Recovery Act was crafted in the Senate. And both Reid and Obama were eager for some GOP support.

Majority Leader Reid asked a bipartisan group including Nelson, Joe Lieberman, Susan Collins, and Arlen Specter to work on a streamlined version of the plan.[51] Collins insisted that the size of the stimulus be reduced significantly, that the amount of assistance to the states be reduced, and that the monies for construction of schools be deleted.[52] The somewhat smaller package garnered Nelson's vote, plus three crucial votes from Republican senators (Olympia Snowe, Susan Collins, and Arlen Specter). With the help of the Republican crossovers, the package overcame the filibuster threat in the Senate by a vote of 61–37.[53]

Since the House and Senate plans were different, a conference committee was formed. The final conference committee version, which was estimated to cost $787 billion, passed the Senate 60–38, again with support from the same three Republican senators and all Democrats. In the House it passed 246–183, with zero Republican votes and seven Democratic defections.

Up until the day before the final Senate vote, Specter of Pennsylvania, a state that Obama won handily in 2008, was elusive. Obama had spent weeks courting him, including an invitation to Obama's Super Bowl party and a one-on-one meeting with the president in the Oval Office. The Republican Senate leadership also wanted Specter's vote and made that clear to the senator. Specter ultimately indicated that he would vote for the stimulus, but only after being assured that the package would contain a large increase in cancer research funding at the National Institutes of Health. Specter's pro-stimulus vote was one of his last votes as a Republican. Three months later he made one of the rarest political moves in Washington, DC: he switched from the Republican to the Democratic Party.[54]

In some ways the 2009 Recovery Act was five landmark pieces of legislation combined in one bill.[55] First, it involved the largest tax cuts since the presidency of Ronald Reagan. Second, it contained the largest investment in infrastructure since the Interstate Highway Act of the 1950s. Third, it was the biggest investment in education since the first federal program launched during the LBJ administration. Fourth, it was the largest public research and development (R&D) infusion in forty years. Finally, it was the largest public investment in clean energy ever.

The Congressional Budget Office estimated that the economic impact of the Recovery Act was favorable but modest. By the second quarter of 2011, the GDP was 0.8 to 2.5 percent higher than it would have been without the stimulus. Between 1.4 and 4.0 million full-time-equivalent jobs were created; the rate of unemployment was 0.5 to 1.6 percentage points lower than it would have been otherwise. As intended, the stimulus was temporary, and its impact was barely detectable by 2013.[56]

Conservative critics of the Recovery Act saw something very different. The spending was seen as primarily base-pleasing rewards, with little stimulus rationale. The focus on temporary tax credits rather than a permanent reduction in tax rates meant the tax relief would do little to stimulate the economy in the long run.[57] The two most successful stimulus programs in modern American history—the first under Kennedy and LBJ and the second under Reagan—both included permanent reductions in the rates of corporate and individual income tax rates.[58]

When Obama signed the stimulus package in March 2009, a national survey found 54 percent of respondents favoring the stimulus and 44 percent opposing it.[59] Over the next year, public support deteriorated gradually as the public learned more about some of the details of the package and as the economic recovery proved to be sluggish. By January 2010 a national survey found 56 percent of respondents opposed to the stimulus and only 42 percent supporting it. Substantial fractions of the respondents perceived that much of the money was being wasted and had been included in the package for purely political reasons.[60]

For the White House the degree of public misunderstanding was distressing. Fewer than 10 percent of survey respondents were aware that they had received a tax cut from President Obama's stimulus policies. In absolute terms the tax cuts in Obama's first year were larger than delivered by any previous president, including Ronald Reagan.[61] The heavy emphasis on government spending in the Recovery Act helped fuel the emergence of the Tea Party movement, as it seemed to lend credence to the frame of Obama as a "left wing radical."[62]

In summary, the first fiscal stimulus was a legislative victory for Obama, as his cross-partisan strategy in the Senate succeeded. However, the extent of bipartisanship was not enough to lead the Republican Party to share political accountability for the consequences of the act. The package was highly controversial when it passed and became more unpopular over time.

Stimulus #2

The second round of stimulus was enacted in December 2010, soon after the midterm elections that resulted in Obama and the Democratic Party losing nine Senate seats and their coveted majority in the House of Representatives. Motivating the need for action was the scheduled expiration of the Bush tax cuts in January 2011, because the two parties were divided on whether to renew the cuts for everyone or to renew them only for households with incomes less than $250,000. Since the economy was sluggish in recovery, neither party was interested in the de facto tax increase that would result if the Bush tax cuts were not renewed at all.

At the direction of House Speaker Nancy Pelosi, the House passed (234–188) a plan to extend the Bush tax credits for all households with incomes under $250,000, consistent with the position President Obama was taking. But the plan was known to have poor prospects in the Senate, and it did not come close (53–46) to attracting the sixty votes necessary to limit debate and overcome a filibuster threat.

The Republicans were unified in opposition, and five Democratic senators defected from the White House position.[63] More importantly, all forty-two of the Republican senators informed President Obama in writing that no business in the lame-duck session would be permitted to occur until the Bush tax cuts were renewed for all Americans.

The Obama White House promptly cut its losses and negotiated a two-year extension of the Bush tax cuts, thereby ensuring that they would not expire until after the November 2012 elections. Republicans also won: two years of relief from the Alternative Minimum Tax, a large reduction in estate taxes, and some targeted business tax cuts. In exchange, Obama won a thirteen-month extension of unemployment benefits for the long-term unemployed and a temporary cut in payroll taxes from 6.2 percent to 4.2 percent. In the end the plan mushroomed into an $858 billion stimulus package, even larger than the one enacted in early 2009. The mix was $700 billion in tax cuts and $158 billion in additional spending.[64]

Despite some intense opposition in Congress from the far left and far right, the $858 billion package passed the Senate (81–19) and the House (277–148).[65] President Obama was clearly on the defensive, but he displayed agility in cutting his losses and getting a second stimulus for a fragile economy that was barely recovering. This was a rare case where, through rapid negotiations with the Republican and Democratic leaders in Congress, Obama accomplished a major bipartisan piece of legislation.

Stimulus #3

In September 2011, with the economy still anemic, President Obama proposed yet a third stimulus effort: a $447 billion "jobs bill" comprised of $272 billion in tax relief (largely payroll tax cuts) and $175 billion in new spending (e.g., public works projects, aid to states for public schools, and further extension of unemployment benefits). This time, however, he faced a Republican majority in the House and a smaller Democratic majority in the Senate.

The plan was considered dead on arrival in the Republican House, as it was widely seen as Obama taking an issue stance in support of his forthcoming reelection bid. There was certainly not much political value for Republicans in granting the president another stimulus victory less than a year before his reelection contest.

Even in the Senate, Majority Leader Reid faced a filibuster threat and thus needed sixty votes to limit debate and bring the plan to the floor. That motion failed miserably (50–49), as two Democratic senators (Ben Nelson and Jon Tester) joined all forty-seven Republican senators in opposition to limiting debate. Another two Democratic senators (Jim Webb and Joe Manchin) gave Obama their vote on the procedural issue but announced their intention to vote against the $447 billion plan if it came to a vote on the merits.[66] Thus, it is doubtful whether Obama's third stimulus package would have won even a simple majority in the Senate, since the Obama White House had no indications of any Republican crossover votes. What the president did win was a campaign issue to buttress his bid for a second term.

AUTO AND HOUSING SECTOR BAILOUTS

As the economy crashed in 2008, President George W. Bush worked with a Democratic Congress to rescue portions of the automobile and housing industries. Obama went much further than Bush in the auto sector, using executive powers in unprecedented ways to rescue General Motors and Chrysler. This section begins with the housing sector and then turns to the automotive sector.

Home Owner Assistance

Not appreciating the gravity of what was unfolding, the Bush White House started with "FHA Secure," a modest program designed to help home owners reset the terms of their mortgages. The program had limited impact because many troubled home owners could not meet the program's down payment and income requirements. Bush followed with another modest initiative, "Hope Now," aimed at encouraging market actors to set new mortgage terms for distressed home owners. The Great Recession deepened so rapidly in 2008 that it was obvious that more potent medicine was required.

Bush then reversed his earlier stance and supported larger lending authority for the federal government. When it became clear that Fannie Mae and Freddie Mac were going down (both companies lost 80 percent of their stock value from July 2007 to July 2008), Bush asked the Democratic Congress for unlimited authority to lend them money, including authority to purchase their stock, a position that some Democrats in Congress had taken much earlier. Unlike TARP, the resulting rescue of Fannie Mae and Freddie Mac proved to be a big financial loss for the federal government. Although this fiscal debacle did not occur on Obama's watch, it become intertwined and confused with the plethora of bailouts, loans, and subsidies that were executed in 2008–2009.

When Obama took office, mortgage foreclosures were continuing to proliferate. In March 2009 he announced a $75 billion plan to end the foreclosure crisis by keeping defaulting owners in their homes. The goal was to modify permanently the mortgages of at least three million home owners. Called the "Making Home Affordable Program," the aim was to modestly reward lenders when they modified the terms of mortgages in an effort to assist home owners. Financing came from TARP monies at the Department of the Treasury.

The program did not achieve its goal.[67] By July 2010 only 390,000 mortgages had been permanently modified. The program was crippled by weak oversight, conflicts of interest, and low rates of bank participation. When banks did play, they denied participation to many home owners on the grounds that they were not eligible for the program. After-the-fact studies found that some of these home owners were indeed eligible. It was estimated that only $4 billion of the original $30 billion dedicated to the program was spent. In March 2011 the Republican House voted to eliminate the program, but Senate Democrats, while irritated by Treasury's incompetent management, blocked the repeal effort.

In October 2011 President Obama announced a new effort to fix the program, including an explicit goal to help an additional one million home owners who might otherwise foreclose.[68] Implementation was slow, but by late 2011 housing prices had stabilized and the slow economic recovery was beginning to curb the number of new mortgage foreclosures.

Auto Sector Relief

One of President George W. Bush's last acts was a response to the grave financial difficulties faced by the Big Three automakers (General Motors, Ford, and Chrysler). Although these companies had been losing market share to the Japanese, Koreans, and Germans for many years, the severe credit crunch in

2007–2008 virtually shut off the availability of affordable car loans. Without a loan, most families cannot afford to buy a car. The national rate of car sales plummeted from a peak rate of seventeen million in 2006 to eleven million in 2008.[69]

In the second quarter of 2008 alone, GM reported a loss of $15.5 billion. And the company was rapidly running out of cash. Ford had much more cash on hand due to asset sales in 2006 but had incurred an $8.7 billion loss in the second quarter of 2008. Chrysler was in deep trouble as well and was predicted to be the first of the Big Three to declare bankruptcy, despite the efforts of the Wall Street firm Cerberus to save it. Conditions were so bad in the auto industry that even the profitable Japanese automakers were piling up red ink because of the credit crunch and the large dip in car sales.

The imminent failure of the Detroit-based automakers sent shivers throughout Wall Street, because the Big Three owed $100 billion to banks and bondholders. If the Big Three collapsed, the potential ripple effects were frightening: parts suppliers, car dealers, car financing firms, insurance companies, hedge funds, and pension funds were all at risk. Even if the Japanese, Koreans, and Germans could fill the void quickly with more cars and trucks, they have different supplier networks than the Big Three, and thus numerous suppliers linked to the Big Three might fold. The United Auto Workers (UAW), which represents workers at the Big Three and their suppliers, had already made major concessions to the Big Three in 2007 and yet were facing a potentially large loss of current members if the companies entered unstructured bankruptcy proceedings. The UAW was and continues to be a core constituency of the Democratic Party.

In the fall of 2008 the Big Three and UAW requested that Bush and Congress establish a loan program to help the industry (especially GM and Chrysler) weather the Great Recession. Ford supported the request—even though GM and Chrysler are competitors and Ford did not need a loan—because Ford shared a supplier base with GM and Chrysler. If the supplier base folded, Ford might fold as well. An initial industry request for $25 billion was later enlarged to $34 billion. And those requests were on top of $25 billion in low-interest loans that Congress had already authorized in 2007 to help finance "green" engines and fuels. The 2007 program, however, was restricted for use by financially sustainable firms, and the Big Three were not looking very sustainable.

Bush initially expressed skepticism but ultimately relented in the face of urgings from a wide range of advocates inside and outside the Bush administration. One of those advocates was President-elect Barack Obama, as Bush and Obama proceeded to build on previous auto-sector rescue operations by Jimmy Carter and Ronald Reagan.[70]

Bush began by suggesting that some of the $25 billion authorized in 2007 be redirected to help General Motors and Chrysler relieve their cash crunch. House Speaker Nancy Pelosi, backed by environmentalists, objected that these funds were intended for the development of green technologies. Pelosi countered that some of the TARP monies should be used for this purpose, but Bush saw those monies as dedicated for the financial sector.

As a result, the Bush White House worked with congressional leaders on a new emergency loan program for GM and Chrysler. A plan passed the House 237–170, with far more support from Democrats (205–20) than Republicans (32–150). President-elect Obama helped unify the Democrats.[71] Headwinds in the Senate were far stronger, and it was obvious that sixty votes would be required for such a controversial bailout. When the roll-call vote was taken, the plan fell eight votes short (52–35).[72] Senate Democrats supported the plan 42–4, but Senate Republicans opposed it 31–10. The opponents cited multiple reasons for their votes, but the fact that the plan did not call for significant concessions from the UAW was a contributing factor. And some opponents felt that GM and Chrysler deserved no special treatment and should enter regular bankruptcy proceedings. Among many Republicans, the idea of the government bailing out GM and Chrysler was deeply unpopular.

Facing a defeat in the Senate and urgent pleas from the industry, Bush agreed to allocate some TARP monies to GM and Chrysler, thereby ensuring that President-elect Obama had enough time to consider how the dire situation should be handled. The Treasury Department began with a $13.4 billion loan to GM and a $4 billion loan to Chrysler. Later Bush approved an additional $5 billion and $1.5 billion, respectively, for the lending arms of GM and Chrysler. And just before leaving office in January 2009, Bush's Treasury leadership started the process of opening up TARP monies for the faltering suppliers of the Big Three.

As Obama took office it appeared that GM and Chrysler had enough cash to make it through March 2009 but not much further. It was only a question of when the two companies would enter Chapter 11 bankruptcy proceedings.

In February 2009 President Obama's new Presidential Task Force on the Automobile Industry—an unprecedented White House entity—began to meet regularly and soon became involved in the day-to-day decisions of running General Motors and Chrysler. The task force reviewed financial and operational restructuring plans that would be implemented before, during, and after the two companies emerged from bankruptcy. Obama's view was that "the executives in Detroit were aware of the problems and chose not to deal with them."[73] His sympathies were with rank-and-file workers and consumers, who were afraid that the warranties on their GM and Chrysler vehicles might not be honored.[74]

In exchange for continued financial support of GM, the Obama task force set down some strict terms: the CEO of GM, Rick Wagoner, must be replaced; the company must enter and exit bankruptcy in a forty-day period; two thousand GM dealers would be dropped; the company would terminate all brands except for Chevrolet, Cadillac, Buick, and GMC; many preferred creditors would not have their claims honored; stockholders would lose all or most of their investment; and the UAW would not take an additional wage cut and would salvage most of their retirement and health-care benefits.[75]

The "new" GM that emerged from bankruptcy has been a profitable company. In 2013, for example, GM's worldwide profit was $3.8 billion, driven by a $7.5 billion profit in the company's North America operations that far exceeded losses elsewhere. Those results were good enough to trigger $7,500 profit-sharing checks to 48,500 GM UAW employees.[76] More profits at GM were reported in 2014 and 2015.[77] Although GM's turnaround has not been based on the smaller, more fuel-efficient cars that candidate Obama envisioned,[78] the corporation has been quite successful with its sport-utility vehicles (SUVs) and pickup trucks. The big question marks at GM have been its troubled operations in Europe, which persistently lose money and were not shed in the 2009 restructuring, and its limited profitability in China. Overall, when the Department of the Treasury sold its last shares of GM stock in late 2013, the company's stock price was at a new high of $40.90 per share.[79]

In 2009 Obama's advisors were divided on whether an effort should be made to rescue Chrysler. The company's new vehicle sales plummeted from 2.3 million in 2005 to less than 1 million in 2011.[80] Daimler had not been successful integrating Chrysler into its global operations and thus chose to sell the company at a loss to Cerberus, which was looking for a deal.

Obama insisted that Chrysler should be saved from destruction, a decision made much easier by the appearance of the Italian firm Fiat, which was looking for a merger to become a global automaker. Fiat was awarded minority ownership of Chrysler (with no cash payment) plus managerial control of the company, based on a complex restructuring plan that allowed Fiat to gradually assume 100 percent ownership if certain performance milestones were met.

Critics of the Chrysler bailout had plenty of provisions to complain about. The company's first-line secured creditors got only twenty-nine cents on the dollar; the second-line secured creditors got zero. The UAW incurred no wage cut and salvaged most of their health and retirement benefits. Fiat was compelled to launch a new fuel-efficient small car (what emerged as the Dodge Dart), even though the US market for small cars was intensely competitive and not very profitable.

The State of Indiana pursued litigation against the Chrysler sale on the grounds that the Obama administration and the bankruptcy judge short-changed the interests of preferred creditors, such as the pension funds for state teachers and police. The Supreme Court refused to block the sale of Chrysler on those grounds.[81] Five years later, however, the success of the Fiat-Chrysler merger has exceeded the wildest dreams of analysts, based largely on the sales of the Grand Cherokee SUV and Ram pickup truck. The merged company is now the seventh-largest automaker in the world,[82] and its North American operations are financially so profitable that they are compensating for Fiat's dismal performance in Europe.[83] The company is now selling more than four million cars per year worldwide, and the North American products have not yet—due to long lead times and capital constraints—fully benefited from Fiat's respected engine technologies.

It would be wrong to say that the American taxpayer made a net gain from the auto bailouts.[84] Even the Center for Automotive Research (in Ann Arbor, Michigan), which is a think tank sympathetic with the Big Three, estimates that the net cost of the bailouts of GM and Chrysler will be almost $14 billion. The same firm estimates that roughly 1.2 million jobs were saved in 2009.[85] The Bureau of Labor Statistics reported that the number of US employees working in motor vehicle and parts manufacturing actually rose from 624,000 (when GM filed for bankruptcy in 2009) to 822,000 in 2012.[86]

Politically, the auto bailouts were not harmful to Obama's reelection bid and may have helped win votes in the contested Midwest. At the time the bailout decisions were being made, surveys showed a clear majority of Americans opposing taxpayer support for GM and Chrysler. A late 2008 survey showed 61 percent opposed to taxpayer support, while an early 2009 survey showed that 54 percent of respondents thought the loans to GM and Chrysler were "mostly bad for the economy."[87]

Opposition to the bailouts, however, was concentrated among Republicans.[88] A majority of Democrats backed use of taxpayer support from the outset (55 percent in one survey). The majority opposition of independents was certainly a concern for Obama, but those views evolved as the practical ramifications of the bailouts began to be experienced. Not surprisingly, the overall level of opposition was much lower in the Midwest (53 percent opposed) than it was in the South or West. A detailed analysis of the disaggregated results would likely show that a majority of Democrats and Independents in the Midwest favored the bailout from the outset.

Surveys also show that opposition to the auto bailouts thawed over time.[89] By early 2012 (Obama's reelection year), the impacts on the economy were viewed differently (see table 3.1). From October 2009 to February 2012, the percentage of respondents perceiving the loans to GM and Chrysler as "mostly good for the economy" rose from 37 percent to 56 percent, while the percentage perceiving "mostly bad for the economy" fell from 54 percent to 38 percent. Politically, the favorable perceptions among respondents in the Midwest were particularly significant.[90]

In order to boost car sales, the Obama administration also worked with the Congress on the enactment of a new program that had been tried in several European countries: "cash for clunkers." Details of the programs vary, but the basic approach is for government to provide a financial incentive for owners of old cars to buy a new one. Sometimes the plans were used exclusively for stimulus purposes; in other cases they were used to clean the environment by replacing old, dirty cars with cleaner new ones.

The US Cash for Clunkers program was not a high-profile legislative priority of the White House, because it emerged from congressional initiative. The Obama White House quietly encouraged the congressional activity, as it was complementary to the efforts to rescue GM and Chrysler.

The House of Representatives passed a $1 billion Cash for Clunkers plan by a strong bipartisan vote of 298–119.[91] Fifty-nine House Republicans defected from the stance of their House leadership and voted for the plan. Only nine

Table 3.1. Public Opinion about the Loans to GM and Chrysler, 2009 versus 2012

Respondents	The Economic Effects of the Loans to GM and Chrysler Were Mostly:			
	October 2009		February 2012	
	Good	Bad	Good	Bad
Total	37%	54%	56%	38%
Republicans	23	70	44	52
Democrats	53	37	72	23
Independents	33	59	54	40
Northeast	39	51	66	27
Midwest	38	49	61	33
South	39	53	53	43
West	32	62	48	43

Source: Pew Research Center, "Majority Says Auto Bailout Was Mostly Good for the Economy," October 30, 2012, http://www.pewresearch.org/daily-number/majority -says-auto-bailout-was-mostly-good-for-economy.

House Democrats voted against it. The plan ran into trouble in the Senate, however. Republican senator Judd Gregg of New Hampshire objected to attaching the plan to a $106 billion war-spending bill that was moving through the Senate. Gregg's objection forced a sixty-vote margin on the procedural issue, and that proved to be a challenging task for the Senate Democratic leadership. With the assistance of the Obama White House, exactly sixty votes were found to overcome the procedural hurdle: all Senate Democrats (except for Ben Nelson) plus four crucial crossover Republicans: Kit Bond of Missouri, Thad Cochran of Mississippi, Susan Collins of Maine, and George Voinovich of Ohio.[92]

Once the plan was enacted, the US Department of Transportation received a flood of applications by interested consumers and the $1 billion fund was quickly exhausted. Consequently, Obama and the congressional leadership worked on a new measure to expand the program with an additional $2 billion. Once again, the plan passed easily in the House (316–109), but opposition was strong in the Senate. Sixty votes were found again (60–37),[93] but this time the defection of four Senate Democrats was overcome by the recruitment of seven crossover Republicans.[94]

The "Consumer Assistance to Recycle and Save" (CARS) program processed credits ($3,500 or $4,500, depending on the fuel efficiency of the new vehicle) for 401,000 cars and 275,000 light trucks. The average mileage rating of the new vehicles (24.9 miles per gallon) was significantly higher than the average mileage rating of the old vehicles (15.8 miles per gallon).[95]

Subsequent studies found that CARS did more to move up the date of vehicle purchases than it did to increase overall vehicle sales.[96] In other words, new vehicle sales were boosted temporarily, but after the program was terminated, sales were lower than they would have been if the program had never been adopted. Nonetheless, the earlier recovery of sales volume was seen as a positive in the depressed industry and further improved Obama's reputation as an ally of the automotive industry and its workers.

COUNTERFACTUALS

When his campaign positions were devised in 2007, President Obama certainly had no reason to foresee that his initial policy actions in January 2009 would focus on the rescue of failing financial institutions and auto companies.[97] Obama claimed that voters repudiated the economic policies of the Republican Party, but he had no electoral mandate for short-term economic policies.[98] Under the circumstances his track record enacting short-term economic policy should be judged as impressive.

Obama's deployment of executive powers in this period was masterful. He worked the informal collaboration with Fed chairman Bernanke to help forestall a repeat of the Great Depression, to boost confidence on Wall Street, and to lower interest rates enough to help revive car sales and home construction. He also secured continuity in monetary policy by helping win Bernanke's confirmation to a second term.

There is a plausible critique that Bernanke, Obama, and the Congress should have done more to help troubled home owners rather than focus primarily on Wall Street. None of the federal government's mortgage-assistance efforts were scaled appropriately for the scope and severity of the problems experienced by home owners.

Meanwhile, Obama's auto industry task force overcame the widespread cynicism that GM and Chrysler could not be saved. With an eye to the battleground states of the Midwest, the White House turned what seemed like unpopular auto bailouts into a political asset. Indeed, challenger Mitt Romney's repeated efforts in 2012 to attack the auto bailouts in Michigan and Ohio were unsuccessful.[99] It is notable that Obama's successes with GM and Chrysler were accomplished almost entirely with innovative uses of executive power.

Some Obama critics argue that the fiscal stimulus should have been much larger than it was, given the dire condition of the US economy.[100] Even some conservative economists now acknowledge that "increasingly [the Obama stimulus] appears to have been a poor match for the severity of the downturn and the magnitude of the required boost."[101]

It was not President Obama, however, who constrained the size of the fiscal stimulus, as Congress was given the flexibility to determine its size and he and his economic advisors certainly would have welcomed a larger one. The political reality is that the president barely achieved the sixty-vote margin in the Senate with a $787 billion package, and he could not have retained the votes of Nelson, Lieberman, Collins, Snowe, and Specter if the package had ballooned near or above $1 trillion. A much larger stimulus may also have caused even more dissension among the Blue Dogs in the House and thereby created bigger obstacles to House passage of the plan.

A different criticism is that Obama should have insisted on a plan for long-term fiscal constraint in conjunction with the short-term stimulus. Had he done so, some argue, he might have been able to persuade Congress to deliver an even larger short-term stimulus than was enacted.[102] The key flaw in this argument is that the fiscal stimulus needed to be enacted quickly. There was insufficient time to build congressional consensus on long-term deficit reduction measures, because the long-term issues around tax reform and cuts to entitlement programs are quite complex and politically sensitive.[103]

My major criticism of Obama's short-term economic policies is that he permitted the Democrats in Congress to sprinkle the $787 billion package with a variety of spending initiatives that were easily framed by opponents as base-rewarding measures with questionable stimulus effects.[104] (See, for example, my discussion of the federal subsidies to the solar energy firm Solyndra in chapter 4.) It appears that Obama's economic advisors tried (unsuccessfully) to discourage some of the spending measures.[105] Many of the measures did have a base-pleasing political effect, but the deeper political problem with spending so much money so quickly (through transparent governmental channels) is that it is easy for opponents of the White House to find examples of waste. And some of the embarrassing developments during Obama's first term, exposed by Republican senator Tom Coburn of Oklahoma, arose from questionable cases of spending under the 2009 Recovery Act.[106]

The "Obama stimulus" rapidly became unpopular—indeed a symbol of Obama's left-wing tendencies and another sword (after TARP) aimed at the hearts of moderate Democrats in the House—and this opposition did not thaw over time as it did in the case of the auto bailouts.[107] If instead Obama had insisted that most, or at least half, of the stimulus be accomplished through tax policy, he would have been less politically vulnerable on the choice of spending programs and would have made it more difficult for congressional Republicans to deny his collaborative overtures. To pursue this much different strategy, he would have had to persuade the Democratic leadership in Congress that both good economics and good politics justified a tax-dominated strategy—not an easy task, but one that might have worked better for the Democrats in the long run. Even if the GOP leadership in Congress had sustained unified opposition against a tax-dominated strategy, the Republicans would have had more difficulty turning public opinion against the package.

Looking back, the official data suggest that the condition of the US economy improved slowly but substantially during the Obama years. The recovery in GDP from the end of 2009 to 2015 was certainly not rapid. Indeed, it was the slowest on record: 11 percent below the average for recoveries since 1960.[108] An objective assessment requires consideration of a variety of economic indicators, as displayed in table 3.2.

The good news is that the economy grew steadily (if slowly) starting in 2010. The overall rate of unemployment fell toward prerecession levels and reached 5.1 percent in September 2015. Car sales rebounded impressively, and even housing starts began to show signs of life. There are no indications of inflationary pressures. By 2015 some well-respected economists were warning that the US economy would soon be overheated.[109]

Less impressive is the change in a key indicator of the job-producing performance of the economy: the "jobs-to-people" ratio (the number of adults employed divided by the total number of adults). Unlike the rate of unemployment, the jobs-to-people ratio is not influenced by whether adults give up looking for work and leave the labor force. The ratio peaked at 63.4 percent in December 2006 and plummeted to a low of 58.3 percent in December 2010. It recovered only slightly in the next four and a half years, and was recorded at 58.9 percent in December 2014 and 59.2 percent in September 2015. The number of people unemployed for six months or longer in 2015 (2.1 million in September 2015), though down substantially from its peak (more than 6 million), remained at almost double the number in 2006 (1.09 million, annual average).[110]

Table 3.2. Trends in Key Economic Indicators, United States, 2006–2015

Year	2006	2007	2008	2009	2010	2011	2012	2013	2014	2015
GDP Growth Rate (%)	2.7	1.8	−0.3	−2.8	2.5	1.6	2.3	2.2	2.4	1.8[1]
December Unemployment Rate (%)	4.4	5.0	5.3	9.9	9.3	8.5	7.9	6.7	5.6	5.0[2]
Number of Long-Term Jobless (millions)	1.09	1.32	2.61	6.12	6.43	5.60	4.77	3.88	2.79	2.10[2]
Jobs-to-People Ratio	63.4	62.7	61.0	58.3	58.3	58.5	58.6	58.6	59.2	59.3
New Housing Starts (M)	1.84	1.40	0.91	0.58	0.60	0.62	0.83	0.99	1.04	1.21[3]
Car Sales (M)	16.6	16.2	13.2	10.4	11.6	12.8	14.5	15.6	16.4	17.0[4]
Median Household Income ($K)	56.6	57.4	55.3	54.9	53.5	52.6	52.8	54.5	53.7	NA
Poverty Rate (%)	12.3	12.5	13.2	14.3	15.1	15.0	15.0	14.5	14.8	14.8
Consumer Price Change (%)	3.2	2.8	3.8	−0.4	1.6	3.2	2.1	1.5	1.6	1.6[5]

Source: Congressional Budget Office, "The Budget and Economic Outlook, 2015–2025" (2015), 140–41.

[1] Simple average of first three quarters. 0.6 percent, 3.3 percent, 1.5 percent

[2] October 2015

[3] September 2015 (seasonally adjusted annual rate)

[4] Forecast of Alliance of Automobile Manufacturers; www.autoalliance.org./auto-market place/sales-data

[5] Through September 2015

Even more disconcerting are the income data. The jobs that were created in the Obama years carried significantly lower wages than the jobs that were lost due to the Great Recession.[111] Median household income showed few signs of growth.[112] The Fed's Survey of Consumer Finances suggested growing income inequality. Average pretax income among the wealthiest 10 percent of families rose 10 percent from 2010 to 2013, while the bottom 40 percent of the wealth distribution experienced a decline in average pretax income. Median family income fell from 2010 to 2013 for every tax bracket except the top 10 percent of filers.[113]

In political terms the recovery from the Great Recession was too slow to help the Democratic Party in the November 2010 midterm elections (see chapter 10) and barely enough to allow Obama to defeat Romney in the November 2012 presidential election. The economy improved a bit by November 2014, but GDP growth in 2015 was unimpressive. Economists will debate for decades what President Obama and the Democratic Congress could have done to spur a stronger economic recovery. Obama may have faced more of a shortage of economic science than political science when it came to engineering a robust recovery.[114]

4

PROMOTING LONG-TERM
GROWTH, REDUCING INEQUALITY

President Obama's track record in economic policy was not confined
to the enactment of short-term measures aimed at averting a depression and
launching a recovery. He was determined to facilitate long-term economic
growth and reduce the extent of income inequality in America. What Obama
was not able to do was initiate some pro-growth legislative initiatives that were
appealing to congressional centrists in both parties, so appealing that they
overcame the natural tendency of congressional Republicans to oppose any
initiative coming from the Obama White House. As a result, Obama's strong
record of legislative accomplishment in 2009–2010 came to an abrupt halt
when the Republicans took control of the House in 2011 and the Senate in 2015.

In this chapter I examine the fate of Obama's long-term economic policies, specifically Wall Street reform, repeal of the Bush tax cuts for high earners, long-term fiscal policy (deficit control through reform of entitlement programs and the tax code), federal minimum-wage policy, free-trade policy, and

regulatory reform. Obama did have significant accomplishments in long-term economic policy, but his track record in that area was much more mixed than it was in short-term economic policy (see chapter 3).

With regard to the theory in chapter 2, readers are encouraged to consider the following issues: How well did Obama deliver for his progressive base on Wall Street reform, repeal of the Bush tax cuts for high earners, and increased federal revenue from corporate tax reform? Was Obama wise to frame fiscal discipline as a key policy goal during the economic recovery? Why were Republican leaders in Congress willing to collaborate with Obama on fast-track trade authority but not on a higher federal minimum wage? Should Obama have put moderate Democrats in the lead on a regulatory reform legislative proposal in 2009–2010 or 2013–2014? Those questions are explored at the end of this chapter and in chapter 11.

WALL STREET REFORM

Obama supported the bailout of banking institutions through the Troubled Asset Relief Program, but was more enthusiastic about a new legislative effort to rein in the Wall Street practices that were seen as contributors to the Great Recession. The animosity toward Wall Street was palpable and included Tea Party Republicans as well as progressive Democrats. Thus, Wall Street reform was engineered with general support from public opinion.

In June 2009 the Obama administration released an eighty-nine-page legislative blueprint called "A New Foundation: Rebuilding Financial Supervision and Regulation."[1] In a related speech calling for "a sweeping overhaul of the financial regulatory system," President Obama highlighted the "culture of irresponsibility" that had developed on Wall Street, including excessive executive compensation and the abuse of consumers.[2] He was particularly interested in a stronger regulatory system that would ensure soundness of the overall financial system. Among other provisions, the blueprint called for regulatory coverage of all financial entities (including hedge funds, money market funds, and venture capital funds as well as banks), a new bureau to protect consumers from financial fraud and poor mortgage practices, and mandatory cuts in the fees that banks may charge for debit and credit cards.

In Congress, Democratic senator Christopher J. Dodd of Connecticut and Democratic representative Barney Frank of Massachusetts assumed responsibility for leading the legislative effort. The "Dodd-Frank" initiative ultimately became a twenty-three-hundred-page law that is quite complex. More formally known as the Wall Street Reform and Consumer Protection Act, Dodd-Frank calls for the issuance of 533 new regulations, 60 studies, and 94 reports.[3] Nonetheless, the plan "closely resembles" the blueprint that Obama unveiled in June 2009.[4]

The pathway to passage of Dodd-Frank was by no means assured. Many Wall Street firms sought to derail the initiative, and the US Chamber of Commerce opposed it bitterly. Moreover, Republican leaders in the House and Senate joined their business allies in opposition to the plan. In collaboration with congressional Democrats, the Obama White House executed a classic "crosspartisan" strategy (see chapter 1) by attracting a limited number of Republican votes in the Senate combined with overwhelming Democratic support in the House and Senate.

The final version of the Dodd-Frank bill passed the House by a 237–192 margin. Only three House Republicans supported it; nineteen Democrats voted against it. Passage in the Senate required sixty votes. However, Democrats could not deliver sixty votes for the final version, because Senator Robert Byrd of West Virginia passed away before the vote and Senator Russ Feingold of Wisconsin voted against the bill, believing it was not strong enough. The key to passage was crossover votes from three Republican senators: Olympia Snowe and Susan Collins of Maine and Scott Brown of Massachusetts (who earlier in the year had won Ted Kennedy's seat in a special election). Interestingly, all three Republican senators represented states that Obama had carried handily in 2008.

Since it was passed less than six months before the November 2010 midterm elections, one might have thought that enactment of the popular Wall Street reform would have boosted the approval ratings of both President Obama and the Democrats in Congress. It did not have this effect, however, in part because of the complexity of the legislation and in part because of media focus on the current state of the economy and health care reform. Indeed, surveys showed that public understanding of Dodd-Frank was quite limited: 38 percent of Americans had never heard of it, 33 percent had heard of it but knew little about what the law entailed, and the remainder of Americans were divided about it.[5] The House Republicans might have garnered more political mileage out of Dodd-Frank than Obama did, since they made an issue of the burdensome regulations in the bill and raised campaign funds from investors who sought to simplify it.[6]

Federal agencies have run into some trouble in the courts trying to implement the Dodd-Frank law.[7] Several rule makings have been overturned on the grounds that the agency involved (typically the SEC) failed to perform required analyses or misinterpreted the statute.[8] It remains to be seen how damaging the judicial setbacks will be to Obama's Wall Street reforms.[9]

In summary, Dodd-Frank was a legislative victory for President Obama. In the difficult Senate, Obama combined a unified Democratic caucus with just enough crossover support from Senate Republicans to ensure passage. However, implementation of Dodd-Frank has been slower than anticipated, and the hundreds of authorized rule makings may not be completed by the end of Obama's second term.[10]

REPEAL OF THE BUSH TAX CUTS FOR HIGH EARNERS

Obama's pledge to repeal the Bush tax cuts for high earners was a signature initiative in his efforts to reduce income inequality. In order to appreciate why the repeal was so difficult to accomplish, this chapter begins with a brief review of the politics of the Bush tax cuts and then addresses Obama's handling of the issue.

In 2001 President George W. Bush persuaded Congress to enact a ten-year, $1.35 trillion package of income tax cuts. The Republicans had slim majorities in the Senate (50–50), as the vice president is authorized to cast the tie-breaking vote, and in the House (221–214); thus Bush chose to design a ten-year temporary "reconciliation" package (i.e., the tax cuts would expire if not renewed within ten years). Since it was temporary and adopted under rules of reconciliation, it bypassed the filibuster threat and required only a simple majority. Bush also worked hard to persuade some Democrats to support his signature initiative, since he knew that his support among some Senate Republicans was soft.

Bush did not negotiate with the House Democratic leadership but reached out to some of the Blue Dog Democrats. Twenty-nine House Democrats ultimately joined a unanimous group of House Republicans in passing the Bush tax cuts.

In the Senate, Bush made up for the loss of two Republican votes (John McCain of Arizona and Lincoln Chafee of Rhode Island) by attracting twelve votes from Democratic senators. John Breaux of Louisiana and Max Baucus of Montana played influential roles in building support among moderate Democrats. Bush, however, was never successful in persuading Congress to make the tax cuts permanent, and thus they were scheduled to expire in 2010.[11]

A key issue in the presidential campaign of 2008 was whether the Bush tax cuts should be allowed to expire or should be extended or made permanent. In the Democratic primary season both Hillary Clinton and Barack Obama pledged not to allow taxes to rise for individuals with incomes less than two hundred thousand dollars per year, but they pledged higher tax rates on high-income Americans. Candidate Obama was particularly insistent that the Bush tax cuts for high earners be rescinded in 2009, even before they were scheduled to expire (at the end of 2010). In the general election Republican nominee John McCain reversed his position as senator and campaigned to make all the Bush tax cuts permanent. Given Obama's decisive victory in November 2008, the expectation was that he would insist on repeal of the Bush tax cuts for high earners.

In the weeks after his victory but before his January 2009 swearing-in ceremony, Obama decided not to honor his campaign pledge, purportedly due to the fragile state of the economy. He indicated that he would delay repeal of the Bush tax cuts for high earners until 2010. This unexpected reversal led to an early public disagreement between Obama and his progressive Speaker of the House, Nancy Pelosi.[12] In the design of the 2009 Recovery Act, Pelosi's view did not prevail. All of the Bush tax cuts were retained.

The plot thickened in the summer of 2010 when former Federal Reserve Board chairman Alan Greenspan went public with a case for complete repeal of the Bush tax cuts. As a lifelong Republican and supporter of the Bush tax cuts in 2001, Greenspan's view stunned leaders of both parties. As expressed on NBC's *Meet the Press*, Greenspan said that fiscal discipline was a higher priority than the need for additional stimulus through tax cuts.[13] Although Greenspan's view did not have any direct legislative impact, it did draw more attention to deficit spending and the need for fiscal discipline.

Political fears led some Democrats in Washington, DC, to think quite differently from Greenspan. As the November 2010 midterm elections approached, Obama and the Democrats were acutely aware of the fact that the

Bush tax cuts were scheduled to expire soon after the election. The conflict between Obama and key congressional Democrats unfolded gradually.

Obama had begun the year by recommending that the tax cuts be extended for all taxpayers except for those with incomes above $250,000 per year (about 2 percent of tax filers). And the revenue ramifications were not trivial: ending the Bush tax cuts for high earners was projected to raise $678 billion in badly needed revenue from 2011 to 2020. In fiscal year 2010 alone, Obama was looking at a projected deficit in excess of $1 trillion.

Before the November 2010 elections, a small but growing cadre of Democrats in Congress began to question the wisdom of Obama's plan. More than thirty Blue Dog Democrats in the House urged Speaker Pelosi to support extension of the Bush tax cuts for all Americans. In the Senate one of the early signs of resistance came from Democratic senator Evan Bayh of Indiana, who had already announced his plans to retire after the election. Veteran Democratic senator Ben Nelson of Nebraska, who had voted for all of the Bush tax cuts, did not believe they should be rescinded. Perhaps most significant were the public stances of Democrat Kent Conrad of North Dakota of the Senate Budget Committee and Democrat Max Baucus of the Senate Finance Committee. They were also signaling that the White House should reconsider its position.

Sensing tough headwinds for Democrats in the midterm elections, Senate majority leader Harry Reid decided to set aside Obama's request for action and postpone floor debate on the Bush tax cuts until after the election. Pelosi reluctantly followed suit, wisely seeing little purpose in making vulnerable House Democrats take a difficult vote on a contentious issue when the Senate was passing on the issue.

The November 2010 elections were an earthquake for Democrats, as the party lost sixty-four seats in the House and five in the Senate. Although the Democrats were in disarray, they needed to act promptly, because *all* of the Bush tax cuts were scheduled to expire in January 2011.

In the House, Pelosi corralled Democrats into passing, by a 234–188 margin, a tax plan that extended all of the Bush tax cuts for households with incomes less than $250,000, as Obama requested. But the House plan died in the Senate (53–46), in part because four Democratic senators (Joe Manchin, Joe Lieberman, Jim Webb, Russ Feingold) defected from the White House position. More importantly, the forty-two Republican senators unanimously informed the White House in writing that—using the filibuster threat—no business would be conducted in the lame-duck session until the Bush tax cuts were extended for all Americans.

The Obama White House promptly reversed course, instituting a quick-concession strategy. Obama negotiated a two-year extension of the Bush tax cuts for all Americans. The bipartisan nature of the deal gave the president a needed boost in his low job-approval rating.[14]

The reversal annoyed progressives,[15] who began to fear that Obama was too inclined to compromise when the political heat was turned on. But Obama would have the last word, as he used his 2012 reelection campaign against Mitt Romney as a vehicle to shift political momentum against the Bush tax cuts for high earners.

In the Obama-Romney race a signature issue for Obama was a refusal to endorse an extension of the Bush tax cuts for households with incomes above $250,000. Obama did pledge that there would be no income tax increase for most Americans but, as a measure of his determination to increase federal revenue and reduce income inequality, he called for higher taxes on America's most prosperous individuals and households. Romney, on the other hand, called for not only a permanent extension of the Bush tax cuts but deeper tax cuts for individuals and corporations as well.

In the lame-duck session after the November 2012 elections, House Speaker John Boehner opted for a quick concession on taxes rather than a confrontation with a victorious Obama. In the ensuing negotiation, President Obama won an increase in the personal income tax rate from 35 percent to 39.6 percent for households with incomes greater than $450,000. He also won an increase in the estate tax from 35 to 40 percent for some taxpayers and a hike in the rate of taxation on capital gains and dividends from 15 percent to 20 percent.[16] Obama's payroll tax cuts were allowed to expire, but both parties were pleased to win permanent relief from the Alternative Minimum Tax. Obama, the Senate leadership, and Boehner also agreed to a two-month delay in cuts in spending at the Defense Department and other agencies.[17] Much to the dismay of House Republicans, the package included no additional cuts in social spending and no reform of entitlement programs.[18]

The postelection package passed easily in the Senate, 89–8, but Boehner had difficulty mustering Republican votes in the House. The package ultimately passed 257–167, with a 172–16 margin among Democrats but with opposition from a majority of Republicans (85–151). Boehner and Paul Ryan voted in favor of the package, but most of the Republican leadership and Tea Party Republicans voted against it.

The fate of the Bush tax cuts for high earners was a big issue for progressive Democrats, and Obama finally delivered a significant victory to them. It was the first time in more than twenty years that a tax-increase package cleared the Congress with significant Republican Party support.

LONG-TERM FISCAL POLICY

Under the George W. Bush administration, the Clinton-era budget surpluses vanished and were followed by eight consecutive years of deficit spending. The red ink in Bush's first term was attributable primarily to the 2000–2002 recession, the expensive operations in Afghanistan and Iraq, the Bush tax cuts, and the unrestrained growth of entitlement spending. In Bush's second term the annual deficits began to diminish as the economy grew, in part because of a surge in tax revenues. The growth in both entitlement and discretionary spending also slowed a bit. Nonetheless, the Bush years witnessed almost a doubling in the nation's accumulated federal debt, a fact that was emphasized in 2008 by Democratic presidential candidate Barack Obama.[19] Obama's campaign rhetoric in 2008 was that of a traditional fiscal conservative. His campaign website referred to the nation's debt as "a hidden domestic enemy." In speeches he lamented the fact that "we have become a debtor nation."[20]

The need for fiscal discipline was a central issue in the 2008 contest between Obama and his Republican opponent, John McCain. McCain pledged a balanced budget within four years, including an immediate across-the-board freeze in federal spending. Obama countered that a "scalpel" would be used to cut spending selectively to offset his spending initiatives—a "pay as you go" philosophy.[21] Obama also expected more revenue from repeal of the Bush tax cuts for high-income Americans while McCain was proposing even more tax cuts.

The Great Recession of 2007–2009 was disastrous for the nation's fiscal outlook. It was accompanied by a collapse in the flow of tax revenues to the federal government and an explosion of federal spending, primarily through the automatic operation of entitlement programs such as unemployment insurance, Medicaid, the Supplemental Nutrition Assistance Program (SNAP, or

Table 4.1. The Annual US Federal Deficit, Absolute Amount and Share (%) of the Gross Domestic Product, Fiscal Years 2006–2015

Fiscal Year	Amount of Deficit ($B)	Share of GDP (%)
2006	−248	1.8
2007	−161	1.1
2008	−459	3.1
2009	−1,413	9.2
2010	−1,294	8.2
2011	−1,300	8.0
2012	−1,087	6.5
2013	−680	3.9
2014	−483	2.7
2015	−439	2.5

Sources: Congressional Budget Office, "The Budget and Economic Outlook 2015–2025," (2015), 140–141; Julie Hirschfeld Davis, "Stronger Economy Cited as U.S. Reports Lowest Budget Deficit of Obama's Tenure," *New York Times*, October 16, 2015, A21.

food stamps), and Supplemental Security Income for the disabled. Obama's first major initiative, the 2009 Recovery Act, accentuated the surge in federal spending.

As table 4.1 indicates, the annual federal budget deficit ballooned at the end of the Bush administration and during President Obama's first term. The increase was from a prerecession low of $161 billion in fiscal year 2007 (about 1.1 percent of GDP) to a peak of $1.4 trillion in fiscal year 2009 (about 9.1 percent of GDP). As a share of GDP, the nation's deficits during Obama's first term were larger than they had been at any time since World War II. It was not until fiscal year 2013 that the recovery produced enough revenues to help the deficit decline rapidly, well below the politically sensitive $1 trillion mark. And President Obama's second term saw the annual deficit decline much further, to levels (measured as a percent of GDP) that are average for the post–World War II period.

To economic experts the near-term deficits were of far less concern than the long-term deficit problem that the Congressional Budget Office projected for 2020 and beyond.[22] Due primarily to the aging of the US population, a rapid growth of entitlement spending was forecast to outstrip the anticipated growth in GDP and federal revenues, resulting in ballooning federal deficits from about

2020 through 2040. Medicare was the big culprit, followed by Medicaid and, eventually, Social Security.

CBO had made the same dismal long-term projection during the Clinton and Bush administrations, yet Congress did not address the issue and in fact made it somewhat worse. Bush's outpatient prescription drug benefit to Medicare was added (with no dedicated revenue source), and the federal personal income tax was cut several times at Bush's request.[23] Thus, the long-term deficit problem that Obama encountered was a separate issue from the huge near-term deficits that were caused primarily by the force of the Great Recession and the temporary 2009 Recovery Act.

Ben Bernanke, chair of the Federal Reserve Board, argued that the near-term focus should be fiscal stimulus, without as much concern about deficit control, but there should also be focus on long-term deficits through reform of entitlement programs.[24] However, this was a complex message to communicate effectively to the public, as concern about the huge near-term deficits became conflated with the projected long-term deficits.

President Obama came under significant public pressure in 2009 to address the federal deficit issue, and he sought to dispel the impression that he might be a fiscally irresponsible politician. He promptly signaled that he was concerned about the size of the federal deficit and, in particular, the adverse economic impact of rapid growth in interest costs from the accumulated debt of the federal government.

In his first budget proposal, Obama called for a 50 percent decrease in the annual federal deficit by the end of his first term (fiscal year 2013). The target deficit of $533 billion (3 percent of GDP)—compared to the $1.4 trillion annual deficit he inherited from Bush in fiscal year 2009—would be accomplished largely by troop withdrawals from Iraq and higher taxes on the wealthy (including a repeal of the Bush tax cuts for high-income Americans). Obama's budget team was also assuming a significant recovery in revenues from a growing economy and savings from the scheduled expiration of the temporary stimulus package.[25]

As Obama sought to seize the high ground on fiscal issues, his credibility was tainted early in his first term. Under pressure from Majority Leader Reid in the Senate and Majority Leader Steny Hoyer in the House, President Obama chose not to stand behind a prominent campaign promise against earmarks.[26] He instead allowed his first budget to contain 8,570 earmarks for numerous purposes, totaling $7.7 billion.[27] Had Obama been able to reduce such earmarks, his credibility might have been buttressed.

The budget resolution crafted at Obama's request was another failure of bipartisanship. It passed the Congress with zero Republican support but only after some embarrassing defections on the Democratic side of the aisle. The House vote was 233 to 196, with twenty Democrats defecting; the Senate vote was 55–43, with Democratic senators Evan Bayh and Ben Nelson defecting. Thus, confidence in the Obama administration on fiscal issues did not get off to a strong start in 2009, especially when it became apparent that the administration—which was focused on the near-term economic mess—did not have a plan to resolve the country's long-term fiscal dilemma.

Thus, for much of 2010–2014 President Obama was drawn into a protracted series of deliberations on possible solutions to the long-term fiscal challenges that both President Clinton and President George W. Bush had sidestepped. Neither Obama nor the congressional leadership had any particular electoral mandate to solve the complex long-term challenge, yet enormous amounts of political energy were expended. The unfortunate result for Obama was disappointment, due to ineffectiveness, and diversion of political energy from more modest, yet plausible, pro-growth initiatives. It all began with pressure from an influential centrist from the president's party in the Senate.

PRESSURE FOR A BIPARTISAN FISCAL COMMISSION

One of the most respected fiscal policy experts in the Congress was Democratic senator Kent Conrad, chair of the Senate Budget Committee. In November 2009 Conrad met with President Obama to explain the urgent need for a grand fiscal deal to curtail deficits in the long run.[28] He explained that bipartisan momentum was building in Congress for creation of a fiscal commission to recommend a package of spending and tax reforms to tame the long-term deficit. Fed chairman Ben Bernanke was also supporting the idea.

There was plenty of reason for Obama to be skeptical of the commission concept. The Kerry-Danforth Commission established by President Clinton in the 1990s failed to persuade Congress to address the long-term-deficit issue. And there were several private efforts at bipartisanship that produced no tangible congressional action on long-term fiscal issues (e.g., the nonpartisan Concord Coalition for fiscal discipline).[29]

Despite the failure of previous efforts, a bipartisan commission bill in the House (cosponsored by Democrat Jim Cooper of Tennessee and Republican Frank Wolf of Virginia) was introduced in March 2009 and eventually attracted more than one hundred cosponsors.[30] Senator Conrad and Republican senator Judd Gregg of New Hampshire also developed a commission bill with more than thirty cosponsors, but Reid was not inclined to bring it to the Senate floor for consideration.

Conrad appealed for Obama's support, warning him that if his commission bill did not receive Senate floor consideration, then he and his bipartisan group of senators would not support the increase in the debt limit that was requested by the Department of the Treasury.

Conrad's linkage of spending to the debt limit was unusual, since Congress had raised the debt ceiling almost one hundred times without any link to spending. Indeed, most legislatures in the world do not vote regularly on debt limits, since annual legislative decisions on taxing and spending are seen as authorizing the necessary debt. Thus, the first pressure on Obama with regard to the debt ceiling came not from conservative House Republicans, but from a bipartisan coalition of senators led by a senior and well-respected Democrat.[31]

The commission bills in Congress called for an eighteen-member commission (including two members from the Obama administration) to issue tax and spending recommendations by the end of 2010, after the November midterm elections. If at least fourteen of the eighteen members agreed on a plan, the House and Senate would be required to take an expedited vote on the plan, with no amendments allowed. Passage would require sixty votes in the Senate and a 60 percent majority vote in the House. The departures from normal congressional procedures (e.g., reduce floor debate and diminished roles for relevant committees) were seen as necessary to address the severity of the long-term fiscal dilemma.[32]

The commission idea, though popular among centrists, drew significant opposition from interest groups on the left and right of the spectrum. The left feared cutbacks to vital government programs, fears that were registered with President Obama by a coalition of thirty national organizations such as the AFL-CIO, Progressive Democrats of America, NOW, NAACP, and the Alliance for Retired Persons.[33] The right feared tax increases, as explained by groups such as the Heritage Foundation and Club for Growth.[34]

The White House was sympathetic with the idea of a fiscal commission but preferred that it be implemented by executive order rather than legislation. That position pleased Speaker Pelosi, who was cool to the idea of a legislated commission.[35] Obama, however, ultimately supported a legislated commission, in part because of Conrad's insistence but also because of the stunning Republican victory in the contest in Massachusetts to replace the late Democratic senator Ted Kennedy.[36] The Tea Party was beginning to be heard in the White House.

Obama dispatched Vice President Joe Biden to work with the Senate on passage of a mandated commission. The sixty-vote threshold would not be easy to meet, because the commission idea drew opposition from both the left and right in Congress. Senate majority leader Harry Reid reluctantly agreed to bring the measure to the floor for debate, but some of his reasons for reluctance began to surface.[37] The first danger sign appeared when Democrat Max Baucus, the potent chair of the Senate Finance Committee, refused to support the commission. Baucus was an influential centrist in the Senate with a strong record of collaboration with Republicans. He was also a champion of Medicare and agricultural subsidies, neither a form of spending likely to be spared by a bipartisan commission on deficit control. More importantly, creation of a commission was likely to dilute the legislative influence of the key committees in Congress, and the Finance Committee has jurisdiction over the key tax issues that would be placed in the purview of the commission. The second danger sign was the reaction of Senate Republicans to Obama's reversal in favor of the commission. What was once a bipartisan initiative of Conrad and Gregg was now seen as an Obama initiative. If the commission passed and was successful, Obama could take credit for it and all of the deficit control that resulted. Moreover, it was hard to imagine that a bipartisan commission would not call for higher taxes as part of a fiscal package, and the antitax groups would be able to characterize any Republican vote for the commission as a vote for an Obama initiative that led to a tax hike.

When the roll-call vote was taken on Conrad-Gregg, the vote for passage (53–46) fell six votes short of the sixty required votes. (Republican senator Lisa Murkowski of Alaska, a supporter, missed the vote due to illness.) Twenty-three Democratic senators—mostly from the left of the Democratic caucus—joined an equal number of Republican senators in opposition to the commission.[38]

What transpired on the Republican side was a classic case of strategic (as opposed to ideological) political behavior. Six Republican cosponsors of the Conrad-Gregg bill (Sam Brownback, Mike Crapo, John Ensign, Kay Hutchison, James Inhofe, and John McCain) reversed their position and voted against passage. Senate minority leader Mitch McConnell also voted against the measure, despite having made public statements in favor of it.[39] As explained in chapter 2, strategic behavior of this sort is a form of "opposition politics," where the party opposing the president takes a position against the president precisely because they seek to obstruct what might be seen as a presidential accomplishment.[40]

The defeat of the legislative commission was a significant setback for Obama. He appeared incapable of marshaling enough bipartisan support for a good-government initiative, and the Republicans sidestepped a potential commitment to consider tax increases as a contribution to deficit control.

THE SIMPSON-BOWLES COMMISSION

Given the failed vote in the Senate, Conrad reluctantly supported what Obama had suggested originally: an executive order creating a bipartisan fiscal commission. The order was issued on February 18, 2010, and mirrored the Conrad-Gregg proposal with two key exceptions: there was no guarantee that the recommendations of the commission would receive a floor vote in the House and Senate, nor was there any bar to amendments during debate in Congress.

The order called for the commission to present its plan to the president and Congress by December 1, 2010, after the midterm congressional elections. The eighteen members of the National Commission on Fiscal Responsibility and Reform were to be selected by the president and the party leaders in Congress. In exchange for setting up the commission, congressional leaders agreed to pass a large increase in the debt limit from $12.394 trillion to $14.294 trillion. However, without any tangible progress toward deficit reduction, it was not easy to find the necessary rank-and-file votes. The House vote for passage was 218–214 (with thirty-nine Democratic defectors joining the unanimous Republicans), while the Senate vote was 60–39, as congressional leaders were forced to rely entirely on Democratic votes to raise the debt ceiling.[41]

As cochairs of the commission President Obama selected former Republican senator Alan Simpson of Wyoming and Erskine Bowles, former chief of staff to President Bill Clinton. Thereafter referred to as Simpson-Bowles, the commission met five times from April to September 2011. But the commission ran into trouble; its recommendations attracted the support of only eleven of its eighteen members, short of the fourteen required in order to submit the plan formally to the president and Congress.

The majority of the commission recommended a plan to reduce the deficit by $4 trillion over ten years. The plan included higher taxes (predominantly on wealthier taxpayers); elimination of many loopholes in the tax code (including the popular deduction for mortgage interest payments); and cutbacks in projected spending under military programs, Medicare, Medicaid, and Social Security.[42]

The seven votes against the commission recommendations were comprised of three liberal members (Andy Stern, former president of the Service Employees International Union, and Democratic House members Xavier Becerra of California and Jan Schakowsky of Illinois); three conservative members (House members David Camp of Michigan, Jeb Hensarling of Texas, and Paul Ryan of Wisconsin); and centrist senator Max Baucus.[43] Although five of six US senators voted in favor of the recommendations, only one of six House members voted to support the plan, and that supportive member (conservative Democrat John Spratt of South Carolina) was defeated in his bid for reelection in November 2010.[44]

Since the commission's plan did not achieve the required fourteen of eighteen votes, it was not submitted to Congress. President Obama, although under no obligation to respond to the plan, faced a political decision as to how to respond. Interestingly, he chose not to endorse the Simpson-Bowles recommendations or even to speak favorably about them. Indeed, his 2012 State of the Union address barely mentioned the commission, and his fiscal year 2012 budget contained only a few of the commission's recommendations.[45]

Obama's silence about the conclusions of the fiscal commission led to much criticism that he was more of "a typical liberal than a post-partisan reformer."[46] Conrad, however, believes Obama made the right decision, because any Obama blessing of the commission's recommendations would have made it more difficult for Republicans to consider and support them.[47] Alan Simpson agrees with this political analysis.[48] At the time, Obama perceived that the House would soon initiate a budgetary process that would inevitably lead to a negotiation on many of the issues addressed by Simpson-Bowles; thus there was little reason for the White House to reduce its flexibility in the forthcoming negotiation by taking a stance on specific recommendations.

Moreover, Obama had little incentive to endorse a plan that contained tax increases and controversial cuts to entitlement programs without any assurance that Republican leaders in Congress would join in the effort.[49] Obama had not campaigned on such a platform in 2008, had no mandate to propose such a plan, knew segments of his base detested the plan, and also was told—based on his party's recent debacle in the 2010 midterm elections—that he faced a difficult reelection bid in 2012, where fiscal issues would be even more hotly disputed than they had been in the 2008 contest against McCain.

The lack of political appeal in Simpson-Bowles was vividly disclosed on the House floor in March 2011 when the commission's plan was proposed as an alternative to the conservative budget plan put forward by Republican Paul Ryan. On the left, a potent coalition of interest groups led by the AFL-CIO and the National Committee to Preserve Medicare and Social Security called for rejection of Simpson-Bowles. On the right, the Club for Growth and Americans for Tax Reform signaled that a vote for Simpson-Bowles would count against a member's rating as a conservative.[50]

Simpson-Bowles was slaughtered by a vote of 382–38; only sixteen Republicans and twenty-two Democrats cast votes in favor of the plan. The only fiscal plan that received fewer votes than Simpson-Bowles was Obama's 2012 budget request, which Republicans debated on the House floor for political theater (it was defeated 414–0).[51]

Rather than rally around Simpson-Bowles, Obama seized on the opportunity to criticize the Ryan budget plan, which contained large cuts to entitlement programs and no new revenues. In one of the most awkward moments in Obama's first term, the president delivered harsh criticism of Ryan's plan without realizing that Ryan was in the audience.[52] Obama was able to energize his progressive base in opposition to Ryan, and that energy later proved crucial when the president entered his 2012 reelection dogfight against Mitt Romney.

Overall, though, Obama accomplished virtually no policy reform through Simpson-Bowles. He raised expectations that he would be a leader of long-term fiscal reform and then did not deliver on the expectations.

THE BIDEN DEFICIT CONTROL TALKS

After Democrats lost control of the House in November 2010, the Department of the Treasury became concerned that it might be difficult for

Congress to muster the votes to raise the debt limit in 2011. According to Treasury's calculations, the debt ceiling needed to be raised by August 2, 2011, or the government would have to stop making payments on the debt.

The Treasury Department explained to Congress that Treasury securities sit at the base of the global financial system and, historically, those securities were considered extremely safe.[53] If Treasury were to default, the reputational damage for the United States could be large, triggering catastrophic damages in the global financial system. Some Republican leaders regarded the Treasury view as a bit melodramatic, but most parties agreed that a halt to debt payments would be damaging to the credibility of the United States.

In February 2011 the White House faced massive negative publicity over OMB's fiscal year 2011 deficit estimate of $1.65 trillion, the largest amount in the history of the country. Measured against GDP, the estimated deficit share was 10.9 percent, the largest share since World War II. The CBO's projected deficit was somewhat smaller ($1.29 trillion) but still enormous.[54]

House Republican leaders made it clear to the White House that they would not support an increase in the debt ceiling without large reductions in the growth of federal spending. Thus, the technique that Conrad used to bring the White House to a bipartisan fiscal commission was now being used by House Republicans to bring the White House to restraints on federal spending.

In April 2011 President Obama delivered a speech wherein he outlined a process for achieving long-term deficit control.[55] Vice President Biden would chair bipartisan talks on the subject. Congressional participants in the talks included four Democrats (senators Max Baucus and Daniel Inouye and representatives Chris Van Hollen and James Clyburn) and two Republicans (Senator Jon Kyl and Representative Eric Cantor).[56] The schedule was to produce a plan by June 2011, allowing sufficient time for the House and Senate to debate and vote on the plan before Treasury's August 2 deadline. Biden indicated that his goal was to find $4 trillion in deficit control over ten years through a mix of spending reductions and revenue enhancement.[57]

At the second meeting of Biden's group, House Speaker Boehner addressed the group and made it clear that higher taxes were off the table. The Democrats were insisting that major reforms of the Medicare program were off the table. Progress in the Biden talks was slow, as much time was devoted to relatively small budget items such as agricultural subsidies and federal retirement programs. Experts doubted progress could be made, since several of the participants had already voted against the Simpson-Bowles recommendations and large amounts of deficit control were unlikely to be accomplished if revenues and health programs were off the table.

With the Biden talks consuming much of May and extending into June, skepticism about the process deepened, in part because the participants were working with a high degree of secrecy. Democratic senator Kent Conrad was quoted in mid-June as saying, "I'm concerned that they will come up with a plan that doesn't fundamentally change the trajectory of our debt but just gets by the debt limit vote."[58] Republican senator Bob Corker of Tennessee and Democratic senator Dick Durbin of Illinois showed public impatience with the Biden group, both requesting that Biden supply a report to Congress on its progress.[59]

The Biden talks collapsed in late June 2011 when the two Republican members pulled out of the process. Cantor explained that the group had reached an impasse over the tax issue, since, in Cantor's view, "there is not support in the House for a tax increase." He urged President Obama to forcefully lead the negotiations to a conclusion.[60] Democrats characterized Cantor as the culprit for blowing up the Biden talks, which they said had already found a pathway to $2 trillion in spending cuts over ten years.[61] Overall, though, the collapse of the Biden talks did not signal to the public that President Obama was in control of fiscal issues.

THE GANG OF SIX

Without authorization from congressional leaders or President Obama, six US senators began to meet informally throughout 2011 in an effort to develop a long-term fiscal plan. The effort was an outgrowth of Simpson-Bowles and included Democratic senators Mark Warner of Virginia, Dick Durbin of Illinois, and Kent Conrad of North Dakota; and Republican senators Saxby Chambliss of Georgia, Tom Coburn of Oklahoma, and Mike Crapo of Idaho.

Dozens of sessions were hosted at Senator Warner's home in Virginia. By May 2011 the group seemed to be struggling, primarily because it was difficult to bridge the divergent views of liberal Durbin and conservative Coburn. Coburn actually left the group in May in order to work on his own plan.[62] The "Gang of Six" exposed itself to harsh criticism from interest groups on the left and right, the latter fearing a recommendation for higher taxes and the former fearing a recommendation to cut vital government programs.[63]

OBAMA AND BOEHNER NEGOTIATE

Despite the rapidly approaching August 2 deadline, Speaker Boehner began negotiations with President Obama by expressing interest in a much bigger deal than participants in the Biden talks were discussing.[64] Boehner put on the table comprehensive reform of the tax code, reform of entitlement programs, and control of discretionary spending. Obama expressed the view that a grand deal might be easier to move through Congress than an incremental plan, a view that Boehner shared.[65]

Neither Boehner nor Obama was encouraged to negotiate by their apparent allies. Eric Cantor, with the support of many rank-and-file Tea Party members in Congress, tried to discourage Boehner from seeking a grand deal. They argued that a grand deal would only make Obama appear to be effective (prior to his 2012 reelection bid), and it was better to focus on defeating Obama in 2012 rather than make a grand deal with him.[66] By all accounts, however, Boehner was sincere in his effort to find a deal.

Democratic leaders in Congress feared that Obama was too inclined to compromise with House conservatives as he had in the December 2010 concession on extending the Bush tax cuts.[67] They also feared that the president was so determined to accomplish a big bipartisan deal that he might sign on to a plan that would be offensive to many rank-and-file Democrats in Congress.[68]

Significant progress was made in the negotiations, and the final offer from Obama to Boehner contained the following provisions: (1) $1.2 trillion in discretionary spending cuts over ten years; (2) $250 billion in Medicare savings over ten years plus an additional $800 billion in Medicare savings in the next decade; (3) a large cost-saving change in the cost-of-living formula used in Social Security; and (4) additional revenue of at least $1.16 trillion over ten years. The last Obama offer also included some controversial triggers (i.e., repeal of the Bush tax cuts for high earners and $425 billion in automatic cuts to Medicare and Medicaid) that would take effect if Congress failed to enact specified portions of the agreement.[69]

The last round of the Obama-Boehner negotiations was complicated by the unexpected release of an ambitious outline from the Gang of Six. That outline appeared to include more revenues than Boehner had included in his last offer to Obama, an offer that Boehner had thought the president was prepared to accept.[70] Obama upped the revenue requirements in his final offer out of a fear that Boehner's revenue offer seemed low compared to what the Senate Republicans in the Gang of Six were prepared to accept.[71]

In reality, the technical details of the plan prepared by the Gang of Six were never worked out, and their entire approach to revenue, which seemed to be based on a budget resolution model rather than definitive legislation, was developed without input from the chairman of the Senate Finance Committee, Max Baucus.[72] A budget resolution can define revenue targets, but the Senate Finance Committee (and its House counterpart) has discretion under a budget resolution to define how the revenues are raised. Thus, the specific revenue measures in the plan, which were part of the appeal of the plan to Republican senators, were of uncertain relevance. But there is no question that the release of the Gang of Six's plan, and the favorable reactions of dozens of senators from both parties, had an influence on Obama's final offer and indeed he went out of his way to publicly praise the work of the Gang of Six.[73]

Speaker Boehner ultimately phoned President Obama and called off the negotiations, indicating that the revenue goalpost had been moved too far and that it was better to seek a more modest resolution of the debt-ceiling dilemma. Obama indicated he was willing to return to a discussion of Boehner's final offer, but Boehner responded that it was too late to find a grand fiscal agreement. The failure of the negotiations was clearly a source of major disappointment to both men.

Although some press stories have suggested that Obama and Boehner were close to a historic deal, the reality is that it is unlikely that a deal would have ever been enacted. Significant doubt exists as to whether rank-and-file Republicans would have voted for a package with $800 billion in new revenues (Boehner's last offer), and many House Democrats would have had difficulty voting for the changes to Medicare and Social Security.[74] More importantly, it is not clear how much of Boehner's revenue offer was hard revenue as opposed to induced revenue based on the assumption that tax reform (with lower rates and a broader base) would increase tax compliance and stimulate the economy, thereby boosting revenues further. Boehner never offered an increase in tax rates (corporate or individual), although he did seem amenable to closing tax loopholes.

Boehner appeared to be assuming that Congress would accept a "dynamic scoring" approach to revenues that are induced by tax reform, an approach that accounts for the indirect effects of economic impacts on governmental revenue. The Congressional Budget Office does not typically employ dynamic scoring.[75] Many rank-and-file Democrats and their allies in the liberal think tank community were skeptical of the validity and reliability of dynamic scoring.[76] They saw it as "cooking the books."[77] Without dynamic scoring, it is hard to believe that Republicans in Congress would have even considered the magnitude of enhanced revenue that Boehner was offering.

The collapse of the Obama-Boehner talks was bad for both politicians, again since they raised expectations and then failed to deliver anything. The collapse seemed to provide further evidence that the government in Washington, DC, was dysfunctional, a perception that certainly did not strengthen President Obama's political hand. The more general implication is that it is not wise for the president to raise expectations on a big issue unless he can deliver.

SUPERCOMMITTEE AND SEQUESTRATION

Once Boehner realized that a grand fiscal deal with President Obama was not feasible or advisable, he initiated discussions with Senate leaders on how to proceed. What emerged, much to Obama's dismay, was legislation to propose another bipartisan "supercommittee" on deficit reduction. If the supercommittee process failed (either because the committee could not produce a plan or because Congress did not pass the plan), then automatic cuts in discretionary spending (defense and domestic) would be triggered. The theory was that the automatic cuts, so-called sequestration, were so distasteful to Republicans and Democrats that the supercommittee would have strong incentives to reach a deal.

The pathway to the "Supercommittee and Sequestration" (S+S) was not smooth. The House, in May 2011, defeated an amendment-free rise of the debt ceiling by a vote of 318–97. The House did pass a higher limit 234–190 but only with a huge condition: Congress would submit a constitutional amendment to the states requiring a balanced budget in the future. The Senate promptly tabled that idea 51–46.

The S+S combination has complex parentage, but Harry Reid was a principal architect of the bipartisan supercommittee. Senate minority leader Mitch

McConnell was also enthusiastic, insisting that the supercommittee have extraordinary procedural authority: a direct pathway to an "up or down" vote on the House and Senate floors, with no amendments and no opportunity to filibuster.[78] In exchange for an increase in the debt ceiling, the supercommittee was charged with finding $1.5 trillion in debt reduction (through spending reduction or new revenues) over ten years. Deadlines for the supercommittee were set as follows: a ten-year plan by November 23, 2012, and a vote in Congress by December 23, 2012.

The key challenge for the supercommittee was how to create a real incentive for negotiation and compromise, especially given the failure of Simpson-Bowles, the failure of the Biden-led talks, and the recent breakdown in the Obama-Boehner negotiations. The White House appears to have been the first to suggest automatic triggers and sequestration, modeled loosely after the 1985 Gramm-Rudman-Hollings budgetary procedures.[79] If the supercommittee process failed, the automatic sequester dictated $2.1 trillion in discretionary spending cuts over ten years, including $84 billion in fiscal year 2013, $109 billion in fiscal year 2014, and even deeper cuts in later years.[80] The cuts, evenly divided between military and domestic programs, would be across the board, except statutory exemptions from sequestration were provided for entitlement programs (e.g., unemployment compensation, Medicaid, Medicare, SNAP, Social Security, and SSI).

President Obama acquiesced to the S+S plan, the Budget Control Act of 2011, after it passed the House 269–161 (Republicans: 174–66; Democrats: 95–95) and the Senate 74–26. Those votes occurred less than forty-eight hours before Treasury's August 2 deadline. At this stage there was optimism that the supercommittee would avert sequestration.

The appointed members of the supercommittee from the Senate were Democrats Patty Murray, Max Baucus, and John Kerry, and Republicans Jon Kyl, Pat Toomey, and Rob Portman; from the House they were Republicans Jeb Hensarling, Dave Camp, Fred Upton, and Democrats James Clyburn, Xavier Becerra, and Chris Van Hollen. The group did include some new faces, but four had served on Simpson-Bowles and, ominously, all four had voted against the majority recommendations.

Some analysts have suggested that the supercommittee process was not serious and was simply a delaying tactic to move the fiscal dilemma until after the November 2012 elections.[81] It is certainly true that neither Obama nor congressional party leaders put any public pressure on the supercommittee to find an agreement. Strong interest groups on the left and right were not supporting the process, and the public at the time was tilting only slightly toward the view that the Republicans in Congress deserved more blame for the fiscal impasse than the Democrats in Congress. Not surprisingly, only about one-third of Americans approved of President Obama's handling of the nation's fiscal affairs.[82]

The supercommittee made little progress during its months of negotiations. A surprise occurred late in the discussions when Republican senator Pat Toomey made a complex proposal that included $400 billion in increased revenue. (Toomey was a former leader of the antitax Club for Growth and was perceived as one of the few Republicans in Congress whose antitax credentials rivaled those of activist Grover Norquist.) Although Toomey's offer was the only sign from a supercommittee Republican of willingness to entertain revenue enhancement, the Democrats dismissed the proposal on the grounds that it did not phase out the Bush tax cuts for high earners but in fact extended and enlarged them in conjunction with removal of a variety of deductions/loopholes in the tax code.[83]

The indiscriminate pain that the supercommittee was supposedly motivated to avoid began to take effect in early 2013. The budget cuts moved fiscal policy in exactly the opposite direction from Obama's preferred course: it was more of the McCain "freeze" than the Obama "scalpel." It also called for near-term spending reductions rather than additional fiscal stimulus and infrastructure support, and it explicitly exempted entitlement programs from any cuts or reforms, the latter being the kind of long-term fiscal discipline that experts such as the Fed's Ben Bernanke were recommending. The Congressional Budget Office warned Congress that the spending cuts induced by sequestration were misdirected and should have been directed at the programs that Obama and Boehner had discussed.[84]

Some of the automatic cuts ultimately hit discretionary (non-entitlement) programs that hurt one of Obama's most important constituencies: low-income Americans. There were cuts to housing assistance for the poor; Head Start; child care assistance for low-income mothers; job training assistance; a nutrition program for women, infants, and children; family planning services; community health centers; services for special education students; financial assistance for college students; and energy bill assistance for low-income households.[85] Perversely for President Obama, the second round of automatic cuts in the sequester included appropriations to the Department of Health and Human Services that are used to administer the Affordable Care Act (ACA). Moreover, much of the domestic discretionary spending is "pass-through" support for state and local governments, which in turn is used to support education, health, criminal justice, and social services.

Not surprisingly, President Obama has acknowledged that he should never have allowed himself to negotiate fiscal policy with Congress under the deadline of a debt-ceiling hike.[86] The result for Obama was counterproductive. The alternative was to let Congress make the first moves on long-term fiscal issues and then react when necessary.

THE 2013 GOVERNMENT SHUTDOWN

Good presidents capitalize on the errors of their partisan opponents, and that is precisely what Obama did in 2013, after his reelection in November 2012. Most House Republicans were also reelected, and they were determined to force Obama to make major policy concessions.

Failing to learn the lesson from Newt Gingrich's confrontation with President Clinton in the 1990s (when the government was shut down and the Republicans were blamed), the House Republicans, led by their Tea Party faction, staged a fall 2013 dispute that led to a sixteen-day shutdown of the federal government. Boehner reluctantly went along with his hard-line conservatives and saw Obama, who certainly knew how to communicate, blame the Republican Party and tear congressional Republicans into disarray.

In exchange for continued funding of the federal government (and a related increase in the debt ceiling), the House Republicans started by asking for repeal of the Affordable Care Act. Some intimated that they would accept a weakening of the ACA. Alternatively, some Republicans called for withdrawal of the Environmental Protection Agency's (EPA) climate regulations or repeal of the Dodd-Frank legislation on Wall Street reform.[87] Having learned his lesson the hard way in 2011, Obama had a simple response: I will not negotiate with Republicans who have a gun to my head. He dared them to shoot. When the government shut down, the Gingrich public-relations fiasco was revisited.

A *Washington Post*/ABC News survey found that eight out of ten respondents disapproved of the shutdown. Two out of three Republicans (and independents who lean Republican) disapproved of the shutdown. A majority of respondents who support the Tea Party disapproved of the shutdown. The public split 50–50 on whether they approved of President Obama's handling of the matter.[88] The results of a *Wall Street Journal*/NBC survey were not quite as strong but still crystal clear: a 22 percentage point difference between those who blamed the House Republicans and those who blamed Obama.[89]

Internationally, the 2013 shutdown damaged the credibility of the US government, with critics drawing analogies to fiscal problems in unstable third world regimes. To ratings agencies such as Standard and Poor's and Fitch, it was further evidence of a need to downgrade America's credit rating.

For the Republican Party the shutdown exposed a deep rift between younger and established conservatives in the House of Representatives. The online *Cook Political Report* downgraded the reelection prospects of twelve Republican House members, thereby encouraging Democratic challengers and inviting money to flow to challengers.[90] And the win for President Obama was an opportunity to "reboot" his second term, which had accomplished virtually nothing in its first year.[91] Fortunately for Republicans, the 2014 midterm elections were a year away, and they had ample time to recover from their self-inflicted wounds.

What did the House Republicans accomplish through the shutdown? As a face-saving measure, Democrats conceded this provision: officials in the Department of Health and Human Services were required to check the incomes of people receiving subsidized health insurance through the exchanges under the ACA.

When Boehner and the House Republicans conceded defeat, the government was funded through January 15, 2014, and the debt ceiling was raised through February 7, 2014. The legislation passed the Senate 81–18. It passed the House 285–144 as Boehner and the establishment Republicans joined with House Democrats to isolate the Tea Party Republicans.[92]

For the rest of his second term the Republicans knew that Obama could not be pressured on the debt ceiling. When the president wanted a "clean" hike (i.e., no amendments) in the debt ceiling, he got it, although sometimes the House passed it with a combination of votes from establishment Republicans and Democrats rather than with votes from Tea Party Republicans.[93] In short, Obama capitalized on a tactical error committed by his partisan opponents.

EASING THE SEQUESTER

The S+S was such a debacle that much political energy was invested by both parties to repeal or fix it. One path to a fix was a grand fiscal deal along the lines that Boehner and Obama had strived but failed to achieve in 2011. The second path, which ultimately carried the day, was a modest two-year budget pact—an old-fashioned budget resolution—engineered by Democratic senator Patty Murray and Republican congressman Paul Ryan. The pact did not repeal the sequester, but it did ease some of its perverse effects.

At the outset there was much speculation about a grand fiscal deal. Obama reached out to some rank-and-file Republicans searching for such a deal, trying to bypass Boehner and McConnell.[94] The president's team also worked quietly with a "Group of Eight" senators to fix the sequester, borrowing some of the ideas from the Boehner-Obama talks.[95] Obama proposed a trade: smaller cost-of-living increases under Social Security and larger Medicare premiums for the high-income elderly in exchange for a tax increase to finance more stimulus and infrastructure.[96] The trade attracted little interest.

Republican senator Lindsey Graham, who was determined to soften the defense cuts, said that he might be willing to accept $600 billion in new revenue in exchange for some entitlement reform and defense support.[97] Most of this discussion proved to be irrelevant, because the votes for a tax increase in the House of Representatives could not be found. Unlike Graham, Ryan was determined to focus on something achievable.[98] Obama ultimately agreed that the solution would not involve a tax increase.[99]

Murray and Ryan led the meaningful discussions.[100] They found a path to $22 billion in deficit reduction over ten years, comprised of $65 billion in additional spending over the next two years and $85 billion in spending reduction and revenue enhancement over ten years. The deal eased some of the automatic cuts in defense and domestic spending by targeted measures such as slowing the growth of military pensions and enacting higher fees on airline passengers.[101]

The package was not huge or elegant, but it was the first semblance of bipartisan collaboration on budgetary issues during the Obama years, although it occurred with only limited input from the president. The House passed the deal 332–94, including a 169–62 vote among House Republicans.[102] The key Senate vote for Murray-Ryan was 64–36, with nine Republican senators joining all fifty-five Democratic senators. Another three Republican senators helped on a prior procedural vote that dodged a filibuster; they then voted against the pact on the merits.[103]

Late in 2015, Obama worked with the Republican leaders in Congress on a two-year bipartisan budget deal that raised the spending caps, further eased the sequester, raised the debt limit, and avoided another government shutdown. It passed the House 266–167 and the Senate 64–35. It was a positive outcome for Obama but widely seen as House Speaker Boehner's last triumph before stepping down.[104]

The political energy devoted to easing the S+S diverted attention from Obama's second-term agenda. From 2013 to 2015, Congress did virtually nothing on Obama's second-term lawmaking priorities.

THE PIVOT: DEFICIT REDUCTION
TO INEQUALITY REDUCTION

During Obama's first term, progressives expressed public frustration that the president rarely used the bully pulpit to highlight the growing problems of poverty and inequality in America. The Obama rhetoric was much more typically about the middle class, and the president's political advisors may have preferred this rhetorical focus for reelection purposes.

The trends in the official poverty statistics during the Obama years were sobering, as the number of Americans recorded as poor grew steadily: 36.5 million in 2006, 37.3 million in 2007, 39.8 million in 2008, 43.6 million in 2009, 46.2 million in both 2010 and 2011, 46.5 million in 2012, 45.3 million in 2013, and 46.7 million in 2014.[105] But these figures do not account for America's safety net.[106] In fact there is little analytic basis for the belief held by some progressives that Obama's 2009–2010 policies were harmful to low-income Americans. The Federal Reserve Board produced the most definitive study of this question.

Family finances for a representative sample of American families in 2007 were compared to a representative sample of American families in 2010. Reflecting the distress of the Great Recession, the nation's median (average) family income, adjusted for inflation, declined 7.7 percent (11.1 percent). When the data are broken down into income groups, only one group did not experience a drop in family income: families in the bottom 20 percent of the income distribution. Among those families, median (average) family income was $12,900

($12,900) in 2007 and $13,400 ($12,900) in 2010. A sub-analysis by the Fed researchers found that low-income families did experience a decline in income from wages, but they also experienced a larger increase in government transfer payments.[107] This is suggestive evidence that the government's safety net, buttressed by the Recovery Act, did its job. In 2012 alone another study estimated that tax and transfer policies in the United States lowered the rate of poverty by 12 percentage points.[108]

Low-income people do not necessarily face hardships if they have access to significant wealth (assets). An elderly couple, for example, may report low income but be gradually spending down a substantial savings account or other forms of liquid assets. Analysts also examined how the Great Recession impacted households at the bottom of the wealth distribution.

Among families in the bottom quartile (25 percent) of wealth, median family income dropped from $24,600 in 2007 to $23,700 in 2010, while average family income increased from $30,500 in 2007 to $32,600 in 2010. The average, though, is strongly skewed by those with high incomes. Families in the middle of the wealth distribution experienced the largest relative decline in family income, a much larger drop in income than experienced by households at the bottom quartile of the wealth distribution.

Low-income Americans did not fare nearly as well from President Obama's second year in office (2010) to his fifth year (2013) in office. During this period, the Recovery Act ended, states cut some social services to help balance their budgets, the rate of long-term unemployment was stubbornly high, the federal sequester began to hit some antipoverty programs, and the average wages for new jobs were lower than for jobs destroyed by the Great Recession. In effect, the "recovery" proved more difficult for low-income Americans than the Great Recession itself.[109]

Median family income in the United States fell 5 percent from 2010 to 2013 (see table 4.2). For the median family in the bottom 20 percent of the income distribution (less than $15,000/year), it fell 4 percent. For nonwhite Hispanic families, it fell 9 percent. For families in the bottom quarter of the wealth distribution (less than $25,000 in net worth), median income fell 7 percent from 2010 to 2013. All of these figures are adjusted for inflation, using constant 2013 dollars.[110]

In 2013 the Census Bureau data finally began to show some progress against poverty, primarily due to growth in the number of full-time workers

Table 4.2. Trends in U.S. Family Income from 2010 to 2013

	Median Income ($k)		
Family Characteristic	2010	2013	% Change
All families	$49.0	$46.7	−5
Families in lower 20% of usual income	$15.8	$15.2	−4
Families without a high school diploma	$24.6	$22.3	−9
Nonwhite or Hispanic families	$37.1	$33.6	−9
Families in bottom 25% of net worth	$25.4	$23.7	−7

Source: Jesse Bricker, Lisa J. Dettling, Alice Henriques, Joanne W. Hsu, Kevin B. Moore, John Sabelhous, Jeffery Thompson, Richard A. Windle, "Changes in US Family Finances from 2010 to 2013: Evidence from the Survey of Consumer Finances," *Federal Reserve Bulletin* 100, no. 4 (2014): 9–13.

and higher earnings among parents with children. The poverty rate for children under age eighteen declined for the first time since 2000.[111] Even the rate of SNAP (food stamp) use, which had grown steadily from 2007 to 2012, began to fall in 2013 and 2014.[112]

In the first year of his second term, Obama continued a strong focus on the welfare of the middle class;[113] he also began a focus on the need to reduce inequality in America. During both terms, he spoke only rarely about poverty or the poor.[114] In his 2013 State of the Union address, President Obama emphasized not deficit reduction but the urgent need for infrastructure investments (e.g., repairs of roads and bridges and modernization of the electrical grid), a large increase in the federal minimum wage, and new public investments in early childhood education.[115] In his 2014 State of the Union address, the inequality theme was even stronger, and some analysts suggested the theme was designed to energize progressives before the November 2014 midterm elections.[116] One of the president's concrete proposals was to expand the Earned Income Tax Credit for the 13.5 million childless workers living significantly below the middle of the income distribution.[117] And he continued to advocate assistance for the long-term unemployed.[118]

Obama's diminished focus on near-term deficits was amply justified by budgetary trends. It is true that he was not able to meet his first-term goal of cutting the annual deficit in half over four years. His fiscal year 2013 budget called for a $901 billion deficit, down from $1.3 trillion in fiscal year 2011 and

$1.15 trillion in fiscal year 2012, but the 2013 budget fell short of his earlier pledge of $650 billion.[119] However, when fiscal year 2013 was over, the deficit had fallen much faster than expected, to $680 billion.[120]

The annual deficit began to plummet faster as the recovery intensified. By the end of fiscal year 2014, CBO estimated a deficit of $483 billion (2.8 percent of GDP), the smallest deficit since 2007 (when the Great Recession began). The 2.8 percent share is actually smaller than the 3.2 percent average since 1980.[121] The deficit fell again in fiscal year 2015 to $439 billion, or about 2.5 percent of GDP.[122]

The progress against deficits under President Obama is a well-kept secret, at least if you believe the results of opinion surveys. Several months after he was reelected (early 2013), Bloomberg News surveyed Americans as to whether they think the deficit is growing, holding about the same, or declining, and the respondents split 62 percent, 28 percent, and 6 percent, respectively. In fact, the annual federal deficit, as reported by the Congressional Budget Office, was lower at the end of fiscal years 2013 and 2014 than it was when Obama took office, and it was far lower as a share of GDP.[123] The legitimate concern is that Obama, like his predecessor, did little to address the projected long-term deficits. In early 2015 CBO projected a deficit of $960 billion in 2024, assuming current policies continue.[124]

Despite Obama's shift from deficit reduction to inequality reduction, some progressives were not impressed. Senator Bernie Sanders of Vermont, one of the most progressive voices in the Congress, succinctly summarized a prevalent sentiment among progressives: "The president is not a fighter."[125] In order to appreciate Sanders's statement and the limits of his perspective, it is useful to trace the fate of Obama's pledge to raise the federal minimum wage.

RAISING THE FEDERAL MINIMUM WAGE

In July 2008 Congress passed the first increase in the federal minimum wage since 1997, raising it from $5.15 per hour to $7.25 per hour. This action received wide bipartisan support in Congress because it was coupled with a substantial package of tax breaks for small businesses favored by President Bush, congressional Republicans, and moderate Democratic senators such as Max Baucus. In the 2008 presidential contest, Obama and John McCain took sharply different positions on the federal minimum wage. McCain opposed a higher minimum on the grounds that it would hurt small businesses and exacerbate unemployment. Obama advocated a further increase in the minimum from $7.25 per hour in 2009 to $9.50 per hour by the end of 2011. He added that future hikes in the minimum should occur automatically—through a process called indexation—to keep pace with the rate of inflation in the economy. Once elected, however, the Obama White House chose not to make the minimum wage a first-year legislative priority. Nor did the president make it a priority in 2010, 2011, or 2012, much to the dismay of organized labor and other progressive interest groups.[126]

In the 2012 contest between Mitt Romney and Obama, Romney advocated a policy of indexation in both the Republican primaries and the general election. Because of Obama's inaction from 2009 to 2012, the president was not in a strong position to champion the issue. Thus, the differences between Romney and Obama were not great on this issue.

In his 2013 State of the Union address, Obama—for the first time—indicated a serious intent to seek an increase in the federal minimum wage.[127] He called for a gradual increase in the minimum from $7.25 to $9.00 per hour by 2015, coupled with a policy of indexation. To progressives, this stance hardly seemed aggressive, since his 2008 position was to reach $9.50 per hour by the end of 2011. Organized labor was irked because they were already working on a plan in Congress to raise the minimum to $10.10 per hour.[128] The White House was reluctant to go as high as $10.10 per hour, in part because of concerns raised by several Democratic senators from the South.[129] For example, Mark Pryor of Arkansas was up for reelection in November 2014 and voiced concerns about the larger increase to $10.10 per hour.[130]

The uphill battle facing the Obama White House was revealed in March 2013. In the course of deliberations on a GOP-favored job training bill, House Democrats were able to force a floor vote on an amendment to increase the federal minimum wage to $10.10 per hour. The amendment was defeated 223–184, as six House Democrats joined all House Republicans in opposition.

In July 2013 Obama devoted a major public address to the issue. At about the same time, fast-food workers in seven cities went on strike to draw attention to their low wages. Nonetheless, the White House found no pathway to bring the House Republican leadership into a negotiation on the issue. Recognizing that the House was opposed, the Senate chose not to take a vote on the issue in 2013, preferring to force votes closer to the November 2014 midterm elections. In order to help unify the Democrats, President Obama ultimately revised his stance and favored the $10.10 proposal.[131]

In his 2014 State of the Union address, Obama again called for an increase in the federal minimum wage as one of several initiatives that congressional Democrats advanced as their "fair share" initiative. In the House of the Representatives, Minority Whip Steny Hoyer orchestrated a discharge petition to force John Boehner to bring the issue to a vote on the House floor. A majority House vote for a discharge petition is necessary to force the Speaker's hand. Although Hoyer obtained 195 signatures from House Democrats, no House Republicans supported the petition and the initiative died in the House.[132]

The Senate deliberations of 2014 were complicated by two intervening developments. In February 2014 the Congressional Budget Office released a comprehensive analysis of both Obama's original proposal to raise the minimum to $9.00 per hour and the congressional Democratic proposal to raise the minimum to $10.10 per hour. Democrats pointed to CBO's finding that the $10.10 minimum would lift nine hundred thousand Americans out of poverty. Republicans highlighted CBO's determination that the $10.10 minimum would induce a loss of five hundred thousand jobs.[133] In addition, only 18 percent of the wage gains from the higher minimum would go to families in poverty.[134] The large magnitude of the raise was sensitive because some senators, including Republican Susan Collins of Maine, supported a raise but felt that $10.10 per hour was too large for businesses in their states.[135]

Meanwhile, due to the sustained inaction in Congress, many state legislatures acted to raise the minimum wage for workers in their states.[136] By the summer of 2014 there were only eight states left that had no minimum wage or had a minimum below the federal minimum.[137] And those states (Alabama, Arkansas, Georgia, Louisiana, Mississippi, South Carolina, Tennessee, and Wyoming) were in predominantly Southern or rural states where the cost of living was significantly below the national average.[138]

Frustrated with the inability to enlist bipartisan support in the Senate, Harry Reid decided in April 2014 to force a floor vote on the issue before the November midterm elections. The proposal brought to the floor was not President Obama's original proposal, but a plan devised by Democratic senator Tom Harkin. It called for a gradual increase in the minimum to $10.10 per year over a thirty-month period coupled with indexation thereafter. The proposal had strong support from organized labor but comparably strong opposition from the business community.

Harkin's proposal required sixty votes to overcome the filibuster threat from the Senate Republican leadership. Reid and Harkin rallied all of the Democrats to support the bill, but only one Republican senator (Bob Corker) crossed over to support the higher minimum wage. Thus, the proposal fell five votes short of the sixty-vote threshold.[139]

Overall, Obama made no legislative progress on the federal minimum wage, which made it a "broken promise" among many progressives.[140] He did issue an executive order in 2014 raising the minimum for federal workers and some government contractors, but only a small portion of America's workers were covered by the order.[141] And he helped persuade some large employers to raise their minimum wages voluntarily, although the number of affected workers was relatively small.[142] Nevertheless, he frustrated progressives by making a proposal with no apparent determination to see it enacted.

FREE TRADE AGREEMENTS

Expanded trade through free-trade agreements is widely seen as an essential ingredient to long-term economic growth. A key to any president's efforts to liberalize trade with one or more countries is referred to as "fast-track authority" (FTA). Such authority gives the White House the power to negotiate the details of a trade agreement with leaders of foreign countries, knowing that Congress must vote "up or down" on the entire agreement. No amendments on specific aspects of an agreement are permitted.

During the 2008 campaign, Obama appeared to oppose free-trade agreements and sharply criticized Hilary Clinton's support of the North American Free Trade Agreement (NAFTA). Once elected president, he portrayed himself around the world as a free trader, like all of his twelve predecessors have.[143] And he encouraged work on two ambitious new trade agreements: the Trans-Pacific Partnership (TPP) with Asian countries and the Transatlantic Trade and Investment Partnership (TTIP) with the European Union. Neither initiative was seen as likely to succeed unless Obama obtained FTA from the Congress.

FTA was first used by the White House in 1974, but the authority needs to be reauthorized periodically by the Congress. It was most recently reauthorized in 2002 for five years. Bush used the authority to make progress on several trade agreements, including deals with Columbia, Panama, and South Korea that were completed by the Obama administration in 2011.[144] However, during his first term Obama did not give any priority to renewing FTA, even though it was a high priority of the business community and a promising issue for collaboration between Republicans and some moderate Democrats in the Congress.[145] In his 2014 State of the Union address, President Obama finally made a strong pitch for FTA.

The politics of FTA are complex, especially for a Democratic president. Democratic votes are hard to find for free-trade agreements, because organized labor and environmental groups actively oppose them. An agreement with low-wage Asian countries is especially controversial among unions, because they see their jobs as threatened by low-wage Asian firms. Environmentalists see Asian firms as less green than American firms.[146] An agreement with Europe is less controversial among unions, but the White House gave higher priority to a Pacific agreement.[147]

In 2002 FTA squeaked through the House of Representatives on a vote of 215–212, as only twenty-five Democrats were willing to join most Republicans (195 out of 222) in passing the measure for the Bush administration. In the Senate only twenty-one of fifty Democrats voted for FTA in 2002. In fact, Congress rejected President Clinton's request for FTA in 1998, in large part because only twenty-nine Democrats in the House were willing to vote for it.[148]

The Obama White House nonetheless saw a possible path forward. In 2013 Senator Max Baucus began preparing an FTA bill, at Obama's request, for consideration in the Senate.[149] Baucus was collaborating informally with Republican congressman Dave Camp, who was preparing a similar bill in the House. The initiative was a high priority of the business community, but organized labor (especially AFL-CIO and the Communications Workers of America) and environmental groups moved quickly to generate opposition.

In November 2013 Democrat Sander Levin obtained signatures from 151 House Democrats indicating opposition to FTA. In the Senate 7 Democratic senators publicly signaled their opposition to FTA.

An unexpected complication arose from the other end of the political spectrum: the Tea Party. Conservative Republicans in Congress were sympathetic to three Tea Party concerns: (1) trade arrangements can harm US workers (e.g., NAFTA); (2) international agreements compromise the sovereignty of the United States; and (3) Obama cannot be trusted to negotiate fair agreements.[150] Speaker Boehner recognized the power of the Tea Party and estimated publicly that a much larger number of House Republicans would vote against FTA in 2014 (perhaps 60 of 247) than did so in 2002 (27 of 222).[151]

Thus, Boehner alerted the White House that Democratic support in the House would be necessary to pass FTA, and, accordingly, the White House seemed to be focusing on the moderate coalition of "New Democrats."[152]

Soon after Obama's 2014 State of the Union address, Harry Reid delivered a damaging blow to the president's trade agenda by publicly announcing his opposition to FTA. At one level Reid's opposition was not surprising. He has always been skeptical of free-trade agreements; he voted against FTA in 2002; and he voted against the specific agreements with Colombia, Panama, and South Korea in 2011. On the other hand, it is hard to imagine an FTA bill reaching the Senate floor when the Senate is controlled by Democrats and led by Reid. In fact, FTA made little progress in the Senate in 2014.

The tide turned in favor of FTA when the GOP took control of the Senate in 2015. Obama seized the opportunity by making passage of FTA a 2015 legislative priority. With Obama a lame duck, McConnell and Boehner had diminished incentives to engage in strategic opposition. Business-oriented Republicans in Congress were also motivated to deliver for a core constituency of the GOP.

Obama collaborated with a bipartisan group of lawmakers that included Republican Orrin Hatch of Utah and Democrat Ron Wyden of Oregon (from the Senate Finance Committee) and Republican Paul Ryan (House Ways and Means Committee). Wyden's leadership is notable, since Democratic activists threatened to run a primary challenger against him in 2016, when his current term expired.[153] Both McConnell in the Senate and Boehner in the House pledged to move FTA quickly through the Congress.[154] To facilitate passage, Wyden persuaded Hatch that two bills should be moved in parallel: one granting Obama FTA and the other providing displaced workers trade adjustment assistance (TAA). The current TAA program, supported by organized labor, was scheduled to expire in 2015. Obama made an aggressive public case for FTA, in addition to meeting with key Democrats in Congress.[155]

In the Senate sixty votes were necessary, but McConnell was leading a Republican caucus of only fifty-four members. Obama and Wyden would need to deliver more than a handful of Democrats, despite intense opposition from organized labor and progressive groups. On the key procedural motion to limit time for debate, pro-FTA forces won 62–38 by enlisting forty-nine of fifty-four Republicans and thirteen of forty-four Democrats. Obama played a crucial role prior to the vote by threatening to veto an amendment aimed at punishing foreign governments that engage in currency manipulation. That amendment was framed as a "poison pill" for FTA.[156] The Senate later passed both the FTA bill and the TAA bill.

The package ran into some trouble in the House when organized labor persuaded many Democrats to join the GOP in voting against the TAA bill. Without TAA, Senate support of the package was considered unlikely. But Boehner and McConnell worked around the problem by passing an FTA bill in both chambers and then daring the Democrats in the House or Senate to vote against the TAA bill. Obama won this unusual collaboration with the GOP when both the House and Senate passed TAA as well as FTA. The key vote in the House on FTA passed 218–208. For Obama, it was perhaps his most significant second-term legislative win.[157]

REGULATORY REFORM

Soon after his election in November 2008, President Obama raised expectations in the business community by calling publicly for suggestions on how to modernize the federal regulatory process. The White House signaled interest in buttressing a key federal executive order (#12866) that had been used by presidents Clinton and Bush 43 to coordinate the activities of federal regulatory agencies, ensure the cost-effectiveness of regulatory actions, and provide regulatory relief to businesses. After receiving numerous public comments, the Obama White House did nothing with the initiative in 2009 or 2010. The silence only lent credence to a chorus of criticism from conservatives and the US Chamber of Commerce that much of Obama's policy agenda—from Dodd-Frank to the Affordable Care Act—was antibusiness in its regulatory burdens.

After the Democratic Party's stinging electoral defeat in November 2010, President Obama reversed course by making significant overtures to the business community.[158] A politically prominent banker, William M. Daley, was named chief of staff in the White House, and Obama established a new "Jobs and Competitiveness Council" chaired by General Electric CEO Jeffrey Immelt.

Obama followed with Executive Order #13563, titled "Improving Regulation and Regulatory Review" (January 18, 2011). Each federal agency was required to prepare, within 120 days, a plan for retrospective review of regulations that may be outmoded. In rolling out the order, Obama insisted that agencies must avoid "unreasonable burdens on business."[159] In August 2011 the

White House followed up with a plan to save businesses $10 billion over five years by reforming more than five hundred regulations at twenty-six different federal agencies. In March 2012 Obama followed with an OMB memorandum aimed at curtailing the "cumulative effects of regulation."[160]

The president "infuriated" the EPA and environmental groups in April 2011 by publicly rejecting a proposal to tighten the health-based air quality for ozone (smog).[161] The EPA's proposal had the backing of independent public health scientists on a key EPA advisory board. By deferring the matter to 2013 (after his reelection), Obama responded to economic concerns that the EPA proposal would push hundreds of counties into "non-attainment" status, which means those counties would need to go through more EPA procedures before they could attract new or expanded factory investments. Democratic governor Bev Perdue of North Carolina as well as the major national business groups praised the decision.

Obama also used his new Jobs and Competitiveness Council to work with Republicans in Congress on a regulatory relief measure for the financial sector of the economy.[162] The "Jumpstart Our Business Startups" (JOBS) Act was aimed at repairing Obama's relationships with Wall Street investors who were annoyed by passage of the 2010 Dodd-Frank legislation. It was also aimed at easing some of the excessive regulatory burdens induced by the 2002 Sarbanes-Oxley legislation, which Congress enacted in response to public outrage over the Enron scandal.

The JOBS Act contains two key provisions.[163] It allows entrepreneurs to raise funds from numerous small investors on the Internet, a process called "crowd-funding." It also eases Securities and Exchange Commission (SEC) regulations to allow companies to go public more quickly and with less expense.

The initiative annoyed many progressives in Congress who feared that the loosened regulations would lead to more defrauding of investors. To oppose the JOBS Act publicly was awkward for progressives, because President Obama had endorsed the idea and House Republicans were eager to collaborate with him on the issue. The AFL-CIO nonetheless opposed the bill on the grounds that it would allow companies to sell stock without adequate internal controls.

The Senate Democratic Caucus split on whether to support Obama on the JOBS Act. Veteran senators Dick Durbin and Carl Levin signaled serious concerns about the bill. When a few Democratic senators threatened to filibuster the bill, Harry Reid (who was hardly enamored of the initiative) persuaded his colleagues that they should not be filibustering an initiative of their Democratic president.[164]

The JOBS Act became a rare bipartisan victory for President Obama. It passed the House 380–41 and the Senate 73–26 (with all twenty-six opponents being members of the Senate Democratic Caucus). Politically, the JOBS Act was significant because it showcased the White House collaborating with the business and financial communities prior to Obama's 2012 reelection bid. Obama found himself cooperating with a most unexpected partner: Virginia congressman and House majority leader Eric Cantor.

Obama's entire regulatory reform initiative drew criticism from the right (as too timid and weak) and left (as dangerous to the welfare of consumers, workers, and the environment). However, it was well timed to buttress his economic credentials as his November 2012 reelection bid approached. In short, regulatory reform helped the White House counteract the allegation that President Barack Obama was antibusiness.

COUNTERFACTUALS

Progressives argue that President Obama never should have encouraged a shift in congressional focus from fiscal stimulus to deficit reduction (short-run or long-run).[165] This criticism has merit.

The economic recovery from the Great Recession in 2009–2015 was so sluggish that Obama could have credibly argued that the focus should remain on fiscal stimulus (including infrastructure investments) rather than deficit control. Even though Congress might have refused to enact more stimulus measures, the president's rhetorical position could have been that deficit control should wait until the economy recovered. He would have been well positioned to blame the weak recovery on the refusal of Congress to enact additional stimulus. Instead, he gave credence to the call for austerity measures, which in turn set expectations for large-scale budgetary and tax reforms that he could not deliver. Obama ultimately advocated a focus on infrastructure and higher business taxes in 2014, but by then his popularity was so low that his ability to be an effective leader on those issues was compromised.[166]

By allowing the debate to shift from stimulus to deficit control, Obama set in motion expectations for a grand fiscal deal that the White House and the Republican leaders in Congress were in no position to deliver.[167] Democratic senator Patty Murray and Republican congressman Paul Ryan stated publicly the reality of the fiscal situation: Congress will not face big, long-term budget issues until there are some clear election results that respond to candidates taking different positions on the long-term issues.[168] Obama did not campaign on a grand fiscal deal (in 2008 or 2012) and was never authorized by his base to put reform of entitlement programs on the table. Likewise, Boehner should have realized that there was no way that rank-and-file House Republicans, especially the dozens linked to the Tea Party, would support a grand fiscal deal that included substantial revenue growth.

Obama's decisions to allow fiscal policy to be negotiated in the context of the debt ceiling—first in 2009–2010 in response to Senator Conrad and again in 2011 in response to House Republicans—were mistakes. Based on previous experiences with commissions and related bipartisan procedural gimmicks, there was little reason to expect that a bipartisan commission would produce a viable long-term fiscal plan that both parties could support. History shows that meaningful long-term fiscal policy is not likely to be adopted unless it emerges from the responsible House and Senate committees. The resulting three-year quest for an elusive "grand fiscal bargain" was counterproductive. By undermining trust, it further poisoned the political environment in Washington and diverted White House and congressional leaders from more practical, pro-growth initiatives with a chance for serious consideration.[169]

Obama missed an opportunity to foster bipartisan collaboration on corporate tax reform, especially a lower corporate rate coupled with closing loopholes and exemptions. The politics of dealing with specific business groups would not have been easy, but centrists in both parties (Democrat Max Baucus in the Senate and Republican Fred Upton in the House) were ready to work with the president. Obama showed interest in the idea on multiple occasions but always coupled that interest with a progressive twist: an overall increase in tax revenues from business. That twist was hard to sell in a sluggish economy and served to discourage bipartisan collaboration in the Congress.[170]

Regulatory reform was not a high priority at the start of the Obama administration, but enough reforms were made before the 2012 election to neutralize the criticism that Obama was ignoring the issue and exacerbating unnecessary regulatory burdens on business. Greater priority to regulatory reform throughout the Obama years might have been helpful to the president and the Democrats politically, even though it might offend some elements of the Obama base. It certainly could have helped hiring in the small-business sector, where uncertainties about Obama's regulatory intentions contributed to lower rates of confidence among owners of small businesses.[171] For example, a modest legislative initiative on regulatory reform in 2009–2010 or 2013–2014 might have attracted significant bipartisan support in Congress and allowed moderate Democrats to show their pro-business inclinations and their ability to collaborate with some congressional Republicans.

Obama's push for FTA occurred later in his presidency than was ideal because Democrats would have been more likely to support his request for FTA if had been designated as a White House priority before his reelection in 2012. Instead of leading with the more controversial Asian agreement, Obama should have led with the European agreement and sought FTA for the European deal before opening the more controversial Asian trade debate. Once the GOP took control of the Senate in 2015, Obama was effective at seizing the opportunity to work with the GOP on FTA, with an emphasis on the Pacific deal.

President Obama missed an opportunity to stimulate bipartisan support in Congress for a Trans-Atlantic Energy Pact with Europe aimed at reducing European dependence on Russian energy and expanding US oil and gas production.[172] The program might have included removal of the ban of US exports of oil and gas, limited government support for the infrastructure costs of liquefied natural gas export terminals, and technical assistance to help Europe launch its own shale gas industry. An energy deal with Europe would have complemented Obama's expansion of the US oil and gas industry. Chapter 8 takes a more in-depth look at President Obama's energy policies, which had both economic and environmental ramifications.

5

THE AFFORDABLE CARE ACT: LEGISLATIVE VICTORY

Barack Obama accomplished what other modern Democratic leaders (Jimmy Carter, Ted Kennedy, and Bill Clinton) could only dream about: he persuaded the US Congress to pass a major health care reform bill that is significantly reducing the number of Americans who have no health insurance.[1] The magnitude of this presidential achievement tends to be lost in public dialogue for a variety of reasons. The proposal was not popular when it was passed, and it became even more unpopular when serious implementation snafus ensued. The reform did not fully address the issues of public concern (e.g., the high cost and uneven quality of health care) and did not accomplish what progressive activists desired most (e.g., a single payer system or at least a public option to obtain Medicare-like insurance for coverage). There are some defeated Democratic politicians around the country who have good reason to believe that the priority given to "Obamacare" resulted in their political careers ending prematurely. As we explore in chapter 10, the political price of the Affordable Care Act was quite high, but it is certainly one of the most significant pieces of legislation enacted by Congress since the 1930s.

With respect to the theory in chapter 2, readers are encouraged to consider the following issues: Given that health care reform was primarily a base-pleasing measure, did Barack Obama make too many compromises to please moderates and conservatives? Could modifications have been made to the ACA that would have made it less controversial, without compromising policy progress? Was it wise for Obama and Nancy Pelosi to force House Democrats to vote on a bill with controversial features (e.g., public option and $1 trillion cost) that were unlikely to pass the Senate? Was the policy value of the individual mandate worth the controversy that it generated? Would Obama have been better off delaying health care reform until his second term, when the economy would likely be in better shape? The end of this chapter considers these issues, as does chapter 11.

For scholars of the presidency, Obama's quest for health care reform is rich with insights into the promise and limitations of presidential leadership. I begin this chapter by linking Obama's achievement to lessons learned from the failure of the 1993 Clinton health care initiative and to pledges made by candidates Hillary Clinton and Barack Obama in the 2008 presidential campaign. The chapter then dissects the messy legislative politics that culminated in the enactment of the ACA. Finally, some counterfactuals are explored, particularly some of the harshest criticisms that have been launched against Obama's decision to give priority to passage of the ACA.

THE 1993 CLINTON REFORM PLAN

After defeating incumbent president George Herbert Walker Bush in the November 1992 election, Bill Clinton declared that health care reform would be his signature legislative priority. He named his wife, Hillary Clinton, leader of the task force that ultimately prepared a 1,342-page proposal for consideration by the Congress. As a "new Democrat," Clinton rejected the single payer approach favored by progressives and instead advanced market-oriented reforms coupled with regulation. His plan to control costs through caps on provider fees triggered unified opposition from physicians groups, insurers, hospitals, and pharmaceutical companies.[2]

The Clinton plan proved to be highly controversial.[3] Conservatives stoked fears about government bureaucrats deciding for families which insurance plans and doctors they would be permitted to use. The Health Insurance Association of America countered Clinton's proposal with some of the most effective thirty-second television advertisements in modern political history. The "Harry and Louise" ads featured a couple sitting at the kitchen table complaining that their insurance had been cancelled and that they had been forced to buy replacement insurance that they didn't want and that cost them more money. It has been estimated that the ads stimulated more than 250,000 phone calls of protest.[4]

Despite numerous presidential speeches from Bill Clinton and a Congress strongly controlled by the Democratic Party, Clinton's health plan never made it to the Senate floor for a vote and was not considered in the House. Clinton's popularity declined steadily in 1993–1994 as voters questioned his health plan and whether his presidency was focusing on the appropriate issues. In the November 1994 midterm elections, the Democratic Party suffered large losses in both the House and Senate. In fact, the Democratic Party lost majorities in both the House and Senate for the first time in four decades.[5]

The sobering story of the 1993 Clinton plan is remembered by veteran leaders of the Democratic Party. Nonetheless, problems in America's health care system steadily worsened in 1995–2008, fueling an even stronger perception in the Democratic Party that reform was urgently needed.

2008 PRESIDENTIAL CAMPAIGN

Health care was a central issue in the 2008 presidential campaign. An estimated forty-six million Americans were without health insurance. Health care costs were rising faster than family incomes. Companies were beginning to drop or scale back insurance coverage to reduce costs and remain economically competitive. And serious questions were being raised about the quality of care received by patients and the seemingly endless amounts of bureaucracy in the system.

In the Democratic nomination contest, candidates Barack Obama and Hillary Clinton each offered ambitious reform proposals. The plans had many similarities, but there were also enough differences to draw some fire.

The Clinton plan contained a legal requirement that all individuals be insured, but the Obama plan did not include such an individual mandate. Clinton attacked Obama's plan on the grounds that the absence of an individual mandate would leave many Americans uninsured, which in turn would drive up the cost of care for the insured. Obama countered that an individual mandate would hurt lower-income Americans who cannot afford health insurance but are not poor enough to qualify for Medicaid. As the Obama campaign sensed that Clinton's position was more persuasive among some voters, the Obama position evolved to the stance that those who choose not to be insured should pay a penalty of unspecified size.[6]

On the Republican side the focus of John McCain's plan was more on cost control than universal access. He called for elimination of favorable tax treatment of employer-sponsored health insurance. In its place the McCain plan provided tax rebates to help cover the cost of health insurance for any individual ($2,500) or family ($5,000). The result would likely have been more use of high-deductible, low-premium plans, which are believed to lead consumers to be more cost-conscious in making health care choices. Details about the financing of McCain's plan were sketchy.

Since both Obama and McCain were touting major health care proposals, voters had good reason to expect that the winner of the November 2008 election would choose health care as a first-term policy priority. Thus, it was no surprise when President-elect Obama called on Congress to pass comprehensive health reform as part of his first budget in January 2009.

THE "PUBLIC OPTION"

When progressives talk health care reform, they typically mean the single payer system that is widespread in Europe. A more modest idea, the "public option," was developed in 2001–2002 by a group of health care leaders convened by the University of California at Berkeley.[7] A government-backed insurance plan would be made available to individuals and families, with the purpose of competing with private insurance plans. It was seen as a compromise between a single payer system and private-market insurance system.

In 2007 Senator John Edwards of North Carolina was the first Democratic presidential candidate to publicize a health care plan. It contained a public option that was available on state insurance exchanges. The Obama and Clinton plans also contained public options, although they were designed somewhat differently (e.g., one plan made Medicare-like coverage available as an option). Proponents of the public option argued that it would lower costs by putting pressure on private insurers and facilitating negotiations with providers that would induce lower unit costs of care. Opponents argued that a public option, although it sounded nice, was really a step toward the single payer system, since private insurers would not be able to compete with a government-subsidized insurer.

Early in 2009 House Speaker Nancy Pelosi announced that the House plan would contain a public option. Opinions in the Senate were highly variable. Public opinion polls typically found that a large majority of respondents favored a public option. Americans like choices. However, most of those who were polled didn't know much about the public option, and responses varied depending on the order of the questions, the language used, and whether pro and con arguments were provided. One survey posed a public option question differently in split samples: half were told the federal government was involved in administering the plan, and half were not told about the federal government. The former version attracted only 50 percent support; the latter attracted 75 percent support.[8]

As Tea Party activists and conservative Republicans geared up to attack health care reform, the public option became an appealing target. The subtext was this: it seems like an "option," but it is really, the argument goes, a step on the path to socialized medicine. And that was another way, in addition to Wall Street and bank bailouts, to frame Obama as a socialist.

PRINCIPLES RATHER THAN A DETAILED PLAN

Learning a key lesson from the 1993 Clinton debacle, the Obama White House did not prepare a detailed health care plan and instead issued principles to guide congressional deliberations. Obama's fiscal year 2010 budget request to Congress set a target of $634 billion in additional federal spending over ten years was coupled with eight reform principles: protect families from medical bankruptcy; make health care affordable; seek universal coverage; accomplish portability of coverage; guarantee patient choice; invest in prevention and wellness; improve patient safety and quality of care; and ensure long-term fiscal sustainability.

The advantage of proposing principles is that the White House provides congressional leaders ample flexibility to negotiate the details of the final package. Congressional negotiations are not always pretty affairs, but they have the practical effect of giving individual members of Congress a stronger stake in the outcome. A similar approach was used by President George W. Bush to secure passage of several of his major legislative victories (e.g., tax cuts and energy).[9]

BUILDING A COALITION, DEFUSING OPPOSITION

The primary beneficiaries of the ACA have been the millions of Americans who lacked health insurance, had inadequate coverage of key services, or were paying more in premiums than they could really afford. Those people were difficult for Obama to mobilize as a political force, because they are not organized for other reasons, they lack resources, they may not fully appreciate their need for coverage or reform, and some were opposed to mandatory coverage because they did not want to pay for it. Moreover, some senior citizens feared that the ACA would be so expensive that Medicare would not be there to pay for their care.[10] In short, the primary beneficiaries of the ACA were not likely to be a loud and influential counterweight to organized interests who might oppose reform, and opposition was likely.[11]

There are a variety of well-organized interest groups with a strong stake in any major reform: labor unions, senior citizens, providers (physicians and nurses), hospitals, makers of pharmaceuticals and medical devices, insurers, and businesses. If too many of these groups aligned together in opposition to health care reform, the prospects of favorable congressional action would plummet. Labor unions became an important advocate of the ACA in large part because they had a strong stake in the success of Obama's presidency. If Obama failed to succeed as a politician, the Republican Party would likely gain politically, and Republican policies tend to be hostile to the interests of organized labor. On the other hand, many labor unions had already secured excellent health care coverage for their members, and thus unions sought— and received—assurance from President Obama that union-negotiated health insurance plans would not be adversely affected by the ACA. As we shall see, the ACA implementation process led to accusations that Obama did not honor his assurances to labor unions, but there is no question that labor unions used their political muscle in an effort to help pass the ACA.[12]

The largest group representing senior citizens is the American Association of Retired Persons (AARP), a politically active group with forty million members. Since all senior citizens are eligible for coverage under Medicare and since many of the uninsured are young, one might speculate that AARP would be indifferent to passage of the ACA. Obama and his allies in Congress transformed AARP into a stalwart supporter by fixing the "doughnut hole"—an obscure gap in coverage under Medicare Part D's support for outpatient prescription drugs. Under the 2003 law that established Part D, a gap in coverage was left for beneficiaries with annual outpatient drug expenses between $2,700 and $6,154.[13] Obama worked with Congress to eliminate this gap in coverage for seniors, who are heavy users of prescription drugs on an outpatient basis.

The pharmaceutical industry showed its resources and political muscle in the successful coalition against the 1993 Clinton health plan. Obama was determined to defuse their potential opposition to his plan. The White House negotiated a deal with the Pharmaceutical Research and Manufacturers of America (PhRMA) that transformed the industry from a likely opponent to an unexpected supporter. Under the deal, members of PhRMA agreed to moderate drug prices (but avoided direct government control of their pricing), pay ACA fees of $85 billion over ten years, and devote $100 million in advertising and other efforts to promote the ACA. In exchange, PhRMA won new protections against generic drugs that compete with patent-protected brand-name drugs and new protections against importation of cheaper medications from other countries. (This latter concession was painful to Obama because it entailed reversal of a 2008 campaign pledge by the Obama-Biden campaign.) Perhaps most importantly, the expansion of the insured population under the ACA was projected to create millions of new customers for pharmaceutical companies.[14]

The deal between Obama and PhRMA was offensive to progressives in Congress. They objected to the substance of the deal and the secret process. They pointed to Obama's pledge during the campaign to bring all stakeholders to the table in a transparent manner.[15] The PhRMA deal was the first in a series of compromises that tempered the enthusiasm of liberals for the ACA.

In one of the most surprising developments, the Obama White House also persuaded the American Medical Association (AMA) to support the ACA. The AMA had opposed the creation of Medicare in 1965 and had opposed the concept of national health insurance for decades. To appease physicians, Obama and Congress delivered $228 billion in new payments for physicians over a ten-year period.[16] The AMA did not win any major progress on tort reform. Although the organization did not support all of the provisions in the ACA, it strongly supported the individual mandate and supported passage of the ACA as a whole.[17]

The hospital industry aligned itself with Obama for similar reasons. Hospitals received $171 billion in new payments over ten years and strongly supported the individual mandate.[18] The American Hospital Association did not support all aspects of the ACA, but, like the AMA, they too supported passage of the ACA as a whole.[19]

Physicians, hospitals, and drug makers were dissuaded from being opponents for yet another reason: the ACA ultimately contained few mandatory cost-control provisions.[20] The most innovative cost-control features (e.g., pricing of bundles of services) were relegated to limited demonstration projects.

The most elaborate interest-group dialogue occurred between the Obama administration, Congress, and the health insurance industry. The Obama White House engaged the insurers, through the American Health Insurance Plans (AHIP), in many months of negotiation before AHIP became a public opponent of the ACA in October 2009. AHIP is the successor organization to the Health Insurance Association of America (HIAA), which was instrumental in defeating the Clinton plan in 1993–1994. AHIP's biggest fears were the single payer idea and the public option, but they also feared a tax on health insurance plans, a requirement that all plans offer a minimum set of benefits, and new restrictions on factors (e.g., age) that may be used in the setting of premiums.[21] AHIP also believed that the large coverage expansion in the ACA was not fiscally sustainable without strong cost controls in the delivery system. The White House did succeed in delaying public opposition from AHIP, which reduced the time available for that association to influence voting in Congress.[22]

Despite this impressive work with interest groups, from the outset the Obama administration faced determined opposition from influential business groups, especially the US Chamber of Commerce and the National Federation of Independent Businesses. Business groups did not simply fear a legislative mandate that businesses offer health insurance to their employees; they feared that new taxes would be levied on businesses to pay for the ACA. And that is exactly what ultimately happened: about one-third of US employers, those who offer generous ("Cadillac") health plans to their employees, will be subject to a new excise tax on insurance plans starting in 2018. The tax is estimated to raise over $100 billion per year.[23]

Business opposition was a serious challenge for the Obama White House. What Obama's plan did not face was the huge unified coalition of interest groups that amassed against the 1993 Clinton plan.

OUTREACH TO REPUBLICANS

President Obama made multiple efforts, both low-key private overtures and highly visible public efforts, to enlist the support of Republican
members of Congress for passage of the ACA. Some authors have characterized Obama's outreach to Republicans as a personal preference for consensus
building and cooperative engagement.[24] On the other hand, the substance of
the ACA was so redistributive in nature (i.e., such a base-oriented proposal)
that it was not a particularly promising issue on which to generate significant
Republican support.

Obama nonetheless obtained public statements of Republican support
for health care reform from several prominent specialists on health care.
They included surgeon and former US senator Bill Frist and George W. Bush's
health policy specialist Mark McClellan.[25] Previous chiefs of the Department
of Health and Human Services' (HHS) Centers for Medicare and Medicaid
Services (CMS), including Tom Scully of the George W. Bush administration,
also endorsed the need for reform.

Republican moderates such as California governor Arnold Schwarzeneg-
ger and New York City mayor Michael Bloomberg joined the many voices
favoring reform. But these statements did not necessarily endorse the specifics
of the Democrat-authored versions of health care reform that were moving
through the Congress at Obama's request, and none of them came from the
influential conservative wing of the Republican Party.

MAX BAUCUS AND CHARLES GRASSLEY

The Senate Finance Committee possessed jurisdiction over health
care reform because of its authority over taxation, Medicare, and Medicaid.
Obama's biggest hope for bipartisan support was in the Senate Finance Committee, where Democratic chair Max Baucus had many years of collaborative experience—and a close personal relationship—with ranking Republican
Charles Grassley of Iowa.[26] If a Baucus-Grassley bill emerged from the Senate
Finance Committee, the prospects for multiple Republican votes on the floor
of the Senate seemed to be promising.

Max Baucus was first elected to the Senate in 1978 and served on its Finance Committee longer than anyone in American history. He comes from a

well-known ranching family in Montana, and his voting record was generally on the conservative-moderate end of the continuum for Senate Democrats. He was considered one of the "most influential" members of Congress because he had a long track record of working effectively with Republicans and Democrats in producing bipartisan legislation.[27] Baucus was viewed with suspicion by many progressives because of his close ties to many industries and his willingness to work with conservative Republicans on issues. He was reelected as senator so many times that he became the longest sitting senator in Montana's history. In 2008 John McCain defeated Barack Obama in Montana by a margin of 50–47 percent; Baucus won reelection in 2008 by a margin of 73–27 percent.

Charles Grassley was first elected to the Senate in 1980 and describes himself as "just a farmer from Butler County." His voting record in the Senate is quite conservative, but he is best known in Congress as an "independent-minded deal-maker."[28] Although Grassley has strong ties to the health care industry, he has not been reluctant to take on the pharmaceutical industry—for example, when he felt their relationships with the US Food and Drug Administration were "too cozy."[29] Grassley served two stints as chair of the Finance Committee, one briefly in 2001 and another from 2003 to 2005. Unlike Baucus, who was starting a new six-year term in 2008, Grassley was up for reelection in November 2010. In 2008 Barack Obama defeated John McCain in Iowa 54–44 percent; in 2004 Grassley won reelection 70–28 percent.

The Obama White House knew that Baucus and Grassley had many legislative accomplishments under their belts. Under George W. Bush, the two senators were instrumental in passing the multiple rounds of Bush tax cuts, the new benefit for prescription drugs under Part D of Medicare, the energy bill of 2005 (including the requirement that gasoline be blended with corn-based ethanol), and repeal of the Alternative Minimum Tax, which affected many middle-income as well as wealthy taxpayers.[30] At the start of the Obama administration, Grassley helped Baucus and Obama secure significant Republican support for expansion of the federal Children's Health Insurance Program (CHIP) for children in low-income families that are not covered by Medicaid.

In the first half of 2009 it appeared that a pathway for a Baucus-Grassley reform bill was available. At the White House Forum on Health Care in March 2009, Grassley emphasized the importance of bipartisanship, even though the Democrats would soon have sixty votes in the Senate. He also made it clear that he could not support a public option, even though a majority of citizens in Iowa and the United States as a whole seemed to support the idea.[31] But Grassley reportedly favored a requirement that all Americans have health insurance and believed that serious reform needed to include subsidies to address affordability, new regulations of the insurance industry, and new sources of revenue to support expanded coverage.[32] Grassley's opposition to a public option irritated progressives, who believed that the public option was a minimum essential feature of meaningful reform.[33] It later became clear, however, that several key Democrats, including Baucus, had doubts about a public option.

To conservative Democrats such as Nebraska's Ben Nelson, the fact that Baucus was taking time to seek support from Grassley and other Republicans was reassuring. McCain had defeated Obama in Nebraska 57–42 percent, and Nelson surprised no one in Congress when he warned: "It would be hard to support a bill that had no Republican support."[34]

CONGRESSIONAL COMMITTEE ACTION

At Obama's request, Democratic leaders in Congress worked on three separate bills in different committees: two in the Senate and one in the House. The key points of contention were (1) whether all individuals should be required to have health insurance, (2) whether employers should be required to offer health insurance, (3) whether an option for government insurance (i.e., a Medicare-like plan for non-elderly people) should be made widely available to compete with private plans, (4) the overall cost of the plan, (5) the sources of program savings, and (6) new revenues to pay for the plan.

The Senate Committee on Health acted first on July 15, 2009. Cosponsored by acting chair Christopher Dodd of Connecticut and Ted Kennedy of Massachusetts, the Dodd-Kennedy plan included an individual mandate, an employer mandate, an expansion of Medicaid, a public option, new regulations of the private insurance industry, and generous public subsidies to lower the price of insurance premiums for all families with incomes less than four times the official poverty line ($88,200 for a family of four). The plan's cost was an eye opener: $1 trillion over ten years, and that figure did not include some of the more expensive provisions in the plan.[35] With Kennedy ailing from a brain tumor, Dodd was on his own to find Republican support. It never emerged, and the plan passed the Health Committee on a 13–10 party-line vote.[36]

The House Energy and Commerce Committee acted next, following the lead of seasoned chair Henry Waxman of California. (Waxman had already collaborated with the chairs of three other interested House committees.) Waxman's plan was similar in magnitude to the Dodd-Kennedy plan. It pleased progressives but engendered significant concerns among Blue Dog Democrats as well as Republicans. Waxman made some concessions to reduce opposition until it was passed by the slim margin of 31–28; five Democrats joined all Committee Republicans in opposition.[37]

As the Congress's August 2009 recess approached, President Obama called on the Senate Finance Committee to finish its work. Senator Grassley expressed irritation with Obama's statement that "it's time to deliver," because Obama was traveling in Paris when he and Baucus received the president's reprimand. Grassley was also annoyed by a letter from the White House encouraging a public option when it was apparent that the idea did not have adequate support in the Senate.[38]

Baucus knew that he had potent bipartisan opposition to a public option on his committee: moderate Democrat Kent Conrad of North Dakota was aligned on this point with moderate Republican Olympia Snowe of Maine. Both coming from rural states, they opposed a public insurance option because it might force rural hospitals out of business (since rural hospitals receive lower reimbursement rates under Medicare compared to private insurance).[39] Baucus was highly attentive to Snowe because she had stated publicly that she wanted to be part of a health care reform bill and was willing—unlike most other Senate Republicans—to collaborate with Baucus, President Obama, and other Senate Democrats.[40]

Disagreements were also emerging over sources of revenue for Obama's plan. Unlike Senator Dodd in the Health Committee, who was opposing taxes on health insurance plans to help pay for reform, Baucus sought such tangible sources of revenue. He did not trust speculative estimates of program savings from prevention, and he opposed large cuts in payments to those delivering care, the providers. In order to buy more time to find a committee consensus, Baucus delayed his committee vote until after the 2009 August recess. The White House was concerned; progressive advocates were deeply worried.

Progressives were already suspicious of Baucus because of his strong financial ties to the health care industry and his decision to take a single payer plan off the table at the start of his committee's deliberations.[41] Moreover, Baucus had previously irritated progressives by collaborating with George W. Bush on several sensitive issues (e.g., the Bush tax cuts). Progressives complained that it was unfair that Baucus was in effect deciding the future of health care in America.[42]

PAINFUL AUGUST RECESS

The Senate GOP leadership (Majority Leader Mitch McConnell and Majority Whip John Kyl) reportedly pressured Grassley and Republican senator Mike Enzi of Wyoming of the Finance Committee to avoid any deals with Baucus.[43] Some speculated that if Grassley collaborated with Baucus and Obama, he would never be a committee chairman again if the Republicans were to win a future Senate majority.[44]

Perhaps more importantly, Grassley, who was up for reelection in November 2010, was hearing more from conservatives in Iowa than he was hearing from home-state supporters of Obama-style health care reform.[45] At a town meeting in Winterset, Iowa, during the August 2009 recess, Grassley was "chastened" by constituent hostility to health reform.[46] Conservatives in Iowa apparently threatened him with a Republican primary challenge in 2010 if he collaborated with Baucus.[47] The *Des Moines Register* polls on health care reform also reported declining support for the kinds of reforms being discussed in Congress.[48] A radio ad in Iowa was sponsored by the conservative Coalition for Patients' Rights and run on local Fox News channels in Iowa: "Now they're at it again with a government-run health care plan. It'll cost more than a trillion dollars and raise taxes $600 billion. Worse, it could put a bureaucrat in charge of your medical decisions, not you or your doctor. Tell Senator Grassley to put patients first, and say 'no' to a government-run health care plan."[49]

Opponents of reform seized on the extra time in August 2009 to mobilize and protest in the districts and states of numerous members of Congress. The Tea Party also staged a large September protest in Washington, DC, that attracted thousands of participants.[50] It was timed to undercut a September 9 joint session of Congress in which President Obama urged Congress to act promptly on health care reform.

THE BELATED BAUCUS PLAN

In March 2009 Baucus formed a "Gang of Six" on the Finance Committee to search for common ground. Those six included Democrats Baucus, Conrad, and Jeff Bingaman and Republicans Grassley, Snowe, and Enzi. As a group, the six were well-established senators, as their last reelection percentages had averaged 72 percent. None had ever confronted a challenger who captured more than 39 percent of the vote.[51] On the other hand, neither Grassley nor Baucus were applauded at home for their work on health care. Surveys showed that Grassley's approval rating in Iowa had declined from 75 percent in January 2009 to 57 percent in September 2009. The largest drop in support was among Democrats. Baucus's approval rating had fallen to about 50 percent, although he was six years away from an election. Grassley needed to make sure that his base was with him. By the end of August 2009, he was sending out fund-raising letters for his reelection touting his determination to fight "Obamacare."[52]

Senator Baucus unveiled his reform plan (without any Republican cosponsors) in mid-September while drawing intense criticism from conservative and liberal activists.[53] The plan tracked Obama's principles, except it did not include a public option. Of the forty-six million uninsured people in the United States, the Baucus plan left twenty-five million uninsured by 2019 (one-third of those were illegal immigrants). By way of contrast, the Waxman plan left seventeen million uninsured. But the Baucus plan was more affordable, with an estimated cost of $774 billion over ten years—below the politically sensitive $1 trillion mark.

In October a somewhat more expensive ($829 billion) version of Baucus's plan passed the Senate Finance Committee on the strength of votes from all of the Democrats and Republican senator Snowe. The Snowe vote elated Baucus, the Senate Democratic leadership, and the White House. The feeling was that if Snowe could vote for it, moderate Senate Democrats might also have the cover they need to vote for it.[54] Snowe, however, was cautious in her support. She warned that if the Baucus plan was modified before it reached the Senate floor, she might vote against reform on the floor.[55]

DEALING WITH WAVERING DEMOCRATS

As public support for Obama's initiative deteriorated in mid-2009, the president engaged in a variety of attempts to reassure the public and pressure Democrats, particularly Democratic moderates in Congress. President Obama gave numerous speeches on behalf of the ACA, often reassuring audiences that if they liked their current insurance plans and doctors they could keep them.[56] This theme was designed specifically to counteract the fears that had been stimulated in 1993 by the Harry and Louise advertisements against Clinton's health care plan.[57] Despite Obama's best efforts, there is no evidence that his speechmaking was effective in boosting public support for the ACA.[58]

Meanwhile, a dispute erupted within the Democratic Party over the tactics that should be used to enlist Democratic support for reform. In the summer of 2009 the Democratic National Committee ran television and radio advertisements aimed at persuading Democratic members of Congress to vote for the ACA. The advertisements were targeted at moderate Democrats Kent Conrad, Evan Bayh, Bill Nelson, Mary Landrieu, Blanche Lincoln, and Ben Nelson. Blue Dog Democrats in the House were targeted as well. Health care activist groups with strong ties to the Democratic Party also pressured congressional Democrats to remain loyal to Obama on the health care issue.[59]

Obama's private advocacy group, Organizing for America (OFA), went a step further by organizing confrontational tactics aimed at the fifty-two Blue Dogs in Congress, including public demonstrations outside their district offices. The progressive MoveOn.org even sponsored attack ads on television against members of Congress who were not yet supporting President Obama on health care.[60] All of this activity occurred before it was clear whether a public option would be included or excluded from the final bill, and some uncommitted Democrats were holding out due to uncertainty about the public option issue.

Much of this activity came to an abrupt halt because of public criticism from Senate majority leader Harry Reid and White House chief of staff Rahm Emanuel. They exhorted allies to stop the "stupidity" of Democrat-on-Democrat attacks.[61]

OFA shifted its emphasis to countering the increasingly effective attacks of the Tea Party. Critics claimed that the ACA would create "death panels" of experts under Medicare to decide which patients would live and which would die without health care. OFA countered by purchasing ads on Google to accompany the outcome of a search on the phrase "death panel." The ads stated: "They [death panels] don't exist. Obama's plan will protect seniors. Get the facts now!" A link was provided to an OFA website with facts to use to dispel the rumor.[62]

As the ACA issue headed for roll-call votes in late 2009, moderate Democrats in Congress could not have been more cross-pressured. They knew a vote for the ACA was expected by Obama, Pelosi, and the Democratic Party. They also knew that many voters in their districts were not simply concerned about the ACA, but strongly opposed—to the point of political activism.

FINDING VOTES ON THE HOUSE FLOOR

Heading into the end of Obama's first year (2009), Speaker Nancy Pelosi faced a difficult challenge finding votes for the ACA on the House floor, but finding votes on tough issues was one of her specialties. She had been an avid fund-raiser for House Democrats in 2006 and 2008, and she knew how to work the rank-and-file members to generate votes.

House Democrats had already cast a difficult vote on emissions trading, or cap and trade (climate policy) with no assurance that the Senate would act (see chapter 7). Now Pelosi was planning to ask for their support of an unpopular health care bill with a public option, a provision that the Senate might never consider on the floor (given the known opposition to the public option in the Senate Finance Committee). Pelosi's task was not an easy one.

When the first version of the ACA was debated on the House floor in November 2009, the opposition was intense. Numerous arguments were made: (1) the public option is a dangerous step toward socialized medicine, (2) the individual mandate is coercion by "big government," and (3) the package is huge and costly: $1.1 trillion over ten years. Only one House Republican (Anh Cao of Louisiana) voted for it; thirty-nine rank-and-file Democrats, mostly Blue Dogs, defied the wishes of Speaker Pelosi and President Obama by voting against it. In closed-door discussions before the House floor vote, Obama apparently played an important role in converting a few final holdouts into supporters.[63]

The House ultimately passed its first version of the ACA in November 2009 on a vote of 220–215. Of the thirty-nine defectors, twenty-two were from the South, seventeen were freshman or sophomores, and thirty-two were representing districts that had awarded Obama less than 50 percent of the vote in 2008. All but one of the defectors ran better in his or her district than Obama did in 2008.

BIGGER SENATE CHALLENGE

The challenge in the Senate was even greater, because with Grassley's support unobtainable, Obama saw only two possible Republican votes (Susan

Collins and Olympia Snowe). A sixty-vote margin was required to overcome the anticipated filibuster. Since there were sixty Democrats and forty Republicans at the time, Obama needed one Republican vote to compensate for each defecting Democrat.

Senate majority leader Harry Reid was responsible for merging the Baucus and Dodd-Kennedy plans into a single bill that could attract sixty votes. The Senate moderates urged Reid to release his merged plan before votes were taken on time limits for debate on amendments. The implication was clear: if Reid released a plan that moderates found unacceptable, they might not vote to limit the time for debate, which could expose the reform effort to a filibuster.

Reid responded to pressure from progressives by announcing that he intended to include a public option in the merged plan. This announcement pleased independent senator Bernie Sanders, who was threatening to vote against reform if a public option was not included in the bill. To address the concerns of critics of the public option, Reid suggested a compromise where individual states would be entitled to opt out of the public insurance option.

Reid's compromise offer did not impress Senate moderates. In November 2009 independent senator Joe Lieberman went on national television and claimed that he would vote against Reid's plan if the public option—any form of public option—remained in the bill.[64] Moderate Democratic senators Evan Bayh, Ben Nelson, and Blanche Lincoln of Arkansas had similar concerns.[65]

Senators Snowe and Conrad suggested an alternative compromise. The idea was to permit a public insurance option only in geographic areas of the country where it could be demonstrated that the private market failed to supply affordable health insurance.[66] Although Senate moderates were interested in Snowe's compromise, Reid decided he could not risk the uncertain path to some GOP support and instead chose a path to reform without any Republican votes.[67]

In Reid's defense, Snowe may not have been "gettable" anyway. Even after making some concessions to her on small business provisions, Reid realized that Snowe could not accept the overall cost of the final bill or the additional taxes added to pay for the cost of ACA.[68] And Snowe's colleague from Maine, Republican Susan Collins, was objecting to the cuts in provider payments that Reid used to help pay for the coverage expansion.

Reid worked hard to marshal support from each of the remaining undecided Senate Democrats. As predicted, the wavering members were primarily senators from states where—with the exceptions of Indiana and Connecticut —Obama had performed relatively poorly in 2008 (Arkansas, Nebraska, Louisiana, and Montana).[69] Removal of the public option clinched support from Bayh, Lieberman, and Lincoln, but special deals were necessary to enlist support from Mary Landrieu of Louisiana and Ben Nelson of Nebraska.

For Senator Landrieu, Reid added a minor provision that ensured more federal funding for Medicaid in states with severe natural disaster problems. Landrieu declared proudly that the provision, which only Louisiana could qualify for due to Katrina and the stringent criteria, promised an additional $300 million for her state.[70] Once made public, this provision became known as a contemporary Louisiana Purchase.

For Senator Nelson, Reid made two concessions. He included compromise language on abortion (providing limited but not certain assurance that federal funds would not be used for abortions). Reid added a permanent provision calling for 100 percent federal funding of the cost to Nebraska of expanding the state's Medicaid program. No other state was granted such generous treatment under the ACA.[71] The Tea Party, Senate conservatives, and many reporters dubbed this provision the "Cornhusker Kickback."

The ACA was unpopular before Senate floor action, but more negative publicity accompanied the allegedly corrupt deals that Reid made to secure passage in the Senate.[72] The Cornhusker Kickback became so unpopular that in subsequent reconciliation legislation after passage of the ACA, the House leadership removed the language that Nelson had negotiated, with Nelson's support.[73]

A few days before Christmas 2009, the Senate voted on a strictly party-line basis, 60–39, to pass the Affordable Care Act. Republican senator Jim Bunning of Kentucky, an outspoken opponent of the ACA, did not vote. The bill has been characterized as the least popular major domestic policy passed in the last century of American politics.[74]

But the path to legislative victory for Obama was far from secured. In order to become law, the House and Senate versions of the ACA needed to be reconciled. Since the House version contained a public option at the insistence of House progressives, the negotiation between the House and Senate was expected to be sensitive. Soon after Christmas a stunning development in the state of Massachusetts cast a big cloud of uncertainty over the future of the ACA.

A WAKE-UP CALL IN MASSACHUSETTS

When Ted Kennedy died from brain cancer in August 2009, a special election was scheduled for January 18, 2010, to replace him. An interim Democratic senator, Paul Kirk, served in the vacated seat until a new senator was elected, thus allowing the Democrats to retain a filibuster-proof 60–40 advantage in floor voting.

The Obama White House had good reason to be confident about the outcome of the special election. The Democratic Party dominates state politics in Massachusetts, and Obama carried the state 62–38 percent in November 2008. The Democratic primary winner for the vacant seat was state attorney general Martha Coakley, who was considered to be a competent (if low-key) candidate. The Republican nominee was Scott Brown, a state senator from southern Massachusetts who had never run for statewide office and was unknown in much of the state. In short, Coakley was a (clear) "prohibitive favorite."[75]

In a stunning upset, however, Brown defeated Coakley 52–47 percent when many Massachusetts Democrats and independents joined Republicans in voting for Brown. Exit surveys showed that voters were angry about the big spending in Washington, DC, the controversial health care bill that was consuming all the energy of politicians, and the depressed state of the economy. Ironically, under Republican governor Mitt Romney, Massachusetts had already enacted health insurance reform that was similar to some of the provisions in the ACA. But Brown campaigned successfully against Obama's unpopular initiative, and his surprise victory was widely interpreted as a rejection of Obama's leadership and his health care initiative. In fact, Brown pledged to voters that he would go to Washington and cast the crucial vote to sustain a filibuster against the ACA. The Democratic margin had diminished to 59–41, and there appeared to be no plausible way to find a Republican senator to vote for Harry Reid's version of the ACA.

OBAMA TAKES CHARGE

Obama summoned Reid and Pelosi to the Oval Office to assess the future of his signature initiative. There were few viable options for moving forward. Reid argued that the House Democrats must accept his version of the ACA because it had already passed the Senate by a vote of 60–40 and because any version that was modified to please the House would not attract sixty votes. Pelosi reminded Reid and Obama that the House version of the ACA had passed by the slim margin of 220–215 and only after she had twisted the arms of many nervous Democrats. She doubted that she could pass Reid's version of the ACA on the House floor.

Obama thought differently. He worried that he had given too much discretion to Congress to fashion the bills. The result was a process full of secrecy and deal making coupled with little bipartisan collaboration. Under the circumstances, Obama favored yet another campaign to attract Republican votes, even though the health issue was energizing the Tea Party movement.[76] Some bipartisan support, Obama envisioned, would cleanse the process.

He started in Baltimore on January 29, 2010, in a rare appearance with House Republicans. It was a televised exchange of views on health care. On February 3 he made a televised appearance with Senate Democrats to show solidarity on health care. On February 28 a bipartisan group of twenty-eight lawmakers discussed health care reform with Obama for seven hours at Blair House, next to the White House.[77] The president was eager to insert some of the ideas of Republican lawmakers into the ACA, but he could not find any Republican votes for the bill.[78]

The unified GOP opposition to reform baffled some observers. Two key provisions of the ACA—the health insurance exchanges and the individual mandate—were originally Republican ideas. Insurance exchanges originated in reforms championed by Republican governors Jon Huntsman of Utah and Mitt Romney of Massachusetts. And a 1989 report by the conservative Heritage Foundation suggested the individual mandate as a way to lower the cost to business of providing insurance to everyone. Together, the exchanges and individual mandate operationalized the conservative notions of markets and personal responsibility.[79]

Conservatives knew, however, that there was much more in the ACA than insurance exchanges and the individual mandate. There was a costly employer mandate, a large expansion of Medicaid, new premium subsidies for people of modest incomes who were not eligible for Medicaid, a multitude of new regulations on the insurance industry, and a government-appointed commission that would determine how much reimbursement would be provided for different services. Rank-and-file Republicans in Congress also were aware of a stark reality: a big bipartisan win for Obama on health care would boost his credibility as a politician and create more headaches for Republicans down the road. Thus, few Republicans in Congress were cross-pressured—they perceived little value in collaborating with Obama on health care.

Ultimately, a frustrated Obama came to accept that there would be no Republican support. He therefore instructed Pelosi that the Senate version of the ACA must be passed in the House, even though it did not have the public option that the House and Obama preferred. He also pledged to help Pelosi find the votes.[80] Once the House passed the Senate version, the president could then sign it with no need for another Senate deliberation. The legislative strategy was to make any final changes that the House wanted through the budget reconciliation process, which could be enacted later in 2010 by simple majority votes in both chambers.

After an intensive campaign of retail (member-to-member) politics on Capitol Hill, Obama and Pelosi found that some moderate Democrats would not budge in their opposition to the ACA. Democratic congressman Jason Altmire of western Pennsylvania withstood many efforts at persuasion by the White House, believing he could not justify the vote to his middle-class constituents in suburban Pittsburgh. And Obama and Pelosi knew they were losing the one Republican vote from Louisiana they had acquired the first time around.

The full-court Obama-Pelosi press was successful in curbing the number of defecting Democrats from 39 to 34, and thus the ACA passed 219–211.[81] A key step in attracting votes from moderate Democrats was Obama's commitment to issue an executive order with the following clarification: federal funds may not be used for abortions.[82] Obama and Pelosi also turned around some progressives who were leaning against the ACA because it was not ambitious enough (i.e., no single payer plan). Thus, it was a creative combination of promised executive action and rank-and-file lobbying that delivered the necessary votes for the ACA. And Pelosi's endless expenditure of energy in search of votes was a key factor in helping the president.

The competitiveness of a House member's district was a strong predictor of whether a Democratic congressperson voted against the ACA.[83] In the twelve Democrat-held congressional districts where Obama had won less than 40 percent of the vote in 2008, none of the representatives voted for the ACA. Only 13 of the 30 Democrats in districts that voted 40–49 percent for Obama in 2008 voted for the plan. On the other hand, all but 7 of the 195 Democrats running in districts that Obama won in 2008 voted in favor of it.

Table 5.1. The Profile and Fate of House Democrats
Who Voted against the Affordable Care Act

Name	State/ District	Years of Service	Obama Share (2008)	Member's Share (2008)	Political Career
Bright	AL/2	2	37	50	defeated 2010
Davis	AL/7	8	74	99	resigned, lost 2010 race for governor; seat stayed Democrat
Ross	AR/4	10	39	86	won 2010; retired 2011; now held by GOP
Marshall	GA/8	8	43	57	defeated 2010
Barrow	GA/12	6	55	66	reelected 2010; won 2012 (despite redistricting); defeated 2014
Minnick	ID/1	2	36	51	defeated 2010
Chandler	KY/6	6	43	65	won 2010; defeated 2012
Kratovil	MD/1	2	39	49	defeated 2010
Peterson	MN/7	20	47	72	reelected 2010, 2012, 2014
Childers	MS/1	2	38	54	defeated 2010
Taylor	MS/4	20	32	75	defeated 2010
Skelton	MO/4	34	38	66	defeated 2010
Adler	NJ/3	2	52	52	defeated 2010
Teague	NM/2	2	49	56	defeated 2010
McMahan	NY/13	2	49	61	defeated 2010
McIntyre	NC/7	14	47	69	reelected 2010, 2012; resigned 2014; GOP won
Kissell	NC/8	2	42	55	won 2010; defeated 2012 after redistricting
Shuler	NC/11	4	47	62	won 2010; retired 2012; redistricting, seat won by GOP in 2012
Boren	OK/2	6	34	70	won 2010, retired 2012; GOP won 2012

Finding the votes in the House and Senate for the reconciliation package was not much easier. The March 2010 package passed the House 220–211 (with thirty-four Democrats defecting) and the Senate 56–43 (as senators Ben Nelson, Blanche Lincoln, and Mark Pryor defected).[84] Thus, Obama won passage of the ACA (and reconciliation) entirely due to the loyalty of most congressional Democrats.

Table 5.1 supplies the profile of the twenty-eight House Democrats who voted against the Affordable Care Act (the original and final versions) and the

Table 5.1. (*cont.*)

Name	State/ District	Years of Service	Obama Share (2008)	Member's Share (2008)	Political Career
Altmire	PA/4	4	44	56	reelected 2010; lost Democratic primary after redistricting in 2012
Holden	PA/17	18	48	64	reelected in 2010; lost 2012 Democratic primary after redistricting, challenger from left won
Sandlin	SD-AL	6	45	68	defeated 2010
Davis	TN/4	8	35	59	defeated 2010
Tanner	TN/8	22	43	100	retired 2010; GOP won 2010
Edwards	TX/17	20	32	53	defeated 2010
Matheson	UT/2	10	40	63	won 2010; won in 2012 after redistricting in UT/4; retired 2014; GOP won 2014
Nye	VA/2	2	51	52	defeated 2010
Boucher	VA/9	28	40	97	defeated 2010

Source: Michael Barone and Chuck McCutcheon, *The Almanac of American Politics, 2012* (Washington, DC: National Journal Group, 2011).

Notes: AL means "at large." Table includes only House Democrats who voted against the original House version of the ACA, the final version, and the reconciliation package. An additional sixteen House Democrats split their votes on the three measures: Griffith, Markey, Boyd, Kosmas, Murphy, Massa, Boccieri, Kucinich, Baird, Gordon, Space, Acury, Lynch, Lapinski, Berry, and Cooper.

related reconciliation package. The twenty-eight ACA defectors were predominately from the South (17 out of 28). Ten represented districts where Obama won less than 40 percent of the vote against McCain in 2008. Nine were freshmen members of the House and thus were vulnerable to reelection defeat due to their limited recognition and congressional experience.

Of the twenty-eight defectors, fifteen were defeated for reelection in 2010. Another two retired and their seats were captured by the GOP in 2010. Seven won reelection in 2010, but the GOP captured their seats in 2012 (due to resignation, redistricting, or electoral defeat). Only two of the twenty-eight seats were held by Democrats in 2015–2016.

One is tempted to infer that the vote against the ACA did not help the reelection prospects of this group of House Democrats. That inference is incorrect. House Democrats from GOP-leaning districts who voted for the ACA fared even worse (see chapter 10). Moreover, those who lost in 2012 or 2014 after redistricting might have survived longer if Obama's popularity had not plunged and if their state legislatures (which orchestrated redistricting) had not been dominated by the GOP in 2011–2012 due to the wave of Democratic losses in 2010.

COUNTERFACTUALS

The central ACA-related questions raised by critics of the Obama administration are (1) whether Obama should have delayed pursuit of health care reform until the economy recovered from the Great Recession, (2) whether Obama compromised too much in his quest to attract GOP support, (3) whether Obama gave adequate consideration to reform ideas suggested by Republicans, (4) whether the public option and individual mandate were worth the political controversy they generated, (5) whether the ACA was unpopular because Obama devoted insufficient effort to advocating it, and (6) whether the ACA lacked adequate cost-control provisions to be affordable and therefore created a political liability—either long run or short run—for Obama and the Democratic Party. As we consider each of these criticisms, recognize that "Obamacare" was so unpopular among independent and Republican voters that it ultimately became a liability for dozens of Democratic candidates for Congress in 2010 and 2014 (see chapter 10). The high political cost of voting for Obamacare may not have been apparent to rank-and-file Democrats in the early days of 2009, but it became increasingly clear as the debate unfolded and was crystal clear after the 2009 August recess. By the time the Democrats lost Ted Kennedy's Senate seat to Republican Scott Brown in early 2010, everyone knew that the ACA was radioactive. Thus, it is useful to consider more ways that Obama could have made the reform palatable or at least less provocative (e.g., Pelosi and Waxman made the sensible decision to not include a single payer plan in the bills that were voted on in the House, even though progressives generally wanted such a plan).

Public opinion about the ACA did fluctuate to some extent in 2009–2010, making it difficult for the White House and members of Congress to assess the political costs of pushing forward. Obama did not propose a detailed plan (which facilitated bargaining and avoided the 1994 Clinton problems), but the vacuum led several plans to be proposed by Democrats in Congress. The Tea Party was free to allege, though, that socialized medicine was coming, since it was not entirely clear what Obama was proposing or which version of reform would be voted on. Thus, it was not easy in 2009 for pollsters to gauge public opinion on an ACA that was not yet well defined.

National surveys showed that health care reform was a top domestic issue for voters in 2007 and much of 2008. All major presidential candidates in both parties produced health care reform plans, although they varied considerably in substance. When Lehman Brothers collapsed on September 14, 2008, and the financial crisis intensified, public opinion changed rapidly and the depressed state of the economy emerged as the dominant issue, far more important than health care.[85] Using concern about the Great Recession as an explanation, some critics argue that Obama should have deferred his health care ambitions until the state of the economy improved.[86]

Despite the rapid change in circumstances since his campaign pledges were made, the Obama White House in early 2009 honored its campaign pledges by putting into play three large domestic legislative initiatives (health care reform, cap and trade for climate protection, and immigration reform). Obama started with health care and climate legislation as equal priorities but gradually gave more priority to health care. He did so even though several of his trusted White House advisors urged him in the summer of 2009 to scale back his health care plan, perhaps settling for a national insurance program for children. Obama had already won bipartisan support for legislation to expand CHIP for lower-income households. The argument was that rather than seek a program for all age groups, he should seek some bipartisan support for an expanded version of CHIP.

The case for moving forward with a large ACA was more compelling. Obama's partisan margins in Congress created an opportunity that was unlikely to be matched for decades to come. A president's influence, especially on members of his own party, tends to be greatest soon after his election. The economy might take a long time to recover, and the president's party typically loses seats in the Congress at the midterm elections. Thus, it was correct for Obama to surmise that it might be much more difficult to pass health care reform in 2011 or 2012 than it would be in 2009.[87] Moreover, the Democratic Party was more unified on health care than on climate change and immigration, and thus the prospects for success in the House and Senate were greatest on health care. And perhaps most importantly, Obama's base would have been outraged at his timidity if he had backed off from all of his major campaign pledges.

It was outrage from base voters that stimulated the damaging insurgent campaigns that Ted Kennedy ran against Jimmy Carter in 1979–1980 and that Pat Buchanan and Ross Perot ran against George Herbert Walker Bush in 1991–1992. At the beginning of his first term Obama was correct that it was crucial for him to please his base from the outset. Moreover, his decision pleased the many Democrats who saw health care reform as necessary to produce a robust economy, although that connection was not apparent to many voters.[88]

As events unfolded, Obama was criticized harshly by segments of his base for compromising too much in an effort to win the support of Republicans in Congress. The argument goes like this: Obama gave away the single payer idea; he even gave away a public option. Despite these giveaways, the president attracted no Republican votes for the ACA.

The flaw in this line of argument is that Obama was forced to make the same compromises to ensure support from moderate Democrats and independents.[89] The chairman of the Senate Finance Committee, Max Baucus, indicated publicly that he would not support a single payer plan.[90] Senator Joe Lieberman made it clear that he would not vote for a plan with either a single payer plan or a public option.[91] The concessions made to Snowe were also important to Conrad. If even one of the Democrats or Lieberman had defected, Obama and Majority Leader Reid would not have had the votes necessary to overcome a filibuster threat. There are few (if any) provisions in the ACA that were included only because they were seen as attractive to the few wavering Republicans.

A related criticism is that Obama devoted too much time and political energy in an effort to attract Republican support for reform. The argument goes that he deferred for too long to Senator Baucus's dubious courting of Republican senator Charles Grassley, resulting in the issue's extending past the 2009 August recess. And, it is argued, he made too many public efforts to reach out to Republicans, thereby suggesting to the public that the health care issue was more important to him than economic recovery.[92] According to this view, Obama and his allies in Congress should have pushed reform through on a partisan vote before the August recess and then circled back to the economy or other issues.

With the benefit of hindsight, this line of criticism has some merit, but it overlooks some delicate questions. Would moderate Democratic senators (Baucus, Conrad, Landrieu, Nelson) and independent Lieberman have been less likely to support the president on health care if he had made no effort to attract Republican votes and simply counted on their votes for passage of his polarizing initiative? Would Baucus have supported reform if Obama had tried to steamroll him? It is precisely because the president made extensive efforts to attract Republican support—and had a plausible case that the GOP was opposing him strategically (rather than substantively)—that he had a strong rationale to insist on the support of all senators who caucused with the Democrats. Moreover, Baucus and Grassley had an extensive record of successful collaboration on many issues, and thus there was ample reason to defer to Baucus for a significant period of time. And the Democrats could not afford to lose a single Democrat, because they needed every vote to get to sixty.

A better criticism is that Obama did not make adequate use of the bully pulpit in local media markets where he was popular and a Republican politician was representing a competitive or Democratic-leaning state. George W. Bush pursued this strategy with considerable success in his 2001 campaign for a large cut in personal income taxes. Called "ginning up support in the provinces," Bush spent much of his time from inauguration to early April 2001 traveling to states where moderate Democratic senators (e.g., Max Baucus of Montana, John Breaux of Louisiana, and Ben Nelson of Nebraska) represented competitive or GOP-leaning electorates. Bush even traveled to Maine to ensure that Republican senators Susan Collins and Olympia Snowe and their supporters were aware of Bush's need for their support.[93] On health care Obama needed to be more aggressive with his "outside game" rather than relying primarily on talks with GOP politicians inside the Washington beltway.

Some critics have suggested that Obama never expressed serious interest in the key reform ideas that might have attracted support from some Republicans.[94] Those ideas include reform of medical malpractice litigation, market-based approaches to health insurance (e.g., health savings accounts), and more encouragement of low-cost, high-deductible plans such as those touted by McCain. The reality is that the addition of some conservative reforms in the ACA would not have changed the fact that the Obama plan was offensive to most

Republicans. It included a coercive individual mandate (that the idea's original authorship came from the Heritage Foundation was not effective immunity from this charge), more government control of the health care system, a large expansion of government spending, and higher taxes. The Tea Party's influence was growing rapidly, and any congressional Republican who chose to collaborate with Obama on health care would have been a sitting duck for a conservative primary challenge. Moreover, rank-and-file Republicans shared a strategic interest with their leadership in blocking passage of Obama's signature domestic priority, even if it contained a few conservative reforms. Thus, while it was arguably important for independents and moderate Democrats to see Obama reaching out for Republican support, the prospects of attracting Republican votes were minimal, regardless of the precise provisions of the ACA.

Proponents of the ACA expressed frustration that many Americans were uninformed and confused about the actual provisions of the ACA.[95] The act does not give undocumented migrants access to taxpayer subsidies for insurance, but a plurality of Americans thought it did (43 percent yes, 38 percent no, 19 percent don't know). The ACA does not establish government panels to make end-of-life decisions for people on Medicare, but many Americans thought it did (41 percent yes, 41 percent no, 19 percent don't know). When Congress tries to pass a complex, one-thousand-plus-page bill in a highly adversarial environment, misimpressions are easy for opponents to create and difficult for proponents to eradicate.

A key error in the original House bill was inclusion of the public option, even though Obama and the progressives clearly wanted it. It was obvious by November 2009 that a bill with a public option would never arise from the Senate, as there was bipartisan and entrenched opposition to it in the Senate Finance Committee. The White House chief of staff, Rahm Emanuel, was already signaling to moderate Democrats that the White House would not insist on the public option.[96] There was no good reason to ask moderate House Democrats to vote for a bill with a public option, and in fact that provision cross-pressured far more House Democrats than it did House Republicans. Removal of the public option was not dictated by national opinion polls (the idea had majority support in those polls); it was dictated by the need to protect moderate Democrats in Republican-leaning districts from the charge that they were voting for socialized medicine (or a public option that would lead the country in that direction). A coordinated decision by Obama, Pelosi, and

Reid to drop the public option would have been politically prudent for House moderates. But it would have offended the base, since "the public option was the darling of the progressive wing of the Democratic Party."[97]

More importantly, the inclusion of the individual mandate in the Affordable Care Act became a lightning rod for criticism against Obama, for it was used as a symbol of his preference for "big government" solutions. Of all of the major provisions in the ACA (the health insurance exchanges, the premium subsidies, the Medicare expansion, the employer mandate, and the individual mandate), the only one that was viewed unfavorably by the majority of Americans was the individual mandate. Unfortunately for Obama, that mandate was also the provision in the complex law that voters were most aware of.[98] Some progressives argue that the individual mandate generated more controversy than it was worth.[99] Others counter that removing the individual mandate would have left too many healthy young people uninsured, causing insurance premiums to rise for everyone else, thereby raising doubts about the fiscal viability of the entire plan.

A less expensive ("copper") insurance plan (e.g., no coverage of mental health, maternity care, and so forth) should arguably have been permitted, since the diminished expense might have softened some of the individual and corporate opposition to the ACA. More generous premium subsidies should also have been made available to lower-middle-income people who lacked access to employer-based health insurance. Under those conditions,, the individual mandate could have been removed, because more people would have been attracted to coverage without the threat of a mandate. Even with the individual mandate in place, it appears that millions of people will choose the exemptions or waivers or choose to pay the fine and remain uninsured (see chapter 6). If the individual mandate was seen as essential, the penalty for not being covered should have been hefty at the outset, since Obama was already being clubbed politically for using a coercive mechanism. Given that he was not committed to enforcing the individual mandate with any vigor (see chapter 6), it was a politically costly mistake to include it in the final House bill (even though it was favored by hospitals, insurers, and physicians).

Finally, some people argue that there is a good government rationale for refraining from passing sweeping new legislation on a partisan vote.[100] Such legislation might be poorly crafted, might serve a narrow range of interests, and might not be durable as partisan winds change. While this view of American politics may have been feasible in 1950–1990, when political parties were less potent and bipartisan coalitions were common, it is no longer viable. Presidents serving in periods of intense polarization will accomplish far too little if they act only when they can find bipartisan support.

A pragmatic version of this argument is that passing the ACA under reconciliation rules is a gimmick that invites repeal of the act through the same mechanism if the Republicans gain control of the Congress in the future.[101] Of course, in 2009–2010 President Obama had no reason to envision a Republican Congress in the foreseeable future. The more telling argument is that he would hold the veto power for at least three years (first term) and perhaps seven (if reelected). Repealing the ACA would have drawn an Obama veto that could not possibly be overturned, since a two-thirds' margin would be required in both the House and Senate. The Republicans could not win repeal in Congress until Obama left the White House and was replaced by a Republican president. By then, the argument goes, millions of Americans would have insurance linked to the ACA, and thus the political risks of repeal to the Republican Party would be enormous. This line of thinking helps explain why the Tea Party–affiliated Republicans felt it was crucial to repeal the ACA as soon as possible, before the key implementation date in 2014.

A prevalent criticism of Obama on health care is that "he signed it, but he never sold it."[102] That may be true, but the unpopularity of the ACA was not attributable to a lack of speechmaking by President Obama. From March 2009 to March 2010, Obama delivered about one speech or public statement per week on health care.[103] He also claimed an electoral "mandate" to reform health care, but he had already used the mandate argument on his good government reforms, the economy, and foreign policy—before the real debate on health care began.[104] Obama certainly spoke more about the economy than health care, but when one considers his radio and TV addresses as well as his speeches, he spoke more about health care than any noneconomic issue.[105]

A more plausible criticism is that Obama did not play a sufficiently aggressive outside media campaign in those specific towns, cities, and states where Republican senators were representing electorates that had voted for him in November 2008. He certainly made sufficient "inside Washington" overtures to Snowe, Collins, and Grassley. As explained in chapter 2, presidents sometimes need to supplement direct cultivation of key senators with personal visits to their states. Future research should examine whether Obama's travel schedule in 2009 gave adequate priority (both in frequency of visits and explicitness about need for support on health care) to Iowa (Grassley), Maine (Snowe and Collins), New Hampshire (Gregg), Indiana (Richard Lugar), Ohio (George Voinovich), and Florida (Mel Martinez). All of these senators were aware that their constituents had voted for Obama in November 2008.

A more cogent argument is that the design of the ACA was inherently divisive (e.g., the public option in the House plan, the individual mandate, and the absence of a "copper" plan), and thus no bully pulpit strategy could make it popular or tolerable. This unpopularity was not restricted to Republicans and conservative-leaning independents. The antagonism toward the ACA was shared by some key groups in Obama's base: the uninsured, heads of households making under thirty thousand dollars a year, young adults, and suburban women.[106]

Finally, consider the impact of the ACA on the federal deficit, an issue that was an important part of the legislative debate in Congress. The final bill was primarily an access-enhancing measure, for little meaningful cost control was included in order to neutralize the opposition of organized interest groups such as the pharmaceutical industry, hospitals, and physicians. The fine print of the ACA does include a promising new approach to paying doctors called "bundled payments"—all costs for an episode of care are bundled together into one price—that reduces the incentive to order unnecessary services. But the bundling provision was limited to ten demonstration projects.[107]

What helped Obama on the fiscal arguments is that Baucus had insisted on real revenue to pay for the ACA. Since the Congressional Budget Office scored the ACA as a net deficit-reducing measure in the long run, the president did not face a powerful argument from members of Congress and constituents interested in a balanced budget. There is no evidence that he was harmed politically on the fiscal aspects of his advocacy of the ACA, although the expected large expansion in the size of the federal government was certainly objectionable to conservatives.

Passage of the ACA was an enormous accomplishment for President Obama and the Democratic Party. However, it was more controversial than it should have been, and the ACA is partly responsible for the ultimate loss of Congress to the Republican Party in 2010 and 2014 (see chapters 6, 10, and 11). In other words, Obama and the Democratic Party paid a much higher political price for the ACA than they needed to pay.

6

THE AFFORDABLE CARE ACT: IMPLEMENTATION NIGHTMARE

The Obama administration proved to be more adept at moving the Affordable Care Act through the Congress than at implementing the complex piece of legislation. The president and his advisors seemed slow to realize that competent implementation of the ACA required a team with different skills than the team required for passing the law. As a result, the Obama administration exhibited symptoms of weak public administration, which supplied the Republicans political ammunition and further complicated the president's quest to build public confidence in the ACA.

One can argue that a different kind of reform, such as one with a single payer plan for all health care, might have been more simple for the public to understand and easier for the federal government to implement. But the ACA does not replace the current system with a single payer plan. It leaves much of America's pluralistic health care system in place and superimposes a variety of reforms on what is already a complex system.

The outcomes of weak administration were generally not permanent damage to the president's policies; most of the implementation problems proved to be fixable. The significant damage was political in nature: to the president's reputation for honesty and competence, to the popularity of the ACA, and to the Democratic Party's electoral fortunes in November 2014. Although Barack Obama's name would not again appear on the ballot after November 2012, his plunge in popularity in 2013–2014, which was exacerbated by ACA implementation snafus, put fellow Democrats at an elevated risk of defeat in the 2014 midterm elections.

My assessment of implementation of the ACA begins with the credentials and experience of Obama's health policy team. I then consider the challenges and strategic options facing the president's adversaries, especially the conservative activists. The key components of the ACA are then explored to determine how well the Obama team implemented them. The chapter highlights how Obama, recognizing his team's mistakes, made aggressive use of executive powers to correct the errors and minimize, as much as possible, the collateral damage to Democrats who were up for reelection in 2014. A key complication is the simultaneous fights Obama waged in the courts and the Congress to sustain the ACA. The chapter concludes with some counterfactuals that might have better secured Obama's policy agenda, protected his own popularity, and reduced the vulnerability of his party in the 2014 midterms.

LEADERSHIP OF OBAMA'S HEALTH POLICY TEAM

There is a tendency for a newly elected president, after a hotly contested election, to perceive that the key expertise he will need for effective governance is political in nature. Presidents certainly need advisors who understand the Congress, the media, public opinion, and the powerful interest groups in Washington, DC. But a president also needs to appreciate the importance of various apolitical aspects of public administration, since skills of public management are often what determine whether a president's policy agenda is actually implemented successfully on the ground.[1]

In the 2009–2010 legislative battle to secure passage of the ACA, Obama was guided by a small team of seasoned advisors inside the White House: Nancy-Ann Min DeParle, the first director of Obama's White House Office of Health Reform, who was a former head of the Health Care Financing Administration in the Clinton administration; OMB director Peter Orszag, a health policy analyst from the Urban Institute; and Phil Schiliro, director of White House Legislative Affairs, a twenty-seven-year veteran of Capitol Hill who worked previously for both Congressman Henry Waxman and Senate majority leader Tom Daschle. It is difficult to dispute the claim that this was a well-qualified team to seek passage of the ACA.

Obama got off to a slower start building his executive team at the critical Department of Health and Human Services, a huge cabinet agency with a budget of almost $1 trillion and a workforce of more than eighty thousand civil servants.[2] He began by nominating Daschle as secretary of HHS, but Daschle ultimately withdrew his nomination to avoid controversy. Daschle had made errors on his tax returns and amended three years of returns on January 2, 2009, for unreported income, including a payment of $140,000 in back taxes plus interest.

After some delay, Obama ultimately nominated and secured Senate confirmation of Kathleen Sebelius as his HHS secretary. A career politician and former governor of the state of Kansas (2003–2009), Sebelius knew how to communicate and defend the president's health care reform agenda. She stepped down in 2014 after the worst of the ACA implementation problems were being fixed and was succeeded by Sylvia Mathews Burwell, who previously had served as OMB director and brought deep management experience from the private as well as public sectors.[3]

The most revealing indication of the White House's neglect of the ACA implementation challenge was the mishandling of the leadership of the Centers for Medicare and Medicaid Services (CMS), a critical yet little-known agency within HHS that had primary responsibility for implementing the new law. Effective leadership of CMS requires not simply knowledge of health care, policy insight, and political skills but also hands-on managerial skills. The leader of CMS must oversee numerous crucial administrative tasks: the development of technically complex health care regulations; the creation of a large new website with a consumer front end and a back end with links to insurers and other organizations; the oversight of complex contracts with information technology and public outreach providers; the coordination of CMS activities with other health agencies of the federal and state governments; and the development of a modified insurance industry built around the types of private insurance plans envisioned in the ACA.

When Obama took office, it was well known that CMS was a troubled federal agency. The agency had suffered from a lack of Senate-confirmed leadership during the last two years of the George W. Bush administration. It had recently lost some of its best civil servants, was plagued by poor staff morale, and was reputed to have some of the most antiquated information technology systems in the federal government. In fact, to compensate for these known problems, the Obama administration created, pursuant to the ACA, a small health care reform office that reported directly to the secretary of HHS.

President Obama did not even nominate a candidate to lead CMS until April 2010—sixteen months after he was sworn into office, eight months after the congressional committees were marking up the ACA, and four months after the ACA was passed by Congress and signed into law by the president. If Obama had appreciated the challenges of ACA implementation and understood the value of including the key public administrator in the development of the legislation, he would have nominated a CMS administrator soon after the nomination of his HHS secretary in 2009.

By the time Obama made his CMS nomination in April 2010, the ACA was already highly politicized and the Republicans in Congress were looking for ways to exploit the law's unpopularity for partisan political benefit. The president's belated nominee for the post, Dr. Donald Berwick, was a highly accomplished and well-known innovator in the field of health care quality and had decades of experience in the Harvard medical complex in Boston. What Berwick lacked that Obama needed was strong management experience at a public agency or in the health care industry. Nor was Berwick well versed on the information technology and contracting issues that would soon confront CMS.[4]

The Republicans in the Senate saw nothing but partisan opportunity in the Berwick nomination. He proved to be a juicy target for criticism because he was an admirer of the British health care system (which the GOP tagged "socialized medicine") and had a track record of provocative speeches and writings that Senate Republicans could readily exploit in a detailed confirmation process.[5]

Senate Republicans did not take long in sending a message to Obama. Within two months of the official Berwick nomination, all forty-two Republicans in the Senate signed a letter to the president requesting withdrawal of the Berwick nomination.[6] The Democratic chair of the relevant confirmation committee was moderate committee chair Max Baucus, who presumably was not eager to schedule a confirmation hearing, knowing the controversy that would ensue. Both Baucus and the White House could count votes and knew there was no plausible pathway to the sixty votes that would be required to confirm Berwick over a filibuster threat, despite his Harvard credentials and record of health care innovation.

At about this time (May 2010), one of the president's closest White House advisors, Harvard professor Larry Summers, was alerted—in what later became a leaked and widely publicized memorandum—that the Obama health care policy team was not properly staffed in the White House or at HHS to accomplish implementation of the ACA.[7] Rather than move Berwick into a White House staff role or a key advisory role to the HHS secretary, where his innovative thinking on health care quality could have been quite valuable, the White House stubbornly made a "recess appointment," which allowed Berwick to serve as CMS administrator without Senate confirmation for a brief period, from July 2010 to December 2011.

As a result, Berwick assumed a most challenging assignment on the president's signature initiative while all of the stakeholders in Washington, from the American Medical Association to the insurance industry, including the CMS staff, knew that his days at CMS were numbered. After Berwick departed CMS, Obama did not accomplish a successful Senate confirmation of a CMS administrator until May 2013, more than four years after he was inaugurated.[8] In the final analysis, President Obama relied upon a troubled agency without effective leadership to implement his signature initiative, and his political opponents in Congress happily exploited the forthcoming mishaps at CMS for partisan gain.

The White House health care policy team was also less equipped to accomplish implementation than to navigate legislative politics with the Congress. When DeParle was promoted from director of the White House Office of Health Reform to deputy White House chief of staff for policy (January 2011–January 2013), she was replaced for a brief period by her deputy, Professor Jeanne Lambrew, a health policy academic from the University of Texas who had previous experience serving President Clinton in the Executive Office of the President. Obama later obtained ACA implementation assistance from Washington political veterans Chris Jennings and Phil Schiliro, but during the key stages of ACA implementation, the White House health care policy team never had strong leadership with public administration, insurance, or business experience, let alone proficiency with information technology or experience overseeing large-scale online initiatives.[9]

THE COMPLEXITY OF THE AFFORDABLE CARE ACT

The primary goal of the ACA is to provide insurance coverage for almost fifty million uninsured Americans while making sure that those with substandard coverage are shifted to adequate plans. What makes the law so complicated is that the coverage expansion is to be accomplished through multiple interacting reforms: an expansion of Medicaid for low-income Americans that requires action in the fifty states; a requirement on large- and medium-size employers to offer adequate coverage for their employees; creation of new federal and state insurance exchanges where individuals and small businesses can purchase affordable insurance, often with the benefit of premium subsidies supplied by the federal government; requirements on insurers to refrain from a variety of discriminatory practices (e.g., refusing to cover applicants with preexisting conditions) that make it difficult for some consumers to obtain insurance and stay insured; and a requirement that the residual uninsured purchase adequate insurance with their own resources or pay a fee to the federal government, the so-called individual mandate. There was also a wide range of other ACA provisions unrelated to insurance coverage. They addressed issues such as the quality of care in hospitals, prescription drugs and medical devices, long-term care, incentives for physicians to locate in underserved areas, community health centers, preventive services, new quality oversight and pricing demonstrations, and flexible savings accounts for future medical expenses.

It is not common for Congress to pass laws that are almost 1,000 pages in length. In fact, the ACA legislation is 961 pages long with 381,517 words. Ultimately 109 implementing regulations were issued by the federal government—mostly by CMS—with a total of 11,588,500 words. Thus, for every word in the ACA, there were roughly 30 words from CMS explaining what Congress did and did not intend.[10] It should not be surprising, then, that there was litigation about whether CMS was correct about what Congress meant.

The ACA includes ninety distinct policy provisions that have an implementation schedule from 2010, the year of enactment, to 2018. Almost half of the provisions were to be implemented by the end of 2011, but some of the most important provisions—the Medicaid expansion, the state and federal insurance exchanges, the employer mandate, and the individual mandate—were not scheduled to take effect until January 2014.[11]

The implementation schedule, at first glance, seems well designed to advance President Obama's political interests. The provisions scheduled for implementation prior to his 2012 reelection were expected to be popular: a requirement that insurers allow children to stay on their parents' insurance until age twenty-six; a temporary insurance program for high-risk people with preexisting conditions to tide them over until they can take advantage of the insurance exchanges; and more generous subsidies for outpatient prescription drugs under Part D of Medicare, a popular program among senior citizens. Withheld until after Obama's 2012 reelection were the launch of the insurance exchanges, the Medicaid expansion, the employer mandate, and the individual mandate. While the timing seemed favorable to Obama, it proved to be quite unfavorable to the Democrats in Congress who ran for reelection in 2014.

CONSERVATIVES COUNTERATTACK

When Obama chose to proceed with passage of the ACA in the face of polarized public opinion and without Republican support in Congress, he created an issue for the both the Tea Party and Republican Party to rally around. The opposition strategy was designed not by big business but by small-government conservatives and their allies among think tanks, conservative philanthropists, and Republicans in the House and Senate.[12] The political counterattack unfolded on several fronts. First, small-government groups and their allies among attorney generals in the fifty states filed twenty-six separate cases opposing the ACA in federal courts around the country. Conservative constitutional scholars, amplified by multiple think tanks, created what has been termed an intellectual "permission structure" for Republican judges to rule against the ACA.[13] Republicans in Congress, amplified by FOX News and talk radio, also attacked the constitutionality of the law. The prospects of winning in the federal judiciary were highly uncertain, but the multiyear process of litigation drew continued media coverage to aspects of the ACA that were not popular (e.g., the individual mandate). Moreover, as conservative judges in some lower courts ruled against the Obama administration, Republicans were encouraged and genuine uncertainty was created about the future of the ACA.

Second, in 2010 conservative donors and business-affiliated political action committees poured money into campaigns against the incumbent Democrats in Congress, especially those who had voted in favor of the ACA and were representing districts or states where John McCain had won or been competitive in 2008. Many of the televised attack ads before the November 2010 midterm elections focused on the evils of "Obamacare." The attacks continued prior to the November 2012 election and, more importantly, after the implementation snafus of 2013–2014 and before the November 2014 midterm elections (see chapter 10).

Third, once the Republican Party took control of the House of Representatives in January 2011, Republicans explored various legislative strategies to obstruct, weaken, defund, or repeal the ACA. The best tactics to employ became, as we shall see below, a matter of severe internal disagreement among congressional Republicans.

As long as Barack Obama was president, the Republicans were not going to win repeal of the ACA, since Obama had veto power. What the Republicans gained was an issue that they could rally around, and the anti-ACA movement became so potent that some Democrats in Congress became worried about their positioning relative to the ACA. As implementation problems surfaced and the popularity of the ACA deteriorated after passage, some Democrats in Congress began to shift their position. They did not call for repeal of the ACA, which was the GOP position. What emerged were bipartisan efforts aimed at "fixing" the ACA. Even though the fixes did not pass the Congress, they kept the ACA—and its alleged flaws—in the public eye, which Republicans believed was in their partisan interest.

PUBLIC ATTITUDES TOWARD THE ACA

At the time the Affordable Care Act was enacted by Congress and signed into law by President Obama (spring 2010), public opinion on the reform was quite polarized. The results of various national polls varied from a slight majority favoring the ACA to a slight majority opposing it. The intensity of opinion was generally stronger among the opponents, since the ACA did not accomplish the key reforms sought by many progressives (i.e., no single payer plan, no public option), and thus the degree of enthusiasm among progressives was tempered.

Public opposition was not restricted to conservatives or self-declared Republicans. Among self-declared independents, opinion about the ACA was about equally divided in the spring of 2010, but opposition grew steadily and became more intense toward the end of that year and throughout 2011. Opposition among independents declined modestly in 2012 during Obama's reelection year but mushroomed in 2013 as implementation problems surfaced in the media. By the end of 2013 and throughout 2014, the percentage of independents opposed to the ACA were running 10–20 points higher than the percentage of independents supporting the ACA.[14] It was not until 2015 that the ratio of favorable to unfavorable attitudes toward the ACA began to approach 1:0.[15]

The fact that a majority of respondents were opposed to the ACA did not mean that the majority of Americans favored repeal. In fact, polling consistently showed a majority of respondents opposed to the Republican-led efforts to repeal the ACA.[16] As implementation issues surfaced, the key question became how to "fix" the ACA, a conversation that unfolded on each of the major provisions: the individual mandate, the employer mandate, the Medicaid expansion, and the health exchanges. Here is where efforts at public administration of the ACA intersected with partisan politics.

THE INDIVIDUAL MANDATE

The ACA requires uninsured individuals to purchase insurance or pay a fee to the government—"the individual responsibility requirement." A fee is applicable if an individual is uninsured for more than three months in a calendar year.

Some of the angriest opposition to the ACA was directed at the individual mandate. The uninsured displayed particularly unfavorable attitudes. One survey found that only 24 percent of the uninsured under the age of sixty-five had a favorable view of the ACA; 47 percent had an unfavorable view. The uninsured complained that the ACA did not simply require coverage for unexpected catastrophic expenses; the law compels coverage of routine medical expenses (including psychiatric visits) that many individuals perceived they would not need.[17] Single men and some women, for example, did not want to pay for coverage of maternity and newborn care.

In order to soften the coercive impact of the individual mandate, the Obama administration was highly permissive with exemptions. Congress authorized only a few narrow exemptions for religious groups, Native American tribes, illegal immigrants, and prisoners.[18] On top of those statutory exemptions, HHS issued a "hardship" form that allows uninsured applicants to claim one or more of fourteen possible sources of hardship. One of the largest exemptions is applicable to people living in states where Medicaid was not expanded as envisioned in the original design of the ACA. HHS also exempted the uninsured if the cost of insurance would be so burdensome that serious deprivation would result (e.g., food, shelter, and so forth). The details of when the hardship exemptions apply were vague when they were announced in 2013, emerging during the botched rollout of the insurance exchanges (discussed below).[19]

The fee for noncompliance with the individual mandate starts low and grows rapidly over two years.[20] For the 2014 tax year the fee was set at $95 per adult (plus $47.50 per child or a maximum of $285 per family) unless an income-related calculation is higher: 1 percent of the portion of the person's adjusted gross income that exceeds the federal income tax filing threshold ($10,150 for a single person). In 2016 the fee is $695 per adult (plus $347.50 per child or a maximum of $2,085 per family) or 2.5 percent of family income, whichever is larger.[21]

Adding to the public irritation, the process of avoiding the fee by obtaining an appropriate exemption was complex, bureaucratic, and involved a change in the tax forms submitted to the Internal Revenue Service. Some exemptions are administered by a tax return declaration (possibly with a requirement for supporting documents); other exemptions (no affordable insurance options, recent foreclosure, recent death of a family member, unpaid medical bills, eviction, religious beliefs) require mailing a letter to an ACA insurance exchange. For the latter exemptions, online requests are not permissible. Those with approved exemptions receive "an exemption certificate number" that must be entered on the IRS tax return.[22]

Recognizing that IRS enforcement of the individual mandate would be politically sensitive, House Republicans looked for a creative way to curb IRS enforcement of the mandate. In April 2011 the House considered a bill to block any new money for IRS to hire agents to enforce the ACA. The provision passed the House on a vote of 260–167, with many Democrats supporting the measure.[23] In the Senate, however, Majority Leader Harry Reid blocked a floor vote on the measure.

The ACA was designed with almost a three-year delay between when the law was enacted and when the individual mandate was scheduled to take effect (January 1, 2014). In fact, the first penalty for violators did not have to be paid until April 15, 2015, as part of a personal income tax return. And the effective date for coverage was delayed until May 1, 2014, due to the startup problems with the federal insurance exchange.

The statutory delay had a good policy rationale, since extensive outreach by HHS, IRS, and the states was required to make sure that the millions of uninsured understood their choices and the penalty for not complying. The delay also offered some political protection for President Obama, because the controversial compulsion to buy insurance was not scheduled to take effect until after the November 2012 presidential election. For conservatives, however, the three-year delay created some opportunities. On the litigation front, conservatives had sufficient time to file creative constitutional challenges to the ACA that featured arguments against the individual mandate.

The opinions of federal courts splintered on the constitutional questions, a confusing development that added more uncertainty to the implementation process and more adverse publicity for the ACA. The US Supreme Court was compelled to resolve the issue in the summer of 2012. The Supreme Court ruled 5–4 in favor of the Obama administration, reasoning that the individual mandate is an application of the Congress's power to tax. Conservative chief justice John Roberts joined with the four liberal members of the Court to form the majority.[24] The outcome of the case was much closer than many experts expected, and segments of the conservative community were repulsed by Roberts's vote and rationale in the case.[25] For President Obama the decision was seen as a major victory.

When the famous HealthCare.gov (website) fiasco occurred in the fall of 2013, pleas from Congress for delay of the individual mandate proliferated. In October 2013 ten Democratic senators signed a letter urging HHS to delay the deadline for people to carry health coverage or pay a penalty.[26] Obama refused to give individuals the same delay that he granted employers (discussed below), a discrepancy that Republicans in Congress criticized with vigor.[27]

After the 2014 elections, the Obama administration continued to worry about new anger that could result when uninsured consumers learn they must pay a penalty to the government.[28] The Treasury Department estimated that as many as six million taxpayers might have to pay a fee. The administration began a concerted effort to get the word out about the numerous types of exemptions from the penalty for not having insurance.[29]

Due the burgeoning number of exemptions, the Congressional Budget Office projected in 2014 that almost 90 percent of the thirty million uninsured in 2016 will be eligible for at least one exemption and thus will not face a penalty under the ACA. CBO's estimate of the number of uninsured not subject to a penalty (due to exemptions) was increased from eighteen million in 2012 to twenty-three million in 2014.[30]

In summary, the Obama administration reaped only limited policy benefit from the individual mandate but incurred large political costs trying to enact it and then implement and defend it. Ironically, all of this controversy was related to a policy—the individual mandate—that candidate Obama had vigorously opposed in 2008 primary debates against Hillary Clinton and Senator John Edwards.

THE EMPLOYER MANDATE

The ACA requires all large- and medium-size employers to offer affordable health coverage to their employees or pay a fine of two thousand dollars per employee. An affordable plan is defined as one that does not cost the employee more than 9.5 percent of his or her income. An employer must also pay for the equivalent of 60 percent of the actuarial value of the employee's coverage, thereby limiting the employee's financial obligation. Small employers with fewer than fifty employees are exempted from the employer mandate.

Republicans were eager to link the ACA's employer mandate to financial hardships for business, layoffs, and overall damage to the economy. Even some proponents of the ACA feared that businesses currently offering insurance might drop their coverage and pay the ACA fee, since they could pay their employees cash that could then be used by employees to help sign up for subsidized plans on the ACA exchanges.[31] Conservative critics focused on two different arguments: the employer mandate would encourage companies to stop hiring full-time workers in order to avoid the costs of health insurance; and small companies would be discouraged from growing, since they must offer health insurance if they pass the fifty-employee threshold.[32]

In February 2014 the Congressional Budget Office stirred the pot with a complex report on the possible effects of the employer mandate. The key CBO finding was that ACA coverage will cause a 1.5 percent to 2.5 percent decline in work hours from 2017 through 2024, an effect that is equivalent to removing two and a half million workers from the US labor force in 2024. The largest impact was among older workers who no longer need to work in order to obtain health insurance, are not yet eligible for Medicare, and might prefer to spend time with family or pursue other interests. Moreover, some low-wage workers will be encouraged to leave the workforce entirely or cut back their hours of work in order to ensure a low enough income to become eligible for Medicaid or for the premium subsidies on the exchanges.[33]

Republicans seized on the CBO report as support for their position that the employer mandate would harm the economy. Democrats spun the report as a positive, since employees were no longer locked into their current jobs simply to obtain health insurance.[34] In reality, a shift of Americans from employer-based insurance to Medicaid or federally subsidized private insurance was not the intended effect of the ACA, and the result would be higher-than-expected federal spending.[35] The entire line of reasoning in the CBO report ran contrary to what the Obama administration had been arguing since 2009.

As mentioned above, the ACA stipulates that if affordable employer-based coverage is available, a worker is not entitled to premium subsidies on the federal exchange. Affordable employer plans are those that cost the employee less than 9.5 percent of their household's income. This key provision is intended to discourage flight from employer plans to the exchanges.[36]

In what has been described as a "drafting error," the authors of the ACA seem to have overlooked the fact that many employees have spouses and children and therefore need access to affordable family coverage. ACA does require employers to allow a worker's dependent children to enroll in a family plan, but the cost of a family plan (covering spouse as well as children) can exceed the 9.5 percent threshold established in the ACA. For a worker earning $30,000 per year (or $2,500 per month), the employee contributions to family coverage can easily exceed $237.50 per month. Employees also face co-payments and deductibles under some employer-sponsored plans. The average deductibles under employer plans have risen rapidly from $828 per individual in 2009 to $1,217 in 2013.[37] In other words, the worker may not be able to afford to cover his spouse and children through the employer's plan, and he may also be barred from applying for premium subsidies on the exchanges.

Uninsured children are a special concern. There were seven million of them when the ACA was passed in 2009. About 75 percent are estimated to be eligible for Medicaid, CHIP, or premium subsidies on the exchanges. The other 25 percent are either noncitizens, are in families with ample incomes, or have access to affordable employer insurance. The US Government Accountability

Office (GAO) estimates, though, that almost 500,000 children are caught in the "family glitch" that occurs when the employee cannot afford to add them to his or her employer-based plan but is barred from using the exchanges.[38]

The employer mandate was supposed to take effect on January 1, 2014. Senate Democrats up for reelection in November 2014 did not want to be put in a position of defending the costly requirement, especially since the economic recovery was sluggish.[39] The average cost of employer-provided insurance was $16,834 per employee (2014) and rising.[40] Recognizing the political realities of the situation, Obama took prompt action to address the issue. For the largest employers (100+ employees), the Department of the Treasury began by delaying the mandate to 2015 and then softened the mandate: instead of requiring that 95 percent of full-time employees be covered by 2015, the requirement was reduced to 70 percent by 2015. For medium-size employers (50–99 employees), the Department of the Treasury first delayed the requirement until 2015 and then for another year, until 2016.

The ACA does not require small employers (those with fewer than 50 employees) to offer health insurance. Still, HHS was authorized to create a new small-business exchange where affordable policies could be found, but the administration delayed creation of the small-business exchange.[41] Small businesses were concerned that the broad range of benefits required to be covered under the ACA would lead to only expensive plans being made available on the small-business exchange.[42] Moreover, the ACA provision allowing plans to set premiums based on age (but not health status) was seen as a cost booster: one estimate was that it would cause 65 percent of small businesses to face higher premiums for covering their employees than they would have faced without the ACA.[43] Opposition to the ACA among small business owners simmered and helped fuel sustained business opposition to the entire program.

EXPANSION OF MEDICAID

The ACA took a seemingly straightforward approach to expanded insurance coverage for low-income Americans. The federal government required each state to provide Medicaid coverage to all people living in households with incomes less than 138 percent of the official federal poverty line. It was a major policy change, since in many states Medicaid did not even cover all people below the poverty line.

Since Medicaid coverage is expensive and state budgets are strained, the ACA authorized HHS to reimburse states for most of the cost of expanded coverage. Specifically, ACA called for the federal government to pay the states 100 percent of the cost of new eligible enrollees through 2016, with the subsidy gradually declining to 90 percent of cost in 2020. The Medicaid program represents such a large and rapidly growing share of most state budgets that the deal seemed attractive, so enticing that some experts could not imagine that a state would refuse it.[44] If a state nonetheless refused to expand Medicaid, HHS was given a decisive club: the ACA empowered HHS to withhold federal funds from the state's existing Medicaid obligations. The loss of federal funds for the existing Medicaid program would create a big hole in any governor's budget.

The ACA's top-down approach to Medicaid expansion was upset by litigation launched by conservatives. Many health law experts were stunned in 2012 when the US Supreme Court, in an opinion otherwise highly pro-ACA, held 7–2 that the ACA's Medicaid-expansion provision is unconstitutional. The Court had no quarrel with Congress enticing states to expand their Medicaid coverage by offering generous federal subsidies to pay for the expansion. What the Court struck down was the threat that HHS might remove funds from the state's existing Medicaid program if the state did not agree to expand the program as required under the ACA. In the Court's view, this form of coercion was a violation of the constitution's concept of federalism.

The Supreme Court decision created an unexpected challenge for President Obama. Governors and state legislatures were soon pressured by conservatives to refrain from expanding Medicaid for low-income Americans under the ACA. Cautious fiscal analysts in the states were also skeptical: the federal government might renege on the generous subsidies authorized in the ACA, and the states faced a gradual increase in their fiscal obligations to Medicaid under the terms set by the ACA. As a result, the Obama White House and its allies were forced to prepare persuasive cases for Medicaid expansion on a state-by-state basis, and their audiences were often Republican governors and state legislators.

While the Democratic Party was controlling much of Washington politics, the Republican Party was potent in the states (see table 6.1). In fact, with the electoral results in 2010 and 2012, the Republican Party controlled twenty-nine or thirty-one of the fifty governorships in the period from 2011 to 2014, the period when most key ACA decisions were made. The Republican Party also

Table 6.1. GOP Control of State Governments, 2007–2016

	State Legislature	GOP Control of: Governor	Both
2007–2008	14	22	9
2009–2010	14	24	9
2011–2012	27	29	22
2013–2014	26	31	23
2015–2016	30	31	23

Source: National Conference of State Legislature, "State and Legislative Partisan Composition," undated, www.nsl.org.

controlled roughly twice as many state legislatures as the Democratic Party, and the Republicans controlled at least one chamber of the legislature in a majority of states. In 2013–2014 there were twenty-three states where the Republicans had a trifecta: they controlled the governor's office and both chambers of the state legislature. Interestingly, the unpopularity of the ACA and President Obama before the 2010 midterm elections contributed to the strong GOP control of many states (see chapter 10).

Withstanding the pressure from conservatives, Republican governors in some states (e.g., Arizona, Michigan, Ohio, and Pennsylvania) followed through with expansions of Medicaid. Other states (e.g., Indiana) expanded Medicaid but only after overcoming stiff resistance among conservative activists and extracting concessions from HHS (e.g., permission to charge premiums for some families above the poverty line and permission to charge a penalty when patients overuse the emergency room).[45] In some cases (e.g., Wisconsin), states did expand Medicaid to some extent but refused additional federal subsidies in order to avoid the detailed requirements of the ACA.[46]

Conservative activists and business groups were not necessarily on the same page about Medicaid expansion. When a state refuses to expand Medicaid, some low-paid full-time workers are required under the ACA to receive insurance from their employers, since they are not eligible for Medicaid. As a result, state refusals to expand Medicaid shift some of the costs of the ACA from the government to business.[47] Thus, state-level decisions against Medicaid expansion are hardly pro-business in their impact, an argument that the Obama administration deployed in discussions with the states.

Some states considered reforms that would direct families with incomes at 100–138 percent of the poverty line to the private insurance exchanges (see below) rather than to Medicaid. The result was a bigger bill for HHS. The average person enrolled in the exchanges with income just above the poverty line costs the federal government nine thousand dollars in premium subsidies; it costs six thousand dollars for enrollment in Medicaid.[48]

Among state responses, one of the most innovative was creation of the "private option": premium subsidies for low-income families instead of a direct expansion of Medicaid. Arkansas (through collaboration between a Democratic governor and a Republican legislature) was the first state to take this route, and the Obama administration used executive authority to approve it.[49] Iowa also adopted a private option, and as this book goes to press, the idea is being considered in some other states.[50]

The private option has political advantages for Republicans and conservative Democrats who would like to expand coverage for low-income people but would prefer to vote for a market-oriented approach rather than a bigger Medicaid program. For Republican politicians the issue was complex: the private option was framed by some conservatives as an indirect way to support Obama and implement "Obamacare." As a result, some Republican legislators in Arkansas risked losing their seats in Republican primaries due to their support for the private option.[51]

In Pennsylvania the politics worked to persuade a vulnerable Republican governor (Tom Corbett) that Medicaid expansion was advisable. Corbett tried to add a work requirement to the Medicaid expansion, but the Obama administration refused to approve one. Corbett did win a premium structure for families above the poverty line and an eight-dollar copayment for each visit to the emergency room for a nonemergency condition.[52]

As of late 2015, thirty-one states and the District of Columbia had expanded Medicaid pursuant to the ACA.[53] There is no deadline under the ACA for states to decide whether they will expand Medicaid.

The decision of many states not to expand Medicaid put more pressure on the Obama administration to expand the exemptions from the individual mandate. Otherwise, low-income people who could not afford insurance but also could not enroll in Medicaid would have been subject to a financial penalty under the individual insurance mandate. The Obama administration added a hardship exemption to protect the millions of low-income Americans in states that refused to expand Medicaid.[54]

Overall, implementation of the Medicaid expansion proved to be much more complex than anyone predicted. The unexpected Supreme Court decision on the constitutionality of the Medicaid expansion limited the power of HHS and gave conservative activists substantial political leverage in the fifty states. The result was that state implementation of the Medicaid expansion slowed significantly.

THE HEALTH EXCHANGES

The nuts and bolts of a "health exchange" marketplace start with a website that offers comparative information on private health insurance plans and a portal where consumers can sign up for one of the plans. That sounds simple enough, but the guts of the website must have several capabilities: (1) the capacity to process millions of users at roughly the same time (especially near an enrollment deadline); (2) an infrastructure that protects the privacy of users; (3) an automated data-verification process that can access government databases to check the accuracy of personal information submitted by users (e.g., legal residency and other personal identifiers, household size, household income, and the applicant's access to employer-based health insurance); (4) links to each of the fifty states and their (often antiquated) Medicaid computer systems; and (5) links on the back end of the website to numerous insurers who wish to market their plans on the exchange to consumers (i.e., detailed plan-specific information on services covered, premiums, deductibles, copayments, and so forth for the geographic area where the consumer lives). Any information technology (IT) expert will tell you that this can all be done, but it is a huge task. It requires leadership, careful planning, IT expertise, superb contractor management, lots of startup money, and numerous tests and refinements before the site goes live.

The federal website was dubbed "HealthCare.gov" and it went live (without the sign-up portal) in 2012. Some states also elected to have their own websites. In fact, when the ACA was enacted in 2010, the expectation was that most states would have their own exchanges, would do their own outreach to encourage users to enroll, and would receive generous federal subsidies from 2010 to 2015 to develop their own exchanges.[55] The ACA required HHS to decide by January 2013 which states would be capable of running exchanges.[56] About three years after enactment but before the first enrollment period began on October 1, 2013, it was apparent that only fourteen states would run their own exchanges, as the other thirty-six states implicitly defaulted to HealthCare.gov. States shied away from launching their own exchanges for a variety of reasons.

Maintaining such a complex website is costly, and the ACA called for each state to assume the cost of maintaining its exchange after January 1, 2015.[57] The early development experiences with state exchanges were mixed (California and Connecticut made good progress, but Hawaii, Maryland, and Oregon ran into a suite of IT and contractor problems).[58] Many cautious state officials were not inclined to take on this new challenge, especially at a time when states were facing red ink and layoffs due to the Great Recession and the slow recovery. Simply put, a big unexpected bill for a website redesign might require diversion of state funds from road projects, education, or other vital and politically sensitive projects.

For Republican governors and legislators, the decision whether to launch a state exchange also had a partisan dimension. Conservative activists argued to Republican governors: If you launch a successful exchange in your state, doesn't that build public confidence in "Obamacare" and thereby buttress the image of Democratic president Barack Obama? Conservative think tanks, such as the Cato Institute, were openly urging states not to participate in any optional aspect of ACA implementation.[59]

With some Republican leaders in Congress calling for a strategy of letting the ACA kill itself, the best partisan strategy for a Republican governor or legislator might have been to delay and obstruct but eventually default to the federal website. Indeed, in several GOP-controlled states (Florida, Georgia, Missouri, and Ohio) it is alleged that state officials actively obstructed efforts to inform individuals and families of what their options would be when the federal exchange opened.[60]

In the selection of contractors for the federal website, HHS/CMS did not follow best practices. To accelerate the process, CMS limited the number of firms that were eligible to bid. They failed to probe the past performance of CGI Federal Inc. (a subsidiary of a Canadian IT firm) before awarding CGI the key contract. The contracts were also written to relieve CGI of responsibilities for cost overruns, in effect putting the onus on the government for financial performance in the contractor relationship.

Overall, thirty-three companies built the website pursuant to sixty distinct contracts. CMS was under the impression that CGI was the lead contractor, but CGI "did not have the same understanding of its role."[61]

Several months before the first open enrollment deadline (October 1, 2013), Obama administration officials were predicting that HealthCare.gov would open on schedule in October because experts had been working for three years behind the scenes to get ready. Confident claims were made that key deadlines in website design and testing had been met and that plenty of money was available for consumer outreach to the uninsured.[62] Obama acknowledged that there would be "bumps" along the way, but his rhetoric was reassuring.

In the insurance and contracting communities, there was no such confidence. A series of computer problems plagued the rollout of George W. Bush's prescription drug benefit (Part D of Medicare) in 2006. CMS was facing a much larger challenge with rolling out the ACA than the agency had faced in rolling out Part D, for the latter affected only senior citizens and only their prescriptions.[63]

The key contractors informed HHS officials months in advance that computer troubles lay ahead for the rollout. Contractors were working through six hundred hardware and software defects. Also, the contractors were frustrated that the government kept changing the requirements in ways that were far too grandiose, given the limited time available before going live.[64]

An example of one of the "eleventh-hour decisions" by HHS was a design requirement that all visitors to HealthCare.gov create an account in order to browse the insurance plans offered on the site. This requirement was made barely a month before the October 1 deadline and caused a bottleneck as millions of curious visitors overwhelmed the site soon after the October 1 deadline.[65]

A demonstration version of the federal website was shown to White House officials during the summer of 2013.[66] The demonstration recreated the consumer interface but did not cover the underlying mechanics such as the crucial (and politically sensitive) capabilities of user verification and eligibility determinations. Those were the mechanics that failed when the site launched. As a result, the White House demonstration did not generate the warning that President Obama sorely needed: that the key federal website was not ready to be rolled out on October 1, 2013.

The Senate Finance Committee, chaired by Democrat Max Baucus, was suspicious that HHS was not ready for the rollout. At one public oversight hearing in the spring of 2013, Baucus bluntly warned HHS secretary Kathleen

Sebelius that the ACA was headed for a "train wreck" unless federal officials improved their state of preparation.

Inside the executive branch, there was bureaucratic infighting, diffuse accountability arrangements, and a serious lack of leadership.[67] Months after the ACA was enacted, a new Office of Consumer and Insurance Oversight was established to oversee implementation of the ACA, particularly as it relates to private health insurance. The new office, though it had access to the secretary of HHS, had four leaders in three years and never developed a sound working arrangement with the IT specialists in CMS. The new office was ultimately subsumed into CMS to shield its operations from congressional budget cuts.[68]

Delays in rule making also slowed preparation for the October 1 rollout. CMS was ready in May 2012 to issue a final rule that defined how the federal and state exchanges would operate, including crucial information that influenced design of the website. This key final rule was delayed five months by the White House and was not published by CMS until after President Obama's November 2012 reelection, presumably to avoid any adverse publicity associated with the huge ACA regulation.

Real-world testing of the website with insurers was scheduled for the third week of July 2013 but did not begin until the third week of September. Dozens of system features were behind schedule, but no adjustment was made to the rollout date.

On October 1, 2013, the federal health exchange opened and nearly three million interested consumers across America accessed the primitive site. It promptly crashed when the first big wave of users sought to create accounts. It was almost three months (until December 23, 2013) before a restart could occur, and adverse press for the administration was widespread. For President Obama it had to be enormously frustrating to observe a botched rollout of his signature domestic policy initiative. He informed reporters that he had not been informed "directly that the website would not be working the way it was supposed to."[69]

The president's entire health policy team pleaded ignorance about the website fiasco. Inside the White House, Obama's health policy advisors said they had focused on interagency coordination issues, not computer issues.[70] Sebelius confessed she was unaware of the website problems and, had she known, she would have delayed the launch. In December 2013 she said the federal online exchange needed five years of design/construction and a year of testing;

instead it had been done in two years with virtually no testing.[71] The temporary CMS administrator, Don Berwick, who was in charge when the key contracts were issued, said he considered the design of the marketplace computer network a staff-level function. He was focused on broader policy issues.[72] By the time a new CMS administrator was confirmed by the Senate in mid-2013, the website fiasco was about to occur. A former White House aide who helped draft the ACA stated simply: "This was the president's signature project and no one with the right technology experience was in charge."[73]

CANCELLATION OF "SUBSTANDARD" INSURANCE POLICIES

The ACA was designed to provide affordable insurance to the uninsured, but it was also designed to eliminate limited plans that subject individuals to large out-of-pocket costs for health care. About fourteen million consumers were buying their insurance individually, and about 50–75 percent of those consumers had policies that did not meet the "minimum essential" standards established in the ACA. To protect these consumers from an abrupt halt to their coverage, the ACA contained a grandfathering clause that allowed insurers to continue offering these limited plans if the policy had been in existence as of March 2010. In a CMS rule making, the administration clarified and narrowed the grandfathering clause by stating that (1) the limited policies could not be offered to any new customers, and (2) a policy would not be grandfathered if it had changed in any significant way since March 2010 (i.e., the deductible, the required co-payments, the benefits covered, and so forth).[74]

As was anticipated under the ACA, insurers informed millions of consumers that their insurance plans were being cancelled and that they needed to find an alternative insurance policy. In many cases the cancellation was caused directly by the ACA while in other cases the insurer was cancelling the offering because the plan was expected to die out due to the lack of new customers. In what proved to be a "perfect storm," the cancellation notices were issued at the same time the federal exchange was shut down due to website problems.[75] As a result, millions of consumers were uncertain about whether they would obtain coverage, what their coverage might be, and when they would be able to obtain new coverage. Angry protests of the cancellations were registered with both the White House and Congress.

President Obama's use of the word "substandard" to describe the cancelled plans inflamed many consumers who felt strongly that they had made the best possible selection for their family. About 45 percent of consumers who buy their own insurance are self-employed or small business owners; another 25 percent are working but do not have access to (or cannot afford) employer-provided insurance; 11 percent are retired but not yet eligible for Medicare; and most of the others are young, part-time workers.[76]

The cancellations triggered some of the worst publicity President Obama experienced during his presidency. Since the 2009 debate about passage of the ACA, Obama had been insistent that under the ACA people who were content with their existing insurance policies would be entitled to keep them. His precise words in August 2009 were: "If you like your private health insurance plan, you can keep your plan. Period."[77] A speech at the 2012 Democratic National Convention by Kathleen Sebelius contained the same theme. And Obama himself echoed the same pledge in 2013 on the third anniversary of the Affordable Care Act.

The cancellation notices seemed to be a direct contradiction to the pledge Obama had made. Recognizing the oversimplification in his previous statements, Obama shifted his rhetoric significantly in a key 2013 speech in Boston. "So if you're getting one of those [cancellation] letters, just shop around in the new marketplace. . . . For the vast majority of people, you can keep it [your current policy]."[78]

The House of Representatives acted quickly to capitalize on the anger. They passed a bill authored by Republican Fred Upton of Michigan that permitted insurers to offer the cancelled policies for another year to both new and existing customers. The White House threatened a veto on the grounds that there was no reason to permit the substandard policies to be offered to new customers. Despite the Obama veto threat, 39 Democrats joined all 222 Republicans in a vote in favor of Upton's bill.[79]

Democratic senator Mary Landrieu, facing a tough reelection contest in November 2014, was determined to separate herself from President Obama while solving this problem. Joined by five of her Democratic colleagues in the Senate, she introduced a bill that would compel insurers to continue offering the cancelled policies to existing customers.

Recognizing the political realities, the Obama White House signaled that it was open to a fix of the troubled rollout.[80] Before the Senate could address the issue, President Obama announced a one-year executive delay in the cancellation of substandard policies but indicated that insurers would not be permitted to issue the substandard policies to new customers. Under the president's plan, the final decision on whether to allow insurers to continue selling limited plans would be left to the insurance regulatory bodies in each of the fifty states.[81] Many state insurance commissioners and industry executives were annoyed by the president's announcement because they had not been consulted and doubted that the executive plan was workable.[82]

Like Senator Landrieu, Democratic senator Kay Hagan of North Carolina was up for reelection in November 2014. She personally informed President Obama that "A one-year fix is not enough and we need to do more."[83] She called for extending the enrollment deadlines further and an investigation into the causes of the botched rollout. At about this time, the conservative organization Americans for Prosperity was spending $1.7 million on TV advertisements in North Carolina linking Senator Hagan to passage of the ACA.[84] More than anything else, Senate Democrats wanted to shift the conversation away from the ACA to the improving economy, but Obama's handling of the ACA implementation was making the shift impossible.

THE "TECH SURGE"

President Obama did not stand still in the face of the website problems. He promptly appointed Jeffrey Zients, a former OMB official, to lead a project to repair HealthCare.gov. In collaboration with a team of outside IT experts, Zients launched what became known as the "tech surge."[85] Improvements in the federal exchange occurred in two stages: a first step was to make the site operational for the first enrollment period, which was delayed several months; a second step was to make more fundamental improvements before the start of the second enrollment period starting November 1, 2014. Daily reports on the "tech surge" were reported through Sebelius to President Obama in the White House.

The first stage of improvements, which entailed only refinements to the site, was so successful that 5.4 million people (in thirty-six states) picked insurance plans on the federal exchange during the first enrollment period. Another 2.6 million people (in fourteen states) signed up for plans on state exchanges.[86] For the second enrollment period, portions of HealthCare.gov were revamped or replaced altogether. The most progress was made on the consumer-facing front end of the portal while progress on the back end that faced insurers was delayed into 2015. The front end displayed a new home page with a visual design and tools to help users compare options without having to register, thereby facilitating an electronic form of window shopping. Software changes were made to support users who created an account and logged into the system.[87] The application for an insurance plan was slashed from seventy-six web pages in 2013 to sixteen pages in 2014. Special efforts were made to streamline the identity verification portal and to make the system work better for consumers using mobile devices.[88]

The insurance industry expressed a concern that consumers who signed up during the first enrollment period may have difficulty renewing their plan during the second enrollment period. CMS responded with a feature that automatically renews insurance plans and premium subsidies in 2015 unless a consumer takes affirmative action on the site to modify or switch their plan.[89]

Further, HHS officials believed that the fall 2013 outage was not a flaw of HealthCare.gov but partly due to a limitation of the Verizon server. In 2014 Verizon upgraded its server and expanded its staffing to support it. About 75 percent of new enrollees in 2014 were also transferred from the Verizon server to a streamlined Amazon-designed portion of the site. CMS developed a plan to move the site from its Verizon platform to a Hewlett-Packard platform, but decided to retain the Verizon platform since there was not enough time in 2014 to test the H-P platform.[90]

Overall, the second enrollment period ran much more smoothly than the first. The improved performance was partly a "learning by doing" phenomenon, but President Obama and his health policy advisors also brought in an entirely new team with operational skills and hands-on IT experience from the early Massachusetts and Connecticut state-developed exchanges.[91]

THE BIG UNKNOWN: WHICH OF THE UNINSURED WILL SIGN UP?

In order for an insurance plan to work, there must be enough healthy people paying premiums to cover the treatment costs for those who are sick plus provide some profit to the insurer. Analysts argued that the big unknown for the new exchanges was the rate of sign-up among young, healthy uninsured Americans. Insurers feared that the premium subsidies would have a larger incentive effect on the older versus the younger uninsured.[92]

The ACA addressed this issue by requiring that insurers offer three plans called bronze, silver, and gold. The bronze plan was intended to be attractive to healthy young people because it was the lowest-priced coverage. The total out-of-pocket costs for the bronze plan were capped at $6,350 for an individual and $12,700 for a family of four.[93] For example, in 2013 the insurer Moda Health offered a twenty-six-year old nonsmoker in Oregon a bronze plan at a premium of $133 per month, with a maximum of $45 in co-payments and a $6,350 deductible.[94]

The best estimate is that roughly 11.6 million Americans between the ages of eighteen to thirty-four are uninsured at any given time. The ACA uses a carrot-and-stick approach to get these young people insured. Federal premium subsidies are offered to lower-income workers who lack access to employer-provided insurance, and those who choose not to enroll in any insurance plan must pay an annual penalty based on their income that starts at $95 and climbs rapidly thereafter.[95] Even strong advocates of the ACA were worried that the carrot-and-stick strategy might not work with young people.[96]

The exchanges were plagued with adverse media publicity in their first year, because it appeared that too few young people were signing up. In order for the exchanges to be fiscally sustainable, it was estimated that 40 percent of the new enrollees needed to be young, but only 20 percent of those enrolling in the early stages of the first enrollment period were young (ages 18–34).[97] In fact, early estimates were that there were more 55–64 year olds signing up on the exchanges than young people ages 18–34.[98] But as more effort was made to enlist young people, their rate of enrollment increased.[99]

The Hispanic population, the largest uninsured racial/ethnicity group, was also slow to sign up for coverage. In the first year only 2.6 million of 10.2 million uninsured and eligible Hispanics enrolled in coverage. Despite the knowledge that this population was heavily dependent on ERs and community health centers for its care, the Spanish version of the HHS website did not launch until December 2014, and there was a shortage of Spanish-speaking "navigators" around the country. (A navigator is a trained advisor who helps households understand the alternative plans in the marketplace and helps them enroll in their preferred plan). Some Hispanic leaders have speculated that the hostile atmosphere around immigration and deportation also had "a chilling effect on enrollment."[100]

Even more concerning was that sick people seemed to be signing up on the exchanges at a more rapid rate than expected. One study found that people enrolling in new plans under the ACA reported serious health conditions at double the rate (24 percent) of those who held on to their existing plans (12 percent). Media stories raised fears that the bad mix of new policyholders would force insurance companies to raise premiums rapidly in future years.[101]

The designers of the ACA anticipated that insurers would face an uncertain mix of policyholders. The ACA allowed insurers to charge older policyholders three times the premium that young policyholders must pay. Moreover, the ACA has a creative scheme called "risk corridors"—or "industry bailouts," according to GOP critics—that protect insurers from the unknown.[102] Specifically, the law authorizes CMS to make extra payments to insurers in the early years of the exchanges if those insurers can show that they were stuck with an especially unhealthy pool of enrollees; insurers who enlist an unexpectedly healthy pool of enrollees are required to pay some of their windfall back to the federal government.

Using executive power, Obama also issued rules that require insurers to report their premiums annually for inspection by Treasury and CMS, thereby providing data on exactly what consumers are facing in the insurance marketplace.[103] Thus, there were safeguards in the ACA that discouraged a rapid rise in premiums in the early years of the new exchanges but did not completely dispel the fear of the unknown.

THE VERIFICATION CHALLENGE

When consumers apply for insurance and premium subsidies on the federal and state exchanges, they self-report various types of information that may not be consistent with data contained in federal databases. If there is a discrepancy between what the consumer reports and what federal databases report about the same person, a resolution of the discrepancy may be necessary.

One source of potential discrepancy is the applicant's residency status. The ACA bars people living in the United States without authorization from obtaining insurance coverage through HealthCare.gov. If necessary, documentation typically entails copies of a US passport or certificate of naturalization. A second source of potential discrepancy is the applicant's Social Security number. Documentation may be needed in the form of a copy of the applicant's Social Security card. A third source of potential discrepancy is the applicant's reported income and eligibility for premium subsidies. The maximum income that is allowed for those seeking premium subsidies is $94,200 for a family of four, or four times the official poverty line.[104] If necessary, documentation can be tax returns, wage statements, tax statements, pay stubs, or letters from employers. A fourth source of potential discrepancy is the applicant's access to health insurance supplied by his or her employer. The aca does not permit people to obtain premium subsidies on exchanges if their employer offers "affordable" health insurance, where affordable is defined as costing less than 9.5 percent of annual household income.

Of the original eight million people who signed up for private health plans on the federal and state exchanges, 85 percent received premium subsidies under the aca. Two million of those who received subsidies submitted information that differed from information in federal databases.[105] All of the applicants with discrepancies were notified that additional documents would be necessary to support their application. cms and its contractor (Serco) took a long time to resolve the two million discrepancies. Until late May 2014 the contractor was using manual processes to resolve discrepancies, because the systems for scanning and transferring documents electronically were not developed in time to support aca implementation.[106]

In September 2014, after much tedious work, cms determined that the discrepancies could not be resolved for about 400,000 consumers who applied during the first enrollment period. Specifically, 279,000 received notices from cms that their incomes could not be verified. Another 115,000 received notices that their citizenship or immigration status could not be verified. In order to avoid a termination of their insurance or a reduction in premium subsidy, new information had to be supplied by September 30, 2014.[107] In December 2014 hhs cut off premium subsidies to 120,000 households that had not responded to income verification requests; another 112,000 were terminated from subsidies because legal residence in the United States was not verified.[108]

cms never resolved exactly how they would verify family size, which influences the size of the premium subsidy. Verifying an applicant's access to affordable, employer-provided health insurance is also a challenge.[109] When the Obama administration delayed the employer mandate until 2015, they also delayed a requirement for employers to inform HHS of the insurance plans they offer to their workers.[110] Thus, as of mid-2015 the verification challenge under the ACA was still a work in progress.

PREMIUM SUBSIDIES AND TAX OBLIGATIONS

The HHS policy was to enroll as many people as possible into insurance plans and provide the approved premium subsidy, given the applicants' estimations of their incomes. It was understood that a correction might be necessary on their 2015 tax return if an applicant's estimated income—which triggered the amount of premium subsidy—was determined to be incorrect. Since an applicant for subsidies was asked to estimate their household's income for the forthcoming year (2014), it was understood that some of the premium subsidies would prove to be too large and some too small because of unanticipated changes in the applicant's income during the year.

The ACA envisioned that corrections would be necessary but capped the total amount of repayment that could be required of any applicant. For those with incomes less than 400 percent of the poverty line, the required repayment could be no larger than $2,500 for a year.[111]

In early 2015 administration officials were worried that the ACA might cause more anger among the newly insured, since they might be surprised to learn that their tax liability was unexpectedly large. And the process of reconciling premium subsidies and tax refunds can be quite a burden for an inexperienced tax filer. To appreciate the political sensitivities of this matter, consider how the IRS process works with respect to premium subsidies. If a filer is insured without a premium subsidy, they simply check a box on line 61 of the 1040 tax return (indicating that they are insured). If they have received a premium subsidy, by January 31 they should receive from the IRS a 1095-A form ("Health Insurance Marketplace Statement") that documents the amount of premium subsidies that were received for the previous year.[112]

Filers who receive premium subsidies must submit a special Form 8962 with their tax return. The form facilitates a reconciliation of any differences between the applicant's estimated income and associated premium subsidy, and their actual 2014 income and the correct 2014 subsidy. The differences are smaller for diligent applicants who adjust their estimated income on the exchanges as changes in their incomes occurred during the year.

If the subsidy has been too small, the tax refund will be larger than it would have been otherwise. If the subsidy has been too large, the filer must pay back the excessive subsidy to the IRS, either in the form of a diminished refund or a check to the IRS. The cap on the size of the repayment ($2,500) is applicable only to those with incomes below 400 percent of the poverty line; those whose actual income is above 400 percent of the poverty line must repay the entire subsidy (with no cap).

The families in this range of America's income distribution may not be able to afford experienced tax consultants. They can call the customer assistance line at IRS, but long delays have been experienced, likely due to budget cuts and staffing shortages at IRS. It is estimated that only half of those calling IRS in early 2015 got through; of those who waited and got through, they were on hold for an average of thirty minutes.[113] Under these circumstances it is understandable that HHS was encouraging states and navigators around the country to promote applications for the hardship exemptions under the ACA.

LEGISLATIVE EFFORTS TO REPEAL, DELAY, OR FIX THE ACA

When the Republican Party regained control of the House of Representatives in November 2010, one of the many issues before them was how to create a legislative expression of their intense hostility toward the ACA. Many of the victorious Republicans in the House had campaigned on a platform to repeal the ACA. But the practical reality was that the Democratic Party continued to control the Senate, and President Obama, with his veto power, could kill any legislative effort to repeal the ACA.

The House responded by scheduling numerous votes on legislation aimed at repealing the ACA. Those votes were only symbolic, since the Democrats controlled the Senate and the White House, but they were seen as useful "messaging" to the base.[114] The majority votes for repeal in the House were typically comprised of unanimous voting from GOP members combined with a handful of nervous Democrats who did not want their voting records to be aligned with the ACA.[115]

After Obama's reelection the Tea Party faction in the House became more militant about repeal of the ACA and sought new legislative tactics to accomplish that objective. The preferred methods revolved around using the House's power on budgeting to force the president into a negotiation over the future of the ACA.[116] The conservative House Republicans had allies in the Senate, such as Ted Cruz of Texas and David Vitter of Louisiana, who were seeking prompt legislative action to restrict or repeal the ACA.

The Republican establishment in Congress, including House Speaker John Boehner, was skeptical of the militant approach. Boehner was fond of arguing: If you perceive your opponent to be committing suicide, get out of the way! According to this view, the proper strategies for House Republicans were to engage in vigorous oversight hearings, expose the technical and design flaws of ACA, and await the 2014 midterm elections to cash in on the unpopularity of the ACA.[117] Influential Senate Republicans supported Speaker Boehner's stance. Florida senator Marco Rubio, for example, urged organization of a grassroots rebellion that would make the ACA a signature issue in the 2014 midterms. A unified Congress, he argued, would then act against the ACA in 2015.[118]

In 2013 the Tea Party faction won the tactical dispute inside the Republican Party. They wanted to go beyond some targeted cuts to the Independent Payment Advisory Board and the nonprofit Consumer Oriented and Operated Plans.[119] The debt-ceiling vote was targeted as the best forum to force Obama into a negotiation over the future of the ACA. In effect, the House Republicans threatened to vote against raising the debt ceiling—or even passing a budget to fund the federal government—until President Obama agreed to repeal or scale back the ACA.

As explained in chapter 4, President Obama held his ground. The federal government was ultimately shut down for sixteen days over the dispute, but public opinion was much more critical of the stance of the Republicans in Congress than the stance of President Obama. The ACA was certainly unpopular, but the public did not approve of "extortion" tactics to repeal it.

The House Republicans were forced to capitulate, winning only a new legislative requirement that reports to Congress be prepared on how income verification on the exchanges was handled by HHS. The inspector general was required to report on the effectiveness of the procedures and safeguards put into place to police fraud in the exchanges.[120]

Once President Obama prevailed against budget-linked efforts to repeal the ACA, he confronted a proliferation of more subtle "reforms" that attracted bipartisan support. Senator Mary Landrieu, who was up for reelection in November 2014, described the nuanced approach to the unpopular ACA: "It needs to be fixed, not repealed."[121] Actually, one of the "fixes," which called for repeal of the ACA's new tax on medical devices, was first proposed soon after the ACA was passed, and momentum for its adoption developed gradually over several years. As one of the significant funding sources for the ACA, the 2.3 percent tax on medical devices was estimated to generate $30 billion in revenue over a ten-year period. But industry opponents argued that the tax encourages the movement of medical device production outside of the United States.

The House took the first action against the medical device tax in June 2012. A bill to repeal the new tax passed 270 to 146, as thirty-seven Democrats ignored President Obama's veto threat and voted for repeal.[122] The bill called for a reduction in premium subsidies in order to pay for the foregone revenue.

There was much speculation that Senate majority leader Harry Reid would not allow for a vote to repeal the medical device tax.[123] Both Reid and Obama knew that the ACA could be easily unraveled, especially if funding sources for the ACA were stripped away one at a time.

Backers of repeal flexed their muscle during Senate deliberations in 2013 on the fiscal year 2014 appropriations package. Repeal of the medical device tax was added as an amendment to the appropriations package and passed comfortably 79–20, as thirty-four Democrats joined Republicans in the vote. Reid knew, however, that the vote was largely symbolic for two reasons. The fine print of the amendment required that new revenues be identified to replace the loss of the medical device tax, but there was no consensus in the Senate on where the revenues could be found. More importantly, the larger Senate appropriations bill contained so many provisions that were offensive to Republicans that the bill had no chance of passage in the House.[124] The move to repeal the medical device tax faltered.

A larger source of funding for the ACA was the projected savings in Medicare achieved through lower payments to insurers under the Medicare Advantage program. Over ten years those savings were estimated at $700 billion. The insurance industry feared that this provision would cause private Medicare Advantage insurance to lose its competitive edge over traditional Medicare coverage. About 30 percent of Medicare beneficiaries choose Medicare Advantage plans because of their low out-of-pocket costs and generous benefits compared to traditional Medicare. The industry helped engineer a bipartisan coalition of House and Senate members seeking to remove the diminished payments for Medicare Advantage plans. More than twenty House Democrats and several Democratic senators expressed interest in protecting the Medicare Advantage plans.[125] But Reid blocked any floor consideration of this idea.

Verification of income was also a sensitive issue in Congress. In 2013 HHS tried to quietly back off an original plan to verify the income of each applicant for premium subsidies. HHS was planning to undertake verification on anyone who reported income 10 percent or more lower than the income in IRS's database for the previous year. HHS planned instead to implement an honor system of self-reporting, with double-checking of only a statistically significant sample of deviations.[126] Members of Congress from both parties were outraged about this change.

In October 2013 the House of Representatives responded with a bill that would require an effective income verification system being put into place before premium subsidies could be implemented on the exchanges. Despite a veto threat from the White House (where there was fear that it might be impossible to demonstrate an effective verification system), the law passed the House on a strong bipartisan vote of 285–144. Senator Reid blocked consideration of a similar measure in the Senate.

A second fix that generated some bipartisan support in the Senate was a proposed amendment that would allow individuals and small businesses to purchase "copper" plans, a lower level of coverage than the ACA "bronze" minimum. The goal was smaller premiums and higher deductibles. The copper plan was sponsored by Democratic senators Mark Begich of Alaska and Mark Warner of Virginia, both whom were up for reelection in November 2014.[127] The copper plan fix was not supported by Reid or the Obama administration and never reached the Senate floor for a vote.

Another bipartisan coalition formed in favor of a change in the ACA's definition of a full-time worker from thirty to forty hours per week. The House voted easily in favor of this fix, as 18 Democrats joined all 230 Republicans. In the Senate, Democrats Joe Donnelly of Indiana and Joe Manchin of West Virginia signed on to a similar measure, but momentum died due to a veto threat from the White House.[128]

Finally, bipartisan support emerged in Congress to abolish the ACA's Independent Payment Advisory Board (IPAB). The purpose of the board was to set physician reimbursement rates under Medicare and help decide which procedures and drugs would be covered and at what prices. Providers and industry opposed the board because they saw it as a form of price control and rationing.

Former Vermont governor Dr. Howard Dean led the charge against IPAB and enlisted support from twenty-two Democrats in the House and Senate. Like most of the other fixes, the bill to abolish IPAB never reached the floor of the Senate for a vote.

Given the bipartisan interest in "fixing" the ACA, the Obama White House was fortunate that Harry Reid was determined to avoid any surgery to the ACA on the Senate floor. Without Reid's control of the agenda in the Senate, the White House might have lost control of the issue. The downside of Reid's strategy was felt by Democrats in the November 2014 midterm elections (see chapter 10).

MORE LITIGATION ROADBLOCKS?

Having lost most of their constitutional challenges to the ACA in the Supreme Court, conservative litigators shifted to a new line of argument that could cripple the federal exchange. Conservatives argued that the strict wording of the ACA allows federal subsidies to be offered only on the state exchanges and thus the Obama administration went beyond its statutory authority when it allocated subsidies to applicants on the federal exchange.[129]

At issue is a 2012 rule making by the Internal Revenue Service in which the IRS made the following interpretation of the ACA: premium subsidies may be offered on both the federal exchange and the state exchanges.[130] Since 80–90 percent of consumers shopping on the exchanges become eligible for premium subsidies, the legality of the IRS ruling is a crucial question. Without those subsidies, many consumers could not afford insurance or would choose to remain uninsured. As of mid-2014, more than five million people received coverage on the federal exchange, about 40 percent of those newly insured under the ACA.[131]

A federal district court judge in the District of Columbia ruled, in *King v. Burwell*, against a conservative challenge, arguing that the overall structure of the ACA suggests that Congress intended the premium subsidies to be available on the federal exchange as well as the state exchanges.[132] A three-judge panel for the DC Circuit Court of Appeals overturned the ruling of the district court judge, voting 2–1 that the plain language of the ACA authorizes the premium subsidies only on the state exchanges.[133] On the same day, a unanimous three-judge panel in the Fourth Circuit Court of Appeals (Richmond) upheld the legality of premium subsidies on the federal exchange.

The Obama administration appealed the ruling of the DC Circuit panel to the entire DC Court of Appeals, where a majority of the judges were Democrats due to a string of Obama appointments. The US Supreme Court would normally await a decision by the full DC Circuit but decided instead, in November 2014, to take the case and resolve the issue, presumably by the summer of 2015.[134]

Some argued that the case is not important, because additional states might decide to operate their own exchanges in order to secure the federal premium subsidies. Proponents of the ACA argued that this scenario was not plausible, because there would not be enough time between when the Court ruled (spring-summer 2015) and the final deadline for state exchanges under the ACA (2016).[135]

Any new state exchanges would need to be ready in October 2015 in order for plans to be sold for 2016. In such a short period it is doubtful that states could authorize exchanges through executive or federal action and establish the necessary components of an exchange (a staff, contractors, a website, a call center, and implementation regulations and guidelines). Exchanges typically take anywhere from twelve to eighteen months to become operational.

State exchanges are also expensive to establish, with one-time costs running in the vicinity of $40 million per state. The ACA authorized federal grants to pay for such one-time costs, but the authorization expired at the end of 2015 and the deadline for grant applications passed before the Supreme Court case was resolved. Moreover, all state exchanges are required to be financially self-supporting by 2015, and few states are eager to pay the ongoing operation and maintenance costs associated with a complex insurance exchange. For a variety of such practical reasons, both Illinois and Arkansas decided they could not transform their federally run exchanges into state exchanges.[136] In effect, the states decided to wait for the Court's decision and any subsequent congressional or administration actions.

In late June 2015 the US Supreme Court ruled 6–3 in favor of the Obama administration's interpretation that the ACA authorizes premium subsidies on both the federal and state exchanges. The Court's decision brought needed clarity and certainty to the future of the ACA's insurance marketplace and reassured millions of consumers that they were in fact entitled to the premium subsidies they had applied for and received.

Even before the Court's 2015 decision, House conservatives were frustrated that because of Obama's veto power, Congress could not overturn or weaken the ACA. They persuaded Speaker John Boehner to sue President Obama for illegal actions during the implementation phase. Authorization for the lawsuit was obtained by a vote of 225–201 in July 2014 (five Republicans and all House Democrats voted against authorization).[137]

Initially the focus of the suit was an allegation that Obama delayed the employer mandate without any authorization to do so under the ACA.[138] Recall that conservatives were frustrated that Obama refused to give individuals the same delay that was provided to employers. A second, more important allegation was that the Obama administration violated the Constitution when HHS allocated funds to cover some of the out-of-pocket health expenses (e.g., deductibles, co-payments) incurred by low- and middle-income families. Under the ACA, cost-sharing subsidies were authorized for families with incomes between 100 and 150 percent of the poverty level.

Boehner argued that Obama requested appropriations for cost-sharing subsidies from Congress in April 2013, but Congress did not appropriate the monies. Lacking a special appropriation, HHS used money from a separate account that Congress had established for the premium subsidies (tax credits and refunds) on the exchanges. The account established for the premium subsidies is permanent, but no account was established by Congress to finance the cost-sharing for out-of-pocket expenses.[139] It may take years to resolve this and other lawsuits against the ACA.

SOME GOOD NEWS ABOUT THE ACA

As the Obama administration worked hard to recover from the botched rollout, some positive signs about the effects of the ACA emerged. Some of those signs were telling because they contradicted prominent critiques of the law that had been touted by Obama's adversaries.

First, critics argue that the ACA is not reducing the number of uninsured, because most of those signing up for coverage on the exchanges were already insured.[140] However, by the middle of 2014, suggestive evidence emerged that the ACA was accomplishing its primary objective. Gallup, for example, used large sample surveys in numerous states to determine whether the number of uninsured was declining faster in states that expanded Medicaid and operated exchanges than in states that took only one of these two measures or neither of them. They found that the twenty-one states adopting both measures reduced the rate of uninsured by almost twice the amount as the other states. For example, from 2013 to mid-2014 Arkansas and Kentucky saw their percentage of uninsured drop from 22.5 percent (20.4 percent) to 12.4 percent (11.9 percent), respectively.[141] By the end of 2014, 11.4 million Americans had selected health insurance plans through the federal and state exchanges.[142]

Second, critics forecasted that overall spending on health care in the United States would balloon under the ACA. Recent trends suggest otherwise. The average annual growth rate in health care spending was 6 percent per year from 2000 to 2009; the growth rate declined to 3.8 percent in 2009 and 2010, 3.6 percent in 2011, 3.7 percent in 2012, and 3.6 percent in 2013.[143] There are many possible explanations for the slowdown (e.g., the weak economy), but the data do not yet indicate a big growth in spending after enactment of the ACA.[144]

Finally, critics speculated that the plans on the insurance exchange would limit the choices of physicians and hospitals available to consumers through "narrow networks" that reduce costs to insurers. Experience in the first year of the federal and state exchanges provided some evidence to support this fear.[145] In the second year of the exchanges, the trend reversed itself a bit as more insurers offered plans on the exchanges and the average number of physicians and hospitals in plans seemed to be increasing.[146]

Overall, it is too early to know how well the ACA will work, since some of the key provisions are not yet fully implemented (e.g., the individual and employer mandates). Based on what is apparent so far (in late 2015), it seems likely that Obama will finish his presidency with much of the new law in operation and with only a small risk that it will be repealed by a future Congress, though significant modifications are quite possible in the years ahead.

COUNTERFACTUALS

The implementation of the ACA could have proceeded much more smoothly if Obama's health policy leadership team had been comprised, preferably in 2009 but no later than 2011, of leaders who possessed the necessary skills and experience relevant to implementation. It is unreasonable to expect a single person to touch all the bases, but the leadership team as a whole needed to include the following: public administration experience, especially managerial experience overseeing a large career civil service engaged in complex implementation activities; management experience coordinating the work of multiple large contractors under strict deadlines and resource constraints;

information technology expertise; business experience, preferably in the insurance sector, where the ACA was seeking to launch an entirely new suite of plans; and knowledge of numerous state governments, especially connections to key leaders of state health agencies and their legislators. Some of this expertise presumably existed among senior career staff at CMS or in other parts of HHS, but President Obama should have ensured that such expertise was available for implementation of his signature initiative.

Another straightforward correction one can imagine is a presidential appointment of a CMS administrator with strong public management or business experience, a leader who would be seen as largely apolitical by members of Congress, stakeholders, and the media. Although many presidents do not give any particular urgency to the CMS nomination, it was imperative that President Obama elevate the priority of this appointment, because the CMS administrator was responsible for implementation of the ACA.

With regard to communications, the president should have used more nuanced language when he said that people can keep their existing insurance policy if they are satisfied with it. The purpose of the ACA is to make sure everyone has an insurance policy that meets certain minimum federal standards. It was obvious that some current policies offered in the private sector did not meet the standards of the ACA, and President Obama and the Congress were determined to upgrade those policies. President Obama still could have reassured most people about their existing insurance, but his language needed to acknowledge that people with inadequate coverage were going to have to upgrade their policies.

A common criticism of President Obama is that he did not "sell the ACA," particularly in the crucial year (2013) after his reelection and before the rollout of the exchanges. Obama's speeches in 2013 tended to focus on the economy, with only brief messages on the ACA. The flaw in this criticism is the assumption that Obama would have made a difference by spending more time speaking about the ACA—that he could have been a persuasive advocate of the ACA among the many diverse segments of the public who were opposed to it: young adults, suburban women, self-described independents, and Republicans.[147] What he really needed was ACA backing from credible third-party sources, but that kind of support is difficult to arrange from the White House.

A big problem for the ACA was the relative amount of TV and radio advertising devoted to attacking it versus supporting it. In the four years after it passed the Congress, $418 million was spent on advertising attacking it compared to $27 million defending it.[148] The health insurance industry, in 2012 alone, allocated much of its $600 million advertising budget to offering help to people who thought the ACA was "confusing" or "intimidating." Those advertisements, though designed for a commercial purpose, did not boost public confidence in the ACA. It should be no surprise that public support for the ACA deteriorated steadily in the weeks and months after the law was enacted.[149] Given the way the ACA was designed (see chapter 5) and given the communications resources available to the opponents of the ACA, it was crucial for the White House to persuade sympathetic philanthropists who support the ACA to make large investments in public information and social marketing about it.

One cannot fault President Obama for the somewhat unexpected Supreme Court decision of 2012 that strengthened the hands of governors and state legislators in the ACA implementation process. The Court ruled 7–2 for a weakening of the mandatory Medicaid expansion while using legal reasoning that was not predicted by many federalism specialists.[150]

On the other hand, the Obama administration did not adequately adjust its approach to ACA implementation in light of the Supreme Court's decision. On July 1, 2012, President Obama and his advisors knew (1) that the Republican Party was controlling the governor's office or the state legislature in the majority of states, (2) that the Tea Party faction of the Republican Party was determined to block or slow implementation of the ACA at the state level and to punish Republican state officials who collaborated with the Obama administration, and (3) that many states were therefore unlikely to promptly implement state exchanges or Medicaid expansions. As a result, the rollout of HealthCare.gov in October 1, 2013, was likely to take on even greater significance than was expected in March 2010, and the media, Congress, and the public were unlikely to tolerate a botched rollout.

Under these circumstances it would have been prudent for HHS to reconsider the pace of implementation of the federal exchange, since it would now be the centerpiece of the ACA's new private health insurance system. Moreover, when the administration delayed CMS's final rule making on the exchanges for six months, until after the president's reelection in November 2012, the IT specialists in CMS and in the contractor community had less than ten months to design, fully test, and refine HealthCare.gov. A complex IT task of this sort is a multiyear endeavor.

A public decision in January 2013 should have been made to delay the rollout of the exchanges until January 2015 (after the November 2014 midterm elections), thereby providing ample time to adjust to the new circumstances, design and test HealthCare.gov, and relieve nervous Senate Democrats who were likely to face a tough midterm election in 2014. An alternative idea, which Secretary Sebelius suggested at a congressional hearing, was some form of gradual phase-in period instead of an all-or-nothing rollout of HealthCare. gov on October 1, 2013.

Obama did make extensive, belated use of executive power in late 2013 and 2014 to delay numerous provisions of the ACA.[151] Some commentators have questioned whether the president actually possessed the authority to delay so many rollout deadlines.

A legal vulnerability may be exploited only when a litigant can demonstrate to a court that harm to them has occurred due to delay and only if the litigant is motivated to expend resources in a judicial resolution.[152] No such litigation ever occurred, although the protestations of conservative leaders are a hint that the delays were politically advantageous for Democrats in the 2014 midterm elections.[153] It would have been much better for Obama and congressional Democrats if the rollout had not even been attempted in late 2013 and instead have occurred smoothly at the start of 2015.

The political damage caused by the nightmarish rollout of the ACA was temporary but significant. The debacle took a big toll on Obama's popularity for two independent reasons: it questioned the competence of Obama and his team, and it exposed doubts about Obama's honesty/candor in light of his shifting statements about whether people who like their current health insurance plan can keep it. According to veteran political analyst Charlie Cook, the president's public image was boosted by the way congressional Republicans forced a temporary government shutdown. Before Obama could benefit from the boost, mismanagement of the ACA caused a late 2013 "collapse" in his image. Cook describes it as "one of the most dramatic shifts I've ever seen in 40 years of politics."[154] Obama recovered some of his popularity in 2015, but by then the damage had been done in the 2014 midterm elections (see chapter 10). Some of this damage was preventable through wiser executive decision making by the president in collaboration with his health policy team.

7

GLOBAL WARMING WARRIOR

Under the leadership of President Barack Obama, the United States enacted binding regulatory programs to reduce the greenhouse gas emissions that are linked to global climate change. One program covers the transportation sector, primarily emissions from cars, light trucks, and heavy long-haul trucks. The second program covers stationary sources such as electric power plants. Taken together, the two initiatives cover the largest sources—and a majority—of greenhouse gas emissions in the US economy.[1]

The progress Obama made on climate policy was not through a request that Congress pass new legislation. Obama used executive power, drawing upon legal authority that the Congress had already assigned to the US Environmental Protection Agency (EPA) and the US Department of Transportation (DOT). For the transport initiative, Obama adapted a vehicle mileage program that the George W. Bush administration had revitalized for energy security purposes and Congress had expanded late in the Bush administration for climate change purposes. The stationary-source program evolved out of litigation that led the US Supreme Court to affirm the power of the EPA, under the Clean Air Act, to regulate greenhouse gases. The international credibility that Obama earned from his executive policies set the stage for a bilateral diplomatic break-through on climate policy for the United States with the Chinese government. It also set the stage for US influence at the 2015 Paris climate negotiations.

In contrast to his successful use of executive power, Obama was notably unsuccessful in delivering on one of his major campaign pledges of 2008: new legislation to create an economy-wide cap and trade program to reduce greenhouse gases. Such a program did pass (narrowly) the House of Representatives in 2009 but never had sufficient support in the Senate to justify floor debate. For congressional Democrats the 2009–2010 flirtation with "cap and tax" proved to be a debacle.

With regard to the theory in chapter 2, readers are encouraged to consider several issues in this chapter's case study: Did Obama choose the best mix of legislative and executive initiatives? Was the conventional House-first strategy on climate legislation the wisest political choice? Should the climate and energy proposals have been separated or combined? How vulnerable are Obama's climate polices to reversal by the courts or a future president? Answers to these questions are explored at the end of this chapter and in chapter 11.

I begin the discussion with Obama's 2007–2008 campaign commitment on climate change and the administration's decision after the election to make climate policy a legislative priority, much like Obama designated health care reform and immigration reform as first-year priorities. Then I review how and why Obama's climate proposal failed to pass the Congress in 2009–2010. Next is an exploration of how Obama used executive powers to regulate greenhouse gas emissions from mobile and stationary sources. The chapter concludes with a consideration of some counterfactuals, explaining why an executive-first strategy on climate change in 2009–2010 could have accomplished much of Obama's policy while also offering some protection to the electoral fortunes of moderate Democrats in Congress.

FULFILLING A CAMPAIGN PLEDGE

Those who know Obama's career as a politician may have been surprised to see him emerge as a "global warming warrior."[2] As a state senator from Illinois, Barack Obama built good relationships with the state's booming coal industry and its unionized coal miners. Joined by most Illinois politicians, he voted for a resolution in the Illinois state Senate urging politicians in Washington, DC, to refrain from implementing the Kyoto Protocol on climate change negotiated by Vice President Al Gore during the Clinton administration.[3]

As scored by the League of Conservation Voters, Senator Obama earned an excellent rating on environmental issues, but there were some notable exceptions. He irritated some environmentalists by advocating for "clean coal," the notion that advanced technology—if supported with sufficient federal subsidies—might permit coal to be used as an energy source without significant adverse effects on the environment. Skeptical environmentalists argue that the entire concept of "clean coal" is a myth—Robert F. Kennedy Jr. calls it a "dirty lie"—designed to perpetuate the use of coal instead of renewables in the global energy system.[4]

Obama went beyond the pro-coal view that favored public subsidies to demonstrate carbon capture and storage technology at coal-fired electric power plants. In collaboration with Republican senator Jim Bunning of Kentucky, Obama introduced legislation calling for public subsidies to develop and demonstrate coal-to-liquid (CTL) technology, which would allow coal (instead of oil) to be used in making liquid fuels that power cars and trucks. Variants of CTL were used to power German tanks in World War II, are now in widespread use in South Africa, and are promoted for application in the United States by analysts from the RAND Corporation and the US Air Force.[5]

Efforts to promote CTL in the United States, though supported by Peabody Energy (a large coal company) and the United Mine Workers, were blocked in Congress by politicians aligned with national environmental advocacy groups.[6] CTL, critics argued, created even more greenhouse gas emissions than burning coal to make electricity, because large amounts of energy are consumed capturing carbon dioxide at the smokestack.

In the race for the 2008 Democratic presidential nomination, the three major candidates (Barack Obama, Hillary Clinton, and John Edwards) each criticized George W. Bush's inaction on climate change. They countered with ambitious pledges to reduce the man-made contributions to global warming.

Obama's climate plan was announced early in the campaign, in October 2007. It called for an economy-wide program to reduce greenhouse gases by 80 percent below 1990 levels by 2050. The near-term goal was to reduce emissions to 1990 levels by 2020. A so-called cap and trade system of emission allowances would be launched through a 100 percent auction of allowances to corporate emitters of greenhouse gases. The cap and trade scheme was to be accompanied by $150 billion in federal subsidies for the development of clean energy. Other provisions of the plan included a new international partnership agreement on climate change, a national low-carbon fuel standard (aimed at promoting biofuels in the transportation sector), a renewable electricity standard (to promote wind, solar, and hydropower), and a doubling of federal auto mileage standards over the next eighteen years (from twenty-five to fifty miles per gallon). It was an ambitious, multifaceted plan.

CAP AND TAX

The path to Republican support of cap and trade of carbon dioxide rested on an analogy of Obama's plan to a GOP plan to control acid rain through sulfur-allowance trading that was championed by President George H. W. Bush and codified in the 1990 Clean Air Act amendments. The auctioning of allowances, although favored on efficiency grounds by professional economists, later became a political headache for Obama. When his 2009 budget documents disclosed the huge revenue-raising potential of auctioned permits, critics from industry were quick to note that the 1990 acid rain plan had distributed the permits to industry free of charge. The auction approach became a target of determined business and GOP opposition.[7]

The Tea Party seized on Obama's proposed auction as evidence that the scheme was another ploy to enhance the size of the federal government. (The budget documents tried to defuse this charge by calling for use of auction revenues to help finance tax cuts). The Obama cap and trade plan was no longer embraced as a Republican innovation; it was dubbed "cap and tax."[8]

Progressives were pleasantly surprised and enthusiastic about Obama's climate plan.[9] He seemed to be as environmentally "green" as Clinton and Edwards. Obama's climate plan did not play a major role in the presidential campaign, because Republican candidate John McCain had a progressive track record on climate change and was touting his own plan.[10] In fact, McCain was well known in environmental circles for having co-sponsored an ambitious cap and trade plan with Senator Joe Lieberman.

Once elected president in November 2008, Obama was urged by some industry leaders and members of Congress to delay action on climate change until the economy recovered. He did not take this advice. He instead made climate change the subject of the second speech (after one on economic recovery) that he made as president-elect. Speaking by video to a climate conference with representatives from twenty-two countries, Obama reaffirmed his campaign pledge to act on climate change without delay.[11]

President Obama's first speech to a joint session of Congress, in February 2009, also featured climate policy. He called on Congress to enact a cap and trade bill to help spark economic recovery through investments in clean energy. During the speech an environmental reporter noticed that the president's call for a cap and trade policy led to a standing ovation from much of the audience, including most Senate Democrats and five Republican senators (Susan Collins and Olympia Snowe, Lindsey Graham, Mel Martinez of Florida, and John McCain).[12] Thus, the prospects of some Republican crossover votes on climate change, at least in the Senate, seemed plausible.

WHERE ARE THE SIXTY VOTES?

Passing economy-wide legislation to reduce greenhouse gases is, politically, an enormous task. The legislation impacts numerous key sectors of the economy, including agriculture, autos, chemicals, mining, power generation, steel and other metals, transportation, and virtually any form of manufacturing. Large and small companies in each of these sectors would be affected due to higher energy prices. As a result, businesses were expected to either oppose such legislation or seek some special form of relief due to the projected financial burdens.

Obama was hardly the first politician to call for legislative action on climate change. On three occasions, from 2001 to 2008, bills were proposed on the Senate floor that would have placed binding limits on the amount of greenhouse gases emitted in the United States. Two votes were taken on the McCain-Lieberman plan (2003 and 2005). Democratic senator Barbara Boxer and Republican John Warner led the third effort in 2008, several months after Obama released his plan on the presidential campaign trail.

The basic structure of the three Senate plans was the same as Obama's plan: a national cap on greenhouse gas emissions coupled with a trading system that would allow companies facing high compliance costs to purchase emissions allowances from companies that could reduce emissions at low cost.

Once trades occurred each year, investments in emissions reduction would be made by those companies that could do so at least cost. A similar system for carbon dioxide control was launched in Europe in 2005.

The three carbon cap and trade plans were never close to reaching the required sixty votes in the Senate.[13] In 2008, the most recent vote (48–36), proponents of cap and trade fell twelve votes short of the sixty required to limit the amount of time for debate and bar a filibuster. It was a procedural vote on a cloture motion, not a direct vote on the merits of cap and trade. Proponents claimed to have fifty-four votes, since six absent senators (Biden, Clinton, Gregg, Kennedy, McCain, and Obama) submitted written statements for the record in favor of the Boxer-Warner plan. (Democrats voting "no" included Mary Landrieu, Sherrod Brown of Ohio, Byron Dorgan of North Dakota, and Timothy Johnson of South Dakota.) Thus, proponents argue, the shortfall was only six votes.[14]

It is risky to infer much from a procedural vote taken when it was fully expected that the motion would fail. The procedural motion would have taken on more substantive importance if it had been seen as being close to passage (since then the substantive bill could pass with a simple majority). Four Democratic senators who voted in favor of the procedural motion to limit debate indicated they were inclined to vote against the Boxer-Warner plan on the merits: Ben Nelson, Jon Tester, Mark Pryor, and Jay Rockefeller.[15] From this perspective, there were potentially ten Democratic defectors.

When Obama won the 2008 election against McCain, the Democratic margin in the Senate grew from 51–49 to 59–41 (and eventually to 60–40), and the theory was that it was now much easier to find sixty votes for climate policy. Besides, with Obama's leadership instead of Bush's opposition, the political atmosphere would change, making Republican senators less reluctant to cross over and discouraging defections by moderate Democratic senators. The Obama White House decided, at least initially, to make climate change a first-tier legislative priority along with health care reform.[16]

A closer look at the 2008 elections reveals that the prospects of reaching sixty votes for climate legislation were not increased by as much as the change in partisan margin suggests (see table 7.1). Of the eight Republican-held seats captured by the Democrats in 2008, four of them were held by senators who voted in favor of the Boxer-Warner plan (Elizabeth Dole, Gordon Smith, John Sununu, and John Warner). Consequently, there was no good basis for

Table 7.1. Votes on Previous Climate Plans (2005, 2008) by GOP Senators Who Were Defeated in 2008 or Switched Parties in 2009

Senator/State	Vote on 2008 Boxer–Warner	2005 Vote on McCain–Lieberman
Ted Stevens/AK	Did not vote	No
Wayne Allard/CO	No	No
Norm Coleman/MN	Did not vote	No
John Sununu/NH	Yes	No
Pete Domenici/NM	No	No
Elizabeth Dole/NC	Yes	No
Gordon Smith/OR	Yes	No
John Warner/VA	Yes	No
Arlen Specter/PA	Did not vote	No

projecting any more than fifty-four to fifty-eight votes in 2009 for a big cap and trade bill (either 50 + 4 or 54 + 4, depending on the votes of Democrats Nelson, Tester, Pryor, and Rockefeller). Moreover, Arlen Specter of Pennsylvania voted against the McCain-Lieberman plan in 2005 and did not vote in 2008 on Boxer-Warner. Counting Specter as a vote for Obama's climate plan was a stretch. The difference between fifty-eight and sixty votes in the Senate cannot be finessed; the latter is legislative success (like the sixty votes for the Affordable Care Act); the former signifies presidential failure to accomplish a first-tier legislative priority.

OPPOSITION FEARS

The opponents of cap and trade in Congress and their allies in the business community knew that the required sixty votes would be difficult to find in the Senate. What they feared was an effort to pass a climate bill under budget reconciliation procedures, which requires only a simple majority vote. Democratic leaders in Congress were still smarting from George W. Bush's use of reconciliation procedures to pass large cuts in income taxes in 2001, 2003, and 2006.[17] From a parliamentary perspective, the climate bill could plausibly be designated a fiscal measure, because the auctioning of permits to polluters was included in Obama's first budget as a big new source of federal revenue.

Before the relevant committees in the House and Senate could get moving on a climate bill, a bipartisan coalition in the Senate killed the idea of passing a cap and trade bill under reconciliation procedures. In early April 2009, by a 67–31 margin, the Senate prohibited the use of reconciliation "for climate change legislation involving a cap and trade system." Although the measure was introduced by conservative Republican Mike Johanns of Nebraska and supported by all forty-one Republican senators, it was also supported by twenty-six crossover Democrats. Virtually all Democratic senators from the Midwest and South crossed over. One of the few Midwestern Democratic senators to vote against the procedural measure was Sherrod Brown of Ohio, but he went out of his way to stress that he might ultimately vote against a climate bill on the merits.[18]

The large Democratic crossover vote is not necessarily an indication that so many Democrats were opposed to a climate bill. Many of them may have been objecting, as a procedural matter, to treatment of climate policy as budgetary/tax policy, since that treatment could set a bad precedent, with unpredictable consequences for other legislation unrelated to climate change. Nonetheless, by foreclosing the reconciliation option, opponents of climate legislation won a key battle: they forced the Obama White House to seek the elusive sixty votes in the Senate.

EXECUTIVE OR LEGISLATIVE ACTION?

When Obama took office in 2009, the EPA had already taken the legal position under George W. Bush that greenhouse gases could be lawfully regulated under the Clean Air Act. That view, published in an "advance notice of proposed rulemaking," built on the Supreme Court's 2007 decision in favor of EPA authority.[19] But that view was controversial. The legal reasoning was crafted by the Bush administration, and the incoming Obama team had their sights set on ambitious climate legislation.

Soon after the April 2009 vote against the reconciliation procedure, a report from the liberal Institute for Policy Integrity at New York University suggested a creative pathway for the Obama administration.[20] Using legal authority under the Clean Air Act, the administration—through an EPA rule making—could create an economy-wide trading system complete with auctioning of permits. The trading system could be coordinated with other countries through a nonbinding international agreement. The authors of the report made the case that all of this policy could be accomplished without seeking legislation from Congress. President Obama already had the power to do it.[21]

The NYU report undercut a key talking point of the Obama administration: the notion that any effort to regulate carbon under the existing Clean Air Act was destined to be a regulatory nightmare. The flaw in the administration's reasoning was a legal assumption that carbon dioxide would have to be declared a "criteria" (localized) air pollutant and regulated on a county-by-county basis as if it were a public health hazard. The NYU team found alternative legal authority in the Clean Air Act that allowed implementation of a national cap and trade system without making the criteria pollutant determination.

From the start of his first term, Obama believed that legislation on climate change would deliver a more durable solution than executive action.[22] He did indicate publicly that his administration was working on executive policies and that should Congress not act, he would move forward on his own.[23] When he reached his second term without a legislative solution, executive action did not look like such a nightmare.

HOUSE-FIRST STRATEGY

Recognizing the uphill climb in the Senate, the Obama White House and Democratic leaders in Congress decided to move a climate bill in the House first. With House Speaker Nancy Pelosi and Henry Waxman (chairman of the relevant Committee on Energy and Commerce) eager to move a climate bill, the House-first strategy had much to recommend it.

The theory went as follows: a big favorable vote in the House on climate policy would please the base and might pressure the Senate to act. Once the Senate acted, the White House could help engineer a successful House-Senate conference, leading to successful final votes in both chambers. The whole strategy made moderate House Democrats nervous, as they were already worried about the forthcoming vote on health care.[24] Some rank-and-file House Democrats wondered why they were being asked to cast a risky vote on climate legislation when the Senate might never get the required sixty votes to pass the measure.[25]

What concerned Obama was Waxman's decision to move the climate bill through his committee before a health care bill. Obama feared that acting on climate first would delay consideration of health reform and ultimately make it more difficult to find the votes for the Affordable Care Act in the House.[26] Nonetheless, Obama pledged to lawmakers that he would be flexible on the precise provisions of the climate bill (e.g., allowing some of the allowances to be awarded to companies without charge instead of a 100 percent auction of allowances) in order to facilitate bargaining among legislators.[27]

WAXMAN BARGAINS WITH BOUCHER

Before Obama's climate initiative could reach the House floor, it required a majority vote from the large and diverse Committee on Energy and Commerce. Chairman Waxman's original draft was unacceptable to a substantial coalition of Blue Dog Democrats and virtually all of the committee's Republicans. Particularly problematic was that the Blue Dogs were a large enough group to block Obama's health care and climate plans.[28]

Democrat Rick Boucher of southwestern Virginia was a twenty-eight-year veteran of the House with a moderate voting record and a strong reputation for constituent service. He was an expert on climate legislation due to his work in 2008 as chair of a House subcommittee on air quality. Rather than oppose President Obama's climate initiative, Boucher decided to work with Blue Dogs on Waxman's committee to revise the bill so that it would be acceptable to coal-fired electric utilities.[29] Boucher had developed strong ties to the electric utility industry (e.g., the Edison Electric Institute), and his district featured significant coal production and coal-related employment. Boucher emerged as the leader of a loose coalition of Blue Dogs who were worried about Waxman's legislative ambitions.

Although Boucher was not successful in persuading Waxman to significantly relax the near-term 20 percent emissions reduction target, he won several major concessions. First, most of the allowances were issued free of charge to utilities rather than auctioned off to the highest bidder. Second, coal-fired utilities were permitted to offset their emissions with 2 billion tons per year of off-site control measures (e.g., planting trees). Third, public subsidies of $10 billion over ten years were provided to underwrite some of the cost of installing carbon capture and storage (CCS), an innovative yet expensive way to control carbon emissions for power plants. Finally, about $150 billion in special emission allowances was made available to utilities that chose to comply with CCS. The concessions were so substantial that the Edison Electric Institute (but not the coal mining industry) decided to support the revised Waxman bill. Boucher argued that the revised legislation was economically better for coal-related industries than the regulatory options available to the EPA under the Clean Air Act. He apparently believed that cap and trade was not permissible under the Clean Air Act.[30]

On May 21, 2009, the revised version of Waxman's climate bill passed the committee on a vote of 33–25. All but four of the committee Democrats (John Barrow, Jim Matheson, Charlie Melancon, and Mike Ross) joined Waxman and Boucher in support of the bill. Only one GOP member (Mary Bono Mack) voted for the bill in committee.[31]

Whether or not Boucher realized it in May 2009, he had placed his political career on the line. In 2010 he was challenged by Republican state representative Morgan Griffith, who made Boucher's stance on the climate issue the centerpiece of his attack on Boucher.[32] (Boucher later voted against the Affordable Care Act, perhaps sensing strong opposition in his district.) Griffith's message was simple: "Boucher betrayed coal." Cap and tax was the issue that enabled Griffith to tie Boucher to Waxman, Pelosi, and Obama.[33]

Boucher lost his reelection bid to Griffith by a vote of 52–48 percent, but he was not alone. There were other House Democrats who voted against the Affordable Care Act but in favor of cap and trade on the House floor. As chapter 10 reveals, they were easy targets for GOP challengers.[34]

OVERCOMING ECONOMIC CONCERNS

The condition of the American economy in the spring of 2009 was horrible. The Great Recession was deepening. The rate of unemployment was 8.9 percent and rising.[35] Two large industrial states in the Midwest, Michigan and Ohio, were suffering disproportionate hardships with jobless rates of 12.9 percent and 10.2 percent, respectively.

Critics of Obama argued that 2009–2010 was not a prudent time to consider a complex and expensive bill that would raise electricity and fuel prices for ordinary Americans. The Waxman bill would also impose relatively greater costs on the Midwest and South (where coal is widely used) than on

the East and West coasts (where use of low-carbon energy is more prevalent). For the first time in twenty-six years of Gallup polling, a majority of the
public preferred a focus on economic growth rather than on environmental
protection.[36]

The Obama White House, led by "climate/energy czar" Carol Browner
(an Al Gore protégé who served as EPA administrator under Bill Clinton), was
working with an unusual coalition of Fortune 500 companies and national
environmental groups called the US Climate Action Partnership (USCAP).
Launched in 2007, USCAP included Duke Energy, Dow Chemical Company,
and a few dozen other big companies as well as the Natural Resources Defense
Council and the Environmental Defense Fund. The role of USCAP was to work
with key legislators on a climate bill that could pass the Congress with bipartisan support.

USCAP's work was loosely coordinated with the public relations efforts
of two other organizations. Al Gore's Alliance for Climate Protection was ex-
pending $80–$100 million annually in public messaging and mobilization. In
the summer of 2009 Clean Energy Works was launched with two hundred field
organizers in twenty-eight Midwestern, Western, and Southern states. About
$50 million was spent on mass advertising of the theme "Better Jobs, Less
Pollution, and More Security."[37] In response to economic concerns, the global
warming warriors countered with the "green jobs" argument: the idea that jobs
would be created in new clean technology industries such as wind farms and
solar panel manufacturing plants.[38]

Countering Browner's coalition was a well-heeled network of trade associations ranging from the US Chamber of Commerce and the National Association of Manufacturers to the American Petroleum Institute and the American
Iron and Steel Institute. In fact, some of the large companies in Browner's
coalition were also dues-paying members of large associations working against
climate legislation. Meanwhile, for coal companies and their employees, the
fight against cap and tax was seen as a struggle for survival.[39]

FLOOR FIGHT IN THE HOUSE

When Waxman delivered his climate bill to the House floor for debate,
passage was by no means assured. In fact, "the legislation squeaked through the
House during a very unusual moment—in which a large Democratic majority

was directed with near-Leninist discipline by one of history's strongest House leaders, Speaker Nancy Pelosi."[40]

The Clean Energy and Security Act of 2009 called for an 80 percent reduction in greenhouse gas emissions by 2050. The near-term mandate was for a 17 percent reduction in emissions below 2005 levels by 2020. The cap and trade system allocated 85 percent of the allowances to industry for free; the remainder was auctioned. Power producers were required to make at least 20 percent of their electricity from renewable sources by 2020. Federal subsidies included $90 billion for renewables, $60 billion for clean coal (primarily CCS), $20 billion for plug-in electric vehicles, and $20 billion in basic research and development (R&D) for new energy technology.

The day before the final floor vote, Pelosi and her colleagues could not find enough votes for passage. A substantial number of pro-labor Democrats from Rust Belt districts were concerned that rising energy costs in the United States would trigger layoffs of workers in the steel, aluminum, auto, paper, and glass industries. Led by veteran Democrat Sander Levin of Michigan, the Rust Belt lawmakers insisted that a new provision be added to protect American workers.

In the middle of the night before the final vote, an internationally provocative provision was inserted into the complex bill. It required the president, starting in 2020, to impose a "border adjustment" (tariff) on selected goods from countries that do not limit their emissions of greenhouse gases. The president can waive the tariffs, but only if he obtains explicit permission from Congress to do so. The intent of the provision was to protect the competitiveness of American industry from imported goods made with cheap, dirty energy.

After the House bill passed, President Obama issued a strongly worded statement against this provision, which he described as protectionism.[41] Obama's ambitions for free-trade agreements around the world would be compromised if this provision became law. The Obama administration was already beginning to plan ambitious new free-trade agreements with nations in Asia and Europe (see chapter 4).

Pelosi delivered the climate bill to Obama on June 26, 2009, on a vote of 219–212. Eight Republicans voted in favor of it; forty-four Democrats defected. The majority of the defecting Democrats represented districts that Obama had lost to McCain in 2008. Of the forty-four defectors (see table 7.2), twenty were from the South, eighteen were freshmen or sophomores, thirty-one were representing districts that awarded Obama less than 50 percent of the vote in 2008, and all had earned a higher 2008 vote share than Obama in their district. Twenty-eight of the defectors resigned before 2010 or lost in 2010. Only six of the districts were represented by a Democrat in 2015, although seven survived 2010 but lost in 2012 after unfavorable redistricting. As bad as those outcomes were, the losses were even worse for House Democrats from GOP-leaning districts who voted for cap and trade (see chapter 10).

For the White House, the narrow win in the House should have been a stark warning about the dim prospects in the Senate, where the composition of membership is more heavily weighted with politicians from states in the South, the Midwest, and the Rocky Mountain West and where the sixty-vote hurdle should have been seen as formidable.

DEATH KNELL FROM SENATE DEMOCRATS

If the demise of Obama's climate bill was not already obvious, the death knell occurred in August 2009. Ten Democratic senators cosigned a letter to President Obama stating that they could not support the sort of climate legislation that was favored by the president, passed by the House of Representatives, and under consideration by the chair of the Senate Committee on Environment and Public Works (Barbara Boxer). Those senators included Evan Bayh, Sherrod Brown, Robert Byrd, Jay Rockefeller, Bob Casey, Arlen Specter, Russ Feingold, Al Franken, Carl Levin, and Debbie Stabenow. The letter should not have come as a complete surprise, as a similar letter was disseminated publicly in July 2008 prior to Senate voting on the cloture motion related to the Boxer-Warner plan.[42]

The letter called specifically for inclusion of the "border adjustments" that President Obama had publicly opposed as protectionism. Businesses, the letter said, should also receive rebates for their increased energy costs. And the letter called for any international agreement on climate change to include emissions monitoring in other countries. All of these provisions were seen as necessary to protect the welfare of the American worker from international competition. The issues raised by the letter were so fundamental and complex that they effectively put the entire legislative initiative on hold.

In October 2009 the White House conceded publicly that a new climate law would not be enacted prior to the December 2009 international climate

**Table 7.2. Profiles of House Democrats (N = 44)
Who Voted against 2009 Climate Cap and Trade Bill**

Name	State/ District	Years of Service	Obama Share[1] (2008)	Member's Share[2] (2008)	House Career
Bright	AL/2	2	37	50	defeated 2010
Griffith	AL/5	2	38	51	defeated 2010
Davis	AL/7	8	74	99	defeated 2010 for Governor; Democrats won seat
Kirkpatrick	AZ/7	2	44	56	defeated 2010; after redistricting, won 2012; 2014
Mitchell	AZ/5	4	47	53	defeated 2010
Berry	AR/1	14	38	100	retired 2010; GOP won
Ross	AR/4	10	39	86	won 2010; retired 2011; GOP won 2012
Stark	CA/13	38	74	76	won 2010; after redistricting lost to Democrat in 2012
Costa	CA/20	6	60	74	won 2010; after redistricting won in CA/16 in 2012, 2014
Salazar	CO/3	6	48	62	defeated 2010
Marshall	GA/8	8	43	57	defeated 2010
Barrow	GA/12	6	55	66	won 2010; 2012 (despite redistricting); defeated 2014
Minnick	ID/1	2	36	51	defeated 2010
Costella	IL/12	2	56	71	won 2010; resigned 2012; Democrats won seat
Foster	IL/14	2	36	58	lost 2010; won IL/11 in 2012, 2014
Visclosky	IN/1	26	62	71	won 2010, 2012, 2014
Donnelly	IN/2	4	50	67	won 2010; resigned 2012 for senate; GOP won seat
Ellsworth	IN/8	4	48	65	resigned 2010; won by GOP
Melancon	LA/3	6	37	100	resigned 2010; won by GOP
Childers	MS/1	2	38	54	defeated 2010
Taylor	MS/4	20	32	75	defeated 2010
Arcuri	NY/24	4	50	52	defeated 2010
Massa	NY/29	2	48	51	resigned 2010; GOP won seat
McIntyre	NC/7	14	42	69	won 2010; won 2012 despite redistricting; resigned 2013: GOP won
Kissell	NC/8	2	42	55	won 2010; defeated 2012 after redistricting

Table 7.2. (*cont.*)

Name	State/ District	Years of Service	Obama Share[1] (2008)	Member's Share[2] (2008)	House Career
Pomeroy[3]	ND-AL	18	45	62	defeated 2010
Wilson	OH/6	4	48	62	defeated 2010
Kucinich	OH/10	14	49	57	won 2010; redistricting, and primary defeat 2012 for OH/9
Boren	OK/2	6	34	70	won 2010, retired; GOP won 2012
DeFazio	OR/4	24	54	82	won 2010, 2012, 2014
Dahlkemper	PA/3	2	46	51	defeated 2010
Altmire	PA/4	4	44	56	won 2010; lost 2012 after redistricting
Carney	PA/10	4	45	56	defeated 2010
Holden	PA/17	18	48	64	won in 2010; lost 2012 Democratic primary after redistricting, Democrats won seat
Sandlin	SD-AL	6	45	68	defeated 2010
Davis	TN/4	8	35	59	defeated 2010
Tanner	TN/8	22	43	100	retired 2010; GOP won 2010
Edwards	TX/17	20	32	53	defeated 2010
Rodriguez	TX/23	10	51	56	defeated 2010
Ortiz	TX/27	28	53	58	defeated 2010
Matheson	UT/2	10	40	63	won 2010; won in 2012 after redistricting in UT/4; retired 2014; GOP won
Nye	VA/2	2	51	52	retired 2010; GOP won
Mollohan	WV/1	2	42	100	lost Democratic primary in 2010; GOP won
Rahall	WV/3	6	42	67	won in 2010, 2012; lost 2014

Source: Michael Barone and Chuck McCutcheon, *The Almanac of American Politics, 2014* (Washington, DC: National Journal Group, 2013).

[1] Obama's share is the percentage of the district vote won by Obama in November 2008.

[2] Member's share is the percentage of the district vote won by the member in November 2008.

[3] AL means at-large seat.

meeting in Copenhagen.[43] In fact, climate legislation was not even introduced in the Senate until three months after Nancy Pelosi moved climate legislation through the House.

THE TEA PARTY INTIMIDATES MODERATE REPUBLICANS

The brain trust of USCAP was well aware that some Democratic senators would vote against Obama's climate initiative because their states were heavily dependent on coal or energy-intensive manufacturing. The theory was that the loss of some Democratic votes could be compensated for via crossover Republican votes. What USCAP did not fully appreciate was the emergent power of the Tea Party.

During the August 2009 recess, members of Congress returned to their states and districts to witness some of the best-attended town hall and protest meetings in modern American history. Organized by the Tea Party, the activities had a single dominant purpose: to signal that the Obama agenda must be stopped. The two Obama initiatives most frequently highlighted by the grassroots protesters were health care reform and cap and tax. The Tea Party put GOP politicians on notice that collaboration with Obama on health care or climate policy would not be tolerated.[44]

The most promising Republican collaborators on climate legislation were senators John McCain, Lindsey Graham, Olympia Snowe, and Susan Collins. McCain had previously sponsored legislation in this area, and, as mentioned earlier, he campaigned in favor of cap and trade as Obama's opponent for the presidency. McCain, though, was up for reelection in 2010, and his home state of Arizona was a hotbed of grassroots Tea Party activity. Not surprisingly, in 2009–2010 he became invisible on the climate issue.

Graham met with Obama numerous times on climate change and worked diligently with Democratic senator John Kerry on some alternative climate plans. Graham contended that Obama fumbled the issue by unilaterally making public proposals (subsidies for nuclear power plants, new leases for offshore drilling, and delay of EPA regulation of carbon until 2011) that Graham had intended to use quietly as bait to attract additional Republican collaborators. Graham was also irritated when the White House erroneously implicated him as an advocate of higher gasoline taxes. On the home front he was publicly chastised for collaborating with Kerry and Obama: "You are a traitor Mr. Graham."[45] When in 2010 Reid decided to put immigration reform ahead of climate change without consulting Graham, the South Carolina senator backed out of the climate discussions.[46]

Senator Snowe joined some of these discussions, showing limited interest in a cap and trade plan that would cover only electric utilities.[47] Similar to her positioning on health care, Snowe was always as elusive as she was interested in collaboration. To protect herself politically, she sensed she needed to keep talking to both sides but remain on the fence as long as possible.

Meanwhile, Republican Susan Collins was co-sponsoring with Democrat Maria Cantwell of Washington a different legislative approach called "cap and dividend." The idea was to auction off the pollution permits but rebate the revenues to individual citizens on a yearly basis ($1,100 for each family of four under the 2009 version of the Cantwell-Collins plan).[48] Since businesses were cool to this idea, it had difficulty gaining traction.

Other Senate Republicans with interest in the climate issue favored alternatives to cap and trade. Senator Lamar Alexander was interested in measures to promote nuclear power and plug-in cars but insisted that cap and trade had to be taken off the table. Senator Judd Gregg was more interested in a limited bill focused on renewable energy and energy efficiency in buildings.[49]

The bottom line was that among the forty-one Republican senators, Obama was finding no collaborators for his climate legislation. Since the extent of Democratic opposition was less on health care than on climate, it is hardly surprising that Obama and his White House political advisors began to give much more priority to health care than to climate legislation. Some Obama critics were confused about the causation, perceiving that climate legislation was moving slowly because Obama was preoccupied with health care.[50]

LAST-DITCH WHITE HOUSE PUSH

In the summer of 2010 the White House responded to a chorus of criticism from progressives that Obama was not giving enough priority to climate change legislation.[51] The president summoned twenty-three senators, Republicans as well as Democrats, to the White House to search for a path forward. He repeated his call for cap and trade legislation but also indicated openness to a fee on greenhouse gas emissions. Kerry and Snowe discussed a scaled-back cap and trade plan that would cover only electric utilities. Most of the attendees were apparently unmoved by the discussion.[52]

In July 2010 Harry Reid made a public announcement that the Senate would not take up climate legislation. He said: "We know we don't have the votes."[53]

OBAMA SURRENDERS ON CAP AND TRADE

Election Day November 2010 was devastating to congressional Democrats, especially in the House, where sixty-four seats switched to the Republican Party. The nervousness in 2009 about the climate vote among some House Democrats seems to have been justified.[54] In hindsight it appears that several prominent House Democrats who voted against the climate bill may have, at least temporarily, saved their seats: John Barrow of Georgia, Joe Donnelly of Indiana, Jason Altmire of Pennsylvania, Jim Matheson of Utah, Mike Ross of Arkansas, and Dan Boren of Oklahoma. Some postelection analyses suggested that the climate vote mattered little in most races, but as we shall see in chapter 10, the climate vote did contribute to the 2010 massacre of House Democrats.[55]

When veteran Democrat Rick Boucher was defeated in a close 2010 election, he acknowledged that his climate vote was a factor but emphasized that the wave of sentiments against Nancy Pelosi and Barack Obama were bigger factors.[56] Others disagree, since Boucher had positioned himself against Obama on health care. Boucher's former chief of staff put it simply: "I don't think there's any question about it, cap and trade was the issue in the campaign. . . . If Rick had voted 'no,' he wouldn't have had a serious contest [in 2010]."[57] Analysis of his district's voting behavior did reveal that Boucher forfeited his historically big margins in the coal counties of southwestern Virginia.[58]

After the November 2010 election, Obama recognized the political reality. He indicated that cap and trade climate legislation would not be pursued any further. In fact, from 2011 to early 2013 the phrase "climate change" was virtually absent from Obama's speeches, especially his State of the Union addresses.[59] Obama learned from the fate of the Blue Dogs and went silent on cap and tax prior to his 2012 reelection.

PROGRESS WITH EXECUTIVE ACTIONS

In contrast to the failure of his legislative initiative on climate change, President Obama used his executive powers to make more progress reducing greenhouse gases (GHG) than any previous president. He began with the transportation sector in his first term. He also used executive power during his first term to lay the technical groundwork for GHG regulations (e.g., a GHG emissions reporting system). Later, mostly in his second term, Obama issued regulations covering the biggest source of emissions: the coal-fired electric power sector.

MOBILE SOURCES

About 25 percent of greenhouse gas emissions in the US economy are emitted from the transportation sector. Light-duty passenger vehicles (cars and light trucks) account for about two-thirds of those emissions; heavy trucks account for another quarter of them.[60]

The Obama administration capitalized on executive actions taken by the Bush administration from 2001 to 2007 as well as the new legislative authority that Congress had enacted in 2008 in collaboration with the Bush administration.[61] When Obama took office in 2009, modest steps had already been taken—legally and technically—to help set a foundation for Obama's ambitious initiative. Indeed, a 2007 Supreme Court decision made a definitive holding that the EPA possesses the power to regulate greenhouse gas emissions as an air pollutant under the Clean Air Act.

President Obama began work on climate change in 2009 by instructing the DOT and EPA to develop a multiyear plan to increase the mileage (miles per gallon, or mpg) of cars and light trucks. The agencies began with a rule making to increase light-duty vehicle mileage from an average of 29 mpg in model year 2012 to 34.5 mpg in model year 2016.[62]

The bigger step was the establishment of an aggressive regulatory plan for model years 2017–2025; it boosted vehicle mileage to an average of 54.5 mpg by 2025. (Those figures are compliance values based on laboratory tests and assumptions that differ from the mpg figures posted for consumers on the window stickers of new vehicles. A 54.5 mpg compliance figure corresponds to about 40 mpg on the window sticker.) The long-term plan was negotiated by the administration in collaboration with automakers, the United Auto Workers union, environmental advocacy groups, and the State of California. The plan was proposed in 2011 and finalized in August 2012, before the presidential election.[63]

The final plan did entail some compromises in order to build a broad consensus. The ambitious mpg figures reflected the influence of the State of California and environmental groups. In exchange for the ambitious targets, California agreed to coordinate its carbon-emission standards with the new DOT/EPA standards. (Under the Clean Air Act, Congress gave California authority to set more stringent tailpipe standards than the federal government in order to address the severe smog in Los Angeles.) As a result, automakers will not have to comply with conflicting California and federal standards, as it is expensive for them to design different engines or platforms for different states. On the other hand, the automakers won some flexibility in the near-term standards for light trucks and some new compliance credits for innovations, such as hybrid engines for light trucks and start/stop engine technology.[64]

The mpg figures are binding through model year 2021 while the targets for 2022–2025 are aspirational. A midterm review was scheduled for 2017 in order to make sure that the regulatory requirements are feasible and cost-effective. A key assumption of the plan is that fuel prices will continue to rise, possibly to as high as six dollars per gallon.[65] That assumption will have to be revisited, for the unexpected growth in US oil production and the decline in China's rate of economic growth caused world oil prices to drop and fuel prices in the United States to decline below three dollars per gallon in late 2014. The aspirational 2022–2025 mpg figures are to be finalized only after the 2017 midterm review.

The Obama administration also used executive powers to establish the first-ever mpg requirements for heavy-duty trucks.[66] Such vehicles comprise only 4 percent of registered vehicles on the road but account for 25 percent of greenhouse gas emissions from the US transportation sector. In 2011 the DOT/EPA mandated a 20 percent reduction in greenhouse gas emissions from heavy trucks by model year 2018. That will be accomplished by raising the average truck fuel efficiency from 6 mpg to 8 mpg. President Obama also instructed the DOT/EPA to establish heavy-truck mpg standards through model year 2025. A schedule was established for a proposed rule by March 2015 and a final rule by March 2016.[67]

Not all stakeholders were enthusiastic about Obama's executive actions. The National Automobile Dealers Association (NADA) feared that the plan could raise new vehicle prices by more than three thousand dollars per vehicle, leading many households to delay their purchase of a new vehicle or shift to a used vehicle.[68] President Obama's vision that automakers can profit by selling more small cars instead of suvs and pickup trucks has not been validated so far; automakers have responded with lightweight materials and turbochargers rather than reducing vehicle size or shifting to a mix of vehicles with more small cars than large. Toyota is not convinced that consumers will appreciate the new vehicles produced under the Obama plan. According to Jim Lentz, head of Toyota North America: "I appreciate the vision of the administration wanting to lead the industry and consumers to higher mileage cars. Consumers have to be willing to do that. . . . There's going to be a disconnect."[69]

Nonetheless, a virtue of an executive plan is that it can be modified over time, based on real-world experience, without having to go back to Congress and request new legislation. For example, when the price of natural gas plummeted in the United States, the Obama administration promptly made a subtle adjustment to compliance credits in order to encourage the production and sale of vehicles powered by natural gas.[70] Some observers have gone so far as saying that Obama's green-car program is a model of industry-government collaboration that should be applied to other industries.[71]

Some progressive critics of the administration make a sweeping allegation that President Obama made little progress on global climate change during his first term.[72] On a global basis, cars and trucks sold in the United States are a relatively small contributor to the climate change problem and are becoming even smaller as the economies of China and India grow. Others realize that Obama's executive actions on vehicle fuel efficiency are a relatively major climate policy accomplishment. Dan Becker, director of the Safe Climate Campaign offers an interesting international perspective: the DOT/EPA regulatory target of 54.5 mpg by 2025 "is the single biggest step any nation has taken to cut global warming."[73] By the spring of 2011, automakers were offering 27 hybrid and plug-in electric models plus more than 160 high-mpg cars.[74] Obama's push for green cars was a key climate strategy, enacted with executive power, although its sustainability may be hurt if the global price of oil does not increase significantly in the years ahead (since it is difficult for dealers to sell green cars with gasoline prices below three dollars per gallon).

STATIONARY SOURCES

During his first term President Obama treated executive action on stationary sources (i.e., electric power plants, steel plants, oil refineries, chemical plants) as a backstop in case Congress did not move promptly to enact his legislative proposal. It was his "trump card."[75] When it became clear that Congress would not pass cap and trade, the administration was very slow to play its trump card, especially as it relates to the electric power sector. It was not until his second term, when Obama brought new blood (John Podesta) into the White House to jump-start his executive strategy on climate change, that significant progress was made.[76] Obama did, however, set the stage with some important technical actions.

The cornerstone of any policy to reduce greenhouse gas emissions is a practical system for measuring greenhouse gases that can be applied to all significant facilities and, where appropriate, aggregated at the company, state, regional, or federal level.[77] Without facility-specific measurements, there is no way of knowing whether a control activity is effective in reducing emissions. The technical challenge is not simple, because there are multiple greenhouse gases (e.g., carbon dioxide and methane) that can be emitted from numerous physical locations at a stationary facility that are not easy to monitor.

Once a measurement system exists, it can be used in numerous ways: to operate a cap and trade system, to monitor compliance with performance standards, to facilitate implementation of voluntary standards, to bring objectivity to audits of corporate sustainability reports, and so forth. No such measurement system existed when President Obama took office in January 2009.

In December 2007 Congress required that the EPA create a national greenhouse gas registry through establishment of mandatory emissions reporting. The EPA issued a regulation to establish the registry in October 2009, covering sources of 80–90 percent of all GHG emissions in the US economy. The registry covers an estimated thirteen thousand facilities that emit more than twenty-five thousand metric tons per year of GHGs. Small businesses are exempt from the requirement to report emissions. Although the registry received little publicity, it is one of the Obama administration's fundamental contributions to national climate policy.

The Obama administration then took several executive actions that established the legal foundation for regulation of GHG emissions from stationary sources. In December 2009 the EPA made an "endangerment" finding, indicating that GHG emissions from mobile and stationary sources are a threat to public health and welfare. In March 2010 the agency indicated in its "timing rule" that regulation of GHG emissions would not take effect any earlier than

January 2, 2011. In June 2010 the EPA issued a "tailoring rule" establishing which sources of GHGs are subject to regulation. And in December 2010 it established that significant emitters of GHGs must obtain permits from the EPA or a state agency whenever a new facility is constructed or modified. The permit process triggers a requirement that sources implement "best available control technology" (BACT). Much of this important yet quiet progress was made while lots of noise was made in Congress about possible climate legislation.

The tailoring rule is of practical importance because it enabled the EPA to focus on large stationary sources (e.g., electric power plants and refineries) rather than small sources (e.g., schools and restaurants). Instead of using the 100–250 ton/year threshold that is used for conventional air pollutants, the agency adopted a much higher threshold (75,000–100,000 tons/year) for greenhouse gases. Under this scheme, the EPA estimated that 550 sources would need to obtain GHG permits for the first time.[78] Had the agency not raised the threshold, an estimated six million facilities in the United States would have required a permit to operate, a number that would have overwhelmed the EPA's ability to monitor and enforce compliance with the rule.

A coalition of states and industries challenged in federal court the EPA's efforts to regulate GHG emissions from mobile and stationary sources. A federal court consolidated into one case the separate challenges to the endangerment finding, the mobile source regulation, the timing rule, and the tailoring rule.

A unanimous federal appeals court upheld all four of the EPA's regulatory actions in June 2012.[79] On appeal, however, the US Supreme Court in June 2014 struck down parts of the agency's tailoring rule. Basically, the Court did not allow the EPA to apply certain regulatory requirements (e.g., BACT) to large stationary sources solely on the basis of their GHG emissions. If a large source was already being regulated due to its emissions of conventional air pollutants, the Court permitted the EPA to extend GHG regulations to those sources. The Court did not resolve how large the GHG emissions must be in order to trigger regulatory requirements, leaving that issue for the agency to resolve.[80] The practical impact of the Court's decision is limited, because most large sources of GHG emissions are also large emitters of conventional pollutants.[81] Overall, the Obama administration's initial executive actions on climate change held up fairly well in the courts.

BELATED REGULATION OF
COAL-FIRED POWER PLANTS

By the end of his first term, President Obama had made some technical progress but had not used his executive authority to regulate the single largest source of man-made greenhouse gas emissions: the hundreds of power plants around the country that produce electricity for consumers and businesses. Specifically, electric power plants account for 38 percent of annual GHG emissions in the United States, and two-thirds of those emissions are from coal-fired power plants.[82]

During Obama's first term, the EPA did propose a regulation governing the construction of new power plants, aimed primarily at reducing greenhouse gases from new coal plants. This rule was seen as having little practical significance, because the availability of cheap natural gas was causing most new plants to be gas-fired. The EPA nonetheless proposed the rule in April 2012 but later withdrew it. It was not until September 2013 that the rule was re-proposed, following release of the "President's Climate Action Plan" in the first year of his second term.[83]

In the electric-power industry the 2013 proposal was seen as a prohibition of construction of new coal-fired power plants unless carbon capture and storage systems were applied to the plants. CCS entails capturing the carbon dioxide at the stack, compressing the gas, and burying it underground permanently. New gas-fired power plants can generally meet the rule's requirements, because the carbon content of natural gas is about 50 percent less than the carbon content of coal. Critics argue that the rule is legally vulnerable because it requires utilities to employ a technology (CCS) that has not yet been successfully demonstrated on a commercial scale.[84]

The failure of Congress to block Obama on climate policy illustrates why it is difficult for them to stop a president who is determined to exercise his executive power: Obama also had unused veto power, so even if bipartisan opposition to his executive actions was mustered, a two-thirds vote was required to override him.

It was not until June 2014 that the Obama administration took the crucial step of establishing a separate EPA rule covering GHG emissions from existing power plants, especially coal-fired power plants. The proposal mandates a 30 percent reduction in carbon dioxide emissions from existing coal plants by 2030, compared to 2005 levels.[85] It calls for state-by-state implementation, with the EPA reviewing each state's implementation plan. In order to achieve the 30 percent reduction, states and utilities may modernize plants, retrofit CCS, improve energy efficiency, switch from coal to natural gas, promote use of renewable energy offsite ("outside the fence"), or join a regional cap and trade program (such as those operating in the Northeast or in California). The off-site measures may be necessary to meet the 30 percent requirement, but those measures are also the most vulnerable legally, since the Clean Air Act does not specifically authorize their use.[86] Obama's rule covering existing power plants was a big deal on the international stage. Connie Hjelmgaard, the European Union's climate commissioner, put it simply: "EPA's carbon rule is the strongest action ever taken by the U.S. government to fight climate change."[87]

The EPA rule makes innovative use of a regulatory program in the Clean Air Act (section 112d) that has not been used extensively in the past.[88] The section generally authorizes the EPA to set performance standards for the best available emission-control systems. Thus, the anticipated litigation against the section rule was expected to be complex and will take several years to reach resolution. (Twelve states and a coal mining company, Murray Energy, initiated litigation against the proposal in 2014, but the court ruled that the issue should not be resolved until after the final rule.[89]) Since the final EPA rule was issued in the fall of 2015, the states will have a year to submit their implementation plans to the EPA, with the deadline a few months before Obama leaves office. The EPA will then need to review each state's plan and approve it, disapprove it, or require revisions to the plan. The states may request up to two years of additional time from the EPA, and the numerous states led by Republican governors are likely to slow down the process of implementation—not unlike what has happened under the Affordable Care Act.[90] Thus, it seems apparent that the state actions and litigation under this rule will not be resolved until after Barack Obama has left the White House.[91]

A bipartisan coalition in Congress also fought to strip the EPA of its authority to regulate carbon emissions at coal-fired power plants. President Obama threatened a veto of the bill (which was an amendment to another bill), effectively forcing a two-thirds margin in Congress. The House voted 255–172 in favor of the amendment; the Senate split 50–50, ten votes short of the filibuster margin (sixty) and seventeen short of the two-thirds margin required to overturn a presidential veto. Four Democratic senators (Landrieu, Manchin,

Nelson, and Pryor) voted in favor; only one Republican (Collins) voted against it. In 2015 the House took a different approach and by a vote of 247–180 passed a measure that would allow each state to decide whether they wanted to opt in to Obama's "Clean Power" plan. As this book goes to press, this bill has little promise due to a filibuster threat in the Senate or an Obama veto.[92]

A key assumption of President Obama's climate policy is that a shift from coal to natural gas in the electric power sector will cause a reduction in greenhouse gases. Recent studies have called this assumption into question, since methane emissions from natural gas production, transport, and distribution are greater than previously thought.[93] Methane is a highly potent greenhouse gas, much more potent than carbon dioxide in the near term. To address the methane concern, in March 2014 President Obama directed the EPA to consider voluntary measures and, if necessary, rule making to reduce methane emissions from the entire life cycle of natural gas production, transportation, distribution, and use.[94] Once again, this initiative—and related litigation—is unlikely to be completed until the next administration, given the normal lengths of rule-making and judicial processes.

A CLIMATE TEST FOR FUTURE ENERGY ACTIONS

In late 2014 the White House launched a creative executive action aimed at enhancing the role of climate considerations in federal energy decisions covered by the National Environmental Policy Act (NEPA).[95] Currently, federal agencies such as the Department of the Interior and the Federal Energy Regulatory Commission are required to consider local environmental impacts, but there is no explicit requirement to consider global concerns such as climate change.

The White House Council on Environmental Quality issued proposed guidelines in December 2014 that, as finalized in 2015, expanded the scope of NEPA review to include global environmental concerns. Final guidance is expected in mid-2015, after refinements to the guidelines are made based on public comment. Although this action does not change any particular energy policy, it sets in motion a process whereby President Obama has ensured stronger consideration of climate concerns in future energy decisions (e.g., approval of new interstate pipelines) by federal agencies. In a related executive action, in 2015 Obama also issued an executive order calling for federal agencies to reduce their carbon dioxide emissions by 40 percent over the next decade compared to 2008 levels.[96]

SURPRISE: A US-CHINA PACT ON CLIMATE CHANGE

In late 2014 the leadership of the United States and China stunned the world with the announcement of a nonbinding agreement to take aggressive steps to address global warming. Obama went beyond his 2009 Copenhagen pledge of a 17 percent emission reduction (relative to 2005 levels) by 2020; he pledged instead a 26–28 percent reduction by 2025 (relative to 2005 levels). In exchange, China made its first-time pledge of a cap on its absolute amount of emissions, beginning in 2030 and declining thereafter. China also pledged a large expansion of nuclear power and renewable sources of energy.[97]

The US-China agreement was a masterful use of executive power. Since it was not a binding treaty, it did not require ratification by the Senate. It nonetheless represented a significant diplomatic breakthrough in bringing China into the mainstream global dialogue on climate policy. The timing of China's shift in position could not have been better, just before the 2015 United Nations Climate Change Conference in Paris. The agreement also undercuts the GOP argument that the United States should not act unilaterally, because there is no assurance that China will act to address climate change. Moreover, if implemented, the agreement provides a greater degree of investment certainty for the future of the global clean energy market.[98]

Skeptics can certainly point to weaknesses in the US-China deal. The nonbinding nature of the agreement means that the numerical goals may have little significance when the leaderships of the countries change. Even if the Paris agreement in 2015 reaffirms the goals, the GOP-controlled Congress is unlikely to cooperate with the new policies necessary to meet the 2025 goal.[99] Moreover, a pledge to address climate change does not ensure that the pledge will be backed up with meaningful emission controls on the ground. For example, for years Mexico has been a highly progressive voice for policies to slow the rate of global climate change. Meanwhile, the country has been notably unsuccessful on the ground in the implementation of climate policy.[100] China faces a big challenge in honoring its pledge, and the Obama administration faces a big challenge in that both the Congress and a majority of states are controlled by the GOP.

COUNTERFACTUALS

At the 2009 Copenhagen climate conference, President Obama made a pledge to the United Nations that the United States will curtail GHG emissions by 17 percent below 2005 levels by 2020.[101] The United States needs to make progress on this pledge in order to persuade China, India, and other countries to get serious about GHG emissions control.

US emissions were down 10 percent by 2014, but some of this reduction was related to the Great Recession, and more emissions were projected as the US economy recovers. To help achieve the 2009 pledge, the Obama administration employed executive powers to launch a series of new regulations aimed at reducing GHG emissions from mobile and stationary sources.

The regulations covering mobile sources have already been upheld in the federal judiciary, and automakers are making significant progress with increasing the fuel efficiency of new cars, light trucks, and heavy trucks.[102] In contrast, some of the regulations covering stationary sources are completed, but others are still under development (as of late 2015). It will be several years before they are finalized and all litigation is resolved. If they are fully implemented, it is possible that Obama's regulatory actions will be sufficient to meet his 2009 Copenhagen pledge.[103]

Progressive critics of the Obama administration claim that the president gave insufficient priority to his 2009 legislative proposal to create an economy-wide cap and trade program to curtail greenhouse gases. They complain that Obama was preoccupied with health care reform, to the detriment of his climate proposal.[104] This critique is not very persuasive. The Obama administration collaborated with the Democratic leadership in moving climate legislation through the House. The key reason that the White House gave lower priority to climate legislation in 2009 and 2010 is because it was quite apparent that the required sixty votes in the Senate could not be enlisted. Ten Democratic senators from the South and the Midwest were strongly opposed to Obama's policy direction, a level of opposition that was much greater—in both number and intensity—than Obama faced on health care reform. Moreover, the emergence of the Tea Party and its focused opposition to climate legislation discouraged moderate Republican senators from collaborating with Obama on the climate issue. Had the president pursued climate legislation instead of health care reform, he likely would have accomplished neither of them.

A more cogent critique of the Obama administration is that an executive-first strategy should have been pursued in 2009 rather than following through with the campaign pledge for a first-year legislative initiative. As a rationale for shifting course, the White House could have pointed to the April 2007 Supreme Court decision affirming the EPA's authority to regulate GHG emissions as an air pollutant under the existing Clean Air Act. When Obama's campaign team crafted and announced his cap and trade plan in October 2007, the ramifications of the Supreme Court's decision were not fully appreciated. Obama would have been criticized for taking "czar-like" steps in response to climate change, but his response could have been that the steps already have been authorized by Congress and the Supreme Court.

Under this counterfactual scenario, moderate Democrats in the House would have been spared the risky 2009 roll-call vote on cap and tax. Some of them might have been reelected rather than defeated. The Obama White House could also have tolerated Blue Dog criticism of the administration's climate regulations, because Congress, in light of the presidential veto power, was not in any position to stop Obama's executive actions on climate change.

Obama's early use of executive powers on climate change would certainly have triggered legal challenges from industry, but his regulators would have had plenty of time to refine the rules and correct any legal errors uncovered by the judiciary. A downside of Obama's delayed use of executive powers is that resolution of the key legal issues may not occur until after he leaves the White House in early 2017.[105] If the Republicans take the White House in 2017 while the litigation is still under way, it will be much easier for a Republican administration to modify, weaken, or repeal Obama's regulatory framework for the electric power sector. If a new administration were to attempt a repeal of a regulatory program that was finished and upheld in the courts under the Obama administration, the federal judiciary would likely review the abrupt change of course with a high degree of scrutiny.[106]

Some might argue that an executive-first strategy would leave the White House vulnerable to public criticism that Obama is engaging in "Caesarism." This critique had some bite in the president's second term, since he had claimed in his first term that he lacked such authority from the Congress and since he was using executive authority to bypass a GOP-controlled Congress. The executive route would have been much easier in the first term, as Obama would not have made the claim that he lacked legal authority. Moreover, a key advantage of executive action is that it is a simpler and quieter process for the White House than a big legislative proposal.

Insofar as a legislative proposal was necessary to please Obama's environmental base, a more modest proposal at the start might have passed the Congress. One option was to propose a cap and trade program in the electricity sector only, since it was the largest source of greenhouse gas emissions in the economy. By excluding the manufacturing sector, Obama would have reduced opposition from industrial labor unions and an influential segment of the business community. Alternatively, he could have proposed a mandate of renewable energy in the electricity sector, building on the mandates that have already been adopted in numerous states. That approach would have deprived the Tea Party of the "cap and tax" motto. Either of these proposals would have attracted significant support among environmental advocates while curbing the intensity of opposition from the business community.[107] For both alternatives, the task of finding sixty votes in the Senate would have been easier (though by no means a sure thing). The fundamental reason that climate policy is difficult to legislate is that both influential labor unions (e.g., coal miners and steelmakers) and business groups will unite against the proposal, thereby stimulating bipartisan opposition in Congress.

8

DRILLER IN CHIEF

In the 2008 presidential campaign against Senator John McCain, Barack Obama took several clear stances on energy policy: pro-renewables (wind and solar energy), pro-biofuels (conventional and advanced forms), and pro–clean coal. In contrast, he was more nuanced and cautious in his stances toward oil and gas production and nuclear power.

The big surprise during the Obama presidency was the rapid increase in oil and gas production in the United States, largely through unconventional methods such as hydraulic fracturing and horizontal drilling (often called "fracking" for short). On Obama's watch the United States emerged as the number one producer of oil and gas in the world, surpassing both Saudi Arabia and Russia.[1] The most recent projections are that the United States will soon be a significant net exporter of both oil and gas, accomplishing the seemingly elusive goal of energy independence that has stumped every president since Richard Nixon.[2]

There is a view, popular in conservative circles, that oil and gas production boomed during the Obama administration for reasons that have nothing to do with Obama himself. Congress certainly did not pass any major oil and gas legislation at the president's request to spur the industry. (In fact, he sought unsuccessfully to enact a windfall profits tax on the industry.) Moreover, the permit processes for oil and gas production in the United States are the responsibility of the fifty states, not the federal government. Nonetheless, in this chapter I demonstrate how President Obama's use of executive power, primarily soft (rhetorical) power, facilitated the remarkable expansion of oil and gas production by undermining the anti-fracking positions of the organized environmental movement.

Likewise, the Obama presidency proved to be much more supportive of nuclear power than would have been predicted based on his 2008 campaign positions. In fact, in the aftermath of the tsunami-induced nuclear disaster in eastern Japan, Obama had the opening to do what Angela Merkel did in Germany: call for the phase-out of civilian nuclear energy. Instead, he used his soft executive power to reaffirm the future of nuclear power in the United States; he went further and advocated large public subsidies for the construction of new nuclear plants and expanded R&D into innovative, small nuclear reactors for community use. He did not persuade Congress to make all of these pro-nuclear moves, but he kept America's nuclear option open for the future.

On the other hand, coal production and use in the United States did not thrive during the Obama administration. Overall coal production declined by 20 percent from 2008 to 2014 and by almost 50 percent in West Virginia and Eastern Kentucky.[3] The decline is partly attributable to Obama's regulatory policies (the alleged "war on coal"), but more so to the expansion of affordable natural gas supplies (which he encouraged). Progress toward President Obama's vision of clean coal was agonizingly slow. Some US plants are now demonstrating the new technology of carbon capture and storage (CCS), a development that could have important global ramifications in the long run.

With regard to the theory in chapter 2, readers are encouraged to consider the following issues: Given that Obama decided to annoy his progressive base with a pro-fracking stance, should he have looked for a bipartisan legislative measure on fracking or gas exports that would have boosted the fortunes of moderate congressional Democrats? Should Obama have made greater efforts to achieve consistency between his climate agenda and his fracking agenda? Was Obama better off politically with a clean coal or "anti-coal" agenda? Was a renewable sources of electricity mandate a missed legislative opportunity in 2009–2010? Both the end of this chapter and chapter 11 explore these issues.

I begin this chapter with a discussion of the revival of oil and gas production in the United States. The fates of coal and nuclear power are then considered. Obama's enthusiasm for renewable energy and biofuels is examined next, and the chapter concludes with consideration of some counterfactuals.

NUMBER ONE GLOBAL PRODUCER OF OIL AND GAS

During the 2008 presidential campaign, Obama appeared skeptical of expanded oil and gas production. He questioned the need to lease more public land for exploration and drilling, arguing that companies had not yet fully developed the sixty-eight million acres of land that were already leased to them. That "use it or lose it" position, coupled with Obama's call for a new windfall profits tax on the oil industry, seemed to portend a radical departure from the pro-oil policies of President George W. Bush.[4]

In June 2008 Obama gave a speech in Florida that appeared to favor a moratorium on offshore drilling. Two months later, following public criticism from John McCain (who was calling for lifting the moratorium), Obama clarified that he would be willing to allow some offshore drilling if it were part of a coherent energy plan.[5] The fine print of Obama's campaign statement includes a call to "promote responsible domestic production of oil and natural gas."[6]

Soon after taking office the Obama administration delayed the Bush administration's plan to permit oil exploration and production activities on the Outer Continental Shelf (ocs), especially the waters off the East and West coasts.[7] Obama shifted course in his 2010 State of the Union address, signaling more openness to expanded drilling. Then, in March 2010, he made a major announcement calling for the opening of vast expanses of the ocs to exploration and production.[8] The details of the Obama plan were similar to the Bush plan except for the exclusion of Bristol Bay, an ecologically sensitive region of southwestern Alaska.[9] In effect, much of the Atlantic coastline, the eastern Gulf of Mexico, and the north coast of Alaska were eligible for possible exploration and production, a total of about 167 million acres of ocean.

Obama's plan appalled some environmental groups. The Sierra Club, for example, warned that the plan would "only jeopardize beaches, marine life, and coastal tourist economies, all so that the oil industry can make a short-term profit."[10] The progressive Center for Biological Diversity lamented that Obama "has pursued the same offshore program as the Bush administration, even while playing a smoke-and-mirrors game."[11]

Obama's team tried to mollify environmentalists by suggesting that the offshore oil-drilling plan was part of a broader strategy to encourage the GOP to help pass his stalled climate bill in the Senate.[12] Republican senator Lindsey Graham of South Carolina and oil state Democratic senators Mark Begich of Alaska and Mary Landrieu of Louisiana supported Obama's effort to link offshore drilling to climate legislation. Other Democrats did not see the linkage as favorable. Democratic senators Robert Menendez and Frank Lautenberg of New Jersey quickly announced that they would oppose any climate bill that was linked to an expansion of offshore drilling.[13]

DISASTER IN THE GULF

Obama's luck on his pivot toward offshore drilling could not have been worse. A few weeks after his public announcement of the initiative, on April 20, 2010, a catastrophic explosion occurred at British Petroleum's (BP) Deepwater Horizon rig in the Gulf of Mexico. Large quantities of oil flowed from the ruptured well into the gulf for more than three months.[14] A shutdown of drilling in the gulf could be a damaging shock to the US economy, since 25 percent of US oil output and 15 percent of US gas output came from drilling activities in the gulf.[15]

Democratic senators from Florida and New Jersey immediately called on Obama to drop his offshore drilling plan. The reactions from Capitol Hill were especially important because congressional approval was required for expanded leasing in the eastern part of the Gulf of Mexico. Congress would also need to remove a large no-drilling buffer off the Florida coast that was scheduled to be in place until mid-2022.[16]

In the face of public outrage over the largest oil spill in the industry's history, the Obama administration reversed course and imposed a temporary suspension on deepwater drilling operations. Meanwhile, a presidential commission performed an in-depth investigation of the causes of the disaster.[17]

By the end of 2010 the Obama administration had flip-flopped and decided against allowing offshore drilling in the eastern Gulf of Mexico or off the Atlantic and Pacific coasts.[18]

Investigations revealed that the Interior Department office responsible for oil and gas regulation, the Minerals Management Service (MMS), was riddled with problems: scandals involving rigged contracts, drug use by employees, sex between industry representatives and MMS employees, and a perception of pro-industry bias.[19] The Obama administration believed that before lifting the suspension on gulf drilling, it needed to revitalize the MMS or replace it.

For investors in the energy sector the signals from the Obama administration were not very predictable. On the one hand, the administration was slow in lifting the suspensions on leases that had been instituted after the BP oil spill. A 2011 federal court order, at the request of industry, was ultimately necessary to force reconsideration of the suspensions.[20] On the other hand, the Obama administration did not want Congress to force its hand. New legislation passed by the GOP-controlled House was aimed at accelerating oil and gas production; bipartisan support for such legislation was also building in the Senate.

Obama preempted the legislative efforts by using his executive powers. He announced plans for expanded drilling in Alaska and the possibility of new areas of exploration off the Atlantic Coast. He also indicated that he would extend the leases for drilling in Alaska and off the Gulf of Mexico that had been frozen after the BP spill in 2010.[21] By the end of 2011, with new safeguards and a revamped federal agency in place to prevent a repeat of that spill, the Obama administration was again moving to reopen some promising areas for development.[22] In early 2015 the Interior Department issued a 2017–2022 blueprint for offshore leasing that called for new sales of leases in the Atlantic Ocean (from Virginia to Georgia), in the central and western regions of the Gulf of Mexico, and in parts of the Arctic Ocean near Alaska.[23]

For the big oil companies Obama's more permissive policy toward exploration and development was welcome. In 2012, for example, the Interior Department granted Shell Oil Company permission to begin work on the company's first production well in the Arctic Ocean off the coast of Alaska. Shell had already spent six years and $4 billion on exploratory activity. Located in the Chukchi Sea, the well required fourteen hundred feet of casing to bring oil and gas to the surface without causing water contamination.[24]

The Obama administration strived to respond with a regulatory posture that protected the environment but allowed responsible exploration and development to proceed.

THE DRAMATIC ONSHORE PROGRESS

The seesaw nature of Obama's policy toward offshore development overshadowed a much more profound innovation at onshore development sites. A growing number of state-level permits were awarded for application of advanced methods of hydraulic fracturing coupled with horizontal drilling. The advances made it economical for energy service companies to access the plentiful reserves of oil and gas trapped in shale deposits thousands of feet below the earth's surface. Such unconventional methods, as applied in Texas, Arkansas, Oklahoma, Colorado, North Dakota, and Pennsylvania, proved to be more commercially successful than anyone could have predicted.[25]

In a 2011 speech at Georgetown University, President Obama modified his energy plan to take a broader view of clean energy than just renewables. The plan did include renewables (such as wind, solar, and biofuels), but the modification was to include nuclear power, natural gas, and clean coal.[26] In total, the president called for 80 percent of electricity to come from clean sources by 2035. The authors of the White House's 2011 energy plan, "Blueprint for a Secure Energy Future," were aware of the recent industry success in shale gas production.[27] Building on that success, Obama's plan borrowed from the playbook of financier T. Boone Pickens and called for expanded use of natural gas to power heavy trucks on US highways.[28]

Globally, the 2011 plan sanctioned the State Department's Global Shale Gas Initiative, which called for sharing American fracking technology with other countries that were considering shale gas development, including China. Shale gas is now an important feature of Chinese energy policy, although geological and political obstacles in China are significant.[29]

Obama also recognized that shale gas development must be done responsibly. The 2011 plan called for voluntary measures by the industry to reduce methane emissions from oil and gas operations, since methane is one of the most potent greenhouse gases linked to climate change. Thus, the Obama administration embraced expanded onshore production of oil and gas from shale, urging that it be done safely.

The legislative aspects of President Obama's 2011 plan stalled promptly in the Congress, but he saw a role for executive power. In a bold stroke of political poaching, he made unconventional gas a centerpiece of his 2012 State of the Union address. Citing America's one-hundred-plus-years' supply of natural gas, Obama linked the future of natural gas production to the creation of six hundred thousand new jobs in the United States.[30] He also called for the expanded use of natural gas for electricity, truck travel, and factory production.[31]

Obama followed up the address with a new presidential executive order calling for White House coordination of natural gas policy. Rather than ordering an expanded role for the EPA in natural gas regulation (which is what some in industry feared), Obama designed a federal interagency coordination group that made the EPA only one of thirteen departments and White House offices with a seat at the table. The premises of the order are that natural gas production should be expanded safely to create jobs, enhance energy security, and improve the national economy. Recognizing the point of the special organizational arrangement, leaders of the oil and gas industry publicly praised the executive order.[32]

Republicans in Congress were furious. They fretted about the political value of the 2012 address for a vulnerable president seeking reelection in a fragile economy. They countered publicly that Obama was saying one thing yet doing something else: the Keystone pipeline from Canada to the Gulf of Mexico was delayed indefinitely (see chapter 10), and the EPA was giving credence to citizen complaints of drinking-water contamination near natural gas drilling sites.[33] Nonetheless, oil and gas became a central rhetorical feature of Obama's new "all-of-the-above" energy push.[34]

For national environmental groups, the president's embracement of fossil fuels was—with the possible exception of the moderate Environmental Defense Fund—unacceptable. They waited until after Obama's 2012 reelection to take aim at the all-of-the-above strategy. Beginning in 2013, their criticism of his energy policies became quite biting. Documentary filmmaker and activist Josh Fox insisted: "Obama is the guy who presided over more fracking than Bush," calling Obama's record on energy "extremely disappointing."[35]

When Obama toured upstate New York in August 2013, approximately five hundred anti-fracking protesters were waiting for him. They protested outside a town hall event where the president spoke on energy policy. Organized by the advocacy groups Food and Water Watch and New Yorkers Against Fracking, the protesters insisted that fracking cannot be done safely, that it will "poison" water and people, and that it spells disaster for the global climate. On the same day, a full-page advertisement in the *Binghamton Press and Sun* led with the command "President Obama: Stop Covering Up the Science on Fracking."[36]

In a 2013 speech in Pittsburgh on climate change, Obama pointedly rejected the arguments of environmentalists against fracking. He aligned himself as a collaborator with industry to make fracking safer and cleaner.[37] And he portrayed the growth of fracking as a personal achievement of his administration.[38]

In an open letter to the president, more than a dozen environmental groups (including Sierra Club, Earthjustice, Environmental Defense Fund, League of Conservation Voters, and Natural Resources Defense Council) urged the White House to drop the all-of-the-above strategy and favor energy resources that will help focus the country on progress against climate change.[39]

Obama was not convinced. In his 2014 State of the Union address, he publicly reaffirmed his all-of-the-above energy strategy and praised natural gas as a "bridge fuel" that can power the American economy until the country is able to make the transition to renewable energy. He called for industry and communities to collaborate on environmentally protective shale gas development.[40] Later in 2014 he did call for more environmental regulation of the oil and gas sector but all within a framework of responsible expansion of US oil and gas production.[41]

Much to the dismay of environmentalists, Obama also took his message to Europe, where Russia's use of natural gas supplies as a political weapon was sparking fear in the Ukraine and throughout Europe. In Brussels key European Union officials inquired whether the United States would be willing to give Europe special preference for an expanded program of natural gas exports. At the time, the US Department of Energy had already approved construction of seven export terminals for liquefied natural gas (LNG). Another twenty-four applications for LNG terminals were pending.[42]

President Obama indicated that the United States would consider the EU's request, but he went out of his way to urge Europe to diversify its gas supplies by developing its own shale gas resources.[43] France, Germany, and several other European countries were enforcing restrictions or prohibitions on shale gas development due to environmental concerns. As a result, the price of natural gas was several times higher in Europe than in the United

States, a price differential that was penalizing the European industrial sector and exacerbating Europe's economic problems. Obama, making a geopolitical argument, was seeking to put more pressure on Russian president Vladimir Putin by upping gas production in Europe as well as in the United States. Russia was substantially dependent on gas exports to Europe for jobs and public revenues.

Upon returning to the States, in May 2014 President Obama released a revised energy plan titled "The All-of-the-Above Energy Strategy as a Path to Sustainable Growth." Expanded production of oil and gas from shale was portrayed as a way to spur the American economy and curb greenhouse gas emissions. Shale gas was framed as an important feature in a long-run path to low-carbon energy for a clean energy future.[44]

The political consequences of a progressive Democratic president using the bully pulpit to promote oil and gas production should not be underestimated. Given that Obama's position was so close to the GOP position, organized environmental groups were left with no plausible way to use national legislative or regulatory powers to restrict or block the growth of oil and gas production. And Democratic politicians in the states as well as the Congress witnessed the pro-fracking stance of their national party leader, lending credence to the legitimacy of industry's position on fracking. Interestingly, the Democratic governors of California, Colorado, and Illinois refused to support a ban on fracking, even though environmental groups had marshaled widespread support for a ban among Democratic-controlled legislatures.[45]

In summary, the Obama presidency not only witnessed but also fostered a dramatic change in the US oil and gas industry. A long-term decline in conventional production was replaced by explosive growth in unconventional production.

An important positive in the sluggish 2009–2015 recovery was linked to fracking. Rising natural gas prices from 1997 to 2008 compelled gas-intensive manufacturers to move their operations abroad. The Obama years brought low natural gas prices and the siting of numerous new manufacturing operations in the United States.[46] In effect, the recent renaissance of manufacturing in the United States is linked—at least in some sectors—significantly to low natural gas prices.

Overall, oil and gas production grew 60 percent and 25 percent, respectively, from 2008 to 2014, as the United States became the number one producer

Table 8.1. Leading National Producers of Oil and Gas, 2008 and 2013

Countries	2008 (mbpd equiv)	2013 (mbpd equiv)
United States	19	25
Russia	21	22
Saudi Arabia	12	13

Source: Energy Information Administration, "International Energy Data and Analysis," US Department of Energy, 2015, http://www.eia.gov/beta/international.

Note: Annual mbpd = millions of barrels per day equivalent. Gas converted to mbpd equivalent assuming 5.55 million British thermal units of natural gas equals 1 barrel of oil equivalent.

in the world.[47] The "shale revolution" is now projected to last for decades as the cost of unconventional methods continues to decline, new shale deposits are being identified, and the industry is spreading, at various paces, to other parts of the world from Australia and China to Poland and the United Kingdom.

By 2020 the United States is projected to be the world's leading exporter of oil and gas, a position that strongly favors the country in future geopolitical struggles. By 2020 the size of the US GDP may be 2.8 percent higher than it would have been without the shale gas revolution, and three million additional jobs may be created as a result. For the ordinary consumer, the benefit has been felt at the pump, as diminished gasoline prices in 2015 are acting like a $750–$1,000 per-year tax cut for ordinary motorists.[48] Through his use of soft executive power, Obama played a major role in this (somewhat unexpected) accomplishment.

CLEAN COAL OR WAR ON COAL?

Southern Illinois is home to some of the largest coal-producing mines in the United States. Barack Obama's home was Chicago, and as an elected official from Illinois, he was proud of Illinois coal and eager to tell people about it.

In the 2008 presidential primary contest against Hillary Clinton, Obama faced an uphill battle in the states of Kentucky and West Virginia, where labor unions and working-class voters were more sympathetic toward Clinton than Obama. The Obama campaign did not concede without a fight, running radio advertisements and using direct mail highlighting Obama's support for clean coal and his record as a pro-coal politician in the state of Illinois. Clinton defeated Obama in the coal states, but Obama's campaign stance on clean coal foreshadowed some of his tendencies as president.

Subsidizing CCS

One of Obama's early presidential decisions was a reversal of Bush's decision to cancel a large clean coal project in southern Illinois called "FutureGen."[49] The phrase "clean coal" generally means capture of carbon dioxide when coal is burned coupled with the permanent storage of carbon dioxide deep underneath the earth's surface.

The US Department of Energy (DOE) pledged $1.073 billion for the FutureGen project, all but $73 million transferred from the 2009 Recovery Act. Industry partners were expected to contribute $500 million, and a site in southwestern Illinois was selected for the permanent storage of carbon dioxide.[50] Since the DOE plan called for the retrofit of CCS on an existing plant, a timeline—accounting for a complex environmental impact statement—led to a 2017 startup date. And after a very slow start, a first-ever EPA permit for carbon dioxide injection was awarded to the sponsors of FutureGen, allowing construction of the CCS facility in southern Illinois to move forward.[51] Unfortunately, during his second term Obama was compelled to terminate federal support for FutureGen when the project did not meet a statutory deadline for use of stimulus funds.[52] The demise of the Illinois CCS project was a significant setback for Obama's clean-coal agenda.

Obama went beyond the revival of FutureGen to promote clean coal. In 2009 DOE allocated $3 billion of Recovery Act monies to cofinance CCS projects at six sites in Texas, North Dakota, California, West Virginia, and Alabama.[53] In early 2010 Obama followed with creation of an Interagency Task Force on CCS to help speed the development and deployment of clean coal technologies. The administration's goal was to ensure that five to ten commercial-scale demonstrations of clean coal plants are up and running by 2016.[54] To date, Obama has not accomplished that goal. The failure of Congress to pass cap and trade legislation, coupled with the improved economics of gas-fired electric power, resulted in several clean coal projects being cancelled. But some projects did move forward.

In 2014 the Sierra Club dropped its six-year litigation battle against Southern Company's large new clean coal plant in Kemper County, Mississippi.[55] In Houston, Texas, NRC Energy used some DOE funds to help plan a 2016 CCS retrofit of an existing coal plant. The project entailed capturing 1.6 million tons of carbon dioxide per year and then injecting the compressed gas underground to enhance oil recovery (from five hundred to fifteen hundred barrels of oil per day).[56] If the projects prove commercially successful, coal may have a brighter future in the United States and around the world.

Given Obama's support for clean coal, it may seem surprising that he was repeatedly accused of launching a "war on coal" during his presidency. It was the exercise of executive power against companies in the coal sector that induced much of the industry's fear of Obama and its intensified criticism of his regulatory policies. Those regulations, explored below, relate to the mining of coal as well as to the use of coal in the production of electricity.

Curbing Mountaintop Mining

In June 2009 the EPA frightened the West Virginia coal sector with a press release titled "Obama Administration Takes Unprecedented Steps to Reduce Environmental Impacts of Mountaintop Coal Mining, Announces Interagency Action Plan to Implement Reform."[57] The EPA then vetoed—for the first time ever—a decision by the Army Corps of Engineers to approve a mountaintop mining project. Citing concerns about water quality, the EPA asserted authority under the Clean Water Act and terminated a 2,300-acre mining operation planned for Logan County, West Virginia.[58] The EPA's position was that a permit should not be provided unless the measured amount of water pollution near a mining operation was kept below a stringent level.

The industry argued that it was impossible to conduct a mountaintop removal project without some adverse effect on natural ecosystems. When explosives are employed to remove the rock and soil from the top of mountains (thereby creating access to rich seams of coal), the neighboring valleys are filled with the debris. Rivers that run through the valleys are inevitably at risk of contamination, and the best that mining companies can do is reclaim the disturbed area and rechannel the rivers. The long-run ecological health of an area affected by mountaintop removal depends critically on the quality of the reclamation work, and the industry, although it touted some successes in reclamation, had an uneven track record (e.g., reforestation efforts at some sites were inadequate).[59]

The Logan County permit rejection was not an isolated decision. From 2000 to 2008 federal and state authorities permitted 511 mining operations in

West Virginia. Under the Obama administration, this practice slowed substantially.[60] The Obama EPA took more than a year (2009–2010) to make decisions on 175 proposed mining sites and ultimately signed off on only 48 (the latter usually approved only after congressional pressure from pro-coal politicians).[61]

The industry sued the EPA in an effort to block the Obama administration's actions at the Logan County mine. The complex, multiyear litigation was a seesaw affair that the EPA ultimately won in a federal appeals court, prior to Obama's reelection bid.[62] As this book goes to press, another round of litigation on mountaintop mining regulation is under way.

The Democratic governor of West Virginia (Joe Manchin) joined with the state's senior Democratic senator (Jay Rockefeller) in registering concerns with the Obama White House, arguing that the president's clean water policies were threatening the future of the state's coal industry.[63] In 2008 coal production generated about 15 percent of West Virginia's state budget.[64]

The industry in Appalachia charged that the Obama administration was anti-coal, but an entirely different opportunity was unfolding for the Western coal industry. Mining in the West does not require mountaintop removal, because huge coal seams are easily accessible near the surface of relatively flat, often barren terrain. About 40 percent of US coal production occurs on public land, primarily in the West.

Expanding Leasing in the West

Accelerated leasing of public land for coal mining became a priority of the Obama administration. In 2011, for example, the Bureau of Land Management of the US Department of the Interior leased more than 7,400 acres of public land in Wyoming's Powder River Basin to coal companies, with the aim of reaching 758 million tons of coal. Despite vocal opposition from environmental groups, an additional 14,000 acres (with up to 1.6 billion tons of mineable coal) were considered for active leasing. The local media in Wyoming described federal regulatory policy as "signaling strong Obama administration support for Western coal mining."[65]

Progressives criticized the Obama administration not only for the vast amount of land that was leased for coal mining but also for the "bargain basement prices" placed on the leases.[66] After years of trying unsuccessfully to persuade the administration to slow down the leasing of public lands, Friends of the Earth and the Western Organization of Resource Councils (an organization representing the interests of farmers and ranchers) filed a lawsuit in 2014 against the Department of the Interior, alleging failure to conduct proper environmental impact assessment before making leasing decisions. Overall, if President Obama was waging a war on coal, it was not apparent from the Interior Department's coal leasing policies in the West.

EPA Coal-Related Regulations

The biggest concern of the national coal industry and its workers was a "regulatory train wreck" predicted to result from four EPA regulations that the Obama administration developed.[67] The proposal and finalization of these complex and controversial rules extended through Obama's first and second terms.[68]

The "Clean Air Interstate Rule" was designed to force hundreds of existing coal-fired power plants in the South and Midwest to adopt pollution controls for sulfur and nitrogen pollution. Uncontrolled emissions from coal burning cause the release, transformation, and long-range transport of harmful pollutants into the Great Lakes region and the northeastern United States. The EPA estimated that the environmental benefits of this rule were far greater than the compliance costs to industry and consumers. After split decisions in the lower federal courts, the Supreme Court upheld this rule on a 6–2 vote.[69]

The "Mercury Rule" compelled existing coal plants to achieve a 90 percent reduction in emissions of mercury and other toxic air pollutants, thereby curbing the nearby deposition of mercury in rivers and lakes as well as the long-range transport of mercury around the world. The EPA also prepared a cost-benefit justification for this rule, based largely on the argument that control of mercury leads to the control of several other harmful pollutants. But the cost-benefit case was not nearly as strong as the Clean Air Interstate Rule. In a legal challenge by industry, the DC Circuit Court of Appeals upheld this rule on a 2–1 vote,[70] but the Supreme Court ruled 5–4 that the rule should be remanded to the EPA for reconsideration.[71]

The "Coal Waste Rule" reclassified coal wastes at power plants in a way that requires more expensive treatment and disposal techniques by utilities. Due to a lack of sufficient cost-benefit rationale, this EPA rule languished for more than a year at the White House Office of Management and Budget. In December 2014 the rule was finalized with more cost-effective provisions aimed at protecting water quality.[72]

And the EPA's "Ozone Rule" was intended to tighten the legal definition of healthy air, which would have resulted in many regions of the country being reclassified as in "nonattainment" for smog. The noncompliant status forces states and localities to implement additional smog controls, but, ominously, it also makes it more difficult for businesses to expand operations or build new plants. Investors certainly think twice about building new industrial plants or lengthening the operational life of an existing coal plant in a nonattainment area. The Ozone Rule was so controversial that President Obama forced the EPA to reconsider the rule, a process that kicked the controversy past his reelection date. Three weeks after the 2012 election, the EPA re-proposed the rule.[73] It has been finalized and is in litigation as this book goes to press.

For an electric utility company, each of the four rules posed a significant compliance challenge. Complying with all four at the same time was seen as a regulatory nightmare.[74] Planners in the utility industry began to make a practical determination that gas-fired electricity was more economical and free of burdensome regulation than coal-fired electricity. The addition of carbon regulation at coal plants in 2013–2014 exacerbated the situation, contributing to the decisions by some utilities to retire old coal plants (rather than renovate them) and shelve plans for construction of new coal plants.[75]

From 2008 to 2012 coal's share of US electricity production fell from 48 percent to 38 percent. With utilities demanding less coal, fewer miners were needed at the mines. The biggest coal producer in Appalachia, Alpha Natural Resources Inc., laid off 10 percent of its workforce due to mine shutdowns in Virginia, West Virginia, and Pennsylvania.[76]

The GOP-controlled House of Representatives passed a variety of bills aimed at blocking Obama's alleged overregulation of coal. A bill to overturn the Interior Department's restrictions of mountaintop mining passed 229–212, with ten Democrats crossing over to join the Republican majority. A bill was also passed to limit the EPA's authority to regulate carbon and coal wastes.[77] Although the House bills were highly publicized, they were of little practical significance because the Democratic leadership in the Senate did not consider them, and Obama had a potent veto weapon if he should need to use it.

Curbing Coal Subsidies Abroad

During his second term Obama took another step against coal by authorizing the Department of the Treasury to end US support for public financing of coal-fired power plants around the world. In collaboration with countries from Europe and elsewhere, the US government used its influence to block funding for new coal plants through the World Bank, the Asian Development Bank, and the Inter-American Bank. Although only about 10 percent of the twelve hundred proposed coal plants in the world were expecting public funding, the stance of the United States was also intended to dissuade private investors from supporting coal.[78]

The coal industry argued that the halt of US support for coal was bad policy. Economically, it allegedly hurt all coal-exporting countries (Australia, Indonesia, Russia, South Africa, and the United States). It also restricted the market for US coal mining equipment and machinery produced by companies such as Caterpillar. But there was little the industry could do to stop the administration, since Obama was acting unilaterally with executive power. The best the Republicans could do was to make President Obama and the Democratic Party pay politically. In addition to West Virginia, the GOP publicized Obama's alleged "War on Coal" in Virginia, Ohio, and Pennsylvania. They did so in both 2012 and 2014.

The Electoral Politics of Coal

In the state of West Virginia, Obama's approval rating in 2012 was at best in the 30 percent range. In the state's 2012 Democratic primary for president, 40 percent of voters cast their ballot for convicted felon Keith R. Judd rather than vote for Obama. During the general election campaign, the Democratic-leaning United Mine Workers of America (which had campaigned aggressively for Obama in his 2008 contest against McCain) virtually withdrew its support of Obama.[79] Meanwhile, Mitt Romney made appearances at coal rallies in Virginia and West Virginia, seeking to capitalize on Obama's unpopularity in coal country.[80]

Romney captured West Virginia in 2012, but the state had been trending to the GOP in presidential elections since 2000, when George W. Bush upset Vice President Al Gore. That was the first presidential win in the state by a GOP candidate in many years. Obama, however, did not lose Ohio, Virginia, or Pennsylvania, despite aggressive campaigns by Romney in each of these states.

The GOP may have extracted a larger political price for Obama's anti-coal policies in 2014. Three of the top coal-producing states (Kentucky, Montana, and West Virginia) featured competitive Senate races in which his unpopularity played a significant role. A credible Democratic challenger in Kentucky to GOP leader Mitch McConnell, Alison Lundergan Grimes, was compelled to attack Obama on coal issues but ultimately could not shake her association with Obama. Democratic senator Max Baucus of Montana, damaged by his lead role in the Affordable Care Act, accepted an ambassadorship to China rather than face reelection, and thus his seat flipped to the GOP. And veteran Democratic senator Jay Rockefeller chose not to run for reelection in West Virginia, which effectively ceded the seat to popular Republican representative Shelley Capito, who became the first Republican US senator from West Virginia in fifty-five years.

Overall, President Obama accomplished much (if not all) of his agenda on coal. Only limited progress was made in demonstrating climate-friendly technology (CCS) for making electricity from coal. Obama accelerated the shift of coal mining from the East to the West, where it is ecologically less disruptive. He put in place multiple controls on air pollution from coal-fired power plants, which are expected to produce significant human health and environmental benefits. And he encouraged a shift from coal to natural gas in electricity production, which will produce similar benefits. The GOP tried but did not succeed in punishing Obama politically in 2012, but the president's coal policies played a role in the GOP's ability to capture the Senate in 2014 (see chapter 10).

PRESERVING THE NUCLEAR OPTION

In one of the early Democratic primary debates in 2008, the candidates were asked a question about the future of nuclear energy in the United States. Senator John Edwards answered first and indicated that he was opposed to nuclear power. Obama answered second and disagreed: "I actually think we should explore nuclear power as part of the mix."[81] Obama was familiar with nuclear power. His home state of Illinois has more nuclear reactors than any other state in the nation. Chicago is headquarters for the company Exelon, which operates the largest fleet of civilian nuclear reactors. As an elected official from Illinois, Obama had developed a good relationship with Exelon.[82]

In the 2008 general election both McCain and Obama took pro-nuclear stances, but Obama was much more cautious. McCain called for a crash program to build 45 reactors by 2030, expanding on the 104 reactors—20 percent of US electricity supply—operating in 2008.[83] Obama criticized the nuclear expansion plan because McCain offered no proposal for dealing with the expanded volume of nuclear wastes. McCain supported but later hedged on whether to proceed with the permanent waste storage facility at Yucca Mountain, Nevada; Obama opposed the Yucca project.

Obama insisted that he did not favor shutting down nuclear plants. Nor did he oppose extending the licenses for existing plants. He urged efforts to find ways to "safely harness" nuclear power and stressed that our nation could not meet aggressive climate goals without nuclear energy. Unlike McCain, Obama was cautious about building new nuclear plants. He emphasized that the security of nuclear fuel, waste storage, and nonproliferation goals must be addressed before expansion could occur. Notably, Obama's rhetoric was much more optimistic about the future of renewable sources of energy than nuclear power.[84]

Throughout much of 2009 the Obama White House gave relatively little attention to the future of nuclear energy. When the president's climate initiative passed the House but ran into stiff opposition in the Senate, the White House began to reconsider its nuclear position. Senate Republicans were generally supportive of nuclear energy, especially Lindsey Graham and Lamar Alexander.

In December 2009 the US Department of Energy issued a report pledging to approve loan guarantees for three to four new nuclear reactors by the end of 2010. Once DOE approval is secured, the US Nuclear Regulatory Commission (NRC) must give a green light for construction.[85] The NRC process was quite cumbersome, but there was optimism that the Southern Company would build two more reactors near Augusta, Georgia (Burke County), adjacent to a site where two reactors were already operating.

In his 2010 State of the Union address, President Obama stunned both Senate Republicans and his Democratic base by proposing to the Congress a massive expansion of federal loan guarantees for nuclear reactors from $18.5 billion to $54.58 billion, enough to finance six or seven new nuclear plants. Federal loan guarantees were considered crucial because private financiers considered the plants too risky to underwrite.[86] Obama's proposal was timed to give a boost to a bipartisan climate bill being written by senators John Kerry, Joe Lieberman, and Lindsey Graham.[87] Obama also called for a large expansion in DOE's nuclear energy research program. The innovative feature of the plan was a $495 million request for R&D work on small, modular nuclear reactors and reprocessing of nuclear wastes.[88]

Obama's plan to triple support for nuclear energy sparked a "near open revolt" among organized environmentalists, a significant element of his political base.[89] To address doubts about nuclear waste disposal, he established a new Blue Ribbon Commission on America's Nuclear Future, which was tasked to recommend solutions.

In March 2011 the Japanese government and nuclear industry were caught unprepared for one of the most serious nuclear plant accidents in history.[90] The incident started with an earthquake that caused a tsunami to strike the Fukushima nuclear facility in northeastern Japan. The tsunami broke the plant's connections to the power grid, causing several reactors to overheat. The ensuing reactor meltdowns led to uncontrolled radiation releases and the displacement of more than 160,000 people in Japan.

The long-term ramifications of the Fukushima disaster are not fully understood, but the incident sparked anti-nuclear protests around the globe. The mass demonstrations were quite prevalent in Germany, where Chancellor Angela Merkel—with elections approaching—responded with a plan to close all of Germany's existing nuclear reactors by 2022. Japan, Italy, and Switzerland also announced plans to scale back nuclear energy.[91]

The pressure mounted on Barack Obama to take a position. Senator Lieberman went on national television and urged the United States to "put brakes" on the nuclear industry until the ramifications of the Japanese disaster were understood. Congressman Waxman, chair of the House Energy and Commerce Committee, called for an independent evaluation of the safety of the US nuclear industry, noting that a recently relicensed nuclear reactor in Vermont is of the same design as several of the Japanese reactors.[92] Progressive congressman Edward Markey of Massachusetts called for a moratorium on the construction of new nuclear power plants, a stance directly contrary to Obama's 2010 State of the Union position.[93]

In one of the most significant uses of soft executive power in his presidency, Obama reaffirmed his support for nuclear power in the United States. He expressed deep concern about the tragedy in Japan and called for a safety investigation of the one-hundred-plus nuclear reactors in the United States. But his message was unambiguous: there would be no moratorium or phase-out.

Nuclear energy was not a salient issue in the 2012 presidential election. Both Obama and Romney took pro-nuclear positions, and both called for a "consent-based" approach to permanent disposal of nuclear wastes. The consent-based approach symbolized the right of Nevada or any future state to decide whether it wanted to be host to a permanent nuclear waste repository.

During his second term Obama used executive power to enhance the commercial viability of existing nuclear power plants. The initiative came in an EPA proposal to regulate carbon dioxide emissions from electricity-generating plants. However, the proposal was also seen as discouraging new nuclear plants, since those states with nuclear plants under construction would face more stringent carbon-control targets. Depending on how the rule is finalized, Obama's policies may be seen as more or less pro-nuclear than his stance during his first term.[94]

As this book goes to press the near-term commercial future of nuclear power is not bright. The Great Recession (2007–2009) and sluggish recovery have slowed the rate of growth in electricity demand, leading many utilities to scrap plans for new plants. The collapse of natural gas prices has prompted most utilities to move to gas-fired power instead of nuclear or coal for new construction. The absence of a price for emitting carbon dioxide, which would have existed under Obama's failed cap and trade plan (see chapter 9), undermined one of the big advantages of low-carbon nuclear power. Obama was certainly much more enthusiastic about renewable sources of energy than nuclear power but, because of his use of soft executive power, the nuclear option remains open for the United States in the future.[95]

WIND AND SOLAR POWER

President George W. Bush was much more of a nuclear and clean coal advocate than a champion of wind and solar energy. Nonetheless, the 2000–2008 period witnessed a rapid growth in private investments in commercial applications of renewables. Dozens of states enacted or considered legislation mandating the use of renewable sources of electricity. And the federal government offered generous tax credits for producers of wind and solar. By the end of the Bush administration (early 2009), about 40 percent of new electricity capacity was based on wind energy, far more than either nuclear or coal.[96]

Candidate Obama's plans for the future of wind and solar power were quite ambitious. The economy-wide cap and trade program was designed to give all low-carbon sources, especially renewables, a competitive edge in the electricity industry. Moreover, Obama advocated a 25 percent renewable electricity standard by 2025, a proposal that was more aggressive than most of the state mandates for renewables. Further, he advocated an expansion of tax incentives and subsidies to accelerate R&D and deployment of renewable energy.

Much of Obama's renewables agenda crumbled in 2009–2010 when his climate initiative (cap and trade plus the national renewables mandate) failed to pass the Senate. But his contributions to the growth of wind and solar were significant, rooted in federal spending and tax initiatives. As we shall see, Obama paid a stiff political price for his support of wind and solar, a price related to the Solyndra scandal that, as explained below, could have been avoided.

Before Obama took office, Bush and the Democratic Congress had already put into place a generous investment tax credit (ITC) to encourage investments in wind and solar energy projects. In October 2008 Congress extended a 30 percent commercial solar investment credit to residential applications, both through 2017. The same legislation provides a similar federal tax credit to help consumers purchase small wind turbines for home, farm, or business uses.[97]

As established by Congress in 1992, a "production tax credit" (PTC) is also made available to companies that make renewable energy available to consumers. The PTC is made available for the first ten years of production and is generous enough to make renewable electricity competitive in many regions of the country. The credit stimulated substantial growth in the wind turbine sector in the decade following its adoption.[98]

Obama's 2009 Recovery Act was designed explicitly to give the renewables industry an even bigger boost. First, the PTC was extended through 2012.[99] Second, the act added a cash-grant option to the investment tax credit, an option that has been quite useful to the solar industry. If eligible for an ITC, a recipient may request, instead of a tax credit, cash through the Department of the Treasury's 1603 Program: Payments for Specified Energy Property in Lieu of Tax Credits. Up to 30 percent of the project's cost may be covered. The cash option can be exercised immediately after a construction project is complete rather than waiting for an offset on the next year's tax bill.[100] The cash-grant option stimulated $32.9 billion of renewable energy projects but expired at the end of 2011. Renewal of the credit was complicated when the Republicans took control of the House.

Where the 2009 Recovery Act ran into political trouble was in the large expenditure of funds for the support of clean energy projects. The act gave DOE $37 billion to dole out in clean energy grants and another $38.5 billion in loan guarantees. Each of those two figures was much larger than DOE's typical annual appropriation for all of its activities combined.[101] Whenever such huge amounts of money are expended quickly, the opportunities for mistakes, inefficiencies, and fraud in government and industry are significant.

Consequently, Obama's support of renewable energy became embroiled in a firestorm of controversy associated with the bankruptcy of Solyndra, a California-based solar company. Solyndra's business model was never capable of competing with China's heavily subsidized producers of solar panels. After years of cash problems, Solyndra defaulted on $535 million in federal loan assistance intended to help finance a plant to make solar panels. Although the vast majority of DOE loan recipients did not default, the Solyndra debacle became the "poster child" of wasted stimulus money and dubious investments in "green jobs." The story of Solyndra shows a self-inflicted wound by the Obama administration through poor public administration at the Department of Energy and questionable political intervention from the White House.

As background, the purpose of the 2005 DOE green technology program was to help finance promising green-energy technologies that were not developed enough to attract adequate private capital. When the so-called 1703 program was announced in 2006, Solyndra, which submitted one of the 134 preliminary applications, was deemed by DOE to be one of the sixteen finalists. After a full application was submitted in 2008, a final decision on Solyndra was unresolved when the Obama administration took office in early 2009.

Under the 2009 Recovery Act, Congress added the new "1705 program" to enable DOE to provide support for "commercially available technologies." The 1705 support was more generous than the 1703 support, because the recipient does not have to pay a credit-subsidy cost representing the cost of the loan to the taxpayer if the recipient defaults. DOE pays the credit-cost subsidy for the recipient.[102] The Obama administration decided to support Solyndra under the 1705 program.[103]

As the DOE prepared to finalize the Solyndra loan, the White House was planning for President Obama to travel to California for an official announcement of the loan. For White House communicators, this looked like a great base-pleasing opportunity. The trip was cancelled when an analyst at the US Office of Management and Budget informed key officials that "this deal is NOT ready for prime time."[104] In fact, the president's economic advisors and OMB had serious doubts about the wisdom of the entire 1705 program, because, in effect, it required DOE to act as a venture capital firm, a role that a cabinet agency of the federal government is not well designed to play.

It was later revealed that the White House's interest in Solyndra was rooted at least partly in campaign politics. One of Solyndra's primary private investors was the George Kaiser Family Foundation. Kaiser was a Tulsa, Oklahoma, billionaire who was a "bundler" (major fund-raiser) for Obama in the 2008 presidential campaign. White House logs show that Kaiser was a frequent visitor to the White House in 2009, but it was never demonstrated that he or the administration engaged in any illegal activity.[105]

The White House did express concern to OMB and DOE that the Solyndra loan application was moving too slowly, and DOE officials reported that they felt "tremendous pressure" from both the White House and Congress.[106] DOE ultimately overcame OMB's objections and the 1705 loan to Solyndra was approved. Both President Obama and Vice President Biden hailed Solyndra publicly as a model of green innovation and clean energy jobs. Since Solyndra was the first recipient of Recovery Act support under the 1705 program, Solyndra was considered the prototype of clean energy support under Obama's 2009 stimulus efforts.

In December 2010 Solyndra came back to DOE seeking more cash to pay its worsening debts. DOE declined but created another form of political vulnerability for Obama. DOE changed the terms of the Solyndra loan agreement in February 2011 so that private investors could recoup $75 million—ahead of the government—if the company went bankrupt.[107] In the spring of 2011 Solyndra declared bankruptcy and laid off its eleven hundred employees. Most of the $535 million loaned to Solyndra was never recouped.

The Obama administration's handling of the Solyndra application became the subject of sobering congressional hearings led by Representative Cliff Stearns, chairman of the Oversight and Investigations Committee of the House Committee on Energy and Commerce. Using his powers as committee chair to call witnesses, request documents, and issue subpoenas, Stearns obtained seventy thousand documents from the Obama administration, including numerous e-mails from DOE, OMB, and the White House. He then generated massive negative publicity about Solyndra, in effect exposing it as an illustration of administration incompetence or corporate cronyism. The liberal group Center for American Progress counted 190 mentions of Solyndra from August 31, 2011, to September 23, 2011, spanning ten hours of major TV network coverage (ABC, NBC, CBS, Fox News, CNN, and MSNBC).

The conservative group Americans for Prosperity took the Solyndra story directly to voters in two rounds of television advertisements (one minute each). The first ad purchase, for $2.4 million (late 2011), was run in Florida, Michigan, New Mexico, and Virginia. A second buy, for $6 million (early 2012), was run in North Carolina, Ohio, Wisconsin, Iowa, Virginia, and Michigan. The advertisement put the spotlight on the Obama administration's "cronyism and blind ideology."[108] By August 2012 the number of Americans who thought the loan to Solyndra was a bad idea outnumbered the number who thought it was a good idea by more than three to one.[109]

DOE and the White House defended the Solyndra loan. They pointed to the fact that investments in innovative technology firms will inevitably lead to some failures. Were it not for the risk of failure, private investors would offer plenty of capital without government assistance. Moreover, defenders of the 1705 program noted that most of the DOE loan recipients did not default.[110]

Despite massive adverse publicity, Obama did not let the Solyndra debacle slow his support for the solar sector. In September 2011 DOE approved four more solar energy loans worth several billion dollars, hours before the loan program was set to expire. A month later Obama announced an executive plan to establish "solar energy zones" where large-scale industrial projects can be implemented through streamlined environmental reviews and permitting procedures.[111]

As the GOP took greater control of the Congress from 2011 through 2016, the Obama administration ran into increasingly effective opposition to the efforts to use tax credits, subsidies, and loan guarantees to boost wind and solar. The tax credit for wind became so politicized that in 2014 investors had no confidence that it would exist until the very end of the tax year. President Obama used his executive power through IRS guidance to sustain tax credits for renewable energy projects as long as possible.[112] As this book goes to press, the tax credits for wind and solar are being renewed. Despite the policy uncertainty, both wind and solar grew rapidly as sources of electricity during the Obama administration.[113]

ETHANOL

Working with senators Charles Grassley and Max Baucus, President George W. Bush engineered a legislative compromise that led to rapid growth in the use of corn-based ethanol as a motor fuel additive in the United States. It was the 2005 Bush energy bill that authorized the EPA to compel refiners to blend ethanol with gasoline.[114] The result was growing use of E10 fuel (10 percent ethanol, 90 percent gasoline) throughout the country.

In a second legislative deal in January 2007, Bush and the Democratic Congress agreed to a rapid expansion of ethanol blending from 4 billion gallons per year in 2005 to 36 billion gallons per year in 2022.[115] Throughout his term Bush also supported an array of federal subsidies, tax incentives, and tariffs on imported ethanol that boosted the commercial success of US corn farmers and ethanol makers.

Although corn-based ethanol is a renewable fuel, it drew significant criticism during the Bush years. First, the need to grow large amounts of corn for ethanol production caused corn and food prices to rise substantially. The result was heightened concern about hunger and malnutrition in developing countries (e.g., food riots in Mexico). Internationally, the United States was widely criticized for subsidizing a corn-based motor fuel instead of preserving agricultural land and corn for use in food production. Second, although once favored by environmentalists as a smog-reducing fuel, corn-based ethanol became seen as a negative for environmental quality and climate protection. Adverse effects ranged from water pollution near farms to release of greenhouse gases from soil when land is cleared for corn production.[116]

Hillary Clinton and Barack Obama were both in the Senate in 2005 when Bush's original ethanol mandate was debated on the Senate floor. Senator Obama voted in favor of Bush's ethanol mandate while Senator Clinton voted against it.[117] In the Democratic primary for president in 2008, Obama was the only candidate to speak with unqualified enthusiasm about ethanol. He argued that ethanol is a national security plan that reduces dependence on petroleum from hostile regions of the world.[118]

In the summer of 2007, VeraSun Energy rolled out its new ethanol processing plant in Charles City, Iowa. Senator Obama, then a little-known presidential aspirant, surprised locals when he traveled from Chicago to appear at the opening ceremony.[119] It was both an opportunity to make an early presence in Iowa (the first caucus state) and to show his support for corn-based ethanol. Seven months later, Obama stunned the Democratic establishment by winning the Iowa caucuses.

In the general election campaign, Obama and McCain took diametrically opposing positions on ethanol. Obama supported the Bush policies, and in fact argued that the mandated market for ethanol should be enlarged. McCain, in contrast, called for elimination of both federal ethanol subsidies and the tariff on imported ethanol. In August 2008 the American Corn Growers Association endorsed Barack Obama for president, only the second time in the association's twenty-two-year history that a presidential endorsement was made.[120]

Soon after his general-election victory in November 2008, Obama found that organized environmentalists, a key group in his political base, were seeking a reversal of his campaign position on corn-based ethanol. Friends of the Earth argued that ethanol is a "false solution."[121] The group called for a cut in federal ethanol subsidies, stricter greenhouse gas regulation of ethanol production, and more funding for advanced biofuels research.

Despite such criticisms, President Obama continued his pro-ethanol policies. He also rejected a request from Luíz Inácio Lula da Silva, the president of Brazil, to lift the $0.53 per gallon tariff on imported ethanol, even though ethanol made from sugar cane has a better environmental profile than ethanol from corn. To facilitate use of even larger blends of ethanol with gasoline, Obama's EPA issued rules allowing the ethanol share to climb to as high as E15 (15 percent ethanol; 85 percent gasoline) in recent-model vehicles. And Obama used his executive power to soften a legislative requirement that was intended by Congress to ensure that ethanol production did not worsen global climate change.[122]

Proponents of ethanol point to Brazil, where millions of cars run each day on high ethanol blends such as E85 (85 percent ethanol, 15 percent gasoline). Obama also favored E85. Due to auto regulations initiated during the Bush administration, about 25 percent of new vehicles sold each year in the United States are capable of running on either E85 or gasoline. Overall, about sixteen million motor vehicles on the road—about 7 percent of the total—were capable of running on E85 in 2014.[123]

The problem Obama faced was that only 1,600 of the 160,000 motor fueling stations in the United States offered E85. Obama deployed resources at the US Department of Agriculture (USDA) to promote the availability of E85 to motorists. USDA funds covered up to 75 percent of the cost of installing pumps at refueling stations that deliver E85. Obama's goal was to increase the number of E85 pumps in the States from 1,600 in 2008 to 10,000 by 2014. However, only 2,625 were available by the end of 2013, as Obama's ethanol agenda ran into opposition in Congress.[124]

Opposition became serious as early as 2011 when the White House was confronted by a potent interest-group coalition seeking to halt government support of corn-based ethanol. The bipartisan coalition included fiscal hawks, free-market advocates, environmentalists, the oil industry, and hog and poultry farmers who depend on corn feed for their animals.

The House voted 283–128 to block any additional public spending on E85 pumps but, in the Senate, a similar measure sponsored by John McCain was defeated (59–41). Five Democrats defected and joined thirty-six Republicans in voting against the subsidies.[125]

The White House was less successful in its effort to block a measure calling for repeal of the ethanol tax credit ($0.45 per gallon) and the tariff on imported ethanol ($0.53 per gallon).[126] The Senate voted 73–27 for an amendment to repeal such support for the domestic ethanol industry.[127] It did not become law, however, but only because the parent bill was never passed in the House for unrelated reasons.

At the end of 2011, when the ethanol support (credits and tariff) was scheduled for expiration, the ethanol industry and the White House reluctantly decided to let the support expire. They feared that the mandated market for ethanol, which was engineered by Bush and the Democratic Congress in 2007 and implemented by Obama, might be put at risk if a legislative debate were waged on subsidies and tariffs.[128]

In the 2012 election campaign for president, ethanol was not a significant issue, because both candidates (Romney and Obama) supported the EPA's ethanol-blending requirements. However, those requirements proved to be more politically feasible than technically and economically realistic. The Obama administration ultimately recognized that the schedule for increased corn-based ethanol established by Congress in 2007 was not tenable. Gasoline consumption was increasing less rapidly than expected, and the efforts to expand use of E15 and E85 were not very successful. As a result, executive power was deployed at the EPA to relax the 2014 ethanol-blending requirements from 18.15 billion gallons to 15.21 billion gallons.[129]

From his days as a US senator, Obama recognized that corn-based ethanol was only a bridge fuel designed to reduce petroleum dependence until advanced biofuels (also known as cellulosic ethanol) became commercially competitive. The 2007 ethanol mandate enacted by Congress required that a majority of ethanol produced in 2022 be advanced (cellulosic), and a multiyear cellulosic mandate on refineries was to be phased in gradually by the EPA.[130] In 2015 the EPA proposed 17.4 billion gallons of ethanol blending for 2016 but 3.4 billion must be cellulosic.[131]

Federal financial support was expended to accelerate R&D and demonstrations of cellulosic ethanol. Using authority contained in the 2008 Farm Bill, Obama implemented the Biomass Crop Assistance Program, the first project aimed at dedicated production of switchgrass for use in making cellulosic ethanol. DOE supported advanced techniques that made use of inputs such as corn stover (stalks, leaves, and husks) and wood chips instead of corn. Despite the boost, progress in cellulosic ethanol production was so slow (for both technical and economic reasons) that the EPA was forced to diminish the legal requirements on refiners to blend gasoline with cellulosic ethanol.[132] Three relatively small cellulosic-ethanol plants were launched in the fall of 2014, but it is not yet clear if the processes being demonstrated (e.g., a joint venture of the ethanol producer Poet and the life-science company DSM to produce ethanol from corn stover) will be commercially competitive.[133]

Overall, in 2007–2008 Obama reaped significant political gain for his pro-ethanol position, as it helped distinguish him from the other Democratic candidates in the all-important Iowa caucuses. From 2009 to 2014 Obama was less successful on policy making and implementation, but he remained pro-ethanol. The federal tax credit for corn-based ethanol production and the tariff on imported ethanol were eliminated over Obama's objection, due to pressure from a bipartisan coalition in Congress. Obama helped protect the ethanol-blending requirements from congressional opposition but was forced, for technical and economic reasons, to relax the implementation schedule for both corn-based and cellulosic ethanol.

COUNTERFACTUALS

Obama's record in energy policy is much more accomplished than is commonly realized. Some analysts contend, with justification, that he was more accomplished on energy than he was on more high-profile issues such as the minimum wage and immigration.[134]

The boom of oil and gas production during the Obama administration is a giant step toward energy independence in the United States, a trend with profound economic and geopolitical ramifications.[135] It is a larger step in this direction than achieved under any modern president and will change the country for decades to come. The accomplishment was not without its challenges for the Obama White House: low oil and gas prices caused fossil fuel consumption to increase, which worked against Obama's climate agenda. And oil and gas production continue to cause some environmental damages, although the administration has used regulatory power to reduce some of those damages.[136]

Obama's centrist stance in 2010 on offshore oil production proved to be highly unlucky, as it ran into the unexpected public outrage associated with the Deepwater Horizon oil spill in the Gulf of Mexico. With the benefit of hindsight, Obama should have staked out his pro-oil and pro-gas stance early in his administration (2009), when he was looking for ways to find legislative collaboration with congressional Republicans.

Critics on the right insist that the oil and gas boom occurred on private land with state-level permits, and thus Obama's policies had nothing to do with it.[137] This critique ignores the fact that the president's rhetorical position on fracking was important in legitimizing unconventional methods in the public eye and undermining the anti-fracking campaigns of several environmental groups.[138] If Obama's position on unconventional gas can be criticized, it is that he did not move aggressively enough with executive power to control methane emissions from gas production and distribution, a step that would have strengthened the compatibility of his pro-gas agenda with his climate agenda.

Critics on the left insist that Obama's support for unconventional methods of oil and gas production was inconsistent with his climate change agenda.[139] This critique confuses production with consumption, as Obama clearly took steps to reduce oil consumption in the United States (e.g., through the mandate for more fuel-efficient cars and trucks). The primary effect of US oil and gas production is to compete with foreign producers in the global market, an effect with significant geopolitical advantages for the United States and our allies around the world.

What Obama needed to do to strengthen his climate legacy was not ban oil and gas production in the United States, but implement cap and trade with executive power in 2009–2010 and strengthen control of methane emissions from oil and gas production with executive power in 2013–2014. Obama's energy policy was predominantly pro-gas and pro-renewables. Critics on the left do not make a convincing case that Obama did not do "the best that was possible politically."[140] Public opinion about climate change was certainly not where it needed to be to support a strongly green, low-carbon legislative policy.[141]

On nuclear power Obama did not accomplish a large increase in the number of nuclear power plants as he proposed in 2010. The nuclear disaster in Japan and low natural gas prices complicated pro-nuclear ambitions and motivated a cautious nuclear policy. Obama deserves credit for not overreacting to the Japanese tragedy and instead preserving a future for nuclear power in the United States, which was basically his 2008 campaign position. For pro-nuclear advocates, the president reached a much more promising outcome than Germany did under Prime Minister Angela Merkel, where nuclear energy is being phased out and rising electricity prices are hurting the competitiveness of German industry.[142]

Using executive power, Obama accomplished a significant shift of coal mining from the East to the West, a favorable environmental trend that is consistent with his 2008 campaign stance against mountaintop mining.[143] The political price Obama paid for this accomplishment was in the Senate, where the Democratic Party's hopes to compete for Senate seats in West Virginia and Kentucky dwindled. The boost for coal mining in the West did not generate any compensating political benefit for Obama or the Democrats.

Obama campaigned in 2008 in favor of clean coal, defined as coal-fired electricity accompanied by CCS. He used executive power through the EPA to insist that any new coal-fired power plant must be equipped with CCS, and he worked with Congress to make generous federal subsidies and loan guarantees available for CCS. A few commercially significant CCS facilities are under way. President Obama's rhetorical shift away from clean coal in 2012–2013 is questionable, since it implies that he is conceding the anti-CCS criticisms of environmentalists rather than setting an example for the world, which remains highly dependent on coal and will eventually need to move toward CCS.[144]

The Obama years were a big boost for developments in wind and solar energy, but it is possible that Obama could have accomplished even more with a clean electricity mandate. When the Democratic Party enjoyed large voting majorities in the House and Senate in 2009–2010, a tactical decision was made by the White House and congressional leaders to keep the cap and trade plan and the renewables mandate together in one huge piece of legislation. When the Tea Party successfully indicted the mammoth climate bill as "cap and tax," thereby scaring off potential Republican supporters, Obama had no way to overcome the determined opposition from Democratic senators from the South and Midwest.

A plausible case can be made that Obama and the congressional Democratic leadership should have pursued a clean electricity mandate through separate legislation in 2009–2010. The argument is not based solely on hindsight reasoning, as the Obama White House had good reason to believe the necessary votes might have been obtainable.

In June 2007 Democratic senator Jeff Bingaman proposed legislation that required 15 percent of electric power in the United States to be derived from renewable sources (primarily wind, solar, and geothermal) by 2020. At the time, those sources accounted for less than 5 percent of the total. The Bingaman proposal appeared to have at least sixty votes in the Senate but, by all accounts (including his own), Senate majority leader Harry Reid erred in not calling for a vote on the Bingaman amendment. As a result, the 2007 energy bill was enacted into law without a renewables electricity requirement.[145]

If as incoming president Obama had pursued cap and trade with executive authority (as described in chapter 9), he could have focused the Congress on a renewable electricity mandate. Under that scenario his prospects of attracting significant Republican support would have been greater. By adding nuclear and clean coal to the renewables package, Obama would have made the mandate even more attractive to Republicans in the Senate. Although progressives would have objected to nuclear and clean coal, the broader clean electricity mandate would have been consistent with Obama's 2008 campaign positions in favor of clean coal and nuclear power. Moreover, the attacks from progressives would have had the salutary effect of positioning the White House in the middle of the debate while showcasing moderate congressional Democrats in negotiation with moderate Republicans.

The Republican leadership—and the Tea Party—would surely have sought to marshal unified opposition to a clean electricity mandate as they did against cap and tax. But opposition to clean energy is more difficult to organize, especially in a setting where each state is permitted to choose the mix of clean electricity sources that is most cost-effective for residents and businesses of the state. The prospects of success might have been much improved compared to the cap and tax debate, especially since the industries behind each of the clean sources of electricity likely would have lobbied moderate Republicans as well as Democrats to help move the bill to passage.

The promise of this approach is validated by the fact that President Obama himself proposed the clean electricity mandate in his 2011 State of the Union message, after his climate bill was declared dead in 2010. By then, however, the Republicans had taken control of the House, blocking any possible consideration of such a sweeping regulatory mandate.

9

DEPORTER IN CHIEF?

The immigration issue has been politically explosive in the United States for at least a century. Republican senator Henry Cabot Lodge of Massachusetts persuaded Congress to override President Woodrow Wilson's veto and enact the Immigration Act of 1917. Alarmed by the rapid flow of immigrants from eastern and southern Europe, Congress barred immigrants over the age of sixteen from entering the country if they were illiterate, as determined by a forty-word reading test in the immigrant's native language. In 1924 Congress added an absolute cap on the number of immigrants permitted to enter the country, responding to an unusual advocacy coalition of Ivy League elites in the Northeast and the AFL-CIO.[1]

The most recent legislative overhaul occurred in 1986 when Republican president Ronald Reagan and a Democratic Congress agreed to a significant liberalization of immigration law. Under a process referred to as "amnesty" by conservatives, about 1.7 million undocumented migrants became permanent residents of the United States and roughly 1 million farmworkers were permitted to apply for a higher level of legal status.[2] In the House of Representatives an anti-amnesty amendment fell only seven votes short of enactment, illustrating the divisiveness of the issue.[3]

The influx of Mexican immigrants into California in the early 1990s was seen as imposing significant burdens on the state's public schools, medical facilities, and criminal justice system. California voters enacted a ballot initiative, "Proposition 187," 59–41 percent with the express purpose of denying public benefits to illegal immigrants (e.g., withholding public school access to undocumented students). Although the vote was overturned by the judiciary due to legal deficiencies, the movement for Proposition 187 revealed a strong anti-immigrant sentiment that has continued to this day.[4]

Republican president George W. Bush, who developed a pro-immigrant reputation as governor of Texas, captured an unusually high share (39–44 percent, depending on the exit poll) of the Hispanic vote in his successful 2004 reelection bid against Massachusetts senator John Kerry.[5] By way of comparison, Republican senator Robert Dole captured only 21 percent of the Hispanic vote in his loss to Bill Clinton in the 1996 presidential election.

Bush followed up his reelection by working with a bipartisan coalition in the Senate to pass—by a vote of 62–36—a comprehensive immigration reform bill. It called for enhanced border security; a guest worker program for two hundred thousand workers interested in three-year, renewable, nonagricultural jobs; permanent legal residency for 1.5 million agricultural workers; and a pathway to permanent residency for millions of undocumented immigrants. However, the initiative died in 2006 when the House Republican leadership refused to participate in a conference committee that would merge the Senate plan with a House "enforcement only" plan. House Republicans insisted that the border must be secure before any liberalization measures would be considered. Thus, it was the House Republicans who blocked passage of Bush's immigration reform initiative, a dynamic that would also complicate the reform ambitions of Barack Obama.

Although immigration is not the only issue of concern to Hispanics, it is an important one, both pragmatically for millions of immigrants and their families and symbolically for how politicians are perceived by the Hispanic community. Thus, politicians with aspirations to attract Hispanic votes are inclined to consider a liberalization position, even though such a position annoys populist white conservatives in both parties.

I begin this chapter by exploring how Obama positioned himself on immigration policy as a US senator from Illinois and as a presidential candidate competing against Hillary Clinton and John McCain. I then expose Obama's perplexing first term, highlighting why he became known among Hispanic activists as "deporter in chief." The administration's handling of the child refugee crisis, one of the administration's low points, is then covered. After reviewing Obama's strong (but judicially vulnerable) executive move on immigration in late 2014, the chapter concludes with some promising counterfactuals.

With regard to the theory in chapter 2, issues that arise in this case study include the following: At the start of his first term should Obama have lowered expectations about comprehensive legislative reform? Would an executive-first strategy on reform have been more productive for the Hispanic community? Why did Obama use his executive power to crack down on illegal immigrants? Did Obama give adequate attention to the public administration aspects of the child refugee crisis? Answers to these issues are explored at the end of this chapter and in chapter 11.

CLINTON VERSUS OBAMA

In the 2008 Democratic primaries, both Hillary Clinton and Barack Obama eagerly courted the Hispanic vote. Their voting records on immigration reform were similar, if not identical. As senators both Clinton and Obama voted in favor of the 2006 bipartisan reform plan requested by President Bush.

In the eyes of Hispanic groups, Obama's voting record was not perfect. In 2005 then Senator Obama (along with John McCain) voted in favor of the Secure Fence Act of 2006, which authorized a fence to be built on the border between Mexico and the United States. Hispanic advocacy groups did not view this vote favorably. Moreover, during the effort to amend the 2006 reform package favored by Bush, Obama voted for two floor amendments (one passed, one failed) that called for weakening the guest worker program. These votes were seen as favoring labor union positions over Hispanic interests, as the labor movement was lobbying against the guest worker program.[6] Obama also sided with labor interests in the aborted effort at immigration reform in 2007.

All of the presidential candidates knew that the early contests in Iowa and South Carolina would feature few Hispanic voters, but many working-class white voters perceived that immigrants take jobs from Americans. In states like Iowa immigration ran far behind the Iraq War, health care, and the economy among the most important issues to voters.[7] Accordingly, none of the major presidential aspirants gave much priority to immigration in their stump speeches.

Obama and Senator John Edwards did attack Hillary Clinton for waffling on an unexpected aspect of the immigration issue. New York governor Eliot Spitzer was advocating a plan to allow undocumented migrants access to driver's licenses in his state. Reporters began asking the presidential candidates to comment on Spitzer's plan. In a Democratic primary debate on October 30, 2007, Obama and Edwards supported Spitzer's plan and criticized Clinton for ducking the issue. Clinton's equivocal stance was seen as an effort to curry favor with rank-and-file labor union members.[8]

Jorge Ramos, the popular anchor at the Spanish-language network Univision, drew more than two million viewers for his nightly newscast. During the Univision primary debate, Ramos extracted a commitment from Obama that, if elected president, Obama would tackle immigration reform as a first-year priority.[9] Obama's immigration pledge proved difficult to deliver on and set the stage for some testy relations with Hispanic activists. When the smoke cleared, the contest between Obama and Clinton among Hispanics was not close. Exit polls found Clinton defeating Obama by nearly two to one among Hispanic voters. In both California and Texas, Clinton lost the contest among non-Hispanic voters but won both states due to her strong performance among Hispanics.[10] Thus, when Obama entered his general election contest against Republican nominee John McCain, he did so with more enthusiasm among African Americans and young people than among Hispanics. Fortunately for Obama, in the Republican primaries McCain moved significantly to the right to appeal to conservative voters with anti-immigration sentiments.

McCAIN VERSUS OBAMA

Among Republicans in the Senate, McCain built one of the strongest records in favor of liberalization of immigration law.[11] McCain was a long-time cosponsor of the DREAM Act, an unsuccessful legislative proposal aimed at liberalization of the law for undocumented young immigrants.[12] More importantly, McCain championed the 2006 bipartisan bill that Bush had requested and worked hard—in collaboration with Senator Ted Kennedy—to defeat floor amendments that would have diminished or eliminated the guest worker program and the pathway to citizenship.[13]

In January 2007, during his quest for the Republican nomination, McCain appeared to shift his position. He indicated that he did not favor liberalization until effective steps were taken to secure the border with Mexico, a position that was consistent with the stance of the House Republican leadership.[14] Mc-Cain stated specifically that the governors of New Mexico, Arizona, and Texas must certify that the border is secure before liberalization measures could be implemented.[15] During the 2007 Senate deliberations on reform, McCain—then seeking the GOP nomination for president—was virtually invisible, in stark contrast to his 2006 leadership role.

In the general election campaign, neither Obama nor McCain highlighted immigration reform.[16] McCain tried to move back to the center by indicating, in a June 2008 speech to Hispanic business leaders, that he favored a comprehensive approach to immigration reform.[17] He also ran television advertisements in three Southwestern states with large Hispanic populations indicating that Senator Obama had been an obstacle in 2007 to passage of bipartisan reform legislation in the Senate. Obama countered with advertisements linking McCain to the anti-immigrant stance of Rush Limbaugh.[18]

The Hispanic share of the presidential vote was 9 percent in 2008, up from 8 percent in 2004. In the crucial battleground states of Colorado, Florida, Nevada, and New Mexico, the Hispanic shares of the vote were much higher than the national average.[19] Exit polls indicated that Obama defeated McCain decisively among Hispanics, with a national margin of victory of 67–31 percent. Hispanic voters played a crucial role in Obama's capture of the Electoral College votes from Colorado, Florida, Nevada, and New Mexico. Two thousand eight was the first year since exit polls began in 1988 that the Democratic presidential nominee won a majority of the Latino vote in Florida (where the numerous Cuban Americans are typically quite conservative in their voting behavior).[20]

In summary, Obama did not enlist the same degree of support among Hispanics that Hillary Clinton did, but he was able to convert the Clinton voters into Obama voters in the general election campaign against McCain. In his quest for Hispanic votes, Obama pledged—in the most public of ways that he would pursue reform legislation on immigration during his first year as president. Before turning to how President Obama handled his campaign pledge and why he never accomplished legislative reform, I examine the big surprise: the massive increase in immigration enforcement launched by the Obama administration.

CRACKING DOWN ON ILLEGAL IMMIGRANTS

When House Republicans blocked Bush's immigration reform initiative in 2006, they stipulated that liberalization measures for the estimated eleven million undocumented migrants living in the United States would not be considered until the US border with Mexico was secured. A proliferation of new federal enforcement measures ensued: some aimed at migrants caught crossing the border and some aimed at businesses caught hiring undocumented migrants. A key objective was to deter migrants from making attempts to enter the country.

In 2006 the Bush administration initiated the key policy change: illegal reentry was designated as a crime punishable by a prison term of two years (or longer in cases of other criminal offenses). Prior to this policy, most illegal border crossings were handled as minor civil offenses, leading to a permissive "catch and release" policy. The new criminal policy was combined with "Operation Streamline," a strategy of fast-track prosecutions, including court hearings for multiple offenders at one time. The goal of the US Border Patrol was to obtain prompt six-month jail terms through guilty pleas that were extracted in as little as twenty-four hours from the time of arrest.

The strategy began in late 2005 in the Border Patrol's Del Rio sector in West Texas. It was then expanded throughout Texas and Arizona by the Bush and Obama administrations.[21] In 2012 more than two hundred thousand offenders were processed under Operation Streamline, nearly half of all immigration prosecutions along the border that year.[22] Sentences were served in federal prisons, county jails, and private detention centers that operate under contract with the government.[23] The Department of Homeland Security (DHS) released data suggesting that Operation Streamline was deterring reentry efforts, thereby reducing by 50 percent the number of reentry attempts by undocumented migrants.[24]

The intensified enforcement sparked numerous objections from the Hispanic community. They argued that apprehended crossers were imprisoned before they understood their rights, as some may have qualified for asylum or refugee status. They also expressed concerns that the intensified focus on undocumented migrants was diverting enforcement resources from the lethal drug cartels operating near the border.[25]

Drug-related violence was widespread in Mexico, often concentrated in border towns as cartels struggled to control smuggling routes into the United States. From 2006 to 2009 an estimated 22,700 people died in Mexico in drug-related violence.[26] In March 2010 a gunman crossed the border into El Paso and killed three employees of the US consulate. Later that month an Arizona rancher named Robert Krantz was killed after reporting that drug-smuggling activity occurred on his land. As the violence provoked anger and fear throughout the Southwest, local politicians pointed the finger at the Obama administration, since border security is the responsibility of the federal government. The Obama administration responded that they were devoting more resources to border security than were allocated by the Bush administration. Politicians in Arizona were not satisfied and decided to take matters into their own hands.

The Arizona legislature, with support from Republican governor Jan Brewer and 70 percent of Arizona residents, enacted Senate Bill (SB)170, the most stringent anti-immigration measure in the history of the United States. The centerpiece of SB170 was the now famous "show me your papers" provision: failure of a migrant to show immigration papers upon official request was classified as a misdemeanor crime. Specifically, the law required police to question the immigration status of anyone stopped for other reasons who might be in the country illegally. SB170 also made it a crime for undocumented migrants to seek or hold a job and allowed police to make arrests without warrants in some circumstances.[27]

Hispanic groups expressed deep concerns about the new law, fearing it would facilitate discriminatory police activity against all Hispanics. President Obama joined in the criticism, opining that the Arizona law threatened to "undermine basic notions of fairness."[28] The US Supreme Court ultimately (in 2012) struck down some of the law's ancillary provisions, on the grounds that they are preempted by federal immigration policy, but unanimously upheld the "show me your papers" provision.[29] The Court did not address allegations that the law could lead to racial profiling.

In the spring of 2010 the Republicans in Congress criticized Obama for failing to build on Bush's efforts to secure the border. From 2006 to 2008 President Bush had launched "Operation Jump Start," as 6,000 National Guard troops were dispatched to the Mexican border. The operation contributed to the arrest of 162,000 illegal migrants and 305,000 pounds of illicit drugs. The Bush initiative was temporary, operating while the Border Control was upping the number of agents from 12,000 in 2006 to 16,700 in 2008.[30] Obama was urged to launch a similar operation.[31]

The pressure on the Obama administration went beyond requests from Republican politicians. Democratic congresswoman Gabrielle Giffords of Arizona wrote the DHS and requested that National Guard troops be deployed once again on the border. A similar request from several legislators was submitted directly to President Obama. The governors of Arizona, New Mexico, and Texas joined in the pleading for more troops. Meanwhile, Arizona senators John McCain and Jon Kyl developed an amendment to a defense appropriations bill that was aimed at forcing the Obama administration to deploy the National Guard. The amendment passed the Democrat-controlled Armed Services Committee.

With the 2010 midterm elections only a few months away and emotions running high in the Southwest, President Obama ordered 1,200 National Guard troops to the Mexican border to join the 340 troops already assisting Border Control agents. Instead of engaging in direct enforcement, the National Guard troops were authorized to engage in intelligence gathering, surveillance, and training.[32]

Obama's troop deployment was responsive to the perceived security concerns but was also seen as accomplishing several political objectives.[33] It preempted the McCain-Kyl effort in Congress. It also responded to the political needs of Democratic politicians serving constituencies in the Southwest. And it was seen as a stage-setting move to help accomplish Obama's larger ambition: liberalization of federal immigration law. Until the border was secured, any legislative approach to liberalization was seen as implausible.

Hispanic groups could not believe that President Obama was undertaking a virtual militarization of the border with Mexico. Pablo Alvaredo, director of the National Day Laborer Organizing Network, put it simply: "We are outraged."[34] To make a horrible situation worse, Hispanic activists learned through a news leak that the US Immigration and Customs Enforcement (ICE) was issuing new internal guidance aimed at accelerating the number of deportations. Ambitious deportation quotas were established for each border agent, and more detention space was made available along the border to hold apprehended migrants before their court hearings. In contradiction to the instructions from the secretary of DHS, ICE sought a "surge" in the detection and punishment of migrants, including those whose only offense was lying on immigration or visa applications.[35]

ICE also launched a new approach aimed at firms employing illegal immigrants. Instead of the high-profile raids at factories and farms conducted during the Bush administration, ICE under President Obama began a quieter but more effective strategy: ICE agents examined the I-9 forms that all new hires must fill out and then cross-checked them with Social Security databases. The result was mass firings of illegal immigrants who did not have proper Social Security documentation. From the summer of 2009 to the summer of 2010, ICE conducted audits of more than twenty-nine hundred firms and levied a record of $3 million in civil fines against companies that were found employing illegal migrants.[36]

When confronted by Hispanic activists requesting justification of the administration's punitive enforcement policies, the Obama administration indicated that legislation was the only solution. This response seemed hollow, since there was no evidence that the Obama administration was making progress on its pledge to achieve comprehensive reform legislation. Thus, I now turn to an exploration of how President Obama handled his campaign pledge on immigration-reform legislation.

STICKING TO HIS CAMPAIGN PLEDGE

Since the US economy was collapsing in January 2009, newly elected president Obama had a plausible argument for delaying immigration reform legislation.[37] The lack of job opportunities in the United States was rapidly reducing the flow of undocumented migrants through the Mexican border. Stated simply, the US economy already had too many, not too few, job seekers already in the country. Moreover, two of Obama's most enthusiastic base groups, African Americans and labor union members, are potentially harmed by liberal immigration policies. Historically, surges in migration tend to lead to declines in the average real wages of black workers as well as increased rates of unemployment and incarceration among young blacks.[38] And union members are historically skeptical of uncontrolled immigration, because they see it as potentially causing loss of jobs and wages for working-class Americans.[39]

In the near term Obama's dilemma was not what to do about future un-skilled migrants. The key question was what to do about the ten to twelve million immigrants who were living in the United States illegally. They were typically young and working and frequently had left their families behind when they came to the States.[40]

Given the administration's early signals, leaders of the Hispanic commu-nity fully expected that health care reform and energy/climate efforts would be higher priority issues than immigration during Obama's first year. None-theless, they also expected Obama to honor his 2008 campaign pledge to ac-complish immigration legislation in his first year.

President Obama chose not to lower expectations and instead sent clear public signals in both the spring and summer of 2009 that the White House in-tended to deliver on immigration reform.[41] In fact, in June 2009 Obama hosted Senator McCain and other congressional leaders at the White House to discuss a possible initiative on immigration reform. The White House recognized that some Republican support was necessary in the Senate, since Obama could not count on all of the Democratic senators to vote for immigration reform.[42] Mc-Cain claimed that the White House did not follow up with a specific request for help.

When Obama and the Democratic-controlled Congress failed to deliver on immigration reform in 2009, leaders of the Hispanic community were frus-trated and angry. Jorge Ramos of Univision was perhaps the most outspoken: "When [Obama] had a hold on Congress, when he had 60 votes in the Senate, he could have done it. And he didn't. He chose other issues. And that's why Latinos are so frustrated."[43] Also of concern to Hispanic activists was Presi-dent Obama's virtual silence on immigration in his 2009 and 2010 State of the Union addresses.[44]

On March 21, 2010, the day the House passed the last piece of the Afford-able Care Act, more than two hundred thousand people marched in Wash-ington, DC, to draw attention to the need for immigration reform. Hispanic activists warned national Democratic leaders that a low turnout of Hispanic voters in November 2010 could be harmful to the reelection campaigns of numerous Democratic politicians.[45]

In the spring of 2010 the White House upgraded immigration reform as a legislative priority, placing it ahead of the president's sagging energy/climate initiative.[46] The White House sought to quell the frustration among Hispanic activists and voters in advance of the fall 2010 midterm elections. Moreover, Senate majority leader Harry Reid was facing a tough reelection himself and was eyeing the large bloc of Hispanic voters (15 percent of the total) in his home state of Nevada. Democratic senators Barbara Boxer and Michael Bennett were also concerned about seeking reelection in 2010 without delivering on immigration reform. Given the political situation, Reid decided to make a public commitment to bring immigration reform to the Senate floor for a vote in 2010. Reid made the bold commitment at a campaign rally in Nevada.

Some of Reid's centrist Democratic colleagues in the Senate saw his pledge as a ploy to strengthen his own reelection prospects at the expense of their futures.[47] Senate insiders, however, knew that Reid was far short of the sixty votes that would be required to pass comprehensive immigration reform, and thus he could not legislate.[48] Since centrist Democrats tended to represent competitive states with small Hispanic populations, Reid's commitment to force a vote on immigration reform made them uneasy. Those senators included, at a minimum, Claire McCaskill, Ben Nelson, Blanche Lincoln, and Mark Pryor.

Obama followed suit by calling the new Republican senator from Massachusetts, Scott Brown, seeking bipartisan support for immigration reform. Brown responded cautiously.[49] The White House also reached out to other Republican moderates such as Senator Lindsey Graham, a good friend of John McCain's. Graham was already working on a bipartisan reform framework with Democratic senator Charles Schumer.

The Schumer-Graham framework was similar to the Bush-inspired plan that had failed to pass the Republican-controlled House in 2006. In order to enhance their legal status, undocumented migrants in the United States would be required to (1) admit they broke the law, (2) pay fines and back taxes, (3) prove they could speak English, and (4) go to the "back of the line" among those seeking permanent residency in the United States. The conditional liberalization was coupled with enhanced border security and interior enforcement against businesses that hired undocumented workers. A controversial feature of the framework was the issuance of Social Security cards with biometric data such as fingerprints or retinal patterns that could be used to ensure that only documented immigrants obtain employment.[50]

Graham, though, struck a note of pessimism, especially about Obama's renewed interest: "No one has spent any political capital laying the groundwork for this [initiative]."[51] Moreover, neither of the two Arizona senators (McCain nor Kyl) was prepared to collaborate on an initiative that would so directly antagonize the Tea Party. McCain was already embroiled in a primary challenge from former congressman J. D. Hayworth, one of America's most passionate and conservative orators on immigration policy. Among many Republicans, Graham was seen as a maverick, with limited ability to attract other Republicans. And Graham began to lose interest as it became apparent that he would have no Republican collaborators.[52]

House Speaker Nancy Pelosi took a more cautious stance than Reid and Obama. She recognized that Democrats were holding dozens of House seats with few Hispanic voters. Highly conservative white voters dominate some of the electorates represented by the Blue Dog Democrats, and those voters do not favor what they see as amnesty for illegal immigrants. As a result, Pelosi told Obama and Reid that the House would act on immigration reform in 2010 but only if the Senate acted first.[53] Insofar as Obama and Reid were staking out a political stance (rather than trying to legislate), Pelosi did not need to worry about whether the Senate would act before November 2010.

In April 2010, sensing the frustration of Hispanic activists with the Obama administration, Democratic senator Dick Durbin of Illinois urged President Obama to consider using executive authority to implement a DREAM-like policy for young student immigrants.[54] Rather than go this route, Obama decided to embrace legislative efforts at comprehensive reform.

It was not until late June 2010 that Barack Obama delivered his first presidential speech devoted exclusively to immigration policy.[55] He praised the framework for reform crafted by senators Schumer and Graham. However, Obama's speech was seen by some as more of a political strategy than a legislative one, as neither the White House nor the Congress seemed to be gearing up to push reform through the Congress in the remaining months of 2010.[56] The speech was seen as serving other purposes: a plug for the president's ally Harry Reid, a reassurance for Hispanic groups that he shared their view on the need for liberalization, and a stage-setter for blaming the Republicans in Congress for the lack of tangible legislative progress.

Obama's handling of the immigration issue did not help matters for congressional Democrats. Exit polls in 2010 revealed that Hispanics voted for Democratic House candidates 60–38 percent, a winning margin significantly smaller than the margin in the 2006 midterm elections (69–30 percent).[57]

In the lame-duck session of Congress (December 2010), President Obama and the Democratic leadership did make a last-ditch effort to pass reform legislation. Instead of an uphill battle for comprehensive reform, they rushed consideration of the more modest Development, Relief, and Education for Alien Minors (DREAM) Act. DREAM provides a pathway to citizenship for those who entered the country illegally before the age of sixteen and have worked in the military or attended college for at least two years. They must also have lived in the United States for five years, have graduated from high school, and have no criminal record. Several hundred thousand young immigrants are believed to satisfy the DREAM criteria. President Obama called wavering members in both parties in an urgent bid to secure passage of the bill. He knew such a proposal would be much more difficult to pass when the more conservative new Congress began in 2011.

In December 2010 the House passed the DREAM Act 216–198, with eight Republicans voting for it and thirty-eight Democrats voting against it.[58] In the Senate proponents of the DREAM Act fell five votes short of the sixty needed to overcome a filibuster threat (55–41). Three Republican senators (Robert Bennett, Richard Lugar, and Lisa Murkowski) voted for the DREAM Act, but five Democrats voted against it (Max Baucus, Jon Tester, Kay Hagan, Ben Nelson, and Mark Pryor).[59] Despite the legislative failure, Frank Sharry, of the immigration reform group America's Voice, said, "Obama and the White House fought hard for the DREAM Act and won points for doing so" among Hispanics.[60]

REPOSITIONING FOR REELECTION IN 2012

Once the Republican Party captured a majority of the seats in the House of Representatives (2011–2012), the prospects for passage of liberalization legislation sank to virtually nil. Republican members of the House typically held seats with relatively few minority voters, a trend that was accentuated when congressional districts were reshaped for a decade after the 2010 election.[61]

The distribution of Hispanic voters in the country is not favorable to immigration reform legislation.[62] Half of all voting-eligible Hispanics live in just 65 (out of 435) congressional districts, and most of those districts are politically noncompetitive. More than 70 percent of the districts represented by

Table 9.1. Geographic Distribution of Hispanic Population by State and Congressional District, 2009, 2013

Percent Hispanic Population	Democrats Number of Senators		Republicans	
	2009	2013	2009	2013
< 5%	17	17	15	15
5–10%	21	16	13	18
10–15%	8	8	6	6
15+%	14	13	6	7
	Number of **Representatives**			
	2009	2013	2009	2013
< 5%	91	29	68	88
5–10%	45	43	41	57
10–15%	269	27	23	30
15+%	92	104	46	57

Source: Michael Barone and Chuck McCutcheon, *The Almanac of American Politics, 2014* (Washington, DC: National Journal Group, 2013).

House Republicans have fewer than 10 percent Hispanic populations. Those with more than 10 percent are often highly conservative districts in California and Texas.[63] In districts represented by Republicans, Hispanics average 6.7 percent of eligible voters. Among House races that were considered competitive in 2014, Hispanics averaged 7.6 percent of the eligible voters. (See table 9.1)

Moreover, the Tea Party was eager to run challengers against incumbent Republicans in Congress who chose to collaborate with Obama on immigration or other issues. Of the three Republican senators who voted for the DREAM Act in December 2010, all three lost to Tea Party challengers at their next Republican primary election (though Lisa Murkowski survived by running in the general election as an independent).

Despite the dim prospects of legislative action, President Obama continued his advocacy of comprehensive immigration-reform legislation. In April 2011 he convened stakeholders and administration officials at the White House to explore reform possibilities. Hispanic activists and lawmakers urged him to use executive authority to halt deportation proceedings against young migrants and others facing extreme hardship or other extraordinary circumstances. Obama's response was "I know some here wish that I could just bypass Congress and change the law myself. But that's not how a democracy works."[64]

In El Paso, Texas, in the spring of 2011, Obama unveiled a comprehensive framework for reform legislation similar to the one inspired by Bush that passed the Senate in 2006. It was released in May 2011 under the title "Building a 21st-Century Immigration System." Although there was no near-term hope of passage, the political value of the framework was that it drew a sharp contrast with punitive Republican policies and positioned Obama to appeal to Hispanic voters in 2012.

For the most part, Republicans in Congress were skeptical of comprehensive reform legislation. Republican senator Marco Rubio did reach out to immigration activists in April 2012 in an effort to stimulate interest in a modest bill similar to the failed DREAM Act of 2010. The Obama administration did not take up Rubio's initiative, in part because Obama was planning executive action to accomplish many of the goals of the DREAM Act.[65]

In the summer of 2011 ICE took modest steps that appealed to Hispanic activists. Border agents were instructed that pregnant women and family breadwinners should be low priorities in deportation actions. The idea was to focus enforcement on illegal immigrants with criminal records. Enforcement priorities under the Secure Communities program did move in this direction, but the effect of the change was not as dramatic as Hispanic activists sought. ICE included as "criminals" immigrants who forged an ID, a common practice by immigrants who looked for work, and a practice that many employers tacitly sanctioned.[66] Nonetheless, the number of deportation actions declined significantly in fiscal year 2013 compared to fiscal year 2012.[67]

In early 2012 the Department of Labor also proposed modest changes to the H-2B guest worker program, which allows employers to hire temporary nonagricultural workers from outside the United States. The changes called for establishment of a nationwide electronic registry where employers must post all jobs for which they sought H-2B workers. The existing business-favored self-certification process was replaced with a formal requirement that employers consult with state workforce agencies to ensure that no suitable Americans were available to do the needed work.

Business groups objected to several aspects of the proposal. A business seeking a guest worker was required to cover the worker's visa fees and transportation costs to and from the worker's home country. Firms were also required to pay for foreign workers for at least 75 percent of the period of their contract, even if no work was required during significant parts of the period. The National Guestworker Alliance favored the proposal as a strategy to reduce exploitation of foreign workers.

As the general election campaign between Obama and Mitt Romney geared up, Latino leaders and progressive Democrats in Congress warned Obama that, despite his modest efforts, support among Latinos was lagging. Obama was advised to use his executive authority, as Democratic senator Dick Durbin had suggested in April 2010, to help as many as 1.4 million young immigrants become eligible for two-year renewable work permits. Obama did not have the legal authority to provide a pathway to citizenship for such students, but he could accomplish many of the other benefits of the DREAM Act. The work permit opens the door to obtaining a Social Security number, a driver's license, professional certificates, and financial aid for college expenses.[68]

Obama decided to take this executive step. An estimated 950,000 young undocumented migrants were made eligible to apply for the work permits and protection from deportation.[69] While the largest number of eligible students live in California, New York, and Texas, many of the students live in the battleground states of Colorado, Florida, Nevada, and New Mexico. The students did not become eligible to vote, but the action was favored by 90 percent of Latinos in the United States.[70] For Obama's political future, the June 2012 timing of the pro-Latino policy—five months before his reelection date—could not have been better.

Meanwhile, in the highly competitive Republican primaries, immigration was a major issue in the contest to select the Republican nominee for president. Governor Mitt Romney positioned himself on the far right on immigration in order to appeal to the Tea Party and conservative white voters. Romney attacked Governor Rick Perry for his state's policy of providing affordable in-state tuition rates to illegal migrants attending Texas colleges and universities. He also attacked Newt Gingrich for advocating a pathway to legal status for those living in the United States without proper documentation. In one of Romney's awkward moments in the primaries, he described a vague policy of "self-deportation" for the millions of illegal immigrants already living in the States.[71]

By the time Romney won the Republican nomination, his stance on immigration was so far to the right that he was poorly positioned to exploit

Obama's vulnerability among Hispanics. In fact, in the second presidential debate against Obama, during which immigration was discussed explicitly, Romney seemed to be less interested in appealing to Hispanic voters than in energizing his conservative base. As one journalist noted, "Politically, Obama was fortunate in 2012 that Hispanics didn't see another option."[72]

When Obama defeated Romney in November 2012, Hispanics played a significant role in the victory. Latino enthusiasm was certainly down, as indicated by the fact that Latino turnout was 2 percentage points lower in 2012 than it was in 2008. But among those who turned out, the message was clear: Obama won by a commanding 71–27 percent margin.[73] Romney was badly hurt in several battleground states with large Hispanic populations. His performance among Hispanics was the worst by a Republican presidential candidate since Bob Dole in 1996.

2013–2014: OPPORTUNE TIME FOR REFORM LEGISLATION?

Proponents of reform felt that 2013–2014 looked like an opportune time for the two political parties to come together around a comprehensive redesign of federal immigration law. For Obama, reform was a high political and legacy-defining priority. He emerged from the 2012 elections with some political leverage, having helped expand the Democratic Party's majority in the Senate and reduce GOP Speaker John Boehner's majority in the House. For the Republican Party, Romney's drubbing among Hispanics sent a clear message that the party needed to shift its position.

Obama did not deliver on this reform opportunity. As was the case with his visions of a grand fiscal bargain on spending and taxes, he did not come close to delivering on it. Like George W. Bush, he was successful in moving a reform package through the Senate in 2013, but he was then stonewalled in the GOP-controlled House. Part of the problem was the White House's underestimation of the remaining strength of the Tea Party, coupled with the sobering reality that most seats controlled by House Republicans contained relatively few Hispanic constituents and that congressional Republicans, in contrast to the national GOP, were not inclined to moderate on this issue. Moreover, an unexpected child refugee crisis surprised both the White House and the Congress and undermined the notion that the Obama administration was prepared to secure the border as part of a broad-based immigration deal. And a fundamental disagreement was simmering about whether illegal immigrants who have been living in the United States for years should be provided a special pathway to citizenship.

A GOOD START

The 2013 State of the Union address was a good forum for Obama to frame the debate as he used stringent rhetoric on immigration, in some ways similar to the rhetoric used by many Republican politicians. He stressed the importance of border security as a precondition to liberalization measures. He endorsed a pathway to citizenship but only under strict conditions—immigrants already here must "learn English" and "go to the back of the line" in the application process.[74] Cuban American and Republican senator Marco Rubio delivered the Republican response to Obama. He challenged the president on many issues but echoed Obama's themes on immigration reform.

President Obama also released a 2013 immigration reform plan that was similar to his May 2011 plan and the plan of the Senate's "Gang of Eight," a bipartisan group of eight senators working to find common ground on the issue (Democrats Dick Durbin, Charles Schumer, Michael Bennett, and Robert Menendez and Republicans John McCain, Jeff Flake, Marco Rubio, and Lindsey Graham).[75] The four prongs were enhanced border security, employer crackdowns, conditions for the pathway to citizenship, and streamlining of the immigration system.[76] The administration also prepared a detailed written plan that was leaked to the press during the executive branch process of interagency review. The bipartisan groups working in the House and Senate were irritated because release of the administration's views did not help build consensus in the Gang of Eight.[77]

In March 2013 the national Republican Party formally endorsed the principles of comprehensive immigration reform, effectively revitalizing the position it had espoused in 2004 at the request of President George W. Bush. The ninety-seven-page report commissioned by the Republican National Committee repudiated the "self-deportation" stance that had served Mitt Romney so poorly in 2012.[78]

The White House helped Hispanic activists organize a formidable coalition of interest groups favoring reform.[79] Those groups included religious, business, farm, gay rights, and human rights groups as well as Silicon Valley companies and investors.[80] Unlike 2006–2007, when reform advocates confronted potent opposition from national labor unions, the Obama White House helped recruit the support of the AFL-CIO and the Service Employees International Union (SEIU). Union leaders committed to advertising, rallies, and letter-writing campaigns on behalf of reform. The message to the rank-and-file union member was that reform would help reverse the thirty-year decline in union membership, since many undocumented workers avoid membership in unions because they fear deportation.[81] The AFL-CIO and SEIU also played hardball: they ran advertisements (mostly in Spanish) pointing to the inflammatory language on immigration coming from many GOP officials; instead they urged viewers to "fight the hate." Unions also launched a voter-contact program in nine GOP-held congressional districts, seeking to put pressure on the House GOP.[82]

Bipartisan groups of legislators began work earnestly in both the Senate and House. The Gang of Eight in the Senate included Rubio while the House Republican leadership encouraged the efforts of the informal House group. Thus, there was no question that the GOP's participation in the bipartisan talks was serious.

In the spring of 2013 Rubio unveiled elements of a bipartisan proposal for the Senate. He followed through with an energetic television blitz, including seven Sunday news shows that covered immigration. Rubio argued for the economic benefits of immigration while insisting that until they became American citizens immigrants would not receive government benefits such as food stamps and health care subsidies under the Affordable Care Act. He emphasized that each immigrant seeking legal status must pass criminal background checks, pay fines, and work for twelve years before becoming eligible for a green card. And the entire proposal was framed in the context of stronger border security, including aggressive use of new computer capabilities under DHS's E-Verify (an Internet-based system) to ensure that employers do not retain or hire illegal immigrants.

Secretly, Obama and John Boehner began what became a full year of discussions aimed at finding common ground on reform legislation. Without Boehner's support, a bill could not reach the floor of the House. To facilitate progress, Obama agreed to restrain his anti-GOP rhetoric on immigration while Boehner sought to find a way to move reform legislation through the

House. A rough deadline of summer 2014 was set for congressional action. If the deadline was not met, the White House insisted, Obama would exploit executive authority to accomplish as much as he could.[83]

THE SENATE DELIVERS REFORM

Much of the heavy lifting in the Senate was performed by the Gang of Eight. Their outline was refined based on extensive bipartisan discussions in the Senate Judiciary Committee. When a detailed bill was voted out of committee on a strong bipartisan vote of 13–5, it was apparent that immigration reform had legs in the Senate.

On the floor, numerous amendments were debated, but votes on two proposals were seen as critical. Republican senator Charles Grassley proposed an amendment that would have required a secure border for six consecutive months before any immigrant could take the first steps in the process toward citizenship. Fearing indefinite delay in liberalization, Senate Democrats led the way in defeating the amendment 53–47. Later, Republican Bob Corker and Democrat John Hoeven proposed an extensive border security amendment that provided for $40 billion in enforcement monies over the next ten years, twenty thousand Border Patrol agents, and seven hundred miles of fencing along the Mexican border. The amendment also set criteria for determining when the border is considered secure. When it became apparent that passage of this amendment would reassure more than a dozen reluctant senators, the amendment passed 67–27 (with all Democrats joined by fifteen Republicans; six senators did not vote, including two Democrats who likely would have voted "yes").[84]

In its final form the Senate reform bill passed 68–32.[85] All Democrats were joined by fourteen Republicans in a rare showing of bipartisan support for a major piece of legislation.[86] On the other hand, the two top ranking Republicans in the Senate (Mitch McConnell and John Cornyn), both facing possible primary challenges in 2014, voted against the reform package. And most leading conservatives in the Senate, including Rand Paul, voted against it.

Among progressives and pro-immigrant groups, the Senate reform bill drew mixed reactions. In their eyes it provided useful elements such as a guest worker program, enlarged numbers of visas, diminished deportations, and a pathway to citizenship for those already living in the United States. On the other hand, the pathway called for thirteen years of waiting in a diminished legal status, compared to the eighteen-month pathway that President Reagan had negotiated with congressional Democrats in 1986. The millions of people who would obtain "registered provisional immigrants" (RPI) status as a result of the bill were not provided coverage by the Affordable Care Act. As a result, since 70 percent of those people lacked health insurance, emergency rooms might become their place for routine care, which is contrary to the express purpose of the Affordable Care Act.[87] More generally, the concern was that RPIs might become a permanent underclass.

Among many House conservatives, the Senate reform bill was a non-starter. The pathway to citizenship, even though it had conditions, was seen as amnesty.[88] The criteria for determining whether the US border is secure were considered soft.[89] Skepticism was widespread as to how one could ever audit a migrant's claim that he or she did not owe any back taxes, especially since the Internal Revenue Service lacks the capabilities to enforce current tax law.[90]

Even before the Senate reform bill passed, Speaker Boehner stated publicly that the House would not take up a Senate-like reform measure. And he emphasized that any reform measure passed in the House must have the support of a majority of House Republicans. Those words were a stark indication of the difficulties that Obama confronted.[91]

BIPARTISAN HOUSE GROUP COLLAPSES

A bipartisan group of House members began working on immigration reform in 2009. The membership of the group changed over the years, and the deliberations were generally held secret given the sensitivity of the issue.[92] In 2013 the group was comprised of four Democrats (John Yarmouth of Kentucky, Luis Gutierrez of Illinois, and Xavier Becerra and Zoe Lofgren of California) and four Republicans (John Carter and Sam Johnson of Texas; Mario Diaz-Balart of Florida; and Raul Labrador of Idaho).

Among the Republicans, Raul Labrador was the best-known conservative, but John Carter (representing a district in central Texas) was considered a key member in the group. Carter was a Tea Party member who had opposed George W. Bush's reform effort in 2006–2007. As chair of the House Appropriations Committee panel on homeland security, Carter had seen the security of the border improve as a result of House-inspired enforcement innovations from 2004 to 2013. Carter also knew that construction companies in his district needed a guest worker program to provide affordable low-skilled laborers.[93]

As early as late January 2013, Boehner indicated that "they basically have an agreement" and both the US Chamber of Commerce and the AFL-CIO were supportive.[94] However, since the details of the agreement were not publicly available, the statement did not mean much.

The group set a deadline for itself: produce a detailed written plan by the Memorial Day recess, which would allow House committee and floor action to occur before the August recess.[95] Although the entire House leadership, in a rare joint statement, pledged to work toward an immigration plan, the deadline was not met. The sticking point in the group's negotiations was how health insurance for migrants should be handled. Soon after the Memorial Day recess, the most conservative member of the group, Raul Labrador, withdrew from the deliberations, because he did not believe that society is responsible for providing health insurance to illegal immigrants.[96]

There were plenty of national opinion polls indicating that a strong majority of Americans agreed with a package of reforms similar to what passed in the Senate, including a pathway to citizenship.[97] Those national polls were largely irrelevant to the calculus of House Republicans who were concerned with the opinions of their own constituents and especially how Republican primary voters might react to immigration reform. In June 2013 the Tea Party Patriots pledged a primary challenge to any GOP member of Congress who voted for comprehensive immigration reform.[98] A large majority of citizens who identify with the Tea Party opposed giving illegal immigrants an opportunity to earn citizenship.[99]

Republican representative Kenny Marchant of the Dallas, Texas, area expressed a common sentiment: the Senate bill "is very unpopular in my district." He went on to indicate that "Republican primary voters are pretty vocal with me on this subject. . . . If you give the legal right to vote to 10 Hispanics in my district, 7 to 8 of them are going to vote Democratic."[100] A pathway to citizenship is a pathway to a legal right to vote, and that could mean the defeat of many local as well as national Republican candidates.

Nor did the 2014 midterm elections spark much concern among House and Senate Republicans who opposed reform. Although Hispanic voters make up 11 percent of eligible voters, their turnout rate tends to be low, especially in midterm contests. Moreover, as table 9.2 indicates, Hispanics represented 5 per-

Table 9.2. Hispanic Populations in States with Competitive Senate Races, 2014

State	Latinos as Share (%) of Population	Latinos as Share (%) of Eligible Voters
Alaska	6.0	4.9
Arkansas	6.7	2.9
Colorado	21.0	14.2
Georgia	9.1	4.0
Iowa	5.2	2.7
Kentucky	3.1	1.6
Louisiana	4.5	2.8
Michigan	4.6	2.9
North Carolina	8.7	3.1
All USA	16.9	10.7

Source: Mark Hugo Lopez, "Latino Vote Is Small in Nearly All States with Hot Senate Races," *PewResearch.org*, September 8, 2014, http://www.pewresearch.org/fact-tank/2014/09/08 /latino-vote-is-small-in-nearly-all-states-with-hot-senate-races.

cent or fewer of the eligible voters in the key battleground states where control of the Senate would be determined (Colorado being the notable exception). Thus, House Republicans had no reason to believe that blocking immigration reform would compromise their party's ability to capture control of the Senate in November 2014.[101]

In September 2013 John Carter and Sam Johnson withdrew from the bipartisan reform talks in the House, leaving only one Republican and four Democrats. Carter and Johnson, both irritated with Obama about other issues (Affordable Care Act implementation and climate change), indicated that the president could not be trusted to faithfully implement an immigration reform plan.[102]

Pro-reform activists strove to pressure Congress into action. Immigration marches were organized in ninety cities during the second week of October 2013.[103] The rallies were large but did not necessarily have impact on House Republicans or their constituents.

For Democratic congressman Luis Gutierrez and Hispanic groups, the collapse of bipartisanship was extremely frustrating. By some calculations, 40 to 50 House Republicans and 185 to 190 House Democrats were prepared to vote for a comprehensive immigration reform plan.[104] In other words, a plan would be able to win a majority on the floor of the House. Such a plan could not get to the floor without the support of House Speaker John Boehner, who was insisting that no plan would be permitted to pass without majority support from Republicans.

BOEHNER'S PIECEMEAL APPROACH

Instead of passing a comprehensive reform plan and then negotiating with the Senate, Boehner approved a strategy that called for passage of a series of immigration reforms on specific issues.[105] He sought to reassure conservatives with the public statement "We have no intention of ever going to conference on the Senate bill."[106] The piecemeal approach drew support from an unexpected source in the Senate: Florida's Marco Rubio. Having been subject to intense criticism from conservatives on his work on comprehensive reform, Rubio backed off the comprehensive strategy and got behind Boehner's effort.[107]

A majority of Republicans might be able to support a series of reforms, even if they could not vote for a plan that contained a pathway to citizenship. That pathway was politically radioactive for Republicans, particularly due to the views of the Tea Party. Boehner and pro-reform interest groups persuaded Obama that this was the only realistic way forward,[108] and Obama reluctantly agreed to the approach as long as it accomplished all of the reforms that were required.[109] For most of 2013 and early 2014, the president took a low-key approach to immigration reform, recognizing that the GOP might shy away from reform if it was too closely identified with him.[110]

House GOP leaders decided to prepare and release broad principles that would guide the development of each reform measure. When those principles were released, they attracted little opposition from the vast majority of House Republicans.[111] Conservative think tanks provided details on some specific measures.[112] The GOP was planning a pathway to green cards for undocumented migrants but not a pathway to citizenship.[113]

Boehner did not want to expose his incumbents to Tea Party challenges. Thus, detailed bills were planned for debate on the House floor in April 2014, after the deadline for challengers to file paperwork in congressional races.[114]

Building support among Republicans was crucial for another reason: the unanimous support for reform among Senate Democrats could not be replicated among House Democrats. Blue Dogs and moderates such as Representatives Nick Rahall of West Virginia, Daniel Lipinski of Illinois, and Collin Peterson of Minnesota were not sympathetic to a Senate-style reform bill.[115] On the other hand, thirty-nine of fifty-three "New Democrats" (self-described moderates) wrote Obama urging reform that contained a pathway to citizenship.

Boehner and the House Republicans began to question whether it made sense to open up the volatile immigration issue in a midterm election year (2014). Along with Majority Leader Eric Cantor, Boehner believed that although the time would never be ripe, the work must be done. The majority whip, Kevin McCarthy of California, thought that waiting until 2015 might be politically advisable.

In early February 2014 the sentiments at a House Republican retreat shifted strongly against enacting reform prior to the 2014 midterm elections.[116] Trying to collaborate with President Obama on reform was hard to do when attacking him for strategic purposes was one of the GOP's best campaign strategies. Conservative senator Ted Cruz added another downside of collaboration: working on an amnesty bill before the election might demoralize the GOP base, which abhorred the entire notion of amnesty.

Boehner began to express public doubts about immigration reform, even though he acknowledged his personal support for the idea. He indicated that the House was not prepared to move forward in partnership with Obama. In a shift in his public stance, he indicated that House Republicans did not trust the White House to implement any reform faithfully.[117]

One of the authors of the Senate bill, Charles Schumer, offered a solution for Boehner in the national press. He urged the House to pass reform but set the effective date in 2017, when Obama would no longer be president. Boehner countered that he did not want to remove any incentive for the president to enforce the current law for the remainder of his term.[118]

Obama could not remain silent in the face of such partisan criticism. He departed from his months of cooperative messaging on immigration and blasted the House GOP: "House Republicans have failed to take action, seemingly preferring the status quo of a broken immigration system over meaningful reform." The GOP response came from Eric Cantor: "You do not attack the very people you hope to engage in a serious dialogue. . . . After five years, President Obama still has not learned how to effectively work with Congress to get things done."[119]

CANTOR'S STUNNING DEFEAT

Cantor was a six-term member of Congress from Virginia's Seventh District and a well-respected conservative with a national reputation. He had never lost a primary election. Compared to other House Republicans, Cantor's views on immigration were middle-of-the-road. He had not endorsed the Senate reform plan but was working with the House leadership on a reform plan that could pass the House.

In a stunning upset in a low-turnout Republican primary, Cantor was challenged and defeated handily by a little-known economics professor named Dave Bratt, a challenger who was not prominent enough to receive funding from national conservative groups.[120] Bratt based his campaign on the proposition that Cantor was out of touch with his conservative constituents. The biggest single issue raised by Bratt was immigration, and he was proudly associated with the Tea Party.[121]

A variety of non-immigration factors contributed to Cantor's defeat: he did not host town meetings, his staff were said to be incompetent, he was considered arrogant, and his negative advertisements against Bratt were seen as offensive.[122] On the other hand, the take-home message from Cantor's defeat among campaign experts was the immigration issue: it is volatile and provokes anger among many highly conservative voters. A bad place to be in politics is on the wrong side of the immigration issue when faced by a Tea Party challenger in a Republican primary.[123]

In June 2014 Democratic congressman Luis Gutierrez announced he was giving up on a bipartisan House reform bill. The Cantor defeat had exacerbated an already poor climate for bipartisan legislation. Gutierrez decided to shift his efforts to pressuring Obama to take executive actions on immigration.[124]

BORDER UNCONTROLLED: CHILD REFUGEE CRISIS

From October 2012 through the summer of 2014, the Obama administration learned that the border with Mexico was not as well managed as the administration thought (or as was suggested in their public reports to Congress). During this period fifty-seven thousand young immigrants—mostly from Honduras, Guatemala, and El Salvador—were apprehended after crossing the border into the United States. The bulk of these children came through south Texas.

Many of the child immigrants behaved differently from most illegal immigrants who seek to rapidly penetrate the interior of Texas. Instead, the child immigrants cross the border and sit down or simply turn themselves in and allow enforcement officials to decide their fate.[125] Interviews with the minors indicated that they were trying to escape violence instigated by gangs and drug cartels in their home countries. Border Control statistics reveal a strong correlation between cities with high homicide rates (e.g., San Pedro Sula, Honduras) and child refugees coming to the United States.[126] The rate of growth of child migration was much larger among teenage girls than among boys.[127] From 2013 to 2014 the number of female child immigrants crossing the border grew 173 percent to 121,000 while the number of male immigrants (366,022) was virtually unchanged.[128]

The flow of children from Honduras was particularly large, reflecting both violence and poverty. The murder rate in Honduras was ninety per one hundred thousand residents, or about eighteen murders per day, a rate considered the highest in the world outside of a war zone. The would-be immigrants felt they were trapped in neighborhoods overseen by *maras*—well-organized, mafia-like groups. If migrants could escape Honduras and start a life elsewhere, they might be able to send money home to their impoverished families. In 2013 successful migrants sent $3.2 billion back to Honduras, an amount equal to about 17 percent of that country's entire GDP.[129]

The risks migrants took trying to enter the United States were far from trivial. The US Border Patrol reported numerous rapes, robberies, and murders involving unaccompanied children as they made their way from their home countries to the States. Smugglers were paid three thousand to five thousand dollars per person in Central America to take the children and get them to the US-Mexican border. Another fee might be paid to get them across the river and into the States.[130] US data also reveal what migrants perceived to be true: few of the Central American children who make it across the border are sent back home. In fiscal year 2013, of the 47,397 children apprehended, only 3,525 were deported (another 888 were allowed to voluntarily return home without a deportation order).[131] Note this is less than 10 percent of the children.

A 2008 change in federal immigration law set the stage for the unexpected crisis. Congress and the Bush administration decided that children from Central American countries (and all other non-border countries) should be treated differently than children from Mexico and Canada. When unaccompanied Mexican children are apprehended, they may be immediately sent back to

Mexico. Children from other countries must be taken into custody and can be held for up to seventy-two hours, after which they must be transferred to temporary shelters under the purview of the Department of Health and Human Services. According to statistics compiled by the nonprofit group Kids in Need of Defense, more than 90 percent of children are ultimately placed with relatives or sponsors until their court hearings occur.

The 2008 law also requires that the children be interviewed to determine if they are eligible for asylum. The criteria for asylum relate to a "credible fear" of persecution at home for reasons of race, religion, nationality, group membership, or political opinion.[132] The number of "credible fear" claims exploded fourfold from fiscal year 2010 to fiscal year 2013, with 80 percent of the claims ultimately judged to be supportable.[133] Under pressure from the GOP-controlled House Judiciary Committee, the Asylum Division of the DHS toughened the criteria its officers use when conducting interviews. The percentage meeting the credible fear standard fell from 83 percent in January 2014 (before the new criteria) to 63 percent in July 2014 (after the new criteria).[134]

Studies estimate that 40–60 percent of the children are eligible for some form of humanitarian relief, either asylum or special immigrant juvenile status, or visas for victims of crime or trafficking.[135] But a final determination requires a court hearing, and juvenile court cases faced a long backlog. The 2008 law was intended to help children by reducing sex trafficking, but it also made it more difficult to quickly return children who were caught crossing the border.[136]

There were widespread rumors in Central American countries that if the children could get into the United States, they would be safer, because the US government would be lenient to them.[137] Some Border Patrol agents expressed their belief that these rumors were related to the 2008 law, especially the new policy allowing children to be reunited with their parents or other family members.[138]

Republican senator John McCain expressed concern that President Obama was not discouraging the border crossings, stating, "The President of the United States has to openly say: 'If you come here and you enter the country illegally you're going to go back.' That is not the message that's being put out on television and radio in Honduras, El Salvador, and Guatemala."[139] After learning that misinformation was being "deliberately planted by criminal organizations, by smuggling networks" about what migrants can expect if they enter the United States, the White House reluctantly agreed that better communication was necessary.[140]

Some Republicans in Congress expressed concern that Obama's 2012 DREAM-like executive order, Deferred Action for Childhood Arrivals (DACA), sent a signal throughout Central America that immigrant children were welcome in the States. The number of apprehended children near the border grew from 22,000 in 2011 to 31,000 in 2012 and 47,397 in 2013. For the first time, the number of Central American children crossing the border actually outnumbered the number of Mexican children.[141]

The Hispanic group RAICES (Refugee and Immigrant Center for Education and Legal Services) in San Antonio interviewed 3,956 migrant children who crossed the border in 2014. The number of migrants who had heard of DACA was "in the single digits."[142] Nonetheless, the House ultimately passed a bill intended to overturn Obama's 2012 order. A similar bill was not considered in the Senate.

Originally the Obama White House dismissed the linkage to the 2012 order as partisan mischief, but it later became apparent that better communication was required. Vice President Joe Biden was dispatched to Central America with the message that Obama's 2012 DACA program does not apply to children who are new arrivals in the United States. The Obama White House also reached out to the Latino media and developed public service announcements in an effort to dispel any misimpressions that might be fueling the surge in dangerous border crossings being made by children.[143]

What the Obama administration was slow to address was the public administration shortfall on the ground. Border Patrol agents were overwhelmed by dealing with children, leaving less time to address drug cartels and serious criminal matters. Nor were Border Patrol agents well trained to address the needs (e.g., counseling and care) of the children, and only 5 percent of the agents were women.[144] Since many of the teenage girls were sexually assaulted during their trip to the States (60 percent according to one estimate), Border Patrol was struggling to find enough female agents to address their needs.[145] Texas governor Rick Perry called on Obama to deploy an additional one thousand National Guard troops along with Lakota helicopters and Predator drones.[146]

The backlog of juvenile cases that required a court hearing swelled to 41,832 by June 30, 2013.[147] The number of lawyers, asylum officers, and immigration judges was far too small to handle the volume. Children could wait up to two years to have their court hearing, but the United States was not prepared to address their needs in the interim. An acute shortage of detention centers along the border was part of the problem. Some children were moved to military bases in Louisiana, Oklahoma, and Texas. The news reporting of overcrowded detention centers created an image of chaos in the government's handling of the children.[148] Complaints also came from community leaders who felt ill-equipped to serve the children. Public school officials in Florida, Texas, and Georgia struggled to prepare for a surge in school enrollment by unaccompanied minors from Guatemala, Honduras, and Central America.[149] The long-term ramifications were also significant, since federal data showed that one-third of the children do not show up for their court hearings and stay in the United States on an indefinite basis.[150]

The crisis spurred a heated debate in Congress and among the public as to whether the unaccompanied children should be deported immediately or processed in the States. In the summer of 2014 one national survey found that 53 percent of Americans felt that the US government should speed up deportation of the children even if some who were eligible for asylum got deported. Among Republicans, 60 percent favored speeding up the deportation process. Democrats were divided: 46 percent wanted to speed up the process, but 47 percent wanted to slow it down.[151]

The politics of handling the surge of immigrants became "toxic." When the federal government searched for US towns where the immigrant minors might be housed temporarily until their hearing (the average stay was thirty days and rising), many communities volunteered to help. But preliminary shelter plans in California, Connecticut, and New York were scrapped due to widespread opposition from residents and local officials.[152]

For too long the Obama administration tried to manage the child immigrant crisis within existing authority and resources. Republicans in Congress insisted that the 2008 law needed to be modified to permit more immediate deportation of the children. Obama also faced a funding shortage and needed to request more funds from Congress. Funds that normally would serve the needs of refugees from Asia, the Middle East, and Africa were diverted to address the influx of minors from Central America. Fewer resources were available to address the needs of refugees fleeing persecution and war elsewhere in the world.[153]

Reluctantly, President Obama made an emergency request of Congress just a few months before the 2014 midterm election.[154] First, he asked for $3.7 billion to shore up the immigration system and strengthen border security, even though several months earlier he had tried to reassure congressional Republicans that "border security is stronger than it has even been" and thus liberalization measures could be enacted.[155] Specifically, the president sought more funds for temporary detention facilities near the border, overtime pay for Border Control agents, and more foreign aid to Central American countries to help them address the root causes of the problem. Second, Obama pleased Republicans by seeking a modification of the 2008 law that was hampering immediate deportation of children from Central America. The request encountered stiff opposition: Senate Democrats, upholding the position of worried human rights groups, opposed any change to the 2008 law; House Republicans disapproved of much of the spending, especially the foreign aid to Central American countries. The level of trust in President Obama on the immigration issue was remarkably low among both congressional Democrats and Republicans.

Overall, the signs of the child immigrant crisis did not emerge suddenly in the summer of 2014; they occurred gradually in 2012 and 2013 before reaching a peak in 2014. The White House response was very late, and by then the administration had squandered its credibility on the issue. Surveys indicate that Obama's handling of the crisis triggered "one of the lowest ratings for his handling of any issue since he became president."[156]

DEPORTER IN CHIEF?

As the prospects of legislative action dwindled in 2014, reform advocates shifted their focus from Boehner and the House Republicans to President Obama.[157] Activists were "furious" at the president for deporting so many immigrants.[158] Those activists included groups such as the National Day Laborer Organizing Network, the National Immigration Law Center, United We Dream, California Immigrant Youth Justice Alliance, Advancing Justice, and the Asian Law Caucus.

From the day when Barack Obama took office in 2009 and until early 2014, the Obama administration deported more total immigrants than any previous administration. In 2013 alone, 369,000 immigrants were deported.[159] On the basis of such statistics, Janet Murgaria, president of the National Council of La Raza, labeled President Obama "Deporter in Chief." Arturo Carmona, executive director of the liberal activist group Presente.org, was even more blunt: "Obama could go down as the worst president in history toward immigrants." Obama was alleged to be on track to deport three million people in two terms; George W. Bush deported two million; and Clinton deported fewer than a million.[160]

The use of the term "deportation" is an oversimplification. ICE statistics lump together "removals" and "returns." A removal represents departure from the country pursuant to a formal order from a judge, whereas a return is not an official deportation, because the migrant leaves the country without any restriction on when he or she can reenter without a visa. There are no formal consequences of a return, and thus it is a more desirable option for an undocumented migrant than a removal. When removals and returns are lumped together, there is no question that the Obama administration has "deported" the most people. When only returns are counted, the comparison is not as definitive, although the Obama administration was still on track to become one of the "worst" administrations, according to immigration activists.[161]

In April 2014, activists staged protests in more than forty cities to decry the millions of deportations instigated by the Obama administration. The activists made a simple request of the president that did not require congressional action: suspend deportations of all undocumented migrants who have not broken any other laws.[162] The Obama administration claimed that the president could not lawfully take such a sweeping action, but many legal experts argued that he could use his prosecutorial discretion to accomplish this result.[163]

When it became apparent that Boehner could not deliver an immigration reform bill in the House, President Obama pledged to immigration activists that he would do whatever he could, under the law, to curtail deportations. In June 2014 he set a deadline for his administration. If Congress did not act, he said, executive action would be taken during September 2014.[164]

Obama appeared to be responding to a growing rate of presidential disapproval among Hispanics. Polls in the summer of 2014 showed that more than twice as many Latinos were likely to strongly disapprove of President Obama's record on immigration than to strongly approve.[165] When September came, the president annoyed Hispanic activists by deciding to delay executive action on immigration until after the 2014 midterm elections. The political calculus made by the White House was plausible. At least five Democratic candidates for Senate (Kay Hagan, Mark Pryor, Mark Begich, Jeanne Shaheen, and Alison Lundergan Grimes) urged the White House to refrain from energizing the immigration issue less than ten weeks before the November 2014 election.[166] Colorado was the only state where a liberal immigration initiative by the president might benefit a Democratic incumbent in a competitive Senate race.[167]

Hispanic activists were extremely disappointed with Obama's decision. Representative Luis Gutierrez accused Obama of creating "pain and suffering" in the Hispanic community.[168] The Latino organization Presente Action actually went so far as to urge Latinos not to cast votes in any of the Senate elections in which Democratic senators had urged delay in Obama's executive order (Arkansas, Louisiana, New Hampshire, and North Carolina).[169]

From a hard-nosed political perspective, Obama's decision may have been correct. Most of the competitive Senate races were in states with small shares of the Hispanic vote, and the Republican-controlled House districts have relatively small Hispanic populations. But by raising expectations that he would resolve the issue before the elections, and then deciding otherwise, Obama exposed himself unnecessarily to Hispanic criticism.

DEMOCRATIC LOSSES IN 2014

The Democrats lost nine Senate seats and fourteen House seats in November 2014. Exit polls indicate that Hispanics were neither enthusiastic nor unified about the election. The number of eligible Hispanic voters was certainly large—indeed it grew rapidly from 17.3 million in 2006 to 25.0 million in 2014—but the rate of turnout of Hispanic voters was relatively low.[170] The Hispanic share of the total vote remained unchanged at 8 percent in 2014. In House races, Democrats won the Hispanic vote by 62–36 percent, a bit worse than in 2006 but slightly better than 2010. In the battleground states with competitive races for governor and senator, Republican candidates did quite well among Hispanics, at least by historical standards.[171]

Some analysts argue that Obama's mismanagement of the immigration issue contributed to the Democratic Party's loss of the governorship and a Senate seat in Colorado.[172] Yet the president's delay of his executive order on immigration did not succeed in protecting Democratic senators from defeat in competitive elections with relatively low Hispanic vote shares (Alaska, Arkansas, Louisiana, and North Carolina).

Historically, immigration was an issue in Senate races only in GOP primaries and mostly in border states. A new trend emerged in 2014. Republican candidates for Senate went on the offensive against Democratic candidates whose records could be framed as pro-immigration. Successful GOP challenger Tom Cotton deployed this tactic against Democrat Mark Pryor of Arkansas; unsuccessful challengers in Michigan and New Hampshire also used the tactic.[173] Public dissatisfaction about the child immigration crisis, and Obama's alleged mismanagement of the issue, may have created an unusual setting in which Republicans were eager to raise the immigration issue in a general election contest.

OBAMA'S LIBERALIZATION ORDER

President Obama did not wait long after the 2014 election to roll out a major executive order on immigration, issuing it just before the Thanksgiving holiday of 2014. One of the perplexing features of the order is that it was developed and issued without following any of the normal notice-and-comment procedures of the Administrative Procedure Act. This gave opponents grounds for a legal challenge that would not have been available if Obama had started with a proposal and then issued the final order with a statement of response to the public comments that were received. By declining the opportunity to seek public comment (which the administration's lawyers may have thought they could do under "prosecutorial discretion") the administration exhibited indifference to a basic process of public administration.

The most important provision provided legal status for five million undocumented migrants already living in the United States. Each eligible migrant could obtain a work permit and a Social Security number but not a green card or US citizenship. On eligibility for the permit, the order expanded the 2012 DACA by removing the age cap on eligibility (which had been set at thirty-one years) and moving the date of first entrance to the United States from June 15, 2007, to any time prior to January 2010. The order also provided eligibility for parents of US citizens and green card holders.

On enforcement the order refocused the punitive aspects of the immigration system on migrants with criminal records, ties to terrorists or gangs, or those who had entered the United States within the last year. The Secure Communities program, feared by the Hispanic community since launched by the Bush administration, was replaced by the "Priority Enforcement Program" (PEP), which was reassuring to illegal immigrants already living in the United States. The priority-setting aspect PEP was framed as a lawful exercise of prosecutorial discretion, since the Congress had not provided the Obama administration with the resources necessary to enforce against all types of illegal immigration.[174] Federal immigration law already provided the president with the authority to defer enforcement action and issue temporary work permits as appropriate. The regulations to this effect had been in place since 1987 and are supported by a long line of court decisions.[175]

The Hispanic community was largely pleased with the order, even though it did not solve all of the problems faced by illegal immigrants. Obama's order therefore created a political dilemma for the Republican Party, since, going into a 2016 presidential election, the national Republican Party would not benefit from seeking judicial action against millions of Hispanics and their families and friends. But congressional Republicans had a different view, in part because their constituents were not representative of the nation as a whole.

The Republicans in Congress blasted the Obama administration for seeking to rewrite federal immigration law without congressional action. The ranking member of the Senate Judiciary Committee, Charles Grassley, declared the order "unconstitutional" while conservative legal scholars argued the Justice Department's rationale for the order was legally deficient.[176] Within two weeks of Obama's action, twenty states—led by Texas—sued the president in federal court. They argued that he had overstepped his authority and violated his constitutional duty to faithfully enforce the law.

Less than ten weeks later, a federal district judge in Texas blocked the Obama administration by issuing a temporary injunction against the executive order.[177] Judge Andrew Hanen, a 2002 appointee of President George W. Bush, issued a 132-page opinion that surprised many legal experts. Instead of challenging Obama's prosecutorial discretion under the US Constitution, Hanen signaled that litigants had a good chance of winning the argument that the order should have complied with the Administrative Procedure Act.[178] The Obama administration appealed the issue to a higher court, but the Fifth Circuit Court of Appeals in New Orleans, in a two-to-one decision, refused to allow the administration to begin implementation of the order.[179]

It may take years for the litigation against the Obama immigration order to work its way through the federal courts. Opponents of the order may not be able to overturn it, since the states initiating the action must show "specific harms" (in order to establish standing to sue) and at least parts of the order seem to be squarely rooted in the president's prosecutorial discretion.[180] But the president appears to have exposed the order to unnecessary legal risk by omitting a public comment opportunity.

General public opinion was divided about the wisdom of Obama's order. One national survey taken soon after the order was issued found that 48 percent of respondents opposed the idea of Obama taking executive action on immigration, 38 percent supported it, and 14 percent were unsure or did not have an opinion.[181] Given the plurality that is unfavorable to the action, it probably was wise for Obama to delay it until after the midterm elections.

In early 2015 House Republicans passed an amendment to the DHS appropriations bill nullifying both the 2012 DREAM-like executive order for youth and the broader 2014 order. The amendment passed 236–191, but there were more Republican defections than Democratic crossovers. The House vote may have had some symbolic significance, but the Democrats in the Senate, despite their minority status, had enough strength to block a similar amendment. In fact, several moderate Democrats in the Senate who were concerned about illegal immigration indicated publicly that they did not support the House action (Heidi Heitkamp, Angus King [who is technically an independent], Joe Manchin, Jeanne Shaheen, and Claire McCaskill).[182] When a vote was taken on a similar measure in the Senate, it fell eight votes short of the sixty votes required to take up the House bill.[183] In the final analysis Obama seems unlikely to lose his liberalization initiative due to hostile congressional action.

COUNTERFACTUALS

Obama pledged in 2008 to deliver comprehensive immigration reform during his first year in office. He did not deliver it in the first year or during any year thereafter. Some might argue that President Obama should have pushed the issue harder in early 2009, demanding that Congress vote on comprehensive reform by July 4, 2009. This strategy probably would have failed. Indeed, immigration reform had a much smaller chance of succeeding than health care reform, since there were too many Democratic members of Congress representing states or districts with small Hispanic populations and large numbers of conservative working-class constituents. Moreover, the economy was shedding jobs so rapidly in 2009 that it was implausible to argue that liberalizing immigration law would help people find jobs. The most likely outcome would have been defeat in Congress, another bruise to Obama's credibility, and more risky votes for Obama's progressive agenda cast by centrist Democrats in the House and the Senate. The distribution of Hispanic voters in the United States was simply unfavorable to a comprehensive legislative solution.[184]

A better approach for Obama might have been to make a down payment on immigration reform in early 2009, in the form of a DREAM-like executive order, similar to what he ultimately did in June 2012. Coupled with the order, he should have lowered expectations for comprehensive reform until the economy was in much better condition. This is a stance he ultimately took in 2012 anyway, and he would have had much more credibility taking the hit in 2009 than in 2012. In effect, he should have said that the immigration pledge had been made before the economic meltdown, and the meltdown forced him to give other measures higher priority.[185] Later in his first term he could have taken additional executive actions to reassure Hispanics that he was dedicated to their cause. If his executive actions failed in the judiciary, he then could have contemplated a targeted or comprehensive legislative fix, depending on the details of the judicial opinions.

The wisdom of Obama's decision to clamp down on border security from 2009 to 2012 is also questionable. He seemed to rely on the theory that a secure border would reassure Republicans and pave the way for comprehensive immigration reform legislation. However, he should have questioned this theory, since President George W. Bush had been talked into a crackdown from 2005 to 2006, one that was demonstrated to cause a sharp drop in border crossings, and, despite the progress on border security, Bush was not able to persuade House Republicans to consider the immigration reform measure passed by the Senate in 2006.[186] Obama's "ruthless" enforcement efforts against undocumented migrants ultimately did more harm than good for his own agenda.[187]

It also seems doubtful whether Obama should have entered into secret political negotiations with John Boehner on immigration reform (2013–2014). Boehner's hold on his position as House Speaker was not highly secure, and much of his conservative caucus was especially suspicious of his views on immigration.[188] Under these circumstances Boehner could not possibly have delivered on a package that created a pathway to citizenship, and thus there was no possible legislative win for Obama and the Democrats. The pathway to citizenship was the essential feature of reform sought by progressives; executive action was already available to accomplish much of the desired reform short of the ultimate pathway, assuming Obama was prepared to follow normal notice-and-comment procedures. A saving grace for Obama was that the negotiations with Boehner remained secret as long as they did.

Obama's handling of the child refugee crisis in 2014 again revealed a White House that did not appreciate the importance of public administration to maintaining public confidence in government. The White House reacted to the crisis as primarily a political matter instead of rapidly identifying and delivering the public administration capabilities that were required to address it.

The severity of the crisis undermined Obama's case for comprehensive reform.[189] It suggested that Obama's border policies were not working. Insofar as Congress was persuadable to pass reform once the border was secure—though, as mentioned above, that was also questionable—the child immigrant crisis undermined Obama's claim that he was securing the border.[190]

Obama did well what good politicians must do: capitalize on the errors committed by their adversaries. When Romney moved far to the right on immigration in the Republican primaries, Obama saw the opening and issued his DREAM-like executive order in June 2012. Even though a Republican could have plausibly run against Obama as both a fibber to the Hispanic community and a "Deporter in Chief," what happened is that Romney effectively handed the Hispanic vote to Obama in 2012 and Obama deftly positioned himself to accept the support.

As party leader what Obama did not do was deepen the Hispanic community's trust in the Democratic Party. The liberalization steps that he took were almost always taken when Hispanic activists could apply intense electoral pressure on him, with the possible exception of the unsuccessful effort to pass the DREAM Act in late 2010. As a result, the Hispanic community will move on from the Obama presidency with ties to the Democratic Party that are widespread but not particularly trusting.[191]

10

MIDTERM MASSACRES

When Barack Obama ran for president in 2008 and 2012, he helped the Democratic Party. He generated enthusiasm among the Democratic base, attracted support from independent voters (especially in 2008), and brought record numbers of young people and African Americans to the polls. In the 2008 election the Democrats recorded a net gain of twenty-four House seats and eight Senate seats; an additional eight House seats and two Senate seats were captured in the 2012 election. In these elections Democratic gains were also recorded in many state races for legislature, governor, and other statewide offices. In short, Obama had some significant coattails for the Democratic Party.

Midterm elections present a different challenge for the White House. Naturally, a two-term president experiences two such elections, one in the middle of the first term and the other in the middle of the second term. A president's name is not on the ballot, so it is tempting to think that a midterm election will be dominated by factors that have little or nothing to do with the president.

Numerous factors surely play a role: local or state issues, candidate personalities, whether a race is for an open seat (since incumbents have inherent advantages), the caliber of a challenger, the relative fund-raising prowess of the candidates, and the strategy and tactics used in the competing campaign organizations. Such factors can be important in all elections, including midterm contests.[1] But some midterm elections seem to become a virtual referendum on the performance of the occupant of the Oval Office, a phenomenon that has been accentuated in the recent period of polarized party politics.[2]

The sobering truth for the White House is that a president's party rarely gains House seats at a midterm election. It has happened only three times in the last century (1934, 1998, 2002). In the seven midterm elections after 1980, prior to the Obama presidency, the president's party lost more than ten House seats three times (1982, 1994, 2006); in each case there was a backlash against the incumbent president.[3]

Table 10.1 reports the electoral performance of the president's party in the eighteen midterm elections since World War II. The average House losses by the president's party have been substantial: roughly thirty seats at the first midterm election and forty seats at the second midterm contest.[4] In the Senate the average midterm loss for the president's party is about three seats, which is substantial given that only thirty-three Senate seats are up for grabs at each national election.[5] The averages also conceal huge variability, which suggests that large losses are not inevitable and that specific circumstances matter. In many midterm elections the president's party manages to minimize its losses of House seats to single digits.[6] The strong performances by the Democratic Party in 1998 (during Clinton's second term) and the Republican Party in 2002 (during George W. Bush's first term) illustrate this point.[7]

Presidents of both parties experience midterm electoral setbacks in Congress, but the average losses are larger for the Democratic Party than the Republican Party. In the House, the average midterm losses since World War II were 21 seats for the Republican Party when the GOP occupies the White House; the average loss for the Democrats was 29 seats when a Democrat occupies the White House. In the Senate, the average midterm losses were 3.2 and 5.0 seats, respectively.

Summed over their two midterm elections, the losses of seats in Congress for the parties of some presidents have been staggering. Under President Harry Truman, the Democratic Party lost a total of seventy-four House seats and

Table 10.1. Extent of Midterm Electoral Losses by the President's Party in Congress, by Presidency and Year, Post–World War II

Year	President	Party	Net House seats gained/lost by party	Net Senate seats gained/lost by party
1946	Truman	D	−45	−12
1950	Truman	D	−29	−6
1954	Eisenhower	R	−18	−1
1958	Eisenhower	R	−48	−13
1962	Kennedy	D	−4	3
1966	Johnson	D	−47	−4
1970	Nixon	R	−12	2
1974	Ford	R	−48	−5
1978	Carter	D	−15	−3
1982	Reagan	R	−26	1
1986	Reagan	R	−5	−8
1990	Bush	R	−8	−1
1994	Clinton	D	−52	−8
1998	Clinton	D	5	0
2002	G.W. Bush	R	8	2
2006	G.W. Bush	R	−30	−6
2010	Obama	D	−63	−6
2014	Obama	D	−13	−9

eighteen Senate seats in 1946 and 1950. The Republican Party under President Dwight Eisenhower lost a total of sixty-six House seats and fourteen Senate seats in 1954 and 1958. President Barack Obama also experienced a political massacre of congressional Democrats, as a total of seventy-six House seats were lost in 2010 and 2014, coupled with a loss of fifteen Senate seats. The magnitude of Obama's midterm losses begs for explanation, the key issue addressed in this chapter.

In particular, I explore President Obama's effectiveness as party leader as reflected in his party's performance in two midterm elections, 2010 and 2014. I start by examining what levers a president has to influence midterm elections, in contrast to structural factors that are outside the president's control. Next I examine the dynamics occurring in the Republican Party in 2010 and 2014, including how the Republicans sought to frame the midterm elections as national referenda on Obama's performance. Some Obama-related factors that appear to have influenced the 2010 and 2014 outcomes are then explored. And the chapter concludes with my assessment of some of the ramifications—policy-wise and politically—of the Democratic Party's huge losses in the 2010 and 2014 midterm elections.

It is a mistake for presidents to treat midterm losses as inevitable or completely out of their control. Chapter 11 considers some counterfactuals for Obama that may have mitigated the extent of those Democratic losses. Insights from the counterfactuals offer some guidance to future presidents seeking to better perform as leaders of their national political parties while retaining their effectiveness as policy makers.

THE PRESIDENT'S ROLE IN MIDTERM ELECTIONS

As a successful party leader, a president helps grow his political party in Congress during good times and helps attenuate losses in bad times. He does so through both political activity and policy making, assuming that he does not hand his opponents an ethical issue such as the Watergate debacle under Richard Nixon. To Barack Obama's credit, the Obama presidency was relatively scandal-free.

"Political activity" is defined here to include a variety of activities: fundraising for the party and particular candidates, delivering speeches that energize the base (nationally or locally), and making personal appearances on behalf of candidates or groups in states and districts throughout the country. Some presidents enjoy this activity more than others, and the president's effectiveness on the campaign trail depends on his personal characteristics, his family's campaigning skills, his degree of popularity nationally or in a specific state or district, and how well he connects with party activists, sympathetic interest groups, and donors.

Presidential policy making is often seen as advancing national interests, but it can also help boost the electoral fortunes of the president's party. Policy making influences partisan outcomes at the polls through a variety of mechanisms. Since the president is the leader of his party, his job approval rating and general popularity tend to elevate the attractiveness of all candidates on the ballot who are affiliated with his party. A president's policy making may boost his popularity if his initiatives are broadly popular. Thus, we have seen many presidents give priority to popular initiatives.[8] Even if the president's initiatives are controversial, divisive, or even unpopular, effective policy making on such issues helps fashion an image that the president is an engaged and influential politician (i.e., "he gets things done"). If the president's policy priorities are blocked in the Congress (due to their unpopularity, partisan gridlock, or opposition from powerful interests), his job approval rating will suffer, and indeed there may be collateral damage to the standing of his party.

The notion that through well-timed policies the president can help his party at a midterm election by creating favorable outcomes (e.g., new jobs and income gains) is overrated. It is quite difficult for the president and his policy team to schedule favorable policy outcomes—particularly economic ones—with the precision necessary to influence the outcome of a midterm election. It is particularly difficult to target favorable policy outcomes in the one-third of states with a Senate race or to the ninety or so competitive House seats that could plausibly flip one way or another. An exception might be a midyear tax refund that is timed before a midterm election, but the opposing party in Congress is highly unlikely to cooperate with such strategic policy making.

When a president asks members of his party in Congress to vote for controversial or unpopular initiatives, he cross-pressures his partisan allies in ways that create electoral risks for the party. Cross-pressured members may have some cover if the White House succeeds in attracting bipartisan support for a controversial proposal.

There is now a significant body of evidence that roll-call votes by members of Congress influence congressional election outcomes.[9] A highly risky vote for a presidential initiative is one that antagonizes influential segments of the member's district or state. Party-line votes in favor of unpopular or divisive presidential initiatives are a danger sign for members of Congress from the president's party, since such votes create an opportunity for the opposing party to nationalize a midterm election by making it a referendum on the incumbent president.

THE 2010 MIDTERM ELECTION: SEATS AT RISK

President Barack Obama is not entirely responsible for the Democratic Party's 2010 electoral losses, because some structural factors working against the Democrats were largely or completely outside of his control. The biggest

Table 10.2. Distribution of House Seats Held by Republicans and Democrats in 2009–2010 as a Function of How Well George W. Bush (2004) and John McCain (2008) Fared in the District

Number of Seats Held in District That Bush (2004) Won:	Partisan Mix of House, 2009–2010	
	Democrats	Republicans
< 45%	136	1
45–50%	48	6
51–55%	38	25
> 55%	34	147
Number of Seats Held in District That McCain (2008) Won:		
< 45%	183	8
45–50%	34	36
51–55%	20	47
> 55%	19	88

Sources: Michael Barone and Richard Cohen, *The Almanac of American Politics, 2010* (Washington, DC: National Journal Group Press, 2009); Michael Barone and Chuck McCutcheon, *The Almanac of American Politics, 2012* (Washington, DC: National Journal Group, 2011).

single factor was the imbalance in the number of seats at risk (sometimes called the party's "exposure"), especially the large number of Democratic House members representing districts that were friendly to a Republican challenger. In the House the Democrats were defending 257 seats compared to 178 for the Republicans. The situation was far more balanced in the Senate, where the Democrats were defending only one more seat (19) than the Republicans (18).

Due to the unpopularity of George W. Bush and the Iraq War, the Democrats captured dozens of competitive and Republican-leaning House districts in 2006 and 2008 (see table 10.2). As a result, sixty of the House Democrats up for reelection in 2010 were freshmen or sophomores. Their vulnerability was heightened because of limited experience and recognition in their own district.[10] The GOP needed to win thirty-nine seats to regain control of the House majority, but both parties knew that forty-one incumbent House Democrats were occupying districts in which Republican John McCain won 50 percent or more against Obama in 2008.[11] A different measure of GOP-leaning seats can be comprised from the George W. Bush vote in 2004, for in 2010 there were fifty-seven House Democrats occupying seats that George W. Bush won in 2004. In contrast, the Republican Party was defending few freshmen and sophomores and was occupying few seats that leaned Democratic in their voting behavior.[12]

Thus, given the structure of the 2010 election and the partisan imbalance in exposure to potential losses, it was likely that the Democratic Party would experience significant losses in the House. The structure of the Senate contests was balanced in number, but the Democrats were defending seats in more states that are historically competitive between the two parties.[13] Thus, the prospects of picking up Senate seats were better for the Republican Party than for the Democratic Party.

TEA PARTY ENERGIZES REPUBLICANS

With their large losses in 2006 and 2008, the Republican Party in Congress was becoming so small that it risked becoming irrelevant. On the other hand, the Republican survivors in Congress tended to be markedly conservative, representing states and districts where the Democratic Party is not very competitive. The Republican leaders in the House and Senate were in a strong position to appeal for party unity, since only unified voting by the Republicans had any chance of blocking, slowing, or amending Obama's ambitious policy agenda. And the ideological homogeneity of the Republicans made it easier to unify them.

An important factor was the rapid development of the Tea Party, the loose coalition of populist conservatives and libertarians who rallied around vice presidential nominee Sarah Palin during the 2008 campaign and were seen by liberals as a reactionary wing of the Republican Party.[14] Obama's race, life story, and progressive values, coupled with his ambitious legislative agenda in 2009 (TARP renewal and corporate bailouts, stimulus spending, the Affordable Care Act, cap and trade, and liberalization of immigration), frightened the Tea Party to such an extent that the grassroots movement spread like brushfire in many regions of the country. A common sentiment among "stop Obama" activists was that the country was headed toward socialism (see chapter 1).

Some activists affiliated with the Tea Party saw Obama as a radical Muslim. A related critique that alarmed evangelical Christians was the idea that Obama was anti-Christian, exemplified by his support for gay rights and abortion. Tea Party concerns overlapped with broader concerns in the Republican base that Obama was anti-gun, anti-farmer, anti-business, anti-property, anti-freedom, anti-military, and anti-American. Some observers resorted to ridicule of the Tea Party's simplistic views, but the effects of ridicule may have been to further energize the Tea Party. Social science studies of the Tea Party reveal that the concerns of grassroots members, though sometimes based on falsehoods, were deeply held. Obama triggered widespread fear, anger, and animosity, and the Tea Party rapidly became effective at organized political activity.[15]

The emergence of the Tea Party made it much more difficult for Republican members of Congress to consider collaborating with President Obama. Many conservative GOP voters did not simply oppose Obama; they despised and feared him.[16] As Obama sought bipartisan collaboration in Congress to further legitimize his agenda and legacy, Republicans in Congress sensed political danger and became highly unified in opposition to his policy initiatives, sometimes for completely partisan, strategic reasons.

The electoral impact of the Tea Party was first heard nationally in January 2010 when populist conservative Scott Brown won Ted Kennedy's vacated Senate seat in Massachusetts. Brown ran on a campaign to deny Obama the critical sixtieth vote for enactment of the Affordable Care Act.[17]

In the Republican primaries in 2010, the Tea Party ran its own candidates in numerous elections, often seeking to dislodge incumbent Republicans who were seen as too inclined to compromise with Obama. Casualties among incumbent Republicans included seasoned senators Robert Bennett and Lisa Murkowski (though Murkowski later won reelection as an independent). Even when Tea Party candidates lost in the 2010 Republican primaries, they sent a strong signal to the Republican winners that collaboration with Obama was unacceptable.

Building on the energy of the Tea Party, Republican candidates for Congress in 2010 ran on emotion-laden national themes. The bottom line was that they urged voters to send President Obama a message with their votes by voting against Democratic candidates.[18] Some of the electoral losses the Democrats experiences were not avoidable, but as I explain in chapter 11, Obama's policy agenda in 2009–2010 made the Tea Party's task easier than it could have been.

THE DISMAL STATE OF THE ECONOMY

It is not easy for a challenger to defeat an incumbent member of Congress. The reelection rates for House and Senate incumbents have been 95–99 percent and 80–95 percent, respectively, over the past thirty years.[19] When incumbents do lose reelection, a poor economy is often a contributing factor.[20]

The immense disruption of the economy caused by the Great Recession (December 2007–June 2009) was still working its way through labor markets in the fall of 2010. The 9.6 percent rate of unemployment in October 2010 was down slightly from a peak of more than 10 percent earlier in 2010 but far above the 5 percent rate that economists often consider the rate of full employment in a healthy economy. And the millions of jobless Americans who had given up looking for work were not even counted in the official rate of unemployment.

Public expectations for a speedy recovery were out of proportion to what federal policy makers were able to generate. The agonizingly slow recovery of labor markets was somewhat surprising to macroeconomists: when recessions originate in the financial sector of the economy, the downturn tends to be more severe, but the recovery tends to be more robust.[21]

The policies of the Federal Reserve Board and the Bush and Obama administrations may have averted a repeat of the Great Depression and started a recovery, at least to some extent.[22] Political credit for this accomplishment is not easy to garner. Trained economists were aware of the disastrous consequences of the Great Depression, but since rank-and-file voters did not experience the Great Depression, they had no appreciation of the Depression-scale hardships that may have been avoided.[23]

Polls showed that voters in 2010 were not naively punitive toward Obama. Indeed, they were much more likely to blame Bush than Obama for the dismal state of the economy in October 2010.[24] Nonetheless, voters were not optimistic about the economy or their families' fiscal future. Millions of Americans had been out of work for more than six months, and some economic forecasters were expressing concern about a possible "double-dip" recession.

Exit polls in 2008 found that 63 percent of voters said the economy was the nation's most important issue; exit polls in 2010 recorded almost identical sentiment.[25] In short, the public did not have confidence in the effectiveness of Obama's economic policies and was disturbed by the terrible fiscal condition of the federal government. Economic pessimism was overwhelming the few optimistic signs in the sluggish recovery (see chapter 3).

OBAMA'S FALLING JOB APPROVAL RATING

One of the significant predictors of midterm election outcomes is the president's job approval rating. The stronger (or weaker) the president's rating, the better (or worse) the president's party fares in Congress.[26]

President Obama's job approval rating, as measured by Gallup, dropped steadily from 63 percent during the first three months of his presidency to 45 percent in October 2010 (see table 10.3). The decline was 12 percentage points among liberals and 20 percentage points among moderates and conservatives.[27] Rasmussen and other polling organizations reported similar trends.[28]

The decline among conservatives was difficult to prevent, given Obama's progressive agenda, but the decline among independents was a big cause for concern. Among independents, it seemed that the entrance of Obama into Washington politics had done little to reduce the partisan bickering, despite his 2008–2009 pledge of a "post-partisan presidency" (see chapter 1). Cable TV news channels, newspapers, drive-time radio, and other information sources portrayed the same partisan fights that independents disliked during the presidency of George W. Bush.[29] As a result, independents started to become disenchanted with Obama.

Exit polls in November 2008 estimated that Obama won somewhere between 52 and 56 percent of independents in his contest against John McCain. Obama's job approval rating among independents remained above 50 percent through 2009 and the first half of 2010 but then fell below 50 percent through the fall until the November election.[30]

Overall, Obama's midterm job approval rating (45 percent) is considered "below average" for presidents since World War II. His standing was comparable to Reagan in 1982 (42 percent) and Clinton in 1994 (48 percent), although better than George W. Bush in 2006 (38 percent).[31]

OBAMA AS 2010 CAMPAIGNER

More than any previous president, Obama helped raise money to support the reelection of congressional Democrats. The number of fund-raisers he attended far exceeded the number attended by his predecessors.[32] And, as we shall see below, incumbent Democrats were well funded in 2010.

Tensions erupted over whether congressional Democrats should have access to the thirteen million e-mail addresses that Obama's campaign compiled in 2008. Obama decided not to keep the list at the White House and instead transferred it to his private advocacy group Organizing for America (OFA). Departing from the previous practices of Bill Clinton and George W. Bush, Obama and his 2008 campaign staff did not loan the list to the Demo-

Table 10.3. Barack Obama's approval ratings from January 2009 to April 2015

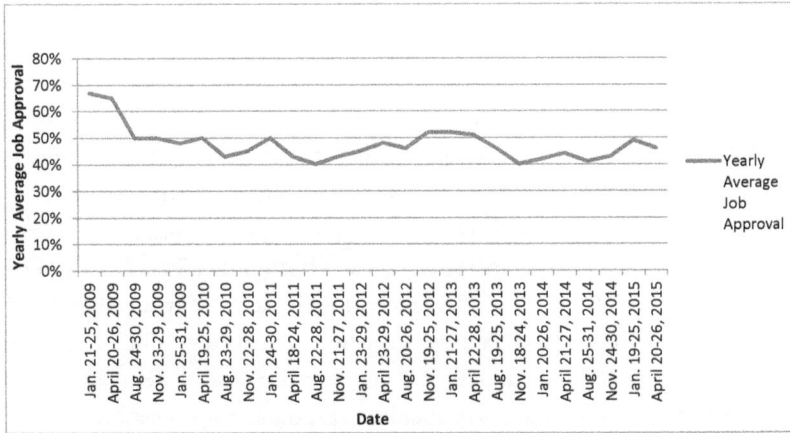

Source: "Presidential Approval Ratings—Barack Obama," *Gallup.com*, 2015,
http:www.gallup.com/poll/116479/barack-obama-presidential-job-approval.aspx.

cratic National Committee. Serious questions were raised as to how effective
OFA was during 2010 in support of either Obama's policies or Democratic
candidates.[33]

Although Obama was a successful fund-raiser, what irritated House Democrats was how he expended his campaign time in 2010 in support of individual
candidates.[34] The perception in the House was that he devoted far more time
making appearances on behalf of Senate Democrats than House Democrats.
President Obama's October 2010 campaign schedule lends some credence to
those concerns, for he appeared locally on behalf of only two House Democrats
compared to four Democratic governors and five Democratic senators.[35] Many
of the vulnerable House Democrats up for reelection in 2010 were freshmen or
sophomores who were not well known in their districts. A visit to their district
by Obama could have been a significant boost in their visibility.

FUND-RAISING AND THE QUALITY
OF REPUBLICAN CHALLENGERS

If the economy is poor and if the majority party in Congress is led
by a president with low job approval ratings, incumbents from the president's

party in Congress are likely to face well-funded and high-caliber challengers.[36] That is what happened in both the House and Senate in 2010.

An indicator of whether a challenger for a House seat is high caliber is whether he or she was previously an elective officeholder. Novices in electoral politics tend to be weak opponents of seasoned incumbents. By this measure of quality the Republican challengers in 2010 were the strongest since 1968.[37]

There were some exceptions to this pattern in which the Tea Party re-cruited and helped nominate Republican candidates for Congress, as some Tea Party candidates proved to be weak general election candidates. According to one estimate, 109 of the GOP challengers for House seats in 2010 had ties to the Tea Party.[38] There is no strong evidence that the Tea Party affiliation either helped or hurt these candidates in 2010. On the other hand, it seems likely that the Tea Party helped nominate Republican candidates for Senate who were virtually unelectable, despite running in otherwise winnable states (Colorado, Delaware, and Nevada).[39]

Money is not considered to have been a decisive factor in the November 2010 House and Senate elections, because both parties had sufficient funds to ensure that every plausible candidate had a hefty war chest. One study found that the average Democrat (Republican) running for the House benefited from $2.83 million ($2.35 million) in spending, "well above the sums needed to fi-nance full-scale campaigns."[40]

THE MIDTERM ENTHUSIASM AND TURNOUT GAPS

Voter turnout is relatively low in nonpresidential elections.[41] Com-pared to turnout rates of 50–60 percent when the presidency is at stake, mid-term congressional elections drew consistently fewer than 40 percent of eli-gible voters from 1990 to 2006.[42] Eligible voters in the lowest income categories are least likely to perceive differences between candidates from the two par-ties, which may help explain why their rates of turnout are disproportionately low.[43]

The soaring rhetoric in Obama's 2008 campaign, coupled with the historic and decisive nature of his electoral victory, contributed to unrealistic public expectations about what he could deliver in the way of change.[44] In his first year, debate over health care reform seemed to go on endlessly, the Senate did not act after the House's prompt action on climate change, and neither the House nor the Senate acted on immigration reform. An early 2010 skit on NBC's *Saturday Night Live* summed up Obama's accomplishments as "jack and squat."[45]

The gap between performance and expectation generated massive disappointment, particularly among young people, Hispanics, women, and self-described independents.[46] Each of these subgroups was an enthusiastic contributor to Obama's 2008 coalition. As Election Day in November 2010 approached, surveys found that 68 percent of Republican respondents expressed a high degree of enthusiasm about the election; only 44 percent of Democrats expressed the same degree of enthusiasm.[47] In close races, party-related differences in turnout can be decisive.

PREELECTION FORECASTS IN 2010

Prior to the 2010 election, experts predicted losses for the Democratic Party in the range of twenty to fifty House seats.[48] Models that give weight to Obama's mediocre job approval rating and weak growth in household incomes supported low-end estimates.[49] Middle-range estimates accounted for two of the key structural variables (the number of Democratic seats at risk and Obama's approval rating) plus early October surveys measuring voter intentions.[50] The higher-end estimates relied more on surveys of what voters said they were likely to do at the polls or alternative indices of the state of the economy.

For the Senate, the forecasts for the Democrats ranged from a loss of one or two seats to a loss of four or five seats. The conventional wisdom was that the Democratic Party did not have enough seats at risk to produce a huge loss. But as we shall see, all of the statistical approaches used by experts under-predicted the damage experienced by the Democratic Party.

RESULTS OF THE 2010 MIDTERM CONTEST

The results were a political earthquake of a magnitude that was far beyond what Democrats feared and Republicans hoped for. It has also stumped political scientists.[51]

The Democratic Party started the evening with a 257–178 House majority. They lost a net sixty-four seats in the House, allowing the Republicans to accomplish a 242–193 majority, the GOP's best showing since 1946. Fifty-five incumbents were defeated, only two of them Republicans. Of the fifteen open seats that switched parties, fourteen switched from the Democratic to the Republican Party.[52] Democrats defended forty-eight seats in districts that John McCain won in 2008; they lost thirty-six of them.[53] In the Senate the Democratic Party started out with a large 59–41 majority. The Republicans accomplished a net gain of six seats, reducing the Democratic margin to 53–47. Two Democratic incumbents were defeated and the Republicans won all four of the open seats.

Turnout on Election Day was surprisingly high, the highest for a midterm election since 1994. The shares of young and minority voters were below midterm averages while the shares of middle-age and older voters were above midterm averages.[54] An election dominated by older voters is bad news for Democratic candidates, because older voters typically allocate a disproportionate share of their votes to Republican candidates.

The voting behavior of self-described independents, as gleaned from exit polls, was a big factor in the 2010 results. Independents voted 57–39 percent for Democratic House candidates in 2006 and 51–43 percent in 2008. The opposite pattern unfolded in 2010 as Republican House candidates captured the independent vote 56–37 percent.[55] Note that this change is partly the result of independent voters switching which party they supported and partly a function of which self-described independents were motivated to vote. Many independents tend to lean heavily toward one party or the other in their voting behavior[56]

CNN's exit poll found that 60 percent of 2010 voters intended their vote to signal their views of President Obama.[57] In short, the Republican Party succeeded in nationalizing the 2010 midterm election, making it a referendum on Obama's performance.

HOW OBAMA'S POLICY AGENDA HURT HIS PARTY

Why did experts seem to under-predict the Democratic Party's losses in 2010? The horrible condition of the economy may be part of the explanation (although it was accounted for by some experts and their statistical models), but it also appears that President Obama's legislative agenda was toxic to the electoral futures of many members of his own party.

Recall that President Obama started his first term with requests that Congress support the TARP bailout for Wall Street and the Recovery Act's fiscal stimulus, both of which became unpopular initiatives that contributed to the GOP narrative that Obama was an old-style big-spending liberal.[58] The $1 trillion Affordable Care Act further underscored Obama's big-government image. Even though it lacked a single payer plan or even a public option, Obamacare included the controversial provision often demonized by the Tea Party: the individual mandate. And the House vote on Obama's cap and trade proposal added a significant complication to the reelection challenge faced by Democrats from coal, oil, and manufacturing states.

The president's most popular legislative success was the regulatory crackdown on Wall Street (the Dodd-Frank law), but, inexplicably, he never garnered much political benefit from the initiative.[59] Indeed, the public debate about Dodd-Frank seemed to reinforce the perception that Obama was anti-business, which in turn helped open the spigots of campaign money from Wall Street to Republican challengers.[60]

Did Democrats do themselves any good by voting against some of the Obama agenda? Casual empiricism says they did. Consider House Democrats representing the forty-eight districts won by McCain in 2008. Of those who voted in favor of the ACA, only 10 percent won reelection; 36 percent of those who voted against the ACA were reelected. A similar pattern exists for the stimulus package. Of the House Democrats (from McCain districts) who voted for it, 23 percent won reelection; 40 percent of those who voted against the stimulus won reelection.[61]

The cap and trade vote does not seem to follow this pattern. Two-thirds of those who voted for cap and trade were defeated, but two-thirds of those who voted against cap and trade were defeated. A confounding variable is the ACA vote, which overlaps with the cap and trade vote. Moreover, some "safe" Democrats voted against cap and trade because it was not "green" enough. If the focus is members from competitive seats who voted for cap and trade but against ACA, there are seven cases, and six of them were defeated. The one who survived (Ben Chandler of Kentucky) did so by six hundred votes but then lost to the same Republican challenger (Andy Barr) in 2012. Cap and trade was a prominent issue in each of the seven races.[62]

Several analysts have employed statistical methods to investigate whether the roll-call votes cast in favor of Obama's policy agenda were associated with smaller shares of the vote for Democratic incumbents in November 2010. Analyses need to control for the fact that incumbent Democrats running in competitive districts face more conservative voters than incumbents running in heavily Democratic districts. In fact, of the incumbent Democrats with overall moderate-conservative voting records, 54 percent were defeated in 2010; only 1 percent of incumbent Democrats with strongly liberal overall voting records were defeated.[63] Thus, district characteristics need to be taken into account.

The first study of this question was released on the Internet soon after Election Day in 2010.[64] The investigator, Eric McGhee, coded each Democratic incumbent in terms of how many "controversial" votes he had made in favor of four Obama proposals: Affordable Care Act, Recovery Act, cap and trade, and TARP. Only 3 House Democrats voted against all four measures; 18 voted for only one of them; 22 voted for two of them; 64 voted for three of four; and 128 voted for all four of them.

The question is whether House Democrats protected themselves at the polls by voting against one or more of Obama's priorities. Using Democratic share of the 2010 vote as the dependent variable, McGhee found that each additional vote cast in favor of Obama's agenda was associated with a loss of two-thirds of one percentage point of the 2010 vote. McGhee's model controlled for the amount of campaign spending in each race and the normal voting pattern in each congressional district (as revealed by the 2008 House vote and the 2008 presidential vote). In an intriguing simulation, McGhee concludes that if all incumbent Democrats had voted against at least one of Obama's four major proposals, the number of seats lost by the Democratic Party in 2010 would have been fifty-two instead of sixty-four. If the four votes had never been scheduled (and thus the bills not passed), the Democrats would have lost only half as many seats (thirty-two instead of sixty-four) as they did.

A questionable assumption of this analysis is that each of the four roll-call votes is equally controversial. Moreover, since the average incumbent Democrat is representing a district that voted 63 percent for Obama in 2008, the analysis might be improved with some focus on competitive or Republican-leaning districts.

A second study, by Gary Jacobson, contained a targeted analysis of forty-four Republican-leaning congressional districts that were represented by an incumbent Democrat in 2009–2010.[65] Six of the forty-four voted against the

Recovery Act; twenty-one voted against the Affordable Care Act; and eleven voted against Dodd-Frank. The cap and trade vote was not analyzed. Jacobson found that voting against each of the three proposals was electorally the best strategy for this subgroup of Democrats. After controlling for presidential and congressional voting in 2008 (to capture the impact of district characteristics), he found that a vote for the Affordable Care Act was associated with a 4.9 percentage point decline in the incumbent Democrat's 2010 share of the vote. Votes for Dodd-Frank and the Recovery Act were associated with reductions in the Democratic vote share of 3.7 and 3.0 percentage points, respectively. When Jacobson enlarged the sample to include some districts without a GOP tilt, the negative effect of a vote for the Affordable Care Act persisted, but the effects of the other controversial votes were not significant.

A limitation of this analysis is that it removes from the data numerous districts that are competitive but not tilting Republican. And the small number of districts in the analysis leads to some imprecision in the reported estimates. Like the first study, it also does not control for whether an incumbent is a freshman or sophomore and thus more vulnerable to defeat.

A third study, by David W. Brady, Morris P. Fiorina, and Arjun S. Wilkins, compensates for the limitations in the previous studies by (1) including a relatively large sample of districts with a Democratic incumbent in 2010 who faced opposition (N = 231), (2) controlling for whether the incumbent was in the first or second term, and (3) accounting for the fact that the adverse effect of voting for Obama's agenda may be greatest in districts where Obama ran poorly in 2008. The latter adjustment is accomplished by modeling interactions between roll-call votes on Obama's issues and Obama's 2008 district performance.

The authors of the study considered only roll-call votes on the Affordable Care Act and cap and trade.[66] The inclusion of the interactions led to an interesting finding: a vote for health care reform and cap and trade exerted a negative impact on an incumbent's 2010 vote share as long as the district awarded Obama less than 72 percent and 62 percent of the vote share, respectively, in 2008. Only in the most heavily Democratic districts, as measured by Obama's 2008 performance, was a vote for Obama's proposals neutral or beneficial for the incumbent's 2010 vote share.

When both proposals are included in the same model, the estimated effects are highly imprecise because of the high degree of correlation between votes for the Affordable Care Act and cap and trade. Seventy-eight percent of the incumbent Democrats voted "yes" on both measures and 8 percent voted "no" on both measures. Five percent voted "yes" on cap and trade and "no" on health care, and 9 percent voted "no" on cap and trade and "yes" on health care. The study's authors argue that too few Democrats voted against TARP and the Recovery Act to permit their inclusion in the analysis.

Considering just those two votes, health care and cap and trade, Brady and his colleagues performed a simulation to determine whether the Democratic Party could have retained its majority under a scenario in which more Democrats voted against the two measures. By uniformly voting down the Affordable Care Act and elevating the number of votes against cap and trade (in those districts where Obama captured less than 60 percent of the 2008 vote), the Democratic Party could have saved forty of the sixty-four seats that it lost. A variety of alternative analyses by the three authors lend credence to the suggestion that House Democrats, with different roll-call voting patterns, could have retained their majority in the House.

I replicated a similar model of Democratic incumbent performance in the 2010 election using the entire sample of House incumbents (N = 257). One version of the model used the Democratic incumbent's 2010 vote share as the dependent variable and was estimated using a method called ordinary least squares (OLS) regression; a second version used incumbent win/loss as a dichotomous dependent variable and was estimated using logistic regression. I also sought to determine the effect of three roll-call votes: the Affordable Care Act, the cap and trade bill, and the 2009 Recovery Act (the stimulus). The vote for/against each bill was treated as a dichotomous independent variable, and I created an interaction term for each bill with the 2008 Obama vote share.

As district-level control variables I used Obama's share of the vote in the district in 2008 as well as the Democratic candidate's share of the House vote in the district in 2008. The estimated coefficients on both of these variables, as expected, are positive and statistically significant in each of the analyses that I performed. When I controlled for whether the incumbent was a freshman (in his or her first term), the estimated coefficient was, as expected, negative and statistically significant.

For the most part, I replicated the findings of previous studies with respect to the adverse effects of voting for the three bills. When a vote for each bill is analyzed separately, each vote appears to hurt the incumbent's 2008 performance. When each of the three bills is included in the same equation, the Affordable Care Act hurts incumbent performance but the other two bills are not statistically significant. If we ignore the individual bills and focus on incumbents who voted for all three of them, the effect on incumbent performance in 2008 is negative and statistically significant in both the OLS and logistic models.

Overall, the key insight from all of these analyses is that Obama's legislative agenda does help explain why the Democratic Party's losses in 2010 were much greater than structural factors would have predicted. On the other hand, such analyses need to be interpreted with caution. One cannot take literally the causal notion that if more Democrats had voted against all three bills, the House majority would have been saved. The flaw in that inference is that other factors would not likely have been constant.

For example, if Obama's signature initiatives had been ignored or rejected by a Democratic Congress, his job approval ratings likely would have fallen to even lower levels than were observed, and those dismal ratings would have put congressional Democrats at even greater risk of defeat in 2010. We would also need to reconsider whether Obama would have been reelected in 2012 if he had accomplished none of his major first-term domestic priorities. He might have been challenged by a prominent Democrat in the 2012 Democratic primary as President Jimmy Carter was challenged by Ted Kennedy in 1980.[67] Nonetheless, it does appear that Obama's agenda (ACA and, to a lesser extent, cap and trade and fiscal stimulus) contributed to the defeat of some of his co-partisans in the House of Representatives.[68]

THE 2014 MASSACRE

Soon after President Obama was reelected in November 2012, the focus of the parties shifted to the November 2014 midterm election. Unlike 2010, where the big story was the GOP takeover of the House, the issue in 2014 was the fate of the Senate. I begin my discussion of this issue with the structural aspects of the 2014 election and then explore the complications faced by Obama and why Obama's job approval ranking slumped. I go on to address the GOP's plan for 2014, Harry Reid's dilemma as Senate majority leader, Obama's role as 2014 campaigner, and the 2014 electoral results. The section concludes by examining the near-term and long-term ramifications of the midterm massacres, both for President Obama and the Democratic Party.

The 2014 Structural Situation

Swing districts in the House can be defined as those where historical voting patterns range from +5 percentage points for the Democratic candidate to +5 percentage points for the Republican candidate. In 1998 there were 164 swing seats, the remainder being solidly Republican (148) or solidly Democratic (123). By 2014 the number of swing seats in the House had dwindled to 90, the remainder being solidly Republican (186) or solidly Democratic (159).[69] The fewer seats in play partly reflected redistricting changes in 2010 (often engineered by Republican officials) and partly demographic changes and migration that put more districts into safe territory for one party or the other.[70]

Among the ninety swing seats in 2014, only a small subset was genuinely in play.[71] Based on 2012 presidential election results, only seventeen were districts held by the GOP but carried by Obama; only nine were districts held by the Democrats but carried by Romney. The Republican Party made a serious effort to challenge about twenty-five of the thirty-six incumbent Democrats holding seats where Obama won 55 percent or less of the vote in 2012. The Democratic Party chose to challenge seriously only about six GOP incumbents, all holding a district that had produced a strong Obama vote in 2012.[72] As a result, the structure of the 2014 House contests seemed unlikely to produce a Democratic House majority, since there were not enough vulnerable and contested Republican incumbents to shift the balance of power to the House Democrats. The real question was whether the Republican Party would retain its margin or increase it.

The Senate situation was entirely different, because the Democratic Party was defending twenty-one incumbents compared to only fifteen for the Republican Party. And many of the incumbent Democrats were running for reelection in GOP-leaning states.

Issue Complications, 2013–2014

As the economic recovery accelerated in 2013–2014, one could reasonably expect that President Obama and the Democratic Party would reap some political benefit from the declining rate of unemployment, the rise in consumer confidence, the surge in car and home sales, and the rising stock market. But it simply did not work out that way, and in fact this period proved to be highly unproductive for the Obama White House and their allies in Congress.

Part of the problem was that gains in the "jobs-to-people" ratio were much more anemic than the substantial declines in the official rate of unemployment, suggesting that the job-producing performance of the economy was damaged. Another problem was that the gains in employment and earnings in 2013–2014 were not particularly impressive for key subgroups in Obama's base: women, young people, blacks, and households with incomes less than thirty thousand dollars per year.[73] Wages for the new jobs in the "Obama economy" were also reported to be far less than wages for the jobs that were destroyed by the Great Recession, and thus income growth in 2013–2014 was slight. Overall, while the economy was recovering, it was not generating much enthusiasm for Obama or the Democrats in Congress.

As the Obama White House sought to focus on the many positives about the recovery and the president's ambitious second-term agenda, public attention was diverted to a series of distracting issues that complicated the picture. Since most of these issues were not easy to resolve, they created additional uncertainty about Obama's effectiveness and ample raw material for partisan attacks by congressional Republicans.

One of the nagging old issues was the proposed north-south Keystone pipeline, which was intended to transport oil from the Canadian tar sands in Alberta to refineries in the Gulf of Mexico. Since the United States was rapidly consuming less Canadian oil (due to advances in US oil production), the Canadians planned to use the pipeline to exploit lucrative export markets in Europe and Asia. Oil producers in the Bakken region of North Dakota would also use the pipeline. For refiners in Louisiana and Texas, the Keystone pipeline promised significant new business.

Obama was cross-pressured by business interests and the Canadian government on one side and organized environmentalists (who saw development of the tar sands as a source of environmental pollution) on the other side. Despite numerous studies of the Keystone issue during Obama's first term, the issue was left unresolved until his second term. Democratic senator Mary Landrieu of Louisiana was up for reelection in November 2014, and the president's handling of the Keystone issue did not help her with her constituents. By refusing to use his executive power to approve or disapprove the pipeline, Obama opened up the issue for a bipartisan group of pro-pipeline members in Congress.

The House easily passed bills calling for approval of the pipeline, but, consistent with Obama's request, Senate majority leader Harry Reid blocked a vote on the issue in the Senate during 2013 and 2014. The Obama-Reid position further undermined Landrieu, who was challenged for reelection by Republican congressman Bill Cassidy.

Another disturbing issue was the inability of the US Veterans Administration to efficiently process requests for medical and other forms of assistance by the thousands of returning veterans from Iraq and Afghanistan. The public did not blame President Obama personally for the poor quality of the VA's public administration, but distressing stories about the VA's incompetence reinforced cynicism about the federal government and drew media attention away from the improving economy and Obama's second-term agenda.

One of the new issues that the Obama administration confronted was the emergence of the deadly Ebola virus in the United States, the first case being reported in September 2014 and a total of four cases by December 2014. Within a few months of the onset of press coverage, 98 percent of Americans had heard or read about the frightening virus, and there was much debate as to whether the federal government was responding properly to the potential emerging crisis.[74] Some critics argued that the Obama administration should have promptly instituted a travel ban from areas (e.g., regions of Africa) where the viral disease was widespread. Backed by public health experts, the president decided against a ban, but the controversy erupted immediately prior to the 2014 midterm elections.

Normally, international issues are not central to elections, but in 2014 they were significant. Events abroad raised unusually difficult challenges for Obama, creating situations that did not buttress his image as an influential or effective leader.[75] Russia's leader Vladimir Putin deftly sidestepped accountability for the Malaysian airliner that was shot down by Russia-supplied forces and later ignored the West as he persistently advanced Russian interests in the conflict with the Ukraine and the European Union. Numerous questions were raised about the Bowe Bergdahl prisoner swap engineered by the Obama administration. A bloody new war broke out in Gaza between Israel and Hamas. And the Middle East extremist group ISIS conquered a large swath of Iraq, forcing a reluctant Obama to resort to air strikes. The foreign policy challenges were quite difficult to resolve and thus planted more seeds of doubt about the competence of the Obama administration.[76]

Surveys also revealed that the public was increasingly concerned about the "gridlock" in Washington, DC. Respondents were asked whether they prefer an elected official who compromises in order to gain consensus or sticks to his or her positions. A 2010 survey showed that 50 percent preferred compromise; 42 percent favored firmness. By 2014 sentiments shifted toward compromise, 57–34 percent. After the big economic issues, respondents saw breaking political gridlock as the second most important issue facing the country. While respondents tended to blame congressional Republicans more than Democrats for gridlock, they did not give Obama high marks as an agent of effective compromise and consensus building.[77]

Failure of Second-Term Legislative Agenda

President Obama started his second term with a job approval rating of 52 percent, much lower than where he started his first term (close to 70 percent) and without the significant bump that previous reelected presidents had experienced.[78] Nonetheless, Obama's standing seemed strong enough to be respected among congressional Democrats and Republicans from competitive districts and states.

Cashing in on an early concession from House Speaker John Boehner, Obama worked the Congress in late 2012 to accomplish repeal of the Bush tax cuts for high-income households (see chapter 4). He then planned to pursue a much bigger agenda: reform of federal immigration law and, somewhat quietly, a grand fiscal deal with Boehner that covered taxes and entitlement programs such as Medicare.

On December 14, 2012, Obama reordered his priorities in the wake of the shooting of twenty children and six school officials at Sandy Hook Elementary School in Newtown, Connecticut. The president placed gun control above his other legislative initiatives, a decision that was clearly opportunistic, as he had given little priority to gun control during his first term and chose not to elevate the issue as a priority in his 2012 reelection campaign.

Capitalizing on the public outcry, Obama requested that Congress enact universal background checks, limits on high-capacity ammunition, an assault-weapons ban, and more severe penalties for people who buy guns and then sell them illegally on the black market. He coupled his legislative request with several months of campaign-style promotion of gun control, including thirteen speeches around the country, multiple interviews with reporters on the issue, and personal calls to key Republican and Democratic senators.[79] He also deployed the resources of Organizing for America to stress the urgency of gun control in America.[80] He was joined by the complementary advocacy efforts of former Republican mayor of New York Michael Bloomberg.

But the president's efforts were unsuccessful, again illustrating the limitations of a "bully pulpit" strategy of lawmaking. Obama's initiative ran into the teeth of one of the better organized and tenacious interest groups in American politics: the National Rifle Association (NRA). The NRA mobilized phone calls, e-mails, and letters to members of Congress and highlighted that roll-call votes on this issue would be scored by the NRA in its official (publicized) ratings of legislators. Republican senator Charles Grassley of Iowa echoed a key argument of pro-gun groups: criminals don't cooperate with background checks.

A bipartisan proposal to expand background checks on gun purchasers was advanced by Republican Pat Toomey and Democrat Joe Manchin, both respected pro-gun conservatives. The measure appeared to have the best chance of passage but ultimately fell five votes short (55–45) of the required sixty votes. Manchin believed that the measure's chances of passage vanished when the NRA announced that it would "score the vote."[81]

Four Republican senators (Toomey, John McCain, Susan Collins, and Mark Steven Kirk) voted in favor of the expanded background checks, but an equal number of Senate Democrats voted against it (Mark Begich, Mark Pryor, Max Baucus, and Heidi Heitkamp). Three of the defecting Democrats were up for reelection in 2014.

Obama's gun-control initiative died in the Senate when none of his requested reforms could reach the required sixty-vote threshold.[82] His proposal was never taken up in the House, where passage would have been even more difficult, so he was forced to resort to a few "small ball" executive actions (e.g., sharing of information on firearm violence among federal agencies).[83] Thus, Obama's first legislative initiative in his second term was a stark failure, an outcome that "was predictable based on the issue's history and the ideological polarization on Capitol Hill." Making things worse, the setback bolstered a second-term narrative that questioned Obama's effectiveness as a domestic policy maker.[84]

Moreover, the failure of gun control frustrated Obama's base and energized his partisan opponents. Some critics argue that the entire effort squandered political capital that Obama should have invested on immigration reform, the legislative priority that he had some electoral mandate to pursue, since it was highlighted in his 2012 campaign against Romney.[85] With hindsight, some have suggested that the gun-control initiative may have moved better in the Senate without White House priority, since Obama's visibility on the issue energized the opposition and helped the NRA bolster its support.[86]

Obama's standing was rejuvenated to some extent later in 2013 when he forced House Republicans to capitulate on the controversial sixteen-day government shutdown. Before he could capitalize on the improved standing, the botched rollout of the Affordable Care Act sent his job approval ratings to new lows.[87] At roughly the same time, the Obama administration was challenged by the burgeoning civil war in Syria, and the president's response was widely criticized as indecisive.[88]

Slumping Job Approval Rating

Overall, 2013 proved to be an unproductive and demoralizing year for President Obama, as nothing he pledged to do with Congress in 2013 was actually accomplished.[89] His job approval ratings slipped into the low forties. In fact, Obama started his sixth year in office with a job approval rating lower than all other presidents (except George W. Bush) since modern polling began in the 1930s.[90]

Among the key group of self-described independents, Obama's job approval was slumping into the range of 30–40 percent.[91] (Although he had defeated McCain among independents in 2008, he lost independents to Romney by a 45–50 percent margin.[92]) Nor was Obama retaining the confidence of the Millennial generation. His job approval rating among eighteen-to-thirty-four-year olds declined from 70 percent in early 2009 to 49 percent in early 2014.[93]

The sharp decline in Obama's ratings in 2013 is partly attributable to lingering economic insecurities (even though the economic recovery was continuing), but the botched rollout of the ACA was also a significant contributor. Obama had also set expectations for legislative progress on an agenda that did not move (i.e., gun control, immigration reform, and a grand fiscal deal).

President Obama's standing slid further in 2014, prior to the November 2014 general election. His overall job approval rating was recorded at 41 percent in both April and June 2014, but the more ominous sign was the asymmetric distribution of intense feelings: of those who disapproved of Obama's performance, 52 percent did so "strongly"; among those who approved, only 23 percent did so "strongly."[94] The year 2014 was a particularly bad one for Obama in foreign policy, where his job approval rating slipped to 37 percent that June. Much was written about his inability to control unsettling events around the world.[95]

The growing disapproval of Obama in 2013–2014 was not rooted in public disagreement with the themes he was emphasizing in his public appearances: job creation through new spending on infrastructure, early childhood education, refinancing student loans, a higher minimum wage, and fair pay for women. Those themes brought a heightened degree of unity between Obama and the Senate Democrats who were up for reelection in 2014. And the public continued to side with Obama on many domestic issues: education, health care, immigration, and the environment.[96] Nor was Obama's problem any public preference for the performance of the two parties in Congress: the House GOP leadership and Senate Democratic leadership were both sporting disapproval ratings in the range of 70–80 percent.[97]

Many Americans were nuanced in their assessment of Obama. He was considered "compassionate" (58 percent) and a good communicator (68 percent). The public was evenly divided on his "competence," but 54 percent no longer felt that Obama "is able to lead the country and get the job done." About 41 percent of respondents felt in June 2014 that his performance was getting worse; only 15 percent felt it was getting better. On a key indicator about the president's ability to be effective (whether Obama is "able to get things done"), his approval rating declined from 57 percent in January 2013 to 43 percent in early 2014, and it never rebounded prior to the November 2014 election.[98]

Early Warning from Tampa, Florida

The Thirteenth Congressional District of Florida encompasses large swaths of St. Petersburg, Tampa, and Clearwater. It is a competitive district that Obama won narrowly in both 2008 and 2012.[99] When forty-year Republican incumbent C. W. Bill Young died in office in October 2013, a special election was scheduled for March 2014 to replace him. The winner of the election would serve for several months and again face voters in the November 2014 midterm election. For the national Democratic Party, Florida's Thirteenth District looked like a promising pickup opportunity.

A credible Democratic candidate, Alex Sink of Clearwater, faced no primary opposition and rapidly built a large war chest for the special contest. She was formerly Florida's chief financial officer and had widespread name recognition from her unsuccessful 2010 campaign for governor against Republican

Rick Scott. In that campaign Sink defeated Scott in the Florida Thirteenth District, even though she lost statewide.

State representative David Jolly won a competitive Republican primary to take on Sink. He was untested as a general election candidate, having served only as a Washington lobbyist and previously as a staffer to Congressman Young. His campaign emerged from the primary broke and Jolly was far behind Sink in name recognition. The national Republican Party backed Jolly but was concerned that his campaign seemed disorganized.[100]

The partisan composition of the district was 37 percent GOP, 35 percent Democratic, and 24 percent independent. Over $11 million was spent on the race, almost $9 million from outside groups. Sink had a modest financial advantage in the race. Bill Clinton and Joe Biden campaigned for Sink; Jeb Bush and Rand Paul for Jolly.[101] Due to the special nature of the election (with nothing else important on the ballot), turnout was expected to be relatively low.

Jolly portrayed himself as a strong conservative, emphasizing anti-immigration themes and criticism of Obama. Sink portrayed herself as a problem solver who could work across party lines. The Jolly campaign spent millions of dollars on television advertisements with a simple message: Sink supports Obamacare and will be another vote for Obama.[102] Sink tried the response recommended by the Democratic National Committee: the Affordable Care Act should be repaired rather than repealed. When the votes were counted, Sink was defeated 48.4 percent to 46.5 percent. She was urged to run again in November against Jolly, but after a period of deliberation she declined. Jolly ultimately was reelected against a weaker opponent.

In summary, Alex Sink was a solid, well-known, and well-financed candidate against a virtual unknown with no campaign experience. The district was evenly balanced. One interpretation of Jolly's victory is that Obama and the Affordable Care Act created a very difficult environment for Sink. It was an early signal of what would happen in November 2014 to more Democratic candidates.[103]

Tea Party versus the Chamber

Given Obama's difficulties in 2013 and early 2014, the midterm election in November was shaping up as an enticing opportunity for the GOP. With Boehner's House majority looking fairly secure, the national Republican Party set its sights on control of the Senate.

Before the primaries in 2014, an internal GOP conflict surfaced over whether to run candidates favored by the Tea Party or stick with candidates favored by traditional leaders of the GOP.[104] Business leaders and national leaders of the Republican Party were convinced that the party had missed an opportunity to seize control of the Senate in 2012 by nominating several Senate candidates who were too conservative to win a general election or were too inexperienced to defeat an entrenched Democratic incumbent.

Business leaders were also irritated that Tea Party conservatives ignored their warnings that closing the government in the fall of 2013 (and risking financial default) would hurt Boehner, the Republican Party, and the Tea Party.[105] They pointed out that the shutdown ultimately accomplished nothing for conservatives.

The Tea Party and many conservative House Republicans entertained doubts about Speaker John Boehner, seeing him as a compromiser rather than a principled conservative. Representative Thomas Massie of Kentucky, for example, often voted against Boehner-led priorities and spearheaded an unsuccessful coup of Boehner as Speaker. Massie was connected to a group of a dozen or so devout House conservatives who were not reluctant to use their voting power as a bloc to deny Boehner legislative control. The group effectively forced Boehner to seek Democratic votes for disaster relief after Superstorm Sandy, for the Violence Against Women Act, and for extension of the Bush tax cuts for people making less than four hundred thousand dollars a year.[106]

Tea Party activists and their allies in Congress were suspicious of business groups. Big business advocated positions that the activists found offensive (e.g., liberalization of immigration law, increased highway spending, and reauthorization of the Export-Import Bank).[107] Business groups also spread their campaign contributions around to Democratic members of the House and Senate as well as to Republicans.[108] On the other hand, the major national business groups—the US Chamber of Commerce and the National Federation of Independent Businesses—stood firmly behind Boehner. They trusted and related to him, in part because he was once president of a small plastics company in Ohio. In 1990 Boehner was instrumental in helping the business community craft a consensus against the Clinton health plan. Business leaders saw him as reasonable and practical.

By 2013–2014 the Tea Party had suffered some image blows, including widespread disapproval of the government shutdown in the fall of 2013. The share of the public that was sympathetic with the Tea Party was declining and the rate of participation in Tea Party rallies and protests was down. Nonetheless, core membership in the national Tea Party groups remained high (over five hundred thousand), with 42 percent of overall membership in the Southern states. Many more Americans were sympathetic with the positions of the Tea Party, especially as they related to illegal immigration and the high rate of federal spending.[109]

The National Republican Senatorial Committee collaborated with the US Chamber of Commerce to identify, recruit, and support the most promising possible candidates for Senate races. In the Republican primaries, potential Senate candidates from the more conservative wing of the GOP were bypassed or defeated in Georgia, Iowa, Kentucky, North Carolina, Oklahoma, and Oregon.

The Tea Party and allied groups (e.g., FreedomWorks for America, Senate Conservatives Fund, Tea Party Patriots Citizens Fund, and Club for Growth) made a determined, multimillion-dollar effort to oust Senator Thad Cochran, the incumbent establishment Republican from Mississippi. The US Chamber of Commerce countered with $455,910 on behalf of Cochran. Cochran also made effective overtures to the African American community in advance of the state's open primary. The successful defense of Cochran was a big victory for the national GOP, and he went on to win reelection without difficulty.[110]

While the GOP was recruiting effective candidates, the independent super PACs (political action committees that work on issues independently of campaigns), led by Americans for Prosperity, made a $20+ million investment in negative advertisements to expose the voting records of vulnerable Senate Democrats.[111] The focus of the advertisements was the Affordable Care Act, and the key targets were Kay Hagan, Mark Pryor, Mary Landrieu, and Mark Begich.[112] It was well known that the 2010 defeat of conservative Democratic senator Blanche Lincoln was related in no small measure to her vote for the Affordable Care Act.[113] To the dismay of the 2014 incumbents, most of the attack advertisements were left unanswered for months, as the big sources of funding for Democratic candidates were held back until closer to the November election.[114]

Determining what stance to take on the ACA was a dilemma for Democratic candidates. In 2012–2013 few Democratic candidates invested money in political advertisements that mentioned the ACA. In 2014, however, some campaigns shifted from a defensive to an offensive posture. In the spring of

2014, six competitive races for Senate and governor (e.g., North Carolina and Michigan) included pro-ACA television commercials. The focus of the ads was the positive aspects of the ACA: coverage for preexisting conditions, preventive care benefits, and the ban on charging women more for health insurance. The advertisements either supported a pro-ACA member or attacked a member of Congress for opposing the ACA.[115] For the Democratic Party the pro-ACA messages were an encouraging change of pace from the barrage of negative ACA messages from the GOP.

Harry Reid's Dilemma

Senate majority leader Harry Reid was in a difficult position in 2013–2014. He sought to protect President Obama's first-term accomplishments (e.g., the Affordable Care Act) and move his second-term agenda through the Senate. He also sought to protect his 55–45 Senate majority by avoiding any roll-call votes that might be used by the GOP against vulnerable Democratic senators who were up for reelection in November 2014.[116]

During his first term Obama enjoyed a higher degree of roll-call voting support from Democrats in Congress than any president since World War II. The rate of Democratic defection from Obama's agenda increased from 10 percent in 2009 to 23 percent in 2012 but, with Obama's job approval rating slipping in 2013–2014, Reid faced the potential of a much higher defection rate if he did not exercise careful control over which measures made it to the floor for a vote.[117]

Starting in 2012–2013 Reid refined the rules for floor consideration so that only a limited number of amendments were permitted for consideration and he could influence which amendments would be considered. Basically Reid retained for himself the right to offer the first set of amendments, which could potentially consume all of the time available for amendments.[118] In this way Reid exercised the power to block amendments that he did not want debated on the Senate floor.[119] Consequently, the number of Republican-sponsored amendments that were considered declined from 218 in 2007 (Reid's first year as majority leader) to 67 in 2013 (including only 4 from July to December 2013).[120]

Since Obama possessed a potent veto power, there was not much risk that the Senate and House would be able to enact measures into law against Obama's will. Whether blocking the votes on these issues was good for vulnerable Senate Democrats in 2014 is questionable, since it likely would have been good for some of those senators to go on record against President Obama.[121] Given how politically "poisonous" Obama was for Democratic Senate candidates, many of them were looking for opportunities to distance themselves from the president.[122] Reid decided against creating those opportunities and instead sought to minimize the number of roll-call votes and promote party unity.

Reid blocked votes on a variety of issues where a bipartisan group of senators might have embarrassed the Obama administration. Those issues included a binding measure to approve the Keystone pipeline, a measure to delay the EPA's new regulations to limit carbon dioxide pollution, and a measure to expedite approval of export terminals for natural gas. Thus, Senate Democrats went into the November election without much opportunity to separate themselves from the Obama administration.

Obama on the 2014 Campaign Trail

Although Obama was unpopular, he proved again in 2014 that he was an effective fund-raiser for the Democrats. He led dozens of fund-raisers in 2013–2014, most of them in New York or California. By August 2014 he was on track to surpass all recent presidents in midterm fund-raising events except for Bill Clinton in 1998.[123] In 2014 Obama was even more visible at fund-raisers but also as invisible as possible in most races where Democratic candidates for Senate were on the ropes. He was headlined in no public campaign events in the 2014 election cycle, and he appeared for only a few candidates where the race was not in question.[124]

The Democratic plan was to use this fund-raising not only to support vulnerable candidates but also to mobilize the Democratic base to register and vote. Polls in 2014 showed that Democratic candidates performed better among all registered voters than among "likely" voters.[125] Turnout was a weakness for the Democrats in midterm elections, and the Senate Democratic Campaign Committee was determined to compensate for the weakness.[126] Without better outreach, midterm voters would be disproportionately Republican in orientation (i.e., older, white, male).[127] Consequently, the budget for outreach efforts to enhance turnout was set at $60 million in 2014, up from $7 million in 2010.

An awkward problem for the national Democratic Party was that House Speaker Nancy Pelosi's fund-raising machine for House Democrats was also highly effective, drawing large sums of donations to House races. Unfortunately, it did not appear that more money for House races would do much good for the Democratic Party, since few seats were in play. It was control of the Senate that was at stake, and funds donated for the House and Senate are not fungible.[128]

On television the GOP-sponsored advertisements in Senate races were most likely to mention Obama or the Affordable Care Act as key issues. In this way the GOP sought to nationalize the election. The Democratic-sponsored advertisements were divided equally between defense of the Affordable Care Act and the recent progress in creating jobs and reducing unemployment.[129] One point is apparent from the advertisements: Obama and the Affordable Care Act remained big issues in the 2014 midterm election as they were in 2010.

The 2014 Election Results

The composition of 2014 voters followed a familiar pattern: disproportionally fewer youth and minority voters.[130] In the battleground states where the fate of the Senate was determined, the Democratic Party did reduce the anticipated decline in turnout among its traditional voter pool.[131] When all was said and done, however, exit polls revealed that the distribution of voters for Republican House candidates in 2014 was similar to the 2010 distribution: in 2014: 60 percent white, 25 percent Hispanic, 10 percent black; 5 percent other; in 2010: 60 percent white, 28 percent Hispanic; 9 percent black; 3 percent other.[132] Not surprisingly, 2014 again proved to be a dazzling year for the Republican Party.[133]

In the House the Republicans began with a 234–201 majority. They increased that majority to 247–188, the party's largest Republican majority in almost a century. In the Senate the Democratic Party began with a 55–45 majority. The Republicans accomplished a net gain of nine seats, seizing a 54–46 majority starting January 2015.

Last-Ditch Effort to Save Landrieu

The Louisiana race for Senate was not resolved in November, because multiple candidates were on the ballot. Incumbent senator Mary Landrieu, although she ran first in the field, could not muster 50 percent of the vote. A special runoff election was scheduled for December to resolve the competition between the two largest vote getters: Senator Landrieu (seeking a fourth term) and Republican congressman Bill Cassidy.

Prior to the November election, Senate majority leader Harry Reid blocked a roll-call vote on the Keystone pipeline, even though such a vote might have allowed Landrieu to create some distance between her image and that of President Obama. Polls showed that 73 percent of white voters in Louisiana "strongly disapproved" of Obama, and white voters were expected to dominate the midterm contest in the state.[134] Recognizing that Landrieu was on the ropes, Reid allowed a Keystone vote to be scheduled on the Senate floor before the runoff election in Louisiana.

The House easily passed a measure, authored by Cassidy, approving the Keystone project. In the Senate, however, Landrieu worked hard to find the sixty votes necessary to overcome a filibuster threat. She came up one vote short, 59–41, and her constituents voted in the runoff knowing that she was unable to deliver the Keystone pipeline.[135] She lost the runoff 56–44 percent, handing the GOP their ninth pickup in the Senate.

RAMIFICATIONS OF THE MIDTERM MASSACRES

Once the GOP majority took control of the Senate in January, they made the Keystone pipelines their first item of business, despite a veto threat from President Obama. After open debate on forty-one amendments, the Senate voted 62–36 to approve the Keystone pipeline, a strong majority but five votes short of the sixty-seven that would be required to override an Obama veto. Joining a unanimous Republican caucus were nine Democratic crossovers: Michael Bennett, Tom Carper, Bob Casey, Joe Donnelly, Heidi Heitkamp, Joe Manchin, Claire McCaskill, Jon Tester, and Mark Warner.[136]

In summary, once the GOP seized a majority in the Senate in 2014, President Obama was forced for the first time to deal with a Republican majority in both chambers of the Congress. The Keystone saga, however, shows that Obama retained significant negative power through the veto.

For President Obama the most damaging aspect of the two midterm elections was the 2010 loss of a Democratic majority in the House of Representatives. From the moment that Republican John Boehner became Speaker of the House, Obama's aspirations for progressive policy change through legislation were doomed.

If the Speaker of the House does not wish to consider the legislative requests of the president, the House rules enable the Speaker to block such consideration (barring highly unusual circumstances) through the Rules Committee. And Speaker Boehner incurred little political risk from blocking Obama's agenda, especially given the rapid rise of the Tea Party's influence in the Republican Party.

Perhaps the next most important ramification of the midterm massacres was the collateral losses that the Democratic Party experienced in races for governor and state legislature. In 2010 alone the Democrats lost a net 6 governorships (11 losses, 5 wins) and a total of 725 state legislative seats around the nation. As a result, the GOP picked up majorities in 23 legislative chambers, the largest state-level gains for the Republican Party since 1966.[137] The GOP made additional progress at the state level in 2014.[138]

Flowing from the state-level successes in 2010 was a GOP that put itself into a commanding position to control the redistricting process in many states. Constitutionally, districts are required to be redrawn every ten years, and the GOP influenced the redrawing of many district lines prior to the 2012 election. The result was a sharp decline in the number of competitive House seats and an inherent advantage for the GOP until the next redistricting begins after the 2020 elections. Some analysts believe that the Democratic Party has little prospect of regaining a majority in the House of Representatives before 2022.[139] If a Democrat wins the White House again in November 2016, it seems likely that a Republican majority in the House will be in place to frustrate the new president's legislative ambitions.

The Democratic loss of the Senate majority in 2014 is of less consequence than it may seem at first blush. For Obama there are few policy reforms that he has been able to enact into law with fifty-five Democrats in the Senate that he cannot enact with forty-six Democratic seats. The reason is that sixty votes are typically required in the Senate. Moreover, Obama lacks a sympathetic House majority, which means that the switch of the Senate majority is of very limited policy significance.

A Republican majority in the Senate can do serious harm to President Obama's aspirations if he is given one or more additional opportunities to nominate Supreme Court justices before his term expires in January 2017. It is much easier for conservatives in the Senate to defeat a judicial nomination with fifty-four Republicans than with forty-six Republicans. Still, it takes only forty votes in the Senate to defeat a Supreme Court nomination with a filibuster threat.

The loss of the Senate majority in 2014 may also be of less long-term significance than the loss of the House majority in 2010, because the structure of the Senate elections in 2016 creates a distinct possibility that the Democrats could retake the Senate majority in January 2017. The four-seat Senate cushion that the Republican Party won in 2014 diminishes the likelihood that the Democrats will be able to win enough seats in the November 2016 elections to recapture the Senate majority, but a Democratic House majority seems much less likely than a Democratic Senate majority.

Without question, the midterm massacres were devastating to President Obama and the Democratic Party. And Obama's policy agenda and low job approval ratings contributed to the massacres. In the final chapter, the insights from chapters 3 through 9 are combined into a refined version of the Obama presidency that would have curtailed the massacres of congressional Democrats in 2010 and 2014 that have been analyzed in this chapter.

11

A COUNTERFACTUAL
OBAMA PRESIDENCY

President Barack Obama built a significant record of accomplishment in domestic affairs, but, as I demonstrated in chapter 10, his policies and strategies were harmful to the electoral fortunes of the Democratic Party.[1] One is tempted to evaluate the Obama record as a big trade-off, which requires weighing the value of the large policy accomplishments against the large losses that the Democratic Party experienced in 2010 and 2014. The major finding of this book is that the big trade-off issue does not need to be resolved. With more creative and astute leadership, Obama could have lessened the big trade-off.

Chapters 3 through 9 revealed that not all of that harm to the Democratic Party was necessary to accomplish Obama's ambitious agenda. Moreover, with a more politically savvy agenda, and with greater care in choices about use of executive and legislative efforts, Obama could have accomplished even more of his agenda than he did. Thus, in this concluding chapter, I present a refined version of the Obama presidency—a "counterfactual presidency"—that might have achieved *more* of Obama's policy agenda with *less* damage to the Democratic Party.[2]

The "counterfactual" presidency is constructed by appealing to the prescriptive propositions (theory) that I posited in chapter 2. Briefly, the counterfactuals must hold constant the fundamentals that Obama faced, but it is assumed that he could have refined his policy agenda or made different decisions on executive versus legislative action, or he could have chosen different sequences or schedules for policy initiatives. Since the fate of incumbent Democrats in Congress is a critical parameter in the analysis, I also lean heavily on the evaluation in chapter 10 of Obama's two damaging midterm elections.

I begin the present chapter with the good news: the key accomplishments in Obama's domestic record. Then I apply the prescriptive propositions to Obama's track record in domestic affairs, drawing on the issue-specific case studies presented in chapters 3 through 9. Together, the counterfactuals help formulate a coherent view of a refined Obama presidency. The chapter concludes with some general lessons for future presidents based on the Obama experience, assuming that the partisan polarization faced by Clinton, George W. Bush, and Obama persists for many years in the future.

ECONOMIC POLICY

Obama began his presidency with the United States facing its worst economic crisis since the onset of the Great Depression. Without question, improving the US economy was the key issue facing the country throughout his presidency. That was the view expressed by the American people in survey after survey leading up to the 2008, 2010, 2012, and 2014 national elections.[3]

Chapters 3 and 4 revealed that Obama was an activist in economic policy and he often had his way. The accomplishments are concentrated in 2009–2010, but several of them occurred later in his presidency. Arguably his most significant decision—though not particularly memorable outside of Washington and Wall Street—was whether to support the monetary policies of Ben Bernanke or to chart a different direction for the Federal Reserve Board at the end of Bernanke's first term (late 2009). President Obama decided to pursue continuity (easy money, low interest rates, and more liquidity in the financial sector) by reappointing Bernanke, even though he originally had been a Bush appointee and his policies were being questioned. Obama followed through with enough White House support for the controversial renomination to overcome growing opposition from both populist progressives and conservatives in the Senate.

Like his early support of TARP, Obama's support of Bernanke's Senate confirmation as chairman of the Fed underscores that the president was not timid about retaining Bush-era initiatives—even unpopular ones—when he regarded them as the best course.[4] It is too early to write definitive books about economic history, but there is a good chance that both Bernanke, the economic policy maker, and TARP, the rescue package for Wall Street, will be viewed favorably in the long run, since they may have helped prevent the Great Recession (December 2007–June 2009) from becoming a repeat of the Great Depression.[5] A case may also be made that Obama's policies to protect home owners from default ("Main Street") were not nearly as extensive as the policies aimed at protecting financial institutions ("Wall Street").

Obama also charted new ground in fiscal policy, specifically fiscal stimuli for a depressed economy plagued by low consumer demand for goods and services. In 2009 he persuaded Congress to enact a $787 billion package of spending and tax relief. It was accomplished primarily with Democratic votes, but Obama captured just enough Republican support in the Senate to overcome a filibuster threat. He sensed that he needed to act quickly, and he and the Democratic Congress did so. Obama signed the Recovery Act in March 2009.

In late 2010 President Obama, then on the defensive politically, worked with Republicans in the House to deliver an even larger $858 billion stimulus, this time with a strong emphasis on tax relief as well as a thirteen-month extension in unemployment benefits for the long-term unemployed. Thus, Obama ultimately collaborated with Congress on a total of $1.6 trillion in fiscal stimuli that were timed to coincide with the early stages of a fragile economic recovery.

In 2011–2012 Obama was unsuccessful in persuading Congress to enact a $447 billion "jobs bill," although widespread Republican opposition to the package gave the president and his fellow Democrats some useful talking points going into the 2012 reelection campaign. That may have been the intended use of the jobs bill from the outset.[6] If so, it may have been a strategic success even if not a legislative one.

From the perspective of presidential studies, Obama's handling of the depressed auto industry was one of his most accomplished areas of economic policy. The bailouts of General Motors Corporation (GM) and Chrysler were partly a continuation of Bush's policy, but they were much more than that. And while these actions were unpopular at the outset, the revived companies and their supply chains proved to be an asset for Obama in Ohio and Michigan when he battled Mitt Romney for reelection in 2012.

The rebirths of GM and Chrysler flowed from remarkably aggressive uses of executive power. Obama and his task force ultimately fired the CEO of GM, helped arrange a new owner (Fiat) for Chrysler, put the welfare of some employees ahead of preferred creditors, reorganized the companies—including their product mixes—prior to formal bankruptcy, secured the future of their suppliers and car loan companies with TARP funds, set in motion a regulatory path to fifty-mile-per-gallon vehicles by 2025, and preserved the United Auto Workers of America (UAW) as a potent economic and political force in American society. The vast majority of the rescue operation was undertaken without legislation (Cash for Clunkers being a notable but minor exception). The Treasury Department ultimately sold its shares of both companies at a modest loss, but the overall narrative proved to be more positive than negative for Obama and congressional Democrats.

Obama's handling of the GM and Chrysler bankruptcies has been heavily criticized by advocates of limited government.[7] It was nonetheless a clear success story in economic policy in that the president accomplished what he set out to do, even though it is possible that GM or Chrysler-Fiat could fold during a future downturn. This innovative story of Obama's auto task force belongs in any serious textbook of American politics where creative use of executive power is covered.

In 2011–2012 President Obama was also quite agile in moving to the center on economic policy prior to his reelection. He began with another stimulus, the $858 billion package that, in contradiction to his 2008 campaign pledge, extended the Bush tax cuts for high earners until after the 2012 election. He deployed OMB on a mission to streamline overly burdensome business regulations while publicly delaying the EPA's costly new ozone standard. And he effectively deployed his new Presidential Commission on Jobs and Competitiveness. The result was the Jumpstart Our Business Startups (JOBS) Act, which passed the Congress in 2012 with strong bipartisan support and offered some regulatory relief to the financial industry. By the time he confronted Romney in the fall campaign of 2012, Obama had accomplished several pro-business initiatives, which helped address a vulnerability he had relative to Romney.

An important facet of the US economic recovery from 2009 to 2016 was the rapid expansion of US oil and gas production and the unexpected collapse of the price of world oil. Consumers enjoyed tangible benefits from the lower world oil price. After rising rapidly from under $1.50 per gallon in 1990 to almost $3.50 per gallon in 2007–2008, the average national price of gasoline actually declined for several years during the Obama administration and was below $2.00 per gallon at the end of 2015.[8]

The drop in the world oil price was partly related to a slowdown in the growth of the Chinese economy and a depressed European economy. It also reflected Saudi Arabia's decision to maintain current levels of oil production despite depressed levels of global demand. On the other hand, the rapid growth of oil and gas production in the United States was also part of the explanation as technological innovation spurred the "shale revolution."[9] Most forecasters are not predicting a return to $100 per barrel oil any time in the foreseeable future.

Chapter 8 revealed how President Obama, using soft executive power, provided a national political environment in which large investments in unconventional production methods were encouraged. Several national environmental groups were seeking a moratorium or prohibition on shale gas production, but their positions, so far to the left of the Obama administration, were not plausible in Washington, DC. The surge in US oil and gas production in the Obama years may have long-lasting economic and geopolitical benefits for the United States. Some fear that environmental regulations late in the Obama presidency could hurt this accomplishment but, if done wisely, those regulations might help promote long-term public acceptance of unconventional methods and help natural gas be seen as compatible with responsible US climate policy. Indeed, one can argue that Obama should have been more aggressive about controlling greenhouse gas emissions from the oil and gas sector, thereby reducing a possible contradiction between his climate and energy policies.

As Obama's second term winds down, there are some notable positives in US economic performance. The official rate of unemployment has declined dramatically from a peak of 10.6 percent in January 2010 to less than 5.1 percent in September 2015. The stock market has surged past its 2007 high point, with the Dow Jones average hovering near record levels in the vicinity of eighteen thousand. Car sales are at all-time highs in 2014–2015, and even the depressed housing industry is beginning to show signs of life as prices of homes are on the rise again. The annual rates of inflation and interest remain low, and the

Federal Reserve Board is starting to taper the stimulus that dominated monetary policy since the 2007 crash. The annual federal deficit in fiscal year 2015 is estimated at $439 billion, or 2.5 percent of GDP, below the fifty-year average for the United States.[10] Levels of consumer and business optimism are at higher levels in 2014–2015 than at any time since January 2008.[11]

Despite the many positive signals, the US economy has some severe weaknesses, and commentators on both the left and right have pointed these out.[12] The rate of GDP growth was very sluggish from 2010 to 2015. It was stronger in the second half of 2014, despite a slowdown in Asia's growth and a depressed European economy, but the economy's performance in 2015 was disappointing (an actual decline of GDP in the first quarter).[13] The persistent weak spots in the US economy are the slow growth in GDP, little growth in the jobs-to-people ratio (perhaps the best indicator of the job-producing proficiency of the economy), a lack of significant growth in median household income, and little progress against poverty.[14]

President Obama did not speak much about poverty in America during his presidency,[15] but his safety-net policies were remarkably effective at protecting low-income Americans against an incredibly troubling period in America's economic history. What Obama was not able to do—indeed did not even try to do—is to propose a suite of antipoverty policies that might put America on a path to reducing poverty dramatically. Obama did spend much of his second term talking about inequality, with a mixed record of accomplishment. He ultimately won removal of most of the Bush tax cuts for high earners but did not persuade Congress to raise the federal minimum wage.

Conservative economists have a variety of plausible criticisms of Obama's economic policies and suggestions of alternative policies that might have triggered a faster, more robust recovery.[16] Liberal critics have their own plausible prescriptions.[17] For politicians seeking consensus guidance, the economics profession did not offer much. Truth be told, Obama may have faced more of a shortage of economic science than political science, as the Obama years exposed many shortcomings in the knowledge base of the economics profession.[18]

In my view, Obama's major mistake in economic policy was the design of the 2009 stimulus, with its heavy emphasis on public spending and subsidies for specific businesses and technologies. A stimulus that was more heavily weighted toward tax relief for the bottom quartiles of the income distribution might have worked out better for Obama, both politically and economically.[19]

Obama's decision to make deficit control an administration priority was also unwise. He was certainly under pressure to do so, with annual deficits exceeding $1 trillion, centrist Democrats seeking White House leadership on the issue, and Republicans warning that Obama was taking the United States down the path of Greece. President Obama chose to highlight deficit control not only in his State of the Union addresses but also in his dialogue with congressional leaders on a grand fiscal bargain.[20] A string of activities (the Simpson-Bowles Commission, the Biden deficit control talks, the Obama-Boehner negotiations, and the supercommittee and sequestration) highlighted what he was not able to accomplish. In fact, the sequestration program actually ran counter to the president's policy agenda and did not address the long-term deficit problem. Obama was compelled to expend political energy in 2013–2015 to reverse some of the perverse sequestration cuts that the White House had helped enact before the 2012 election.

In the course of pursuing a grand fiscal deal, Obama raised expectations on sensitive issues (entitlement and tax reforms) on which he had no electoral mandate and little leverage. Not surprisingly, he did not deliver anything significant, and that hurt his image, at least among political elites but also among some voters.[21] Perhaps more importantly, the preoccupation with big fiscal issues undermined the potential for enactment of modest pro-growth reforms.

The foregone opportunities that were legislatively realistic include an expansion of the Earned Income Tax Credit favored by both Obama and House conservative Paul Ryan,[22] corporate tax reform (a lower rate coupled with a broader base) favored by Senate Democrat Max Baucus and House Republican Dave Camp, and an energy pact between the United States and Europe.[23]

In sum, Obama would have been better off focusing on near-term economic performance and pro-growth measures and letting the Republicans and Democrats in Congress lead on long-term deficit control, if they were inclined and able to do so. A challenge for this approach is that he would have had to communicate effectively the different causes of the near-term and long-term deficits. Insofar as Congress made significant progress on the long-term challenge, there would be ample opportunity for Obama to enter the debate and garner some collaborative credit for whatever was accomplished. The near-term deficit issues were primarily caused by the Great Recession, and those deficits declined rapidly as the economy recovered. Thus, with regard to near-term fiscal management, the record of the Obama administration—with an assist from the fiscal hawks in Congress—is one of progress compared to the fiscal mess that the Bush administration left behind.

HEALTH CARE REFORM

The ACA is widely cited by journalists as Obama's signature accomplishment, and it certainly represents the largest change in US social policy since the administration of Lyndon B. Johnson. I have downgraded it from this "signature" designation because it was more controversial than it should have been both in design and in its rollout. It also remains vulnerable to legal, legislative, and implementation challenges.

The US Supreme Court in 2012 upheld the constitutionality of the ACA's individual mandate. In 2014 the Court upheld the premium subsidies on the federal exchange, but the resolution of some other legal issues remains murky. The Medicaid expansion has already been weakened by one Supreme Court decision. Still another legal challenge is brewing because the federal government is using funds that (allegedly) were not properly appropriated by the Congress. It may be several years before all of the ACA litigation is resolved.

Should the ACA survive all of the remaining legal challenges (which is certainly possible), it will still be vulnerable to a Republican White House in 2017, assuming the Congress remains in the hands of the Republicans. If a Republican president cooperates with a Republican Congress, they can use "reconciliation" authority to strip away much of the ACA without the need for sixty votes in the Senate. The individual and employer mandates are particularly vulnerable to repeal. If the Democrats win the White House in 2017, a veto threat can stymie any Republican effort to repeal the ACA or weaken its key provisions—assuming the ACA is not too politically toxic for a new Democratic president to defend. The most recent polling (mid-2015) on the ACA shows some improvement, but at best the number of people who are favorable toward the plan is about equal to the number who are unfavorable.[24]

Even if the Democrats win the White House in November 2016, there will be bipartisan pressure to "fix" the ACA in various ways (e.g., pare back the employer mandate by redefining a full-time worker, eliminate the new tax on medical devices, allow lower-cost "copper" plans, and delay the tax on "Cadillac" health plans). Indeed, a prudent position for a new Democratic president might be that the ACA needs to be refined rather than repealed. On the other hand, the longer the ACA remains in place, the more difficult it will be for Republicans to disrupt it—without electoral retribution—as millions of Americans are enjoying subsidized insurance coverage. Indeed, in 2014 only about a third (35 percent) of Americans told pollsters that they favor repeal of the ACA; a majority (58 percent) of them are seeking "improvements."[25] Thus, there is no question that, to Obama's credit, the ACA was a large-scale accomplishment in social policy that responded to the priorities of the Democratic Party.[26] The political price for the ACA was extraordinarily high but could have been diminished by more politically astute presidential leadership.

CLIMATE CHANGE POLICY

Compared to the George W. Bush administration, the Obama White House was successful in changing the course of US policy toward global climate change. The success was not through legislation. Indeed, as explained in chapter 7, Obama's big 2009 legislative proposal on climate policy was blocked in the Senate and became politically damaging with regard to its electoral impact on moderate Democrats in the House of Representatives. The 2009 climate initiative may be a case in which the White House did not exert effective management of the Speaker of House, Nancy Pelosi, who was determined to seek climate legislation as a higher priority than health care, even though there was no plausible road to success for climate legislation in the Senate and even though Obama preferred to give higher priority to health care than to climate.

Obama recovered from his legislative setback in 2009–2010 and used federal rule-making power to mandate major reductions in greenhouse gases in both the transportation and electricity sectors of the US economy. The rule-making contribution is often seen as an element of domestic policy, but the greener positioning of the United States also helped bring China into constructive international dialogue on climate change. As this book goes to press, the United States is well positioned to be a leader at the next international climate conference in Paris.

OBAMA, CONGRESS, AND CROSSOVER VOTING

In a polarized environment the president must minimize defections in Congress from his own party while enlisting support from a limited number of members from the opposing party. In table 11.1, I assemble the crossover voting from 2009 to 2015 on the legislative measures covered in this book. Of the twenty-seven votes taken in the House, nineteen were resolved in favor of Obama's position. In the Senate twenty-one of thirty-two votes were resolved in favor of his position. The number of measures in the two chambers is not equal, because some measures were considered in only one chamber.

If Congress were perfectly polarized on party lines, one would look at table 11.1 and see a column of zeros for Republican crossovers and a column of zeros for Democratic crossovers. Notice, however, that in reality most votes have been characterized by at least some crossover behavior. The votes on the debt limit and the ACA are the only measures where party-line voting was perfect in the Senate. There were no measures with perfect party-line voting in the House.

Since some of the measures induced an unusually high amount of crossover votes (e.g., the seventy-seven House Republicans voting for phase two of Cash for Clunkers) and may be outliers, an informative statistic for the Obama years is the median number of members who crossed over in the sample of votes. In the House the median number of crossover votes was larger among Democrats (thirty-two) than among Republicans (zero), a pattern that is consistent with the fact that Obama-favored measures were more likely to be ideologically progressive than ideologically centrist. Moreover, the Tea Party movement made any pro-Obama vote by a House Republican very dangerous. The comparison is closer in the Senate, where the median number of Democratic crossovers (three) is equal to the median number of Republican crossovers (three).

Overall, the median crossover vote counts are not large, suggesting that rank-and-file members are trying to support their party leadership vis-à-vis the president's policy preferences. But the large variation around the median is a clear indication that the substance of the individual issues matters and that congressional leaders are not always able to deliver 100 percent loyalty from their party caucuses. There are some unusual votes on which Obama is more aligned with congressional Republicans than with congressional Democrats (e.g., fast-track trade authority). With these data as a foundation, I return to the prescriptive foundations for presidential effectiveness advanced in chapter 2.

PRESCRIPTIVE PROPOSITIONS

In order to supply a rigorous evaluation of Obama's domestic policy making, I have compared the decisions of the Obama administration on key issues to the nine prescriptive propositions for presidents operating in a polarized

Table 11.1. Selected Votes on Obama-Related Measures, House and Senate, 2009–2015

Measure	House				Senate				Result for Obama
	Dates	Total	R-Cross	D-Cross	Dates	Total	R-Cross	D-Cross	
Block Phase II of TARP					1/15/09	52–42	6	9	W
Bernanke Confirmation					1/28/10	70–30	22	12	W
Recovery Act Conference	2/13/09	246–183	0	7	2/13/09	60–38	3	0	W
Report Stimulus II									
–Original Version	12/2/10	234–188	3	20	12/04/10	53–36	0	5	L¹
–Final Version	12/17/10	277–148	138	112	12/15/10	81–19	37	14	W
"Jobs Bill"					10/11/11	50–49	0	2	L¹
Cash for Clunkers									
–Phase I	6/9/09	298–119	59	9	6/18/09	60–36	4	1	W
–Phase II	6/30/09	316–109	77	14	8/6/09	60–37	7	4	W
Dodd-Frank	6/30/10	237–192	3	19	7/15/10	60–39	3	1	W
Repeal of Bush Tax Cuts for High Earners	12/2/10	234–188	3	20	1/26/10	53–46	0	5	L¹
Repeal of Bush Tax Cuts for High Earners	1/1/13	234–188	85	16	1/1/13	89–8	40	3	W
2010 Budget Resolution					4/2/09	55–43	0	2	W
Bipartisan Budget					1/26/10	53–46	16	22	L
Raise Debt Limit	12/16/09	218–214	0	39	1/28/10	60–39	0	0	W
Raise Debt Limit–Version #1 –Version w/Constitutional Amendment to Balance Budget	7/19/11	234–190	9	5	7/22/11	51–46	0	0	W
–Version #2	8/1/11	269–161	174	95	8/2/11	74–26	28	7	W

Table 11.1. (cont.)

Measure	House				Senate				Result for Obama
	Dates	Total	R-Cross	D-Cross	Dates	Total	R-Cross	D-Cross	
Raise Debt Limit w/ACA Amendment	10/16/13	284–144	87	0	10/16/13	81–18	27	0	W
Murray-Ryan Ease of Sequester	12/12/13	332–94	169	32	12/18/13	64–36	9	0	W
Raise Minimum Wage –Version #1 $10.10/hr.	3/15/13	184–233	0	6					L
–Version #2 $10.10/hr. w/index					4/30/14	54–42	1	0	L[1]
Affordable Care Act	11/7/09	220–215	1	39	12/24/09	60–39	0	0	W
Affordable Care Act	3/21/10	219–211	0	34					W
3/10 Reconciliation	3/21/10	220–211	0	33	3/25/10	56–43	0	3	W
2013 Upton Amendment on Cancelled Policies	11/15/13	261–157	4	39					W[3]
Repeal Medical Device Tax	6/7/13	270–146	0	37	3/21/13	79–20	0	34	W[3]
IRS Income Verification Bill	10/16/13	235–191	0	5					W[3]
Redefine Full-time Workers (30–40 hours/week)	4/13/14	248–179	0	18					W[3]
Climate Bill	6/26/09	219–212	0	44					L[3]
Ethanol-Block Refueling Stations $	6/16/11	283–128	45	93	6/16/11	41–59	11	5	W
–Repeal of Credit & Tariff					6/16/11	73–27	14	38	L

Table 11.1. (cont.)

Measure	House				Senate				Result for Obama
	Dates	Total	R-Cross	D-Cross	Dates	Total	R-Cross	D-Cross	
Immigration Reform DREAM Act	12/8/10	216–198	8	38	12/18/10	55–41	3	5	L[1]
Comprehensive Immigration Reform –Grassley Amendment on Border Security					6/13/13	53–47	5	2	W
–Corker-Hoeven on Border Security					6/24/13	67–27	15	0	W
–Final Reform Package					6/27/13	68–32	14	0	L[2]
Approve Keystone Pipeline I					11/18/14	59–41	0	14	W
Approve Keystone Pipeline II	2/11/15	270–152	1	29	1/29/15	62–36	0	9	W[4]
Nullify DREAM Executive Order	1/14/15	236–191	10	2	2/27/15	57–42	1	4	W[1]
Fast-Track Trade Authority	6/18/15	218–208	50	170	5/21/15	62–38	5	31	W

Note: R = Republican; D = Democrat; W = win for Obama's position; L = loss for Obama's position.

[1] Fell short of 60 votes

[2] Blocked in House (no vote)

[3] Blocked in Senate (no vote)

[4] Larger bill failed

environment. Recall that these propositions are constructed based on previous theoretical and empirical studies of American politics.

1. The president should begin a four-year term with one or more initiatives that appeal to his base.

President Obama adhered to this proposition, although he often irritated his base when forced to compromise (e.g., no single payer or public option in the Affordable Care Act and multiple delays in repeal of the Bush tax cuts for high earners). In his first term the economic stimulus package contained numerous base-pleasing components (e.g., spending geared to low-income populations and green-technology subsidies) while the health care and climate/energy proposals were both highly responsive to the wishes of Obama's base. In his second term Obama again promoted several base-pleasing proposals, such as gun control, immigration reform, low-carbon electricity, and a higher federal minimum wage. Although he did not accomplish all of these priorities, he was certainly attentive to his base in his construction of priorities.

2. The president should begin a four-year term with one or more legislative initiatives that appeal to centrists, especially initiatives that facilitate collaboration between pragmatists from both parties in the Congress.

President Obama did not follow this prescription at the start of his first term, as none of his first-year legislative initiatives were aimed at appealing to centrists. Some might argue that the 2009 Recovery Act was a centrist initiative, but the numerous base-pleasing subsidies that were included in the act made it easy for Republican congressional leaders to marshal unified opposition. Indeed, many centrist Democrats in the House and Senate were reluctant to vote for the act.

Reacting to his initial agenda, one moderate political commentator described Obama with fear as a "transformational liberal" rather than a "centrist."[27] Obama apparently did not see himself as an ideological figure, but that is certainly the way his initial agenda was received by the public.[28]

Within three months of his inauguration, the partisan gap in Obama's job approval ratings (88 percent of Democrats approved; 27 percent of Republicans approved) was the largest in the modern era (covering Nixon to Obama).[29] The perceptions of Obama's ideology were not driven by his foreign policies, which had overt conservative as well as progressive elements, but by his portfolio of domestic legislative priorities, which were overwhelmingly progressive in nature.[30]

In this respect Obama's presidency started quite differently from the presidency of George W. Bush, who mustered bipartisan support for No Child Left Behind (NCLB) in 2001–2002 and a new prescription drug benefit under Medicare in 2003. Both of those proposals appealed to moderate members of Congress, regardless of party affiliation.

One can argue that Bush was forced to take a more centrist path at the start because the legitimacy of his presidency was in question. Recall that Bush lost the popular vote to Vice President Al Gore, that Bush won the Electoral College by the narrowest of margins, that the Florida outcome was clouded by the "hanging chads" mess, and that the White House was secured by Bush only after a highly controversial decision by the US Supreme Court. Obama assumed office with much stronger political standing than Bush (or so it seemed), and presumably he did not feel the same urgency to put on display centrist aspects of his policy preferences.[31] President Obama also was working with a Democratic Congress in which progressive leaders (e.g., House Speaker Nancy Pelosi) were resisting calls from moderates for a more centrist agenda.

During Obama's entire first term, moderate Democrats in Congress were never put in the lead on a White House legislative priority that might have fostered significant collaboration with the more moderate Republicans in Congress. The predictable result was a highly polarized first term for Obama, an outcome that undermined his appeal as a "post-partisan" politician, disappointed independent voters, put moderate Democrats at electoral risk by dominating the airwaves with progressive policy initiatives, and made it relatively easy for Republican leaders in Congress to accomplish virtually unified opposition to Obama's agenda.[32]

An exception to this characterization is the 2009 Cash for Clunkers automotive legislation that attracted significant Republican as well as Democratic interest in the Congress. Interestingly, one of the reasons the plan may have attracted bipartisan support is that it was never framed as a legislative priority of the White House (although Obama supported it) and thus did not attract strategic opposition from Republican leaders in Congress. It is also notable that Cash for Clunkers was not a measure of social policy; it was a practical measure of economic policy that seemed highly responsive to the horrible conditions in one of America's most important industrial sectors. Whether the program accomplished anything meaningful economically is an entirely different question that is certainly disputed.[33]

Obama's first-term launch could have been politically better for him and the Democrats in Congress if some pro-growth measures had been proposed that had significant appeal among centrists. Pro-growth measures are those that are aimed at boosting economic growth over the next decade or so, measures that could have been framed as complementary to Obama's near-term stimulus efforts.[34]

A variety of measures were promising. Indeed, Obama ultimately supported each of the following concepts: corporate tax reform (a lower rate coupled with a broader base that closes loopholes), regulatory reform (streamlining inefficient regulations adopted prior to Obama's presidency and strengthening cost-benefit review of future regulations), and/or an energy-export agreement with Europe. Some of the energy provisions in Obama's huge 2009 climate/energy initiative might also have worked as separate initiatives, since they were destined for failure when linked to cap and tax. Some options with promise among centrists in both parties include demonstrations of carbon capture and storage technology at coal- and gas-fired electric power plants, loan guarantees for construction of new nuclear power plants, expanded use of natural gas in the transport sector, a renewable electricity mandate, and energy efficiency improvements throughout the economy. Such policies do not have the salience of health care or immigration, but they would provide a foundation for centrists to work together, which, if successful, might have built the foundation for collaboration on higher-visibility issues. It is important for independent voters to see Congress working, even if the issues are not highly salient ones.

In short, Obama was sympathetic with many centrist policy initiatives that might have attracted bipartisan support in 2009–2010, but he never advanced them as stand-alone ventures. When they were proposed they were typically combined with progressive elements that deterred any significant Republican collaboration in Congress (e.g., the 2009 Recovery Act included significant tax cuts but also many progressive spending provisions).

Obama did move to the center on some business issues in 2011–2012 before his reelection. He extended the Bush tax cuts as part of a second stimulus measure. He partnered with Eric Cantor in the House on the regulation-reducing JOBS Act, although the legislation was aimed narrowly at the financial sector. He also used executive power to streamline some burdensome regulations of business and delayed the EPA's tightening of the ozone (smog) standard.

A plausible-sounding critique exists that Obama did not engage in enough personal outreach to members of Congress,[35] but the truth is more complex. As with his first term, the start of Obama's second term was not short on personal outreach to congressional Republicans and Democrats in the form of dinners, coffees, and White House meetings.[36] What was lacking was something promising to talk about: a major legislative proposal with appeal to centrists in both parties. Firearms control came closest to fitting this description, as suburban women—whether Republicans, Democrats, or independents—are particularly sympathetic with the need for gun control. What the White House could not do, despite the opportunistic timing of the initiative, is overcome the predictable and potent opposition mustered by the National Rifle Association (NRA) and other pro-gun groups. Immigration reform attracted significant Republican support in the Senate, but, like his predecessor in the Oval Office, Obama never came close to finding common ground with the House Republicans, who were more sensitive to the Tea Party than the Hispanic vote. And neither firearms control nor immigration control was responsive to the greatest concern of the day: the slow economic recovery. Obama needed to make centrist-oriented proposals on the economic front, for this was the most salient issue in the minds of voters.

A better start to Obama's second term (early 2013) might have occurred if he had made some pro-growth proposals, especially since he saw that most of the House Republicans were reelected at the same time that he was reelected, which squelched any prospects of more legislative progressivism. Once again, corporate tax reform and regulatory reform would have been promising legislative ventures in year five of his presidency. They would have reinforced his strong focus on the economy and would have been difficult for Republicans in Congress to oppose in unison. Obama was willing to pursue regulatory reform to help secure his own reelection in 2011–2012, but he did not request a legislative approach to regulatory reform that might have helped centrist Democrats in the House and Senate in 2010 or 2014.[37]

Defenders of President Obama argue that the sixty-vote threshold in the Senate made it virtually impossible for him to overcome the filibuster threat that a unified GOP could muster. In his most opportune time for legislation, 2009–2010, it is estimated that more than 70 percent of Obama administration priorities faced filibuster-related problems in the Senate, up from 51 percent during the George W. Bush and Bill Clinton presidencies.[38] What Obama needed to do was make one or more pro-growth proposals that would challenge the Republican congressional leadership's ability to orchestrate unified opposition.

3. The president should begin a four-year term with one or more legislative initiatives that have a high probability of enactment.

With a 256–178 Democratic majority in the House and a Democratic margin in the Senate ranging from 58–42 to 60–40, President Obama did not have difficulty finding legislative initiatives that could pass the Congress in 2009–2010. The number of bills passed by the Democratic Congress and signed by Obama in 2009–2010 was large. They covered a wide range of topics: a woman's right to sue for pay discrimination, expanded health insurance for children, strengthened hate crime law, authorizing the Food and Drug Administration to regulate tobacco, protection of more wilderness areas, expansion of the national community service program, foreclosure assistance measures, regulation of abusive credit card practices, extension of the home buyer tax credit, expansion of Pell grants for college students, additional first responders in health sector, and better monitoring of food safety.[39] Obama was also successful on some of his major priorities. When he called for fiscal stimulus and Wall Street reform, he had good reason to believe that Congress would deliver (even though the details were far from clear), and Congress did deliver, though Obama's winning margins in the Senate were—as one might expect under polarization—frequently small (see table 11.1).

Once the Republicans captured a majority in the House (starting 2011–2012), Obama had extreme difficulty adhering to this principle. Since any Obama initiative could not reach the floor of the House without the approval of the Rules Committee and the Speaker of the House, Obama—for the first time—was compelled to negotiate with a Republican congressional leader.

His major effort to collaborate with Speaker John Boehner throughout 2011–2015 was the quest for a grand fiscal bargain covering tax reform and entitlement spending. Chapter 4 explains why this quest never gained traction. It was far too ambitious, given how controversial any package would have been among the bases of the two politicians.[40] Indeed, it is highly questionable whether the two leaders could have delivered the votes necessary to pass the kind of agreement that they were discussing.

Obama would have been better off leading his collaboration with Boehner with a more focused initiative, such as regulatory reform, selected corporate tax reforms, or reform of the Earned Income Tax Credit. If Obama and Boehner demonstrated that they could deliver legislatively on that more modest scale, momentum and trust would have been established. It might have been feasible then to explore more ambitious undertakings. But the window for collaboration was short, as the Republicans were primarily interested not in collaboration but in denying Obama a second term.

The start of Obama's second term, like the start of George W. Bush's second term (when Bush sought a controversial private option under Social Security), suffered from a big flaw: the absence of a major legislative priority with a high probability of enactment. Virtually nothing from Obama's 2013 legislative agenda was accomplished, even though he had recently won reelection to a second term.[41]

Obama cannot be criticized for seeking gun control after the Sandy Hook shooting. Nor was his quest for immigration reform an implausible second-term initiative. But both of these initiatives—for different reasons—were low-probability rather than high-probability initiatives. They needed to be coupled with a proposal with high probability of enactment. Of course, soon after his 2012 reelection Obama did win a quick concession from Boehner that reduced the Bush tax cuts for high-income households. That was a significant victory for Obama linked directly to the Obama-Romney contest and a belated delivery on his 2008 campaign pledge.

Obama also signaled a practical interest in corporate tax reform, building on some promising informal discussions between moderate Democrat Max Baucus in the Senate and moderate House Republican Dave Camp.[42] The Congressional Budget Office estimated that Camp's revenue-neutral tax plan would raise the GDP by as much as 20 percent and create just short of two million new jobs.[43] Baucus was working on a similar plan to close tax loopholes and use the additional revenue to lower the corporate tax rate, thereby ensuring support from business groups and conservative Republicans. His more liberal Senate colleagues, Charles Schumer and Harry Reid, were pressuring Baucus to propose a different plan that would use the additional revenue to reduce the federal deficit, a plan with little support among business groups or GOP members.[44] Here was an opportunity for Obama to side publicly with the centrists instead of the progressives, but he chose instead not to take sides.

The entire initiative fizzled when Baucus, who was first appointed chair of the Senate Finance Committee in 2001, announced in April 2013 that he would not run for reelection in 2014. Facing a tough reelection battle (given his association with "Obamacare") and under constant criticism from liberals in the Senate and the White House, Baucus accepted Obama's nomination to serve as US ambassador to China.[45] With Baucus scheduled to leave the Senate and Camp serving the end of his term (December 2013) as committee chair in the House, the White House lacked the key players to generate a bipartisan agreement. In any event, 2014 was looking like such a Republican year that incentives were created in the business community to wait until 2015 for legislative action, when a more Republican-heavy Congress might deliver a more enticing reform package. In 2015 Obama continued to look for a bipartisan path to corporate tax reform, but progress was slow, because he was beyond his post-election window of opportunity and continued to link his reform interest with a request for higher taxes.[46]

In order to be credible, the president must start a four-year term with at least one legislative victory, even if that means making a proposal that is far more attractive to centrists than to the president's base. Obama, like his predecessor, ignored this prescription or misjudged what was legislatively doable. The error caused damage to his credibility as a politician and to the legacy of his second term.

4. When choosing a small number of legislative priorities, the president should favor those initiatives that cannot be accomplished with executive power and disfavor those initiatives that can be accomplished (in whole or significant part) through executive action.

President Obama adhered to this principle when he belatedly elevated health care over climate change and immigration during 2009–2010. All of the key health care reforms that he sought (Medicaid expansion, new health care exchanges, premium subsidies for lower-income households, and employer and individual mandates) could not have been adopted through executive powers, because Congress had not provided the Department of Health and Human Services with the necessary legal authority or appropriations.

The situation was different for climate change and immigration, because President Obama already possessed substantial legal authority to pursue reforms under previous acts of Congress and the executive powers in the Constitution. As I argue in more detail in the next section, leading with executive action would have been preferable on climate change and immigration, but,

Table 11.2. Judicial Rulings on Key Executive Actions, 2009–2015

Obama Action	Agency	Court	Upheld	Overturned	Comment
Sale of Chrysler to Fiat	Treasury	Supreme Court	✓		Court allowed sale but vacated lower-court's reasoning
Dodd-Frank Regulations	SEC	DC Circuit		✓	
Individual Mandate in Affordable Care Act	HHS	Supreme Court	✓		
Medicaid Expansion in Affordable Care Act	HHS	Supreme Court		✓	Disallowed threat to cut existing federal support under Medicaid.
Federal Subsidies Premium in Affordable Care Act	IRS	Supreme Court	✓		
Limits on Carbon Emissions from Cars and Light Trucks	EPA	DC Circuit	✓		
Limits on Carbon Emissions from Stationary Sources	EPA	Supreme Court	✓		Court limited EPA power to sources already regulated for other pollution
Limits on Mercury Emissions from Power Plants	EPA	Supreme Court	✓		Court did not vacate the rule
Limits on Air Pollution That Travels across State Lines	EPA	Supreme Court	✓		
Work Permits for Millions of Illegal Migrants	DHS	Federal District Court (Texas)		✓	
Restrict Permits for Mountaintop Mining for Coal	EPA	DC Circuit	✓		

even given that Obama was determined to seek legislation on them, he kept the two issues in play for too long in 2009–2010 when it was clear that enactment was impossible.[47] He instigated the squandering of political energy on climate and immigration when the prospects for progress were worse than bleak.

A major argument against executive action is that it is vulnerable to reversal by the federal judiciary. Table 11.2 provides an accounting of the record of President Obama's executive actions that were subject to litigation and reviewed in this book. Overall, the Obama administration won a clear majority of the cases. When the Obama administration lost in federal court, it was typically on a split decision, implying that the outcome of the litigation could have gone either way. Thus, the record shows that the Obama administration was proficient at defending its executive actions when they were challenged in litigation.

5. The president should lean toward executive over legislative action when legislative failure may hurt his job approval ratings or cross-pressure more members of his party than members of the opposing party.

President Obama's tendency was to use a legislative request as an "opening gambit" and turn to executive action only when Congress failed to act.[48] By neglecting to lead with executive action when Democrats in Congress were likely to be cross-pressured, Obama made some politically damaging errors that exacerbated the losses that the Democratic Party experienced in both the 2010 and 2014 midterm elections.

The most egregious error was President Obama's handling of the climate change issue during his first term. As detailed in chapter 7, the Supreme Court ruled in 2007 that the EPA had broad authority to enact measures to address climate change under the Clean Air Act. Obama did not need to obtain legislation to accomplish much of what he desired regarding climate change. By making a far-reaching legislative proposal on climate change in 2009, he unnecessarily cross-pressured dozens of House Democrats, compared with little compensating pressure on House Republicans. He also set himself up for legislative failure, with negative consequences for his credibility and job approval.

What Obama should have done in his first term is what he did in his second term: exploit legal authority under the Clean Air Act to accomplish emissions reductions from the electric power sector, the major source of greenhouse gas emissions in the US economy. Coupled with the first-term executive actions that he took in the transport sector, Obama would have finished his first term with an outstanding record on climate change, all accomplished without subjecting House or Senate Democrats to any controversial roll-call votes. The GOP and their allies would have attacked Obama for taking unilateral action and then litigated the new EPA regulations, but cross-pressured Democrats in Congress would have been much better off.

The White House committed a somewhat similar error on immigration reform, although the legal claim of executive authority is not as secure on immigration as it is on climate change. Nonetheless, the 1986 federal immigration law and subsequent regulations highlight the president's broad authority to defer deportations and issue temporary work permits as part of prosecutorial discretion. Obama did not possess the legal authority to offer a pathway to citizenship, but legislation providing that pathway had little prospect of passing the Congress in the 2009–2016 period for the same reasons that George W. Bush was unable to move legislation.

Moreover, in 2009–2012 the politics of a legislative vote on immigration reform were actually worse for the Democrats than for the Republicans in Congress. Comprehensive immigration reform does not cross-pressure many Republicans in the House because of the geographical distribution of Hispanic votes in the United States. With generally low Hispanic vote shares in House districts represented by Republicans, House Republicans are insulated from the preferences of Hispanic voters. In contrast, many House Democrats represented districts or states with small Hispanic vote shares and large white working-class constituencies. Much to the delight of the GOP, Democrats in Congress were cross-pressured by an issue that is highly emotional and easy for the Tea Party and conservative talk-show hosts to dramatize.

What Obama could have done is signal early in 2009, through a DREAM-like executive order, that he was aligned with Hispanic interests on the subject of immigration. He should have lowered expectations for comprehensive immigration reform early in 2009, explaining that he could not pursue comprehensive reform until the economy recovered, and emphasizing that he had made his campaign pledge on immigration before the economic meltdown occurred, but now economic measures must have higher priority. With comprehensive reform off the table, the president also should have refrained from dialing up enforcement activity, which earned him the perverse title "Deporter in Chief."

Later in his first and second terms, Obama should have followed up with additional executive measures on immigration, similar to those he ultimately adopted in 2014. Had he proceeded in this manner, he would have salvaged some of his credibility with the Hispanic community and helped Democrats in Congress in both 2010 and 2014 by securing undiminished margins of victory among Hispanics. The first-term path Obama chose—intensified enforcement against illegal immigration coupled with little progress on liberalization—ultimately moved federal policy in the opposite direction of his 2008 campaign pledge and hurt his party's credibility with the Hispanic community. His only saving grace is that he capitalized on Mitt Romney's anti-immigration stance in 2012, in effect seizing on an opponent's "unforced error." For that savvy behavior, Obama deserves credit.

6. *The president, in collaboration with his allies in Congress, should consider carefully whether a legislative proposal should start in the House or Senate, making sure that members of his party do not take controversial votes when passage of the proposal in the other chamber is highly unlikely.*

The Obama administration and the Democratic congressional leadership violated this principle on the climate-change issue. Speaker Nancy Pelosi and committee chair Henry Waxman, both elected from progressive districts in California, pushed a huge climate bill through the House in 2009 without any indication that a climate bill could pass in the Senate. It should have been apparent to the White House, based on climate votes taken from 2005 to 2008, that the Senate would not be able to pass a big climate bill in 2009–2010, even though the Democrats had between fifty-eight and sixty seats in the Senate during that time.

It was indeed reasonable for the Obama White House to expect that there might be three to five Republican votes in the Senate for a climate bill. Obama should also have counted at least ten Democratic senators from the Midwest and the South voting against such a bill, as they were already on record against a big climate bill. They represented regions of the country that faced near-term economic hardships from climate legislation. Thus, there was no plausible pathway to obtain sixty votes in the Senate, even though climate legislation was pledged by Obama during the 2008 campaign and even though it was a White House priority in 2009. In many ways Obama's obstacle to climate legislation was as much regional as it was partisan, since the dependence on fossil fuels was greater in the South and Midwest than it was on the US coasts.

Interestingly, journalistic accounts indicate that Obama was irritated that Pelosi and Waxman chose to move the climate bill through the House before the health care bill. Apparently he feared that his higher priority (health care) might never pass the House if the controversial climate vote occurred first. The president also should have been worried that the House climate vote might subject some House Democrats to unnecessary electoral risk. The number of incumbents who lost their seats due to the 2009 climate vote was not enough (by itself) to shift control of the House and was smaller than the damage due to the Affordable Care Act vote, but those who did lose their seats did so for no defensible reason.

Pelosi learned her lesson on proper sequencing of House and Senate votes and acted accordingly on immigration reform. She indicated in late 2009 that the House would not take up immigration reform until the Senate acted.[49] That was a wise stance given the dozens of House Democrats who were representing districts with few Hispanics and large numbers of conservative whites.

7. The president may conclude, on occasion, that a legislative proposal is advisable, even if it is unlikely to be enacted by the Congress.

From 2013 to 2016 Obama made numerous proposals to Congress that were not enacted as he faced a Republican majority in the House (2011–2016) six of his eight years as president. Unsuccessful proposals are often damaging (since they suggest the president is an ineffective leader), but they may have political value for the White House in some circumstances.

Even when a proposal is defeated, it may cross-pressure members of the opposing party and force them to take damaging roll-call votes. An apt illustration of this principle may have been President Obama's unsuccessful proposal to raise the federal minimum wage in 2013–2014.[50] The proposal attracted support from most Democrats but could not attract enough Republican support to pass the House or overcome a filibuster threat in the Senate. Nonetheless, the minimum-wage vote was one that many congressional Republicans might have preferred not to take, since low-wage white voters are an important Republican constituency whose interests do not align with the business interests that oppose a higher minimum wage (e.g., retail and food establishments).[51]

At the end of the Bush administration (2007–2008), President Bush actually supported a minimum wage hike rather than subject his demoralized congressional Republicans to a risky vote against a higher federal minimum wage. (Mitt Romney also favored a higher minimum wage in his campaign against Obama.) Thus, it seems likely that Obama's proposal to raise the federal minimum wage, though never enacted, did not hurt him or his party politically and may have helped it. In fact, the focus he put on the issue may have helped pass higher minimum wages in several state legislatures and local governments where the Democratic Party was in control.[52]

However, since most of Obama's legislative proposals were progressive in character, they rarely cross-pressured a significant number of Republicans. The president's gun control plan cross-pressured some Republican senators but apparently not more than the number of cross-pressured Democratic senators. Thus, if a proposal is likely to fail, the president needs to consider whether his party or the opposing party will have more cross-pressured members of Congress.

8. When seeking to attract (minimize) crossover votes from members of the opposing (president's) party in Congress, the president should target members representing states or districts where voting behavior was favorable (unfavorable) to him.

Some evidence relevant to this proposition is presented in table 11.3, where US senators are rated and ranked according to their propensity to cross over on Obama's agenda. Broadly consistent with the predictions in chapter 2, high crossover rates are reported for senators from states where Obama performed poorly in 2008 and 2012: Democrats Nelson of Nebraska and Manchin of West Virginia; Feingold of Wisconsin, and Sanders of Vermont (who is technically an independent) are surprising exceptions, indicating that the most liberal senators may have some leeway to withhold support from a Democratic president. Among the Republican senators, the high crossover rates were expected from Collins and Snowe of Maine and Voinovich and Portman of Ohio. The crossover rates of Hoeven of North Dakota and Flake of Arizona are so high that they could experience premature electoral defeat in a primary as Lugar of Indiana experienced in 2012.

It is not easy to assess whether the Obama White House did as well as it could have in discouraging Democratic defections and enticing Republican

Table 11.3. Senators Who Most Frequently Cast Crossover Votes on Obama's Agenda, 2009–2015

		Democratic Senators	
Name	State	Crossover Count	Crossover Rate[1] (N)
1. Ben Nelson	NE	9	0.43 (21)
2. Manchin	WV	5	0.33 (15)
3. Feingold	WI	5	0.33 (15)
4. Specter	PA	4	0.27 (15)
5. Sanders	VT	7	0.25 (28)
6. Merkley	OR	7	0.25 (28)
7. Lautenberg	NJ	5	0.25 (20)
8. Byrd	WV	2	0.25 (8)
9. Blumenthal	CT	3	0.23 (13)
11. Harkin	IA	6	0.21 (28)
12. Cantwell	WA	6	0.21 (28)
13. Dorgan	ND	3	0.20 (15)
14. Pryor	AR	5	0.19 (27)
15. Kaufman	DE	2	0.18 (11)

		Republican Senators	
Name	State	Crossover Count	Crossover Rate (N)
1. Hoeven	ND	8	0.62 (13)
2. Flake	AZ	4	0.57 (7)
3. Kirk	IL	7	0.47 (15)
4. Collins	ME	13	0.46 (28)
5. Lugar	IN	9	0.43 (21)
6. Voinovich	OH	6	0.43 (14)
7. Blunt	MO	5	0.38 (13)
8. Portman	OH	5	0.38 (13)
9. Alexander	TN	10	0.36 (28)
10. Corker	TN	10	0.36 (28)
11. Snowe	ME	7	0.33 (21)
12. Bond	MO	5	0.33 (15)
13. Ayotte	NH	4	0.31 (13)
14. Coats	IN	4	0.31 (13)
15. Moran	KS	4	0.31 (13)

[1] In the case of a Democratic (Republican) senator, the crossover rate is defined as the number of votes cast against (in favor of) Obama's legislative positions divided by the number of legislative positions reviewed in this book (N). Excluded from the table due to short periods of service were Kirk (MA), Cowan (MA), Chiesa (NJ), and Gress (NH); excludes FTA vote in 2015.

crossovers. In a 2012 article I compared the rate of crossovers on George W. Bush's domestic agenda to the rate for Barack Obama's domestic agenda. Obama was better than Bush at discouraging defections from his own party but weaker at attracting votes from senators of the opposing party.[53]

Obama's difficulty in attracting Republican crossover votes has a variety of complementary explanations. Mitch McConnell, the leader of the Senate Republicans, stated publicly that he was determined to obstruct Obama's agenda and believed his mission was to ensure that Obama was not reelected in 2012.[54] As a result, McConnell worked hard to unify his caucus against Obama initiatives. The substance of the president's agenda was also too progressive to have much appeal to Republicans, and the emergence of the Tea Party may have intimidated those Republicans who were inclined to support Obama on some issues. In any event, the Senate Republican caucus was so small and ideologically homogenous (in 2009–2010) that it was relatively easy for GOP leaders to make a case for party unity against the president. Nonetheless, Obama was not very effective at courting or pressuring the seven GOP senators who in 2009–2010 were representing states he had won in 2008.

9. The president should give priority to the public administration aspects of governance not only for the good of the country but also because good public administration reassures the public, protects the president's job approval rating, and indirectly protects the political welfare of members of the president's party in Congress.

There are many public administration successes in the Obama years, but they go unnoticed because good public administration solves problems and prevents controversy. For example, the creative use of executive power to restructure and revive General Motors and Chrysler (including their finance arms and suppliers) required careful collaboration between the Obama White House and public-finance administrators in the US Department of the Treasury. What began as an unpopular bailout ultimately became a success story in economic policy for the Obama administration, one that the president was able to defend throughout the Midwest in his 2012 contest against Romney.

However, the priority given to public administration was sorely inadequate in several of the case studies: the botched implementation of the ACA through poor leadership and oversight of contractors; the mishandling of green-technology loans and subsidies by the White House and the US Department of Energy; the belated White House reaction to the child refugee crisis on the Mexican border, coupled with a failure to appreciate the magnitude of the public administration capacities that were necessary to address it; and Obama's perplexing failure to seek public comment on his 2014 immigration initiative, thereby creating unnecessary legal risk for a promising executive policy. Each of these failures was ultimately corrected (to varying degrees), but the political costs of poor administration (e.g., in the 2014 midterm elections) were substantial both for the president's job approval rating and for the Democratic Party.

A REFINED OBAMA PRESIDENCY

Pulling together my counterfactual insights from the case studies, I urge readers to consider a counterfactual Obama presidency. Had his administration proceeded with the following policies and strategic refinements, President Obama could have accomplished even more of his policy agenda than he did, and with less damage to his own job approval rating and to the Democratic majorities in Congress.

1. A 2009 stimulus package in the vicinity of $800 billion should have been enacted, but the composition of the stimulus should have made less use of federal subsidies for specific technologies and businesses and even more use of tax cuts for the lower half of the income distribution.

As designed, the Recovery Act called for too much money to be spent by the federal government in too short a period of time, leading inevitably to embarrassing examples of waste and poorly evaluated federal expenditures (e.g., the bankrupt solar energy firm Solyndra).[55] If instead more than half of the act (instead of only a third) had focused on tax cuts for individuals in the lower half of the income distribution, it might have been more stimulating to the economy, better for Obama's low-income base, more enticing for some Republicans to support at the outset, and much more difficult for Republicans to criticize in the implementation phase. It is much more attractive for Republicans to criticize how federal bureaucrats spend money than it is to criticize how ordinary Americans spend it.

2. A refined Affordable Care Act would have retained the Medicaid expansion, the health care exchanges, and premium subsidies but dropped the individual mandate, the most radioactive element, and softened the employer mandate. After the unexpected 2012 Supreme Court decision, an adjusted implementation schedule should have rolled out the federal insurance exchange in January 2015, allowing ample time for proper preparation and relieving pressures before the November 2014 midterm election.

The controversial roll-call votes for the ACA in Congress played a major role in the loss of the Democratic Party majorities in the House (2010) and Senate (2014).[56] Some of those losses were avoidable. The design of the ACA needed to be less controversial, and its implementation needed to be handled with more sensitivity to the welfare of congressional Democrats. The House version of the ACA included the public option, which allowed conservatives to allege that the ACA was a step toward socialized medicine. The Senate dropped the public option, which was politically prudent, but the House vote was more controversial than it needed to be.

The most unpopular major ACA provision remains the individual insurance mandate, while each of the other major provisions is viewed favorability by 60 percent or more of US citizens (see table 11.4). Given that the Tea Party and conservative Republicans were showcasing the coercive nature of the individual mandate to demonize Obama, the Democrats in Congress should have considered dropping it.[57]

The best argument in favor of an individual mandate is that it improves the functioning of insurance markets by making sure that numerous young, healthy people are included in the insured population. Their insurance premiums help finance the expense of coverage for older, sicker groups of policyholders. Not surprisingly, the health insurance industry, which opposed the ACA, was one of the strongest advocates of an individual mandate. But the concept of a mandate was so controversial among ordinary voters (including the uninsured)—indeed, that is why candidate Obama opposed the mandate during the Democratic nominating process—that it could not be designed, implemented, and enforced with enough vigor to have much policy value. Early studies suggest that the ACA has significantly reduced the size of the uninsured population but primarily because of the premium subsidies on the exchanges and the expansion of Medicaid in many states. With 90 percent of the uninsured exempt or eligible for waivers from the ACA's individual mandate (largely due to executive moves by the Obama administration), it is difficult to argue that the political hit Democrats took for voting for the coercive provision was worth the provision's limited policy value.

Table 11.4. Public Views of Affordable Care Act: Comparison of Key Provisions

| | Percent of Respondents with Favorable Impressions | | | |
	Total	Democrats	Independents	Republicans
Insurance Exchanges	78	91	79	66
Premium Subsidies	76	90	78	55
Medicaid Expansion	75	90	78	52
Employer Mandate	60	78	61	34
Individual Mandate	35	53	31	17

Source: "Kaiser Health Policy Tracking Poll: December 2014," Kaiser Family Foundation, December 18, 2014, http://kff.org/health-reform/poll-finding/kaiser-health-policy-tracking-poll-december-2014.
Note: Poll taken December 2–9, 2014; N = 1,505.

Other than the Tea Party, the other ardent opponents of the ACA were influential segments of the business community, including the US Chamber of Commerce. In order to soften corporate opposition to the employer mandate, less expensive "copper" plans should also have been permitted. Copper plans provide a basic set of coverage for employees without forcing companies to pay for some of the discretionary services (e.g., mental health care) that were included in the ACA's bronze plans.

In effect, congressional Democrats voted for a version of the ACA that was far more controversial than was necessary and certainly more controversial than Obama was willing to implement and enforce on his own. Even without an individual mandate, the Medicaid expansion, insurance subsidies, the employer mandate, and other provisions of the ACA would have produced a sharp decline in the number of uninsured.

The need to drop the individual mandate may not have been obvious in January 2009. However, it was apparent after the August 2009 recess (when the Tea Party dominated town hall meetings around the country) and was crystal clear in January 2010 when Republican Scott Brown took Ted Kennedy's Senate seat in Massachusetts, pledging to cast the deciding vote against Obamacare. During 2009–2010 polls clearly showed that Obama's health care initiative was a source of "the highly polarized response to the Obama presidency."[58]

Once the ACA was enacted the Obama administration needed to perform their public administration tasks with more competence and political sensitivity. The unexpected 2012 Supreme Court ruling that weakened the Medicaid expansion should have been followed by a delay in the launch of the federal insurance exchange. The Department of Health and Human Services should have been given adequate time to do proper testing and refinement of HealthCare.gov before the first round of signups on the federal exchange. That basic step would have protected Obama's job approval rating in 2013–2014 and the viability of incumbent Democrats in the November 2014 midterm elections.

The rollout of the ACA could also have been improved with competent implementation of the insurance exchanges. In chapter 6 the website debacle is traced to Obama's lack of attention to the public administration aspects of implementation of the ACA. With some different staffing decisions in the White House and at the Department of Health and Human Services, the roll-out of the insurance exchanges could have occurred more smoothly, with less damage to Obama's job approval ratings, less damage to the popularity of the ACA, and a more favorable political environment for Democrats running for reelection in 2014.

Most importantly, a managerially strong, apolitical administrator of the Center for Medicare and Medicaid Services would have paid enormous dividends to the Obama administration in both the original design of the ACA and throughout the implementation process. The need for this leadership was foreseeable from the outset and would have complemented the political and communications skills of HHS secretary Kathleen Sebelius.

3. An executive approach to climate policy should have been taken in the first term to accomplish emissions reductions in the two most important sectors of the economy: electric power generation and transportation.

Building on the 2007 Supreme Court decision that upheld the EPA's authority to address climate change, President Obama should have issued an executive order in 2009 calling for federal regulation of the two largest sources of greenhouse gases in the US economy: electric power generation and transportation. The timetable for the necessary rule making should have been spread over three years (2009–2011), allowing sufficient time for the proposals to be vetted and refined based on public comment, stakeholder outreach, and scientific/economic analysis. With a final rule issued well before the 2012 election, Obama's reelection path would not have been compromised.

Showing sensitivity to the horrible condition of the economy in 2009, the effective dates for implementation of the rules should have been linked to a key indicator of economic recovery such as the official rate of unemployment or a minimum number of quarters of significant GDP growth. In this way Obama could have insisted that near-term recovery was a priority over regulatory deadlines, since even worthy rules are costly to businesses, workers, and consumers. In effect, the excellent work that the DOT/EPA did with regulating motor vehicle emissions (2009–2012) should have been paralleled with an EPA rule making on the electric power sector. The electric utility rule could have been either a traditional performance standard that each plant must meet or, if the administration was willing to take more legal risk, a cap and trade system operated through the states.

An executive approach to climate change would have spared the Democrats in Congress a damaging roll-call vote on cap and tax. Obama allowed House Democratic leaders Pelosi and Waxman to push a large cap and tax bill through the House on the slimmest of margins, even though there was no plausible pathway to passage in the Senate. The House climate vote was politically damaging to some House Democrats, although not nearly as damaging as the ACA vote.[59]

4. An executive approach to immigration reform should have proceeded in stages: a DREAM-like reform in 2009 for young people followed by more expansive liberalization for adults in 2012, without any of the intensification of punitive enforcement at employers and the border that dominated much of the Obama presidency.

Early in 2009 President Obama should have put a hold on comprehensive immigration reform legislation until the economic crisis eased. Adding numerous unskilled migrants to the US labor market in 2009–2010 was simply not a viable political or economic stance, given the unusually high rates of joblessness and the low rate of job creation.

To show his sympathy with the Hispanic community, Obama should have issued a DREAM-like executive order in early 2009, thereby allowing young undocumented immigrants who have been living in the United States for several years to hold a job, attend college, obtain a Social Security number, and secure a driver's license. The incremental effect on competition for jobs would have been minimal, since these young immigrants were already in the States and most were already working. In fact, after the order some might have left their jobs and enrolled in college, thereby providing some relief for the horrible job market for young people.

From the outset of the administration, Obama should have been skeptical of the alleged linkage between effective border control and congressional willingness to liberalize immigration policy. A careful legislative analysis of the distribution of Hispanic votes would have revealed that it is very difficult to pass immigration-liberalization measures in a GOP-controlled House. Indeed, even progressive Nancy Pelosi was candid with Obama in late 2009 that she did not intend to bring immigration to the House floor unless the Senate acted first. She knew that dozens of incumbent House Democrats were representing districts where a vote for liberalization of immigration law would have been damaging.

The proper level of enforcement at the border and against employers is also a sensitive issue. Obama allowed himself to be plausibly characterized as "Deporter in Chief" by a set of policies that had little chance of setting the stage for liberalization. Since Obama possessed a wide range of enforcement discretion, he should have restrained enforcement so that it was no greater than practiced under George W. Bush.

Instead of legislation, Obama should have followed his 2009 DREAM-like order with a broader executive order in 2011 or 2012, similar to the one he ultimately issued in 2014. President Obama's decision to delay broad executive action in order to allow time for quiet legislative negotiations with John Boehner was questionable for two reasons: (1) the most Boehner could give, under the best of circumstances, was access to work permits, but Obama could achieve that outcome with appropriate executive action; and (2) the House Republicans were unlikely to vote for a pathway to citizenship for both substantive and strategic reasons, yet citizenship was the key policy feature that Democrats desired. If Boehner was serious about delivering meaningful reform legislation, he could have done so any time before or after Obama's executive order was issued. The stark reality was that Boehner's rank-and-file members had too few Hispanics and too many Tea Party sympathizers in their districts to support a pathway to citizenship for undocumented migrants.

～

Overall, the counterfactual Obama presidency could have accomplished more of Obama's policy goals but with less damage to Obama's job approval ratings and the Democratic Party. The themes of the modified Obama presidency are more strategic use of executive power, some centrist legislative proposals to entice a degree of bipartisan collaboration, less cross-posturing of moderate Democrats in Congress, and more attention to the basics of public administration. Even a seemingly small shift in a president's job approval rating can determine the outcome of a significant number of House seats.[60] Moreover, House Democrats would have cast fewer controversial votes and voted for a much less controversial ACA. Senate Democrats also would have faced a less hostile political environment in 2014. Under the revised circumstances the Democrats still would have lost numerous House seats in 2010, due to the large number of Democrats in Republican-leaning districts, and some seats in the Senate in 2014, but the overall magnitude of losses would have been smaller, perhaps allowing the Democratic Party to retain majorities in the Congress. Under that scenario Obama's legislative prospects from 2011 to 2016 would have been vastly greater than they proved to be.

LESSONS FOR FUTURE PRESIDENTS

Barack Obama did not cause partisan polarization in America. It began in the 1970s after the Watergate affair, intensified around 1990, and has hardened for twenty-five years. It has deep roots in the transformation of politics in the Southern and Northeastern regions of the United States. It has been exacerbated by the fragmentation of day-to-day communications in American life, the proliferation of partisan media outlets and talk shows, and a pattern of residential living that leads to more and more people being exposed primarily to people who are like themselves.

The current bout of polarization took decades to develop and is unlikely to dissipate quickly. Thus, the key question for future presidents is how to accomplish some degree of effectiveness in a polarized environment without exposing their co-partisans in Congress to undue risk. The Obama years provide several instructive lessons.

Lesson #1: Presidents who are blessed with a partisan majority in the House of Representatives should jealously guard that majority, even more than they should guard a majority in the coveted Senate.

This counterintuitive claim does not deny how important Senate votes are to confirmation of a president's nominations to the Supreme Court, lower courts, and federal departments and agencies. Without a Senate majority from his own party, the president is certainly put in a much weaker position. On the other hand, in a polarized environment a president who must face a Speaker of the House from the opposing party is in deep trouble with regard to his entire legislative agenda, a reality that has been vividly illustrated by the Obama presidency.

A Speaker of the House from the opposing party can simply block a president's legislative requests from reaching the House floor, as John Boehner did effectively from 2011 to 2015, and without any significant adverse impact on Boehner's ability to maintain Republican control of the House. The mechanism of the Speaker's control is his party caucus, the chairs of relevant committees and subcommittees, and his influence over the Rules Committee.[61]

One might argue that President Ronald Reagan achieved legislative victories in 1981–1984, despite a Democratic House majority, but he did so in the pre-polarization era. Reagan reached across party lines on several occasions and attracted the votes of dozens of Blue Dog and other moderate Democrats. Reagan even collaborated with Democratic Speaker of the House Tip O'Neill.

In the modern era of polarized politics it is much more difficult for the president to obtain crossover votes in the House and extremely difficult to collaborate with a Speaker from the opposing party. Indeed, John Boehner ultimately lost his position as Speaker in late 2015 due to concerns among conservative Republicans that he was attempting too much collaboration with Obama!

The Senate is different from the House because the Senate majority leader does not have the same degree of agenda-setting control as the Speaker of the House. In 2013 Majority Leader Reid revised the Senate rules temporarily to gain greater control over which amendments were debated on the floor. Senate Republicans punished Reid for this maneuver through unified party voting against Reid-favored measures. Reid only began to allow more GOP-sponsored amendments in 2014 when the GOP allowed more of Obama's executive nominations to be approved.[62] The committee process is also less rigid in the Senate than the House, which means that on some occasions a presidential initiative may be able to get to the Senate floor without a full-blown committee deliberation. Since a Democratic president knows that his party faces especially tough midterm elections, special efforts should be taken to protect a precious partisan majority in the House.

My investigation of the Obama presidency suggests that Obama did not jealously guard his Democratic House majority and often behaved as if his

Democratic majority in the Senate was more important to him. Moderate Democratic incumbents in the House were asked to take risky roll-call votes on progressive initiatives that were unlikely to pass the Senate or could have been accomplished (in whole or in part) through executive action. Moreover, the deliberative sequence of House-first/Senate-second was used on some key issues when a Senate-first sequence might have protected numerous House Democrats from taking risky votes. Some argue that the bad votes in the House are more the responsibility of Speaker Pelosi than they are of the White House.[63] In other words, Obama may not have been as successful managing Pelosi as he needed to be for his own—and his party's—political benefit.

As his party's leader Obama also seemed to give more priority to the Senate than the House. He was highly successful in raising money for Democrats in both chambers, but in 2010 he was, inexplicably, more willing to appear on behalf of Senate incumbents than House incumbents. Many of the House incumbents in tough races in 2010 were freshmen and sophomores who were poorly known among Democratic voters. Although Obama was unpopular among Republicans, his job approval ratings were still high among Democrats. A district visit by Obama would have boosted the incumbent's visibility and credibility while energizing base voters. In 2014 Obama appeared ready to assist House as well as Senate incumbents, but there were few House freshman and sophomores to defend, and the case was made that his popularity was so low that personal appearances with Democratic incumbents were too risky. Had the counterfactual agenda been pursued, Obama's popularity would not have declined so sharply and he might have been a more effective resource on the campaign trails in 2010 and 2014. A campaign model for protecting a partisan House majority may have been George W. Bush in 2002, when, aided by some of his post 9/11 boost in popularity, he campaigned tirelessly for Republican House incumbents and some GOP challengers, and the resulting GOP gains in the House speak for themselves.

Lesson #2: Presidents in a polarized environment should see the cross-partisan strategy as the primary means of working legislative requests through the Congress.

The White House rarely has the option of a partisan approach to lawmaking. A filibuster threat by the minority party is very difficult to overcome because of the sixty-vote Senate threshold. The pattern that worked for both George W. Bush (2001–2006) and Barack Obama (2009–2010) was a partisan approach in the House (i.e., no compromises to leaders or members of the opposing party) and a sixty-plus Senate vote comprised primarily of votes from the president's party, supplemented by a sufficient number of votes from the opposing party (usually in the range of one to fifteen) to limit the time for debate on the floor. The strength of this cross-partisan strategy is that it minimizes the number of compromises that must be made to members of the opposing party.

Contrary to popular belief, Obama did not achieve most of his legislative victories from party-line votes by Democrats. The Affordable Care Act was the only major legislative achievement accomplished with Democratic votes alone. All of the other Obama wins in Congress examined in this book were comprised of at least a small number of votes from Senate Republicans.

Lesson #3: The executive lawmaking route should become more popular among presidents than legislation, because it may be quieter, have a higher probability of success, and create fewer damaging cross-pressures on members of Congress from the president's party.

Like George W. Bush, Barack Obama underutilized executive power as a means to lawmaking, although they both strived to use it in their second terms. The climate and immigration chapters illustrate this point vividly.

In a polarized environment where legislation is difficult to obtain and where controversial votes can threaten the president's partisan majorities in Congress, executive policy making is often a more dependable and party-protective strategy. It is also less "noisy" than legislative debates, which means that the approval-reducing impacts of controversy—especially among independents—are lessened for both the president and his allies in Congress.

Instead of starting with a legislative proposal and treating executive action as either an implementation mechanism or a last resort to lawmaking, a president should begin to consider executive action as the preferred lawmaking approach (whenever feasible) and legislation as the last resort if he runs into insurmountable obstacles. Whenever a president induces controversial roll-call votes on legislation when he could have acted unilaterally, he is not giving adequate attention to his role as party leader. Whether they like it or not, it is crucial—under conditions of polarization—for presidents to see themselves as leader of their political party as well as leader of the country. Executive action may be prudent when a legislative request will cross-pressure more members of the president's party than members of the opposing party in Congress.

◠

President Obama was an effective lawmaker in economic policy, health care, and climate change. He could have been even more effective by integrating his role as party leader into his role as national policy maker and by performing more astute political analyses of the content of his policy agenda and his decisions about executive versus administrative action. The result would have been fewer congressional Democrats "walking the plank" for his progressive agenda. For Obama, the benefit would have been a longer period of service in the White House with the support of a Democratic congressional majority. For future presidents, whether conservative or liberal, the Obama presidency is rich with lessons from victories and setbacks.

NOTES

1. Barack Obama's Assets and Constraints

1. Barack Obama, *Dreams from My Father: A Story of Race and Inheritance* (New York: Three Rivers Press, 2004).

2. Christopher S. Parker and Matt A. Barreto, *Change They Can't Believe In: The Tea Party and Reactionary Politics in America* (Princeton, NJ: Princeton University Press, 2013).

3. Graham G. Dodds, "Unilateral Directives," in *The Obama Presidency: A Preliminary Assessment*, eds. Robert P. Watson, Jack Covarrubias, Tom Lansford, and Douglas M. Brattebo (Albany: SUNY Press, 2012), 343; Erwin C. Hargrove, *The Effective Presidency*, 2nd ed. (Boulder, CO: Paradigm Publishers, 2014), 259; Bert A. Rockman, Eric N. Waltenburg, and Colin Campbell, "Presidential Style and the Obama Presidency," in *The Obama Presidency: Appraisals and Prospects*, eds. Bert A. Rockman, Andrew Rudalevige, and Colin Campbell (Washington, DC: CQ Press, 2012), 259–60, 338–40.

4. Richard Benedetto, "Rookie Senators, Beware," *USA Today*, November 5, 2014, 10A.

5. Hargrove, *Effective Presidency*, 277, 279 (describing Obama as a "progressive communitarian" whose progressive values were most evident in his second inaugural address).

6. John Harwood, "'Partisan' Seeks a Prefix: Bi- or Post-," *New York Times*, December 6, 2008.

7. Bill Adair and Angie Drobnic Holan, "Several Ratings Rank Obama Lower," September 26, 2008, *Politifact.com*, http://www.politifact.com/truth-o-meter /statements/2008/sep/26/john-mccain/several-ratings-rank-obama-lower.

8. John S. Jackson and John C. Green, *The State of Party Elites: The Changing Role of Contemporary American Parties*, eds. John C. Green and Daniel J. Coffey (Lanham, MD: Rowman and Littlefield, 2011), 72–73.

9. James E. Campbell, "Political Forces on the Obama Presidency: From Elections to Governing," in Rockman et al., *Obama Presidency*, 74, fig. 4.1.

10. James E. Campbell, "The Exceptional Election of 2008: Performance, Values, and Crisis," *Presidential Studies Quarterly* 40, no. 2 (2010): 225–46.

11. Shanto Iyengar, *Media Politics. A Citizen's Guide* (New York: W. W. Norton, 2011), 280 (McCain had a slight lead until the economic crisis "fundamentally altered the trajectory of voter preference"); Campbell, "Political Forces," 79–80 (the presidential campaigns were derailed by the economic crisis, since a mid-August survey of forty-seven prominent economists contained no hint of the collapse; McCain's Gallup preference polls dropped six percentage points from September 14 to October 6), 89 ("The basis for Obama's victory over McCain, the turning point in the election, was the Wall Street Meltdown").

12. Hargrove, *Effective Presidency*, 261 ("had there been no financial meltdown, as there was in the fall, Obama still would have won").

13. Scout Tufankjian, *Yes We Can: Barack Obama's History-Making Presidential Campaign* (Brooklyn, NY: PowerHouse Books, 2008). This book includes especially good photographs of key events during the 2008 campaign.

14. Daniel M. Shea, "The Obama Netroots Campaign, Young Voters, and the Future of Local Party Organizations," in Green and Coffey, *State of Party Elites*, 142–43.

15. John Allen Hendricks and Robert E. Denton Jr., *Communicator-in-Chief: How Barack Obama Used New Media Technology to Win the White House* (Lanham, MD: Lexington Books, 2010).

16. Shea, "Obama Netroots Campaign," 143.

17. Charlie Cook, "Shifting Rubble," *National Journal*, December 1, 2012, 56; Gary C. Jacobson, "Polarization, Public Opinion, and the Presidency: The Obama and Anti-Obama Coalitions," in Rockman et al., *Obama Presidency*, 98; Kenneth R. Mayer, "Lessons of Defeat: Republican Party Responses to the 2012 Presidential Election," in *The 2012 Presidential Election: Forecasts, Outcomes, and Consequences*, eds. Amnon Cavari, Richard J. Powell, and Kenneth R. Mayer (Lanham, MD: Rowman and Littlefield, 2014), 111–16; Beth Reinhard, "Southern Democrats Walk a Tightrope with Black Voters," *Wall Street Journal*, October 6, 2014, A1 (in 2012 Obama became the first president in history to stimulate a higher turnout among blacks [66.2 percent] than among whites [64.1 percent], according to exit polls).

18. The monthly rate of unemployment declined from a peak of 10.0 percent in October 2009 to 9.4 percent in 2010, 8.8 percent in October 2011, and 7.8 percent in October 2013. "Labor Force Statistics from the Current Population Survey," *Bureau of Labor Statistics*, http://data.bls.gov/timeseries/LNS14000000. Also see Andrew J. Dowdle, Dirk C. Van Raemdonck, and Robert Maranto, eds., *The Obama Presidency: Change and Continuity* (New York: Routledge, 2011), 13.

19. James E. Campbell, "The Miserable Presidential Election of 2012: A First Party-Term Incumbent Survives," *Forum* 10, no. 4 (2012): 20–28.

20. Bush lost Iowa to Gore in 2000 but won Iowa against Kerry in 2004.

21. See, for example, Richard Waterman, Carol L. Smith, and Hank Jenkins-Smith, *The Presidential Expectations Gap* (Ann Arbor: University of Michigan

Press, 2014), 159 (expectations gap causes lower presidential approval ratings and lower vote for reelection of incumbent president and president's party at midterm elections). Also see Louis Brownlow, *President and the Presidency* (Chicago: Public Administration Service, 1947), 3 (one of the first presidential scholars to address the presidential expectations gap); Stephen Wayne, "Great Expectations: What People Want from Presidents," in *Rethinking the Presidency*, ed. Thomas E. Cronin (Boston: Little, Brown, 1982), 185; Theodore Lowi, *The Personal Presidency* (Ithaca, NY: Cornell University Press, 1985), 11 (due to excessive expectations, "partial success is defined by the mass public as failure"); John Davis, "Assessing the Obama Presidency: A Window into the Future," in *The Barack Obama Presidency: A Two-Year Assessment*, ed. John Davis (New York: Palgrave Macmillan, 2011), 220 ("the reality is that Obama could never live up to those expectations"); Robert P. Watson, "Rating Presidents and Assessing Obama," in Watson et al., *Obama Presidency*, 14; Barbara Sinclair, "Doing Big Things: Obama and the 111th Congress," in Rockman et al., *Obama Presidency*, 198 (expectations for Obama were at "dizzying heights").

22. Dante Chinni, "Second-Term Slips," *Wall Street Journal*, November 23–24, 2013, A4 (Obama-ACA, Clinton-Monica, and GWB-Katrina experienced parallel paths of declining popularity in their second terms, though for very different reasons).

23. Julia Azari, *Delivering the People's Message: The Changing Politics of the Presidential Mandate* (Ithaca, NY: Cornell University, 2014), 158.

24. Michael Hirsh, "George W. Bush: He Gave Rise to the Tea Party," *National Journal*, October 2, 2013.

25. Kate Zernike, *Boiling Mad: Inside Tea Party America* (New York: Henry Holt, 2010), 13–18.

26. Theda Skocpol and Vanessa Williamson, *The Tea Party and the Remaking of Republican Conservatism* (New York: Oxford University Press, 2012), 7–8.

27. Zernike, *Boiling Mad*, 168.

28. Ibid., 163–64.

29. Parker and Barreto, *Change They Can't Believe In*, 35.

30. Gary C. Jacobson. *The Politics of Congressional Elections*, 8th ed. (New York: Pearson, 2013), 222–27, esp. note 121.

31. Zernike, *Boiling Mad*, 192 (the Tea Party movement was more about small-government libertarianism than social issues).

32. Douglas M. Brattebo and Robert P. Watson, "Making History," in Watson et al., *Obama Presidency*, 414–15.

33. The Democrats had fifty-nine seats in the Senate from January to July 2009 because Democratic senator Al Franken of Minnesota (who won a contested race) did not take office until July 2009.

34. The total number of types of unilateral executive action may be twenty-nine. Graham G. Dodds, *Take up Your Pen: Unilateral Presidential Directives in American Politics* (Philadelphia: University of Pennsylvania Press, 2013), 6.

35. On presidential executive orders, see Kenneth R. Mayer, *With the Stroke of a Pen: Executive Orders and Presidential Power* (Princeton, NJ: Princeton University

Press, 2001); and Adam L. Warber, *Executive Orders and the Modern Presidency: Legislating from the Oval Office* (Boulder, CO: Lynne Rienner, 2006). On rule making, see Terry Moe and William G. Howell, "The Presidential Power of Unilateral Action," *Journal of Law, Economics, and Organizations* 15, no. 1 (1999): 132–79; and Cindy Skrzycki, *The Regulators: The Anonymous Power Brokers Who Shape Your Life* (Lanham, MD: Rowman and Littlefield, 2003).

36. Gregory Korte, "How Obama Became the Go-It-Alone President," *USA Today*, December 17, 2014, A1; Kenneth S. Lowande, "The Contemporary Presidency after the Orders: Presidential Memoranda and Unilateral Action," *Presidential Studies Quarterly*, October 27, 2014; Dodds, *Take up Your Pen*, 6.

37. For in-depth evidence of the impact of executive orders on equal employment opportunity, White House review of regulations, and environmental policy, see Ricardo Jose Pereira Rodrigues, *The Preeminence of Politics: Executive Orders from Eisenhower to Clinton* (New York: LFB Scholarly Publishing, 2007). Also see Mayer, *With the Stroke of a Pen*; Phillip J. Cooper, *By Order of the President: The Use and Abuse of Executive Direct Action* (Lawrence: University of Kansas Press, 2003); and Adam L. Weber, *Executive Orders and the Modern Presidency: Legislating from the Oval Office* (Boulder, CO: Lynne Rienner, 2006).

38. "Executive Order 13166," *Limited English Proficiency (LEP): A Federal Interagency Website*, http://www.lep.gov/13166/eo/13166.html.

39. Elena Kagan, "Presidential Administration," *Harvard Law Review* 114, no. 8 (June 2001): 245–385.

40. Dodds, *Take up Your Pen*, 12 (when EOs are challenged in federal court, the president wins about 86 percent of the time).

41. Ibid. (fewer than 10 percent of executive orders are overridden by Congress).

42. US General Accounting Office, "Delay of Effective Dates of Final Rules Subject to Administration's January 20, 2001, Memorandum," GAO-02-370R. Washington, DC, January 2002.

43. Cass R. Sunstein, David Schkade, Lisa M. Ellman, and Andres Sawicki, *Are Judges Political? An Empirical Analysis of the Federal Judiciary* (Washington, DC: Brookings Institution Press, 2006).

44. On the role of supermajority requirements in legislatures, see Manabu Saeki, *The Other Side of Gridlock: Policy Stability and Supermajoritarianism in US Lawmaking* (Albany: SUNY Press, 2010), 12, 13–14. On the history of the filibuster in the US Senate, see Gregory Koger, *Filibustering: A Political History in the House and Senate* (Chicago: University of Chicago Press, 2010); and for a defense of the filibuster, see Richard A. Arenberg and Robert B. Dove, *Defending the Filibuster: The Soul of the Senate* (Bloomington: Indiana University Press, 2012).

45. Thomas E. Mann and Normal J. Ornstein, *The Broken Branch: How Congress Is Failing America and How to Get It Back on Track* (New York: Oxford University Press, 2006), 10, 93; Barbara Sinclair, "The President and the Congressional Party Leadership in a Hyperpartisan Era," in *Rivals for Power: Presidential-Congressional Relations*, 5th ed., ed. James A. Thurber (Lanham, MD: Rowman and Littlefield, 2013), 116.

46. Matthew N. Beckmann, *Pushing the Agenda: Presidential Leadership in U.S. Lawmaking, 1953–2004* (New York: Cambridge University Press, 2010), 7, table 1.1; see generally Jon R. Bond, Richard Fleisher, and Glen S. Krutz, "Malign Neglect: Evidence That Delay Has Become the Primary Method of Defeating Presidential Appointments," *Congress and the Presidency* 36, no. 3 (2009): 1–18.

47. E. Scott Adler and John D. Wilkerson, *Congress and the Politics of Problem Solving* (New York: Cambridge University Press, 2012), 139.

48. Sinclair, "President and Congressional Party Leadership," 146–59; John H. Aldrich, *Why Parties? A Second Look* (Chicago: University of Chicago Press, 2011), 244–46, 247.

49. "Presidents are not legislators—in chief or otherwise." Beckmann, *Pushing the Agenda*, 5.

50. "The Constitution remains largely silent on the nature and extent of presidential authority, especially in domestic affairs." Terry M. Moe and Scott A. Wilson, "Presidents and the Politics of Structure," *Law and Contemporary Problems* 57, no. 2 (1994): 23.

51. Dodds, *Take up Your Pen*, 36–38, 43–44.

52. Mann and Ornstein, *Broken Branch*, 14, 19–20.

53. Dodds, *Take up Your Pen*, 30–31, 33.

54. On the process of agenda setting in the legislature, see Gary W. Cox and Matthew D. McCubbins, *Setting the Agenda* (Cambridge: Cambridge University Press, 2005). On vote-centered strategies, see Beckmann, *Pushing the Agenda*, 17.

55. Beckmann, *Pushing the Agenda*, 46–47.

56. On agenda setting, see Beckmann, *Pushing the Agenda*, 19; on vote-centered influence, see Marc J. Hetherington and Bruce A. Larson, *Parties, Politics, and Public Policy in America*, 11th ed. (Washington, DC: CQ Press, 2010), 184, fig. 5–5. From 1949 to 2006 the record shows that presidents won about 60 percent of their formal requests to Congress, surprisingly similar rates during unified and divided government. David R. Mayhew, *Partisan Balance: Why Political Parties Don't Kill the U.S. Constitution System* (Princeton, NJ: Princeton University Press, 2011), 57–58; David W. Brady and Craig Volden, *Revolving Gridlock: Politics and Policy from Jimmy Carter to George W. Bush*, 2nd ed. (Boulder, CO: Westview Press, 2005), 39–40.

57. William A. Galston, "Obama and the Limits of Unilateral Action," *Wall Street Journal*, January 29, 2014, A15.

58. Beckmann, *Pushing the Agenda*, 19.

59. Jacob S. Hacker and Paul Pierson, *Off Center: The Republican Revolution and the Erosion of American Democracy* (New Haven, CT: Yale University Press, 2006), 171.

60. The notion of a "cross-partisan" strategy, and how it is distinct from bipartisanship, was advanced in Charles O. Jones, *The Presidency in a Separated System*, 2nd ed. (Washington, DC: Brookings Institution Press, 2005); seeds of the idea are apparent in Charles O. Jones, *Separate but Equal Branches: Congress and the Presidency* (Chatham, NJ: Chatham House Press, 1995).

61. A key feature of "cross-partisanship" is that collaboration with members of the other party may not occur until late in the process and may occur in only one of the two chambers (where votes are short). See Jones, *Presidency in a Separated System*, 26–30.

62. Frances E. Lee, *Beyond Ideology: Politics, Principles, and Partisanship in the US Senate* (Chicago: University of Chicago Press, 2009), chapter 4.

63. Mann and Ornstein, *Broken Branch*, 124.

64. John D. Graham, *Bush on the Home Front: Triumphs and Setbacks* (Bloomington: Indiana University Press, 2010), 316–20.

65. Graham, *Bush on the Home Front*.

66. Brady and Volden, *Revolving Gridlock*, 31.

67. Mayhew, *Partisan Balance*, 61; Hetherington and Larson, *Parties, Politics, and Public Policy*, 183.

68. Bob Woodward, *The Price of Politics* (New York: Simon and Schuster, 2012); Ron Suskind, *Confidence Men: Wall Street, Washington, and the Education of a President* (New York: Harper, 2011); Michael Grunwald, *The NEW New Deal: The Hidden Story of Change in the Obama Era* (New York: Simon and Schuster, 2012); Richard Wolffe, *Revival: The Struggle for Survival Inside the Obama White House* (New York: Crown, 2010).

69. Lawrence R. Jacobs and Theda Skocpol, *Health Care Reform and American Politics: What Everyone Needs to Know* (New York: Oxford University Press, 2012).

70. Theda Skocpol, "Naming the Problem: What It Will Take to Counter Extremism and Engage Americans in the Fight against Global Warming," paper prepared for the symposium on "The Politics of America's Fight against Global Warming," co-sponsored by the Columbia School of Journalism and the Scholars Strategy Network, Tsai Auditorium, Harvard University, Boston, Massachusetts, February 14, 2013.

71. Watson et al., *Obama Presidency*; Rockman et al., *Obama Presidency*; John Davis, ed., *The Barack Obama Presidency: A Two-Year Assessment* (New York: Palgrave-MacMillan, 2011); Dowdle et al., *Obama Presidency*; Carol McNamara and Melanie M. Marlowe, eds., *The Obama Presidency in the Constitutional Order: A First Look*, rev. ed. (Lanham, MD: Rowman and Littlefield, 2011).

72. Brenden J. Doherty, *The Rise of the President's Permanent Campaign* (Lawrence: University of Kansas Press, 2012), 171; Daniel J. Galvin, *Presidential Party Building, Dwight D. Eisenhower to George W. Bush* (Princeton, NJ: Princeton University Press, 2010), 7.

73. Gary C. Jacobson, *A Divider, Not a Uniter: George W. Bush and the American People* (New York: Pearson Education, 2007).

74. Harwood, "Partisan Seeks a Prefix."

75. James Q. Wilson, "How Divided Are We?" *Commentary* 121, no. 2 (February 2006): 15–21; Sunil Ahuja, *Congress Behaving Badly: The Rise of Partisanship and Incivility and the Death of Public Trust* (Westport, CT: Praeger, 2008).

76. George C. Edwards III, *Overreach: Leadership and the Obama Presidency* (Princeton, NJ: Princeton University Press 2012), 20 (Obama's legislative agenda in 2009 lent credence to the Tea Party frame that he is a "left wing radical").

77. Parker and Barretto, *Change They Can't Believe In*, 55 (Tea Party belief that Obama is on his way to destroy the country with socialism); Azari, *Delivering the People's Message*, 163 (Tea Party denounced Obama and his policies as "socialist"); John Drew, "How I Confronted Obama Biographer David Maraniss," *American Thinker*, November 2, 2012 (arguing from firsthand experience with Obama at Occidental College in California "that young Obama was 100% committed to preparing for a Communist revolution in the United States"), http://www.americanthinker.com /articles/2012/11/how_i_confronted_obama_biographer_david_maraniss.html.

78. Charlie Cook, "Colossal Miscalculation on Health Care," *National Journal*, January 16, 2010; Charlie Cook, "Too Much All at Once," *Off to the Races*, February 2, 2010 (the public wanted a focus on jobs and the economy; proposals on health care and climate change were too much); Edwards, *Overreach*, 10 (Obama should have told the public that he could not afford health care or the environment because he was pouring money into the economy, nursing it back together).

79. Paul C. Light, "Less Room for Breakthrough Ideas," *Washington Post*, November 11, 2008; Edwards, *Overreach*, 119 (in 2009 Obama deferred a fight over the Bush tax cuts, opposed a commission on interrogation tactics, declined to engage on guns or gays in the military, deferred on immigration reform, and disengaged on the union "card check" issue).

80. William A. Galston, "Barack Obama's First Two Years: Policy Accomplishments, Political Failures," in Dowdle et al., *Obama Presidency*, 195.

81. Beckmann, *Pushing the Agenda*, 12–13; Brandice Canes-Wrone, *Who Leads Whom? Presidents, Policy, and the Public* (Chicago: University of Chicago Press, 2006), 49; Azari, *Delivering the People's Message*, 140.

82. Canes-Wrone, *Who Leads Whom?* 49, 51–81.

83. Richard M. Skinner, "Barack Obama and the Partisan Presidency," in Green and Coffey, *State of the Parties*, 319–20 (Obama "has advanced an agenda that has so far proved to have little cross-party appeal").

84. Edwards, *Overreach*, 46 (reporting but not sharing these sentiments); Joel D. Auerbach, "'Change We Can Believe In' Meets Reality," in Rockman et al., *Obama Presidency*, 29–30 ("liberals see [Obama] as much too prone to compromise"); Stephen J. Wayne, "Obama's First Term, Legislative Presidency," in Thurber, *Rivals for Power*, 27, 35–36 (critics on the left say Obama compromised too much and too soon in his first year; he was not sufficiently supportive of the left's core concerns).

85. Michael Barone and Chuck McCutcheon, *The Almanac of American Politics, 2012* (Washington, DC: National Journal Group, 2011) (read the narratives on each of these veteran Senators and their periodic disputes with the Obama administration).

86. Galston, "Barack Obama's First Two Years," 195 (Obama's 2009 agenda "reinforced the narrative that the Republicans wanted to promote anyway, which was [that] Obama is not a different kind of Democrat—he's the same old tax-and-spend liberal").

87. Ibid., 187–200.

88. Aaron Wildavsky, "The Two Presidencies," *Trans-Action*, December 4, 1996, 7–14.

89. For temporal comparisons of public opinion as to whether the president should be active in world affairs or "mind [his] own business internationally," see Janet Hook, "Americans Want to Pull Back from World Stage," *Wall Street Journal*, April 30, 2014, A1 (citing data from both WSJ/NBC and the Pew Research Center surveys); also see Susan Page and Kendall Breitman, "Sanction Russia, Don't Arm Ukraine," *USA Today*, April 29, 2014, 1A, 5A (more detail on Pew Research Center Survey: by 72 percent to 13 percent, respondents said president should focus more on domestic policy, a margin that was up ten percentage points from previous years).

90. "The Blueprint for Change: Barack Obama's Plan for America," *On the Issues*, 2008, http://www.ontheissues.org/Blueprint_Obama.htm.

91. Hargrove, *Effective Presidency*, 279.

92. James Mann, "Obama Isn't Finished Yet," *New York Times*, September 23, 2014, A27 (some of Reagan's, Clinton's, and Bush's accomplishments came in their last two years, but mostly in foreign policy); Thomas F. "Mack" McLarty, "How Obama Can Salvage His Last Two Years," *Wall Street Journal*, October 21, 2014, A15 (last two years of second term are easier in foreign than domestic affairs).

93. Steven G. Calabresi and Christopher S. Yoo, *The Unitary Executive: Presidential Power from Washington to Bush* (New Haven, CT: Yale University Press, 2008).

94. Philip E. Tetlock and Aaron Belkin, eds., *Counterfactual Thought Experiments in World Politics* (Princeton, NJ: Princeton University Press, 1996); Joseph S. Nye Jr., *Presidential Leadership and the Creation of the American Era* (Princeton, NJ: Princeton University Press, 2013), 62.

95. B. Fischhoff and R. Beyth, "'I Knew It Would Happen': Remembered Probabilities of Once Future Things," *Organizational Behavior and Human Performance* 13 (1975): 1–16; Neal J. Roese and Kathleen D. Vohs, "Hindsight Bias," *Perspectives on Psychological Science* 7, no. 5 (2012): 411–26.

96. For a popular introduction to decision analysis, see John S. Hammond, Ralph L. Keeney, and Howard Raiffa, *Smart Choices: A Practical Guide to Making Better Decisions* (Boston: Harvard Business Review Press, 1999).

97. Nye, *Presidential Leadership*, 62.

2. Presidential Effectiveness When Congress Is Polarized

1. Terry M. Moe and William G. Howell, "Unilateral Action and Presidential Power: A Theory," *Presidential Studies Q.* 29, no. 4 (1999): 850–73.

2. Eric A. Posner and Adrian Vermeule, *The Executive Unbound: After the Madisonian Republic* (New York: Oxford University Press, 2011).

3. Brandice Canes-Wrone, *Who Leads Whom? Presidents, Policy, and the Public* (Chicago: University of Chicago Press, 2006), 181.

4. James Mann, "Obama Isn't Finished Yet," *New York Times*, September 23, 2014, A27.

5. Paul Light, *The President's Agenda: Domestic Policy Choice from Kennedy to Carter* (Baltimore, MD: Johns Hopkins University Press, 1999).

6. Jon R. Bond and Richard Fleisher, *The President in the Legislative Arena* (Chicago: University of Chicago Press, 1990).

7. David R. Mayhew, *Partisan Balance: Why Political Parties Don't Kill the U.S. Constitution System* (Princeton, NJ: Princeton University Press, 2011), 57–58.

8. Ibid., 37.

9. On "position taking" by elected officials, especially legislators, see generally David R. Mayhew, *Congress: The Electoral Connection* (New Haven, CT: Yale University Press, 1974).

10. Frances E. Lee, *Beyond Ideology: Politics, Principles, and Partisanship in the US Senate* (Chicago: University of Chicago Press, 2009), 70.

11. A cross-pressured legislator is sometimes defined as one who feels party leadership pressure to vote one way and constituent (or interest group, activist, or donor) pressure to vote another way. See Jamie L. Carson, "Electoral Accountability, Party Loyalty, and Roll-Call Voting in the US Senate," in *Why Not Parties?*, eds. Nathan W. Monroe, Jason M. Roberts, and David W. Rohde (Chicago: University of Chicago Press, 2008), 29.

12. Matthew J. Lebo and Andrew J. O'Geen, "The President's Role in the Partisan Congressional Arena," *Journal of Politics* 73, no. 3 (2011): 718–34.

13. Ibid.

14. Joseph S. Nye Jr., *Presidential Leadership and the Creation of the American Era* (Princeton, NJ: Princeton University Press, 2013), 89.

15. Ibid., 76.

16. Morris P. Fiorina, *Disconnect: The Breakdown of Representation in American Politics* (Norman: University of Oklahoma Press, 2009), 8–9.

17. William A. Galston, "Americans Are as Polarized as Washington," *Wall Street Journal*, June 3, 2014.

18. One national exit poll during the November 2012 presidential general election reported 35 percent self-declared conservatives, 25 percent liberals, and 40 percent moderates (or unable or unwilling to classify). See James E. Campbell, "The Miserable Presidential Election of 2012: A First Party-Term Incumbent Survives," *Forum* 10, no. 4 (2012): 27, table 6.

19. On the importance of moderate voters in American politics, and how they differ from party activists, see Fiorina, *Disconnect*.

20. Fiorina, *Disconnect*, 12–14; George C. Edwards III, *Overreach: Leadership and the Obama Presidency* (Princeton, NJ: Princeton University Press 2012), 14, table 1.1.

21. James E. Campbell, "Political Forces on the Obama Presidency: From Elections to Governing," in *The Obama Presidency: Appraisals and Prospects*, eds. Bert A. Rockman, Andrew Rudalevige, and Colin Campbell (Washington, DC: CQ Press, 2012), 75.

22. Ibid., 82.

23. George C. Edwards III, *Strategic Assessments: Evaluating Opportunities and Strategies in the Obama Presidency* (Washington, DC: CQ Press, 2012), 44–45 (citing Gallup surveys showing roughly twice as many self-declared conservatives as

self-declared liberals; in 2009 no state in the USA—not even Vermont, Hawaii, or Massachusetts—had a majority or even plurality of people who called themselves liberals). Also see Edwards, *Overreach*, 126.

24. Campbell, "Political Forces," 77 (averaged ANES data from 2004 and 2008: 45 percent of strong Democrats describe themselves as liberal; 85 percent of strong Republicans describe themselves as conservative).

25. Fiorina, *Disconnect*, 170–73.

26. Christopher Ellis and James A. Stimson, *Ideology in America* (New York: Cambridge University Press, 2012).

27. Campbell, "Political Forces," 70.

28. Shanto Iyengar, *Media Politics: A Citizen's Guide* (New York: W. W. Norton, 2011), 307–308.

29. Ibid., 313.

30. Nye, *Presidential Leadership*, 6.

31. Nicholas Henry, *Public Administration and Public Affairs*, 11th ed. (New York: Longman, 2010); John Mikesell, *Fiscal Administration*, 8th ed. (Boston: Wadsworth, 2011).

32. Woodrow Wilson, "The Study of Administration (1887)," in *Classics of Public Administration*, eds. Jay Shafritz and Albert Hyde, 4th ed. (Fort Worth, TX: Harcourt Brace, 1997).

33. Robert Dahl, "The Science of Public Administration: Three Problems," *Public Administration Review* 7, no. 1 (1947): 1–11; David Rosenbloom, "The Politics-Administration Dichotomy in US Historical Context," *Public Administration Review* 68, no. 1 (2008): 57–60.

34. Daniel J. Galvin, *Presidential Party Building, Dwight D. Eisenhower to George W. Bush* (Princeton, NJ: Princeton University Press, 2010), 7.

35. Ibid.

36. John H. Aldrich and David W. Rohde, "The Consequences of Party Organization in the House: The Role of Majority and Minority Parties in Conditional Government," in *Polarized Politics*, eds. John R. Bond and Richard Fleisher (Washington, DC: CQ Press, 2000), 67–69; Richard M. Skinner, "Barack Obama and the Partisan Presidency," in John S. Jackson and John C. Green, *The State of Party Elites: The Changing Role of Contemporary American Parties*, eds. John C. Green and Daniel J. Coffey (Lanham, MD: Rowman and Littlefield, 2011), 309, 313.

37. Galvin, *Presidential Power Building*, 30–31, 257.

38. Ibid., 25.

39. On Obama's role as a fund-raiser, see Brendan J. Doherty, "Presidential Re-election Fundraising from Jimmy Carter to Barack Obama," *Political Science Quarterly* 129, no. 44 (2014–15): 585–612.

40. Galvin, *Presidential Power Building*, 5.

41. Ronald Brownstein, "Running Into the Wind," *National Journal*, January 15, 2014, 6.

42. Marc J. Hetherington and Bruce A. Larson, *Parties, Politics, and Public Policy in America*, 11th ed. (Washington, DC: CQ Press, 2010), 6–7, table 1–17.

43. The term "Bush 41" refers to George Herbert Walker Bush, the forty-first president of the United States. "Bush 43" refers to Bush 41's son George W. Bush, the forty-third president of the United States.

44. The tension between being a good presidential policy maker and being a good party leader is sometimes called the "leadership dilemma." See Julia R. Azari, Lara M. Brown, and Zim G. Nwokora, "A Rock and A Hard Place: Between a Party and the People," in *The Presidential Leadership Dilemma: Between the Constitution and a Political Party*, eds. Julia R. Azari, Lara M. Brown, and Zim G. Nwokora (Albany: SUNY Press, 2013), 2–4.

45. Lebo and O'Geen, "President's Role," 718–34.

46. Jeffrey E. Cohen, Jon R. Bond, and Richard Fleisher, "The Implications of the 2012 Presidential Election for Presidential-Congressional Elections: Change or More of the Same?" in *The 2012 Presidential Election: Forecasts, Outcomes, and Consequences*, eds. Amnon Cavari, Richard J. Powell, and Kenneth R. Mayer (Lanham, MD: Rowman and Littlefield, 2014), 158–59, 161.

47. Fiorina, *Disconnect*, 152.

48. Marty Cohen, David Karol, Hans Noel, and John Zaller, *The Party Decides: Presidential Nominations Before and After Reform* (Chicago: University of Chicago Press, 2008), 350–51.

49. Hetherington and Larson, *Parties, Politics, and Public Policy*, 39, table 2-1.

50. Sean M. Theriault, *Party Polarization in Congress* (New York: Cambridge University Press, 2008), 113.

51. Barbara Sinclair, *Party Wars: Polarization and the Politics of National Policy Making* (Norman: University of Oklahoma Press, 2006), 23, 29–30.

52. Fiorina, *Disconnect*, 87; David Louter, "Partisan Divide More Entrenched, Study Finds," *LA Times*, June 13, 2014 (quoting Pew Research Center results of survey of ten thousand adults; ideologically strident voters have increased level of antipathy toward other major ideology; strident voters have more influence because they engage more in the process, vote more, volunteer more, and give more money to candidates).

53. John H. Aldrich, *Why Parties? A Second Look* (Chicago: University of Chicago Press, 2011), 169–201.

54. Sinclair, *Party Wars*, 29–30.

55. James N. Druckman and Lawrence R. Jacobs, *Who Governs? Presidents, Public Opinion, and Manipulation* (Chicago: University of Chicago Press, 2015), 11, 13.

56. James P. Pfiffner, *The Strategic Presidency: Hitting the Ground Running* (Lawrence: University Press of Kansas, 1996), 113.

57. Carl Hulse and Adam Nagourney, "Senate GOP Leader Finds Weapon in Unity," *New York Times*, March 16, 2010.

58. James A. Thurber, ed., *Rivals for Power: Presidential-Congressional Relations*, 5th ed. (Lanham, MD: Rowman and Littlefield, 2013), 7–9.

59. For the formal theory of "pivotal" legislative politics, see Keith Krehbiel, *Pivotal Politics: A Theory of US Lawmaking* (Chicago: University of Chicago Press, 1998), esp. 23–24.

60. David W. Brady and Craig Volden, *Revolving Gridlock: Politics and Policy from Jimmy Carter to George W. Bush*, 2nd ed. (Boulder, CO: Westview Press, 2005), 207; Matthew N. Beckmann, *Pushing the Agenda: Presidential Leadership in U.S. Lawmaking, 1953–2004* (New York: Cambridge University Press, 2010), 48.

61. Donald F. Kettl and James W. Fesler, *The Politics of the Administrative Process*, 4th ed. (Washington, DC: CQ Press, 2009), 365–408.

62. Jeffrey E. Cohen, Jon R. Bond, and Richard Fleisher, "Placing Presidential-Congressional Relations in Context: A Comparison of Barack Obama and His Predecessors," *Polity* 45, no. 1 (2013).

63. Manabu Saeki, *The Other Side of Gridlock: Policy Stability and Supermajoritarianism in US Lawmaking* (Albany: SUNY Press, 2010), xiv, 9.

64. Erwin C. Hargrove, *The Effective Presidency*, 2nd ed. (Boulder, CO: Paradigm Publishers, 2014), 227.

65. Julia Azari, *Delivering the People's Message: The Changing Politics of the Presidential Mandate* (Ithaca, NY: Cornell University, 2014), 140, 148; Barbara Sinclair, "The President and the Congressional Party Leadership in a Hyperpartisan Era," in Thurber, *Rivals for Power*, 113.

66. Sinclair, *Party Wars*, 5, 7, fig. 1.1.

67. Mayhew, *Partisan Balance*, 142.

68. Sarah Binder, "The Disappearing Political Center: Congress and the Incredible Shrinking Middle," *Brookings Review* 14, no. 4 (1996): 36–39; Sarah Binder, "Going Nowhere: A Gridlocked Congress," *Brookings Review* 18, no. 1 (2000): 16–19; Sarah A. Binder, "Elections, Parties, and Governance," in *The Legislative Branch*, eds. Paul J. Quirk and Sarah Binder (New York: Oxford University Press, 2005), 148–70, esp. 153–54; Theriault, *Party Polarization in Congress*, 226.

69. Michael Barone, "Washington Is Partisan—Get Used to It," *Wall Street Journal*, October 18, 2013, A13.

70. Matthew Levendusky, *How Partisan Media Polarizes America* (Chicago: University of Chicago Press, 2013), 135, 148, 152.

71. Geoffrey C. Layman and Thomas M. Carsey, "Party Polarization and 'Conflict Extension' in the American Electorate," *American Journal of Political Science* 46 (2002): 786–802.

72. Theda Skocpol and Vanessa Williamson, *The Tea Party and the Remaking of Republican Conservatism* (New York: Oxford University Press, 2012), 183–88.

73. James E. Campbell, *Polarized: The Reality of American Politics* (Princeton, NJ: Princeton University Press, in press) (available in prepublication draft form, June 20, 2015).

74. Alex Roarty, "Getting to Yes," *National Journal*, February 23, 2013, 11–12. Also see Sinclair, *Party Wars*, 13.

75. S. M. Theriault, *The Gingrich Senators* (Oxford, UK: Oxford University Press, 2013); Frances E. Lee, "How Party Polarization Affects Governance," *Annual Review of Political Science* 18 (2015): 15.1–15.22, 15.5.

76. See generally Thomas E. Mann and Normal J. Ornstein, *The Broken Branch: How Congress Is Failing America and How to Get It Back on Track* (New York: Oxford University Press, 2006).

77. Bond and Fleischer, *Polarized Politics*, 3–4.

78. Lee, *Beyond Ideology*, 70.

79. Cohen, Bond, and Fleisher, "Implications," 153; Sinclair, *President and the Congressional Party Leadership*, 116 (members of the opposing party see POTUS success as a threat to their electoral goals; by blocking legislative goals of the POTUS, leaders of the opposing party in Congress advance the electoral interests of rank- and file members).

80. Hetherington and Larson, *Parties, Politics, and Public Policy*, 189.

81. Thomas E. Mann, "Polarizing the House of Representatives: How Much Does Gerrymandering Matter?" in *Red and Blue Nation? Characteristics and Causes of America's Polarized Politics*, eds. Pietro S. Nivola and David W. Brady (Washington, DC: Brookings Institution Press, 2006), 279–80.

82. William A. Galston and Pietro S. Nivola, "Delineating the Problem," in Nivola and Brady, *Red and Blue Nation?* 26 ("the dreaded chance of being ousted in a primary, however long the odds, now chills the would-be centrists in both parties").

83. Nolan McCarty, Keith T. Poole, and Howard Rosenthal, *Polarized America: The Dance of Ideology and Unequal Riches* (Cambridge: MIT Press, 2006), 165, 181.

84. David Orentlicher, *Two Presidents Are Better Than One* (New York: New York University Press, 2013), 90–91.

85. Mann and Ornstein, *Broken Branch*, 94.

86. Lee, "Party Polarization," 15.11.

87. Frances E. Lee, "Presidents and Party Teams: The Politics of Debt Limits and Executive Oversight, 2001–2013," *Presidential Studies Quarterly* 43, no. 4 (2013): 775–76.

88. Frances E. Lee, "Dividers, Not Uniters: Presidential Leadership and Senate Partisanship, 1981–2004," *Journal of Politics* 70, no. 4 (2008): 914, 915.

89. Stephen Skowronek, *The Politics Presidents Make: Leadership from John Adams to George Bush* (Cambridge, MA: Belknap Press, 1993), 20 (presidents as the "lightning rod" of American politics); Lee, "Dividers, Not Uniters," 915.

90. Lee, "Dividers, Not Uniters," 921.

91. John B. Gilmore, *Strategic Disagreement: Stalemate in American Politics* (Pittsburgh: University of Pittsburgh Press, 1995).

92. Lee, "Presidents and Party Teams," 778.

93. Ibid., 777.

94. Beckmann, *Pushing the Agenda*, 49.

95. George C. Edwards III, "Presidential Electoral Performance as a Source of Presidential Power," *American Journal of Political Science* 22 (February 1978): 152–68.

96. Jacob S. Hacker and Paul Pierson, *Off Center: The Republican Revolution and the Erosion of American Democracy* (New Haven, CT: Yale University Press, 2006), 173.

97. Andrew J. Dowdle, Dirk C. van Raemdonck, and Robert Maranto, "Barack Obama: A Reagan of the Left?" in *The Obama Presidency*, eds. Andrew J. Dowdle, Dirk C. van Raemdonck, and Robert Maranto, 10.

98. Beckmann, *Pushing the Agenda*, 56.

99. George C. Edwards III, *The Strategic President: Persuasion and Opportunity in Presidential Leadership* (Princeton, NJ: Princeton University Press, 2009).

100. Druckman and Jacobs, *Who Governs?*, 12.

101. Samuel Kernell, *Going Public: New Strategies of Presidential Leadership*, 4th ed. (Washington, DC: CQ Press, 2007).

102. Azari, Brown, and Nwokora, *Presidential Leadership Dilemma*, 11–14.

103. Canes-Wrone, *Who Leads Whom?*, 55–56, 186.

104. James N. Druckman and Justin W. Holmes, "Does Presidential Rhetoric Matter? Priming and Presidential Approval," *Presidential Studies Quarterly* 34 (2004): 755–78.

105. Canes-Wrone, *Who Leads Whom?*, 76, 79.

106. George C. Edwards, *On Deaf Ears: The Limits of the Bully Pulpit* (New Haven, CT: Yale University Press, 2003).

107. Edwards, *Strategic President*; Jeffrey E. Cohen and Costas Panagopoulos, *Going Local: Presidential Leadership in the Post-Broadcast Age* (New York: Cambridge University Press, 2010).

108. Kent Tedin, Brandon Rottinghaus, and Harrell Rodgers, "When the President Goes Public: The Consequences of Communication Mode for Opinion Change across Issue Types and Groups," *Political Research Quarterly* 64, no. 3 (2011): 506–19; Charles Cameron and Jee-Kwang Park, "Going Public When Opinion Is Contested: Evidence from Presidential Campaigns for Supreme Court Justices," *Presidential Studies Quarterly* 41, no. 3 (2011): 442–70; Edwards, *Strategic President*.

109. Canes-Wrone, *Who Leads Whom?* 51.

110. Druckman and Jacobs, *Who Governs?* 15.

111. Beckmann, *Pushing the Agenda*, 12–13; Sinclair, *Party Wars*, 251–54; Robert S. Erikson and Christopher Wlezien, *The Timeline of Presidential Elections: How Campaigns Do (And Do Not) Matter* (Chicago: University of Chicago Press, 2012), chapter 9.

112. Azari, *Delivering the People's Message*, 140.

113. Druckman and Jacobs, *Who Governs?* 117.

114. Canes-Wrone, *Who Leads Whom?* 35, 49, 89, 177.

115. Ibid., 186.

116. Ibid., 26.

117. Ibid.

118. Mann and Ornstein, *Broken Branch*, 124–28; George C. Edwards III, "Riding High in the Polls: George W. Bush and Public Opinion," in *The George W. Bush Presidency: Appraisals and Prospects*, eds. Colin Campbell and Bert A. Rockman (Washington, DC: CQ Press, 2004), 32–34.

119. Hacker and Pierson, *Off Center*, 172.

120. John D. Graham, *Bush on the Home Front: Domestic Policy Triumphs and Setbacks* (Bloomington: Indiana University Press, 2010), 320–24.

121. Lee, "Presidents and Party Teams," 789.

122. "Gridlock" may be defined generally as the impossibility of significantly changing the status quo or, more narrowly, as a lack of movement toward solving

the nation's problems. Sometimes formal models of the legislature define "gridlock" more narrowly as the absence of legislative change in spite of the fact that a majority of legislators favor change. George Tsebelis, *Veto Players: How Political Institutions Work* (Princeton, NJ: Princeton University Press, 2002), 6, 26–27.

123. William Mayer, ed., *The Swing Voter in American Politics* (Washington, DC: Brookings Institution, 2008), 9–12.

124. Shanto Iyengar, *Media Politics*, 277, 285.

125. Amy Walter, "The Myth of the Independent Voter," *Cook Political Report*, January 15, 2014.

126. Alan I. Abramowitz, *The Disappearing Center: Engaged Citizens, Polarization, and American Democracy* (New Haven, CT: Yale University Press, 2010), 56, 87.

127. On the roughly equal strength of the Republican and Democratic parties in 2004 and 2008 (based on self-identification by voters), see Campbell, "Miserable Presidential Election," 20–28. In 2008, 89 percent of self-identified Democrats voted for Obama; 90 percent of self-identified Republicans voted for McCain; see Skinner, "Barack Obama," 15. On the powerful role of partisan identity on voter choice, see Donald Green, Bradley Palmquist, and Eric Schickler, *Partisan Hearts and Minds: Political Parties and the Social Identities of Voters* (New Haven, CT: Yale University Press, 2002).

128. Amnon Cavari, "The Interplay of Macropartisanship and Macrohandling, and the 2012 Electoral Success of the Democratic Party," in *The 2012 Presidential Election: Forecasts, Outcomes, and Consequences*, eds. Amnon Cavari, Richard J. Powell, and Kenneth R. Mayer (Lanham, MD: Rowman and Littlefield, 2014), 83, 90 (the Democratic identification advantage eroded from 1960 to 1980, and the two parties have been roughly equal in partisan identification since 1980); Abramowitz, *Disappearing Center*, 90–91 (exit polls from 2006 and 2008 suggest that the Democratic Party retains a small advantage in party identification).

129. The increasing strength of the Republican Party in the South is more related to economic changes than to race. Byron E. Shafer and Richard Johnson, *The End of Southern Exceptionalism: Class, Race, and Partisan Change in the Post-War South* (Boston: Harvard University Press, 2006); the demise of Republicans in the Northeast during the 1990s was pleasing to many conservatives who saw these members as Republican in Name Only (RINOs). Howard L. Reiter and Jeffrey M. Stonecash, *Counter Realignment: Political Change in the Northeastern United States* (New York: Cambridge University Press, 2011), 162.

130. Morris P. Fiorina, *Culture War? The Myth of a Polarized America*, 2nd ed. (New York: Pearson Education, 2006), 61; Abramowitz, *Disappearing Center*, 69.

131. Abramowitz, *Disappearing Center*, 104, 108 (mobilizing core supporters can be a more effective use of campaign resources than trying to persuade swing voters).

132. Green, Palmquist, and Schickler, *Partisan Hearts and Minds*, 46, 48, 218; Morris P. Fiorina, et al., *America's New Democracy*, 3rd ed. (New York: Pearson-Longman, 2006), 126; Abramowitz, *Disappearing Center*, 87 (rates of turnout among pure independents have declined from around 80 percent in the 1950s to just over

50 percent in recent years); 23, 26 (independents tend to be less informed and less politically engaged than self-identified Republicans and Democrats).

133. Karl Rove, "Winning Independent Voters Will Win 2014," *Wall Street Journal*, January 16, 2014, A13.

134. On how pure independents differ from partisans, see Steven Greene, "Understanding Party Identification: A Social Identity Approach," *Political Psychology* 20, no. 2 (1999): 393–403.

135. Azari, *Delivering the People's Message*, 154; also see John Harwood, "'Partisan' Seeks a Prefix: Bi- or Post-,'" *New York Times,* December 6, 2008.

136. Jeffrey E. Cohen and Costas Panagopoulos, "Presidential Leadership and Public Opinion in an Age of Polarization," in Dowdle et al., *Obama Presidency*, 34.

137. Ibid., 40–41 (pure independents and moderates found Obama's "post-partisan" rhetoric appealing but became disenchanted when he had to pass his policies on partisan votes).

138. George C. Edwards, *Strategic Assessments*, 55.

139. Adapted from Aldrich, *Why Parties?* 225.

140. See generally Mayhew, *Congress*.

141. Theriault, *Party Polarization in Congress*, 143, 145.

142. Sinclair, *Party Wars*, 130; Lee, *Beyond Ideology*, 18.

143. Sinclair, *Party Wars*, 238, 240.

144. See generally Theriault, *Party Polarization in Congress*.

145. Lebo and O'Geen, *President's Role*, 718–34.

146. Cohen, Bond, and Fleisher, "Implications," 164.

147. Richard E. Neustadt, *Presidential Power* (New York: New American Library, 1964), chapters 4 and 5; Paul Gronke, Jeffrey Koch, and J. Matthew Wilson, "Follow the Leader? Presidential Approval, Presidential Support, and Representatives' Electoral Fortunes," *Journal of Politics* 65 (2003): 785–808; Mayhew, *Congress*, xx, 43, esp. note 67.

148. Lebo and O'Geen, *President's Role*, 718–34.

3. Preventing Collapse, Stimulating Recovery

1. National Bureau of Economic Research, "US Business Cycle Expansions and Contractions," http://www.nber.org/cycles.html.

2. Kristin S. Seefeldt and John D. Graham, *America's Poor and the Great Recession* (Bloomington: Indiana University Press, 2010), 8–10.

3. In this discussion I draw heavily from the discussion in John D. Graham, *Bush on the Home Front: Triumphs and Setbacks* (Bloomington: Indiana University Press, 2010).

4. See generally Robert J. Schiller, *The Subprime Solution* (Princeton, NJ: Princeton University Press, 2008), 5, 32–33; Mark Zandi, *Financial Shock* (New York: Pearson Education, 2009), 15–16.

5. Zandi, *Financial Shock*, 147.

6. Schiller, *Subprime Solution*, 50–51.

7. For more detail on TARP, see Graham, *Bush on the Home Front*, 283–86.

8. Mark Peters, "Leaders Parse Government Moves to Stem Financial Crisis," *Wall Street Journal*, October 30, 2013, A7; Alan S. Blinder and Mark Zandi, "Don't Look Back in Anger at Bailouts and Stimulus," *Wall Street Journal*, October 16, 2015, A13.

9. Erwin C. Hargrove, *The Effective Presidency*, 2nd ed. (Boulder, CO: Paradigm Publishers, 2014), 264 (referring to the bonuses provided to officers of American International Group [AIG], the bankrupt insurance company).

10. Peters, "Leaders Parse," A7.

11. Martha Joynt Kumar, *Before the Oath: How George W. Bush and Barack Obama Managed a Transfer of Power* (Baltimore: Johns Hopkins University Press, 2015), 87–88.

12. Deborah Solomon and Damien Paletta, "US Seeks Rest of Bailout Cash," *Wall Street Journal*, January 13, 2009.

13. Ryan Tracy, "TARP Watchdog Isn't Ready to Pack It," *Wall Street Journal*, February 4, 2015, C3.

14. A *Wall Street Journal*/NBC poll in January 2010 found that a majority of respondents opposed the bank bailouts orchestrated by Bush and Obama, and 65 percent disapproved of the bailouts of General Motors and Chrysler. Peters, "Leaders Parse," A7.

15. Lor Montgomery and Paul Kane, "Senate Votes to Release Bailout Funds to Obama," *Washington Post*, January 16, 2009.

16. David Goldman, "Senate Vote Fails, Obama Gets $350B," *CNN.com*, January 15, 2009, http://money.cnn.com/2009/01/15/news/economy/senate_tarp_vote.

17. Gary C. Jacobson, "Polarization, Public Opinion, and the Presidency: The Obama and Anti-Obama Coalitions," in *The Obama Presidency: Appraisals and Prospects*, eds. Bert A. Rockman, Andrew Rudalevige, and Colin Campbell (Washington, DC: CQ Press, 2012) (citing July 2010 survey by Pew Center for the People and the Press).

18. Chris Isidore, "TARP Bailout Close to Breaking Even," *CNN.com*, December 19, 2012, money.cnn.com/2012/12/19/news/economy/tarp-breaking-even.

19. US Department of the Treasury, "TARP Tracker from September 2008 to date," January 24, 2014, www.treasury.gov/initiatives/financial-stability/reports/Pages/TARP-Tracker.aspx.

20. Jonathan Weisman, "US Declares Bank and Auto Bailouts Over, and Profitable," *New York Times*, December 20, 2014, B1–2.

21. David Weidner, "TARP: The Bailout Success Story That Wasn't," February 12, 2013, www.moneywatch.com/story/losses-mounting-in-bank-bailouts-2013–02–12.

22. Edmund L. Andrews, "Obama to Nominate Bernanke to Second Term at Fed," *New York Times*, August 24, 2009.

23. Jon Hilsenrath, "Meltdown Averted, Bernanke Struggled to Stoke Growth," *Wall Street Journal*, December 18, 2013.

24. Neil Irwin, "Bernanke Confirmed by Senate for 2nd Term as Fed Chairman," *Washington Post*, January 29, 2010.

25. Edmund L. Andrews and David M. Herszenhorn, "Bernanke Is Said to Support Stimulus," *New York Times*, January 17, 2008.

26. Julia Werdigier and Edmund L. Andrews, "Bernanke Says Obama Stimulus Plans Are Good but Not Enough," *New York Times*, January 13, 2009.

27. Andrews, "Obama to Nominate."

28. Neil Irwin, "Obama Picks Bernanke for a Second Term as Federal Reserve Chairman," *Washington Post*, August 26, 2009.

29. Michael Grunwald, "Why Obama Reappointed Bernanke to the Fed," *Time*, August 25, 2009, http://content.time.com/time/politics/article/0,8599,1918422,00 .html.

30. Liz Peek, "Tea Party Rallying Cry: Abolish the Federal Reserve!" *Fiscal Times*, November 10, 2010, http://www.thefiscaltimes.com/Articles/2010/11/10/Tea-Party -Calls-for-Abolishing-the-Fed.

31. Sewell Chan and David M. Herszenhorn, "Bernanke's Bid for a Second Term at the Fed Hits Resistance," *New York Times*, January 22, 2010.

32. Irwin, "Bernanke Confirmed."

33. Congressional Budget Office, "Estimated Impact of the American Recovery and Reinvestment Act," August 2011, updated February 21, 2014, https://www.cbo .gov/publication/45122.

34. Jeff Zeleny and David M. Herszenhorn, "Obama Seeks Wide Support in Congress for Stimulus," *New York Times*, January 6, 2009.

35. Dan Balz, "Why Did Barack Obama Fail to Bring the Change He Promised?" *Washington Post*, September 2, 2012.

36. Obama's political advisor David Axelrod acknowledges that the White House may have been "naïve" in their pursuit of a bipartisan stimulus package. George C. Edwards III, *Overreach: Leadership and the Obama Presidency* (Princeton, NJ: Princeton University Press 2012), 188 (quoting Axelrod).

37. Paul Kane and Michael D. Shear, "Obama Seeks GOP Backing for Stimulus," *Washington Post*, January 24, 2009.

38. Bob Woodward, *The Price of Politics* (New York: Simon and Schuster, 2012), 13.

39. Jackie Calmes and David M. Herszenhorn, "Obama Presses for Quick Jolt to the Economy," *New York Times*, January 23, 2009.

40. Ibid.

41. Michael Grunwald, *The NEW New Deal: The Hidden Story of Change in the Obama Era* (New York: Simon and Schuster, 2012).

42. Barbara Sinclair, "Doing Big Things: Obama and the 111th Congress," in Rockman et al., *Obama Presidency*, 204.

43. Carl M. Cannon, "Bracing Lesson of Eric Cantor's Loss," *Real Clear Politics*, June 13, 2014, http://www.realclearpolitics.com/articles/2014/06/13/bracing_lessons _of_eric_cantors_loss_122975.html.

44. Sandra Fabry, "Senator Coburn Details 'Stimulus' Waste in New Report," *Americans for Tax Reform*, June 16, 2009, www.atr.org/sen-coburn-details -stimulus-waste-new-a3380 (detailing one hundred examples of waste in the 2009 Recovery Act).

45. Alan K. Ota, "GOP Moderates See Political Benefits in Opposing Obama's Economic Agenda," *Congressional Quarterly Today*, February 6, 2009.

46. Woodward, *Price of Politics*, 19.

47. Ibid., 20–21.

48. Ibid., 23.

49. J. Calmes, "House Passes Stimulus Plan with No GOP Votes," *New York Times*, January 28, 2009.

50. Trish Turner, "Influential Senate Democrat Questions Party Support for Stimulus Bill," *Fox News*, January 30, 2009, http://www.foxnews.com/politics/2009 /01/30/influential-senate-dem-questions-party-support-stimulus.

51. Carl Hulse, "Maine Senators Break with Republican Party on Stimulus," *New York Times*, February 10, 2009; Sinclair, "Doing Big Things," 204–205.

52. Barbara Sinclair, "The President and the Congressional Party Leadership in a Hyperpartisan Era," in *Rivals for Power: Presidential-Congressional Relations*, 5th ed., ed. James A. Thurber (Lanham, MD: Rowman and Littlefield, 2013).

53. D. M. Herszenhorn, "Recovery Bill Gets Final Approval," *New York Times*, February 13, 2009.

54. Scott Wilson, "Bruised by Stimulus Battle, Obama Changed His Approach to Washington," *Washington Post*, April 29, 2009.

55. Jonathan Alter, *The Promise: President Obama, Year One* (New York: Simon and Schuster, 2010), 131.

56. Congressional Budget Office, "Estimated Impact."

57. Ted Gayer, "Economic Policymaking During the Great Recession," in *The Obama Presidency*, eds. Andrew J. Dowdle, Dirk C. van Raemdonck, and Robert Maranto, 146.

58. Allan H. Meltzer, "Why Obamanomics Has Failed," *Wall Street Journal*, June 30, 2012.

59. Paul Steinhauser, "CNN Poll: 56% Oppose Stimulus Program," *CNN Politics*, January 24, 2010, http://politicalticker.blogs.cnn.com/2010/01/24/cnn-poll-56 -percent-oppose-stimulus-program.

60. Ed Hornick, "Stimulus Created Jobs, Controversy, Backlash," *CNN Politics*, February 17, 2010, http://www.cnn.com/2010/POLITICS/02/17/economic.stimulus .2010.

61. Richard Waterman, Carol L. Smith, and Hank Jenkins-Smith, *The Presidential Expectations Gap* (Ann Arbor: University of Michigan Press, 2014), 126.

62. Edwards, *Overreach*, 20.

63. R. Pear, "President's Jobs Measure Is Turned Back in Key Senate Test," *New York Times*, October 11, 2011.

64. David M. Herszenhorn, "House Set to Follow Senate in Approving Tax Deal," *New York Times*, December 15, 2010.

65. J. Hook and J. McKinnon, "Congress Passes Tax Deal," *Wall Street Journal*, December 17, 2010; Associated Press, "Senate Passes Package Extending Bush Tax Cuts," *MSN.com*, December 15, 2010, http://www.nbcnews.com/id/40675581/ns /politics-capitol_hill/t/senate-passes-package-extending-bush-tax-cuts.

66. Alexander Bolton, "Obama's Job Plan Blocked in the Senate," *The Hill*, October 11, 2011, http://thehill.com/blogs/floor-action/senate/188969-senate-deals-second-defeat-to-obamas-jobs-plan.

67. Prashaut Gopal, "Obama Blocked by Banks on Mortgage Plan to Stimulate Economy," *Bloomberg.com*, August 16, 2011, http://www.bloomberg.com/news/articles/2011-08-16/banks-block-obama-on-mortgage-stimulus-plan.

68. Zachary A. Goldfarb and Scott Wilson, "Government Announces New Program to Help 'Underwater' Homeowners," *Washington Post*, October 24, 2011.

69. This subsection draws heavily from material in Graham, *Bush on the Home Front*, 281–91.

70. Steve A. Stuglin, "US Auto Industry Rescue," in *The Obama Presidency: A Preliminary Assessment*, ed. Robert P. Watson (Albany: SUNY Press, 2012), 145, 147; Kumar, *Before the Oath*, 87–91.

71. Jackie Calmes, "Obama Asks Bush to Provide Help to Automakers," *New York Times*, November 10, 2008; Deborah Charles, "Obama Urges Congress to Quickly Pass Rescue Plan," *Reuters.com*, November 5, 2008, http://www.reuters.com/article/2008/11/15/us-usa-obama-sb-idUSTRE4AE1RH20081115.

72. Business Review, "Auto Bailout Talks Collapse in the Senate," *New York Times*, December 12, 2008.

73. Stuglin, "US Auto Industry," 155.

74. Ibid., 156.

75. Damien Paletta and Jeff Bennett, "US to Sell Rest of GM Stake by Year-End," *Wall Street Journal*, November 22, 2013, A1.

76. Nathan Bomey, "GM Earnings Down 22% for 2013, but Profit-Sharing Up to $7,500," *Detroit Free Press*, February 6, 2014.

77. Greg Gardner, "GM Profit Exceeds Expectations on Strength of North America," *USA Today*, October 21, 2015.

78. Mike Spector and Jackie Calmes, "In Detroit, Obama Slams Auto Makers," *Wall Street Journal*, May 18, 2007, A8.

79. Jeff Bennett and Eric Morath, "US Remaining Stake in GM," *Wall Street Journal*, December 10, 2013, B3.

80. Alex Taylor III, "The Chrysler-Fiat Reversal of Fortune," *Fortune*, May 2, 2013, http://fortune.com/2013/05/02/the-chrysler-fiat-reversal-of-fortune.

81. Roger Parloff, "Supreme Court Clears Way for Chrysler," *CNN.com*, June 10, 2009, http://money.cnn.com/2009/06/09/news/economy/supreme_court_chrysler/index.htm?postversion=2009060919.

82. Rachel Abrams, "Fiat Completes Acquisition of Chrysler," *New York Times*, January 21, 2014, http://dealbook.nytimes.com/2014/01/21/fiat-completes-acquisition-of-chrysler.

83. Bill Vlasic, "A Merger Once Scoffed at Bears Fruit," *New York Times*, January 9, 2012; James R. Healey, "Done Deal: Fiat Owns Chrysler," *USA Today*, January 21, 2014.

84. Weisman, "US Declares," B1–2 (Treasury reports that the auto bailouts were a net loss to the taxpayer of $9 billion but more than 1 million jobs were preserved).

85. Bennett and Morath, "US Remaining," B3.

86. Paletta and Bennett, "US to Sell," A1.

87. Paul Steinhauser, "Six in Ten Oppose Auto Bailout, Poll Shows," *CNN Politics.com*, December 3, 2008, http://www.cnn.com/2008/POLITICS/12/03/auto.poll.

88. Dennis Jacobe, "Republicans, Democrats, Differ over US Automakers Bailout," *Gallup Economy*, February 23, 2012, http://www.gallup.com/poll/152936/republicans-democrats-differ-automaker-bailout.aspx; Gregory Wallace, "Auto Bailout Still Largely Unpopular," *CNN Money*, June 12, 2014, http://money.cnn.com/2014/06/12/news/economy/poll-auto-bailout.

89. Annie Lowery, "Auto Bailout Is Looking Better to the Public," *New York Times*, March 13, 2012, http://economix.blogs.nytimes.com/2012/03/13/auto-bailout-is-looking-better-to-the-public/?_r=0.

90. Pew Research Center for the People and the Press, "Auto Bailout Now Backed, Stimulus Divisive," February 23, 2012, http://www.people-press.org/2012/02/23/auto-bailout-now-backed-stimulus-divisive.

91. Jennifer Liberto, "House OKs $4 Billion 'Clunker' Bill," *CNN.com*, June 6, 2009, http://money.cnn.com/2009/06/09/news/economy/cash_for_clunkers/index.htm?section=money_topstories&utm_source=feedburner&utm_medium=feed&utm_campaign=Feed%3A+rss%2Fmoney_topstories+%28Top+Stories%29.

92. "Congress Approves 'Cash for Clunkers' Program," *Fox News.com*, June 18, 2009, http://www.foxnews.com/politics/2009/06/18/congress-approves-cash-clunkers-program.

93. Matthew L. Wald, "Senate Adds Cash to 'Clunker' Plan," *New York Times*, August 6, 2009.

94. James R. Healey and C. Woodyard, "House Adds Cash to 'Clunkers' Program; Senate Vote Needed," *USA Today*, August 2, 2009.

95. US Department of Transportation, 2009, www.cars.gov.

96. Atif Mian and Amir Sufi, "The Effects of Fiscal Stimulus: Evidence from the 2009 'Cash for Clunkers' Program," *Quarterly Journal of Economics* 127, no. 3 (2012): 1107–42.

97. Edwards, *Overreach*, 11.

98. Azari, *Delivering the People's Message*, 156–58.

99. Micah Cohen, "In Ohio, Polls Show Benefit of Auto Rescue to Obama," *New York Times*, November 5, 2012, http://fivethirtyeight.blogs.nytimes.com/2012/11/05/in-ohio-polls-show-benefit-of-auto-rescue-to-obama.

100. See, for example, Noam Scheiber, *The Escape Artists: How Obama's Team Fumbled the Recovery* (New York: Simon and Schuster, 2012).

101. Glenn Hubbard, "The Unemployment Puzzle: Where Have All the Workers Gone?" *Wall Street Journal*, April 5–6, 2014, C1.

102. Louis Fisher, "Obama: Performance in Office," in *The Barack Obama Presidency: A Two-Year Assessment*, ed. John Davis (New York: Palgrave-MacMillan, 2011), 20.

103. Balz, "Why Did Barack Obama Fail?"

104. Tom Cohen, "GOP Senators List What They Say Are the 100 Worst Stimulus Projects," *CNN Politics*, August 3, 2010, http://politicalticker.blogs.cnn.com/2010 /08/03/gop-senators-list-what-they-say-are-the-100-worst-stimulus-projects.

105. Woodward, *Price of Politics*, 11.

106. For a list of one hundred examples of alleged waste in the Obama stimulus plan, see Fabry, "Senator Coburn."

107. Edwards, *Overreach*, 50; Pew Research, "Auto Bailout."

108. Peter J. Wallison, "Four Years of Dodd-Frank Damage," *Wall Street Journal*, July 21, 2014, A13.

109. Martin Feldstein, "The Fed Needs to Step up Its Pace of Rate Increases," *Wall Street Journal*, March 31, 2015. A17.

110. Bureau of Labor Statistics, "The Employment Situation," 2015, www.bls.gov /news.release/pdf/empsit.pdf.

111. Catherine Rampbell, "Majority of Jobs Added in the Recovery Pay Low Wages, Study Finds," *New York Times*, August 31, 2012, B1, B5.

112. Neil Irwin, "Why the Middle Class Isn't Buying the Talk about a Recovery," *New York Times*, August 22, 2014, B3; Nick Timiraos, "Incomes End a 6-Year Decline, Just Barely," *Wall Street Journal*, September 17, 2014, A2; Carmen DeNavas-Walt and Bernadette D. Proctor, "Income and Poverty in the United States: 2014," September 2015, P60–252, vii, US Census Bureau, https://www.census.gov/content /dam/Census/library/publications/2015/demo/p60–252.pdf.

113. Ben Leubsdorf, "Fed: Gap between Rich, Poor Americans Widened during Recovery," *Wall Street Journal*, September 5, 2014, A2.

114. In mid-2015, leading economists such as Ben Bernanke and Larry Summers were in sharp disagreement about why the economic recovery was so slow. See Greg Ip, "On Secular Stagnation, Ben Bernanke's Theory Meets Larry Summers's Evidence," *Wall Street Journal*, April 8, 2015, A2.

4. Promoting Long-Term Growth, Reducing Inequality

1. Wall Street Journal Staff, "Obama's Financial Reform Plan: The Condensed Version," *Wall Street Journal*, June 17, 2009.

2. Wall Street Journal Staff, "Obama's Remarks on Financial Regulatory Reform," *Wall Street Journal*, June 17, 2009.

3. Andy Sullivan and Kevin Drawbaugh, "Wall Street Reform Clears Congress," *Reuters.com*, July 15, 2010, http://uk.reuters.com/article/2010/07/15/us-financial -regulation-idUKTRE66E0MD20100715.

4. Brady Dennis, "Obama Signs Financial Overhaul into Law," *Washington Post-Politics*, July 22, 2010.

5. Sullivan and Drawbaugh, "Wall Street Reform."

6. Victoria McGraine, "House Republicans Take Aim at Dodd-Frank," *Wall Street Journal*, July 21, 2014, C1.

7. Dina ElBoghdady, "Courts Taking up Opposition to Dodd-Frank," *Washington Post*, October 5, 2012.

8. Eugene Scalia, "Why Dodd-Frank Rules Keep Losing in Court," *Wall Street Journal*, October 3, 2012.

9. Paul Rose and Christopher J. Walker, "The Importance of Cost-Benefit Analysis in Financial Regulation," Report for US Chamber of Commerce, March 2013, Ohio State Public Law Working Paper No. 208, http://ssrn.com/abstract =2231314.

10. Peter J. Wallison, "Four Years of Dodd-Frank Damage," *Wall Street Journal*, July 21, 2014, A13.

11. John D. Graham, *Bush on the Home Front: Domestic Policy Triumphs and Setbacks* (Bloomington: Indiana University Press, 2010), 33–39.

12. Alexander Mooney, "Pelosi, Obama Disagree on Bush Tax Cuts, Bush Investigations," *CNN.com*, January 19, 2009, http://politicalticker.blogs.cnn.com/2009 /01/18/pelosi-obama-disagree-on-tax-cuts-bush-investigations.

13. Sewell Chan, "Greenspan Calls for Repeal of All of Bush Tax Cuts," *New York Times*, August 6, 2010.

14. Douglas M. Brattebo and Robert P. Watson, "Making History," in *The Obama Presidency: A Preliminary Assessment*, ed. Robert P. Watson (Albany: SUNY Press, 2012), 402–403.

15. Bob Woodward, *The Price of Politics* (New York: Simon and Schuster, 2012), 75 (the left viewed the 2010 stimulus as "betrayal" on the part of Obama).

16. Janet Hook, Corey Boles, and Siobhan Hughes, "Congress Passes Cliff Deal," *Wall Street Journal*, January 2, 2013.

17. Lori Montgomery and Rosalind S. Helderman, "Congress Approves Fiscal Cliff Measure," *Washington Post*, January 1, 2013.

18. Jennifer Steinhauer, "Divided House Passes Tax Deal in End to Latest Fiscal Standoff," *New York Times*, January 1, 2013.

19. Brad Haynes, "Obama Calls McCain Deficit Plan Absurd," *Wall Street Journal—Washington Wire*, July 10, 2008, http://blogs.wsj.com/washwire/2008/07/10 /obama-calls-mccains-deficit-plan-absurd.

20. Ibid.

21. Stephen Brown, "Both Candidates Face Deficits, Economists Say," *Los Angeles Times*, October 23, 2008.

22. Austan Goolsbee, "Washington Isn't Spending Too Much," *Wall Street Journal*, January 6, 2012, A13.

23. Graham, *Bush on the Home Front*.

24. MarketWatch, "Fiscal Stimulus Still Needed, Bernanke Says," *Wall Street Journal*, July 21, 2010.

25. Jackie Calmes, "Obama Planning to Slash Deficit, Despite Stimulus Spending," *New York Times*, February 21, 2009.

26. Dan Balz, "Why Did Barack Obama Fail to Bring the Change He Promised?" *Washington Post*, September 2, 2012 (Obama states that he regrets signing the first budget with numerous earmarks).

27. Woodward, *Price of Politics*, 21.

28. Ibid., 29.

29. Joshua Green, "Why Won't Americans Listen to Alan Simpson and Erskine Bowles," *Bloomberg Business Week*, February 28, 2013, http://www.businessweek.com/articles/2013-02-28/why-wont-americans-listen-to-alan-simpson-and-erskine-bowles.

30. Jeanne Sahadi, "Leading Senators Call for Commission," *CNN Money*, December 20, 2009, http://money.cnn.com/2009/12/09/news/economy/fiscal_commission.

31. Joseph White, "Presidents, Congress, and Budget Decisions," in James A. Thurber, ed., *Rivals for Power: Presidential-Congressional Relations* (Lanham, MD: Rowman and Littlefield, 2013), 194 (Obama's budget struggles were as much a conflict with centrist Democrats [led by Conrad] as a conflict with congressional Republicans).

32. Committee for a Responsible Federal Budget, "Fiscal Commission Gains Momentum," December 17, 2009, http://crfb.org/blogs/fiscal-commission-gains-momentum.

33. Sahadi, "Leading Senators."

34. Stuart M. Butler, "Conrad-Gregg Commission Is Wrong Approach to Fiscal Crisis," *Heritage Foundation Backgrounder #2360*, January 13, 2010, http://www.heritage.org/research/reports/2010/01/conrad-gregg-commission-bill-is-wrong-approach-to-fiscal-crisis.

35. Jackie Calmes, "Obama Endorses Bill to Create Panel on Deficit," *New York Times*, January 23, 2010.

36. Ed Henry, Dana Bash, and John King, "Under Pressure, Obama Backs Fiscal Commission," *CNN Politics*, January 23, 2010, http://politicalticker.blogs.cnn.com/2010/01/23/under-pressure-obama-backs-fiscal-commission/comment-page-1.

37. Woodward, *Price of Politics*, 60.

38. Lori Montgomery, "Senate Rejects Plan to Create Commission on the Deficit," *Washington Post*, January 27, 2010, A8.

39. J. Taylor Rushing, "Gregg Calls for Re-Vote on Fiscal Plan," *The Hill*, February 3, 2010, http://thehill.com/homenews/senate/79599-gregg-calls-for-re-vote-on-fiscal-commission.

40. See generally Frances E. Lee, *Beyond Ideology: Politics, Principles, and Partisanship in the U.S. Senate* (Chicago: University of Chicago Press, 2009).

41. D. Andrew Austin and Mindy R. Levit, "The Debt Limit: History and Recent Increases," *Congressional Research Service Report 7-5700*, October 15, 2013, 28–31; Jackie Calmes, "Senate on Party-Line Vote, Raises Debt Limit," *New York Times*, January 28, 2010.

42. Green, "Why Won't Americans Listen?"

43. Louis Jacobson and J. B. Wogan, "Ryan and Simpson-Bowles Commission: The Full Story," *PolitiFact.com*, August 30, 2012, http://ec2-23-20-167-227.compute-1.amazonaws.com/truth-o-meter/article/2012/aug/30/ryan-and-simpson-bowles-commission-full-story.

44. Woodward, *Price of Politics*, 67.

45. Ibid., 68; Carrie Budoff Brown, "Simpson, Bowles Come in from Cold," *Politico*, April 14, 2011, http://www.politico.com/news/stories/0411/53242.html.

46. Ezra Klein, "The Reason the White House Didn't Embrace Simpson-Bowles," *Washington Post*, February 27, 2012, http://www.washingtonpost.com/blogs/wonk blog/post/the-reason-the-white-house-didnt-embrace-simpson-bowles/2011/08/25 /gIQAqlj2dR_blog.html.

47. Woodward, *Price of Politics*, 172–73.

48. Balz, "Why Did Barack Obama Fail?"

49. Green, "Why Won't Americans Listen?"

50. Jonathan Weisman, "Budget Plan's Defeat Shows Hurdle to Compromise," *New York Times*, April 3, 2012, http://mobile.nytimes.com/2012/04/04/us/politics /in-a-budget-plans-defeat-lessons-on-the-difficulty-of-compromise.html.

51. Stephen Dinan, "House Rejects Bowles-Simpson, Obama Budgets," *Washington Times*, March 28, 2012.

52. Balz, "Why Did Barack Obama Fail?"; Jackie Calmes, "Obama's Deficit Dilemma," *New York Times*, February 27, 2012.

53. Ariana Eunjung Cha, Ezra Klein, and Dylan Matthews, "What's the Debt Ceiling, and Why Is Everyone in Washington Talking about It?" *Washington Post*, April 18, 2011.

54. Damian Paletta and Corey Boles, "White House Expects Deficit to Spike at $1.65 Trillion," *Wall Street Journal*, February 14, 2011.

55. Christi Parsons and Michael A. Memoli, "Amid Fresh Barbs, Biden Is 'Optimistic' about Deficit Talks," *Los Angeles Times*, May 10, 2011.

56. Eric Wasson, "Cantor, Kyl to Represent Republicans at Biden Deficit-Reduction Talks," *The Hill*, April 19, 2011, http://thehill.com/blogs/blog-briefing -room/news/156837-cantor-kyl-will-join-biden-debt-talks.

57. Brian Faler and Heidi Przybyla, "Biden Says U.S. Deficit Talks Seek Signal with $4 Trillion in Savings," *Bloomberg.com*, June 17, 2011, http://www.bloomberg .com/apps/news?pid=newsarchive&sid=aUQ8KWXclHgM.

58. Ibid.

59. David Welna, "Senators Impatient over Biden Group's Debt Plan," *NPR.org*, June 22, 2011, http://www.npr.org/2011/06/22/137349383/senators-impatient-over -biden-groups-debt-ceiling.

60. Lisa Mascaro, "Rep. Eric Cantor Pulls Out of Biden Deficit Talks," *Los Angeles Times*, June 23, 2011.

61. Woodward, *Price of Politics*, 153.

62. Matt Bai, "Obama vs. Boehner: Who Killed the Debt Deal?" *New York Times*, March 28, 2012.

63. Jackie Calmes, "'Gang of Six' in the Senate Seeking a Plan on Debt," *New York Times*, April 16, 2011.

64. Woodward, *Price of Politics*, 211.

65. Bai, "Obama vs. Boehner."

66. Woodward, *Price of Politics*, 181, 189.

67. Ibid., 332.

68. Bai, "Obama vs. Boehner"; Barbara Sinclair, "The President and the Congressional Party Leadership in a Hyperpartisan Era," in Thurber, *Rivals for Power*,

130 (Obama craved a big fiscal deal; his Democratic allies in Congress feared that he would compromise too much to get it).

69. Bai, "Obama vs. Boehner."

70. Peter Wallsten, Lori Montgomery, and Scott Wilson, "Obama's Evolution: Behind the Failed 'Grand Bargain' on the Debt," *Washington Post*, March 17, 2012.

71. Jeanne Sahadi, "What 'Gang of Six' Plan Would Do," *CNN.com*, July 19, 2011, http://money.cnn.com/2011/07/19/news/economy/gang_of_six_budget.

72. Keith Hennessey, "Understanding the Gang of Six Plan," July 20, 2011, http://keithhennessey.com/2011/07/20/understanding-the-gang-of-six-plan.

73. Jackie Calmes and Carl Hulse, "Debt Ceiling Talks Collapse as Boehner Walks Out," *New York Times*, July 22, 2011.

74. Bai, "Obama vs. Boehner."

75. Congressional Budget Office, "Processes: What Sort of Behavioral Responses Are Included in Your Estimates?" http://www.cbo.gov/sites/default/files/cbofiles/attachments/2014-IntroToCBO-2.pdf.

76. Paul N. Van de Water, "Budget Plans Should Not Rely on 'Dynamic Scoring,'" Center on Budget and Policy Priorities, June 21, 2012, http://www.cbpp.org/cms/index.cfm?fa=view&id=5246.

77. Kristina Peterson, "Party Preparations: Senate Maneuvering Begins," *Wall Street Journal*, October 23, 2014, A4.

78. Woodward, *Price of Politics*, 339, 344.

79. Ibid., 360–61, 363–64.

80. Suzy Khimm, "The Sequester, Explained," *Washington Post*, September 14, 2012, http://www.washingtonpost.com/blogs/wonkblog/wp/2012/09/14/the-sequester-explained; Fred Barnes, "The Upside of the GOP Shutdown Defeat," *Wall Street Journal*, October 22, 2014, A17.

81. James A. Thurber, "Agony, Angst, and the Failure of the Supercommittee," *Extensions*, Summer 2012, http://www.american.edu/spa/ccps/upload/Agony-Angst-and-theFailure-of-the-Supercommittee.pdf.

82. Wallsten et al., "Obama's Evolution."

83. Ted Barrett, Kate Bolduan, and Deirdre Walsh, "'Super Committee' Fails to Reach Agreement," November 21, 2011, *CNN.com*, http://www.cnn.com/2011/11/21/politics/super-committee; Naftali Bendavid and Janet Hook, "Deficit Effort Nears Collapse," *Wall Street Journal*, November 21, 2011.

84. Jackie Calmes, "Budget Office Warns that Deficits Will Rise Again Because Cuts Are Misdirected," *New York Times*, September 18, 2013, A13.

85. Kristin S. Seefeldt and John D. Graham, *America's Poor and the Great Recession* (Bloomington: Indiana University Press, 2010), 90–93.

86. Jackie Calmes, "Signs Indicate that Obama's Debt Ceiling Gamble May Be Paying Off," *New York Times*, October 16, 2013, A18.

87. "The Debt-Ceiling Deal," *Economist*, October, 19, 2013, 32.

88. Dan Balz and Scott Clement, "Poll: Major Damage to GOP after Shutdown, and Broad Dissatisfaction with Government," *Washington Post*, October 22, 2013.

89. "Debt-Ceiling Deal," 31.

90. Barnes, "Upside of GOP Shutdown."

91. Dan Balz, "Can Obama Seize the Moment and Make Washington Work?" *Washington Post*, October 18, 2013, A4.

92. Jonathan Weisman and Ashley Parker, "Republicans Back Down, Ending Crisis over Shutdown and Debt Limit," *New York Times*, October 16, 2013.

93. Janet Hook and Kristina Peterson, "GOP Backs Off Fight on Debt Limit," *Wall Street Journal*, February 12, 2014, A1; Kristina Peterson and Janet Hook, "Boehner Strategy Signals a Shift for Party," *Wall Street Journal*, February 13, 2014, A4.

94. Jonathan Weisman, "Seeking Compromise, President Reaches Out to Rank and File," *New York Times*, March 4, 2013, A12.

95. Peter Nicholas and Kristina Peterson, "Grand Bargain Eludes Budget Negotiators," *Wall Street Journal*, July 29, 2013, A4.

96. Heidi Przybla and Mike Dorning, "Obama's Goal of Grand Budget Deal Elusive as Talks Begin," *Bloomberg.com*, October 18, 2013, http://www.business week.com/news/2013–10–18/obama-s-goal-of-grand-budget-deal-elusive-as-talks -begin-taxes.

97. Peter Nicholas and Damian Paletta, "On Spending Cuts, the Focus Shifts to How, Not If," *Wall Street Journal*, February 26, 2013, A6.

98. Susan Davis, "Budget Talks Set Low Expectations for a Deal," *USA Today*, October 20, 2013.

99. Damian Paletta and Janet Hook, "White House Hints at Flexibility on Taxes," *Wall Street Journal*, October 30, 2013, A7.

100. Damian Paletta, "After Shutdown, Focus Turns to Conference Committee," *Wall Street Journal*, October 17, 2013, A4.

101. Janet Hook, "Deal Brings Stability to US Budget," *Wall Street Journal*, December 11, 2013, A1.

102. Paul Kane and Ed O'Keefe, "House Passes 2-Year Bipartisan Budget Deal," *Washington Post*, December 12, 2013.

103. Janet Hook, "Nine GOP Senators Back Budget Bill in Final Passage," *Wall Street Journal*, December 19, 2013, A5.

104. Kelsey Snell, "Senate Approves Two-Year Bipartisan Budget Agreement," *Washington Post*, October 30, 2015.

105. Nick Timiraos, "Incomes End a 6-Year Decline, Just Barely," *Wall Street Journal*, September 17, 2014, A2.

106. Seefeldt and Graham, *America's Poor*, 17–30.

107. Jesse Bricker, Arthur B. Kennickell, Kevin B. Moore, and John Sabelhaus, "Changes in Family Finances from 2007 to 2010: Evidence from the Survey of Consumer Finances," *Federal Reserve Bulletin* 98, no. 2 (June 2012), http://www .federalreserve.gov/pubs/bulletin/2012/PDF/scf12.pdf.

108. Tali Mendelberg and Bennett L. Butler, "Obama Cares: Look at the Numbers," *New York Times*, August 22, 2014, A21.

109. Seefeldt and Graham, *America's Poor*, 84–101.

110. Jesse Bricker, Lisa J. Dettling, Alice Henriques, Joanne W. Hsu, Kevin B. Moore, John Sabelhaus, Jeffrey Thompson, and Richard A. Windle, "Changes in

U.S. Family Finances from 2010 to 2013: Evidence from the Survey of Consumer Finances," *Federal Reserve Bulletin* 100, no. 4 (September 2014): 9–13.

111. Robert Pear, "Number of Children Living in Poverty Drops Sharply, Census Bureau Reports," *New York Times*, September 17, 2014, A19.

112. Neil Shah, "Food-Stamp Use Starting to Fall," *Wall Street Journal*, September 2, 2014, A3.

113. Gerald F. Seib, "Obama's Second Term Agenda: Progressive Ideas, Populist Packaging," *Wall Street Journal*, July 26, 2013.

114. Jeff Shesol, "The 'P' Word: Why Presidents Stopped Talking about Poverty," *New Yorker*, January 9, 2014 (a word search of the last fifty State of the Union addresses turns up few mentions of the words "poor" or "poverty," with the lowest number of mentions attributed to Obama and George W Bush); Dave Boyer, "Obama Gets Poor Ranking on Mentions of 'Poverty': More Abundance for 'Middle Class,'" *Washington Times*, July 8, 2013; Mendelberg and Butler, "Obama Cares"; Jennifer Epstein, "Obama Leaves Out Most Mentions of Poverty," *Politico.com*, September 16, 2012, http://www.politico.com/story/2012/09/obama-leaves-out-most-mentions-of-poverty-081253.

115. Corey Boles, "Obama Proposals Face Long Odds," *Wall Street Journal*, July 30, 2013, A4.

116. Gerald F. Seib, "Obama Seeks Way to Right His Ship," *Wall Street Journal*, January 1, 2014, A1.

117. Damian Paletta, "Obama Scales Back Budget Goals," *Wall Street Journal*, March 5, 2014, A1.

118. Siobhan Hughes, "Senate Passes Bill to Aid Long-Term Unemployed," *Wall Street Journal*, April 8, 2014, A4.

119. Jake Tapper, "Obama's Broken Deficit Promise," *ABC News*, February 13, 2012, http://abcnews.go.com/blogs/politics/2012/02/obamas-broken-deficit-promise.

120. Damian Paletta, "CBO Estimates U.S. Deficit Will Shrink More Than Expected in 2014," *Wall Street Journal*, April 15, 2014, A3.

121. Josh Zumbrun, "US Racks Up Smallest Deficit since 2007," *Wall Street Journal*, January 14, 2015, A1.

122. Nick Timiraos, "US Posts Smallest Annual Budget Deficit since 2007," *Wall Street Journal*, October 16, 2015, A4.

123. Rick Unger, "The Best Kept Secret in American Politics—Federal Budget Deficits Are Actually Shrinking," *Forbes*, February 27, 2013.

124. Zumbrun, "US Racks Up Deficit."

125. Bernie Sanders, United States Senator for Vermont, July 30, 2013, http://www.sanders.senate.gov/newsroom/newswatch/073013.

126. "Falling Behind," editorial, *New York Times*, January 3, 2012, A20.

127. Tami Luhby, "The Impact of a $9 Minimum Wage," *CNN.com*, February 13, 2013, http://money.cnn.com/2013/02/12/news/economy/obama-minimum-wage.

128. Stephen Dinan, "House Defeats Minimum Wage Increase," *Washington Times*, March 15, 2013.

129. Catherine Rampell and Steven Greenhouse, "$10 Minimum Wage Proposal Has Growing Support from the White House," *New York Times*, November 7, 2013.

130. Kristina Peterson and Michael R. Crittenden, "Democrats Consider Smaller Minimum-Wage Increase," *Wall Street Journal*, April 3, 2014, A14.

131. Dave Jamieson, "Obama Gets Behind Democrats' $10.10 Minimum Wage Proposal," *Huffington Post-Politics*, August 8, 2014, http://www.huffingtonpost.com/2013/11/07/obama-minimum-wage_n_4235965.html; Sean Sullivan, "Obama Supports Bill to Bump Wage," *Washington Post*, November 8, 2013, A20.

132. Susan Davis, "Senate Fails to Advance Minimum Wage Hike," *USA Today*, April 30, 2014.

133. Eric Morath, Damian Paletta, and Carol L. Lee, "Wage-Rise Report Sees Fewer Jobs, Less Poverty," *Wall Street Journal*, February 19, 2014, A1; Congressional Budget Office, "The Effects of a Minimum Wage Increase on Employment and Family Income," February 2014, http://www.cbo.gov/sites/default/files/44995-Minimum Wage.pdf.

134. David Neumark, "Who Really Gets the Minimum Wage," *Wall Street Journal*, July 7, 2014, A11.

135. Peterson and Crittenden, "Democrats Consider."

136. Damian Paletta and Eric Morath, "Patchwork of Local Wage Laws Fuels Debate over Raising Federal Minimum Wage," *Wall Street Journal*, November 30–December 1, 2013, A5; Eric Morath, "Minimum Wage Battle Shifting to Local Level," *Wall Street Journal*, April 30, 2014, A5; Eric Morath, "Michigan Becomes Seventh State This Year to Raise Minimum Wage," *Wall Street Journal*, May 29, 2014, A5.

137. Hunter Schwarz, "There Are Eight States Left with Minimum Wages Lower Than the Federal Minimum Wage," *Washington Post*, August 4, 2014, http://www.washingtonpost.com/blogs/govbeat/wp/2014/08/04/there-are-eight-states-left-with-minimum-wages-lower-than-the-federal-minimum-wage.

138. Ibid.

139. Wesley Lowery, "Senate Republicans Block Minimum Wage Increase Bill," *Washington Post*, April 30, 2014, http://www.washingtonpost.com/blogs/post-politics/wp/2014/04/30/senate-republicans-block-minimum-wage-increase-bill.

140. Matt Stoller, "The Progressive Case against Obama," *Salon*, October 27, 2012, http://www.salon.com/2012/10/27/the-progressive-case-against-obama.

141. Richard McGregor, "Obama Seeks to Revive Presidency with State of the Union Minimum Wage Vow," *Financial Times*, January 29, 2014, 1, 3.

142. Eric Morath, "Workers Try a Tactic in Minimum Wage Fight," *Wall Street Journal*, May 21, 2014, B1.

143. George E. Condon Jr., "The Reluctant Fighter," *National Journal*, February 8, 2014, 54.

144. Tom Raum, "Foes of Obama Trade Pacts Mostly Fellow Democrats," Associated Press, January 25, 2014, http://bigstory.ap.org/article/foes-obama-trade-pacts-mostly-fellow-democrats.

145. Robert B. Zoeller, "Leading from the Front on Free Trade," *Wall Street Journal*, January 13, 2014, A15; Myron Brilliant, "Why Harry Reid Must Reconsider on Trade," *Wall Street Journal*, February 19, 2014, A11.

146. William Mauldin and Siobhan Hughes, "Obama Seeks to Woo Fellow Democrats," *Wall Street Journal*, January 22, 2015, A4.

147. Nicholas Kulish and Jackie Calmes, "Obama Bid for Europe Trade Pact Stirs Hope on Both Sides," *New York Times*, February 13, 2013.

148. William A. Galston, "A Fight Obama Needs to Have With Democrats," *Wall Street Journal*, January 14, 2015, A13.

149. Laura Litvan and Kathleen Hunter, "Reid Says He Opposes Renewing Fast-Track Authority," *Bloomberg.com*, January 29, 2014, http://www.bloomberg.com /news/articles/2014–01–29/reid-says-he-opposes-renewing-fast-track-trade -authority; William Mauldin and Siobhan Hughes, "Reid Deals Body Blow to Obama on Trade," *Wall Street Journal*, January 30, 2014, A1.

150. William Mauldin and Siobhan Hughes, "Trade Bill's Prospects Become Bumpier," *Wall Street Journal*, February 7–9, 2014, 6; Tea Party, "Uprising Swells against Obama's Plans to Skirt Congress on 'New World Order,'" http://www.tea party.org/uprising-swells-obamas-plans-skirt-congress-new-world-order-32652; William Mauldin, "Tea-Party Resistance Clouds Push for Major Trade Pacts," *Wall Street Journal*, December 16, 2013, A4; Condon, "Reluctant Fighter," 54.

151. William Mauldin and Siobhan Hughes, "Fast-Track Trade Bill's Path in Congress Gets Bumpier," *Wall Street Journal*, February 5, 2014.

152. Mauldin and Hughes, "Obama Seeks to Woo."

153. Susan Davis, "Trade Pact Gets a Boost," *USA Today*, April 17, 2015, B1.

154. William Mauldin, "Lawmakers Introduce 'Fast Track' Trade Bill, Triggering Democratic Discord," *Wall Street Journal*, April 28, 2015, A1.

155. Gerald F. Sieb, "Obama Presses Case for Trade Pact," *Wall Street Journal*, April 28, 2015, A1.

156. William Mauldin, "White House Threatens to Veto Trade Bill over Currency Measure," *Wall Street Journal*, May 19, 2015, A6.

157. Richard Cowan, "Senate Advances Fast-Track Trade Bill Sought by Obama," *Reuters.com*, May 21, 2015, http://www.reuters.com/article/2015/05/22/us-usa-trade -idUSKBN0O61WJ20150522.

158. Ross K. Baker, *Is Bipartisanship Dead? A Report from the Senate* (Boulder, CO: Paradigm Publishers, 2015), 74.

159. Lori Montgomery, "Obama Orders All Federal Agencies to Review Regulations," *Washington Post*, January 18, 2011.

160. Cass R. Sunstein, "Cumulative Effects of Regulations," Memorandum for the Heads of Executive Departments and Agencies, March 20, 2012, https://www.white house.gov/sites/default/files/omb/assets/inforeg/cumulative-effects-guidance.pdf.

161. John M. Broder, "Re-Election Strategy Is Tied to a Shift on Smog," *New York Times*, November 16, 2011.

162. Mark Lander, "Obama Signs Bill to Promote Start-Up Investments," *New York Times*, April 5, 2012.

163. Andrew Ackerman and Jared A. Favole, "Obama Signs Bill Easing IPO Rules," *Wall Street Journal*, April 5, 2012.

164. Baker, *Is Bipartisanship Dead?* 73–76.

165. White, "Presidents, Congress"; Dean Baker, "The Sequester Is President Obama's Fault," *Truthout.org*, March 4, 2013, www.truth-out.org/news/item/14904 -the-sequester-is-president.

166. Carol E. Lee and Damian Paletta, "Obama to Assert Unilateral Agenda," *Wall Street Journal*, January 27, 2014, A1.

167. For the argument that Obama pivoted too quickly from stimulus/recovery to deficit control, see Noam Scheiber, *The Escape Artists: How Obama's Team Fumbled the Recovery* (New York: Simon and Schuster, 2012).

168. Janet Hook, "Small Budget Deal Makes Bigger One Less Likely," *Wall Street Journal*, December 21–22, 2013, A6.

169. Gerald F. Seib, "Celebrating Small Deals That Can Be Done," *Wall Street Journal*, January 28, 2014, A4.

170. John D. McKinnon, "New Taxes Would Hit Wealthy, Companies," *Wall Street Journal*, February 2, 2015, A4.

171. Andrea Riquier, "Why Small Business Is Reluctant to Hire," *Investor's Business Daily*, May 28, 2015, A1.

172. Bruno Macaes, "Send a Message to Putin with a Trans-Atlantic Energy Pact," *Wall Street Journal*, April 23, 2014, A15.

5. The Affordable Care Act: Legislative Victory

1. K. G. Carman and C. Eibner, "Changes in Health Insurance Enrollment since 2013: Evidence from the RAND Health Reform Opinion Study," RAND Corporation, 2014, http://www.rand.org/pubs/research_reports/RR656.; Sara R. Collins and Petra W. Rasmussen, "New Federal Surveys Show Declines in Number of Uninsured Americans in Early 2014," *Commonwealth Fund*, September 2014, http://www.commonwealthfund.org/publications/blog/2014/sep/new-federal-surveys-show-declines-in-number-of-uninsured-americans-in-early-2014.

2. Michael K. Gusmano, "Health Care Reform," in *The Obama Presidency: A Preliminary Assessment*, ed. Robert P. Watson et al. (Albany: SUNY Press, 2012), 199.

3. For a detailed look at the failure of the 1993 Clinton plan, see Theda Skocpol, *Boomerang: Clinton's Health Security Effort and the Turn against Government in US Politics* (New York: W. W. Norton, 1996).

4. Rance Crain, "Clinton-Era 'Harry and Louise' Campaign Was a Harbinger of Today's Health-Care Mess," *Advertising Age*, November 19, 2013, http://adage.com/article/rance-crain/clinton-era-ads-harbinger-today-s-health-care-mess/245312.

5. George C. Edwards III, *Overreach: Leadership and the Obama Presidency* (Princeton, NJ: Princeton University Press 2012), 4.

6. Paul Krugman, "Clinton, Obama, Insurance," *New York Times*, February 4, 2008.

7. Helen A. Halpin and Peter Harbage, "The Origins and Demise of the Public Option," *Health Affairs* 29, no. 6 (2010): 1117–24.

8. Marjorie Connelly, "Polls and the Public Option," *New York Times*, October 28, 2009, http://prescriptions.blogs.nytimes.com/2009/10/28/polls-and-the-public-option.

9. John D. Graham, *Bush on the Home Front: Domestic Policy Triumphs and Setbacks* (Bloomington: Indiana University Press, 2010).

10. Theda Skocpol, "Flashpoint in Health-Care Reform," *Dissent* 59, no. 2 (2012): 95–101.

11. Lawrence R. Jacobs, "The Privileges of Access: Interest Groups and the White House," in *The Obama Presidency: Appraisals and Prospects*, eds. Bert A. Rockman, Andrew Rudalevige, and Colin Campbell (Washington, DC: CQ Press, 2012), 162–63.

12. Steven Mufson and Tom Hamburger, "Labor Union Officials Say Obama Betrayed Them in Health-Care Rollout," *Washington Post*, January 31, 2014.

13. Jacobs, "Privileges of Access," 163.

14. Ibid.

15. Peter Baker, "Obama Was Pushed by Drug Industry, E-Mails Suggest," *New York Times*, June 8, 2012; Paul Blumenthal, "The Legacy of Billy Tauzin: The White House-PhRMA Deal," *Huffington Post*, May 25, 2011, http://www.huffingtonpost.com/paul-blumenthal/the-legacy-of-billy-tauzi_b_460358.html.

16. Jacobs, "Privileges of Access," 162.

17. "Medicare FAQs," Medicare NewsGroup, www.medicarenewsgroup.com/news/medicare-faqs.

18. Jacobs, "Privileges of Access," 162.

19. "Medicare FAQs."

20. Gusmano, "Health Care Reform," 202.

21. Mark Carl Rom, "President Obama's Health Care Reform," in *The Obama Presidency: Change and Continuity*, eds. Andrew J. Dowdle, Dirk C. Van Raemdonck, and Robert Maranto, (New York: Routledge, 2011), 156.

22. Jacobs, "Privileges of Access," 163.

23. American Academy of Actuaries and Society of Actuaries, "Federal Health Reform: Excise Tax on High-Cost Employer Plans," Technical Report, January 2010, https://www.soa.org/Files/Research/research-fed-health-excise-tax.pdf.

24. Justin S. Vaughn, "No Place for a Community Organizer: Barack Obama's Leadership of Congress," in Dowdle et al., *Obama Presidency*, 113.

25. Michael D. Shear and Ceci Connolly, "Reform Gets Conditional GOP Support: Urged by the White House, Republicans Speak Up for Bipartisan Health Fix," *Washington Post*, November 7, 2009; Edwards, *Overreach*, 142.

26. Ross K. Baker, *Is Bipartisanship Dead? A Report from the Senate* (Boulder, CO: Paradigm Publishers, 2015), 58.

27. Michael Barone, *The Almanac of American Politics* (Washington, DC: National Journal Group, 2014), 997.

28. Ibid., 643.

29. Ibid.

30. Graham, *Bush on the Home Front*, 35–44.

31. Matt Corley, "Grassley: In Order for Health Care to Be Bipartisan, 'We Need to Make Sure There Is No Public Option,'" *think.progress.org*, June 24, 2009 (citing a May 2009 Des Moines Register poll showing 56% favor a public option); Nate Silver,

"Public Support for Public Option," *Fivethirtyeightpolitics.com*, June 20, 2009 (five out of six national polls show majority support for a public option, including by a 68–28 percent margin in the Kaiser tracking poll).

32. John Harwood, "Bipartisan Health Bill Is Possible, Leaders Say," *New York Times*, June 7, 2009.

33. Barbara Sinclair, "Doing Big Things: Obama and the 111th Congress," in Rockman et al., *Obama Presidency*, 208; Dan Balz, "Concern, Doubts from the Left on Obama's Health-Care Plan," *Washington Post*, August 23, 2009.

34. Carrie Budoff Brown and Chris Frates, "Max Baucus to Gang of Six: 'Time Is Running Out,'" *Politico.com*, September 8, 2009, http://www.politico.com/story /2009/09/gang-of-six-could-hold-obamas-fate-026879.

35. K. Phillips, "CBO Releases Estimates on Kennedy-Dodd Health Care Bill," *New York Times*, June 15, 2009, http://thecaucus.blogs.nytimes.com/2009/06/15 /cbo-releases-estimates-on-kennedy-dodd-health-care-bill/?_r=0.

36. David M. Herszenhorn, "Senate Committee Approves Health Care Bill," *New York Times*, July 15, 2009, http://thecaucus.blogs.nytimes.com/2009/07/15 /senate-committee-approves-health-care-bill.

37. Robert Pear and David M. Herszenhorn, "Health Bill Clears Hurdle and Hints at Consensus, *New York Times*, July 31, 2009.

38. Associated Press, "GOP Senator Irked at Obama Over Health Care," *NBC NEWS.com*, June 7, 2009, http://www.nbcnews.com/id/31153130/ns/politics-capitol _hill/t/gop-senator-irked-obama-over-health-care.

39. N. Levey and J. Hook, "Senate Democrats Move to Drop Medicare Proposal," *Los Angeles Times*, December 15, 2009.

40. Baker, *Is Bipartisanship Dead?* 59.

41. A. Goodman, "Report: Senator Max Baucus Received More Campaign Money from Health and Insurance Industry Interests Than Any Other Member of Congress," June 16, 2009, *Democracy Now*, http://www.democracynow.org/2009 /6/16/report_senator_max_baucus_received_more.

42. K. Zeese, "Viewpoint: Max Baucus Should Not Be Deciding Health Care for America," *Baltimore Chronicle*, May 31, 2009.

43. Baker, *Is Bipartisanship Dead?* 47.

44. George C. Edwards III, *Strategic Assessments: Evaluating Opportunities and Strategies in the Obama Presidency* (Washington, DC: CQ Press, 2012), 58.

45. Perry Beacon, "Polite Debate at Grassley's Iowa Town Halls," *Washington Post*, August 12, 2009.

46. Baker, *Is Bipartisanship Dead?* 58.

47. Edwards, *Overreach*, 124; Jonathan Alter, *The Promise: President Obama, Year One* (New York: Simon and Schuster, 2010), 256–57.

48. Heartland Connection, "Poll: Iowans Divided over Health Care Reform," September 25, 2009, http://origin-www.heartlandconnection.com/news/story.aspx ?list=194787&id=354872.

49. David Welna, "Visiting Senator Grassley at Home in Iowa," *NPR.org*, July 3, 2009, http://www.npr.org/templates/story/story.php?storyId=106242754.

50. M. Barabel, "Thousands Gather in DC to Protest Healthcare Overhaul Plan," *Los Angeles Times*, September 13, 2009.

51. Nate Silver, "Health Care Is Hazardous to Poll Numbers for Grassley, Other Senators," *Fivethirtyeight.com*, September 22, 2009, http://fivethirtyeight.com /features/health-care-is-hazardous-to-poll.

52. Ezra Klein, "Chuck Grassley Fundraises against Health-Care Reform," *Washington Post*, August 31, 2009.

53. Robert Pear and David M. Herszenhorn, "Baucus Offers Health Plan but Lacks GOP Support," *New York Times*, September 16, 2009.

54. N. Levey and J. Oliphant, "Healthcare Reform Bill Clears Senate Finance Committee," *Los Angeles Times*, October 14, 2009; Baker, *Is Bipartisanship Dead?* 60.

55. Robert Pear and David M. Herszenhorn, "Republican's Vote Lifts a Health Bill, but Hurdles Remain," *New York Times*, October 13, 2009.

56. Colleen McCain Nelson, Peter Nicholas, and Carol E. Lee, "Aides Debated Obama Health-Care Coverage Promise," *Wall Street Journal*, November 2–3, 2013, A1.

57. Gusmano, "Health Care Reform," 207.

58. Edwards, *Overreach*, 56, table 2.4.

59. Ceci Connolly, "Health-Care Activists Targeting Democrats," *Washington Post*, June 28, 2009; Jeff Zeleny, "Millions Spent to Sway Democrats on Health Care," *New York Times*, March 14, 2010; Edwards, *Overreach*, 175.

60. Barbara Trish, "Organizing for America," in *The State of the Parties: The Changing Role of Contemporary American Parties*, eds. John C. Green and Daniel J. Coffey (Lanham, MD: Rowman and Littlefield, 2011), 169–70.

61. Jonathan Martin, "Rahm Emanuel Warns Liberal Groups to Stop Ads," *Politico.com*, August 6, 2009, http://www.politico.com/story/2009/08/rahm-warns-liberal-groups-to-stop-ads-025900; Peter Wallsten, "Chief of Staff Draws Fire from Left as Obama Falters," *Wall Street Journal*, January 26, 2010.

62. Trish, "Organizing for America," 178.

63. C. Hulse and R. Pear, "Sweeping Health Care Plan Passes House," *New York Times*, November 7, 2009.

64. A. Nagourney, "Reid Faces Battles in Washington and at Home," *New York Times Magazine*, January 12, 2010; Baker, *Is Bipartisanship Dead?* 2; Barbara Sinclair, "The President and the Congressional Party Leadership in a Hyperpartisan Era," in *Rivals for Power: Presidential-Congressional Relations*, 5th ed., ed. James A. Thurber (Lanham, MD: Rowman and Littlefield, 2013), 122.

65. G. Stephanopoulos, "Landrieu 'Skeptical' of Reid Health Care Plan," *ABC News.com*, November 3, 2009, http://abcnews.go.com/blogs/politics/2009/11/land rieu-skeptical-of-reid-health-care-plan; C. Brown and J. Sherman, "Senator Blanche Lincoln Also on Board," *Politico.com*, November 21, 2009, http://www.politico.com /news/stories/1109/29792.html; G. Chaddock, "Healthcare's Dealbreakers: Blanche Lincoln Wants to Focus on Jobs," *Christian Science Monitor*, November 24, 2009.

66. P. Murphy, "All Roads Lead to Olympia Snowe as Reid Looks for Health Care Closer," *politicsdaily.com*, December 9, 2009, http://www.politicsdaily.com

/2009/12/09/all-roads-lead-to-olympia-snowe-as-reid-looks-for-health-care-cl; Halpin and Harbage, "Origins and Demise," 1117–24.

67. David M. Herszenhorn and Robert Pear, "Final Votes in Congress Cap Battle on Health Bill," *New York Times*, March 25, 2010.

68. Robert Pear, "Senate Approves Health-Care Overhaul on Party-Line Vote," *New York Times*, December 24, 2009.

69. Forecasting models made a roughly accurate prediction that the final hold-outs in the Senate would be Nelson, Lincoln, and Landrieu. John H. Aldrich, *Why Parties? A Second Look* (Chicago: University of Chicago Press, 2011), 321.

70. Avik Roy, "The $4 Billion Typo in Obamacare's 'Louisiana Purchase,'" *Forbes*, March 6, 2012.

71. B. Wingfield, "Senate Clinches Votes for Health Care Overhaul," *Forbes. com*, December 19, 2009.

72. William A. Galston, "Barack Obama's First Two Years: Policy Accomplishments, Political Failures," in Dowdle et al., *Obama Presidency*, 196.

73. M. Loffman, "Cornhusker to Give Back 'Kick Back'?" *ABC News*, January 7, 2010, http://blogs.abcnews.com/thenote/2010/01/cornhusker-to-give-back-kick -back.html; P. Overby, "With Health Care Bill, One Day You're In . . .," *NPR.com*, March 19, 2010, http://www.npr.org/templates/story/story.php?storyId=1249 33273.

74. Edwards, *Overreach*, 99.

75. Michael Cooper, "GOP Senate Victory Stuns Democrats," *New York Times*, January 19, 2010.

76. C. Babington, "Obama Invites GOP Leaders to Health Care Reform Talk," Associated Press, February 7, 2010, http://www.timesfreepress.com/news/local /story/2010/feb/07/obama-invites-gop-leaders-health-care-talk/4851.

77. David M. Herszenhorn and Robert Pear, "Obama Offers to Use Some GOP Health Proposals," *New York Times*, March 2, 2010.

78. Babington, "Obama Invites GOP Leaders"; Herszenhorn and Pear, "Obama Offers."

79. Stuart M. Butler, "Assuring Affordable Health Care for All Americans," *Heritage Foundation*, October 1, 1989, http://www.heritage.org/research/lecture /assuring-affordable-health-care-for-all-americans.

80. Peter Grier, "Obama Takes Hands-On Role in Advancing Health Care Reform," *Christian Science Monitor*, January 6, 2010.

81. S. Murray and L. Montgomery, "House Passes Health Care Reform Bill without Republican Votes," *Washington Post*, March 22, 2010.

82. Robert Pear and David M. Herszenhorn, "Obama Hails Vote on Health Care as Answering 'the Call of History,'" *New York Times*, March 21, 2010.

83. Edwards, *Overreach*, 176.

84. Aldrich, *Why Parties?* 321–22.

85. Gusmano, "Health Care Reform," 201.

86. S. Benen, "Clyburn Hitting the Brakes on Healthcare," *Washington Monthly*, January 26, 2009, http://www.washingtonmonthly.com/archives/individual/2009

_01/016615.php; Erwin C. Hargrove, *The Effective Presidency*, 2nd ed. (Boulder, CO: Paradigm Publishers, 2014), 266; Noam Scheiber, *The Escape Artists: How Obama's Team Fumbled the Recovery* (New York: Simon and Schuster, 2012); Michael R. Crittenden, "Schumer: Health Law Took Democrats Off Course," *Wall Street Journal*, November 26, A4, http://blogs.wsj.com/washwire/2014/11/25/schumer-to-democrats-convince-middle-class-were-on-their-side (in a speech at the National Press Club after the 2014 elections, Democratic senator Charles Schumer claimed that the Democrats "blew the opportunity" that voters gave them in 2008 by pursuing health reform instead of focusing on the economy).

87. Obama apparently believed it was now or never. See Bob Woodward, *The Price of Politics* (New York: Simon and Schuster, 2012), 11.

88. Dana Milbank, "Why Obama Needs Rahm at the Top," *Washington Post*, February 21, 2010, A13; Galston, "Barack Obama's First Two Years," 196.

89. Galston, "Barack Obama's First Two Years," 190.

90. Rom, "President Obama's Health Care Reform," 156.

91. Skocpol, "Flashpoint."

92. Edwards, *Overreach*, 169.

93. Noam Scheiber, "Nice Guys Finish Last: What Obama Could Learn from Bush about Bipartisanship," *New Republic*, February 11, 2010.

94. Galston, "Barack Obama's First Two Years," 190–91.

95. Kaiser Health Policy Tracking Poll, Kaiser Family Foundation, http://kff.org/health-reform/poll-findings.

96. Wallsten, "Chief of Staff Draws Fire."

97. Halpin and Harbage, "Origins and Demise," 1117–24.

98. Bianca DiJulio, Jamie Firth, and Mollyann Brodie, "Kaiser Health Policy Tracking Poll: December 2014," December 18, 2014, http://kff.org/health-reform/poll-finding/kaiser-health-policy-tracking-poll-december-2014.

99. Paul Starr, *Remedy and Reaction: The Peculiar Struggle over Health Care Reform* (New Haven, CT: Yale University Press, 2011).

100. Hargrove, *Effective Presidency*, 289–90.

101. Keith Hennessey, "A Strategy to Undo Obamacare," *Wall Street Journal*, July 3, 2012, A15.

102. Gerald F. Seib, "Obamacare's Challenge: A Skeptical Public," *Wall Street Journal*, August 6, 2013, A4.

103. Jonah Goldberg, "Big GOP Win a Rebuke of President," *USA Today*, November 6, 2014, 10A.

104. Julia Azari, *Delivering the People's Message: The Changing Politics of the Presidential Mandate* (Ithaca, NY: Cornell University, 2014), 162.

105. Byron W. Doynes and Glen Sussman, "Environmental Policy and Global Climate Change," in Watson et al., *Obama Presidency*, 162–64; Matthew N. Green, "2010 Midterm Election," in Watson et al., *Obama Presidency*, 135–36 (fig. 9.1) (analysis of Obama speeches from September 2009 to October 2010 shows much more emphasis on economy than health care, especially in 2010, but both topics received extensive coverage). .

106. Seib, "Obamacare's Challenge," A4.

107. Ezekiel L. Emanuel, "Inside the Making of Obamacare," *Wall Street Journal*, March 8–9, 2014, C3.

6. The Affordable Care Act: Implementation Nightmare

1. Frank J. Thompson, "Health Reform, Polarization, and Public Administration," *Public Administration Review* 73, special issue (2013): S3–S12.

2. Louise Radnofsky, "New Head of HHS Brings Key Set of Skills," *Wall Street Journal*, June 6, 2014, A5.

3. Ibid.

4. Tracey Jan, "Don Berwick Reflects on Health Law Woes," *Boston Globe*, October 24, 2013; Sarah Kliff, "Medicare Administrator Donald Berwick Resigns in the Face of Republican Opposition," *Washington Post*, November 23, 2011.

5. Robert Pear, "Obama's Pick to Head Medicare and Medicaid Resigns Post," *New York Times*, November 23, 2011.

6. Jessica Zigmond, "GOP Senators Oppose Berwick Nomination," *Modern Healthcare*, March 3, 2011, http://www.modernhealthcare.com/article/20110303/NEWS/303039977.

7. Robert Pear, "Obama Health Team Turns to Carrying Out the Law," *New York Times*, April 18, 2010; CBS News, "Obamacare: Memo Reveals Health Care Adviser Warned W. H. Was Losing Control 3 Years Ago," November 4, 2013, http://www.cbsnews.com/news/obamacare-memo-reveals-health-care-adviser-warned-wh-was-losing-control-3-years-ago; David Cutler to Larry Summers, Memorandum, "Urgent Need for Changes in Health Reform Implementation," May 11, 2010, http://www.washingtonpost.com/blogs/wonkblog/files/2013/11/Cutler-implementation-memo-1.pdf ("I do not believe the . . . relevant members of the Administration understand the President's vision or have the capability to carry it out").

8. Marilyn Tavenner, who did have some relevant skills, began work at CMS in early 2010 and was nominated by President Obama to lead CMS in late 2011. Democratic senator Tom Harkin of Iowa delayed her nomination for more than a year for unrelated reasons. She was confirmed in the Senate 91–7. Jennifer Haberkorn and Paige Winfield Cunningham, "Marilyn Tavenner Approved by Senate for CMS Post," *Politico*, May 15, 2013, http://www.politico.com/story/2013/05/marilyn-tavenner-cms-91438.html.

9. Jennings lasted less than six months in 2013. Robert Pear, "Clinton Aide Joins Obama on Health Care," *New York Times*, July 7, 2013; David Jackson, "Obama Losing Health Care Adviser," *USA Today*, January 24, 2014. Schiliro returned in early 2014 to help Obama manage relations with Congress, since Democrats were growing uneasy about ACA implementation. Juliet Eilperin, "Phil Schiliro Returns to Help Spearhead White House Health-Care Policy," *Washington Post*, December 7, 2013, http://www.washingtonpost.com/blogs/post-politics/wp/2013/12/07/phil-schiliro-returns-to-help-spearhead-white-house-health-care-policy.

10. Penny Star, "11,588,500 Words: Obamacare Regulations 30 Times as Long as Law," *CBSNews.com*, October 14, 2013, http://cbsnews.com/news/article/penny-starr/11588500-words-obamacare-regs-30x-long-law.

11. "Health Reform Implementation Timeline," Kaiser Family Foundation, 2014, Kff.org/interactive/implementation-timeline.

12. See, for example, the Heritage Foundation's website material on "Obamacare" at *Heritage.org*.

13. Ezra Klein, "How Republicans Made It Possible for the Supreme Court to Rule against the Mandate," *Washington Post*, June 25, 2012.

14. "Health Tracking Poll: Exploring the Public's Views on the Affordable Care Act," Kaiser Family Foundation, retrieved November 1, 2014, Kff.org/international/health-tracking-poll.

15. Abby Goodnough, "Poll on Health Care Law Shows Increased Support," *New York Times*, March 20, 2015, A16 (in early March 2015, the Kaiser tracking poll found 41 percent favorable/43 percent unfavorable to the ACA; in July 2014, it was 37 percent favorable/53 percent unfavorable).

16. Ibid.

17. Michael Barone, "How ObamaCare Misreads America," *Wall Street Journal*, February 3, 2014, A15.

18. Laura Saunders, "Penalty for Not Having Health Coverage Can Be Thousands of Dollars," *Wall Street Journal*, September 27, 2014, B7.

19. Ezra Klein, "The Individual Mandate No Longer Applies to People Whose Plans Were Cancelled," *Washington Post*, December 19, 2013, http://www.washingtonpost.com/blogs/wonkblog/wp/2013/12/19/the-obama-administration-just-delayed-the-individual-mandate-for-people-whose-plans-have-been-canceled.

20. Tara Siegel Bernard, "Health Law Tax Effects Now Loom for Failures," *New York Times*, December 26, 2014, B1, 2.

21. Kaiser Family Foundation, Kff.org/health-reform/faq.

22. Ibid.

23. Ed O'Keefe, "The House Has Voted 54 Times in Four Years on Obamacare. Here's the Full List," *Washington Post*, March 21, 2014, http://www.washingtonpost.com/blogs/the-fix/wp/2014/03/21/the-house-has-voted-54-times-in-four-years-on-obamacare-heres-the-full-list.

24. Adam Liptak, "Supreme Court Upholds Health Care Law, 5–4, in Victory for Obama," *New York Times*, June 28, 2012.

25. See, for example, Mike Lee, *Why John Roberts Was Wrong about Healthcare: A Conservative Critique of the Supreme Court's Obamacare Ruling* (New York: Simon and Shuster, 2013).

26. Colleen McCain Nelson and Peter Nicholas, "White House Races to Quell Health Uproar," *Wall Street Journal*, October 30, 2013, A4.

27. Joseph Shaw, "White House: No Obamacare Individual Mandate Delay," *New York Daily News*, March 16, 2014, http://www.nydailynews.com/blogs/d/white-house-no-obamacare-individual-mandate-delay-blog-entry-1.1733398.

28. Robert Pear, "White House Seeks to Limit Health Law's Tax Troubles," *New York Times*, February 1, 2015, 15.

29. Stephanie Armour, "Six Million May Owe Health-Insurance Penalty," *Wall Street Journal*, January 29, 2015, A3.

30. Stephanie Armour, "Fewer Uninsured Face Fines as Health Law's Exemptions Swell," *Wall Street Journal*, August 6, 2014.

31. James Surowiecki, "The Business End of Obamacare," *New Yorker*, October 14, 2013.

32. Jason Lange, "Obama's Healthcare Program Not Costing Full-time Jobs, White House Says," *Chicago Tribune*, October 22, 2014.

33. Congressional Budget Office, "Labor Market Effects of the Affordable Care Act: Updated Estimates," *Congressional Budget Office*, 2014, http://www.cbo.gov/sites/default/files/cbofiles/attachments/45010-breakout-AppendixC.pdf.

34. Damian Paletta, "Lawmakers Spar over CBO's U.S. Health Law Findings," *Wall Street Journal*, February 6, 2014, A4.

35. "2014 Employer Health Benefits Survey," Kaiser Family Foundation, September 10, 2014, http://kff.org/health-costs/report/2014-employer-health-benefits-survey.

36. Kelley Kennedy, "Glitch in Law May Leave Kids with No Insurance," *USA Today*, September 25, 2013, A1.

37. Stephanie Armour, "More Cost of Health Care Shifts to Consumers," *Wall Street Journal*, December 4, 2014, A1.

38. "Children's Health Insurance: Opportunity Exists for Improved Access to Affordable Insurance," General Accounting Office, June 20, 2012, GAO-12–648, http://www.gao.gov/assets/600/591797.pdf.

39. Juliet Eilperin and Amy Goldstein, "White House Delays Health Insurance Mandate for Medium-Sized Employers until 2016," *Washington Post*, February 11, 2014, A1.

40. Anna Wilde Mathews, "Average Health Insurance Tab: $16,834," *Wall Street Journal*, September 11, 2014, B2.

41. Bob Tita, "Some Factories Stick with Old Health Plans," *Wall Street Journal*, October 31, 2014, B7.

42. Sarah E. Needleman, "Small Firms Caught in Health-Policy Limbo," *Wall Street Journal*, November 16–17, 2013, A5; Adam Janofsky and Louise Radnofsky, "Small Firms Hit Bumps Test-Driving Health Site," *Wall Street Journal*, November 4, 2014, B5.

43. Jennifer Corbett Dooren, "Rising Premiums May Hit Small Firms," *Wall Street Journal*, February 25, 2014, B4.

44. Sherry Glied and Stephanie Ma, "How States Stand to Gain or Lose Federal Funds by Opting In or Out of the Medicaid Expansion," *Commonwealth Fund*, December 2013, http://www.commonwealthfund.org/~/media/Files/Publications/Issue%20Brief/2013/Dec/1718_Glied_how_states_stand_gain_lose_Medicaid_expansion_ib_v2.pdf.

45. Louise Radnofsky and Arian Campo-Flores, "Deal Offers Model for Medicaid Expansion," *Wall Street Journal*, January 28, 2015, A1.

46. Mark Peters and Louise Radnofsky, "A Medicaid Bet in Wisconsin," December 19, 2013, A8.

47. Louise Radnofsky, "In Medicaid, a New Health-Care Fight," *Wall Street Journal*, February 11, 2013, A1.

48. Kyle Cheney and Kathryn Smith, "Medicaid Expansion Decision Looms for Many States," *Politico*, November 11, 2012, http://www.politico.com/news/stories /1112/83787_Page2.html.

49. Ana Campoy, "Tie to Obama's Health Law Proves Risky for Arkansas Republican," *Wall Street Journal*, June 7–8, 2014, A5.

50. Abby Goodnough, "In Arkansas, 'Private Option' Medicaid Plan Could Be Derailed," *New York Times*, February 11, 2014, A12; Louise Radnofsky, "Tennessee Moves to Expand Medicaid," *Wall Street Journal*, December 16, 2014, A6.

51. Ana Campoy and Louise Radnofsky, "Arkansas Fails to Pass 'Private Option' Health Law," *Wall Street Journal*, February 19, 2014, A3.

52. Jason Millman, "Pennsylvania's Republican Governor Expands Medicaid," *Washington Post*, August 28, 2014, http://www.washingtonpost.com /blogs/wonkblog/wp/2014/08/28/pennsylvanias-republican-governor-expands -medicaid.

53. "Current Status of State Medicaid Expansion Decisions," Kaiser Family Foundation, November 2, 2015, kff.org/health-reform/slide/current-status-of-the -medicaid-expansion-decision.

54. Radnofsky, "In Medicaid."

55. Louise Radnofsky, "Obama Sees 'Bumps' for Health Law," *Wall Street Journal*, May 1, 2013, A6.

56. Robert Pear, "States Decline to Set Up Exchanges for Insurance," *New York Times*, November 17, 2012, A13.

57. Stephanie Armour, "Five States' Health-Care Exchanges See Costly Fixes," *Wall Street Journal*, June 4, 2014, A2.

58. Jennifer Corbett Dooren, "States Grapple with Fixing Problem-Plagued Health Exchanges," *Wall Street Journal*, April 4, 2014, A4.

59. Michael F. Cannon, "50 Vetoes: How States Can Stop the Obama Health Care Law," Cato Institute, March 21, 2013, http://www.cato.org/publications/white -paper/50-vetoes-how-states-can-stop-obama-health-care-law.

60. Lizette Alvarez and Robert Pear, "Several States Undercutting Health Care Enrollment," *New York Times*, September 18, 2013, A10.

61. Louise Radnofsky, "Poor Oversight, Work Marred Health Site's Launch, Report Says," *Wall Street Journal*, January 21, 2015, A2.

62. Radnofsky, "Obama Sees 'Bumps,'" A6.

63. Ibid.

64. Eric Lipton, Ian Austen, and Sharon LaFraniere, "Tension and Flaws before Health Website Crash," *New York Times*, November 23, 2013, A1.

65. Lucia Graves, Marina Koren, Brian Resnick, and Alex Seitz-Wald, "Obama: 'There's No Sugarcoating' the Health Care Insurance Exchange," *National Journal*, October 21, 2013.

66. Sarah Kliff, "Obamacare Chief Marilyn Tavenner Heads to the Hill Tuesday: Here's What to Expect," *Washington Post*, October 28, 2013.

67. Ricardo Alonso-Zaldivar, "Probe Exposes Flaws behind HealthCare.gov Rollout," Associated Press, July 31, 2014, http://news.yahoo.com/probe-exposes-flaws-behind-healthcare-gov-rollout-171328973.html.

68. Christopher Weaver and Louise Radnofsky, "Federal Health Site Stymied by Lack of Direction," *Wall Street Journal*, October 28, 2013, A1.

69. Peter Nicholas and Carol L. Lee, "White House Soul Searches as Errors Mount," *Wall Street Journal*, November 16–17, 2013, A4.

70. Weaver and Radnofsky, "Federal Health Site," A1.

71. Monica Langley, "Health Law's Rocky Debut Puts Sebelius in Cross Hairs," *Wall Street Journal*, October 18, 2013.

72. "Don Berwick Reflects on Health Law Woes," *Boston Globe*, October 24, 2013.

73. Quoting Bob Kocher, in Weaver and Radnofsky, "Federal Health Site," A1.

74. Brian Howey, "Obama Knew Millions Could Not Keep Their Policies," *HPI Daily Wire*, October 30, 2013, http://howeypolitics.com/Content/HPI-Daily-Wire/HPI-Daily-Wire/Article/Oct—30—2013-HPI-Daily-Wire/12/31/10537.

75. Colleen McCain Nelson, Peter Nicholas, and Carol E. Lee, "Aides Debated Obama Health-Care Coverage Promise," *Wall Street Journal*, November 2, 2013, A1.

76. Elizabeth Williamson, "Outspoken Group Bears Brunt of Canceled Health-Insurance Policies," *Wall Street Journal*, November 2–3, 2013, A13.

77. For a description of the origins of Obama's reassuring claim and his apology for making it, see Angie Drobnic Holan, "Lie of the Year: 'If You Like Your Health Care Plan, You Can Keep It,'" *Politifact.com*, December 12, 2013, http://www.politifact.com/truth-o-meter/article/2013/dec/12/lie-year-if-you-like-your-health-care-plan-keep-it.

78. Colleen McCain Nelson and Peter Nicholas, "Obama Tempers Insurance Pledge as Health Fight Rages," *Wall Street Journal*, October 31, 2013, A2.

79. NRO Staff, "39 House Dems Vote for Upton Plan," *National Review*, November 15, 2013 (Upton plan passed the House 261–167, with thirty-nine Democrats joining all House Republicans).

80. Siobhan Hughes, Janet Hook, and Colleen McCain Nelson, "Obama Open to Health-Law Change," *Wall Street Journal*, November 14, 2013, A1.

81. Reed Abelson and Suzanne Craig, "After Obama Meeting, Insurers Question Plan's Workability," *New York Times*, November 18, 2013, A12.

82. Nicholas and Lee, "White House Soul Searches," A4.

83. Editorial, "One-Year Delay a Good First Step," *Wilson (NC) Times*, November 14, 2013, http://www.wilsontimes.com/News/Feature/Story/27289730—One-year-delay-is-a-good-first-step.

84. Patrick O'Connor and Valerie Bauerlein, "Democratic Lawmakers Running for Cover," *Wall Street Journal*, November 15, 2013, A5.

85. Aamer Madhani, "Website Could Jinx Obama's Legacy," *USA Today*, October 23, 2013, 4A.

86. Spencer E. Ante, Anna Wilde Matthews, and Louise Radnofsky, "Overhaul of Health Site in the Works," *Wall Street Journal*, June 6, 2014, A5.

87. Ibid.

88. Louise Radnofsky, "HealthCare.gov Shortens Insurance Application," *Wall Street Journal*, October 9, 2014, A2.

89. US Department of Health and Human Services, "HHS Announces Auto-Enrollment Plan for Current Marketplace Consumers for 2015," *HHS Press Office*, June 6, 2014, http://www.hhs.gov/news/press/2014pres/06/20140626a.html.

90. Louise Radnofsky and Stephanie Armour, "HealthCare.gov Delays Web Host Switch," *Wall Street Journal*, October 2, 2014, A3.

91. Stephanie Armour and Louise Radnofsky, "Healthcare.gov Holds Up amid Enrollment Surge," *Wall Street Journal*, December 16, 2014, A6; Stephanie Armour, Louise Radnofsky, and Anna Wilde Mathews, "Health-Care Web Site Users Have Few Problems," *Wall Street Journal*, November 17, 2014, A4; Stephanie Armour and Louise Radnofsky, "Health Site's Chief Braces for New Sign-Ups," *Wall Street Journal*, November 7, 2014, A6.

92. Christopher Weaver and Louise Radnofsky, "Subsidies for Older Buyers Give Health Insurers a Headache," *Wall Street Journal*, August 30, 2013, A1.

93. Leslie Scism and Timothy W. Martin, "High Deductibles Fuel New Worries of Health-Law Sticker Shock," *Wall Street Journal*, December 9, 2013, A1.

94. Christopher Weaver and Louise Radnofsky, "New Health Law's Success Rests on the Young," *Wall Street Journal*, July 2, 2013, A1.

95. Ibid.

96. Alan S. Blinder, "Despite a Botched Rollout, the Health-Care Law Is Worth It," *Wall Street Journal*, November 12, 2013, A12.

97. Louise Radnofsky, "Sign-ups by Young on New Exchanges Remain Sluggish," *Wall Street Journal*, February 13, 2014, A6.

98. Robert Pear, "Health Care Enrollment Falls Short of Goal, with Deadline Approaching," *New York Times*, March 12, 2014, A14.

99. Louise Radnofsky and Anna Wilde Mathews, "Obama Administration Says 28% of Health-Law Enrollees Are 18-to-34 Year Olds," *Wall Street Journal*, May 2, 2014, A1.

100. Arian Campo-Flores, "Latinos Lag under Health Law," *Wall Street Journal*, November 12, 2014, A1.

101. Anna Wilde Mathews and Christopher Weaver, "Sick Drawn to New Coverage in Health-Law Plans," *Wall Street Journal*, June 25, 2014, A1.

102. Sam Baker, "Unleashing the Furies," *National Journal*, February 8, 2014, 56.

103. Robert Pear, "Obama Asks Health Plans to Report Rising Rates," *New York Times*, April 14, 2013, A11.

104. David Lawder, "Obamacare Exchanges Not Properly Verifying Applicant Data: Watchdog," *Reuters.com*, July 1, 2014, http://www.reuters.com/article/2014/07/01/us-usa-healthcare-subsidies-idUSKBN0F65AC20140701.

105. Robert Pear, "Thousands to Be Questioned on Eligibility for Health Insurance Subsidies," *New York Times*, June 6, 2014, A12.

106. Ibid.

107. Louise Radnofsky, "Tens of Thousands Likely to Lose Health Insurance at End of September," *Wall Street Journal*, September 16, 2014, A3.

108. Louise Radnofsky, "Health-Law Enrollment in 2015 Won't Meet Forecast," *Wall Street Journal*, November 11, 2014, A1.

109. Sarah Kliff, "It's Not Just the Employer Mandate: Three Obamacare Delays You Haven't Heard About," *Washington Post*, July 8, 2013, http://www.washington post.com/blogs/wonkblog/wp/2013/07/08/its-not-just-the-employer-mandate-three -obamacare-delays-you-havent-heard-about.

110. Pear, "Thousands to Be Questioned," A12.

111. Ibid.

112. Tara Siegel Bernard, "The New Health Care Rules and Taxes," *New York Times*, December 26, 2014, B2.

113. Pear, "White House Seeks," 15.

114. Ross K. Baker, *Is Bipartisanship Dead? A Report from the Senate* (Boulder, CO: Paradigm Publishers, 2015), 69.

115. O'Keefe, "House Has Voted."

116. Jim DeMint and Mike Needham, "The Only Way to Stop ObamaCare Is to Cut Off Its Funding," *Wall Street Journal*, August 9, 2013, A13.

117. Siobhan Hughes, "Republicans Give Health Law Room to Stumble," *Wall Street Journal*, November 2–3, 2014, A4.

118. Juliet Eilperin, "Fight Over Health Care Law Isn't Over Some in GOP Say," *Washington Post*, October 18, 2013, A6.

119. Catherine Hollander, "How Obamacare Could Suffer Death by a Thousand Cuts," *National Journal*, August 3, 2013, 35.

120. Sarah Kliff, "The 'Concession' Won by the GOP on Income Verification Is Meaningless," *Washington Post*, October 18, 2013, A6.

121. Patrick O'Connor and Kristina Peterson, "Tweaks to Health Law Attract Some Democrats," *Wall Street Journal*, September 27, 2013, A4.

122. Robert Pear, "House Acts to Repeal Medical-Device Tax," *New York Times*, June 7, 2012.

123. Matt Dobias, "House Approves Bill to Repeal Medical Device Tax," *Politico Pro*, June 7, 2012, http://www.politico.com/news/stories/0612/77189.html; Jonathan Weisman, "Reid's Uncompromising Power Play in Senate Rankles Republicans," *International New York Times*, January 9, 2014, http://www.nytimes.com/2014/01/10 /us/politics/reids-uncompromising-power-play-in-senate-rankles-republicans.html ?gwh=C3E4A86C560598F4B728DA78A6F11A6F&gwt=pay.

124. Kristina Peterson and Christopher Weaver, "Medical-Device Tax Repeal Faces Uphill Climb in the Senate," *Wall Street Journal*, March 22, 2013.

125. Kristina Peterson and Anna Wilde Mathews, "Some Democrats Fight Obama over Medicare," *Wall Street Journal*, April 7, 2014, A4.

126. Kliff, "Not Just the Employer Mandate."

127. Louise Radnofsky, "Health-Law Backers Push Skimpier 'Copper' Insurance Policies," *Wall Street Journal*, February 14, 2014, A4.

128. Kristina Peterson, "Health-Law Tweak Redefining Full-Time Worker Gains Bipartisan Traction," *Wall Street Journal*, April 4, 2014, A4.

129. Jonathan H. Adler and Michael F. Cannon, "Another Obamacare Glitch," *Wall Street Journal*, November 16, 2011.

130. Joe Palazzolo, "Health Law Faces New Legal Challenges," *Wall Street Journal*, October 21, 2013, A6.

131. Henry J. Aaron, David M. Cutler, and Peter R. Orszag, "Stop the Anti-Obamacare Shenanigans," *New York Times*, September 11, 2014, A23.

132. Robert Pear, "Federal Judge Upholds Health Care Subsidies," *New York Times*, January 16, 2014, A15.

133. Brent Kendall, "Appeals Court to Revisit Ruling Limiting Health Law Subsidies," *Wall Street Journal*, September 5, 2014, A2.

134. Liptak, "Supreme Court Upholds Law."

135. Margot Sanger-Katz, "Many States Will Be Unprepared if Court Weakens Health Law," *New York Times*, December 11, 2014, A3.

136. Louise Radnofsky, "States Stand Pat ahead of Supreme Court Health-Law Ruling," *Wall Street Journal*, January 16, 2015, A2.

137. Michael R. Crittenden and Colleen McCain Nelson, "House Votes to Authorize Boehner to Sue Obama," *Wall Street Journal*, July 30, 2014.

138. Ashley Parker, "House GOP Files Lawsuit in Battling Health Law," *New York Times*, November 21, 2014.

139. Robert Pear, "Suit on Health Law Puts Focus on Funding Powers," *New York Times*, November 20, 2014, 25.

140. Christopher Weaver and Anna Wilde Mathews, "Exchanges See Little Progress on Insured," *Wall Street Journal*, January 18–19, 2014, A1.

141. Dan Witters, "Arkansas, Kentucky Report Sharpest Drops in Uninsured Rate," *Gallup.com*, August 5, 2014, http://www.gallup.com/poll/174290/arkansas-kentucky-report-sharpest-drops-uninsured-rate.aspx.

142. Louise Radnofsky, "About 11.4 Million Enrolled under Health Law," *Wall Street Journal*, February 18, 2015, A2.

143. Stephanie Armour, "More Cost of Health Care Shifts to Consumers," *Wall Street Journal*, December 4, 2014, A1.

144. Louise Radnofsky, "How the ACA May Affect Health Costs," *Wall Street Journal*, February 24, 2014, R4.

145. Christopher Weaver and Melinda Beck, "Insurers Cut Doctors' Fees in New Health Care Plans," *Wall Street Journal*, November 22, 2013, A1; Reed Abelson, "More Insured but the Choices Are Narrowing," *New York Times*, May 13, 2014, A1.

146. Louise Radnofsky, "U.S. States to Get More Insurers under ACA," *Wall Street Journal*, September 24, 2014, A4; Anna Wilde Mathews, "Insurers Fill Gaps in Health Plans," *Wall Street Journal*, June 10, 2014, B1.

147. Colleen McCain Nelson, "Health Law Puts Obama Legacy on the Line," *Wall Street Journal*, September 27, 2013, A4.

148. Martha T. Moore, "Insurance Ads Play off Obamacare Fears," *USA Today*, October 23, 2013, 4A (citing data from Kantor Media CMAG); Laura Meckler, "Some Democrats Talking Up Health Law on Stump," *Wall Street Journal*, May 28, 2014, A4.

149. Marilyn Werber Serafini, "Writing the Rules for the Health Law," *National Journal*, May 1, 2010, 6.

150. Liptak, "Supreme Court Upholds Law."

151. Timothy W. Martin and Christopher Weaver, "Flurry of Tweaks to Affordable Care Act Leaves Insurers Rattled," *Wall Street Journal*, December 21–22, 2013, A4; Staff Report, "The Do-It-Yourself-Presidency," *National Journal*, October 5, 2014, 23.

152. Jess Bravin, "Obama's Fix for a Political Problem Stirs a Legal Question," *Wall Street Journal*, November 16–17, 2013, A4.

153. Karl Rove, "Behind the White House's Health-Law Dodges," *Wall Street Journal*, February 13, 2014, A11.

154. Charlie Cook, "A Historic Collapse," *National Journal*, December 7, 2013, 36; Neil King Jr., "Poll: Health Law Hurts President Politically," *Wall Street Journal*, December 11, 2013, A4.

7. Global Warming Warrior

1. See generally, National Research Council, *America's Energy Future: Technology and Transformation* (Washington, DC: National Academies Press, 2009); William Nordhaus, *The Climate Casino: Risk, Uncertainty, and Economics for a Warming World?* (New Haven, CT: Yale University Press, 2013).

2. I borrow the term from Theda Skocpol, "Naming the Problem: What It Will Take to Counter Extremism and Engage Americans in the Fight Against Global Warming," report prepared for the symposium on "The Politics of America's Fight Against Global Warming," co-sponsored by the Columbia School of Journalism and the Scholars Strategy Network, Harvard University, February 14, 2013.

3. Ken Dilonian, "Obama Shifts Stance on Environmental Issues," *USA Today*, May 18, 2008.

4. "RFK Jr: Some Leaders Fall for Coal's Lies," ABC News, May 22, 2009, http://www.huffingtonpost.com/2009/04/21/rfk-jr-obama-is-indenture_n_189644.html.

5. See generally National Research Council, *Liquid Transportation Fuels from Coal and Biomass* (Washington, DC: National Academy Press, 2009).

6. Alec MacGillis and Steven Mufson, "Coal Fuels Debate over Obama," *Washington Post.com,* June 24, 2007.

7. "Obama's Final Budget Calls for 100% Auction of Carbon Permits," *Environmental Leader*, May 8, 2009, http://www.environmentalleader.com/2009/05/08/obamas-final-budget-calls-for-100-auction-of-carbon-permits; Lori Montgomery, "Obama Officials Defend Budget," *Washington Post*, March 4, 2009.

8. Sarah Palin, "A 'Cap and Tax' Road to Economic Disaster," *Washington Post*, July 14, 2009.

9. Joe Romm, "Obama's Excellent Energy and Climate Plan," *ClimateProgress*, October 10, 2007, http://thinkprogress.org/climate/2007/10/09/201951/obamas-excellent-energy-and-climate-plan.

10. Andrew C, Revkin, Shan Carter, Jonathan Ellis, Farhana Hossain, and Alan McLean, "On the Issues: Climate Change," *New York Times*, May 23, 2012.

11. John M. Broder, "Obama Affirms Climate Change Goals," *New York Times*, November 18, 2008.

12. Darren Samuelsohn, "Climate Bill Needed to 'Save the Planet,' Says Obama," *New York Times*, February 25, 2009.

13. The 2005 version of the McCain-Lieberman plan was defeated 38–60, as eleven Democrats voted against it and six Republicans voted for it. The defeat was worse in 2005 than in 2003 because the addition of pro–nuclear power provisions in 2005 triggered opposition from four Democratic senators who favor climate legislation. Darren Samuelsohn, "Climate Change: Senate Seesaws on Climate with McCain-Lieberman Defeat, Bingaman Win," *Energy and Environment Daily*, June 23, 2005, http://www.eenews.net/stories/9934.

14. Kate Sheppard, "Climate Security Act Dies, Failing to Muster Enough Votes to Move Forward," *Grist*, June 6, 2008, http://grist.org/article/an-inhospitable-climate.

15. Darren Goode, "Senate Rejects Cloture on Climate Change Bill," *National Journal*, June 6, 2008; David M. Herszenhorn, "After Verbal Fire, Senate Effectively Kills Climate Change Bill," *New York Times*, June 7, 2008.

16. Ryan Lizza, "As the World Burns," *New Yorker*, October 11, 2010.

17. John D. Graham, *Bush on the Home Front: Domestic Policy Triumphs and Setbacks* (Bloomington: Indiana University Press, 2010).

18. Kate Sheppard, "Senate Rules Out Using Budget Process to Pass Cap and Trade," *Grist*, April 2, 2009, http://grist.org/article/2009–04–01-senate-budget-cap-trade; Darren Samuelsohn, "Cap and Trade Advocates Press On after Budget Battle," *New York Times*, April 3, 2009.

19. EPA, "Advance Notice of Proposed Rulemaking: Regulating Greenhouse Gas Emissions under the Clean Air Act," July 11, 2008, EPA-HQ-OAR-2008–0318, *Federal Register* 73, no. 147 (2008): 44354.

20. Inimai M. Chettiar and Jason A. Schwartz, "The Road Ahead: EPA's Options and Obligations for Regulating Greenhouse Gases," Report No. 3, Institute for Policy Integrity, NYU School of Law, April 2009, http://policyintegrity.org/files/publications/TheRoadAhead.pdf.

21. Michael A. Livermore, "Obama Could Create a Cap-and-Trade System without Congress," *Grist*, April 28, 2009, http://grist.org/article/2009-obama-could-create-a-cap-and-trade-syste.

22. Ronald Brownstein, "Under Pressure," *National Journal*, May 17, 2014, 9.

23. Andrew C. Revkin, "Obama Aide Concedes Climate Law Must Wait," *New York Times*, October 2, 2009; Byron W. Daynes and Glen Sussman, "Environmental Policy and Global Climate Change," in *The Obama Presidency: A Preliminary Assessment*, ed. Robert P. Watson et al. (Albany: SUNY Press, 2012), 170.

24. Jonathan Alter, *The Promise: President Obama, Year One* (New York: Simon and Schuster, 2010), 260.

25. Paul Kane, "House Democrats Hit Boiling Point over Perceived Lack of White House Support," *Washington Post*, July 15, 2010.

26. Jonathan Alter, *The Promise: President Obama, Year One* (New York: Simon and Schuster, 2010), 260; George C. Edwards III, *Overreach: Leadership and the Obama Presidency* (Princeton, NJ: Princeton University Press 2012), 152.

27. Jeff Mason, "Obama 'Flexible' on Climate Legislation," *Reuters.com*, April 9, 2009, http://www.reuters.com/article/2009/04/09/us-obama-climate-idUSTRE5378 FN20090409?feedType=RSS&feedName=environmentNews.

28. Naftali Bendavid, "'Blue Dog' Democrats Hold Health-Care Overhaul at Bay," *Wall Street Journal*, July 27, 2009.

29. Steven Mufson, "High-Stakes Quest for Permission to Pollute," *Washington Post*, June 5, 2009.

30. Louis Peck, "A Veteran of the Climate Wars Reflects on U.S. Failure to Act," January 4, 2011, *Environment 360*, http://e360.yale.edu/feature/a_veteran_of_the _climate_wars_reflects_on_us_failure_to_act/2356.

31. Lisa Lerer, "Climate Bill Clears House Committee," *Politico.com*, May 21, 2009, http://www.politico.com/news/stories/0509/22852.html.

32. Darren Samuelsohn and Robin Bravender, "Democrats' Day of Reckoning Comes for Climate Vote," *Politico.com*, November 3, 2010, http://www.politico.com /news/stories/1110/44617.html.

33. Debra McCown, "Analyst Says Cap and Trade Led to Boucher's Defeat," *Tricities.com*, November 4, 2010, http://www.tricities.com/news/article_5a087a3c-e031 -5aca-83c6-b4f223952eb8.html.

34. Andrew Wheeler, "Join the Debate, Cap and Trade Political Kryptonite for Democrats?" The Arena, *Politico.com*, November 4, 2010, http://www.politico.com /arena/energy.

35. Bureau of Labor Statistics, US Department of Labor, "States with the Highest Unemployment Rates, April 2009," http//bls.gov/opub/ted/2009/may/wk4/art02.htm.

36. Edwards, *Overreach*, 100–101, table 3.13.

37. Skocpol, "Naming the Problem," 49–50.

38. Eric Pooley, *Climate War: True Believers, Power Brokers, and the Fight to Save the Earth* (New York: Hyperion, 2011); Keith Johnson, "Green Jobs: Obama, Big Business Stress Upside to Energy and Climate Legislation," *Wall Street Journal*, December 15, 2009, http://blogs.wsj.com/environmentalcapital/2009/12/15 /green-jobs-obama-big-business-stress-upside-to-energy-and-climate-legislation.

39. Brian Wingfield, "Seeing Red on Cap and Trade," *Forbes*, September 28, 2009.

40. Skocpol, "Naming the Problem," 122.

41. John M. Broder, "Obama Opposes Trade Sanctions in Climate Bill," *New York Times*, June 29, 2009.

42. John M. Broder, "Climate Bill Is Threatened by Senators," *New York Times*, August 7, 2009.

43. Revkin, "Obama Aide Concedes."

44. Skocpol, "Naming the Problem," 56–57, 85–87.

45. Lizza, "As the World Burns."

46. Robert Draper, "Lindsey Graham, This Year's Maverick," *New York Times*, July 4, 2010.

47. Joe Romm, "Obama Pushes Senators for Energy Bill with Carbon Price— and so Does Olympia Snowe," *ClimateProgress*, June 29, 2010, http://thinkprogress .org/climate/2010/06/29/206331/obama-carbon-price-utility-cap-olympia-snow.

428 · Notes to Pages 223–227

48. For an optimistic view of the cap-and-dividend idea, see Skocpol, "Naming the Problem," 123–28.

49. Laura Meckler and Stephen Power, "Democrats Step Back on Carbon Cap," *Wall Street Journal*, June 30, 2010.

50. Darren Samuelsohn, "Cap and Trade in Senate Limbo as Obama Makes All-Out Push on Health Care," *New York Times*, September 9, 2009.

51. Tim Dickinson, "Climate Bill, R.I.P.," *Rolling Stone*, July 21, 2010, http://www.rollingstone.com/politics/news/climate-bill-r-i-p-20100721.

52. John M. Broder, "White House Energy Session Changes No Minds," *New York Times*, June 29, 2010.

53. Carl Hulse and David M. Herszenhorn, "Democrats Call Off Climate Effort," *New York Times*, July 22, 2010.

54. William A. Galston, "Barack Obama's First Two Years: Accomplishments, Political Failures," in Andrew J. Dowdle, Dirk C. Van Raemdonck, and Robert Maranto, eds., *The Obama Presidency: Change and Continuity* (New York: Routledge, 2011), 196.

55. John Broder, "Should Democrats Blame Waxman and Markey," *New York Times*, November 5, 2010, http://green.blogs.nytimes.com/2010/11/05/should-democrats-blame-waxman-and-markey.

56. Peck, "Veteran of the Climate Wars."

57. David Mark, "Cap and Trade Political Kryptonite for Democrats?" The Arena, *Politico.com*, November 4, 2010, http://www.politico.com/arena/energy.

58. Michael Barone, *Almanac of American Politics, 2014* (Washington, DC: National Journal Group, 2013), 1746–1748.

59. Maxwell T. Boykoff, "A Dangerous Shift in Obama's 'Climate Change' Rhetoric," *Washington Post*, January 29, 2012, B2.

60. "Sources of Greenhouse Gas Emissions," U.S. Environmental Protection Agency, http://www3.epa.gov/climatechange.

61. Graham, *Bush on the Home Front*.

62. Bill Vlasic, "US Sets Higher Fuel Efficiency Standards," *New York Times*, August 28, 2012.

63. Juliet Eilperin, "Autos Must Average 54.5 MPG by 2025, New EPA Standards Say," *Washington Post*, August 28, 2012.

64. Sharon Terlep and Stephen Power, "White House Offers Concessions to Auto Industry for Fuel-Economy Plan," *Wall Street Journal*, July 27, 2011, A3.

65. Joseph B. White, "Detroit Gallops Again," *Wall Street Journal*, January 17, 2014, B5.

66. Carl E. Lee, Laura Stevens, and Alice Mundy, "Obama Sets Deadline for Trucks' Fuel Economy Standards," *Wall Street Journal*, February 19, 2014, B4.

67. Stephen Edelstein, "Obama Looks to Set Next Heavy Duty Truck Fuel Efficiency Standards," *Christian Science Monitor*, February 21, 2014.

68. Eilperin, "Autos Must Average 54.5."

69. White, "Detroit Gallops Again," B5.

70. Crain Communications, "CAFÉ Rules Are Set, So It's Time to Stop Whining, Get Busy," *Automotive News*, September 3, 2012, 12.

71. Alan M. Webber, "Government and Business Can Be Friends (Really)," *USA Today*, August 30, 2011, 9A.

72. Stephen Stromberg, "Barack Obama: The Climate Change President," *Washington Post*, November 12, 2014, http://www.washingtonpost.com/blogs/post-partisan /wp/2014/11/12/barack-obama-the-climate-change-president.

73. Nick Bunkley, "CAFÉ Guide: A Map through the Maze," *Automotive News*, October 15, 2012, 3.

74. Coral Davenport, "Obama's Stealth Victory," *National Journal*, May 21, 2011.

75. John M. Broder, "Senate Poses Obstacles to Obama Climate Pledge," *New York Times*, December 12, 2009.

76. Colleen McCain Nelson and Carol E. Lee, "Former Clinton Aide Podesta Played Key Role in Developing Carbon Rule," *Wall Street Journal*, June 4, 2014, A5; Ben Geman, "The Audacity of John Podesta," *National Journal*, November 22, 2014, 13.

77. David Rich, "New EPA Rule Establishes Mandatory Greenhouse Gas Reporting," World Resources Institute, *GHG Progocol.org*, March 12, 2009, www .ghgprotocol.org/feature/new-epa-rule-establishes.

78. Robin Bravender, "EPA Issues Final 'Tailoring' Rule for Greenhouse Gas Emissions," *New York Times,* May 13, 2010.

79. Matthew L. Wald, "Court Backs EPA over Emissions Intended to Reduce Global Warming," *New York Times*, June 26, 2012.

80. Thomas Lorenzen, "Supreme Court Invalidates EPA's GHG Tailoring Rule," *Dorsey.com*, June 26, 2014, www.dorsey.com/eu-lorenzen-energy-greenhouse-gas -rule-invalidated.

81. Jonathan H. Adler, "Further Thoughts on Today's Supreme Court Decision on Greenhouse Gas Regulation," *Washington Post*, June 23, 2014.

82. Juliet Eilperin and Steven Mufson, "Everything You Need to Know about the EPA's Proposed Rule on Coal Plants," *Washington Post*, June 2, 2014.

83. Executive Office of the President, "The President's Climate Action Plan," June 2013, https://www.whitehouse.gov/sites/default/files/image/president27s climateactionplan.pdf.

84. Michael B. Gerrard, "Obama's New Emission Rules: Will They Survive Challenges?" *Environment 360*, Yale University, http://e360.yale.edu/feature/obamas _new_emission_rules_will_they_survive_challenges/2776.

85. Eilperin and Mufson, "Everything You Need to Know."

86. Gerrard, "Obama's New Emission Rules."

87. Kim Hjelmgaard, "China Follows USA with Emissions Pledge," *USA Today*, June 4, 2014, 3A.

88. Nathan Richardson, Art Fraas, and Dallas Burtraw, "Greenhouse Gas Regulation under the Clean Air Act," Discussion Paper 10–23, Resources for the Future, April 2010, http://www.rff.org/files/sharepoint/WorkImages/Download/RFF-DP -10-23.pdf.

89. Neela Banerjee, "12 States Sue the EPA over Proposed Power Plant Regulations," *Los Angeles Times*, August 4, 2014.

90. Keith Johnson and Peter Nicholas, "Obama's Climate Plans Face Years Long Fight," *Wall Street Journal*, June 24, 2013, A4; Coral Davenport, "McConnell

Urges States to Help Thwart Obama's 'War on Coal,'" *New York Times*, March 20, 2015, A1.

91. Eilperin and Mufson, "Everything You Need to Know."

92. Mark Clayton, "House Votes to Strip EPA of Power to Curb Carbon Emissions," *Christian Science Monitor*, April 7, 2011; also see Jean Chemnick, "Power Plant Bill Clears House, Capito Says Uphill Senate Fight 'Worth Happening,'" *Energy and Environment Daily*, June 25, 2015, http://www.eenews.net/tv/2015/06/26.

93. Amy Harder, "White House, Calls for New Rules to Cut Methane Emissions," *Wall Street Journal*, March 29–30, 2014, A3.

94. Coral Davenport, "White House Unveils Plans to Cut Methane Emissions," *New York Times,* March 28, 2014.

95. Amy Harder, "White House Proposes Vetting Projects for Climate Change," *Wall Street Journal*, December 19, 2014, A4.

96. Julie Hirschfeld Davis, "Obama Orders Cuts in Federal Greenhouse Gas Emissions," *New York Times*, March 20, 2015, A20.

97. Geman, "Audacity of John Podesta," 13.

98. Fred Krupp, "A Game-Changing Climate Agreement," *Wall Street Journal*, November 13, 2014, A15.

99. Colleen McCain Nelson, "GOP Weighs How to Undercut Obama's Climate Talks," *Wall Street Journal*, April 27, 2015, A4.

100. Victoria Bennett, "A Leader in Climate Change Measures, Mexico Lags on Follow-Through," *New York Times*, November 30, 2014, 10.

101. Michael B. Gerrard and Shelley Welton, "US Federal Climate Law in Obama's Second Term," *Transnational Environmental Law* 3, no. 1 (2014): 111–125.

102. Jerry Hirsh, "Average Fuel Economy of New Autos at New Record; Progress May Stall," *Los Angeles Times*, October 8, 2014; Michael Sivak and Brandon Schoettle, "Fuel-Economy Distributions of Purchased New Vehicles in the U.S.: Model Years 2008 and 2014," Transportation Research Institute, University of Michigan, UMTRI-2015–4, February 2015, http://deepblue.lib.umich.edu/bitstream/handle/2027.42/110907/103159.pdf?sequence=1.

103. Ronald Brownstein, "Time Is Ticking for Obama's Climate Agenda," *National Journal*, June 29, 2013, 7.

104. Lizza, "As the World Burns."

105. Brownstein, "Time Is Ticking," 7.

106. That is the basic holding of the famous *State Farm* case involving the federal airbag requirement. *Motor Vehicle Manufacturers Association v. State Farm Ins.* 463 U.S. 29 (1983).

107. Apparently both options were more appealing to White House chief of staff Rahm Emanuel than what Senator Barbara Boxer was trying to move in the Senate. Lizza, "As the World Burns."

8. Driller in Chief

1. Russell Gold and Daniel Gilbert, "US Is Overtaking Russia as Largest Oil-and-Gas Producer," *Wall Street Journal*, October 2, 2013.

2. Edward L. Morse, "Welcome to the Revolution: Why Shale Is the Next Shale," *Foreign Affairs*, May/June 2014, https://www.foreignaffairs.com/articles/2014-04-17/welcome-revolution.

3. "U.S. Coal Production, 2009–2015," US Energy Information Administration, www.eia.gov/coal/production/quarterly/pdf/t1p01p1.pdf.

4. "The Obama-Biden Plan, 2008" *Change.gov*, http://change.gov/agenda/education_agenda.

5. E. Hornick and A. Marquardt, "Obama Says Offshore Drilling Stance Nothing New," *CNN.com*, August 2, 2008, http://www.cnn.com/2008/POLITICS/08/02/campaign.wrap; "Barack Obama," Council on Foreign Relations, www.cfr/experts/world/barack/obama/b11603.

6. U.S. Department of Energy, "Barack Obama and Joe Biden: New Energy for America," Barack Obama.com, 2008, http://energy.gov/sites/prod/files/edg/media/Obama_New_Energy_0804.pdf.

7. "Congress Allows Offshore Oil Drilling to Expire," ENS-Newswire, September 30, 2008, http://www.nbcnewyork.com/news/green/Congress_Allows_Offshore_Oil_Drilling_Ban_to_Expire.html.

8. J. Eilperin and A. Kornblut, "President Obama Opens New Acres to Offshore Drilling," *Washington Post*, April 1, 2010; M. Clayton, "Gulf of Mexico Oil Spill Imperils Obama's Offshore Drilling Plan," *Christian Science Monitor*, April 30, 2010.

9. John M. Broder, "Obama Shifts to Speed Oil and Gas Drilling," *New York Times*, May 14, 2010.

10. John M. Broder, "Obama on Drilling Plan Draws Critics," *New York Times*, March 31, 2010.

11. Neil King Jr. and Keith Johnson, "Obama Decried, Then Used, Some Bush Drilling Policies," *Wall Street Journal*, July 5, 2010.

12. Broder, "Obama Shifts to Speed Oil."

13. Glenn Hess, "Obama's Energy Plan Stirs Mixed Reaction," *Chemical and Engineering News* 88, no. 18 (2010): 30–33.

14. Matthew A. Williams and Brian Richard, "Response to the Gulf Oil Spill," in *The Obama Presidency: A Preliminary Assessment*, eds. Robert P. Watson, Jack Covarrubias, Tom Lansford, and Douglas M. Brattebo (Albany: SUNY Press, 2012), 225.

15. Glenn Hess, "Obama Pressed to Scrap Drilling Plan," *Chemical and Engineering News* 88, no. 19 (2010): 9.

16. Ibid.

17. "Obama Extends Moratorium on Offshore Drilling," *CBSNews.com*, May 27, 2010, http://www.cbsnews.com/news/obama-extends-moratorium-on-offshore-drilling.

18. Juliet Eilperin, "Obama Administration Reimposes Offshore Oil Drilling Ban," *Washington Post*, December 1, 2010.

19. King and Johnson, "Obama Decried."

20. Laurel Brubaker Calkins, "US in Contempt over Gulf Drill Ban, Judge Rules," *Bloomberg.com*, February 3, 2011, http://www.bloomberg.com/news/articles/2011-02-03/u-s-administration-in-contempt-over-gulf-drill-ban-judge-rules.

21. John M. Broder, "An Energy Plan Derailed by Events Is Being Retooled," *New York Times*, March 30, 2011.

22. "Obama to Expand Oil, Gas Drilling off Alaska and in Gulf," *MSNBC.com*, November 8, 2011, http://www.nbcnews.com/id/45210622/#.ViZ0BNWrSJA; Vanessa Vick, "Offshore Drilling and Exploration," *New York Times*, November 9, 2011.

23. Amy Harder, "Offshore Atlantic Blueprint Part of Five-Year Drilling Blueprint," *Wall Street Journal*, January 28, 2015, A3.

24. John M. Broder, "US Approves an Initial Step in Oil Drilling Near Alaska," *New York Times*, August 31, 2012, B3.

25. Gregory Zuckerman, *The Frackers: The Outrageous Inside Story of the New Billionaire Wildcatters* (New York: Penguin, 2013).

26. Laura Meckler, "Obama Outlines Energy Plan," *Wall Street Journal*, March 31, 2011.

27. "Blueprint for a Secure Energy Future," White House, March 30, 2011, www .whitehouse.gov/sites/default/files/blueprint_secure_energy_future.pdf.

28. Dave Michaels, "Obama Endorses Pickens Plan for Natural Gas Vehicles," *Dallas Morning News*, March 30, 2011.

29. Robert A. Hefner III, "The United States of Gas: Why the Shale Revolution Could Have Happened Only in America," *Foreign Affairs*, May/June 2014, 9, 12.

30. Jim Snyder and Katarzyna Klimasinska, "Obama Pushes Natural Gas Fracking to Create 600,000 Jobs," *Bloomberg.com*, January 25, 2012, http://www .bloomberg.com/news/2012–01–25/obama-backs-fracking-to-create-600–000-jobs -vows-safe-drilling.html.

31. Charles K. Ebinger, "What Does the State of the Union Mean for Energy Policy?" *Brookings.com*, January 27, 2012, http://www.brookings.edu/blogs/up -front/posts/2012/01/27-sotu-energy-policy-ebinger.

32. Nick Snow, "Obama Forms Unconventional Gas Interagency Working Group," *Oil and Gas Journal*, April 13, 2012, http://www.ogj.com/articles/print /vol-110/issue-4c/general-interest/obama-forms-unconventional.html.

33. David Grant, "State of the Union: Why Obama Energy Blueprint Has Republicans Fuming," *Christian Science Monitor*, January 25, 2012.

34. Loren Steffy, "Obama's 'All-of-the-Above' Energy Push Becomes a Strategy of One," *Forbes*, January 29, 2014.

35. Andrew Restoccia and Talia Buford, "'Gasland' Director: Obama Is AWOL on Fracking," *Politico.com*, October 21, 2013, www.politico.com/story/2013/10 /gasland.

36. Kate Sheppard, "Anti-Fracking Groups Greet Obama on New York Tour," *Huff Post Politics*, August 23, 2013, www.huffingtonpost.com/2013/08/23; Bryan Walsh, "As Obama Visits Upstate New York, the Fracking Debate Takes Center Stage," August 22, 2013, *Time*, http://science.time.com/2013/08/22/as-obama-visits -upstate-new-york-the-fracking-debate-takes-center-stage.

37. Kevin Begos, "Obama Fracking Support in Climate Speech Worries Environmental Groups," Associated Press, June 27, 2013, http://www.huffingtonpost.com /2013/06/27/obama-fracking-support_n_3510651.html?utm_hp_ref=green.

38. Suzanne Goldenberg, "2013 in Review: Obama Talks Climate Change—But Pushes Fracking," *Guardian*, December 20, 2013, http://www.theguardian.com /environment/2013/dec/20/2013-climate-change-review-obama-fracking.

39. Ben Geman, "Green Groups to Obama: Choose Climate over Oil," *National Journal*, January 17, 2014; Juliet Eilperin and Lenny Bernstein, "Green Groups Assail Obama on Climate," *Washington Post*, January 17, 2014, A3.

40. Ben Geman, "Obama, in Speech, Defends 'All of the Above' Energy Plan," *National Journal*, January 28, 2014.

41. Amy Harder, "Energy Regulatory Push Is Planned by Administration," *Wall Street Journal*, December 30, 2014, A2.

42. Ewa Krukowska, "Obama Pitches Shale Gas to Europe Seeking to Cut Imports," *Bloomberg.com*, March 26, 2014, http://www.bloomberg.com/news/2014-03 -26/obama-pitches-shale-gas-to-europe-seeking-to-cut-imports.html.

43. Ian Traynor, "European Leaders Ask Obama to Allow Increased Exports of US Shale Gas," *Guardian*, March 26, 2014, http://www.theguardian.com/world /2014/mar/26/europe-asks-obama-increased-exports-shale-gas.

44. "The All-of-the-Above Energy Strategy as a Path to Sustainable Growth," *WhiteHouse.gov*, May 2014, http://www.whitehouse.gov/sites/default/files/docs/aota _energy_strategy_as_a_path_to_sustainable_economic_growth.pdf.

45. Olga Schenk, Michelle H. W. Lee, Naveed H. Paydar, John A. Rupp, and John D. Graham, "Unconventional Gas Development in the US States: Exploring the Variation," *European Journal of Risk Regulation* 4 (2014): 436–458.

46. Hess, "Obama's Energy Plan," 30–33.

47. Stephanie Stamm, "Oil Change," *National Journal*, November 22, 2014, 28.

48. Morse, "Welcome to the Revolution."

49. B. Geman, "DOE Revives FutureGen, Reversing Bush-Era Decision," *New York Times*, June 12, 2009.

50. R. Trager, "Site Chosen for Long-Awaited US Clean Coal Project," *RSC.org*, March 8, 2011, http://www.rsc.org/chemistryworld/News/2011/March/08031102.asp.

51. Michael Bologna, "EPA Grants First Underground Injection Permits to Future Gen for Illinois Project," *BNA.com*, September 4, 2014, http://www.bna.com/epa -grants-first-n17179894408.

52. Manuel Quinones, "Problems That Killed FutureGen Now Threaten other Projects," *EENews.net*, February 5, 2015, http://www.eenews.net/eenewspm/2015 /02/05/1060012965.

53. Louis Jacobson, "Despite Notable Hurdles, Plants That Sequester Carbon Are Advancing," *Politifact.com*, December 6, 2012, http://www.politifact.com /truth-o-meter/promises/obameter/promise/453/create-clean-coal-partnerships.

54. "Obama Announces Steps to Boost Biofuels, Clean Coal," *WhiteHouse.gov*, February 3, 2010, https://www.whitehouse.gov/the-press-office/obama-announces -steps-boost-biofuels-clean-coal.

55. Rebecca Smith, "Sierra Club Ends Opposition to Southern Company Clean-Coal Plant in Mississippi," *Wall Street Journal*, August 5, 2014, B5; Rebecca Smith, "Clean-Coal Plant Costs Soar," *Wall Street Journal*, May 23–24, 2015, B1.

56. Jeff Johnson, "Carbon Capture Ramps Up," *Chemical and Engineering News* 92, no. 35 (2014): 46.

57. "Obama Administration Takes Unprecedented Step to Reduce Environmental Impacts of Mountaintop Coal Mining, Announces Interagency Action Plan to Implement Reforms," EPA Press Release, June 11, 2009, http://yosemite.epa.gov/opa/admpress.nsf/bd4379a92ceceeac8525735900400c27/e7d3e5608bba2651852575d200590f23!OpenDocument.

58. Jeffrey Tomich, "EPA Vetoes Arch Coal Permit," *St. Louis Post-Dispatch*, January 14, 2011, http://www.stltoday.com/business/local/epa-vetoes-arch-coal-permit/article_ee10b5e7-3ee6-594b-a3e9-dda53f6d4079.html.

59. Government Accountability Office, "Surface Coal Mining: Financial Assurances for and Long-Term Oversight of Mines with Valley Fills in Four Appalachian States," GAO-10-126, January 2010, http://www.gao.gov/new.items/d10206.pdf.

60. EPA Office of Inspector General, "Congressionally Requested Information on the Status and Length of Review for Appalachian Surface Mining Permit Applications," Report No. 12-P-0083, November 21, 2011, http://www.epa.gov/oig/reports/specialReportsByType/congressionally_requested_reports.html; Manuel Quinones, "State Officials Fume as Obama Administration Scrutinizes Coal Mining Permits," *New York Times*, May 5, 2011.

61. David A. Fahrenthold, "EPA Crackdown on Mountaintop Coal Mining Criticized as Contradictory," *Washington Post*, January 28, 2010.

62. Ken Ward Jr., "Appeals Court Upholds EPA's Mountaintop Removal Crackdown," *West Virginia Gazette*, July 11, 2014.

63. Darren Samuelsohn, "Sen. Rockefeller Criticizes Obama over Coal Policy," *New York Times*, February 4, 2010.

64. Brad Plumer, "Here's Why Central Appalachia's Coal Industry Is Dying," *Washington Post*, November 4, 2013.

65. Manuel Quinones, "Feds OK Powder River Basin Coal Leases," *Wyofile.com*, November 24, 2011, http://www.wyofile.com/feds-ok-powder-river-basin-coal-leases.

66. Ben Adler, "Could This Lawsuit Force Obama to Fix His Ridiculous Coal-Leasing Program?" *Grist*, December 2, 2014, http://grist.org/climate-energy/could-this-lawsuit-force-obama-to-fix-his-ridiculous-coal-leasing-program.

67. National Mining Association, "EPA's Regulatory Train Wreck, 2014," www.nma.org/pdf/fact_sheets/epa_tw.pdf.

68. Brent Kendall and Amy Harder, "Litigation Awaits New EPA Emissions Rules," *Wall Street Journal*, March 23, 2015, B4.

69. Greg Stohr, "Obama Power-Plant Pollution Rule Upheld by Top US Court," *Bloomberg Business*, April 29, 2014, http://www.bloomberg.com/news/articles/2014-04-29/obama-power-plant-pollution-rule-upheld-by-u-s-supreme-court.

70. Amy Harder and Brent Kendall, "Appeals Court Upholds EPA Rule on Power Plant Emissions," *Wall Street Journal*, April 15, 2014.

71. Adam Liptak and Coral Davenport, "Supreme Court Blocks Obama's Limits on Power Plants," *New York Times*, June 29, 2015.

72. Emmarie Huetteman, "EPA Issues Rules on Disposal of Coal Ash to Protect Water Supply," *New York Times*, December 19, 2014.

73. Amy Harder, "Stricter Ozone Air Pollution Standard," *Wall Street Journal*, November 26, 2014.

74. Coral Davenport, "The Coal Lobby's Fight for Survival," *National Journal*, June 27, 2013.

75. Brad Plumer, "Getting Ready for a Wave of Coal-Plant Shutdowns," *Washington Post*, August 19, 2013, http://www.washingtonpost.com/blogs/wonkblog/post/getting-ready-for-a-wave-of-coal-plant-shutdowns/2011/08/19/gIQAzkZ0PJ_blog.html; Government Accountability Office, "EPA Regulations and Electricity: Update on Agencies' Monitoring Efforts and Coal-Fueled Generating Unit Retirements," GAO-14-672, August 2014, http://www.gao.gov/products/GAO-14-672.

76. Tennille Tracy, "Campaigns Spar over Coal's Future," *Wall Street Journal*, September 24, 2012, A4.

77. Ibid.

78. Coral Davenport, "Long Reach," *National Journal*, November 2, 2013, 35.

79. Andrew Grossman and Kris Maher, "Trouble in Coal Country for Obama," *Wall Street Journal*, May 12, 2012, A6.

80. Keith Johnson, "Campaigns Clash over the Future of Coal," *Wall Street Journal*, October 19, 2012, A4.

81. David Kestenbaum, "Nuclear Power: A Thorny Issue for Candidates," *NPR.org*, July 21, 2008, http://www.npr.org/templates/story/story.php?storyId=92690120.

82. Peter Wallsten and Jia Lynn Yang, "Obama's Support for Nuclear Power Faces a Test," *Washington Post*, March 8, 2011.

83. Bob Drogin, "McCain Pushes Nuclear Power," *Los Angeles Times*, June 19, 2008.

84. Mat McDermott, "The Nuclear Option: McCain v. Obama on Nuclear Power," *Treehugger.com*, September 23, 2008, http://www.treehugger.com/corporate-responsibility/the-nuclear-option-mccain-v-obama-on-nuclear-power.html.

85. Margaret Kriz Hobson, "Guaranteeing Nuclear Power," *National Journal*, January 16, 2010.

86. Ibid.

87. Ibid.

88. Jeff Johnson, "New Jolt for Nuclear Power," *Chemical and Engineering News* 88, no. 10 (2010): 31–33.

89. Mark Clayton, "Obama's Nuclear Power Policy: A Study in Contradictions?" *Christian Science Monitor*, February 4, 2010.

90. Josie Garthwaite, "How Is Japan's Nuclear Disaster Different?" *National Geographic*, March 16, 2011.

91. Mark Clayton, "Germany to Phase Out Nuclear Power, Could the US Do the Same?" *Christian Science Monitor*, June 7, 2011.

92. Jared A. Favole and Tennille Tracy, "Obama Stands by Nuclear Power," *Wall Street Journal*, March 15, 2011.

93. Amanda Carey, "How a Moratorium on Nuclear Power Could Stop Obama's Clean Energy Agenda in Its Tracks," *DailyCaller.com*, March 15, 2011, http://dailycaller.com/2011/03/15/how-a-moratorium-on-nuclear-power-could-stop-obamas-clean-energy-agenda-in-its-tracks.

94. Matthew L. Wald, "EPA Wrestles with Role of Nuclear Plants in Carbon Emissions Rules," *New York Times*, December 26, 2014, B3.

95. John M. Broder, "US Nuclear Industry Faces New Uncertainty," *New York Times*, March 13, 2011.

96. John D. Graham, *Bush on the Home Front* (Bloomington: Indiana University Press, 2010), 146–49.

97. Jenna Goodward and Mariana Gonzalez, "Bottom Line on Renewable Energy Tax Credits," *World Resources Institute*, October 2010, http://www.wri.org /publication/bottom-line-renewable-energy-tax-credits.

98. Bryan Walsh, "Why 2012 Will Be a Bad Year for Renewable Energy," *Time*, December 13, 2011; Union of Concerned Scientists, "Production Tax Credit for Renewable Energy," http://www.ucsusa.org/clean_energy/smart-energy-solutions /increase-renewables/production-tax-credit-for.html#.Vb_IgPlcicU.

99. US Department of Energy, "Economic Stimulus Act Extends Renewable Energy Tax Credits," EERE Network News, February 18, 2009, http://www.energy.gov /eere/geothermal/articles/economic-stimulus-act-extends-renewable-energy-tax -credits; Kate Galbraith, "Future of Solar and Wind Power May Hinge on Federal Aid," *New York Times*, October 25, 2011.

100. Andrew Herndon, "Clean-Energy Funding to Drop after Obama Grant Program Ends," *Bloomberg.com*, November 30, 2011, http://www.bloomberg.com /news/articles/2011-11-30/clean-energy-funding-to-drop-after-obama-grant -program-ends-1-.

101. Steven Mufson, "Energy Secretary Steven Chu, Renowned Physicist, at Center of Solyndra Policy Storm," *Washington Post*, October 27, 2011.

102. Laurence M. Vance, "The Real Problem with Solyndra," *Freedom of Future Foundation*, September 27, 2011, http://fff.org/explore-freedom/article/real-problem -solyndra.

103. D'Angelo Gore and Eugene Kiely, "Obama's Solyndra Problem," *Factcheck. org*, October 7, 2011, http://www.factcheck.org/2011/10/obamas-solyndra-problem.

104. Robert P. Murphy, "Lessons from Solyndra," Library of Economics and Liberty, February 6, 2012, http://www.econlib.org/library/Columns/y2012/Murphy solyndra.html; emphasis in original.

105. Carol D. Leonnis and Joe Stephens, "Top Obama Donor George Kaiser Says He Didn't Play Politics to Win Government Loan," *Washington Post*, September 2, 2011.

106. Katherine Ling, "Probe Links Solyndra Execs' Lies to Loss of $535M," *EENews.net*, August 26, 2015, http://www.eenews.net/greenwire/stories/1060023976 /print.

107. Darren Samuelsohn, "Say DOE Broke the Law on Solyndra—So What?" *Politico.com*, October 21, 2011, http://www.politico.com/news/stories/1011/66592 _Page2.html.

108. Kevin Liptak, "Group Spends $6 Million Linking Obama to Solyndra in Ad," *Politicalticker*, January 16, 2012, http://politicalticker.blogs.cnn.com/2012/01/16 /group-spends-6-million-linking-obama-to-solyndra-in-ad.

109. Rasmussen Reports, "56% Think Loan Guarantees for Solyndra Were a Bad Idea," August 7, 2012, http://www.rasmussenreports.com/public_content/politics /current_events/environment_energy/56_think_loan_guarantees_for_solyndra _were_a_bad_idea.

110. Bill Loveless, "Energy Department Loan Chief Leaves a Shared-Up Office," *USA Today*, July 6, 2015, 2B.

111. Julie Cart, "Obama Administration Announces Desert 'Solar Energy Zones,'" *Los Angeles Times*, October 28, 2011.

112. Ted Mann, "IRS Relaxes Renewable Energy Project Credit Rule," *Wall Street Journal*, August 11, 2014, B2.

113. Saqib Rahim, "Rush Is on to Invest in Solar and Wind Ahead of Tax Credit's End," *EnergyWire*, June 26, 2015, http://www.eenews.net/energywire/2015/06/26 /stories/1060020931.

114. Graham, *Bush on the Home Front*, 149–60.

115. Ibid., 151.

116. Erica Gies, "As Ethanol Booms, Critics Warn of Environmental Effect," *New York Times*, June 24, 2010.

117. Shailagh Murray, "Clinton-Obama Differences Clear in Senate Votes," *Washington Post*, January 1, 2007.

118. Larry Rohter, "Obama Camp Closely Linked with Ethanol," *New York Times*, June 2, 2008.

119. Ibid.

120. Robert Bryce, "Obama: The Senator from Big Corn," *Guardian*, September 4, 2008, http://www.theguardian.com/commentisfree/2008/sep/04/uselections2008 .biofuels.

121. Kent Garber, "Obama under Pressure over Role of Ethanol in Energy Policy," *USNews.com*, November 21, 2008.

122. Jim Tankersley, "Obama Urges Greater Use of Biofuels," *Los Angeles Times*, February 3, 2010; Steven Mufson, "EPA Biofuels Guidelines Could Spur Production of Ethanol from Corn," *Washington Post*, February 4, 2010.

123. Renewable Fuels Association, "E85,"http://www.ethanolrfa.org/resources /blends/e85/.

124. Energy Information Administration, "E85 Fueling Station Availability Is Increasing," March 7, 2014, http://www.eia.gov/todayinenergy/detail.cfm?id=15311.

125. Wendy Koch, "Senate, House Vote to End Some Ethanol Subsidies," *USA Today*, June 16, 2011.

126. Ibid.

127. Steven Mufson and Lori Montgomery, "Senate Approves Cut in Ethanol Subsidies, Votes for Feinstein Amendments," *Washington Post*, June 6, 2011.

128. Robert Pear, "After Three Decades, Tax Credit for Ethanol Expires," *New York Times*, January 1, 2012.

129. David Wogan, "Why the EPA Revised the Renewable Fuel Standards," *Scientific American*, November 19, 2013, http://blogs.scientificamerican.com/plugged-in /2013/11/19/why-the-epa-revised-the-renewable-fuel-standards.

130. Kevin Bullis, "The Cellulosic Ethanol Industry Faces Big Challenges," *Technology Review*, August 12, 2013, http://www.technologyreview.com/news/517816/the-cellulosic-ethanol-industry-faces-big-challenges.

131. Christopher Doering, "Ethanol Groups Blast EPA over Renewable Fuel Mandate," *USA Today*, May 29, 2015.

132. Wogan, "Why the EPA Revised Standards."

133. Christina Nunez, "'Fantasy' of Fuel from Corn Waste Gets Big US Tests," *National Geographic*, September 11, 2014, http://news.nationalgeographic.com/news/energy/2014/09/140911-project-liberty-cellulosic-ethanol-us-test.

134. John Deutch, "Obama's Second-Term Energy Policy Is Working," *Wall Street Journal*, August 16, 2014.

135. Michael Levi, *The Power Surge: Energy, Opportunity, and the Battle for America's Future* (New York: Oxford University Press, 2013); Russell Gold, *The Boom: How Fracking Ignited the American Revolution and Changed the World* (New York: Simon and Schuster, 2014); Daniel Yergin, *The Quest: Energy, Security, and the Remaking of the Modern World* (New York: Penguin, 2011).

136. For example, the Obama administration, through the US Department of the Interior, issued protective regulations covering fracking that occurs on public lands. Joby Warrick, "Obama Administration Tightens Federal Rules on Oil and Gas Fracking," *Washington Post*, March 20, 2015.

137. Travis Fisher and Alex Fitzsimmons, "Fate of the Union: Energy Policy under Barack Obama," *InstituteforEnergyResearch.org*, January 28, 2014, http://instituteforenergyresearch.org/analysis/fate-of-the-union-energy-policy-under-barack-obama.

138. Dina Cappiello and Matthew Daly, "Obama's Energy Strategy Draws Sharp Criticism from Green Groups as Oil and Gas Take Center Stage," Associated Press, January 30, 2014, http://www.huffingtonpost.com/2014/01/30/obamas-energy-strategy-green-groups-climate_n_4696516.html.

139. Naomi Oreskes, "Tomgram: A 'Green' Bridge to Hell" and "Wishful Thinking about Natural Gas: Why Fossil Fuels Can't Solve the Problems Created by Fossil Fuels," *TomDispatch.com*, July, 27, 2014, www.tomdispatch.com/blog/175873.

140. Will Oremus, "The Answer Is Not 'All of the Above,'" *Slate.com*, January 29, 2014, http://www.slate.com/articles/technology/future_tense/2014/01/all_of_the_above_obama_s_energy_policy_isn_t_as_stupid_as_it_sounds.html.

141. Jeffrey Ball, "Obama's Meaningless 'All of the Above' Energy Strategy Is Infuriating Both Environmentalists and Fossil Fuelers," *New Republic.com*, January 30, 2014.

142. Matthew Karnitschnig, "Germany's Expensive Gamble on Renewable Energy," *Wall Street Journal*, August 26, 2014; Pilita Clark, "Energy Price Gap with the US to Hurt Europe for 'at least 20 Years,'" *Financial Times*, January 29, 2014, http://www.ft.com/cms/s/0/80950dfe-8901-11e3-9f48-00144feab7de.html#axzz3nHQZehiH.

143. Robert Pear and Felicity Barringer, "Coal Mining Debris Rule Is Approved," *New York Times*, December 2, 2008; Ken Ward Jr., "McCain, Obama Both Oppose Mountaintop Removal Mining," *Daily Mountain Eagle*, October 1, 2008.

144. Obama did not mention the phrase "clean coal" in his 2012 or 2013 State of the Union addresses.

145. "Energy Overhaul Clears Congress without Tax, Electricity Provisions," in *CQ Almanac 2007*, ed. Jan Austin (Washington, DC: Congressional Quarterly, 2008).

9. Deporter in Chief?

1. Drew Keeling, "In Immigration Debate, Echoes of Ellis Island," *Los Angeles Times*, July 4, 2013.
2. Damien Paletta, "Obama's Plan Seen Affecting Wages, Job Moves," *Wall Street Journal*, November 21, 2014, A4.
3. Graham, *Bush on the Home Front: Domestic Policy Triumphs and Setbacks* (Bloomington: Indiana University Press, 2010), 223.
4. See generally Andrew Wroe, *The Republican Party and Immigration Politics: From Proposition 187 to George W Bush* (New York: Palgrave Macmillan, 2008.
5. Darrell M. West, "How the Politics of Immigration Reform Have Changed," February 5, 2013, www.brookings.edu/research/opinions/2013/02/05-immigration-reform; David L. Leal, Matt A. Barreto, Jongho Lee, and Rodolfo O. de la Garza, "The Latino Vote in the 2004 Election," *Political Science and Politics* 1 (2005), http://journals.cambridge.org/action/displayAbstract?fromPage=online&aid=285530&fileId=S1049096505055770.
6. Angie Drobnic Holan, "John McCain Said That Barack Obama Voted against Part of Immigration Reform," *Politifact.com*, July 7, 2010, http://www.politifact.com/truth-o-meter/statements/2010/jul/07/john-mccain/john-mccain-said-barack-obama-voted-against-part-i.
7. *Washington Post*/ABC News Poll, November 19, 2007, http://www.washingtonpost.com/wp-srv/politics/polls/postpoll_111907.html.
8. Marc Santora, "Immigration Is Fodder for Clinton Rivals," *New York Times*, November 1, 2007.
9. Bryan Curtis, "Latino Media Superstar Trashes Obama," *Daily Beast*, June 27, 2010, www.thedailybeast.com/articles/2010/06/28/univisions-jorge-ramos-obama's-immigration-promise.html.
10. Susan Minushkin and Mark Hugo Lopez, "The Hispanic Vote in the 2008 Democratic Presidential Primaries," *PewHispanic.org*, March 7, 2008, updated June 4, 2008, http://www.pewhispanic.org/2008/03/07/the-hispanic-vote-in-the-2008-democratic-presidential-primaries.
11. Shan Carter, Jonathan Ellis, Farhana Hossain, and Alan McLean, "On the Issues: Immigration," *New York Times*, May 23, 2012.
12. Tyche Hendricks, "McCain, Obama to Avoid Fray on Immigration," *SFGate.com*, October 13, 2008, www.sfgate.com/news/article/McCain-Obama-Seek-to-Avoid-Fray-On-Immigration-3265787.php.
13. Ryan Lizza, "Getting to Maybe: Inside the Gang of Eight's Immigration Deal," *New Yorker*, June 24, 2013.
14. Bill Schneider, "Analysis: McCain's Uphill Battle on Illegal Immigration," CNN Election Center 2008, last modified June 21, 2008, Edition.cnn.com/2008/POLITICS/06/21/mccain.hispanics.

15. Richard Simon, "Both Sides Tout Immigration Reform," *Los Angeles Times*, June 29, 2008.

16. Jennifer Ludden, "Immigration Issue Doesn't Divide McCain, Obama," *NPR.org*, June 10, 2008, www.npr.org/templates/story/story.php?storyId=91323073.

17. Schneider, "McCain's Uphill Battle."

18. June Kronholz, "Obama, McCain Court Hispanics, but Avoid Immigration Issue," *Wall Street Journal*, September 20, 2008.

19. Mark Hugo Lopez, "The Hispanic Vote in the 2008 Election," Pew Research Center Hispanic Trends Project, November 5, 2008, http://www.pewhispanic. org/2008/11/05/the-hispanic-vote-in-the-2008-election.

20. Julia Preston, "In Big Shift, Latino Vote Was Heavily for Obama," *New York Times*, November 6, 2008.

21. Miriam Jordan, "Convictions Surge for Illegal Immigrants Who Try to Return to the US," *Wall Street Journal*, March 19, 2014, A6.

22. Joshua Partlow, "Under Operation Streamline Fast-track Proceedings for Illegal Immigrants," *Washington Post*, February 10, 2014.

23. Fernando Santos, "Detainees Sentenced in Seconds in 'Streamline' Justice on Border," *New York Times*, February 11, 2014.

24. Ibid.

25. Joanna Lydgate, "Operation Streamline: Border Enforcement That Doesn't Work," *Los Angeles Times*, May 14, 2010.

26. Michael D. Shear and Spencer S. Hsu, "President Obama to Send More National Guard Troops to US-Mexican Border," *Washington Post*, May 26, 2010.

27. Randal C. Archibold, "Arizona Enacts Stringent Law on Immigration," *New York Times*, April 23, 2010.

28. Ibid.

29. Adam Liptak, "Blocking Parts of Arizona Law, Justices Allow Its Centerpiece," *New York Times*, June 25, 2012.

30. Muzaffar Chishti and Claire Bergeron, "Political Considerations Surround Decision to Deploy National Guard to Southwest Border," Migration Policy Institute, June 15, 2010, http://www.migrationpolicy.org/article/political-considerations -surround-decision-deploy-national-guard-southwest-border.

31. Randal C. Archibold, "Obama to Send up to 1,200 Troops to the Border," *New York Times*, May 25, 2010.

32. Keith Johnson, "Obama to Send 1,200 Troops to Mexican Border," *Wall Street Journal*, May 26, 2010, A7.

33. Archibold, "Obama to Send up to 1,200 Troops."

34. "Day Laborers React to Chief Beck's Announcement of Scomm Reforms in Wake of Trust Act Veto," National Day Laborer Organizing Network, October 9, 2012. http://www.ndlon.org/en/pressroom/press-releases/item/558-chief-beck-scomm.

35. Spencer S. Hsu and Andrew Becker, "ICE Officials Set Quotas to Deport More Illegal Immigrants," *Washington Post*, March 27, 2010.

36. Julia Preston, "Illegal Workers Swept from Jobs in 'Silent Raids,'" *New York Times*, July 10, 2010.

37. Michael Barone, "Immigration Reform: The New Third Rail," *Wall Street Journal*, April 16, 2010.

38. George J. Borjas, Jeffrey Grogger, and Gordon H. Hanson, "Immigration and African-American Employment Opportunities: The Response in Wages, Employment, and Incarceration to Labor Supply Shocks," NBER Working Paper #12518, August 2006, http://www.academia.edu/7821761/Immigration_and_african_american, 8106; George J. Borjas, Jeffrey Grogger, and Gordon H. Hanson, "Immigration and the Economic Status of African-American Men," January 2009, http://gps.ucsd.edu/_files/faculty/hanson/hanson_publication_immigration_men.pdf.

39. Jagdish Bhagwati and Francisco Rivera-Batiz, "A Kinder, Gentler Immigration Policy," *Foreign Affairs*, November–December 2013, http://www.foreignaffairs.com/articles/140153/jagdish-bhagwati-and-francisco-rivera-batiz/a-kinder-gentler-immigration-policy.

40. Miriam Jordan, "Costs and Benefits of Immigration Overhaul," *Wall Street Journal*, February 4, 2013, A2.

41. Alex Simendinger, "Sharry on the Border Battles," *National Journal*, May 1, 2010, 2 (interview with Frank Sharry, founder and executive director, America's Voice); Julia Preston, "Obama to Push Immigration Bill as One Priority," *New York Times*, April 8, 2009.

42. Lizza, "Getting to Maybe."

43. Curtis, "Latino Media Superstar Trashes Obama."

44. Simendinger, "Sharry on the Border Battles."

45. Ibid.

46. Laura Meckler, "Democrats Revive Immigration Push," *Wall Street Journal*, April 22, 2010, A5.

47. Alexander Bolton, "Desire to Tackle Immigration Reform Splits Reid from Centrist Democrats," *The Hill*, April 14, 2010, http://thehill.com/homenews/senate/92079-immigration-splits-reid-from-centrist-colleagues.

48. Ibid.

49. Kasie Hunt, "Obama Woos Brown on Immigration,"*Politico.com*, April 20, 2010, http://www.politico.com/news/stories/0410/36112.html.

50. Julia Preston, "Two Senators Offer Immigration Overhaul," *New York Times*, March 18, 2010.

51. Hunt, "Obama Woos Brown."

52. Dana Milbank, "Obama's Fatal Flinch on Immigration Reform," *Washington Post*, May 2, 2010.

53. Barone, "Immigration Reform."

54. Julia Preston, "Obama to Permit Migrants to Remain in US," *New York Times*, June 15, 2012.

55. Peter Baker, "Obama Urges Fix to 'Broken' Immigration System," *New York Times*, July 1, 2010.

56. Chuck Todd, Mark Murray, and Carrie Dean, "Why Immigration Reform Died in Congress," *NBCNews.com*, July 1, 2010, http://www.nbcnews.com/politics/first-read/why-immigration-reform-died-congress-n145276.

57. Mark Hugo Lopez, "The Latino Vote in the 2010 Elections," Pew Research Center Hispanic Trends Project, November 3, 2010, http://www.pewhispanic.org /2010/11/03/the-latino-vote-in-the-2010-elections.

58. Julia Preston, "House Backs Legal Status for Many Young Immigrants," *New York Times*, December 8, 2010.

59. Lisa Mascaro and Michael Muskal, "DREAM Act Fails to Advance in Senate," *Los Angeles Times*, December 18, 2010.

60. Tim Gaynor, "Analysis: 'DREAM Act' Failure Kills Immigration Reform Hopes," *Reuters.com*, December 18, 2010, http://www.reuters.com/article/2010/12/18 /us-usa-immigration-idUKTRE6BH1Q720101218.

61. Richard McGregor, "Republican Gerrymander Eases Pressure on Migration Reform," *Financial Times*, July 12, 2013, 3.

62. Nate Cohn, "Why House Deportation Vote Won't Hurt the GOP," *International New York Times*, August 5, 2014, A3.

63. Ashley Parker and Jonathan Martin, "Senate, 68 to 32, Passes Overhaul for Immigration," *New York Times*, June 27, 2013.

64. Aamer Madhani, "Immigration Reform Is Back," *National Journal*, May 12, 2011.

65. Josh Hicks, "Obama's Failed Promise of a First-Year Immigration Overhaul," *Washington Post*, September 25, 2012.

66. Fawn Johnson, "Immigration: Broken Record," *National Journal*, October 12, 2013, 39.

67. Nick Miroff, "Border Town Becomes a Purgatory for Legions of Mexican Detainees," *Washington Post*, January 17, 2014, A1, A8.

68. Julia Preston, "Young Immigrants, in America Illegally, Line Up for Reprieve," *New York Times*, November 17, A13.

69. Mark Hugo Lopez and Jens Manuel Krogstad, "Five Facts about the Deferred Action for Childhood Arrivals Program," *PEWResearch.org*, August 15, 2014, http:// www.pewresearch.org/fact-tank/2014/08/15/5-facts-about-the-deferred-action-for -childhood-arrivals-program/st 15, 2014.

70. Preston, "Obama to Permit Migrants to Remain."

71. Dan Balz, "Obama and Romney on the Issues: Immigration," *Washington Post*, October 5, 2012.

72. Johnson, "Immigration: Broken Record," 39.

73. Mark Hugo Lopez and Ana Gonzalez-Barrera, "Inside the 2012 Latino Electorate," Pew Research Center Hispanic Trends Project, June 3, 2013, http://www .pewhispanic.org/2013/06/03/inside-the-2012-latino-electorate.

74. John Avlon, "Obama's 2013 State of the Union and the Immigration Reform Moment," *Daily Beast*, February 13, 2013, http://www.thedailybeast.com/articles/2013 /02/13/obama-s-2013-state-of-the-union-and-the-immigration-reform-moment.html.

75. Rosalind S. Helderman and William Branigan, "Bipartisan Group of Senators Unveils Immigration Reform Plan," *Washington Post*, January 28, 2013.

76. Ezra Klein, "READ: President Obama's Immigration Proposal," *Washington Post*, January 29, 2013.

77. Alan Gomez, "White House Immigration Plan Offers Path to Residency," *USA Today*, February 17, 2013.

78. Amanda Peterson Beadle, "Republican Party Officially Backs Immigration Reform," American Immigration Council, March 18, 2013, immigrationimpact.com /2013/03/18/republican-party-officially.

79. Sara Murray, "Businesses Push for More Low-Skilled Visas," *Wall Street Journal*, August 9, 2013, A3.

80. Laura Meckler and Kristina Peterson, "Obama Pushing Immigration as New Doubts Emerge in House," *Wall Street Journal*, November 14, 2013, A1.

81. Melanie Trottman, Miriam Jordan, and Kris Maher, "Unions Seize on Immigration Debate," *Wall Street Journal*, February 5, 2013, A6.

82. Laura Meckler and Kristina Peterson, "Advocates for Immigration Bill Are Taking a New Tack," *Wall Street Journal*, November 13, 2013, A4.

83. Carol E. Lee and Peter Nicholas, "Boehner Warns Obama against Unilateral Action on Immigration," *Wall Street Journal*, November 7, 2014; Caroline May, "Report: Boehner's Secret Amnesty Talks with Obama Revealed," *FoxNews.com*, November 8, 2014, http://nation.foxnews.com/2014/11/08/report-boehners-secret -amnesty-talks-obama-revealed.

84. Kristina Peterson, "Senate Backs Plan for Border," *Wall Street Journal*, June 25, 2013, A5.

85. Ashley Parker and Jonathan Martin, "Senate, 68 to 32, Passes Overhaul for Immigration," *New York Times*, June 27, 2013.

86. Ed O'Keefe, "Senate Approves Comprehensive Immigration Bill," *Washington Post*, June 27, 2013.

87. Fawn Johnson, "How Immigration Reform Could Create a New Underclass," *National Journal*, August 3, 2013, 14–21.

88. Charles Babington, "Republican National, House Interests Split by Immigration," Associated Press, June 17, 2013, http://www.huffingtonpost.com/2013/06/17 /republican-immigration_n_3455659.html.

89. Erica Werner, "Senate Immigration Reform: Bipartisan Group Turns Focus to Border Security," Huff Post Politics, January 31, 2013, http://www.huffingtonpost .com/2013/01/31/senate-immigration-reform_n_2594068.html; Laura Meckler, "Defining Border Security Key to Talks," *Wall Street Journal*, February 2, 2013, A4; Werner, "Senate Immigration Reform."

90. Corey Boles, "Taxing Problem for an Immigration Plan," *Wall Street Journal*, May 11, 2013, A5.

91. O'Keefe, "Senate Approves Comprehensive Immigration Bill."

92. Ashley Parker, "House Group Works to Present Its Own Immigration Plan," *New York Times*, February 2, 2013.

93. Kristina Peterson, "GOP Ground Shifts on Immigration," *Wall Street Journal*, June 8, 2013, A5.

94. Helderman and Branigan, "Bipartisan Group of Senators."

95. David Grant, "Immigration Reform Is Stuck in the House, but 'Gang' Is Resolute," *Christian Science Monitor*, May 23, 2013.

96. Rebecca Kaplan, "Raul Labrador Quits House Immigration Group, Bipartisan Effort in Jeopardy," *National Journal*, June 5, 2013.

97. Julia Preston, "Poll Shows Path to Citizenship Favored," *New York Times*, June 10, 2014, A13; Gerald F. Seib, "Polarization Is Not Just in Washington," *Wall Street Journal*, April 16, 2013, A4; Rebecca Ballhaus, "Some Democrats Oppose Overhaul Bill," *Wall Street Journal–Europe*, July 5–7, 2013, 6.

98. William Galston, "An Immigration Challenge for Boehner," *Wall Street Journal*, October 23, 2013, A13.

99. Preston, "Poll Shows Path," A13.

100. Babington, "Republican National."

101. Cohn, "Why House Deportation Vote," A3.

102. David Weigel, "House Bipartisan Group on Immigration Reform Totally Collapses because Barack Obama Is President," *Slate.com*, September 20, 2013, http://www.slate.com/blogs/weigel/2013/09/20/house_bipartisan_group_on _immigration_reform_totally_collapses_because_barack.html.

103. Miriam Jordan, "Nationwide Marches to Press for Action on Immigrants," *Wall Street Journal*, October 5–6, 2013, A5.

104. Laura Matthews, "Immigration Reform 2013: House Gang Preps Comprehensive Bill for October Push," *International Business Times*, August 29, 2013, http:// www.ibtimes.com/immigration-reform-2013-house-gang-preps-comprehensive -bill-october-push-1401634.

105. Laura Meckler, "House GOP Puts Immigration Reform on Back Burner," *Wall Street Journal*, September 4, 2013, A4.

106. Meckler and Peterson, "Obama Pushing Immigration," A1.

107. Laura Meckler and Neil King Jr., "Rubio Backs Off His Immigration Bill," *Wall Street Journal*, October 29, 2013, A6.

108. Carol E. Lee and Peter Nicholas, "Face-Off over Immigration," *Wall Street Journal*, November 7, 2014, A1.

109. Carol E. Lee, "Obama Backs Piecemeal Immigration Overhaul," *Wall Street Journal*, November 20, 2013, A1.

110. Laura Meckler and Kristina Peterson, "Obama Signals He Would Back House GOP Immigration Framework," *Wall Street Journal*, January 31, 2014.

111. Laura Meckler, "House Republicans Cool to Schumer Immigration Proposal," *Wall Street Journal*, February 10, 2014, A4.

112. Edward P. Lazear, "An Immigration Game Plan for the New Congress," *Wall Street Journal*, December 5, 2014, A13.

113. Laura Meckler and Kristina Peterson, "GOP Readies New Immigration Plan," *Wall Street Journal*, January 17, 2014, A4.

114. Laura Meckler, "House GOP Sets New Push to Overhaul Immigration," *Wall Street Journal*, January 25–26, 2014, A1.

115. Kristina Peterson, "Some Democrats Waver on Immigration," *Wall Street Journal*, August 8, 2013, A4.

116. Laura Meckler and Kristina Peterson, "House GOP Cools to Immigration Overhaul," *Wall Street Journal*, February 6, 2014, A6.

117. Jonathan Weisman, "House Leader Cites Doubts over Bill on Immigration," *International New York Times*, February 8–9, 2014, 4.

118. Meckler, "House Republicans Cool," A4.

119. Siobhan Hughes, "Cantor Spars with Obama on Immigration Overhaul," *Wall Street Journal*, April 17, 2014, A4.

120. Patrick O'Connor, "Tea Party's Poll Setbacks Don't Limit Its Washington Clout," *Wall Street Journal*, June 26, 2014, A1.

121. Charlie Cook, "Untended Fences," *National Journal*, June 14, 2014, 32.

122. Rem Rieder, "Cantor Proves Tea-Party Obits Premature," *USA Today*, June 12, 2014, 2B.

123. Cook, "Untended Fences," 32.

124. Laura Meckler, "Immigrant-Bill Backer Gives Up," *Wall Street Journal*, June 26, 2014, A3.

125. Rick Jarvis, "US Policy Lures Kids to Cross Border Illegally," *USA Today*, June 18, 2014, 7A.

126. Frances Robles, "Violence Drives Flow of Young Migrants," *International New York Times*, July 10, 2014, 1, 4.

127. Miriam Jordan, "Rate of Girls Crossing U.S.-Mexico Border Alone Outpaces Boys, Study Finds," *Wall Street Journal*, July 26–27, 2014, A4.

128. Josh Hicks, "Wanted: More Women to Work for Border Control," *Washington Post*, January 1, 2014, A11.

129. Jude Webber, "Life on the Line," *Financial Times*, July 18, 2014, 5.

130. Ana Campoy, "Immigrant 'Stash Houses' Thrive along Texas-Mexico Border," *Wall Street Journal*, June 26, 2014, A3.

131. Laura Meckler and Ana Campoy, "Few Children Are Sent Back," *Wall Street Journal*, July 14, 2014, 6.

132. Brian Knowlton, "The Context of a Crisis," *International New York Times*, July 18, 2014, 5.

133. Ana Campoy, "Illegal Immigrants Seeking Asylum Face a Higher Bar," *Wall Street Journal*, September 29, 2014, A3.

134. Ibid.

135. Molly Hennessy-Fisks, Brian Bennett, and Cindy Carcamo, "Obama Administration Acts to Ease Immigration Crunch at Border," *Los Angeles Times*, June 21, 2014, A1.

136. Manny Fernandez, "US Towns Fight to Avoid Taking Migrant Minors," *International New York Times*, July 18, 2014, 5; Rick Jervis, "US Policy Lures Kids to Cross Border Illegally," *USA Today*, June 18, 2014, 7A.

137. Knowlton, "Context of a Crisis," 5.

138. Byron Tau, "U.S. Is Bracing for Influx of Central American Migrants," *Wall Street Journal*. December 10, 2015.

139. Campoy, "Immigrant 'Stash Houses,'"A3.

140. Hennessy-Fisks et al., "Obama Administration Acts," A1.

141. Ibid.

142. Julia Preston, "Experts See Legal Hazards in State's Immigration Suit," *New York Times*, December 6, 2014, A4.

143. Kathleen Hennessey, "US Pushes to Slow Child Immigration," *Los Angeles Times*, June 17, 2014, AA2.

144. Hicks, "Wanted: More Women," A11.

145. Ibid.

146. Hennessy-Fisks et al., "Obama Administration Acts," A1.

147. Meckler and Campoy, "Few Children Are Sent Back," 6.

148. Knowlton, "Context of a Crisis," 5.

149. Jolie Lee, "Schools Brace for up to 50,000 Migrants," *USA Today*, August 7, 2014, A1.

150. Hennessy-Fisks et al., "Obama Administration Acts," A1.

151. Alan Gomez, "Obama's Border Strategy Not a Hit," *USA Today*, July 18, 2014, 2A.

152. Fernandez, "US Towns Fight," 5.

153. Miriam Jordan, "Migrant Wave Diverts Resources from Refugee Programs," *Wall Street Journal*, August 16–17, 2013, A3.

154. Michael R. Crittenden and Laura Meckler, "Senate Democrats Push Back against Speedy Deportations," *Wall Street Journal*, July 16, 2014, A3; Kristina Peterson and Laura Meckler, "Lawmakers Clash over Fix for Border Crisis," *Wall Street Journal*, July 18, 2014, A3.

155. Klein, "READ."

156. Gomez, "Obama's Border Strategy," 2A.

157. Miriam Jordan, "Immigration Activists Shift Focus to Obama," *National Journal*, October 14, 2013, A6.

158. Laura Meckler, "Impasse over Immigration Fuels New Fight for Obama," *Wall Street Journal*, February 10, 2014, 7.

159. Laura Meckler, "Immigration Impasse Could Rekindle Fight over Deportations," *Wall Street Journal*, February 8–9, 2014, A4.

160. Johnson, "Immigration: Broken Record," 39.

161. Julie Kliegman, "Activist Janet Murguía Calls Obama 'Deporter in Chief,' Says He Has Deported More Immigrants Than Other Presidents," *Politifact.com*, March 17, 2014, http://www.politifact.com/truth-o-meter/statements/2014/mar/17/janet-murguia/activist-janet-murguia-calls-obama-deporter-chief-.

162. Fawn Johnson, "Obama's Options," *National Journal*, April 5, 2014, 28.

163. Associated Press, "Experts: Obama Can Do A Lot to Change Immigration," *Hoosier Times*, August 13, 2014, E2.

164. Laura Meckler, "Obama Aims to Shift Immigration Debate to 2016," *Wall Street Journal*, September 8, 2014, A4.

165. Ross K. Baker, "Liberal Democrats in a Funk over Obama Inaction," *USA Today*, August 11, 2014, 1A, 2A.

166. Laura Meckler and Kristina Peterson, "Obama's Immigration Plans Irk Some Democrats," *Wall Street Journal*, August 26, 2014, A5.

167. Meckler, "Obama Aims," A4.

168. Ibid.

169. Arian Campo-Flores, "Hispanic-Voter Frustration Threatens Democrats Most," *Wall Street Journal*, October 17, 2014, A6.

170. Benjy Sarlin and Alex Seitz-Wald, "Why the Democrats Lost, According to Everyone," *MSNBC.com*, November 7, 2014, http://www.msnbc.com/msnbc/why-the-democrats-lost-midterms-according-everyone#54977.

171. Jens Manuel Krogstad and Mark Hugo Lopez, "Five Takeaways about the 2014 Latino Vote," *PewResearch.org*, November 10, 2014, http://www.pewresearch.org/fact-tank/2014/11/10/5-takeaways-about-the-2014-latino-vote; Julia Preston, "GOP's Inroads with Latinos a Path for 2016," *New York Times*, November 5, 2014.

172. Reid J. Epstein, Laura Meckler, and Dante Chinni, "Democratic Coalition Frays around Edges in Midterm Elections," *Wall Street Journal*, November 6, 2014, A1.

173. Beth Reinhard, "GOP Ads Go on Attack over Border," *Wall Street Journal*, August 11, 2014, A4.

174. David Jackson and Alan Gomez, "Obama's Immigration Order: Some of the Key Changes," *USA Today*, November 21, 2014, 4A.

175. Stephen Legomsky, "The President Is Right on Immigration," *Wall Street Journal*, November 24, 2014, A15.

176. David B. Rivkin Jr. and Elizabeth Price Foley, "Obama's Immigration Enablers," *Wall Street Journal*, November 25, 2014, A13.

177. Laura Meckler and Nathan Koppel, "Obama Administration Dealt Setback on Immigration," *Wall Street Journal*, February, 18, 2015, A1.

178. Michael W. McConnell, "Why Obama's Immigration Order Was Blocked," *Wall Street Journal*, February 18, 2015, A1.

179. Nathan Koppel, "Appeals Court Keeps Block of Obama Immigration Plan," *Wall Street Journal*, May 27, 2015, A4.

180. Preston, "Experts See Legal Hazards," A4.

181. Megan Murphy, "Political Rivals Prime Weapons for Duel over President's Powers," *Financial Times*, November 21, 2014, 3.

182. Laura Meckler and Kristina Peterson, "House Vote to Block Obama's Executive Action on Immigration," *Wall Street Journal*, January 15, 2015, A3.

183. Kristina Peterson and Michael R. Crittenden, "Senate Democrats Block GOP Move on Obama Immigration Policy," *Wall Street Journal*, February 4, 2015, A4.

184. Marc R. Rosenblum, "US Immigration Policy since 9/11: Understanding the Stalemate over Comprehensive Immigration Reform," Migration Policy Institute, Woodrow Wilson International Center for Scholars, August 2011, http://www.migrationpolicy.org/pubs/RMSG-post-9–11policy.pdf.

185. Jake Tapper, "McCain Takes Issue with President Obama Partly Blaming Him for Immigration Reform Failure," *ABCNews*, September 21, 2012, abcnews.go.com/blogs/politics/2012/09/McCain-takes-issue.

186. Graham, *Bush on the Home Front,* 242–50.

187. Bhagwati and Rivera-Batiz, "Kinder, Gentler Immigration Policy."

188. Gerald F. Seib, "Risks, Rewards for Boehner in Rebellion on Right," *Wall Street Journal*, January 6, 2015, A4; Kristina Peterson and Michael R. Crittenden, "Challenges Await Victorious Boehner," *Wall Street Journal*, January 7, 2015, A1, A4.

189. Knowlton, "Context of a Crisis," 5.

190. Laura Meckler and Kristina Peterson, "Border Surge Complicates GOP Pitch to Hispanics," *Wall Street Journal*, July 28, 2014, A5.

191. Julia Preston, "Young Undocumented Immigrants Growing Disenchanted with Both Parties, Study Finds," *International New York Times*, May 21, 2014, A16.

10. Midterm Massacres

1. See generally Gary C. Jacobson, *The Politics of Congressional Elections*, 8th ed. (Upper Saddle River, NJ: Pearson Education, 2013).

2. There are two prominent theories that seek to explain midterm outcomes for the president's party. The referendum model emphasizes the president's popularity and economic conditions in the period before the midterm election. The coattails/ surge theory focuses on the president's performance in the previous election, since his coattails will no longer be available at the midterm. For a classic treatment of the question, see James E. Campbell, "Explaining the Losses in Midterm Congressional Elections," *Journal of Politics* 47, no. 4 (1985): 1140–57. More recently see James E. Campbell, *The Presidential Pulse of Congressional Elections* (Lexington: University of Kentucky Press, 2015). For a journalistic account of the 2014 midterm as a referendum on Obama, see Lindsey Boema, "2014 Elections Look Like a Referendum on Obama," *CBS News.com*, November 4, 2014, http://www.cbsnews.com /news/2014-midterm-elections-becoming-a-referendum-on-obama.

3. Susan Davis, "Why Democrats Won't Take Back the House," *USA Today*, August 11, 2014, 1A, 2A.

4. Vincent A. Pacileo IV, "The Freedom of the Lame Duck: Presidential Effectiveness in the Post 22nd Amendment Era," http://cspc.nonprofitsoapbox.com /storage/Fellows2011/Pacileo-_Final_Paper.pdf.

5. Matthew N. Green, "2010 Midterm Election," in *The Obama Presidency: A Preliminary Assessment*, eds. Robert P. Watson, Jack Covarrubias, Tom Lansford, and Douglas M. Brattebo (Albany: SUNY Press, 2012), 130.

6. Davis, "Why Democrats Won't Take Back the House," 1A, 2A.

7. Gerhard Peters, "Seats in Congress Gained/Lost by the President's Party in Midterm Elections," The American Presidency Project, December 19, 2014, http:// www.presidency.ucsb.edu/data/mid-term_elections.php.

8. Brandice Canes-Wrone, *Who Leads Whom? Presidents, Policy, and the Public* (Chicago: University of Chicago Press, 2005).

9. Gary C. Jacobson, "The 1994 House Elections in Perspective," *Political Science Quarterly* 111 (1996): 203–223; John A. Ferejohn, "A Tale of Two Congresses: Social Policy in the Clinton Years," in *The Social Divide: Political Parties and the Future of Activist Government*, ed. Margaret Weir (Washington, DC: Brookings Institution, 1998), 49–82; Brandice Canes-Wrone, David W. Brady, and John F. Cogan, "Out of Step, Out of Office: Electoral Accountability and House Members' Voting," *American Political Science Review* 96 (2002): 127–40.

10. Dan Balz and Shailagh Murray, "Election 2010: Grim Expectations for Freshman and Sophomore Democrats," *Washington Post*, November 2, 2010.

11. Green, "2010 Midterm Election," 131.

12. Balz and Murray, "Election 2010."

13. Alan Abramowitz, "Can Republicans Take Back the House?" University of Virginia Center for Politics, June 17, 2010, http://www.centerforpolitics.org/crystalball/articles/aia2010061701.

14. Gary C. Jacobson, "Republican Resurgence in 2010," *Political Science Quarterly* 126, no. 1 (2011): 31–34.

15. Theda Skocpol, Vanessa Williamson, and John Coggin, "The Tea Party and the Remaking of Republican Conservatism," Harvard University, March 2011, http://scholar.harvard.edu/files/williamson/files/tea_party_pop.pdf.

16. George C. Edwards III, *Strategic Assessments: Evaluating Opportunities and Strategies in the Obama Presidency* (Washington, DC: CQ Press, 2012), 48.

17. Jay Cost, "Health Care Reform Has Endangered the Democratic Majority," *RealClearPolitics.com*, August 31, 2010, http://www.realclearpolitics.com/horseraceblog/congress.

18. Jacobson, *Politics of Congressional Elections*, 223–32.

19. Marc J. Hetherington and Bruce A. Larson, *Parties, Politics, and Public Policy in America*, 11th ed. (Washington, DC: CQ Press, 2010), 55, tables 2–4.

20. Kevin B. Grier and Joseph P. McGarrity, "The Effect of Macroeconomic Fluctuations on the Electoral Fortunes of House Incumbents," *Journal of Law and Economics* 41, no. 1 (1998): 143–62; Green, "2010 Midterm Election."

21. Michael D. Bordo and Joseph G. Haubrich, "Deep Recessions, Fast Recoveries, and Financial Crises: Evidence from the American Record," June 2012, http://www.nber.org/papers/w18194.pdf (N = 27 cycles since 1882 in USA).

22. "What Accounts for the Slow Growth of the Economy after the Recession?" Congressional Budget Office, November 2012, http://www.cbo.gov/sites/default/files/43707-SlowRecovery.pdf.

23. Jacobson, *Politics of Congressional Elections*, 230.

24. Jacobson, "Republican Resurgence," 30, especially note 8; Jacobson, *Politics of Congressional Elections*, 225, especially note 118.

25. James E. Campbell, "Political Forces on the Obama Presidency," in *The Obama Presidency: Appraisals and Prospects*, eds. Bert A. Rockman, Andrew Rudalevige, and Colin Campbell (Washington, DC: CQ Press, 2012), 86.

26. Paul Gronke and Brian Newman, "From FDR to Clinton: A Field Essay on Presidential Approval," *Political Research Quarterly* 56, no. 4 (2003): 501–512; Joseph Bafumi, Robert S. Erikson, and Christopher Wlezien, "Ideological Balancing: Generic Polls and Midterm Congressional Elections," *Journal of Politics* 72, no. 3 (2010): 705–719.

27. Campbell, "Political Forces," 86.

28. Jeffrey E. Cohen and Costas Panagopoulos, "Presidential Leadership and Public Opinion in an Age of Polarization," in *The Obama Presidency: Change and Continuity*, eds. Andrew J. Dowdle, Dirk C. van Raemdonck, and Robert Maranto (New York: Routledge, 2011), 36, fig. 3.1; Green, "2010 Midterm Election," 134.

29. Richard Waterman, Carol L. Silva, and Hank Jenkins-Smith, "The Presidential Expectations Gap: Public Attitudes Concerning the Presidency," *Congress and the Presidency* 42, no. 2 (2015): 123.

30. Gary C. Jacobson, "Polarization, Public Opinion, and the Presidency: The Obama and Anti-Obama Coalitions," in Rockman et al., *Obama Presidency*, 111 (especially note 58).

31. Jacobson, "Republican Resurgence," 30.

32. Colleen McCain Nelson, "Obama Ramps Up Fundraising, Even on Vacation," *Wall Street Journal*, August 9–10, 2014, A4.

33. Barbara Trish, "Organizing for America," in *The State of the Parties: The Changing Role of Contemporary American Parties*, eds. John C. Green and Daniel J. Coffey (Lanham, MD: Rowman and Littlefield, 2011), 165, 176–77.

34. Paul Kane, "House Democrats Hit Boiling Point over Perceived Lack of White House Support," *Washington Post*, July 15, 2010.

35. Brian Hughes, "Tale of the Tape: Obama's Campaigning a Far Cry from 2010," *Washington Examiner*, November 1, 2014.

36. Gary C. Jacobson and Samuel Kernell, *Strategy and Choice in Congressional Elections* (New Haven, CT: Yale University Press, 1981), 19–34.

37. Jacobson, "Republican Resurgence," 37–38 (including note 29).

38. "Where the Tea Party Candidates Are Running," *New York Times*, October 14, 2010, http://www.nytimes.com/interactive/2010/10/15/us/politics/tea-party-graphic .html?_r=0.

39. Jacobson, "Republican Resurgence," 39.

40. Campaign Finance Institute, "Non-Party Spending Doubled in 2010 but Did Not Dictate the Results," November 5, 2010, http://www.cfinst.org/press/preleases /10–11–05/Non-Party_Spending_Doubled_But_Did_Not_Dictate_Results.aspx; Jacobson, "Republican Resurgence," 40.

41. Drew Desilver, "Voter Turnout Always Drops for Midterm Elections, but Why?" *PewResearch.org*, July 24, 2014, http://www.pewresearch.org/fact-tank /2014/07/24/voter-turnout-always-drops-off-for-midterm-elections-but-why; Brian G. Knight, "An Econometric Evaluation of Competing Explanations for the Midterm Gap," NBER Working Paper No 20311, July 2014, http://www.nber.org /papers/w20311.

42. Hetherington and Larson, *Parties, Politics, and Public Policy*, 225–26.

43. Jan E. Leighley and Jonathan Nagler, *Who Votes Now? Demographics, Issues, Inequality, and Turnout in the United States* (Princeton, NJ: Princeton University Press, 2014), 183–84, 188.

44. Waterman, Silva, and Jenkins-Smith, "Presidential Expectations," 121.

45. Ibid., 122.

46. Ibid., 130–31.

47. Green, "2010 Midterm Election," 136–37.

48. James E. Campbell, ed., "Symposium: Forecasts for the 2010 Midterm Elections," *PS: Political Science and Politics* 43 (October 2010): 625–41.

49. Michael S. Lewis-Beck and Charles Tien, "The Referendum Model: A 2010 Congressional Forecast," *PS: Political Science and Politics* (October 2010): 637–38.

50. Alan I. Abramowitz, "How Large a Wave? Using the Generic Ballot to Forecast the 2010 Midterm Elections," *PS: Political Science and Politics* 43, no. 4 (October 2010): 631–32.

51. John H. Aldrich, Bradford H. Bishop, Rebecca S. Hatch, D. Sunshine Hilly-gus, and David W. Rohde, "Blame, Responsibility, and the Tea Party in the 2010 Midterm Elections," *Political Behavior* 36, no. 3 (2014): 471–91.

52. Jacobson, "Republican Resurgence," 27.

53. George C. Edwards III, *Overreach: Leadership and the Obama Presidency* (Princeton, NJ: Princeton University Press, 2012), 172.

54. Jacobson, "Polarization, Public Opinion," 114.

55. Ibid.

56. Amy Walter, "The Myth of the Independent Voter," *Cook Political Report*, January 15, 2014, http://cookpolitical.com/story/660800.

57. Green, "2010 Midterm Election," 134.

58. Matthew N. Green and Kristen Hudak, "Congress and the Bailout: Explain-ing the Bailout Votes and their Electoral Effect, Extension of Remarks," *Legislative Studies Section Newsletter* 32, no. 1 (2009).

59. Waterman, Silva, and Jenkins-Smith, "Presidential Expectations," 123.

60. Jacobson, "Republican Resurgence," 48.

61. Edwards, *Overreach*, 172.

62. Andrew Wheeler, "Cap and Trade Political Kryptonite for Democrats?" *Politico.com*, November 4, 2010, http://www.politico.com/arena/energy.

63. Jacobson, "Republican Resurgence," 48.

64. Eric McGhee, "Did Controversial Roll Call Votes Doom the Democrats?" *TheMonkeyCage.org*, November 4, 2010, http://themonkeycage.org/2010/11/04/did_controversial_roll_call.

65. Jacobson, "Republican Resurgence," 48–49 (especially table 7 and note 52).

66. David W. Brady, Morris P. Fiorina, and Arjun S. Wilkins, "The 2010 Elec-tions: Why Did Political Science Forecasts Go Awry?" *PS: Political Science and Poli-tics* (April 2011): 247–50.

67. Alan I. Abramowitz, *Disappearing Center: Engaged Citizens, Polarization, and American Democracy* (New Haven, CT: Yale University Press, 2010), 108.

68. Charlie Cook, "The Lessons of 2010," *National Journal*, August 2, 2014, 15.

69. Charlie Cook, "The Big Sort," *National Journal*, April 13, 2013, 44.

70. Patrick O'Connor, "House Districts Keep Getting Safer," *Wall Street Jour-nal*, July 29, 2013, A4.

71. Karl Rove, "Can the Democrats Retake the House in 2014?" *Wall Street Jour-nal*, August 15, 2013, A13.

72. Ronald Brownstein, "More Paralysis Ahead," *National Journal*, October 25, 2014, 11.

73. Jonathan Weisman, "Economic Recovery Yields Few Benefits for the Voters Democrats Rely On," *International New York Times*, May 20, 2014, A14.

74. Janet Hook, "GOP Holds Better Hand amid Wild Cards," *Wall Street Jour-nal*, October 15, 2014, A4; Charlie Cook, "Questions and Possible Answers," *Na-tional Journal*, October 25, 2014, 12.

75. James Oliphant, "Presidential Paralysis," *National Journal*, June 14, 2014, 24; William A. Galston, "A World of Trouble for Obama," *Wall Street Journal*, Septem-ber 13, 2014, A11.

76. Cook, "Questions and Possible Answers," 12; Andrew Kohut, "How Americans View an Unruly World," *Wall Street Journal*, August 5, 2014, A11.

77. Gerald F. Seib, "Voters Show Early Signs of Punishing Political Gridlock," *Wall Street Journal*, October 21, 2014, A4.

78. James D. King and James W. Riddlesperger, "The 2012–2013 Transition to the Second Obama Administration," in *The 2012 Presidential Election: Forecasts, Outcomes, and Consequences*, eds. Amnon Cavari, Richard Powell, and Kenneth Mayer (Lanham, MD: Rowman and Littlefield, 2014), 144.

79. Jonathan Weisman, "Senate Blocks Drive for Gun Control," *New York Times*, April 17, 2013.

80. Philip Bump, "A Political Machine That's Running Out of Gas," *Washington Post*, May 21, 2014, A14.

81. An interest group "scores" a vote when it is judged to be a critical vote in the eyes of the leaders of the interest group. The NRA develops a rating of each member of Congress depending on how he or she rates on votes scored by the NRA. A low rate on the NRA score is a vulnerability in pro-gun regions of the United States, regardless of whether the member is a Democrat or Republican. Ross K. Baker, *Is Bipartisanship Dead? A Report from the Senate* (St. Paul, MN: Paradigm Publishers, 2014), 42–44.

82. Ed O'Keefe and Philip Rucker, "Gun Control Overhaul Is Defeated in Senate," *Washington Post*, April 17, 2013.

83. King and Riddlesperger, "2012–2013 Transition," 138–39.

84. Ibid.

85. George E. Condon Jr., "Obama's Lost Year," *National Journal*, November 9, 2013, 38.

86. Ryan Lizza, "Four Reasons Why the Gun-Control Bills Failed," *New Yorker*, April 18, 2013.

87. John B. Judis, "Here's Why the Democrats Got Crushed—and Why 2016 Won't Be a Cakewalk," *New Republic*, November 5, 2014.

88. Gerald F. Seib, "Democrats Lose Edge on Peace and Prosperity," *Wall Street Journal*, October 14, 2014, A4.

89. Condon, "Obama's Lost Year," 38.

90. Neil King Jr. and Patrick O'Connor, "Poll Finds Americans Anxious over Future Obama's Performance," *Wall Street Journal*, January 28, 2014, A1.

91. Daniel Henninger, "Obama's State of Disunion," *Wall Street Journal*, January 29, 2014, A11.

92. Andrew Kohut, "The Demographics behind the Democrats' 2014 Troubles," *Wall Street Journal*, March 21, 2014, A13.

93. Ibid.

94. Charlie Cook, "Early Days Yet," *National Journal*, May 3, 2014, 40.

95. Patrick O'Connor, "Poll Shows Erosion in President's Support," *Wall Street Journal*, June 18, 2014, A4.

96. Ibid.

97. Charlie Cook, "Message Testing," *National Journal*, April 12, 2014, 60.

98. Kohut, "Demographics," A13.

99. Catalina Camia, "Alex Sink Decides against Florida Rematch for Congress," *USA Today Politics*, April 15, 2014, http://onpolitics.usatoday.com/2014/04/15/alex-sink-rematch-david-jolly-congress-florida.

100. Alex Isenstadt, "David Jolly Defeats Alex Sink in Florida 13th," *Politico.com*, March 11, 2014, http://www.politico.com/story/2014/03/david-jolly-alex-sink-florida-special-election-2014-104543.

101. Arian Campo-Flores, "Republican David Jolly Wins Florida Congressional Race," *Wall Street Journal*, March 11, 2014.

102. Laura Meckler, "Republican Candidates Big and Small Slam Health Law in Ads," *Wall Street Journal*, March 19, 2014, A4.

103. Sean Sullivan, "Republican Jolly Wins Florida Special Election," *Washington Post*, March 11, 2014, http://www.washingtonpost.com/blogs/post-politics/wp/2014/03/11/republican-jolly-wins-florida-special-election.

104. Janet Hook, "Tea Party Faces Test of Its Clout in Primaries," *Wall Street Journal*, February 25, 2014, A1.

105. Laura Meckler, "Business Voices Frustration with GOP," *Wall Street Journal*, October 17, 2013, A1.

106. Patrick O'Connor, "Freshmen GOP Lawmakers Revel in Maverick Power," *Wall Street Journal*, August 2, 2013, A1.

107. Patrick O'Connor, "Tea Party's Poll Setbacks Don't Limit Its Washington Clout," *Wall Street Journal*, June 26, 2014, A1.

108. Gerald F. Seib, "Big Business Rethinks Its Political Game, *Wall Street Journal*, July 1, 2014, A4.

109. Devin Burghart, "The Status of the Tea Party Movement—Part Two," Institute for Research and Education on Human Rights, 2014, http://www.irehr.org/issue-areas/tea-party-nationalism/tea-party-news-and-analysis/527-status-of-tea-party-by-the-numbers.

110. O'Connor, "Tea Party's Poll," A1.

111. Carl Huse, "Ads Attacking Health Law Stagger Outspent Democrats," *New York Times*, January 15, 2014, 1.

112. Ibid.

113. Janet Hook, "Democrats Face Battles in South to Hold the Senate," *Wall Street Journal*, December 3, 2013, A1.

114. Thomas Catan and Rebecca Ballhaus, "Democrats Take Aim at Early Flurry of GOP Ads," *Wall Street Journal*, February 20, 2014, A4; Jonathan Martin and Ashley Parker, "Obama Factor Adds to Fears of Democrats," *International New York Times*, March 16, 2014, A1.

115. Laura Meckler, "Some Democrats Talking Up Health Law on Stump," *Wall Street Journal*, May 28, 2014, A4.

116. Siobhan Hughes, "Harry Reid Remains Power Player as Senate Shifts," *Wall Street Journal*, November 12, 2014, A4.

117. Peter Baker and Jeremy W. Peters, "As Budget Fight Looms, Obama Sees Defiance in His Own Party," *New York Times*, September 18, 2013, A13.

118. Baker, *Is Bipartisanship Dead?* 39.

119. Charlie Cook, "Blocking the Vote," *National Journal*, July 26, 2014, 15.

120. Jonathan Weisman, "Reid's Uncompromising Power Play in Senate Rankles Republicans," *International New York Times*, January 9, 2014.

121. Kristina Peterson, "Midterm Elections 2014: Republicans' Agenda Takes Place," *Wall Street Journal*, November 6, 2014, A4; Cook, "Blocking the Vote," 15; Oliphant, "Presidential Paralysis," 24; Benjy Sarlin and Alex Seitz-Wald, "Why the Democrats Lost, According to Everyone," *MSNBC.com*, November 7, 2014, http://www.msnbc .com/msnbc/why-the-democrats-lost-midterms-according-everyone#54977.

122. Martin and Parker, "Obama Factor," A1.

123. Nelson, "Obama Ramps Up," A4.

124. Carol E. Lee and Colleen McCain Nelson, "On the Trail, Obama's Hard to Find," *Wall Street Journal*, October 11–12, 2014, A4; Carol E. Lee, "For Obama, a Harsh Referendum," *Wall Street Journal*, November 5, 2014, A1.

125. Kohut, "Demographics," A13.

126. Janet Hook, "Democrats Stick to Game Plan," *Wall Street Journal*, March 21, 2014, A4.

127. Gerald F. Seib, "2014 vs. 2012: Two Portraits of American Voters," *Wall Street Journal*, October 24, 2014, A4.

128. Charlie Cook, "Wrong Target," *National Journal*, February 8, 2014, 64.

129. Patrick O'Connor, "Government Shutdown Fades as Campaign Problem for GOP," *Wall Street Journal*, September 26, 2014, A4.

130. Ronald Brownstein, "Shellacking, the Sequel," *National Journal*, November 8, 2014, 12.

131. Nate Cohn, "Democratic Effort Appears to Generate a Better Turnout, if Not Outcome," *New York Times*, November 16, 2014, 19.

132. Brownstein, "Shellacking the Sequel," 12.

133. CNN Politics, "House: Full Results," *CNN.com*, December 17, 2014, http:// www.cnn.com/election/2014/results/race/house#exit-polls; "Exit Polls," http://www .cnn.com/ELECTION/2010/results/polls/#USH00p1.

134. Melinda Deslatte and Bill Barrow, "Last of Senate's Deep South Democrats Defeated," December 7, 2014, http://www.cnsnews.com/news/article/ sen-mary-landrieu-louisiana-defeated.

135. Amy Harder and Siobhan Hughes, "Senate Narrowly Defeats Keystone XL Bill," *Wall Street Journal*, November 19, 2014, A1.

136. Paul Singer, "Senate Passes Keystone Despite Threat of Veto," *USA Today*, January 30, 2015, 3A.

137. Cook, "Lessons of 2010," 15.

138. Allysia Finley, "Behind the GOP Statehouse Juggernaut," *Wall Street Journal*, December 13–14, 2014, A11.

139. Davis, "Why Democrats Won't Take Back the House," 2A.

11. A Counterfactual Obama Presidency

1. Gary C. Jacobson, *The Politics of Congressional Elections*, 8th ed. (Upper Saddle River, NJ: Pearson Education, 2013), 223 ("Obama's legislative successes

were, on the whole, political failures, and his party's congressional candidates paid the price").

2. On the value and limitations of counterfactuals in political science, see James D. Fearon, "Counterfactuals and Hypothesis Testing in Political Science," *World Politics* 43, no. 2 (1991): 169–95.

3. James E. Campbell, "The Midterm Landslide of 2010: A Triple Wave Election," *Forum* 8, no. 4 (2010): Article 3; James E. Campbell, "The Miserable Presidential Election of 2012: A First Party-Term Incumbent Survives," *Forum* 10, no. 4 (2012): 20–28; James E. Campbell, "The Republican Wave of 2014: The Continuity of the 2012 and 2014 Elections," *Forum* 12, no. 4 (2014): 609–26.

4. Bernanke's approach to "quantitative easing" appears to have worked as intended, without causing a material rise in inflation or a devaluation of the dollar. Binyamin Applebaum, "Bond-Buying Reaches the End," *New York Times*, October 30, 2014, B1, B10.

5. For an introduction into the causes and consequences of the Great Recession, see Kristin S. Seefeldt and John D. Graham, *America's Poor and the Great Recession* (Bloomington: Indiana University Press, 2014). For a favorable view of Obama's short-term economic policies, see Alan S. Blinder and Mark Zandi, "Don't Look Back in Anger at Bailouts and Stimulus," *Wall Street Journal*, October 16, 2015, A13.

6. Barack Obama, "The New Economic Patriotism: A Plan for Jobs and Middle Class Security," *ABCNews.com*, October 2012, http://abcnews.go.com/images /Politics/Jobs%20Plan%20Booklet.pdf.

7. Todd Zywicki, "The Auto Bailout and the Rule of Law," *National Affairs* 7 (Spring 2011), http://www.nationalaffairs.com/publications/detail/the-auto-bailout -and-the-rule-of-law.

8. *Statista.com*, "Retail Price of Regular Gasoline in the United States from 1990 to 2014 (in U.S. Dollars Per Gallon)," http://www.statista.com/statistics /204740/retail-price-of-gasoline-in-the-united-states-since-1990; Gary Strauss, "2015 Gas Prices Could Average $2.64, Lowest since 2009," *USAToday.com*, January 6, 2014.

9. Daniel Yergin, *The Quest: Energy, Security, and the Remaking of the Modern World* (New York: Penguin, 2011), 325–44.

10. Nick Timiraos, "CBO: Deficit to Narrow, Then Widen in 2018," *Wall Street Journal*, January 27, 2015, A2; Nick Timiraos, "US Posts Smallest Annual Budget Deficit since 2007," *Wall Street Journal*, October 16, 2015, A4.

11. Floyd Norris, "After a Dismal Quarter, a Rosy Outlook," *New York Times*, June 28, 2014, B3.

12. Jack Rasmus, *Obama's Economy: Recovery for the Few* (London: Pluto Press, 2012).

13. Jessica Menton, "Economic Growth 2015: US GDP Shrinks 0.7% in Q1," *International Business Times*, May 29, 2015.

14. Josh Mitchell, "Job Growth Rebounds, but Wages Lag," *Wall Street Journal*, October 4–5, 2014, A1.

15. Michael D. Shear, "Obama Urges Liberals and Conservatives to Unite on Poverty," *New York Times*, May 12, 2015 (after years of silence about poverty in the United States, Obama spoke directly on the subject at a May 2015 conference at Georgetown University).

16. John B. Taylor, *First Principles: Five Keys to Restoring America's Prosperity*, (New York: W. W. Norton, 2012); *Economics One: A Blog by John B. Taylor*, http://economicsone.com.

17. Rasmus, *Obama's Economy*.

18. James C. Capretta, "Recasting Conservative Economics," American Enterprise Institute, March 26, 2013, http://www.aeiorg/publication/recasting-conservative-economics.

19. See, for example, Owen M. Zidar, "Tax Cuts for Whom? Heterogeneous Effects of Income Tax Changes on Growth and Employment," NBER Working Paper No. 21035, March 2015, http://www.nber.org/papers/w21035.

20. Large-scale tax and entitlement reform were featured, for example, in Obama's 2013 State of the Union address, even though he did not campaign on any specific approach to a grand fiscal deal. Michael Catalini, "Cliff Notes on Obama's 2013 State of the Union Address," *National Journal*, February 12, 2013.

21. The images of both Obama and Boehner were hurt by the collapse of the grand bargain negotiations. Gary Andres and Patrick Griffin, "White House-Congressional Relations in a Partisan Age," in *Rivals for Power*, 5th ed., ed. James A. Thurber (Lanham, MD: Rowman and Littlefield, 2013), 48, 59.

22. Nancy Cook, "A Tax Change Both Parties Can Support," *National Journal*, September 6, 2014, 9.

23. Gerald F. Seib, "Celebrating Small Deals That Can Be Done," *Wall Street Journal*, January 28, 2014, A4; Alan S. Blinder, "A Tax Break Worthy of Bipartisan Cheers," *Wall Street Journal*, March 13, 2014, A15; Jacob Lew, "Treasury Secretary Optimistic on Business Tax Overhaul," *Wall Street Journal*, January 22, 2015, A4.

24. Elizabeth Whitman, "Obamacare Approval Ratings: Popularity of Affordable Care Act Rises, Public Now Evenly Split between Liking and Disliking Law, Survey Shows," *International Business Times*, April 21, 2015.

25. Charlie Cook, "Early Days Yet," *National Journal*, May 3, 2014, 40.

26. Russell Muirhead, *The Promise of Party in a Polarized Age* (Cambridge, MA: Harvard University Press, 2014), 214.

27. David Brooks, "A Moderate Manifesto," *New York Times*, March 2, 2009.

28. Muirhead, *Promise of Party*, 1, 208–210.

29. "Partisan Gap in Obama Job Approval Widest in Modern Era," Pew Research Center, April 2, 2009, http://pewresearch.org/pubs/1178/polarized-partisan-gap-in-obama-approval.

30. For an explanation of why conservatives saw Obama's domestic policies as socialistic in nature, see Matt Shipley, "Obama and Socialism," *AmericanFoundingPrinciples.com*, February 18, 2014, AmericanFoundingPrinciples.com/2014/02/18/Obama-and-socialism.

31. Joel D. Auerbach, "'Change We Can Believe In' Meets Reality," in *The Obama Presidency: Appraisals and Prospects*, eds. Bert A. Rockman, Andrew Rudalevige, and Colin Campbell (New York: CQ Press, 2012), 4.

32. William McGurn, "Let's Face It: Obama Is No Post-Partisan," *Wall Street Journal*, July 21, 2009; Ronald Brownstein, "Parties Trading Places for 2014," *National Journal*, March 6, 2014.

33. For incisive economic critiques of the "Cash for Clunkers" program, see Mark Hoekstra, Steven L. Puller, and Jeremy West, "Cash for Corollas: When Stimulus Reduces Spending," NBER Working Paper 20349, July 2014, http://www.nber.org/papers/w20349; Adam Copeland and James Kahn, "The Production Impact of 'Cash for Clunkers': Implications for Stabilization Policy," *Economic Inquiry* 51, no. 1 (2013): 288–303; Atif Mian and Amir Sufi, "The Effects of Fiscal Stimulus: Evidence from the 2009 'Cash for Clunkers' Program," *Quarterly Journal of Economics* 127, no. 3 (2012): 1107–42.

34. For example, see Martin Feldstein, "A Simple Route to Major Deficit Reduction," *Wall Street Journal*, February 21, 2013, A15.

35. Stephen J. Wayne, *Personality and Politics: Obama For and Against Himself* (Washington, DC: CQ Press, 2012); Stephen J. Wayne, "Obama's First Term, Legislative Presidency: Partisan, Not Personal," in Thurber, *Rivals for Power*, 35.

36. George E. Condon Jr., "When Schmoozing Is Overrated," *National Journal* 45, no. 44 (2013): 28.

37. Brownstein, "Parties Trading Places."

38. Barbara Sinclair, "The President and the Congressional Party Leadership in a Hyperpartisan Era," in Thurber, *Rivals for Power*, 125.

39. See "Staff Report: Accomplishments of 2009," *National Journal*, 2010; Max J. Skidmore, "Legislative Leader," in *The Obama Presidency: A Preliminary Assessment*, eds. Robert P. Watson, Jack Covarrubias, Tom Lansford, and Douglas M. Brattebo (Albany: SUNY Press, 2012), 102; Wayne, "Obama's First Term." (In the 2008 campaign Obama proposed over five hundred new policy initiatives, many of them requiring legislation; about half were accomplished; one quarter compromised; and one quarter left un-enacted.)

40. Janet Hook, "Small Budget Deal Makes Bigger One Less Likely," *Wall Street Journal*, December 21–22, 2013, A6.

41. Carol E. Lee and Damian Paletta, "Obama to Assert Unilateral Agenda," *Wall Street Journal*, January 27, 2014, A1.

42. John D. McKinnon and Colleen McCain Nelson, "Obama Offers New Deal on Corporate Taxes, Jobs," *Wall Street Journal*, July 31, 2013, A1; Laura Sanders, "Will 'Tax Reform' Really Happen?" *Wall Street Journal*, August 3, 2013, B8; John D. McKinnon and Siobhan Hughes, "Baucus to Float Plan on Corporate Taxes," *Wall Street Journal*, November 19, 2013, A4.

43. Dave Camp, "How to Fix Our Appalling Tax Code," *Wall Street Journal*, February 26, 2014, A7.

44. Paul Kane, "Baucus to Retire Rather Than Seek Reelection in 2014, Strategists Say," *Washington Post*, April 23, 2013, http://www.washingtonpost.com

/blogs/post-politics/wp/2013/04/23/baucus-to-retire-rather-than-seek-re-election
-in-2014.

45. Susan Davis and Malia Rulon Herman, "Obama to Nominate Senator Baucus Ambassador to China," *USA Today*, December 19, 2013.

46. Gene Sperling, "Believe It or Not, Corporate Tax Reform Is Doable in 2015,"
Wall Street Journal, October 9, 2014, A17; Lew, "Treasury Secretary Optimistic," A4.

47. William A. Galston, "Barack Obama's First Two Years: Policy Accomplishments, Political Failures," in *The Obama Presidency*, eds. Andrew Dowdle, Dirk C.
van Raemdonck, and Robert Maranto (Philadelphia: Routledge, 2011), 193.

48. Staff Report, "The Do-It-Yourself Presidency," *National Journal*, October 15,
2014, 21.

49. R. Lawrence Butler, "Party Governance under Speaker Nancy Pelosi," in
State of the Parties, eds. John C. Green and Daniel J. Coffey (Lanham, MD: Rowman and Littlefield, 2011), 323–32, esp. 331.

50. Michael D. Shear and Carl Hulse, "World Events Muffle Democrats' Economic Rallying Cry," *New York Times*, September 17, 2014, A17 (arguing that a
higher minimum wage was part of an appealing Democratic message in 2014 but
the message was drowned out by the child-refugee crisis, Ebola, Putin, the terrorist
threat of ISIS, and the VA mess).

51. Patrick O'Connor and Colleen McCain Nelson, "Obama State of the Union
Seeks to Motivate Democrats," *Wall Street Journal*, January 29, 2014, A4.

52. Mark Trumbull, "With 21 States Raising Minimum Wage, 2015 Is a Tipping
Point," *Christian Science Monitor*, January 1, 2015.

53. John D. Graham and Veronica V. Stidvent, "Overcoming a Polarized Congress: The Economic Politics of Bush and Obama," *White House Studies* 12, no. 2
(2012): 167–81.

54. Carl Hulse and Adam Nagourney, "Senate GOP Leader Finds Weapon in
Unity," *New York Times*, March 16, 2010.

55. For an evaluation of the green-energy investments in the Recovery Act, see
Joseph E. Aldy, "A Preliminary Assessment of the American Recovery and Rein-
vestment Act's Clean Energy Package," *Review of Environmental Economics and
Policy* 7, no. 1 (2013): 136–55.

56. See chapter 10. Also see Chris Cillizza, "What Effect Did Health-Care Reform Have on Election?" *Washington Post*, November 7, 2010 (GOP pollster Bill Mc-
Inturff: in the one hundred most competitive House districts, 51 percent of voters
called their vote a message of "no" on Obamacare; 20 percent a "yes"; a majority of
independents said their vote was in opposition to health care reform); Laura Meckler, "Republican Candidates Big and Small Slam Health Law in Ads," *Wall Street
Journal*, March 19, 2014, A4 (anti-Obamacare was the most popular GOP theme
in 2014 political advertisements; the theme was used by candidates running for
Congress, state legislature, state attorney general, and even public utility commissioner); Beth Reinhard and Laura Meckler, "Health Law's Election Impact Is Dim-
ming," *Wall Street Journal*, September 17, 2014, A4 (the percentage of GOP congressional political ads focused on the ACA declined from 42 percent in late 2013/early

2014 to 23 percent in the summer of 2014); Karl Rove, "Obamacare Returns as an Election Albatross," *Wall Street Journal*, October 23, 2014, A17 (citing Gallup data showing that in early October 2014, 54 percent say the ACA hurt them compared to 27 percent who say that it helped them); Laura Meckler, "Some Democrats Talking up Health Law on Stump," *Wall Street Journal*, May 28, 2014, A4 (in the North Carolina Senate race involving Democratic incumbent Ms. Kay Hagan, 95 percent of the ads against her mentioned Obamacare).

57. Dropping the individual mandate would not have neutralized the argument that the ACA is too expensive, but it would have undercut the argument that it was too "intrusive." Gary C. Jacobson, *The Politics of Congressional Elections*, 8th ed. (New York: Pearson, 2013), 230.

58. George C. Edwards III, *Overreach: Leadership and the Obama Presidency* (Princeton, NJ: Princeton University Press, 2012), 185.

59. Charlie Cook, "The Lessons of 2010," *National Journal*, August 2, 2014, 15.

60. Alan I. Abramowitz, "How Large a Wave? Using the Generic Ballot to Forecast the 2010 Midterm Elections," *PS: Political Science and Politics* 43, no. 4 (2010): 632.

61. Wayne, "Obama's First Term," 32–33.

62. Kristina Peterson, "Senate Eases Path to Bipartisan Bills," *Wall Street Journal*, March 14, 2014, A4.

63. Butler, "Party Governance," 323–32, esp. 332.

INDEX

JOHN D. GRAHAM is Dean of the Indiana University School of Public and Environmental Affairs. He is author of *Bush on the Home Front: Domestic Policy Triumphs and Setbacks* (Indiana University Press, 2010) and, with Kristin S. Seefeldt, of *America's Poor and the Great Recession* (Indiana University Press, 2013). From 2001 to 2006 he served as Administrator of the Office of Information and Regulatory Affairs, White House Office of Management and Budget.

www.ingramcontent.com/pod-product-compliance
Lightning Source LLC
Chambersburg PA
CBHW030921150426
42812CB00046B/419